What Everyone Else Is Saying About WillMaker Plus...

"By far the most comprehensive program we reveiwed, offering guidance on everything...."
—**USA Today**

"The most complete of the five products we tried."
—**The Wall Street Journal**

"From a group of tough critics, Nolo's WillMaker got the most praise... superior on every front."
—**Kiplinger's Personal Finance Magazine**

"WillMaker is such an easy-to-use program that users may never need to look at the manual... refreshingly painless."
—**Fortune**

"The most... comprehensive and widely praised of the will writing programs."
—**Chicago Tribune**

"You can complete the documents fairly quickly, or you can spend a great deal of time exploring all the clearly written definitions and explanations...."
—**PC World**

"Even if you know you should see a lawyer... Quicken's question-and-answer technique can help you sort through the options."
—**BusinessWeek**

"The most sophisticated legal software on the market."
—**Worth**

"The level of detail and complexity anticipated by the progam makes WillMaker one of the leading legal-advice programs on the market."
—**Inc.**

Keep Up With the Latest in the Law and in This Product

Use Quicken WillMaker Plus's easy Web Update feature to download the latest legal and software updates (requires Internet access). For plain-English legal information on a broad array of estate planning and personal matters, check out www.nolo.com.

Product support (including Web Update) for Quicken WillMaker Plus 2006 ends on **January 1, 2007**. Be sure to register your product to qualify for special upgrade pricing.

Please note that legal documents created and signed before January 1, 2007 will remain legally valid and enforceable if you have used Web Update regularly. You will need to upgrade your software only if you want to create new documents or update existing documents.

An Important Message to Our Readers

This product is not a substitute for legal advice from an attorney. We've done our best to give you useful, accurate legal information, but that's not the same as personalized legal advice. If you want help understanding how the law applies to your particular circumstances, or deciding which estate planning documents are best for you and your family, you should consider seeing a qualified attorney. Estate planning documents are not valid in Louisiana.

Quicken WillMaker Plus

ESTATE PLANNING ESSENTIALS

2006 EDITION

NOLO

Printing History

Second Edition	OCTOBER 2005
Editor	SHAE IRVING
Illustrations	MARI STEIN
Book Design	TERRI HEARSH
Book Production	MARGARET LIVINGSTON
Proofreading	SHERYL ROSE
Index	BAYSIDE INDEXING SERVICE
Printing	DELTA PRINTING SOLUTIONS, INC.

WillMaker.
    Quicken WillMaker plus : estate planning essentials -- 2nd ed.
        p. cm.
    Includes index.
    ISBN 1-4133-0354-4 (alk. paper)
      1. Willmaker. 2. Estate planning--United States--Popular works. 3. Wills--United
States--Popular works. 4. Estate planning--United States--Forms. 5. Wills--United
States--Forms. I. Nolo (Firm) II. Title.

KF750.Z9W55 2005
346.7305'2--dc22

                          2005047348

For information on bulk purchases or corporate premium sales, please contact the Special Sales Department. For academic sales or textbook adoptions, ask for Academic Sales. Call 800-955-4775 or write to Nolo, 950 Parker Street, Berkeley, CA 94710.

Table of Contents

5 About Your Property

6 How to Leave Your Property

7 Providing Management for Children's Property

8 Choosing an Executor

15 Creating an Individual Trust

16 Creating a Shared Marital Trust

17 Creating an AB Trust

18 Signing, Storing and Registering Your Trust

19 Transferring Property to the Trust

20 Living With Your Living Trust

21 After a Grantor Dies

22 Durable Powers of Attorney for Finances

23 Health Care Directives

24 Final Arrangements

25 If You Need More Help

Users' Manual

Quicken WillMaker Plus Index

Users' Manual Index

What You Can Do With Quicken WillMaker Plus

Many people feel daunted by the thought of making a will, living trust, or other important legal document. Quicken WillMaker Plus is here to help you put your mind at ease by making these tasks as painless as possible. A friendly, step-by-step interview will lead you through the process of making each document you choose, and before you know it, the job will be done.

With Quicken WillMaker Plus, you can create a wide range of documents to help you plan your estate, including a will, living trust, health care directive (living will), and durable power of attorney for finances. We explain each document in detail as you make it, providing lots of help along the way. The program also includes a number of forms that will help the person you've chosen to wrap up your estate (your executor); you can inform your loved ones that these forms will be available on your computer when the time comes.

Finally, we provide many forms that you can use to accomplish a variety of other personal or financial tasks, such as terminating a joint credit card account or making a legal agreement with your child care provider. The rest of this section introduces each form you can make with Quicken WillMaker Plus.

Congratulations for deciding to get your legal affairs in order. Relax and take your time as you select and prepare the documents that are best for you.

Icons Used in This Legal Manual

Throughout the book, the following symbols will help you along.

 Take advantage of an important tip.

 Slow down and consider a critical issue or potential problem.

 Consider talking with an estate planning lawyer.

 You may be able to skip some material that doesn't apply to you.

 Look for related information in another part of this manual.

 Go to a source outside this manual for more information about the particular issue or topic discussed in the text.

A. Using Quicken WillMaker Plus to Plan Your Estate

Estate planning is the process of arranging for what will happen to your property when you die. (Whatever you own at your death is called your estate.) It can also involve making arrangements for the care of your young children in the event of your death, planning for your own care in case someday you can't make decisions on your own and taking steps to avoid probate court proceedings at your death. If you have a large amount of property, you may also be concerned with the bite that federal estate tax may take at your death.

Quicken WillMaker Plus can help you with all of these issues, and a few others as well. What follows is a discussion of the estate planning documents you can create with Quicken WillMaker Plus, so you can see what they accomplish and decide whether or not they fit your situation. Along the way, we'll point out other estate planning strategies you might want to look into.

1. Wills and Basic Trusts

Perhaps the most essential reason to set up an estate plan is to have some say about who gets your property when you die. To accomplish that goal, you need a will or a trust. You can make either one with Quicken WillMaker Plus.

If you don't use a will, trust or other legal method to transfer your property when you die, state law determines what happens to your possessions. (See Chapter 2, Section B.)

a. What Wills and Basic Trusts Can Do

When you make a will or basic trust with Quicken WillMaker Plus, you can specify who will inherit your property. You can also:

- name alternates, in case your first choices die before you do
- choose someone you trust to oversee the distribution of your property after your death, and
- name a trusted adult to manage the property that a child or young adult inherits from you. (We give you several ways to handle this; they're explained in Chapter 7.)

Property That Doesn't Pass Through a Will or Trust

You cannot use a will or trust to leave certain kinds of assets, including:

- bank accounts for which you have named a pay-on-death beneficiary
- life insurance proceeds (they go to the beneficiary you named in the policy)
- stocks and bonds for which you have named a transfer-on-death beneficiary
- property owned as "community property with right of survivorship," which automatically goes to the survivor when one co-owner dies
- property owned in joint tenancy or tenancy by the entirety (it automatically goes to the surviving owners at your death), and
- individual retirement accounts (IRAs, 401(k) plans) and certain pension funds (they go to the beneficiary you named in forms provided by the account custodian).

If you live in the state of Washington, however, there is an exception to this general rule. See Chapter 5, Section A.

b. Comparing Wills and Basic Trusts

Both wills and basic living trusts let you leave your property to the people you want to inherit it. You can revoke or change a will or living trust at any time, for any reason, before you die.

The big difference is that assets left in trust don't have to go through probate court proceedings at your death. This is because when you create a living trust, you must transfer ownership of the designated property to yourself as "trustee" of the trust. During your lifetime, you still have control over all the property transferred to your living trust and can do what you want with it—sell it, spend it or give it away. Then, after your death, the person you named to take over as trustee distributes the property to the family and friends you named.

Why avoid probate? In a nutshell, because for most families it's a waste of time and money. It typically takes from nine to 18 months to file a deceased person's will with the court, gather the assets, pay debts and taxes and eventually distribute what is left as the will directs. Fees for attorneys, appraisers, accountants and probate court can reduce by about 5% the amount left for survivors to inherit. Unless relatives are fighting over who gets what, or there are big claims against the estate, a court-supervised process is seldom necessary.

Making a living trust involves more paperwork than making a will, because you must transfer ownership of the property to yourself as trustee and conduct future personal business in the name of the trust. But there is no need to file a separate tax return for the trust. All transactions, such as the sale of trust property at a profit, are reported on your personal income tax return.

A trust also offers a way that the trust property can be taken care of if someday you can't handle it yourself. If you become incapacitated, the person you appointed in your trust to take over after your death can step in and manage trust property. If you don't have a trust, close family members may have to go to court to get that kind of authority. (You can also arrange for property

management in a durable power of attorney for finances, discussed in Chapter 22.)

A will can do one important thing that a living trust can't: let you name someone (called a personal guardian) to raise your young children in the unlikely event that neither you nor the other parent is available.

Another difference that may matter to you: Unlike wills, living trusts are not made public at your death.

For more detailed discussions of wills and trusts, see Chapters 2 and 13.

What Wills and Trusts Can Do

	Will	Basic Living Trust	AB Living Trust
Avoid probate		x	x
Reduce estate tax			x
Keep your estate plan confidential		x	x
Set up management of property for minors	x	x	x
Arrange for management of some or all of your property if you become incapacitated		x	x
Appoint guardian to raise young children if you can't	x		

Quicken WillMaker Plus's basic trust avoids probate but has no effect on estate taxes. If you think your estate may be large enough to owe federal estate taxes, check out the "AB Trust," discussed below.

c. Choosing Between a Will and a Basic Living Trust

Many people create both a will and a living trust. It's common to use a living trust to leave only some assets and leave the rest by will or by another probate-avoidance method. In fact, even if you make a living trust, you'll still want to make a simple back-up will to handle property you don't get around to transferring to the trust.

Here are some factors to think about when you're deciding whether the centerpiece of your estate plan should be a will or a living trust:

- **Your age.** If you're under 60 and healthy, it often makes sense to prepare a will, use simple probate-avoidance devices such as joint tenancy or pay-on-death bank accounts for some property and leave the more complicated estate planning until later.
- **The size of your estate.** The bigger your estate, the bigger the potential probate cost and the less likely that your estate will qualify for simplified probate proceedings (discussed in Chapter 13). Often it makes good sense to concentrate energy on seeing that major assets, such as real estate or business assets, are owned in a way that will avoid probate.
- **The type of property you own.** You don't need a trust to avoid probate for assets like your bank and retirement accounts—it's a matter of filling out beneficiary forms that your bank or retirement plan administrator can give you. But transferring real estate outside of the probate process usually involves making a living trust. This process may well be worth the work, but there is more effort required—the living trust will have no effect unless you transfer title of your property to yourself as trustee of your living trust.

2. The Estate Tax-Reducing AB Trust

The second kind of trust you can make with Quicken WillMaker Plus is an "AB" or bypass trust, which lets married couples avoid both probate and estate tax.

Estate tax is not a concern for most people. The tax is levied on the property you own at your death—but a large amount of property is exempt from taxation. For deaths occurring in 2006, that amount is $2 million. The exemption amount is scheduled to keep rising until 2010, when the estate tax vanishes completely. But there's another wrinkle: Unless Congress reauthorizes these changes, the estate tax will automatically reappear in 2011, with an exempt amount of $1 million.

Although all this uncertainty makes effective tax planning a near-impossible challenge for the rich, most people don't need to worry about it. If you expect to die leaving less than $1 million in taxable assets, you can forget about the estate tax. It won't be an issue. (For more about whether or not an AB trust is for you, see Chapter 14.)

If you're married, estate tax is most likely to be an issue when the second spouse dies. (When the first spouse dies, everything left to the survivor passes tax-free.) But if the second spouse owns all the couple's property, and it's worth more than the estate tax exemption, estate tax will be due. If that's the case, it's worth doing some tax planning, because the tax is steep.

With an AB trust, you leave property first to your spouse (in trust, with certain restrictions) and then to your children. Because the second spouse never legally owns the deceased spouse's property, her estate won't owe tax on it at her death. With a special kind of AB trust called a disclaimer trust, the surviving spouse decides, after the first spouse dies, whether or not to create the tax-saving trust. A disclaimer trust can be useful for couples who aren't sure whether or not estate tax will be a concern for the surviving spouse. AB trusts are discussed in detail in Chapter 17.

3. Durable Power of Attorney for Finances

It's a good idea for almost everyone with property or an income to sign a durable power of attorney for finances. It's particularly important, however, if you fear that health problems may make it impossible for you to handle your financial matters.

Making a durable power of attorney ensures that someone you trust will be on hand to manage the many practical, financial tasks that will arise if you become incapacitated. For example, bills must be paid, bank deposits must be made and someone must handle insurance and benefits paperwork. Many other matters may need attention as well, from property repairs to managing investments or a small business. In most cases, a durable power of attorney for finances is the best way to take care of tasks like these. See Chapter 22 for more information.

4. Health Care Directives

If you're concerned about the kinds of medical treatment you may receive at the end of your life, and other issues surrounding dying a natural death, you may want a living will, known in most states as a health care directive. (Despite the confusingly similar names, living wills are not related to either wills or living trusts, the two documents most commonly used to pass property at death.)

In conjunction with making a health care directive, you may also pick a trusted person (not necessarily the same one you pick to manage your finances) to make sure your health care wishes are carried out. Depending on your state's law, you may appoint this person in the same document you use to express your wishes or in a separate document called a durable power of attorney for health care.

Although many people make health care directives or powers of attorney for the first time when they are older or become ill, creating a directive is a good idea for anyone. Every day, people are injured in accidents and wind up in hospitals, and if they haven't made their wishes clear, confusion and disagreement may make tough circumstances even tougher for close family members.

You can make these documents, tailored to your state's laws, with Quicken WillMaker Plus. See Chapter 23.

5. Final Arrangements

As you go through the process of creating a will, a living trust or other estate planning documents, your thoughts may turn to how your family will pay for your funeral or other issues surrounding what will happen to you after your death.

With the Quicken WillMaker Plus Final Arrangements document, you can let your loved ones know what kind of disposition (burial or cremation) you want, the commemorative ceremony you have in mind and whether you have already made any arrangements for organ donation. The level of detail is entirely up to you—give your general wishes or specific instructions. You can also choose someone to oversee your wishes.

For more information on the Final Arrangements document, see Chapter 24.

6. Information for Caregivers and Survivors

Finally, you may want to complete Quicken WillMaker Plus's "Information for Caregivers and Survivors" form. With this document, you can provide a comprehensive guide to the details of your life—from information about your bank accounts to people you want contacted in the event of your illness or death—for the person who will care for you in the event of your incapacity or who will deal with your estate after your death.

To prepare this form, the program will systematically walk you through the particulars of your life, asking you about many items, including things your loved ones may not know about—for example, what bank accounts you have, who your doctor is and whether you have life insurance. The result of this interview will be a document that will greatly aid those who need to care for you or manage your estate.

B. Documents for Executors

Quicken WillMaker Plus contains a number of documents you can use if you are named as someone's executor—and you can help your own executor by letting him or her know that these forms are available on your computer when they're needed.

An executor, sometimes called a personal representative. is the person you name in your will to take legal responsibility for safeguarding and handling your property after you die, seeing that debts and taxes are paid and distributing what is left to your beneficiaries as your will directs. If someone dies without naming an executor, a court will appoint someone to take the job. This person is most often called an "administrator."

What follows is a description of each of the documents for executors that you can make with Quicken WillMaker Plus.

1. Executor's Checklist

If you have been named the executor of an estate, you'll want to know what kind of tasks you are expected to perform. The Executor's Checklist tells you what you must do.

Every estate (and state) is different. An executor's duties are different for every estate. The tasks depend on the size of the estate, the kinds of property the deceased owned and other factors, such as the needs and expectations of the family. State laws governing the administration of estates also vary. Use the Executor's Checklist as a guide, tailoring it to your situation. For a more thorough guide to an executor's duties, see *The Executor's Guide: Settling a Loved One's Estate or Trust*, by Mary Randolph (Nolo).

2. Executor's Letter to Financial Institution

If you are the executor or administrator of someone's estate, your tasks include locating and making an inventory of all of the deceased person's property. One category of property you must investigate is bank and other financial accounts held by the deceased. You can use this form to write to financial institutions to find out what accounts or loans the deceased had with that institution, as well as to learn what those accounts were worth at the time of death.

3. Affidavit of Domicile

An Affidavit of Domicile (sometimes called an Affidavit of Residence) is one of the documents used by an executor to transfer ownership of stock or other securities from the name of the deceased person to the new owner. The purpose of the Affidavit of Domicile is to establish the state of residence of the stockholder (in this case, the deceased).

4. Employee Death Benefits Letter

As an executor, one of your duties will be to contact each of the deceased person's former employers to find out whether the estate or survivors are entitled to any death benefits. You can use Quicken WillMaker Plus's Employee Death Benefits Letter to request the information you need.

5. Life Insurance Claim Form Request

Before a life insurance company will pay the proceeds on a policy, it will ask the beneficiary to fill out a claim form that provides information about the beneficiary. The claim form verifies that the person making the claim is the proper beneficiary under the policy.

Use the Request for Life Insurance Claim Form to provide the life insurance company with the information it needs before it will send out an insurance claim form.

6. Life Insurance Request for Proceeds Letter

A life insurance company will pay the proceeds of a policy only after it receives confirmation that the insured person has died. The company also needs to verify that the person requesting the proceeds is the beneficiary who is entitled to receive the benefits under the terms of the policy. That's why you must complete and submit its claim form with a cover letter like this one.

7. Notice to Vehicle Insurance Company of Death

As the executor for someone who owned (or co-owned) an insured vehicle, you will want to be added as a "named insured" to the vehicle insurance policy as soon as possible. This status will give you all the protections and rights that the deceased person had under the policy. It will also give you peace of mind as you manage and care for the vehicle in your role as the executor, and it will ensure that any payments from the insurance company go jointly to you and any other people insured by the policy.

8. Notice to Homeowners' Insurance Company of Death

As with vehicles (above), you will want to be added as a "named insured" to the deceased person's homeowners' insurance policy. This will give you all the rights that the deceased person had under the policy, and it will ensure that any payments from the insurance company go jointly to you as the executor and any other individuals insured under the policy. It will also give you peace of mind as you manage and care for the home and its contents.

9. Notice to Creditor of Death

Use this form to notify each of the deceased person's creditors of the death and to close the deceased person's credit accounts.

10. Notice to Stop Social Security Payments After Death

If a deceased person was receiving Social Security benefits, the executor must notify the Social Security Administration of the death and return checks issued for the month of death and thereafter.

Complete this form to provide the Social Security Administration with the required notice.

11. General Notice of Death

If you are handling the estate of someone who has died, you may want to notify businesses and organizations of the death. For example, you might want to notify charities to which the deceased person has made regular donations. You can use this letter to inform anyone who might need to know of the death.

Requesting Birth or Death Certificates

As you fulfill your duties as executor or carry out other tasks, you may need to obtain copies of a death or birth certificate. It's usually easy to find forms and instructions online. Many county websites offer birth and death certificate request forms that you can print out and send; others allow you to submit your request electronically and pay by credit card. To find out your options, go to the official website of the county where the birth or death occurred. You can usually find it by using this formula, substituting the state postal abbreviation for "XX": www.co .[COUNTY_NAME]. [XX].us. For example, you can find the website for King County, Washington at www.co.king.wa.us.

C. Forms for Home and Family

Quicken WillMaker Plus provides a range of forms you can use to take care of your loved ones, pets and property. For example, there are authorizations you can use to give someone else permission to take care of your child, and agreements you can complete to arrange for home pet care. Here are descriptions of each of the forms for your home and family.

1. Child Care Agreement

If you want to hire someone to care for your children in your home, you should prepare a child care agreement. Your child care provider can be either live in (an au pair or nanny) or live out (a babysitter), part time or full time.

Quicken WillMaker Plus's child care agreement allows you to spell out the exact responsibilities of the position and to specify the child care provider's hours, amount and schedule of payment, benefits and other important aspects of the job.

2. Child Care Instructions

Use this form to provide important information for babysitters and child care providers such as names and phone numbers of doctors and emergency contacts, and instructions about meals, naps and other details of your child's care.

3. Authorization for Minor's Medical Treatment

Creating a medical care authorization allows another adult to authorize necessary medical or dental treatment for your child if he or she is injured or becomes ill while under the care of another adult—for example, while playing on a sports team or staying with a babysitter.

4. Authorization for Foreign Travel With Minor

If your young child will be traveling outside the United States with someone other than his or her parent or legal guardian, you should prepare an authorization for foreign travel. The form provides necessary proof that you have consented to the travel.

5. Temporary Guardianship Authorization for Care of Minor

If you leave your child in the care of another adult for a few days, weeks or months, you should authorize the caretaker to make any necessary decisions about your child's medical, educational and other care. You can do this by preparing a temporary guardianship authorization.

6. Elder Care Agreement

Quicken WillMaker Plus's elder care agreement is for people who wish to sign an agreement with an elder care provider who will take care of their older parent(s) or other elderly relative(s) at home. The agreement allows you to spell out the exact responsibilities of the position and to specify the worker's hours, amount and schedule of payment, benefits and other important aspects of the job.

7. Pet Care Agreement

If you're going on a trip or will otherwise be unable to care for your pet for a period of time, you might leave your animal in the care of a friend, relative or neighbor. If you do so, it's prudent to prepare this written agreement setting out clear instructions for your pet's care and clarifying each party's responsibilities and expectations.

8. Housekeeping Services Agreement

If you hire someone to clean or take care of your house on a regular basis, you can use Quicken WillMaker Plus's housekeeping services agreement. The agreement allows you to spell out the exact responsibilities of the position and to specify the housekeeper's hours, benefits and other details.

9. Housesitting Instructions

Use this form to provide detailed housesitting instructions for a person who will care for your home while you are away. You can specify your wishes about your plants and garden, newspapers and mail, telephone calls, appliances and equipment, lights and security, tools and supplies, vehicles, and other matters. You can also include important information such as how you can be reached while you are away and whom the housesitter can contact for help in your absence.

10. Authorization to Drive a Motor Vehicle

Lending your vehicle to a friend or even a relative isn't always as simple as handing over the keys. If the person who borrows your car is pulled over by the police or is involved in an accident, he or she will want to quickly prove that you agreed to the use. Otherwise, the driver may be detained while police investigate whether the car is stolen.

This simple authorization takes just a few minutes to complete, and it provides important legal proof that you've given someone else permission to drive your vehicle. The form is designed for a car, but it will work fine for a motorcycle, truck or other motor vehicle such as a motorboat.

D. Personal Finance and Consumer Forms

Quicken WillMaker Plus provides a number of forms to help you with basic finance and consumer matters. There are forms to use if you need to borrow or lend money, letters to help you keep your credit in good shape and a few other documents to help with financial tasks—such as a power of attorney you can use to have someone take care of financial transactions if you're unavailable. Here's a little more information about each form.

1. General Bill of Sale for Personal Property

Use this form to record the terms of the sale of personal property, such as a computer, a bicycle or a guitar. When you sell an item with this written bill of sale, you reduce the chance of a dispute arising after the sale.

2. Special (Limited) Power of Attorney for Finances

A limited power of attorney for finances lets you appoint someone (called your "attorney-in-fact") to help you with one or more clearly defined tasks involving your finances or property. For example, you may want to name someone to monitor certain investments for you while you are on vacation —and sell them if necessary. Or you may need someone to sign business or legal papers for you while you are unavailable. This form lets you temporarily delegate authority to someone you trust.

3. Revocation of Power of Attorney

If you've made a power of attorney, you can change your mind and cancel it at any time. Use this notice of revocation to put an end to any power of attorney, including a durable power—that is, one that is designed to remain in effect even after you become incapacitated.

4. Promissory Notes

If you are borrowing or lending money, you should create a promissory note. Like an I.O.U., a promissory note records the terms of the loan, including the period of repayment and the interest rate (if interest will be charged), as well as the borrower's promise to pay back the loan. Quicken WillMaker Plus offers four different kinds of promissory notes.

Installment payments. This type of promissory note requires the borrower to make the same monthly payment for a specified number of months. You can choose whether or not the borrower will pay interest on the loan.

Balloon payment. This promissory note requires the borrower to pay the same amount of money each month for a specified number of months, followed by a large balloon payment at the end of the repayment period. The borrower must pay interest on the loan.

Payments of interest only. With this type of note, the borrower pays only the interest on the loan each month for a specified number of months, with a balloon payment of the principal and any remaining interest at the end of the loan term.

One lump-sum payment. As the name indicates, this note requires the borrower to make a just one payment on a specified date. You can choose whether the borrower will pay interest on the loan.

5. Security Agreement for Borrowing Money

Use this form if you are borrowing or lending money and the borrower agrees to provide the lender with a security interest as collateral for the loan. This security agreement allows the borrower to offer tangible personal property as collateral—that is, physical items of property other than real estate, such as a car, jewelry or furniture.

6. Request for Credit Report

It's important to regularly review your credit report to be sure it's up to date and free of errors. Send this form to any credit reporting agency to request a copy of your credit file.

7. Request Correction of Credit Report

A clean credit report is essential if you want to qualify for a loan or other credit, rent an apartment or maybe even get a job. Using this form, you can ask a credit bureau to fix any mistakes in your credit file, including:

- incorrect personal information
- credit card or other accounts that don't belong to you
- incorrect account status or history
- information that's too old to be reported
- unauthorized credit inquiries, and
- any other errors.

8. Request Correction of Credit Report: Follow-Up

If you've asked a credit bureau to correct mistakes in your credit report using Quicken WillMaker Plus's Request Correction of Credit Report or another form, you may need to follow up to get the action you want. If more than 30 days have passed since you made your request, you can complete this letter to prompt the credit bureau to take care of your request.

9. Request Correction of Creditor's Records

To clean up your credit record, you should first ask the major credit bureaus to correct any mistakes on your credit report. You can do this with Quicken WillMaker Plus's Request Correction of Credit Report.

If you've already asked a credit bureau to correct your file, and the credit bureau tells you that the creditor reporting the information insists that it is accurate, you will need to contact the creditor directly. Use this letter to make a complaint to the creditor and enlist its assistance in correcting your credit record.

10. Creditor Verification Letter

When trying to remove incorrect information from your credit file, you may hit a roadblock if a credit bureau tells you that the creditor reporting the information insists that the information is accurate and complete. If this happens to you, the first thing to do is contact the creditor associated with the inaccurate information and demand that it tell the credit bureau to remove the information or correct any errors. You can do this using Quicken WillMaker Plus's Request Correction of Creditor's Records.

After that, you may get a letter from the creditor, agreeing that the information is incorrect and should be removed. You should send a copy of the creditor's letter to the credit bureau along with this creditor verification letter. The verification letter is a cover letter that confirms the creditor's statement that the information in your credit report is not correct.

11. Dispute Credit Card Charge

If you use a major credit card to purchase an item that you never receive or that turns out to be defective, you can use this letter to inform the credit card company that you will not pay the charge. Before you complete the letter, Quicken WillMaker Plus explains when you are legally permitted to refuse to pay a credit card charge.

12. Notice to Terminate Joint Credit Card Account

If you are separating from or divorcing a spouse or partner, you will want to immediately close any joint credit card accounts. This involves notifying all creditors of your request to close the accounts so that no new charges can be made. Use this form to accomplish this task.

13. Notice to Put Name on "Do Not Call" List

The best way to stop telemarketers from calling you is to enter your telephone number in the national "do not call" registry, available at www.ftc.gov/donotcall. Telemarketers are prohibited from calling numbers listed in the registry. Those who violate the law are subject to stiff fines—up to $11,000 for each offending phone call. A number of states have "do not call" lists as well. You may want to add your number to your state's registry, if it offers one.

Some companies are exempt from the federal registry's rules. These include long-distance telephone companies, airlines, banks and credit unions. Organizations soliciting money for political organizations or charities are also exempt. But even these businesses and organizations are required to keep their own lists of consumers who say that they do not want to be called again. If you ask a company not to call you, but you get another call within 12 months, you can sue for up to $500.

If you wish to contact a business or organization to request that they cease calling you, you can use this "Notice to Put Name on 'Do Not Call' List." If necessary, you can use this form to prove that the company violated the law by calling you after you asked them not to. End every unwanted call by stating, "Put me on your 'do not call' list." Then follow up by mailing the telemarketer this form that states the same thing, thereby generating irrefutable evidence of your request that they cease calling.

14. Cancel Membership or Subscription

Use this form to cancel a magazine subscription or your membership in an organization. The form allows you to state the reason for the cancelation (perhaps you are no longer interested in the subject or cause), although you do not have to provide a reason. You can also use this form to request a refund of your membership or subscription fee, if you believe it is warranted. ■

About Wills

Making a will is an excellent way to ensure that your plans for leaving property to family, friends and organizations of your choice are carried out after you die. You can efficiently and safely write your own legal will using the Quicken WillMaker Plus program. But before you start, it is a good idea to read this chapter and Chapter 3, which explain generally what a will can accomplish and how you can use Quicken WillMaker Plus to meet your needs.

A. Legal Requirements

For a will to be legally valid, both you—the person making the will—and the will itself must meet some technical requirements.

1. Who Can Make a Will

There are a few legal requirements that control who can make a valid will. Before you start your computer and get the Quicken WillMaker Plus program going, make sure you qualify to make a will in the eyes of the law.

a. Age

To make a will, you must either be:
- at least 18 years old, or
- living in a state that permits people under 18 to make a will if they are married, in the military or otherwise considered legally emancipated.

b. Mental Competence

You must also be of sound mind to prepare a valid will. While this sounds like a subjective standard, the laws generally require that you must:
- know what a will is, what it does and that you are making one
- understand the relationship between you and the people who would normally be provided for in your will, such as a spouse or children
- understand the kind and quantity of property you own, and
- be able to decide how to distribute your belongings.

This threshold of mental competence is not hard to meet. Very few wills are successfully challenged based on the charge that the person making the will was mentally incompetent. It is not enough to show that the person was forgetful or absentminded.

To have a probate court declare a will invalid usually requires proving that the testator was totally overtaken by the fraud or undue influence of another person—and that person then benefited from the wrongdoing by becoming entitled to a large amount of money or property under the will.

Interestingly, the great majority of undue influence contests are filed against attorneys who draw up wills in which they are named to take clients' property. If the person making the will was very old, ill, senile or otherwise in poor mental condition when he or she made the will, it is obviously easier to convince a judge that undue influence occurred.

If a contest seems possible. If you have any serious doubts about your ability to meet the legal requirements for making a will, or you believe your will is likely to be contested by another person for any reason, consult an experienced lawyer. (See Chapter 25.)

2. Will Requirements

State law determines whether a will made by a resident of the state is valid. And a will that is valid in the state where it is made is valid in all other states.

Contrary to what many people believe, a will need not be notarized to be legally valid. But adding a notarized document to the will verifying that the will was signed and witnessed can be helpful when it comes time to file the will in probate court. This option is available in all but a handful of states. (See Chapter 10, Section B2.)

There are surprisingly few legal restrictions and requirements in the will-making process. In most states, a will must:

- include at least one substantive provision — either giving away some property or naming a guardian to care for minor children who are left without parents
- be signed and dated by the person making it
- be witnessed by at least two other people (three in Vermont) who are not named to take property under the will, and
- be clear enough so that others can understand what the testator intended. Nonsensical, legalistic language such as: "I hereby give, bequeath and devise" is both unwise and unnecessary.

Handwritten and Oral Wills

In about half the states, unwitnessed, handwritten wills—called holographic wills—are legally valid. And a few states accept the historical holdover of oral wills under very limited circumstances, such as when a mortally wounded soldier utters last wishes.

But handwritten and oral wills are fraught with possible legal problems. Most obviously, after your death, it may be difficult to prove that your unwitnessed, handwritten document was actually written by you and that you intended it to be your will. And it may be almost impossible to prove the authenticity of an oral will.

A properly signed, witnessed will is much less vulnerable to challenge by anyone claiming it was forged or fabricated. If need be, witnesses can later testify in court that the person whose name is on the will is the same person who signed it, and that making the will was a voluntary and knowing act.

B. Dying Without a Will

If you die without a valid will, money and other property you own at death will be divided and distributed to others according to your state's intestate succession laws. These laws divide all property among the relatives who are considered closest to you according to a set formula—and completely exclude friends and charities.

These legal formulas often do not mirror most people's wishes. For example, dividing property according to intestate succession laws is often unsatisfactory if you are married and have no children, because most state laws require your spouse to share your property with your parents. The situation is even worse for unmarried couples. Except in a few states (see Chapter 4, Section E4), unmarried partners receive nothing. And even in the states that offer exceptions, benefits aren't automatic—eligible couples must register their partnerships with the state.

Also, if you have minor children, another important reason to make a will is to name a personal guardian to care for them. This is an important concern of most parents, who worry that their children will be left without a caretaker if both die or are unavailable. (See Chapter 4, Section F.) Intestate succession laws do not deal with the issue of who will take care of your children. When you don't name a guardian in your will, it is left up to the courts and social service agencies to find and appoint a personal guardian.

C. Making Basic Decisions About Your Will

Making a will is not difficult, but it is undeniably a serious and sobering process. Before you begin, get organized and focus on these important questions:

- What do you own? (See Chapter 52.)
- Whom would you like to get your property? (See Chapter 6.)
- If you have minor children, who is the best person to care for them, and who is best suited to manage property you leave them? (See Chapter 4 and Chapter 7.)
- Whom should you name to see that your property is distributed according to your wishes after your death? (See Chapter 8.)

This manual offers guidance on how to use Quicken WillMaker Plus to give legal effect to your decisions in all of these areas. The ultimate choices, however, are up to you.

D. Other Ways to Leave Property

A will is not the only way—and in some cases, not the best way—to transfer ownership of your property to another person upon your death. For a discussion of the different ways to pass property after your death, see Chapter 1, Section A.

E. Making Your Own Will

As a way to decide who gets your property, the will has been around in substantially the same form for about 500 years. For the first 450 years, self-help was the rule and lawyer assistance the exception. When this country was founded, and even during the Civil War, it was highly unusual for a person to hire a lawyer to formally set out what should be done with his or her property. However, in the past 50 years, the legal profession has scored a public relations coup by convincing many people that writing a will without a lawyer is like doing your own brain surgery.

In truth, the hardest part of making a will is figuring out what property you own and whom you want to get it when you die—questions you can answer best. Quicken WillMaker Plus provides you with step-by-step legal guidance along the way.

But you may have a question about your particular situation that Quicken WillMaker Plus does not answer. Or perhaps you have a very large estate—worth over $1.5 million—and want to engage in some sophisticated tax planning. Or you may simply be comforted by having a lawyer give your Quicken WillMaker Plus will a once-over. Whenever you have concerns such as these or simply feel that you are in over your head, it may be wise to consult someone who has knowledge and experience in wills and estate planning. (See Chapter 25.)

Using a Computer for the Job

The computer is an ideal tool for assisting informed consumers with making simple wills. It will never betray your confidences or urge you to do anything you do not feel is right. And it will not charge you a cent to revise your will should your needs change.

The reason computers are such efficient will-making tools is that writing wills involves little more than systematically collecting answers to well-defined questions, then translating the answers into language developed over hundreds of years.

Nolo's will-making program, which has been in wide and successful use for two decades, prompts you to answer the necessary questions—and produces a will that fits your circumstances and is legal in your state. ■

Chapter 3

About Quicken WillMaker Plus Wills

Because they reflect people's intentions of how and to whom they want to leave their property, wills can be as complex and intricate as life. While state laws broadly regulate the procedures for valid will making, you are generally free to write a will to meet your needs. Of course, this freedom can be dizzying to those who are not used to wading in the muck of legal documents.

Quicken WillMaker Plus offers considerable guidance, so that the task of will making will be understandable and legal rules will not be trampled. The program works by having you systematically answer questions. As you will soon see, you either already have enough information to answer them easily, or you can quickly get it.

Keeping track of important information. As you prepare to make your will, you may wish to make a list of financial and estate planning advisers that you have consulted in the past. It may also be a good time to organize other estate planning documents—such as your living trust documents or life insurance policy— and to record their locations so that others will know where to find them.

With Quicken WillMaker Plus you can make an "Information for Caregivers and Survivors" form to help with this task. With this document, you can provide a comprehensive guide to the details of your life—ranging from information about your property and your financial accounts to the names and addresses of people you want contacted in the event of your death—for people who will care for you if you ever become incapacitated and those who will wind up your affairs after death. To find out more, click on the Document List button and select Information for Caregivers and Survivors from the list.

A. What You Can Do With a Quicken WillMaker Plus Will

This chapter gives you a quick survey of what you can and cannot do with the Quicken WillMaker Plus program. Each topic is discussed in greater detail, both in the help screens that run with the program and in other chapters in the manual.

1. Tailor Your Will to Your Needs

Quicken WillMaker Plus provides unique guidance and options for users based on the state in which they live, their marital status, whether they have children and whether the children are minors. Recognizing that some people have very simple wishes for leaving their property while others' plans are more complex, Quicken WillMaker Plus lets the user choose from among several approaches designed to meet these different needs. For instance, a married person may choose to:

- leave all property to his or her spouse
- leave most property to a spouse, with several specific property items going to people he or she names, or
- divvy property among many different people and organizations.

(See Chapter 6.)

2. Name a Guardian to Care for Your Children

You may use Quicken WillMaker Plus to name a personal guardian to care for your minor children until they reach age 18, in case there is no natural or adoptive parent to handle these duties. You may name the same guardian for all your children, or different guardians for different children. (It is important, however, that both parents name the same person as guardian for any particular child;

see example below.) You will also have the opportunity to explain your choices in your will.

If your children need a guardian after your death, a court will formally review your choice. Your choice will normally be approved unless the person you name refuses to assume the responsibility or the court becomes convinced that the best interests of your children would be better served if they were left in the care of someone else. (See Chapter 4, Section F.)

> **EXAMPLE:** Millicent names her friend Vera to serve as personal guardian in the event that her husband, Frank, dies at the same time she does or is otherwise unavailable to care for their three children. Millicent and Frank die together in an earthquake. The court appoints Vera as personal guardian for all three children, since her ability to care for them has not been questioned.
>
> If Frank had written a will naming another person to serve as guardian, however, the court would have to choose between those nominated. For this reason, parents should choose the same people as personal guardians if that is possible.

3. Name Beneficiaries to Get Specific Property

Quicken WillMaker Plus lets you make an unlimited number of separate gifts—called specific bequests—of cash, personal property or real estate. You may choose to leave these bequests to your spouse, children, grandchildren or anyone else—including friends, business associates, charities or other organizations. (See Chapter 6.)

> **EXAMPLE:** Using Quicken WillMaker Plus, Marcia leaves her interest in the family home to her spouse Duane, her valuable coin col-

lection to one of her children, her boat to another child, her computer to a charity and $5,000 to her two aunts, in equal shares.

> **EXAMPLE:** Raymond, a lifelong bachelor, follows Quicken WillMaker Plus's directions and leaves his house to his favorite charity. He divides his personal possessions among 15 different relatives and friends.

> **EXAMPLE:** Darryl and Floyd have lived together for several years. Darryl wants to leave Floyd all of his property, which includes his car, time-share ownership in a condominium, a savings account and miscellaneous personal belongings. He can use Quicken WillMaker Plus to accomplish this.

4. Name Someone to Take All Remaining Property

If you have chosen an approach that lets you divvy your property by making specific bequests, Quicken WillMaker Plus also allows you to name people or organizations to take whatever property is left over after you have made the specific bequests. This property is called your residuary estate. (See Chapter 6, Section F.)

> **EXAMPLE:** Annie wants to make a number of small bequests to friends and charities but to leave the bulk of her property to her friend Maureen. She accomplishes this by using the specific bequest screens to make the small gifts, and then names Maureen as residuary beneficiary. There is no need for her to list the property that goes to Maureen. The very nature of the residuary estate is that the residuary beneficiary—in this case, Maureen—gets everything that is left over after the specific bequests are distributed.

5. Name Alternate Beneficiaries

Using Quicken WillMaker Plus, all beneficiaries you name take the property you leave them under your will only if they survive you by 45 days. The reason that Quicken WillMaker Plus imposes this 45-day rule is that you do not want to leave your property to a beneficiary who dies very shortly after you do, because that property will then be passed along to that person's inheritors. These beneficiaries are not likely to be the ones you would choose to receive your property.

To account for the possibility that your first choices of beneficiaries will not meet the survivorship requirement, Quicken WillMaker Plus allows you to name alternate beneficiaries for any specific bequests and for your residuary property. (See Chapter 6.)

Avoiding Legalese: Per Stirpes and Per Capita

"Per stirpes" and "per capita" are legal jargon for the way children inherit property in place of a deceased parent — for example, one of these terms might govern how a granddaughter would inherit property left to her mother under a will, if her mother died before the will maker. It's not necessary for your will to include these terms. In fact, it's better to avoid them, because they can be interpreted in different ways. Instead, your Quicken WillMaker Plus will lets you set out exactly whom you want to inherit your property, who will take the property if your first choice beneficiary doesn't survive you, and the shares that they will inherit.

6. Name a Manager for Children's Property

You may leave property to your own or other people's children. Or your young children may receive property from some other source. But at your death, property left to minors—especially cash or other liquid assets—will usually have to be managed by an adult until the minors turn 18. And in many cases, it may be most prudent to have property left to minors managed for them until they are even older.

Property management involves safeguarding and spending the property for the young person's education, health care and basic living needs; keeping good records of these expenditures; and seeing that income taxes are paid. Management ends at the age you specify in the will. What is left of the property is then distributed to the child.

Quicken WillMaker Plus allows you to name a trusted person—or, if no one is available, you can name an institution such as a bank or trust company—to manage property left to young beneficiaries. The management methods available are different from state to state. (See Chapter 7, Section D.)

Quicken WillMaker Plus also allows you to name a property guardian who will handle property that other people leave your children or property that you leave them outside of your will. (See Chapter 7, Section E.)

Providing for beneficiaries with special needs. It is common to set up management for property that will pass to a beneficiary who has a mental or physical disability, or who manages money poorly. The management provided under Quicken WillMaker Plus is not sufficiently detailed to provide adequately for people with disabilities or those with special problems such as spendthrift tendencies or substance abuse. If you need this type of management, consult an attorney who specializes in dealing with the needs of disabled people. (See Chapter 25.)

7. Cancel Debts Others Owe You

You can use Quicken WillMaker Plus to relieve any debtors who owe you money at your death from the responsibility of paying your survivors. All you need to do is specify the debts and the people who owe them. Quicken WillMaker Plus will then include a statement in your will canceling the debts. If a debt is canceled in this way, Quicken WillMaker Plus also automatically wipes out any interest that has accrued on it as of your death. (See Chapter 9, Section A.)

> **EXAMPLE:** Cynthia has lent $25,000 at 10% annual interest to her son George as a down payment on a house. She uses Quicken WillMaker Plus to cancel this debt. At Cynthia's death, George need not pay her estate the remaining balance of the loan, or the interest accrued on it.

8. Designate How Debts, Expenses and Taxes Are Paid

Quicken WillMaker Plus allows you to designate a particular source of money or other specific assets from which your executor should pay your debts, final expenses such as funeral and probate costs and any estate and inheritance taxes. (See Chapter 9, Section E.)

> **EXAMPLE:** Brent owns a savings account, a portfolio of stocks and bonds, an R.V. and two cars. He uses Quicken WillMaker Plus to make a will—leaving his R.V. and stocks and bonds to his nephew, his cars to his niece and his savings account to his favorite charity, River Friends. He also designates the savings account as the source of payment of his debts and expenses of probate. Under this arrangement, River Friends will receive whatever is left in the savings account after debts and expenses of probate have been paid.

> **EXAMPLE:** Calvin's estate is valued at over $1.5 million. It is likely that his estate will owe some federal estate taxes when he dies. He uses Quicken WillMaker Plus to specify that any estate tax he owes should be paid proportionately from all the property subject to the tax. If there is estate tax liability, the executor he designates will require that each of Calvin's beneficiaries pay part of the tax in the same proportion their bequest bears to the value of Calvin's estate as a whole.

9. Name an Executor

With Quicken WillMaker Plus, you can name an executor for your estate—that is, the property you own and leave at your death. This person or institution, called a personal representative in some states, will be responsible for making sure the provisions in your will are carried out and your property distributed as your will directs. Quicken WillMaker Plus also produces a letter to your executor that generally explains what the job requires.

The executor can be any competent adult. Commonly, people name a spouse or other close relative or friend or—for large estates or where no trusted person is able to serve—a financial institution such as a bank or savings and loan. You are free to name two or more people or institutions to share the job. (See Chapter 8.)

It is also wise to use Quicken WillMaker Plus to name an alternate executor in case your first choice becomes unable or unwilling to serve.

> **EXAMPLE:** Rick and Phyllis both use Quicken WillMaker Plus to complete wills naming each other as executor in case the other dies first. They both name Rick's father as an alternate executor to distribute their property in the event they die at the same time.

> **EXAMPLE:** Pat and Babs do not wish to burden their relatives with having to take care of their fairly considerable estate. Each names the Third National Bank as executor after checking that their estate is large enough so that this bank will be willing to take the job.

B. What You Cannot Do With a Quicken WillMaker Plus Will

Quicken WillMaker Plus allows you to produce a valid and effective will designed to meet most needs. But there are some restrictions built into the program. Some of the restrictions are designed to prevent you from writing in conditions that may not be legally valid. Others are intended to keep the program simple and easy to use.

1. Make Bequests With Conditions

You cannot make a bequest that will take effect only if a certain condition occurs—an if, and or but such as "$5,000 to John if he stops smoking." Such conditional bequests are confusing and usu-

ally require someone to oversee and supervise the beneficiaries to be sure they satisfy the conditions in the will. If you doubt this, consider that someone would have to constantly check up on John to make sure he never took a puff—and someone would have to wrench away his property if he ever got caught in the act.

So, to use Quicken WillMaker Plus, you must be willing to leave property to people outright; you cannot make them jump through hoops or change their behavior to get it.

> **Takers must survive by 45 days.** To ensure that property goes to people you want to have it, Quicken WillMaker Plus automatically imposes the condition that each of your beneficiaries must survive you by 45 days. If they do not survive you by that amount of time, the property you had slated for them will pass instead to the person or institution you have named as an alternate beneficiary, or it will go to the one you have named to take your residuary estate.

2. Write Joint Wills

In the past, it was common for a married couple who had an agreed scheme for how to distribute all their property to write one document together: a joint will. But time has shown that setup to be crawling with problems.

Quicken WillMaker Plus requires that each spouse make his or her own will, even if both agree about how their property is to be distributed. This limitation is not imposed to annoy people or defeat their intentions; there is solid legal reasoning behind it.

Joint wills are intended to prevent the surviving spouse from changing his or her mind about what to do with the property after the first spouse dies. The practical effect is to tie up the property for years in title and probate determinations—often until long after the second spouse dies. Also, many court battles are fought over whether the surviving spouse is legally entitled to revoke any part of the joint will.

There are still some lawyers who will agree to write joint wills for clients, but they do so in the face of the risk that such wills may become cumbersome or even found invalid in later court challenges. For these reasons, it is best for both spouses to write separate wills—a bit more time-consuming, perhaps, but a lot safer from a legal standpoint.

3. Explain the Reasons for Leaving Your Property

Most of the time, the act of leaving property to people—or choosing not to leave them anything—speaks for itself. Occasionally, however, people making wills want to explain to survivors the reasons they left property as they did. This might be the case, for example, if you opt to leave one of your two children more property than the other to equal out the loan you made during your lifetime to help one of them buy a house. Although the yearning to make such explanations is understandable, Quicken WillMaker Plus does not allow you to do it in your will, because of the risk that you might add legally confusing language to the document.

However, there is an easy and legally safe way to provide your heirs with explanations for your bequests. You can draft a letter that you can attach to your will, explaining your reasons for leaving property to some people—or not leaving it to others. (See Chapter 12.)

4. Name Coguardians for Children or Their Property

Quicken WillMaker Plus allows you to name one personal guardian to care for each of your minor children and one guardian to care for their property. While you may wish to choose different guardians for different children, you may not name two people to share the job of being a personal or property guardian. (See Chapter 7.)

At first glance, it may seem to be a good idea to divide up the job—naming two people or a married couple to agree to take on the responsibility of caring for your children or supervising their property if you die while they are still young. But a closer look reveals that naming coguardians often presents more problems than it solves.

For example, as life unwinds, the loving couple you named to jointly care for your children may divorce—making it impossible for them to be in the same room together, much less agree on the best way to raise a child. In such cases, courts are often called in to decide who is the most fitting guardian—a process that may be long, costly and very often heart-rending.

Review wills to avoid conflicts. People who jointly own property or have children together should review their wills together to be sure they do not provide conflicting information—such as each naming different guardians for the children.

5. Control Property After Death

Property given to others in a Quicken WillMaker Plus will must go to them as soon as you die. You cannot make a bequest by will with the property to be used for a person's life and then be given to a second person when the first person dies. Such an arrangement involves too many variables for both will makers and beneficiaries to handle. You will need to use more complex estate planning strategies to carry out this type of plan. (See Chapter 25.)

> **EXAMPLE:** Emory wants his grandchildren to get his house when he dies but wants his wife to have the right to live in the house until her death. Emory cannot use Quicken WillMaker Plus to accomplish this. Emory would have to leave his house in trust to his spouse for her life and then to his grandchildren upon his spouse's death.

6. Require a Bond for Executors or Property Managers

A bond is like an insurance policy that protects the beneficiaries in the unlikely event that the executor wrongfully spends or distributes estate property. Because the premium or fee that must be paid for a bond comes out of the estate—leaving less money for the beneficiaries—most wills for small or moderate estates do not require one.

Following this general practice, the will produced by the Quicken WillMaker Plus program does not require a bond. Instead, take care to appoint someone you know to be trustworthy.

C. A Look at a Quicken WillMaker Plus Will

You may find it helpful to take a look at a Quicken WillMaker Plus will, but do not be alarmed if the sample will does not match the one you produce. Your Quicken WillMaker Plus will is tailored to your property, circumstances and state laws. Nearly every paragraph, or clause, of the will used as an example here is explained in the brackets following it.

Will of Sally K. Hanson

Part 1. Personal Information

I, Sally K. Hanson, a resident of the State of Texas, Big Sky County, declare that this is my will. My Social Security number is 123-45-6789.

Part 2. Revocation of Previous Wills

I revoke all wills and codicils that I have previously made.

[This provision makes clear that this is the will to be used—not any other wills or amendments to those wills, called codicils, that were made earlier. To prevent possible confusion, all earlier wills and codicils should also be physically destroyed.]

Part 3. Marital Status

I am married to David Lee Hanson.

[Here you identify your spouse if you are married. If you are not married, this provision will not appear in your will.]

Part 4. Children

I have the following children now living: Cosmos Hanson, John Hanson and Katrin Hanson.

[This part of your will should list all of your natural-born and adopted children; your stepchildren should not be included here. By naming all your children, you will prevent a child from claiming that he or she was accidentally overlooked in your will. It will also ward off later claims that any child is entitled to take a share of your property against your wishes.]

Part 5. Disposition of Property

All beneficiaries must survive me for 45 days to receive property under this will. As used in this will, the phrase survive me means to be alive or in existence as an organization on the 45th day after my death.

[This language means that to receive property under your will, a person must be alive for at least 45 days after your death. Otherwise, the property will go to whomever you named as an alternate. This language permits you to choose another way to leave your property if your first choice dies within a short time after you do.

This will clause also prevents the confusion associated with the simultaneous death of two spouses, when it is hard to tell who gets the property they have left to one other. Property left to a spouse who dies within 45 days of the first spouse, including a spouse who dies simultaneously, will go to the person or organization named as alternate.]

All personal and real property that I leave in this will shall pass subject to any encumbrances or liens placed on the property as security for the repayment of a loan or debt.

[This language explains that whoever gets any property under this will also gets the mortgage and other legal claims against the property, such as liens. And anyone who takes property that is subject to a loan, such as a car loan, gets the debt as well as the property.]

If I leave property to be shared by two or more beneficiaries, it shall be shared equally by them unless this will provides otherwise.

If I leave property to be shared by two or more beneficiaries, and any of them does not survive me, I leave his or her share to the others equally unless this will provides otherwise for that share.

[This language provides that for all specific and residuary bequests that are made to two or more people, the property shall be split equally among the people, unless the bequest itself says otherwise. If you want to give property to be split among people in unequal shares, you need to indicate that when you are describing the bequest by including the percentage share in parentheses after each beneficiary's name. Otherwise, it will be presumed that you wanted the property split equally.]

"Specific bequest" refers to a gift of specifically identified property that I leave in this will.

"Residuary estate" means all property I own at my death that is subject to this will that does not pass under a specific bequest.

[These definitions are included so that you and your survivors are clear on their meanings when they appear later in your will.]

I leave $10,000 to Stephen Rose. If Stephen Rose does not survive me, I leave this property to Vera Reynolds.

[This language leaves a specific item of property—$10,000—to a named beneficiary, Stephen Rose. If Stephen Rose does not survive the testator, then Vera Reynolds will get the money.]

I leave my rare stamp collection to Frank Williams, William Williams and Katrina Williams-Post in the following shares: Frank Williams shall receive a 1/4 share. William Williams shall receive a 1/4 share. Katrina Williams-Post shall receive a 1/2 share.

[This language leaves a specific item of property—a stamp collection—to three people in unequal shares.]

I leave my collection of Nash cars to The Hayward City Auto Museum and Graham Healy in equal shares. If Graham Healy does not survive me, I leave his or her share of this property to Althea Simpson.

[This will leaves specific property to an organization and a person equally. Since the testator here was concerned only about providing for the possibility that the person would not survive to take the property, she named an alternate for him.]

I leave my residuary estate to my husband, David Lee Hanson.

[This clause gives the residuary estate—all property that does not pass under this will in specific bequests—to the testator's spouse. Your residuary estate may be defined differently depending on your plans for leaving your property.]

If David Lee Hanson does not survive me, I leave my residuary estate to Cosmos Hanson, John Hanson and Katrin Hanson in a children's pot trust to be administered under the children's pot trust provisions.

[If the person named here to take the residuary estate does not survive the testator, the residuary estate will pass to the three people named: the testator's children. The property will be put in one pot for all of the children to use as they mature. Specifics of how this pot trust operates are explained later in the will. Keep in mind that, in this example, the pot trust will come into being only if the testator's spouse does not survive the testator by at least 45 days.]

If all these children are age 18 or older at my death, my residuary estate shall be distributed to them directly in equal shares.

[This clause makes clear what should happen if the children are older than the age the testator specified the pot trust should end. In this case, no pot trust will be created; the children will get the property directly and divide it evenly.]

If any of these children do not survive me, I leave his or her share to the others equally.

[This clause explains that if any one of the three children here does not survive, the others will get the property directly and divide it evenly.]

If David Lee Hanson, Cosmos Hanson, John Hanson and Katrin Hanson all do not survive me, I leave my residuary estate to Claire Randolph.

Part 6. Custodianship Under the Uniform Transfers to Minors Act

All property left in this will to Claire Randolph shall be given to Mercer Randolph, to be held until Claire Randolph reaches age 21, as custodian for Claire Randolph under the Texas Uniform Transfers to Minors Act. If Mercer Randolph is unwilling or unable to serve as custodian of property left to Claire Randolph under this will, Lynn Randolph shall serve instead.

[This clause provides that all property left to the child named in the clause will be managed by the person named as the custodian until the child turns the age indicated. An alternate custodian is also named in case the first-choice custodian is unable or unwilling to serve when the time comes.]

Part 7. Children's Pot Trust

A.   Beneficiaries of Children's Pot Trust

Cosmos Hanson, John Hanson and Katrin Hanson shall be the beneficiaries of the children's pot trust provided for in this will. If a beneficiary survives me but dies before the children's pot trust terminates, that beneficiary's interest in the trust shall pass to the surviving beneficiaries of the children's pot trust.

B.   Trustee of Children's Pot Trust

Brian Uldrian shall serve as the trustee of the children's pot trust. If Brian Uldrian is unable or unwilling to serve, Roberta Uldrian shall serve instead.

C.   Administration of the Children's Pot Trust

The trustee shall manage and distribute the assets in the children's pot trust in the following manner.

The trustee may distribute trust assets as he or she deems necessary for a beneficiary's health, support, maintenance and education. Education includes, but is not limited to, college, graduate, postgraduate and vocational studies and reasonably related living expenses.

In deciding whether or not to make distributions, the trustee shall consider the value of the trust assets, the relative current and future needs of each beneficiary and each beneficiary's other income, resources and sources of support. In doing so, the trustee has the discretion to make distributions that benefit some beneficiaries more than others or that completely exclude others.

Any trust income that is not distributed by the trustee shall be accumulated and added to the principal.

D. Termination of the Children's Pot Trust

When the youngest surviving beneficiary of this children's pot trust reaches 18, the trustee shall distribute the remaining trust assets to the surviving beneficiaries in equal shares.

If none of the trust beneficiaries survives to the age of 18, the trustee shall distribute the remaining trust assets to my heirs at the death of the last surviving beneficiary.

Part 8. Individual Child's Trust

A. Beneficiaries and Trustees

All property left in this will to Vera Reynolds shall be held in a separate trust for Vera Reynolds until she reaches age 25. The trustee of the Vera Reynolds trust shall be Clarence Reynolds.

[This clause provides that all property given to the child named in the clause shall be held in trust—that is, managed strictly for the benefit of the child—by the person named as the trustee until the child turns the age indicated. An alternate trustee is also named in case the first choice trustee is unable or unwilling to serve when the time comes.]

B. Administration of an Individual Child's Trust

The trustee of an individual child's trust shall manage and distribute the assets in the trust in the following manner.

Until the trust beneficiary reaches the age specified for final distribution of the principal, the trustee may distribute some or all of the principal or net income of the trust as the trustee deems necessary for the child's health, support, maintenance and education. Education includes, but is not limited to, college, graduate, postgraduate and vocational studies and reasonable living expenses.

[This clause lets the trustee spend the trust principal and income for the child's general living, health and educational needs. The clause gives the trustee great latitude in how this is done and what amount is spent.]

In deciding whether or not to make a distribution to a beneficiary, the trustee may take into account the beneficiary's other income, resources and sources of support.

[This clause lets the trustee withhold the trust principal or income from the trust beneficiary if, in the trustee's opinion, the beneficiary has sufficient income from other sources.]

Any trust income that is not distributed by the trustee shall be accumulated and added to the principal.

[Every trust involves two types of property: the property in the trust—called the trust principal—and the income that is earned by investing the principal. This clause assures that the trustee must add to the trust principal any income that is earned on the principal, unless the income is distributed to the trust beneficiary.]

C. Termination of an Individual Child's Trust

An individual child's trust shall terminate as soon as one of the following events occurs:

- the beneficiary reaches the age stated above, in which case the trustee shall distribute the remaining principal and accumulated net income of the trust to the beneficiary

- the beneficiary dies, in which case the principal and accumulated net income of the trust shall pass under the beneficiary's will, or if there is no will, to his or her heirs, or

- the trust principal is exhausted through distributions allowed under these provisions.

[This clause sets out three events that may cause the trust to end. The first is when the minor or young adult reaches the age specified for the trust to end. If the trust ends for this reason, the minor or young adult gets whatever trust principal and accumulated income is left. The trust will also end if the minor or young adult dies before the age set for the trust to end. If the trust ends for this reason, the principal and income accumulated in the trust goes to whomever the young adult named in his or her will to get it or, if there is no will, to the minor or young adult's legal heirs—such as parents, brothers and sisters. A third occurrence that will cause the trust to end is when there is no trust principal left—or so little left that it's no longer financially feasible to maintain it.]

Part 9. General Trust Administration Provisions

All trusts established in this will shall be managed subject to the following provisions.

A. Bond

No bond shall be required of any trustee.

[The trustee will not be required to post bond to ensure that she carries out her duties faithfully.]

B. Court Supervision

It is my intent that any trust established in this will be administered independently of court supervision to the maximum extent possible under the laws of the state having jurisdiction over the trust.

[As a general rule, the management of a trust is a private matter and not subject to very much court supervision. However, to the extent that any state's laws require such supervision, this clause makes clear that supervision is not desired.]

C.   Transferability of Interests

The interests of any beneficiary of all trusts established by this will shall not be transferable by voluntary or involuntary assignment or by operation of law and shall be free from the claims of creditors and from attachment, execution, bankruptcy, or other legal process to the fullest extent permitted by law.

[This important clause removes the trust principal and accumulated income from the reach of the minor or young adult's creditors—while it is being held in the trust. Also, this clause prevents the minor or young adult from transferring ownership of the principal or accumulated interest to others—again, while it is in the trust. Once property is distributed to the minor or young adult, however, there are no restrictions on what he or she can do with it.]

D.   Powers of the Trustee

In addition to other powers granted a trustee in this will, a trustee shall have the powers to:

1) Invest and reinvest trust funds in every kind of property and every kind of investment, provided that the trustee acts with the care, skill, prudence and diligence under the prevailing circumstances that a prudent person acting in a similar capacity and familiar with such matters would use.

2) Receive additional property from any source and acquire or hold properties jointly or in undivided interests or in partnership or joint venture with other people or entities.

3) Enter, continue or participate in the operation of any business, and incorporate, liquidate, reorganize or otherwise change the form or terminate the operation of the business and contribute capital or loan money to the business.

4) Exercise all the rights, powers and privileges of an owner of any securities held in the trust.

5) Borrow funds, guarantee or indemnify in the name of the trust and secure any obligation, mortgage, pledge or other security interest, and renew, extend or modify any such obligations.

6) Lease trust property for terms within or beyond the term of the trust.

7) Prosecute, defend, contest or otherwise litigate legal actions or other proceedings for the protection or benefit of the trust; pay, compromise, release, adjust or submit to arbitra-

tion any debt, claim or controversy; and insure the trust against any risk and the trustee against liability with respect to other people.

8) Pay himself or herself reasonable compensation out of trust assets for ordinary and extraordinary services, and for all services in connection with the complete or partial termination of this trust.

9) Employ and discharge professionals to aid or assist in managing the trust and compensate them from the trust assets.

10) Make distributions to the beneficiaries directly or to other people or organizations on behalf of the beneficiaries.

[This list of powers should cover the gamut of activities that trustees might be called upon to exercise in administering any trust set up in this will.]

E.   Severability

The invalidity of any trust provision of this will shall not affect the validity of the remaining trust provisions.

[This language ensures that in the unlikely event that a court finds any individual part of this trust to be invalid, the rest of the document will remain in effect.]

Part 10. Personal Guardian

If at my death a guardian is needed to care for my children, I name Madelyn Bridges as personal guardian. If this person is unable or unwilling to serve as personal guardian, I name Don Bridges to serve instead.

Reasons for my choice for guardian for all my children: Madelyn Bridges has established a close relationship with all three of the children. She frequently takes care of them when my husband and I must work on weekends—and her training as a doctor makes her especially knowledgeable about handling their health care needs. Best of all, she is a loving and trustworthy friend who has unerring judgment and common sense—an excellent choice to raise the children if David and I cannot.

No personal guardian shall be required to post bond.

[This clause names someone to provide parental-type care for a minor child if there is no natural parent able to provide it. The clause also provides for an alternate to step in if the first choice is not able or willing to act when the moment comes. When making your own will, be aware that if there is a natural parent on the scene, that parent will usually be awarded custody of the children, unless a court concludes that the children would be at

risk of harm. The explanation provided for the choice helps ensure that a court will help follow your reasoning—and often helps ensure court approval of your choice of guardian. The clause also provides that the personal guardian need not provide a bond to guarantee faithful performance of his or her duties.]

Part 11. Property Guardian

If at my death, a guardian is needed to care for any property belonging to my minor children, I name Raymond Oster as property guardian. If this person is unwilling or unable to serve as property guardian, I name Stephanie Oster to serve instead.

No property guardian shall be required to post bond.

[This clause appoints someone to manage property that the testator or other people leave to minor children outside of the will, as in a life insurance policy or living trust. This person will also manage property left to minor children under a will if you or anyone else who leaves them property does not arrange for someone to manage it. You may also appoint an alternate property guardian in case your first choice is not able or willing to serve when the time comes. The clause also provides that the personal guardian need not provide a bond—a kind of insurance of good performance—to guarantee that he or she will act faithfully.]

Part 12. Forgiveness of Debts

I wish to forgive all debts specified below, plus accrued interest as of the date of my death: Joe Hunt, April 6, 1997, $10,000.

[Forgiving a debt is equivalent to making a bequest of money. It is a common way to equalize what you leave to all your children when you have loaned one of them some money— that is, the amount that you would otherwise leave that child can be reduced by the amount of the debt being forgiven.]

Part 13. Executor

I name David Lee Hanson to serve as my executor. If David Lee Hanson is unwilling or unable to serve as executor, I name Madelyn Bridges to serve instead.

No executor shall be required to post bond.

[This clause identifies the choices for executor and an alternate executor who will take over if the first choice is unable or unwilling to serve when the time comes. You have the option of naming more than one.]

Part 14. Executor's Powers

I direct my executor to take all actions legally permissible to have the probate of my will done as simply and as free of court supervision as possible under the laws of the state having jurisdiction over this will, including filing a petition in the appropriate court for the independent administration of my estate.

[This clause sets out the specific authority that the executor will need to competently manage the estate until it has been distributed under the terms of the will. The will language expresses your desire that your executor work as free from court supervision as possible. This will cut down on delays and expense.

When you print out your will, a second paragraph will list a number of specific powers that your executor will have, if necessary. It also makes clear that the listing of these specific powers does not deprive your executor of any other powers that he or she has under the law of your state. The general idea is to give your executor as much power as possible, so that he or she will not have to go to court and get permission to take a particular action.]

Part 15. Payment of Debts

Except for liens and encumbrances placed on property as security for the repayment of a loan or debt, I want all debts and expenses owed by my estate to be paid using the following assets in the order listed: Account #666777 at Cudahy Savings Bank.

[This clause states how debts will be paid. Depending on the choice you make when using Quicken WillMaker Plus, your debts may be paid either from specific assets you designate or from your residuary estate—all the property covered by your will that does not pass through a specific bequest.]

Part 16. Payment of Taxes

I want all estate and inheritance taxes assessed against property in my estate or against my beneficiaries to be paid using the following assets, in the order listed: Account #939494050 at the Independence Bank, Pacific Branch.

[This clause states how any estate or death taxes owed by the estate or beneficiaries should be paid. This will usually apply only to people whose estate has a net value of $1 million or more. Depending on the choice you make when operating Quicken WillMaker Plus, your taxes may be paid from all of your property, from specific assets you designate or by your executor according to the law of your state.]

Part 17. No Contest Provision

If any beneficiary under this will contests this will or any of its provisions, any share or interest in my estate given to the contesting beneficiary under this will is revoked and shall be disposed of as if that contesting beneficiary had not survived me.

[This harsh-sounding clause is intended to discourage anyone who receives anything under the will from challenging its legality for the purpose of receiving a larger share. The clause is often not very effective if a spouse or children are the ones doing the suing but may be enforced against less closely related beneficiaries. A few states have passed laws specifically stating that a no contest clause will not be enforced, but if your will has such a provision, the rest of it will be enforced as written.]

/////

/////

/////

/////

/////

/////

/////

/////

/////

[These hashmarks will automatically appear to fill up the rest of the page so that the witnesses' signatures appear with some text of the will—one way to help guard against an unethical survivor tampering with the document.]

Part 18. Severability

If any provision of this will is held invalid, that shall not affect other provisions that can be given effect without the invalid provision.

[This is standard language that ensures that in the unlikely event that a court finds any individual part of your will to be invalid, the rest of the document will remain in effect.]

SIGNATURE

I, Sally K. Hanson, the testator, sign my name to this instrument, this _____ day of
_____, _____, at _____. I declare that I sign and
execute this instrument as my last will, that I sign it willingly, and that I execute it as my
free and voluntary act. I declare that I am of the age of majority or otherwise legally
empowered to make a will, and under no constraint or undue influence.

Signature: _____

WITNESSES

We, the witnesses, sign our names to this instrument, and declare that the testator
willingly signed and executed this instrument as the testator's last will.

In the presence of the testator, and in the presence of each other, we sign this will as
witnesses to the testator's signing.

To the best of our knowledge, the testator is of the age of majority or otherwise legally
empowered to make a will, is mentally competent and under no constraint or undue
influence. We declare under penalty of perjury that the foregoing is true and correct, this
_____ day of _____, _____, at _____.

Witness #1: _____

Residing at: _____

Witness #2: _____

Residing at: _____

About You and Yours

As you go through Quicken WillMaker Plus, you will first be asked to answer a number of preliminary questions about yourself and where and how you live. This section discusses those questions in the order in which they appear in the program.

A. Your Name

Enter your name—first, middle if you choose, then last—in the same form that you use on other formal documents, such as your driver's license or bank accounts. This may or may not be the name that appears on your birth certificate.

If you customarily use more than one name for business purposes, list all of them in your Quicken WillMaker Plus answer, separated by aka, which stands for "also known as."

There is room for you to list several names. But use your common sense. Your name is needed here to identify you and all the property you own. Be sure to include all names in which you have held bank accounts, stocks, bonds, real estate or other property. But you need not list every embarrassing nickname from your childhood, or names you use for nonbusiness purposes.

B. Your Gender

Quicken WillMaker Plus also asks you to select a pronoun by which you identify your gender. This is not to be nosy, but so that the screens you see while proceeding through the program and the language in your final document will be easier to read, avoiding the awkward "he or she."

C. Your Social Security Number

Quicken WillMaker Plus prompts you to enter your nine-digit Social Security number. This is not a legal requirement, and you may choose not to provide it. However, it is a good idea to supply the information, because the number is often helpful to your executor and others who must track down your records and property after your death. And the information may be especially helpful if you have a common name that may be easily confused with others.

D. Your State

You are asked to specify the state of your legal residence, sometimes called a domicile. This is the state where you make your home now and for the indefinite future. This information is vital for a number of will-making reasons, so it is important to check your answer for accuracy.

Your state's laws affect:
- marital property ownership
- property management options for young beneficiaries
- how your will can be admitted into probate, and
- whether your property will be subject to state inheritance tax.

(See Chapter 13.)

If you live in two or more states during the year and have business relationships in both, you may not be sure which state is your legal residence.

Choose the state where you are the most rooted —that is, the state in which you:
- are registered to vote
- register your motor vehicles
- own valuable property—especially property with a title document, such as a house or car

- have checking, savings and other investment accounts, and
- maintain a business.

To avoid confusion, it is best to keep all or at least most of your roots in one state, if possible. For people with larger estates, ideally this should be in a state that does not levy an inheritance tax. (See Chapter 9, Section E.)

⚠ **Wills valid in continental U.S. only.** Quicken WillMaker Plus produces valid wills in all of the continental United States except for Louisiana—and the program guides you by showing you screens geared specifically to the state of residence you indicate when using it.

Because the property and probate laws in Puerto Rico and Guam, for example, may differ from a state you have selected to use in making your will, we do not guarantee that a Quicken WillMaker Plus will is valid there. However, some users who reside outside the U.S. do use Quicken WillMaker Plus to help draft their wills and then have them looked over by an experienced local professional. In this way, Quicken WillMaker Plus helps users answer questions and organize basic information about their property and beneficiaries that is commonly used in making wills.

1. Living Overseas

If you live overseas temporarily because you are in the armed services, your residence will be the Home of Record you declared to the military authorities.

Normally, your Home of Record is the state you lived in before you received your assignment, where your parents or spouse live, or where you now have a permanent home. If there is a close call between two states, consider the factors listed above for determining a legal residence, or get advice from the military legal authorities.

If you live overseas for business or education, you probably still have ties with a particular state that would make it your legal residence. For example, if you were born in Wisconsin, lived there for many years, registered to vote there and receive mail there in care of your parents who still live in Milwaukee, then Wisconsin is your legal residence for purposes of making a will.

⚠ **If your choice is not clear.** If you do not maintain continuous ties with a particular state, or if you have homes in both the U.S. and another country, consult a lawyer to find out which state to list as your legal domicile when using Quicken WillMaker Plus.

2. Your County

Including your county in your will is optional but recommended, for convenience and as one additional way to help others identify you and to track down your property after your death.

Also, a county name may provide those handling your estate with important direction, because wills go through probate in the court system of the county where you last resided, no matter where you died. The one exception is real estate: that property is probated in the court of the county in which it is located.

E. Marital Status

If you are married, review the property ownership laws affecting married people. (See Chapter 5, Section D.)

For most people, listing their proper marital status does not require much thought. But if you are unsure whether you are married or single according to law, it is important to clarify your status. The information below should help.

1. Divorce

If you're not sure whether or not you are legally divorced, make sure you see a copy of the final order signed by a judge. To track down a divorce order, contact the court clerk in the county where you believe the divorce occurred. You will need to give the first and last names of you and your former spouse and make a good guess at what year the divorce became final. If you cannot locate a final decree of divorce, it is safest to assume you are still legally married.

If the divorce was supposed to have taken place outside the United States, it may be difficult to verify. If you have any reason to think that someone you consider to be a former spouse might claim to be married to you at your death because an out-of-country divorce was not legal, consult a lawyer. (See Chapter 25.)

The Importance of Your Marital Status

You should make a new will whenever you marry or divorce. (See Chapter 11, Section A.)

If your marital status changes but your will does not, your new spouse or ex-spouse may get more or less of your property than you intend. For example, if you marry after making a will and do not provide for the new spouse—either in the will or through transfers outside the will—your spouse, in many states, may be entitled to claim a big share of your property at your death.

Also, if you name a spouse in a will, then divorce or have the marriage annulled and die before making a new will, state laws will produce different, often unexpected, results. In most states, the former spouse will automatically get nothing. In other states, the former spouse is entitled to take the property as set out in the will.

2. Separation

Many married couples, contemplating divorce or reconciliation, live apart from one another, sometimes for several years. While this often feels like a murky limbo while you are living it, for will-making purposes, your status is straightforward: You are legally married until a court issues a formal decree of divorce, signed by a judge. This is true even if you and your spouse are legally separated as declared in a legal document. Note that many separation agreements, however, set out rights and restrictions that may affect your ownership of property.

3. Common Law Marriage

It is uncommon to have a common law marriage. In most states, common law marriage does not exist.

But in the states listed below, couples can become legally married if they live together and either hold themselves out to the public as being married or actually intend to be married to one another. Once these conditions are met, the couple is legally married. And the marriage will still be valid even if they later move to a state that does not allow couples to form common law marriages there.

No matter what state you live in, if either you or the person you live with is still legally married to some other person, you cannot have a common law marriage.

The following states recognize some form of common law marriage:

Alabama
Colorado
District of Columbia
Georgia (if created before 1/1/97)
Idaho (if created before 1/1/96)
Iowa
Kansas
Montana
New Hampshire (for inheritance purposes only)
Ohio (if created before 10/10/91)
Oklahoma
Pennsylvania (if created before 1/1/05)
Rhode Island
South Carolina
Texas
Utah

There is no such thing as a common law divorce; no matter how your marriage begins, you must go through formal divorce proceedings to end it.

4. Same-Sex Couples

The laws affecting same-sex couples are in enormous flux. If you are a member of a same-sex couple and have gone through a marriage ceremony (civil or religious) or registered your partnership with your state or local government, you're probably at least a little bit confused about the legal status of your union.

Fortunately, when it comes to making a will, things are pretty simple. You and your partner can both use Quicken WillMaker Plus to make wills that let you leave your property exactly as you wish. Each of you should just make a will for a single person. (To do that, answer "no" when the program asks whether you are married.) Your will won't identity your partner as your spouse or domestic partner, but you can use your will to leave property to your partner (or others), and to name your partner as the executor of your will if you like.

But if you're legally married (an option currently available only in Massachusetts), why not use the will for married couples? That's because Quicken WillMaker Plus uses the language "husband" and "wife" in a will for a married person. (Each spouse makes a separate will.) This language is not legally necessary—it simply helps to make the document clearer—but obviously it's not appropriate for a same-sex couple.

If you want a will that spells out your relationship with your life partner—whether it's marriage, domestic partnership, civil union or something else—you should see a lawyer.

Same-Sex Partners and the Law

Here's a brief overview of the legal status of lesbian and gay partnerships.

State rules.

- California offers registered same-sex domestic partners most of the same rights that married couples enjoy, including participation in the community property system (see Chapter 5, Section D) and the right to inherit from a deceased partner who didn't make a will.
- Connecticut allows same-sex couples to form civil unions that give partners all the rights of married couples under state law, including inheritance rights.
- The District of Columbia's domestic partnership law does not include inheritance rights.
- Hawaii allows unmarried couples to enter into reciprocal beneficiary relationships, giving each partner most of the inheritance rights of married couples.
- Maine gives registered domestic partners many of the same rights as married couples, including the right to inherit property if a deceased partner didn't make a will.
- Massachusetts is (as of May 2004) the only state that lets same-sex couples enter into marriages that are recognized by the state.

- New Jersey's domestic partnership law does not give a surviving domestic partner the right to inherit from a deceased partner, but it does treat survivors like spouses for inheritance tax purposes.
- Vermont allows same-sex couples to form civil unions that give partners all the rights of married couples under state law, including inheritance rights.

Federal rules. The federal government does not currently recognize any same-sex relationships, no matter what state law says. (This is because of a federal law called the Defense of Marriage Act.) So same-sex couples who enter into marriages or marriage-like relationships are not currently entitled to the federal estate and gift tax benefits married couples enjoy—or to Social Security benefits, immigration privileges or any of the more than 1,000 benefits extended to heterosexual married couples.

 More information for same-sex couples. For complete information about the legal issues that same-sex couples face, see *A Legal Guide for Lesbian and Gay Couples,* by Hayden Curry, Denis Clifford and Frederick Hertz (Nolo).

5. Your Spouse's Name

Quicken WillMaker Plus prompts you to provide your spouse's name by asking for the name of your husband or wife. Enter your spouse's full name. As with your own name, list all names used for business purposes, following the tips suggested for entering your own name in Section A.

F. Your Children

Becoming a parent is what may have motivated you to buckle down to the task of writing your will in the first place.

If you are the parent of young children, your will is the perfect place to address some driving concerns you are likely to have if you die before they are grown. These concerns include:

- who will care for your children, and
- who will manage their property.

Quicken WillMaker Plus lets you make these decisions separately. This gives you the option of placing the responsibilities in the hands of the same person or, if need be, naming different people. First, you are asked to name someone to care for your children. Later in the program, you'll deal with the issue of providing property management for your own or other people's young children. (See Chapter 7.)

1. Identifying Your Children

Quicken WillMaker Plus asks you whether or not you have any children and, if you do, it asks you to name each of them. You are not required to leave property to your children, but it is important that you at least state each child's name. If you don't, it may not be clear whether you intentionally left a child out of your will, or whether the child was accidentally overlooked (called "pretermitted," under the law). A child who is unintentionally omitted from your will—usually because you made your will before he or she was born—has a right to take a share of your estate.

Children Born After a Parent Dies. If a child is conceived before your death but is born after you die, he or she will most likely be entitled to part of your estate even if your will doesn't mention the child. But the law is now rushing to answer a new question posed by advancing medical technology: What happens if a child is conceived *after* the death of his or her father? If sperm or embryos are frozen before the father's death, a child could be born years later.

Individual states are taking different approaches to this matter. Some are giving posthumously conceived children the rights to inherit property and receive other benefits from their deceased dads. Others are refusing such rights. If you are curious about this issue or planning for a posthumously conceived child, you should consult a knowledgeable estate planning lawyer.

When naming your children, you should include:

- children born to or adopted by you while you were married to your current spouse
- children born to or adopted by you when you were married to a previous spouse, and
- children born to or adopted by you when you were not married.

If you are the parent of a child who has been legally adopted by another person—or you have otherwise given up your legal parental rights—then you need not name that child in your will.

You should not name stepchildren that you have not adopted, since they are not entitled by law to a share of your property when you die. The pretermitted heir rule does not apply to them. Also, Quicken WillMaker Plus offers a number of options that include your children as a group, and if you include stepchildren in the list and use one of these options, your will might contain provisions you did not intend.

However, you are free to leave your stepchildren as much property in your will as you wish. If you want to treat your children and stepchildren equally and not differentiate between them, when Quicken WillMaker Plus asks how you wish to leave your property, choose the option labeled "Leave it some other way." (See Chapter 6, Sections A and C.)

To list your children, enter their full names in the sequence and format you want the names to appear in your will.

⚠ Don't use "all my children." Some people are tempted to skimp on naming their children individually and want to fill in "all my children," "my surviving children," "my lawful heirs" or "my issue." Don't do it. That shorthand language is much more confusing than listing each child by name.

2. Your Children's Birthdates

Quicken WillMaker Plus also asks you to enter your children's dates of birth—month, day, year. The program will automatically compute their ages in years—an important consideration when you are asked to name a personal guardian and provide management for property you or others leave them.

G. Grandchildren

Quicken WillMaker Plus asks you to name your grandchildren. Name all of them—including children your child legally adopted and those born while he or she was not married.

This question is asked because the rule that allows unintentionally omitted children to take a share of your estate also applies to grandchildren you may have overlooked in your will if their parent—that is, your child—dies before you do. (See Section F.)

As it does for your own children, Quicken WillMaker Plus automatically provides the statement that if you have not left any property to a grandchild, that is intentional—and therefore eliminates the problem. Again, you are free to leave the grandchild property if you choose. Also, if you have additional grandchildren after making your will, it is wise to make a new will that includes them.

Keep Your Will Current

Here are two situations in which you should make a new will:

- **If a child is born to or legally adopted by you after you make your will.** You should draft a new will to list the new child. If you do not, that child may challenge your will and receive a share of what you leave.

- **If one of your children dies before you do and leaves children of his or her own.** The laws of many states require that you name and provide for the children of deceased children. If you do not, they may be considered accidentally overlooked, and entitled to part of your property. To protect against this, make a new will, naming these grandchildren so that you can signal that you are aware that these grandchildren exist. You are still free to leave them as little or as much property as you wish in your will. (See Chapter 11 for information on updating your will.)

H. Personal Guardians for Your Minor Children

Among the most pressing concerns of parents with minor children is who will care for the children if one or both of them die before the children reach 18.

Although contemplating the possibility of your early death can be wrenching, it is important to face up to it and adopt the best contingency plan for the care of your young children. If the other parent is available, then he or she can usually handle the task.

But life is full of possibilities—some of them rather bleak. You and the other parent might die close together in time. Or you may currently be a single parent and need to come to terms with what will happen if you do not survive until your children reach age 18.

This section discusses using Quicken WillMaker Plus to choose a personal guardian to care for the children's basic health, education and other daily needs. Choosing a person to manage your children's property is discussed in Chapter 7.

1. Reasons for Naming a Personal Guardian

The general legal rule is that if there are two parents willing and able to care for the children, and one dies, the other will take over physical custody and responsibility for caring for the child. In many states, the surviving parent may also be given authority by a court to manage any property the deceased parent left to the children—unless the deceased parent has specified a different property management arrangement in a will.

But there is no ready fallback plan if both parents of a minor child die or, in the case of a single parent, there is not another parent able or willing to do the job. Using Quicken WillMaker Plus, you can cover these concerns by naming a personal guardian and an alternate. The person you name will normally be appointed by the court to act as a surrogate parent for your minor children if both of the following are true:

- There is no surviving natural or adoptive parent able to properly care for the children.
- The court agrees that your choice is in the best interests of the children.

If both parents are making wills, they should name the same person as guardian for each child. This will help avoid the possibility of a dispute and perhaps even a court battle should the parents die simultaneously. But remember, if one spouse dies, the other will usually assume custody and will then be free to make a new will naming a different personal guardian if he or she wishes. In short, in a family where both parents are active caretakers, the personal guardian named in a will cares for the children only if both parents die at the same time or close together.

However, if you feel strongly that the other person is not the best person to care for the children, be sure to explain your reasoning when the Quicken WillMaker Plus program prompts you to do so. (See Section 4, below.)

One guardian and alternate per child. Quicken WillMaker Plus allows you to name only one person as personal guardian and one person as alternate personal guardian for each of your minor children. While it is legally permissible to name coguardians, it is normally a poor idea because of the possibility that the coguardians will later disagree or go separate ways.

Naming Different Guardians for Different Children

One obvious concern when choosing a personal guardian for your children is to keep them together if they get along well with one another. This suggests that it is best to name the same personal guardian for all the children.

There are families, however, where the children are not particularly close to one another but have strong attachments with one or more adults outside the immediate family. For instance, one child may spend a lot of time with a grandparent while another child may be close to an aunt and uncle. Also, in a second or third marriage, a child from an earlier marriage may be closer to a different adult than a child from the current marriage.

In these situations and others, logic dictates other advice: Choose the personal guardian you believe would best be able to care for the child. This may mean that you will choose different personal guardians for different children.

2. Choosing a Personal Guardian

To qualify as a personal guardian, your choice must be an adult—18 in most states—and competent to do the job. For obvious reasons, you should first consider an adult with whom the child already has a close relationship—a stepparent, grandparent, aunt or uncle, older sibling, babysitter, close friend of the family or even neighbor. Whomever you choose, be sure that person is mature, good-hearted and willing and able to assume the responsibility.

3. Choosing an Alternate Personal Guardian

Quicken WillMaker Plus lets you name a back-up or alternate personal guardian to serve in case your first choice for each child either changes his or her mind or is unable to do the job at your death. The considerations involved in naming an alternate personal guardian are the same as those you pondered when making your first choice: maturity, a good heart, familiarity with the children and willingness to serve.

4. Explaining Your Choice

Leaving a written explanation of why you made a particular choice for a personal guardian may be especially important if you are separated or divorced. You may have strong ideas about why the child's other parent, or perhaps a grandparent, should not have custody of your minor children. In an age when many parents live separately, the following predicaments are sadly common:

- "I have custody of my three children. I don't want my ex-husband, who I believe is emotionally destructive, to get custody of our children if I die. Can I choose a guardian to serve instead of him?"

- "I have legal custody of my daughter and I've remarried. My present wife is a much better mother to my daughter than my ex-wife, who never cared for her properly. What can I do to make sure my present wife gets custody if I die?"

- "I live with a man who's been a good parent to my children for six years. My father doesn't like the fact that we aren't married and may well try to get custody of the kids if I die. What can I do to see that my partner gets custody?"

There is no definitive answer to these questions. If you die while the child is still a minor and the other parent disputes your choice in court, the judge will likely grant custody to the other natural parent, unless that parent:

- has legally abandoned the child by not providing for or visiting the child for an extended period, or
- is clearly unfit as a parent.

EXAMPLE: Susan and Fred, an unmarried couple, have two minor children. Although Susan loves Fred, she does not think he is capable of raising the children on his own. She uses Quicken WillMaker Plus to name her mother, Elinor, as guardian. If Susan dies, Fred, as the children's natural parent, will be given first priority as personal guardian over Elinor, despite Susan's will, assuming the court finds he is willing and able to care for the children. However, if the court finds that Fred should not be personal guardian, Elinor would get the nod, assuming she was fit.

Tips on What to Include

When deciding who should become a child's personal guardian, the courts of all states are required to act in the child's best interests. In making this determination, the courts commonly consider a number of facts, which you might want to include when explaining your choice for personal guardian. They include:

- whom the parents nominated to become the personal guardian
- whether the proposed personal guardian will provide the greatest stability and continuity of care for the child
- which person will best be able to meet the child's needs, whatever these happen to be
- the quality of the relationship between the child and the adults being considered for guardian
- the child's preferences to the extent these can be gleaned, and
- the moral fitness and conduct of the proposed guardians.

It is usually difficult to prove that a parent is unfit, absent serious and obvious problems such as chronic drug or alcohol abuse, mental illness or a history of child abuse. The fact that you do not like or respect the other parent is never enough, by itself, for a court to deny custody to him or her.

But if you honestly believe the other natural parent is incapable of caring for your children properly—or simply will not assume the responsibility—you should reinforce that belief by explaining why you elected to name other people as guardians and alternates.

EXAMPLE: Justine and Paul live together with Justine's minor children from an earlier marriage. The natural father is out of the picture, but Justine fears that her mother, Tamira, who does not approve of unmarried couples living together, will try to get custody of the kids if something happens to her. Justine wants Paul to have custody because he knows the children well and loves them. She can use Quicken WillMaker Plus to name Paul as personal guardian and add a statement making the reasons for this choice clear.

If Justine dies and Tamira goes to court to get custody, the fact that Justine named Paul will give him an advantage. If he is a good parent, he is likely to get custody in most states.

Custody Difficulties for Lesbians and Gay Men

Many lesbians and gay men are parents. If only one of the couple is lesbian or gay, and there is later an acrimonious divorce, there may also be a difficult legal battle over who gets custody of the children. In a court fight over custody, judges are supposed to consider all factors and arrive at a decision in the best interests of the child. This means that virtually any information about a parent's lifestyle, sexual orientation and behavior can be brought out in court. In many states, especially in the South and Midwest, evidence of a parent's lesbian or gay sexual identity is still a legally accepted reason for denying custody. If you anticipate a contested custody case, you will find guidance in *A Legal Guide for Lesbian & Gay Couples*, by Hayden Curry, Denis Clifford and Frederick Hertz (Nolo). ■

Chapter 5

About Your Property

This chapter discusses the grist of will making: what you own, how you own it and what legal rules affect how you can leave it. Once you have considered the information about property in this chapter, you will be ready to use Quicken WillMaker Plus to leave it to others—a task discussed in detail in Chapter 6. If you have children, see Chapter 7 for a discussion of their right to inherit property and your right to disinherit them.

Many readers will not need the information in this chapter. If you plan to leave your property in a lump—that is, without giving specific items of property to specific people—it makes little difference what you own and how you own it. That will be sorted out when you die, and the people you have named to take "all" your property will get whatever you own—and they will not get what you do not own.

This chapter is important for you to read if either of the following is true:

- You are married—and this includes everyone who has not received a final decree of divorce—and plan to name someone other than your spouse to receive all or most of your property.
- You plan to leave specific items of property to specific people or organizations.

Keeping track of your property. There are many things your survivors will need to know about your property—and it will help them to learn some relevant information about it, including:

- the specific location of some items
- the location of ownership, warranty and appraisal papers

- the value of some items—especially if they have special significance, and
- guidance about maintaining the property.

You can use Quicken WillMaker Plus's "Information for Caregivers and Survivors" form for this task.

A. Property You Should Not Include in Your Will

In almost all cases, your will does not affect property that you have already arranged to leave by another method. For example, property in a living trust or a pay-on-death account, in joint tenancy or in a retirement account or insurance policy where you have named the beneficiary is not affected by your will. (If you live in the state of Washington, however, there is an exception to this rule. See below.)

1. Property Held in Joint Tenancy

Two or more people can own property—real estate or personal property such as securities or a bank account—in joint tenancy with right of survivorship. When one of them dies, his or her share automatically goes to the surviving owner, called a joint tenant. A joint tenant cannot use a will to leave his or her share of the property to someone else.

EXAMPLE: Laverne owns her house in joint tenancy with her daughter, Linda. Later, she makes a will, leaving all of her property to her son, Philip. At Laverne's death, Linda gets the house.

If, however, you want to end a joint tenancy while you are alive, that's easy to do. You need only sign a new deed changing the way the property is held from joint tenancy to tenancy in common. (See Section B, below.) Each person still owns the same share, but because a tenancy in common does not include any automatic right of survivorship, each owner is then free to leave his or her share of the property by will.

Normally, joint tenancies with right of survivorship are created by language in the document—a deed, title document or bank account certificate—that controls how the property is owned. To find out whether you own property in joint tenancy, examine the title document for the words "joint tenants," "joint tenancy" or "joint tenancy with right of survivorship." If you find just the notation "JT WROS," that too means joint tenancy with right of survivorship. Simply listing the owners' names joined by "and" or "or" is not normally adequate to create a joint tenancy. although a few states allow it.

Finally, in a handful of community property states, married couples can own property in a form very similar to joint tenancy, called "community property with right of survivorship." (For more information, see Section D1, below.)

States That Restrict Joint Tenancy

A handful of states have restricted or abolished joint tenancy. Here are the rules you should know.

Alaska. No joint tenancies for real estate, except for husband and wife, who may own property as tenants by the entirety. (See Section 2, below.)

Oregon. A transfer of real estate to husband and wife creates a tenancy by the entirety, not joint tenancy. (See Section 2, below.)

Tennessee. A transfer of real estate to husband and wife creates a tenancy by the entirety, not joint tenancy. (See Section 2, below.)

Texas. A joint tenancy can be created only if you sign a separate written agreement.

Wisconsin. No joint tenancies between spouses after January 1, 1986. If you attempt to create a joint tenancy, it will be treated as community property with right of survivorship. (See Section D1, below.)

If you are the sole owner when you die. If the other joint owners die before you do, and you end up the sole owner, you can of course change your will, or make a new one, to add the property and name someone to receive it. If you do not, the property will pass to the person or organization named in your will to receive any property that you did not leave to specific people or organizations.

2. Property Held in Tenancy by the Entirety

This form of ownership is basically the same as joint tenancy with right of survivorship discussed above but almost always is limited to married couples. (In Hawaii, unmarried couples with registered "reciprocal beneficiary" relationships can take advantage of tenancy by the entirety ownership. In Vermont, the option is available for lesbian and gay couples with registered civil unions.) The certificate of title for the property must specify that it is held as a tenancy by the entirety for this type of ownership to exist. When one spouse dies, the entire interest in the property goes automatically to the other.

Before tenancy by the entirety property can be changed to some other form of property ownership, both spouses must agree to the change.

Nearly half the states recognize tenancy by the entirety, but several of them—as indicated in the chart below—allow it only for real estate. In Kentucky, the deed must expressly state that there is a right of survivorship. If not, the spouses take the property as tenants in common. (Ky. Rev. Stat. Ann. § 381.050.)

States With Tenancy by the Entirety Ownership	
Alaska*	Missouri
Arkansas	New Jersey
Connecticut	New York*
Delaware	North Carolina*
District of Columbia	Ohio* (only if created before 4/4/85)
Florida	
Hawaii	Oklahoma
Illinois*	Oregon*
Indiana*	Pennsylvania
Kentucky*	Rhode Island
Maryland	Tennessee
Massachusetts	Utah
Michigan	Vermont
Mississippi	Virginia
	Wyoming

* Applies only to real estate.

3. Pay-on-Death Bank Accounts

These accounts are held in your name, but with a direction to pay the balance to another person at your death. You can change this pay-on-death form of ownership while you are alive, but if you die with property owned in this way, the person you designated on the bank's or government's registration form when you set up the account will have the right to take it.

> **EXAMPLE:** Marc opens a bank account and deposits $5,000 in it. He states on the bank's form that whatever funds are in the account at his death should be turned over to his son, Jordan. Later, when Marc makes his will, he leaves the account to his nephew, but he does not change the way the account is registered at the bank. His son, not the nephew, will receive the money in the account.

As long as you are alive, the person you named to take the money in a payable-on-death or P.O.D. account has no rights to it. If you need the money—or just change your mind about leaving it to the beneficiary you named—you can spend the money, name a different beneficiary or close the account.

Don't Create a Joint Account Just to Avoid Probate

If you want to leave money to someone at your death—but not to give it away now—stick to a P.O.D. account. It will accomplish your goal simply and easily. Don't set up a joint account with the understanding that the other person will withdraw money only after you die. This is a common mistake, and it often has unwanted consequences:

- The new co-owner might withdraw money from the account sooner than you wished.
- Creditors can reach the other person's share.
- If you change your mind, you can't erase the other person's name from the account.
- There may be gift tax consequences if you make someone a co-owner of your account.
- After your death, relatives may fight about who should get the money and what you really intended.

4. Registered Government Bonds and Notes

You can also name a beneficiary to take certain kinds of government securities, including Treasury bills, notes and bonds.

To do this, register ownership of the account in your name, followed by the words "pay on death to" and the name of your beneficiary. If the beneficiary is a minor, you must specify that—for example, by writing "payable on death to Jasmine Martin, a minor."

You have complete control over these assets. You do not need the beneficiary's consent to sell or give away the securities, and you can name a different beneficiary at any time by filling out new ownership documents. After your death, ownership will be transferred to the beneficiary you named.

One significant limitation on adding a pay-on-death beneficiary is that there may be only one primary owner and one beneficiary. You can't name a pay-on-death beneficiary if two or more people own the securities together—you and your spouse, for example. In that situation, the best you can do is to create a right of survivorship, so that the surviving co-owner gets the securities when the first co-owner dies. After the first co-owner's death, the survivor could add a beneficiary designation.

EXAMPLE: Marilyn and Richard buy Treasury bonds and notes and hold title to their account as "Marilyn Vanderburg and Richard Vanderburg, with right of survivorship." Many years later, after Marilyn's death, Richard changes the title to add their adult daughter as the beneficiary. Now, the title is held as "Richard Vanderburg, payable on death to Melissa Vanderburg."

Also, you cannot name an alternate beneficiary to take the bonds if your first choice does not survive you.

5. Property You Place in a Trust

Property you place in a trust passes automatically to the beneficiary named in the trust document—you cannot pass this property in your will. This includes property placed in a revocable living trust.

During your lifetime, you retain control over the property you place in trust. After you die, the person you named in your trust document to be the successor trustee takes control of the property. He or she is in charge of transferring the trust property to the family, friends or charities you named as the trust beneficiaries. In most cases, the whole transfer process can be handled within a few weeks at little or no cost.

With property such as bank accounts or securities, the successor trustee will need to show the institution that he or she has the legal right to take possession of the property.

When all the trust property has been transferred to the beneficiaries, the living trust ceases to exist.

6. Property Left in Retirement Accounts

IRAs, Keoghs, 401(k)s and similar retirement plans allow you to name a beneficiary and alternate beneficiary to take what remains in your account at your death. Once you name a beneficiary on the forms provided by the account administrator, your will has no effect on it. If you want to change the beneficiary, you must notify the retirement account administrator.

7. Life Insurance and Annuities

Proceeds of life insurance and annuity policies automatically go to the person or institution you named as beneficiary of the policy. If your first choice dies before you, the proceeds go to any alternate beneficiary you named. Your will does not affect insurance money unless you named your own estate as the beneficiary.

Washington's "Superwill Statute"

The state of Washington has passed a law called the "superwill statute" that varies some of the rules discussed above. If you like, you can leave the following types of property in your will:

- your share of joint tenancy bank accounts
- pay-on-death bank accounts
- property in a living trust, and
- money in individual retirement accounts (but not 410(k)s).

If you set up one of these devices for leaving your property and then later use your will to change the beneficiary, the property goes to the person you name in your will. However, if you designate a new beneficiary after you make your will—for example, by updating the paperwork for a pay-on-death bank account or amending your living trust—the gift in the will has no effect. (Wash. Rev. Code § 11.11.020.)

B. Property You Own With Others

If you are not married, and you own property with someone else, you probably own it in tenancy in common. This is the most common way for unmarried people to own property together. Each co-owner is free to sell or give away his or her interest during life or leave it to another at death in a will. To tell whether or not you own property as tenancy in common, check the deed or other title document; it should specifically note that the property is held as a tenancy in common.

More rules for married people making wills. If you are married, a whole host of legal rules may affect what property you own jointly and separately. (See Section D, below.)

C. Property on Which You Owe Money

Using Quicken WillMaker Plus, if you leave property on which you owe money, the beneficiary who takes it at your death will also take over the debt owed on that property. This means the beneficiary of the property is responsible for paying off the debt. (But your survivors will not inherit your debt, per se. For example, if you die with nothing to your name except credit card debt, your survivors will not be responsible for paying those bills.)

D. Property Ownership Rules for Married People

Most married people leave all or the greatest share of their property to their surviving spouses at death. For them, the nuances of marital property law are not important, since the survivor gets the property anyway.

But if you plan to leave your property to several people instead of or in addition to your spouse, the picture becomes more complicated. Under your state's laws, your spouse may own some property you believe is yours. And if you do not own it, you cannot give it away—either now or at your death. Questions of which spouse owns what property are important if your spouse does not agree to your plan for property disposition.

There are two issues to consider:

- What do you own?

- Will your spouse have the right to claim a share of your property after your death? (See Section E, below.)

This section will help you determine what you own and so can leave to others in your will. To figure it out, you need to know a little about the laws in your state. When it comes to property ownership, states are broadly divided into two types: community property states and common law property states.

Community Property States

Alaska*	Nevada
Arizona	New Mexico
California**	Texas
Idaho	Washington
Louisiana	Wisconsin

* If the couple makes a written agreement stating that they wish their property to be treated as community property.

** Registered domestic partners are also covered by community property laws.

Common Law States

All other states

1. Community Property States

If you live in a community property state, there are a few key rules to keep in mind while making your will:

- You can leave your separate property to anyone you wish.

- You can leave half of the community property (property you and your spouse own together) to anyone you wish.
- After your death, your spouse automatically keeps his or her half of the community property.

Another Option: Community Property With Right of Survivorship

Alaska, Arizona, California, Nevada and Wisconsin allow a form of community property that works just like joint tenancy—in other words, the surviving spouse automatically inherits the property when the other spouse dies. To take advantage of this type of ownership, the property's title document must state that the property is owned "as community property with right of survivorship," or something similar.

---

a. Your Separate Property

The following property qualifies as separate property in virtually all community property states:

- property that you own before marriage
- property that you receive after marriage by gift or inheritance
- property that you purchase entirely with your separate property, and
- property that you earn or accumulate after permanent separation.

In some states, additional types of property—such as personal injury awards received by one spouse during marriage—may also qualify as separate property. (See Subsection c, below.)

Community property states differ in how they treat income earned from separate property.

Most hold that such income is separate. But a number of states take the opposite approach, treating income from separate property as community property.

Normally, separate property stays separate as long as it is not:

- so mixed with marital property that it is impossible to tell what is separate and what is not, or
- transferred in writing by the separate property owner into a form of shared ownership.

Just as separate property can be transformed into shared property, community property can be turned into separate property by a gift from one spouse to the other. The rules differ somewhat from state to state, but, generally speaking, gifts made to transform one type of property into another must be made with a signed document.

b. Community Property

The basic rule of community property is simple: During a marriage, all property earned or acquired by either spouse is owned fifty-fifty by each spouse, except for property received by only one of them through gift or inheritance.

More specifically, community property usually includes:

- All income received by either spouse from employment or any other source (except gifts to or inheritance by just one spouse)— for example, wages, stock options, pensions and other employment compensation and business profits. This rule generally applies only to the period when the couple lives together as husband and wife. Most community property states consider income and property acquired after the spouses permanently separate to be the separate property of the spouse who receives it.

• All property acquired with community property income during the marriage.

• All separate property that is transformed into community property under state law. This transformation can occur in several ways, including when one spouse makes a gift of separate property to both of them or when property is so mixed together that it's no longer possible to tell what property is separate (lawyers call this "commingling").

• As mentioned above, in a few community property states, income earned during marriage from separate property—for example, rent, interest or dividends—is community property. Most community property states consider such income to be separate property, however.

EXAMPLE: Beth and Daniel live in Idaho, one of the few community property states where income earned from separate property belongs to the community. Beth inherits 22 head of Angus cattle from her father. Those cattle go on to breed a herd of more than 100 cattle. All the descendants of the original 22 animals are considered income from Beth's separate property and are included in the couple's community property estate.

Classifying Property in Community Property States: Some Examples

Property	Community or Separate	Why
A computer you inherited while married	Separate; you can leave it in your will	Inherited property belongs only to the person who inherited it.
A car you bought before you got married	Separate; you can leave it in your will	Property owned before marriage is not community property.
A boat you bought with your income while married and registered in your name	Community; you can leave only your half-interest in your will	It was purchased with community property income (income earned during the marriage).
The family home you and your spouse own together	Community; you can leave your half-interest in your will	It was purchased with community property income (income earned during the marriage).
A loan that your brother owes you	Community; you can leave your half-interest in your will	The loan was made from community property funds and belongs half to you and half to your spouse.
A fishing cabin you inherited from your father	Separate; you can leave it in your will	Inherited property belongs only to the person who inherited it.
Stock you and your spouse bought with savings from your spouse's earnings	Community; you can leave your half-interest in your will	It was purchased with one spouse's earnings, which are community property during marriage

c.   Property That Is Difficult to Categorize

Normally, classifying property as community or separate property is easy. But in some situations, it can be a close call. There are several potential problem areas.

Businesses. Family businesses can create complications, especially if they were owned before marriage by one spouse and expanded during the marriage. The key is to figure out whether the increased value of the business is community or separate property. If you and your spouse do not have the same view of how to pass on the business, it may be worthwhile to get help from a lawyer or accountant.

Money from a personal injury lawsuit. Usually, but not always, awards won in a personal injury lawsuit are the separate property of the spouse receiving them. There is no easy way to characterize this type of property. If a significant amount of your property came from a personal injury settlement, research the specifics of your state's law or ask an estate planning expert.

Pensions. Generally, the part of a pension gained from earnings made during the marriage is considered to be community property. This is also true of military pensions. However, some federal pensions—such as Railroad Retirement benefits and Social Security retirement benefits—are not considered community property, because federal law deems them to be the separate property of the employee earning them.

2.   Common Law Property States

Common law property states are all states other than the community property states listed at the beginning of Section D, above.

In these states, you own:

- all property you purchased using your property or income, and
- property you own solely in your name if it has a title slip, deed or other legal ownership document.

In common law states, the key to ownership for many types of valuable property is whose name is on the title. If you and your spouse take title to a house together—that is, both of your names are on the deed—you both own it. That is true even if you earned or inherited the money you used to buy it. If your spouse earns the money, but you take title in your name alone, you own it.

If the property is valuable but has no title document, such as a computer, then the person whose income or property is used to pay for it owns it. If joint income is used, then you own it together. You can each leave your half in your will, unless you signed an agreement providing for a joint tenancy or a tenancy by the entirety. (See Section A, above.)

> **EXAMPLE:** Will and Jane are married and live in Kentucky, a common law property state. They have five children. Shortly after their marriage, Jane wrote an extremely popular computer program that helps doctors diagnose illness. She has received royalties averaging about $200,000 a year over a ten-year period. Jane has used the royalties to buy a car, boat and mountain cabin—all registered in her name alone. The couple also owns a house as joint tenants. In addition, Jane owns a number of family heirlooms which she inherited from her parents. Throughout their marriage, Jane and Will have maintained separate savings accounts. Will works as a computer engineer and has deposited all of his income into his account.

Jane put her unspent royalties in her account, which now contains $75,000.

Jane owns:
- the savings account listed in her name alone
- one-half interest in the house (which, because it is held in joint tenancy, will go to Will at Jane's death)
- the car, boat and cabin, since there are title documents listing them in her name (if there were no such documents, she would still own them because they were bought with her income)
- her family heirlooms.

Will owns:
- the savings account listed in his name alone
- one-half interest in the house (which, because it is held in joint tenancy, will go to Jane at Will's death).

EXAMPLE: Martha and Scott, who are married, have both worked for 30 years as schoolteachers in Michigan, a common law state. Generally, Scott and Martha pooled their income and jointly purchased a house, worth $200,000 (in both their names as joint tenants); cars (one in Martha's name and one in Scott's); a share in a vacation condominium (in both names as joint tenants); and household furniture. Each maintains a separate savings account, and they also have a joint tenancy checking account containing $2,000. In addition, Scott and his sister own a piece of land as tenants in common.

Martha owns:
- her savings account
- half-interest in the house and condo (which, because they are held in joint tenancy, will go to Scott at Martha's death)
- her car
- half the furniture

Scott owns:
- his savings account
- half-interest in the house and condo (which, because they are held in joint tenancy, will go to Martha at Scott's death)
- his car
- half the furniture
- a half-interest in the land he owns with his sister

3. Moving From State to State

Complications may set in when a husband and wife acquire property in a common law property state and then move to a community property state. California, Idaho, Washington and Wisconsin treat the earlier-acquired property as if it had been acquired in the community property state. The legal jargon for this type of property is quasi-community property. Wisconsin calls it "deferred marital property."

The other community property states do not recognize the quasi-community property concept for will-making purposes. Instead, they go by the rules of the state where the property was acquired. If you and your spouse move from a non-community property state into one of the states that recognizes quasi-community property, all of your property is treated according to community property rules. However, if you move to any of the other community property states from a common law state, you must assess your property according to the rules of the state where the property was acquired.

Couples who move from a community property state to a common law state face the opposite problem. Generally, each spouse retains one-half interest in the community property the couple accumulated while living in the community property state. However, if there is a conflict after your death, it can get messy; courts dealing with the issue have not been consistent.

If you move. If you move from a community property state to a common law one, and you and your spouse have any disagreement as to who owns what, it may be wise to check with a lawyer. (See Chapter 25.)

E. Your Spouse's Right to Inherit From You

If you intend to leave your spouse very little or no property, you may run into some legal roadblocks. All common law property states (see Section D2, above) protect a surviving spouse from being completely disinherited—and most assure that a spouse has the right to receive a substantial share of a deceased spouse's property. Community property states offer a different kind of protection.

1. Spousal Protection in Common Law States

In a common law state, a shortchanged surviving spouse usually has the option of either taking what the will provides, called "taking under the will," or rejecting the gift and instead taking the minimum share allowed by state law, called "taking against the will." In some states, your spouse may have the right to inherit the family residence, or at least use it for his or her life. The Florida constitution, for example, gives a surviving spouse the deceased spouse's residence.

Laws protecting spouses vary among the states. In many common law property states, a spouse is entitled to one-third of the property left in the will. In a few, it is one-half. The exact amount of the spouse's minimum share may also depend on whether there are also minor children and whether the spouse has been provided for outside the will by trusts or other means.

EXAMPLE: Leonard's will leaves $50,000 to his second wife, June, and the rest of his property, totaling $400,000, to May and April, his daughters from his first marriage. June can choose instead to receive her statutory share of Leonard's estate, which will be far more than $50,000. To the probable dismay of May and April, their shares will be substantially reduced; they will share what is left of Leonard's property after June gets her statutory share.

Of course, these are just options; a spouse who is not unhappy with the share he or she receives by will is free to let it stand. And in almost all states, one spouse can give up all rights to inherit any property by completing and signing a waiver. If you want to make that type of arrangement, consult a lawyer. (See Chapter 25, Section B.)

Family Allowances

Some states provide additional, relatively minor protection such as family allowances and probate homesteads. These vary from state to state in too much detail to discuss here. Generally, however, these devices attempt to assure that your spouse and children are not left out in the cold after your death, by allowing them temporary protection (such as the right to remain in the family home for a short period) or funds (typically, living expenses while an estate is being probated).

In many common law states, how much the surviving spouse is entitled to receive depends on what that spouse receives both under the will and outside of the will—for example, through joint tenancy or a living trust—as well as what the surviving spouse owns. The total of all of these is called the augmented estate.

While the augmented estate concept is rather complicated, its purpose is easy to grasp. Basically, almost all property of both spouses is taken into account. The surviving spouse gets a piece of the whole pie.

Leaving little to a spouse. If you do not plan to leave at least half of your property to your spouse in your will and have not provided for him or her generously outside your will, consult a lawyer.

2. Spousal Protection in Community Property States

Most community property states do not give surviving spouses the right to take a share of the deceased spouse's estate. Instead, they try to protect spouses while both are still alive, by granting each spouse half ownership of property and earnings either spouse acquires during the marriage. (See Section D1, above.)

However, in just a few states—and in very limited circumstances—a surviving spouse may elect to take a portion of the deceased spouse's community or separate property. These laws are designed to prevent spouses from being either accidentally overlooked—for example, if one spouse makes a will before marriage and forgets to change it afterwards to include the new spouse—or deliberately deprived of their fair share of property. These spousal protections are available only in California (California Prob. Code §§ 6560 and following), Idaho (Idaho Code §§ 15-2-202 and following) and Wisconsin (Wis. Stat §§ 861.02 and following)—and they're complicated. If you want to learn more about them, see a lawyer. ■

Chapter 6

How to Leave Your Property

The heart of will making is deciding who gets your property when you die. For many, this is an easy task: You want it all to go to your spouse, your kids, your partner or your favorite charity. For others, it's a little more complicated—for example, you want most of your earthly possessions to go to your spouse, partner, child or charity, but you also want certain items to go to other people. You may even have a fairly complicated scheme in mind that involves divvying your property among a number of people and organizations.

Chapter 5 introduced some basic concepts about your property and whether you can leave it to others in your will. This chapter explains how to put your plan into effect using the Quicken WillMaker Plus program. If you want to leave all or most of your property to a spouse, loved one or favorite charity, the program offers you some shortcuts. And Quicken WillMaker Plus also accommodates more complex wishes.

After you name whom you want to get your property, Quicken WillMaker Plus lets you name alternates—that is, who should get property if your first choices do not survive you.

You do not need to read all of this chapter to figure out how to write the will you want. Start with the discussion that is tailored to your situation:

- If you are married with children: Section A
- If you are married with no children: Section B
- If you are unmarried with children: Section C
- If you are unmarried with no children: Section D.

A. If You Are Married With Children

Many married people have simple will-making needs. They want to leave all or most of their property to their spouses. As alternates for their spouses, they may want to choose their children, or name another person or organization. Quicken WillMaker Plus lets you choose any of those paths easily. And if you do not want to make your spouse the main beneficiary of your will, that option is available, too.

1. Choosing Beneficiaries

Quicken WillMaker Plus prompts you to choose one of three approaches to leaving your property. You can:

- leave everything to your spouse
- leave most of your property, with some specific exceptions, to your spouse, or
- make a plan that may or may not include your spouse.

The third option offers flexibility. You should choose it if you want to divide up your property more evenly among a number of beneficiaries, or if you want to give all or most of your property to someone other than your spouse. But if you do choose this approach to making your will, be sure that you understand the rules governing what you own and the rights of your spouse. (See Chapter 5, Section D.)

> **EXAMPLE:** Anne and Robert are a married couple with one young child. Anne wants a simple will, in which she leaves all of her property to Robert. She chooses the first option—everything to your spouse—to get a will that reflects her wishes.

EXAMPLE: Arnie wants his wife to receive most of his property when he dies, but he has a valuable violin that he wants to go to his best friend, Eddie, and a coin collection that he wants his nephew to receive. Arnie chooses the second option—most to your spouse. Then, later in the program, he can name Eddie to receive his violin and his nephew to receive his coin collection.

EXAMPLE: Sylvia is married to Fred. She wants to leave him her share of their investment portfolio and family business but also wants to leave a number of specific property items to different friends, relatives and charities. She chooses the third option when using Quicken WillMaker Plus. The program then prompts her to list specific property items and the person or organization she wants to receive each one. Before she does, Sylvia reviews Chapter 5 to make sure she understands what property is appropriate to leave in her will.

When you can skip ahead. If you do not want to name your spouse to receive all or most of your property, skip the rest of this section and go to Section E, below, for a discussion of what comes next.

2. Choosing Alternates for Your Spouse

If you want your spouse to receive all or most of your property, your next task will be to choose an alternate for your spouse.

The will you create with Quicken WillMaker Plus provides that all beneficiaries—including your spouse—must survive you by 45 days to receive the property you leave them. This is a standard will provision, called a survivorship requirement. It is based on the assumption that if a beneficiary survives you by only a few days or weeks, you would prefer the property to go to another beneficiary that you choose and name in your will.

The alternates you choose will receive the property only if your spouse dies fewer than 45 days after you do.

Depending on your previous choices, Quicken WillMaker Plus offers two or three options for alternates. You can name:

• your child or children, or
• alternate beneficiaries.

These two approaches to naming alternates are shortcuts. If your spouse does not survive you by 45 days or more, then alternates will receive all the property that would have gone to your spouse. You need not specify which items go to which beneficiaries.

If you named your spouse to receive all your property, you also have a third option: You can make a completely new plan for leaving your property which will take effect only if your spouse does not survive you by at least 45 days. If you make this choice, you can divvy up your property among a number of alternate beneficiaries.

Each of these approaches to naming alternates is discussed below.

a. Designating Your Children

It is common for married people with children to simply leave all or most of their property to the surviving spouse and name the children to take the property as alternates. This means if your spouse does not survive you by 45 days, the property your spouse would have received will pass to your child or children.

If you have more than one child, you will also need to decide how the children should share the property.

If any of your children are 18 or older, you can specify the share each will receive. Later in the program, you can designate someone to manage a child's share if he or she is still a young adult—that is, between the ages of 18 and 35—when you die. (See Chapter 7.)

> **EXAMPLE:** Meg and Charlie have three grown children. When Charlie makes his will, he leaves everything to Meg and names the children as alternates for her. He directs that all three children should receive equal shares of his property if Meg doesn't survive him and they take it, instead.

If any of your children are minors—that is, under 18 years old—you may:

- specify the share each child will receive; later, you may designate how each child's share will be managed and doled out if a child is under 35 when you die, or
- direct that the property be held in one undivided fund, called a pot trust; under this option, the person you select to serve as trustee will use the assets in the trust for all your children as needed, until your youngest child turns an age you choose.

(See Chapter 7 for a discussion of these methods for managing property left to children.)

> **EXAMPLE:** Julia and Emanuel have three young children. When Julia makes her will, she names Emanuel to inherit most of her property and leaves a few small items to her sister. As alternates for her husband, she picks her children. But because they are too young to manage money or property, later in the program she names her sister to manage any property the children may take under her will while they are still young.

> **EXAMPLE:** Barry and his wife Marta have two young daughters close in age. In his will, Barry leaves Marta all his property and chooses the children as alternate beneficiaries. He also picks the pot trust option and names his mother as trustee. If Marta does not survive him by at least 45 days, all of Barry's property will go into a trust for the two girls, administered by Barry's mother.

Quicken WillMaker Plus also lets you name a second level of alternates—that is, alternates who will take the property a child would have received, if that child does not survive you. You can name an alternate for each child or simply designate that the survivors receive any property that would have gone to a deceased child.

b. Naming Alternates

If you decide to specify alternates to receive the property left to your spouse, you may name whomever you want. You are not constrained, as with the first option, to naming only your children as alternates. For instance, you may name a charity, a friend or just one of your children. If your spouse does not survive you by 45 days, the alternates you name will receive the property your spouse would have received. If you name more than one person or organization, you may specify what share each is to receive.

> **EXAMPLE:** Celeste is married with two grown children. The children have both been provided for nicely with money from trusts and are financially secure. In her will, Celeste leaves her husband most of her property, with a few exceptions of some heirlooms for her children. As an alternate for

her husband, she names the university where she taught for many years.

You can also name a second level of alternates—that is, alternates to take the property should both your spouse and a first level of alternates you name all die before you do. You can name a back-up alternate for each alternate. If you named more than one first-level alternate, you may also designate that the survivors receive any property that would have gone to a deceased alternate.

c.   Making an Alternate Plan

This option—Plan B—is available only if you choose to leave all your property to your spouse.

It lets you create a whole new plan to take effect if, and only if, your spouse doesn't survive you by 45 days. This option is for people who think like this: I want to leave all my property to my spouse, period. But in case my spouse does not survive me, I want to make a whole new plan from the ground up—my Plan B—that does not include my spouse. So, if my spouse survives me, he or she gets all my property. But if not, I'll have been able to divide my property just as if I weren't married.

Your Plan B can include as many specific bequests as you wish. (See Section E, below.) After you have made all your specific bequests, you can also name someone to take the rest of your property. This is called your residuary beneficiary. (See Section F, below.) Again, all of these Plan B bequests will take effect only if your spouse does not survive you by 45 days.

> **EXAMPLE:** Sean wants to leave all his property to Eva, his wife, if she's alive when he dies. But thinking about what he would want to happen if Eva were not around to take everything, he decides that he would want to divide his property among several friends, relatives and charities.
>
> When he sits down with Quicken WillMaker Plus to make his will, Sean names Eva to get all his property. Then, when it's time to name alternates, he chooses the Plan B option and leaves $10,000 to a local food bank, his piano to his niece and the rest of his property to his brother.

B. If You Are Married With No Children

Many married people have simple will-making needs. They want to leave all or most of their property to their spouses. Then, as alternates for their spouses, they may name one or more other people or organizations. Quicken WillMaker Plus lets you choose this path easily. And if you do not want to make your spouse the main beneficiary of your will, that option is available, too.

1.   Choosing Beneficiaries

Quicken WillMaker Plus prompts you to choose one of three approaches to leaving your property. You can:

- leave everything to your spouse
- leave most of your property, with some specific exceptions, to your spouse
- make a plan that may or may not include your spouse.

The third option offers flexibility. You should choose it if you want to divide up your property more evenly among a number of beneficiaries or if you want to give all or most of your property to someone other than your spouse. If you choose it, be sure that you understand the rules governing what you own and the rights of your spouse. (See Chapter 5, Section D.)

EXAMPLE: Mark and Abby are a young married couple with no children. Mark wants simply to leave everything to Abby in his will. He chooses the first option—everything to your spouse—so that his will reflects his intentions.

EXAMPLE: Paul wants his wife to receive most of his property when he dies, but he wants his golf clubs to go to his best friend, Eric, and wants his niece to take his photography equipment. Paul chooses the second option—most to your spouse. Then, later in the program, he can name Eric to receive his golf clubs and his niece to receive the photography equipment.

EXAMPLE: Eleanor is married to William. She wants to leave William her share of their investment portfolio and family business, but also wants to leave a number of specific items to different friends, relatives and charities. She chooses the third option when using Quicken WillMaker Plus—make a different plan. The program then prompts her to list specific property items and the person or organization she wants to receive each of them. Before she does, Eleanor reviews Chapter 5 to make sure she understands what property is appropriate to leave in her will.

When you can skip ahead. If you do not want to name your spouse to receive all or most of your property, skip the rest of this section and go to Section E, below, for a discussion of what comes next.

2. Choosing Alternates for Your Spouse

If you want your spouse to receive all or most of your property, your next task will be to choose an alternate for your spouse.

The will you create with Quicken WillMaker Plus provides that all beneficiaries—including your spouse—must survive you by 45 days to receive the property you leave them. This is a standard will provision, called a survivorship requirement. It is based on the assumption that if a beneficiary survives you by only a few days or weeks, you would prefer the property to go to another beneficiary that you name in your will.

The alternates you choose will receive the property only if your spouse does not live at least 45 days longer than you do.

The simplest ways to provide for an alternate are to name:

- one person or organization to receive everything your spouse would have received, or
- more than one person or organization to share the property. If you go that route, the alternates will receive all the property that would have gone to your spouse. You need not specify which items go to which beneficiaries.

If, however, you named your spouse to receive all your property, you have a second option: You can make a completely new plan for leaving your property—Plan B—which will take effect only if your spouse does not survive you by 45 days. If you choose to make a new plan, you can divvy up your property among several alternate beneficiaries.

These approaches to naming alternates are discussed below.

a. Naming Alternates

You may name whomever you want as the alternate for your spouse. For instance, you may name a charity, friend or relative. If your spouse does not survive you by 45 days, the alternates you name will receive the property your spouse would have received. If you name more than one person or organization, you may specify what share each is to receive.

> **EXAMPLE:** In her will, Sharon leaves most of her property to her husband, Alex, with a few exceptions of some small items for friends. As an alternate for Alex, she names the charity at which she volunteered for many years.

You can also name a second level of alternates—that is, alternates to take the property should both your spouse and alternate not survive you. You can name a back-up alternate for each alternate. If you named more than one first-level alternate, you may designate that the survivors receive any property that would have gone to a deceased alternate.

b. Making an Alternate Plan

This option is available only if you choose to leave all your property to your spouse.

It lets you create a whole new plan to take effect if, and only if, your spouse doesn't survive you by 45 days. This option is for people who think like this: I want to leave all my property to my spouse, period. But in case my spouse does not survive me, I want to make a whole new plan from the ground up—my Plan B—that does not include my spouse. So, if my spouse survives me, he or she gets all my property. But if not, I'll divide my property just as if I weren't married.

Your alternate plan—Plan B—can include as many specific bequests as you wish. (See Section E, below.) After you have made all your specific

bequests, you can also name someone to take the rest of your property. This is called your residuary beneficiary. (See Section F, below.) Again, all of these Plan B bequests will take effect only if your spouse does not survive you by 45 days.

> **EXAMPLE:** Sean wants to leave all his property to Eva, his wife, if she's alive when he dies. But thinking about what he would want to happen if Eva were not around to take everything, he decides that he would want to divide his property among several friends, relatives and charities.

When he sits down with Quicken WillMaker Plus to make his will, Sean names Eva to take everything. Then, when it's time to name alternates, he chooses the Plan B option and leaves $10,000 to a local food bank, his piano to his niece and everything else to his brother.

C. If You Are Unmarried With Children

If you are a single parent, your children probably figure prominently in your plans for distributing your property after your death. With that in mind, Quicken WillMaker Plus offers some shortcuts when making your will.

1. Choosing Beneficiaries

Quicken WillMaker Plus prompts you to choose one of three approaches to leaving your property. You can:

- leave everything to your child or children
- leave most of your property, with some specific exceptions, to your child or children, or
- make a plan that may or may not include your children.

The third option offers flexibility. You should choose it if you want to divide up your property more evenly among a number of beneficiaries, or if you want to give all or most of your property to someone other than your children. If you choose it, be sure that you understand the rules governing what you own. (See Chapter 5, Section D, below.)

> **EXAMPLE:** Raquel is a divorced mother of two young children. She wants to leave all her property to the children, in equal shares. She chooses the first option.

> **EXAMPLE:** Carlo, a widower, has one son, who is now 40 years old. Carlo wants to leave most of his property to his son but also make a few small bequests to charities. He chooses the second option. Then, later in the program, he can name the charities and the amounts he wants to leave to each.

> **EXAMPLE:** Brenda has three children, all of whom are grown and financially healthy. She wants to leave a number of specific property items to her children but also to many different friends, relatives and charities. She chooses the third option when using Quicken WillMaker Plus. The program then asks her to list specific property items and the person or organization she wants to receive each one. Before doing this, Brenda reviews Chapter 5 to make sure she understands what property she can leave in her will.

When you can skip ahead. If you do not want to name your child or children to receive all or most of your property, skip the rest of this section and go to Section E, below, for a discussion of what comes next.

2. Designating Children's Shares

If you have a number of children, you must decide how you want them to share the property they receive through your will.

If any of your children are adults—that is, 18 or older—you can specify the share each will receive. Later in the program, you will have the option of designating someone to manage a child's share if he or she is still a young adult when you die. (See Chapter 7.)

> **EXAMPLE:** Charlie has three grown children. When Charlie makes his will, he names the children to receive everything. He directs that all three children should receive equal shares of his property.

If any of your children are minors—that is, under 18 years old—you may:

- specify the share each child will receive; later, you may designate how each child's share will be managed and doled out if a child is under 35 when you die, or
- direct that the property be held in one undivided fund, called a pot trust; under this option, the person you select to serve as trustee will use the assets in the trust for all your children as needed, until your youngest child turns an age you choose.

(See Chapter 7 for an explanation of all of these methods for managing property left to children.)

> **EXAMPLE:** Tess has three children, two teenagers and one 26-year-old boy. When she makes her will, she leaves the children most of her property and leaves a few small items to her sister. Because her oldest child is self-supporting, she leaves him just a 1/5 share and leaves the two younger children 2/5 each. Later in the program, Tess names her sister to

manage any property the two younger children come to own while they are still young.

EXAMPLE: Frank has two young sons close in age. In his will, he leaves them all his property. He then picks the pot trust option and names his sister as trustee. That means that if the boys inherit Frank's property while they are still young, all of it will go into a trust for them, administered by Frank's sister.

3. Choosing Alternates for Your Children

If you choose your child or children to receive all or most of your property, your next task will be to choose an alternate for your child.

When you can skip ahead. If you do not want to name your child or children to receive all or most of your property, skip the rest of this section and go to Section E, below, for a discussion of what comes next.

The will you create with Quicken WillMaker Plus provides that a beneficiary must survive you by 45 days to receive property through the will. This is a standard will provision, called a survivorship requirement. It is based on the assumption that if a beneficiary survives you by only a few weeks, you would prefer the property to go to another beneficiary that you name in your will.

The alternates you choose for a child will receive the property only if the child does not survive you by at least 45 days.

No alternates necessary for pot trusts. If you chose a pot trust, you don't need to name alternates. If one child does not survive you, the other surviving children will still share the property.

If you have one child, you can either:
- name one or more alternates for that child, or
- make a plan that may or may not include your child and other people or organizations.

If you have more than one child and have designated a share for each child, you can either:
- name one or more alternates for each child, or
- specify that if one child doesn't survive you, the survivors should take the deceased child's share.

If you chose a pot trust, you need not name alternates. If any child does not survive you, the others will share the property.

a. Naming Alternates

You may name whomever you want—for instance, a charity, friend or relative—as the alternate for a child. If the child does not survive you by 45 days, the alternates will receive the property the child would have received. If you name more than one alternate, you may specify the share each is to receive.

EXAMPLE: In her will, Sharon leaves her daughter most of her property and gives the rest to friends. As an alternate for her daughter, she names her daughter's two young children.

b. Surviving Children

Rather than name alternates for each of your children, you may want to provide that whatever property you leave them will go to all the children who survive you.

EXAMPLE: In his will, Patrick leaves his daughter and two sons all of his property. He specifies that each should receive an equal share. When Quicken WillMaker Plus asks him to name alternates for the children, he specifies that the survivors should take the share.

D. If You Are Unmarried With No Children

As a single person, you are free to leave your property to any person or organization you choose. You may have one beneficiary in mind—perhaps a partner or an organization you value highly. Quicken WillMaker Plus gives you the choice of simply leaving everything to that one beneficiary and then choosing an alternate beneficiary as well. If you don't want to name one main beneficiary to take the property under your will, that option is available, too.

1. Choosing Beneficiaries

Quicken WillMaker Plus prompts you to choose one of two approaches to leaving your property. You can:

- leave everything to one person, or
- leave your property to a group of beneficiaries or divide it among several.

The first option gives you a shortcut in the process of making your will. The second option can be more involved. If you choose it, be sure that you understand what kinds of property should be left in a will, and what might be passed to your survivors in other ways. (See Chapter 5, Section A.)

EXAMPLE: Fernando and Robert have been together for many years. When Fernando makes his will, he wants all his property to go to Robert. He chooses the first option—leave everything to one person—to make a will that reflects his wishes.

EXAMPLE: Theresa, whose husband died several years ago, wants to divide her money and possessions among different friends, relatives and charities. She chooses the second option. Quicken WillMaker Plus then asks her to list specific property items and the person or organization she wants to receive each one. Before she does, Sylvia reviews Chapter 5 to make sure she understands what property she is free to leave in her will.

When you can skip ahead. If you do not want to name one beneficiary to receive all or most of your property, skip the rest of this section and go to Section E, below, for a discussion of what comes next.

2. Choosing Alternates

If you specify that one person or organization should receive all or most of your property, your next task will be to choose an alternate for that beneficiary.

The will you create with Quicken WillMaker Plus provides that all beneficiaries must survive you by 45 days to receive the property you leave them. This is a standard will provision, called a survivorship requirement. It is based on the assumption that if a beneficiary survives you by only a few days or weeks, you would prefer the property to go to another beneficiary that you name in your will.

The alternates you choose will receive the property only if your main beneficiary does not survive for at least 45 days after you die.

Quicken WillMaker Plus offers two options for alternates. You can:

- name alternate beneficiaries, or
- make a completely new plan which will take effect only if your main beneficiary does not survive you by 45 days. This way, you can divvy up your property among several alternate beneficiaries.

a.   Naming Alternates

If you decide to specify alternates to receive the property left to your main beneficiary, you may name whomever you want. For instance, you may name a charity or a group of friends. If you name more than one person or organization, you may specify the share each is to receive.

If your main beneficiary does not survive you by 45 days, the alternates you name will receive the property he or she would have received.

> **EXAMPLE:** Christine is not married and has no children. She is very close to her sister Karen, and wants to leave all her property to her.
>
> In her will, Christine names Karen as her main beneficiary. As alternates, she names Karen's two children.

If you name one alternate beneficiary, you can also name a second level of alternates—that is, alternates to take the property should both your main beneficiary and the alternate not survive you by 45 days or more. If you named more than one alternate, however, the survivors will receive any property that would have gone to a deceased alternate.

> **EXAMPLE:** In his will, Michael leaves everything to his friend Denise. As alternates for Denise, he names two other friends, Jeff and Jack. If both Denise and Jeff do not survive Michael, Jack will receive all of Michael's property.

b.   Making an Alternate Plan

This option lets you create a whole new plan to take effect only if your main beneficiary does not survive you by 45 days. Your alternate plan—Plan B—can include as many specific bequests as you wish. (See Section E, below.)

After you have made all your specific bequests, you can also name someone to take the rest of your property. This is called your residuary beneficiary. (See Section F, below.)

> **EXAMPLE:** Sven wants to leave all his property to Jeannette, his companion, if she's alive when he dies. But thinking about what he would want to happen if Jeannette were not around to get everything, he decides that he would want to divide his property among relatives and charities.
>
> When he sits down with Quicken WillMaker Plus to make his will, Sven names Jeannette to take all of his property. Then, when it's time to name alternates, he chooses the Plan B option and leaves $10,000 to a local food bank, his piano to his niece and everything else to his brother.

E.   Making Specific Bequests

This section discusses how to make specific bequests—that is, leave specific property items to specific people or groups. You should read this section if you:

- left most of your property to a main beneficiary but want to leave some items to others
- want to divide your property among several beneficiaries, without leaving most or all of it to one main beneficiary, or
- left everything to one beneficiary, but instead of naming one alternate for that beneficiary,

you want to make a Plan B to take effect if your main beneficiary doesn't survive you.

Quicken WillMaker Plus lets you make an unlimited number of separate specific bequests. For each one, you must provide this information:

- a description of the item—for example, a house, cash, an heirloom or a car
- the names of the people or organizations you want to get the items, and
- if you wish, the name of an alternate beneficiary, who will receive specific property if your first beneficiary does not survive you by 45 days. You can name more than one alternate beneficiary; if you do, they will share the property.

1. Describing the Property

The first part of making a specific bequest is to describe the property you want to pass to a certain beneficiary or beneficiaries you have in mind. For example, if you want to leave your guitar to your best friend, you would begin by entering a brief description of the guitar, such as "my 1959 Martin guitar."

When describing an item, be as concise as you can, but use enough detail so that people will be able to identify and find the property. Most often, this will not be difficult: "my baby grand piano," "my collection of blue apothecary jars" or "my llama throw rug" are all the description you will need for tangible items that are easy to locate. If an item is very valuable or could be easily confused with other property, make sure you include identifying characteristics such as location, serial number, color or some other unique feature.

Tips on Describing Property in Your Will

Here is some help in how to identify different types of property with enough detail to prevent confusion:

- **Household furnishings.** You normally need not get very specific here, unless some object is particularly valuable. It is enough to list the location of the property: "all household furnishings and possessions in the apartment at 55 Drury Lane."
- **Real estate.** You can simply provide the street address or, for unimproved property, the name by which it is commonly known: "my condominium at 123 45th Avenue," "my summer home at 84 Memory Lane in Oakville," "the vacant lot next to the McHenry Place on Old Farm Road." You need not provide the legal description from the deed.
- **Bank, stock and money market accounts.** List financial accounts by their account numbers. Also, include the name and location of the organization holding the property: "$20,000 from savings account #22222 at Independence Bank, Big Mountain, Idaho"; "my money market account #23456 at Beryl Pynch & Company, Chicago, Illinois"; "100 shares of General Foods common stock."
- **Personal items.** As with household goods, it is usually adequate to briefly describe personal items and group them, unless they have significant monetary or sentimental value. For example, items of extremely valuable jewelry should normally be listed and identified separately, while a drawer full of costume jewelry and baubles could be grouped.

⚠ Do not include property that will pass by other means. Before describing the property you wish to leave in a specific bequest, take a moment to reflect on what property you are legally able to pass in your will. If you have already arranged to leave property outside your will by using legal devices such as life insurance, pay-on-death bank accounts or living trusts, you usually should not include that property in a specific bequest. (See Chapter 5, Section A.)

2. Naming Beneficiaries

The second step in making a specific bequest is to name one or more beneficiaries. If you have already entered the name of a beneficiary in the Contact List, select the name from the list and paste it in the beneficiary field. (See the Users' Manual for help.)

a. People

Beneficiaries' names need not be the names that appear on their birth certificates; as long as the names you use clearly identify the beneficiaries, all is well.

b. Minors or Young Adults

If any of the beneficiaries you name is a minor (under 18) or young adult (under 35), you will have a chance, in a later part of Quicken WillMaker Plus, to choose someone to manage the property for them until they are older. (See Chapter 7.)

c. Multiple Beneficiaries

If you name two or more beneficiaries to share a specific bequest, you will later be asked to specify each person's share. To avoid possible tiffs among your beneficiaries, the property you plan to leave them either should be property that is easily divided—a sum of money or an investment portfolio—or property that you intend to be sold so that the proceeds can be split, such as undeveloped real estate or a valuable collection. For property that requires discretion to divide—family antiques, for example—it may be wiser to leave items separately.

d. Organizations

You may want to leave property to a charity or a public or private organization—for example, the American Red Cross, the Greenview Battered Women's Shelter or the University of Illinois at Champaign-Urbana.

The organization you name need not be set up as a nonprofit, unless you wish your estate to qualify for a charitable estate tax deduction. (See Chapter 13.) It can be any organization you consider worthy of your bequest. The only limitation is that the organization must not be set up for some illicit or illegal purpose.

When naming an organization, be sure to enter its complete name, which may be different from the truncated version by which it is commonly known. Several different organizations may use similar names—and you want to be sure your bequest goes to the one you have in mind. Someone at the organization will be more than happy to help you get it straight.

3. Specifying Shares

If you name a group of beneficiaries to receive specific property, Quicken WillMaker Plus will ask you whether you want them to receive equal or unequal shares of the property. If you want it shared unequally, the shares must add up to one. Quicken WillMaker Plus will warn you if your computations are off.

> **EXAMPLE:** Fred Wagner wants to leave an undeveloped real estate parcel to his three children, Mary, Sue and Peter. Because he has already paid for Mary's graduate school education, he wants to give Sue and Peter greater percentages of the property in case they want to go back to school, too. He lists his children and the share of his property to which they are entitled this way: Mary Wagner (1/5), Susan Wagner (2/5) and Peter Wagner (2/5).

Do Not Place Conditions on Bequests

Don't place conditions on any of your bequests; it risks making a confusing and even unenforceable will.

Here are some examples of what not to do:

- "I leave my gold Rolex to Andres, but only if he divorces his current wife, Samantha." Such a bequest would not be considered legally valid, because it encourages the breakup of a family.

- "I leave my dental office equipment to Claude, as long as he sets up a dental practice in San Francisco." The reason this bequest is unwieldy becomes obvious once you think ahead to the need for constant supervision. Who would be responsible for tracking Claude's dentistry career and making sure he ends up in San Francisco? What if Claude initially practices in San Francisco, using the equipment he was willed, then moves to grow grapes in the Napa Valley? Must he give up the equipment? To whom?

- "I leave my vintage Barbie doll collection to Collette, if the dolls are still in good condition." Who is to judge whether the dolls are in good condition? What happens if they aren't?

If you are determined to place conditions on beneficiaries or property, consult a lawyer who is experienced in drafting bequests that will adequately address these potentially complex arrangements.

4. Naming Alternates

To receive property under your will, a beneficiary must survive you by 45 days. Quicken WillMaker Plus assumes that if a beneficiary survives you by only a few days or weeks, you would prefer the property to pass to an alternate or residuary beneficiary named in your will, rather than have the property pass along with the beneficiary's other property.

With Quicken WillMaker Plus, you can name one or more alternate beneficiaries to take the bequest if your first choices do not survive you by the required period.

> **EXAMPLE:** Joan leaves her horse to her brother Pierre. In case Pierre does not survive her by 45 days and so become eligible to receive this bequest, Joan names her sister Carmen as Pierre's alternate beneficiary.

If you name multiple beneficiaries to receive property, you can name an alternate for each beneficiary.

> **EXAMPLE:** Gideon leaves his house to his three nephews—Aaron, Thomas and Zeke—in equal shares. In case Aaron does not survive him by 45 days, Gideon specifies that the house should then go to the survivors, Thomas and Zeke. In case Thomas does not survive him by 45 days, Gideon names his brother Horace to take Thomas's share. In case Zeke does not survive him by 45 days, Gideon specifies that Aaron and Horace should take Zeke's share.

Providing for Pets

You cannot legally name a pet as a beneficiary in your will; the law considers pets to be property. But if you live with animals, you'll want to be sure that they receive good homes and good care after your death. Because of Quicken WillMaker Plus's proscription against leaving bequests with conditions on them, you cannot leave, for example, "$1,000 to Suzy Anderson, to be spent for my cat, Felix."

However, you can leave your pet to another person in your will. It is also permissible—and common practice—to leave some money to the caretaker, explaining in a letter attached to your will that you want the money to be used for the pet's care. Chapter 12, Section B, discusses this and also provides some suggestions about what you might do if you don't know anyone who is willing or able to care for your pet.

 Setting up a trust for your pet. In a majority of states, you can establish a trust for your pet rather than leaving your pet to someone else through your will. The trust is a legally independent entity, managed by a trustee you name. You also define the terms of the trust—how your pet is to be cared for—in the trust document. Pet trusts can be desirable for people who feel they'd prefer not to leave their pet outright to someone. But creating a pet trust is more costly and complicated than simply leaving your pet outright. You'll need to hire an attorney to get the document drafted.

5. Reviewing Specific Bequests

When you complete a specific bequest—that is, you have identified the property, named the beneficiary and named an alternate beneficiary—Quicken WillMaker Plus will display the beneficiary's name on the screen. You can also view this list by property. You can then add a new bequest or review, change or delete any of the bequests you have made.

F. Naming Residuary Beneficiaries

Quicken WillMaker Plus will ask you to name a beneficiary for your residuary estate only if either of the following is true:

- You chose not to name one main beneficiary to receive most or all of your property.
- After leaving all your property to one beneficiary, you chose to create an alternate plan, or Plan B, in case your first choice does not survive you. In this case, you name a residuary beneficiary as part of your alternate plan.

If you left all or most of your property to one or more beneficiaries, they will receive property that does not pass in a specific bequest or by means other than your will. In effect, they will automatically become your residuary beneficiaries.

> **EXAMPLE:** When Mikki makes her will, she leaves all her property to her husband, Tyler. By the time she dies, 15 years later, she has acquired a new car, stocks and other items. Everything goes to her husband.

1. What a Residuary Beneficiary Receives

Your residuary beneficiary receives anything that does not go, for one reason or another, to the beneficiaries you named to receive specific bequests.

Specifically, the residuary beneficiary receives property that:

- you overlook when making your will
- you acquire after you make your will, and
- does not go to the person you named to get it in a specific bequest—for example, because that person died before you did and you did not name an alternate beneficiary, or the alternate also failed to survive you.

> **EXAMPLE:** In her will, Sara, a widow, leaves many different items to many different beneficiaries: books to her daughter, jewelry to a friend, a car to her nephew and so on. She doesn't name alternate beneficiaries for these specific bequests, but she names her daughter as residuary beneficiary.
>
> When Sara dies, some years after making the will, the friend to whom she left the jewelry has already died. The jewelry goes to Sara's daughter, as does the other property that Sara acquired since making her will.

There is no need to describe, in your will, the property the residuary beneficiary will receive. By definition, your residuary estate is the rest of your property that does not pass outside of your will or in a specific bequest, so it is impossible to know exactly what it will include. When your executor inventories your entire estate after your death, he or she will identify your residuary estate.

2. How to Name Residuary Beneficiaries

You can name one or more individuals or organizations, or a combination of both, as residuary beneficiaries. Use the Contact List to select and paste the name if it is already on the list. (See the Users' Manual for help.)

If you name more than one residuary beneficiary, Quicken WillMaker Plus will ask you what shares you want each to receive.

> **EXAMPLE:** After making a large number of specific bequests in his Quicken WillMaker Plus will, Maurice leaves his residuary estate to his four children, Clara, Heinrich, Lise and Wiebke. He wants Lise and Wiebke each to receive 30% (3/10) of the property and the other two children to receive 20% (2/10) each. So he indicates that he wants to leave the residuary estate in unequal shares and enters the desired shares on the screen provided for this purpose.

If any of the beneficiaries you name is a minor (under 18) or young adult (under 35), you will have a chance, in a later part of Quicken WillMaker Plus, to choose someone to manage the property for them until they are older. (See Chapter 7.)

3. Naming Alternates

Quicken WillMaker Plus also asks you to choose an alternate residuary beneficiary, in case your first choice does not survive you by 45 days.

⚠ **When you need not bother naming alternates.** You do not have to name an alternate residuary beneficiary, and not everyone is concerned about this issue. Younger people in reasonably good health are usually confident that they can address a beneficiary's premature death by updating their wills. However, many married people are concerned about what will happen if they die close together in time. And older people in poor health may fear that they won't have an opportunity to update their wills if their first choice beneficiaries die before they do.

> **EXAMPLE:** After making many specific bequests, Alfredo leaves his residuary estate to his daughter, Vanessa. He then specifies that if Vanessa does not survive him, her share should go to her two children—Alfredo's grandchildren. If Vanessa does not survive Alfredo, and Alfredo does not write a new will, Vanessa's children would each take one-half of Alfredo's residuary estate.

> **EXAMPLE:** Jack makes a large number of specific bequests to friends and relatives and then leaves his residuary estate to his friend, Joe. He names another friend, Josette, as alternate residuary beneficiary. Josette will be entitled to take property under Jack's will only if Joe does not survive Jack by 45 days and there is property left over after the specific bequests are distributed. ∎

Providing Management for Children's Property

Except for items of little value, minors are not permitted by law to receive property directly. Instead, that property will have to be distributed to and managed by a responsible adult. It is of vital importance to both your own children and any other young beneficiaries that you arrange for this management yourself, in your will. If you don't, a court may need to appoint and supervise someone. Or, in many states, your executor can name a custodian (discussed below) to manage the property the child inherits. But it's better to make your own choice and state it in your will, instead of leaving the decision to someone else.

Keeping track of children's property. The person you name to take care of your child's property will need access to financial records related to property that the child will own. For help collecting this information, use Quicken WillMaker Plus's "Information for Caregivers and Survivors" form.

A. Property Management for Your Children

Quicken WillMaker Plus enables you to establish management for property that your minor children receive from you:

- under your will, or
- outside of your will—for example, through a living trust or a life insurance policy.

For property received under your will, this management may last until the minor turns an age you choose. For property that your minor children receive outside of your will, the management provided by Quicken WillMaker Plus lasts until the children become adults—18 years old in most states.

If you are a parent, you may choose to leave your property directly to your spouse or partner and trust him or her to use good judgment in providing for your children's needs. Even if you do this, however, you are not necessarily freed from the need to provide property management. To plan for the possibility that your spouse or partner dies close in time to you, you may want to name your children as alternate beneficiaries. You can then appoint a trusted adult as manager for the property they could inherit.

Finally, once you choose a person to manage the property, you must decide what you want to happen when your children reach the age of 18. You can choose to have what property is left by that time handed over in one lump sum or, for property left in your will, you may provide that the property management continue until the children are somewhat older.

Explaining Your Bequests to Your Children

Using Quicken WillMaker Plus, you are free to divide up your property among your children as you see fit. If your children are already responsible adults, your prime concern will likely be fairness—given the circumstances and the children's needs. Often, this will mean dividing your property equally among your children. Sometimes, however, the special health or educational needs of one child, the relative affluence and stability of another or the fact that you are estranged from a child will be the impetus for you to divide the property unevenly.

Doing this can sometimes raise serious angst; a child who receives less property may conclude that you cared for him or her less. To deal with this, you may wish to explain your reasons for dividing your property unequally. Because of the risk of adding illegal or confusing language, Quicken WillMaker Plus does not allow you to make this explanation in your will. Fortunately, there is a sound and sensible way to express your reasons and feelings. Simply prepare a separate letter to accompany your will. (See Chapter 12, Section B.)

B. Property Management for Other Children

It often also makes good sense to establish management for property you plan to leave to other minor children in your will—for example, your grandchildren, nieces and nephews. That way, you free their parents, or other adults responsible for them, from the expensive and time-consuming burden of having to go to court to get legal authority to manage that property. Here, too, you can use Quicken WillMaker Plus to provide property management that lasts until the young beneficiary is 35 years old.

And there also may be a good reason to provide property management for beneficiaries who are 18 or over. For example, those considering young adults as beneficiaries may want to put off the time they can take control of it. You can use Quicken WillMaker Plus to postpone distributing property left to any young adult—yours or someone else's—until the beneficiary reaches an age you choose, up to 35 years old.

C. An Overview of Property Management

This section presents an overview of basic property management considerations. Section D, below, discusses how to use Quicken WillMaker Plus to put your management choices into your will.

Property management consists of naming a trusted adult to be in charge of caring for and accurately accounting for the property that a young beneficiary takes under your will until the beneficiary turns a specific age. The property being managed for the young beneficiary must be held, invested or spent in the best interest of the beneficiary. In other words, someone other than the young beneficiaries will decide if their inheritances will be spent on college tuition or a new sports car.

1. Property Management for Minors

Except for property of little value—worth less than $2,000 or so—minors may not directly control property they get under a will. This legal rule is most important if the property is:

- cash or other liquid assets—for example, a savings account that can easily be spent, or
- property that comes with a title document—for example, real estate.

Property of this type must be managed by an adult for the minor's benefit until he or she turns 18. If you do not provide for this management in your will, the court will do it for you—an expensive and time-consuming alternative requiring court supervision of how the property should be managed or spent.

And from a practical standpoint, it may be important for you to provide management for property you leave to minors where that property is unique or valuable—for example, a collection of rare coins that you do not want squandered or damaged.

In addition, you may want to provide that management for property left to a minor continues beyond age 18—the age at which a court-established guardianship ends. Quicken WillMaker Plus allows this more enduring form of property management.

What Happens If the Minor Does Not Get Property

If you arrange for property management for a minor, but the minor never actually becomes entitled to the property, no harm is done. The management provisions for that minor are ignored. For instance, suppose you identify a favorite niece to take property as an alternate beneficiary and provide management for that property until the niece turns 25. If the niece never gets to take the property because your first choice beneficiary survives you, no property management will be established for her, since none will be needed.

2. Property Management for Young Adults

If you are leaving valuable property to someone who is in his or her late teens or early twenties, you may justifiably wish to delay the time the beneficiary actually gets to use it. Quicken WillMaker Plus lets you extend the time property left to young adults is managed.

D. Property Management Under Quicken WillMaker Plus

Quicken WillMaker Plus offers four approaches to property management for minors and young adults:

- the Uniform Transfers to Minors Act—for property left in your will—in all states except South Carolina and Vermont (see Section D1)
- the Quicken WillMaker Plus child's trust—for property left in your will—as an alternative to the UTMA and as an option for will makers who live in one of the two states that have not adopted the UTMA (see Section D2)
- the Quicken WillMaker Plus pot trust—for property left to your children in your will—if at least one of your children is under 18 (see Section D3), and
- a property guardianship—for property that passes to your minor children outside of your will (see Section E).

1. The Uniform Transfers to Minors Act

The Uniform Transfers to Minors Act (UTMA) allows you to name a custodian to manage property you leave to a minor. The management ends when the minor reaches age 18 to 25, depending on state law.

States are free to adopt or reject the UTMA, which is a model law proposed by a group of legal scholars. The great majority of states have adopted the UTMA, many making minor changes to it. It is likely that the UTMA will be universally adopted in a few more years.

States That Have Not Adopted the UTMA

The UTMA has not been adopted in South Carolina or Vermont.

If you are a resident of one of these states, you can set up property management for any minor or young adult beneficiary using the Quicken WillMaker Plus child's trust, discussed in Section 2, below. If at least one of your children is under 18 years old, you may also use the Quicken WillMaker Plus pot trust, discussed in Section 3, below.

Age Limits for Property Management in UTMA States

State	Age at Which Minor Gets Property	State	Age at Which Minor Gets Property
Alabama	21	Missouri	21
Alaska	18 to 25	Montana	21
Arizona	21	Nebraska	21
Arkansas	18 to 21	Nevada	18 to 25
California	18 to 25	New Hampshire	21
Colorado	21	New Jersey	18 to 21
Connecticut	21	New Mexico	21
Delaware	21	New York	21
District of Columbia	18 to 21	North Carolina	18 to 21
Florida	21	North Dakota	21
Georgia	21	Ohio	18 to 21
Hawaii	21	Oklahoma	18 to 21
Idaho	21	Oregon	21 to 25
Illinois	21	Pennsylvania	21 to 25
Indiana	21	Rhode Island	21
Iowa	21	South Dakota	18
Kansas	21	Tennessee	21 to 25
Kentucky	18	Texas	21
Maine	18 to 21	Utah	21
Maryland	21	Virginia	18 to 21
Massachusetts	21	Washington	21
Michigan	18 to 21	West Virginia	21
Minnesota	21	Wisconsin	21
Mississippi	21	Wyoming	21

If the UTMA has been adopted in your state, you may use it to specify a custodian to manage property you leave to a minor in your will until the age at which the laws of your state require that it be turned over to the minor. Depending on your state, this varies from 18 to 25. Quicken WillMaker Plus keeps track of the state you indicate as your residence and tells you whether the UTMA is available and, if so, the age at which property management under it must end.

Among the powers the UTMA gives the custodian are the rights to collect, hold, manage, invest and reinvest the property, and to spend "it for the use and benefit of the minor." All of these actions can be taken without getting approval from a court. The custodian must also keep records so that tax returns can be filed on behalf of the minor and must otherwise act prudently in controlling the property.

Special Rule for Life Insurance

Often the major source of property left to children comes from a life insurance policy naming the children as beneficiaries. If you want the insurance proceeds for a particular child to be managed, and you live in a state that has adopted the UTMA, instruct your insurance agent to provide you with the form necessary to name a custodian to manage the property for the beneficiary under the terms of this Act.

---

2. The Quicken WillMaker Plus Child's Trust

The Quicken WillMaker Plus child's trust, which can be used in all states, is a legal structure you establish in your will. If you create a trust, any property a minor beneficiary gets will be managed by a person or institution you choose to serve as trustee until the beneficiary turns an age you choose—through age 35. The trustee's powers are listed in your will. The trustee may use trust assets for the education, medical needs and living expenses of the beneficiary. All property you leave to a beneficiary for whom a trust is established will be managed under the terms of the trust.

Because management under the Quicken WillMaker Plus child's trust can be extended through age 35, it is also suitable to use for property left to young adults. (The pros and cons of management options are discussed in Section 4, below.)

3. The Quicken WillMaker Plus Pot Trust

The Quicken WillMaker Plus pot trust is a legal structure you can establish in your will. However, instead of creating a separate child's trust for the property you leave to each child, you create one trust for all the property you leave to your children. You name a single trustee to manage the property for the benefit of the children as a group, without regard to how much is spent on an individual child.

For example, if there are three children and one of them needs an expensive medical procedure, all of the property could be spent on that child, even though the other children would receive nothing. While this potential result may seem unfair, it in fact mirrors the reality faced by many families: Some children need more money than others.

The pot trust will last until the youngest child turns an age you specify. If there is a significant age gap between your children, the oldest children may have to wait many years past the time they become adults before they receive their shares of the property. For instance, if one of your children is 5 and another child is 17—and you specify that the pot trust should end when the youngest turns 18—the 17-year-old will have to wait at least until age 30 to receive a share of the property left in the trust.

All or none must go in pot. The Quicken WillMaker Plus pot trust option is available only for property you leave to all of your children as a group. If you want to use the pot trust for some but not all of your children, you will need to see a lawyer. (See Chapter 25.)

4. Choosing Among Management Options

For each minor or young adult to whom you leave property in your will, you must decide which management approach to use: the UTMA, a child's trust or the pot trust. This section helps you decide which is best for you and yours.

Needs not covered by Quicken WillMaker Plus. The property management features offered by Quicken WillMaker Plus—the UTMA, child's trust and pot trust—provide the property manager with broad management authority adequate for most minors and young adults. However, they are not designed to:

- provide skilled long-term management of a business
- provide for management of funds beyond age 35 for a person with spendthrift tendencies or other personal habits that may impede sound financial management beyond young adulthood, or
- meet a disabled beneficiary's special needs. A physical, mental or developmental disability will likely require management customized to the beneficiary's circumstances, both to perpetuate the beneficiary's way of life and to preserve the property, while assuring that the beneficiary continues to qualify for government benefits.

For all these situations, specific trust provisions tailored to the needs of the beneficiary and your wishes should be drafted by an attorney experienced in this type of work.

a. Using the UTMA

As a general rule, the less valuable the property involved and the more mature the child, the more appropriate the UTMA is, because it is simpler to use than a child's trust or pot trust. There are a couple of reasons for this.

Because the UTMA is built into state law, banks, insurance companies, brokerage firms and other financial institutions know about it and should make it easy for the custodian to carry out property management duties. To set up a child's trust or pot trust, the financial institution would have to be given a copy of the trust document and may tie up the proceeding in red tape to be sure the trustee is acting under its terms.

Also, a custodian acting under the UTMA need not file a separate income tax return for the property being managed; it can be included in the young beneficiary's return. However, in a child's trust or a pot trust, both the beneficiary and the trust must file returns.

Because the UTMA requires that management end at a relatively young age, if the property you are leaving is worth $100,000 or less—or the child is likely to be able to handle more than that by age 21 (25 in Alaska, California, Nevada, Oregon, Pennsylvania or Tennessee), use the UTMA. After all, $100,000 is likely to be used up before management under the UTMA ends.

b. Using the Quicken WillMaker Plus Child's Trust

Generally, the more property is worth, and the less mature the young beneficiary, the better it is to use the child's trust, even though doing so creates more work for the property manager than does the UTMA. For example, in a child's trust, the property manager must keep the beneficiary informed, manage trust assets prudently (meeting the requirements of state law) and file a separate tax return for the trust each year.

However, if a minor or young adult stands to get a fairly large amount of property—such as $200,000 or more—you might not want it all dis-tributed by your state's UTMA cut-off age, which is usually 18 or 21. In such circumstances, you may be better off using the Quicken WillMaker Plus child's trust. Remember, under the child's trust, management can last until an age you choose, through age 35.

c. Using the Quicken WillMaker Plus Pot Trust

As a general rule, the pot trust makes sense only when the children are young and fairly close in age. For instance, if one of your children were 30 and another child of a later marriage were 2, and you specify that the pot trust should end when the youngest child turns 18, the 30-year-old would have to wait until age 46 to receive the property. However, the pot trust option is available to you as long as any of your children is a minor.

Like the trustee of a child's trust, a pot trust trustee must invest trust assets following the rules set out in state law, communicate regularly with the trust beneficiaries to keep them informed and file annual tax returns. The trustee of the pot trust also has the significant added responsibility of weighing competing claims from multiple benefi-ciaries when deciding how to spend trust assets.

E. Property Guardians

The UTMA, Quicken WillMaker Plus child's trust and pot trust are good management options for property that minor or young adult beneficia-ries receive under your will. However, if you have minor children and they receive property of sig-nificant value outside of your will, a court will usually have to step in and appoint a guardian to manage the property under court supervision un-til the children turn 18.

The two most common ways that children receive property outside of a will are from life insurance or through a living trust. (See Chapter 13.) While it is possible to provide for management of this type of property through your life insurance agent under the UTMA or within the living trust itself, often no such management is established and a property guardianship is required.

In addition, property that your children receive from other sources—the lottery, a gift from an aunt or uncle, earnings from playing in a rock band—may also need to be managed by a property guardian.

It is always better to specify who will be managing any such property that your minor children come to own. Otherwise, the court will appoint someone who may or may not have your children's best interests in mind. If you are using the Quicken WillMaker Plus child's trust, a pot trust or the UTMA to provide management for property you are leaving to your children in your will, the person you have named as trustee or custodian would also be a good choice for property guardian. Another possible choice is the person you chose to be personal guardian, if you think he or she will handle the property wisely for the benefit of the minor. You also may wish to choose someone else entirely. (See Section F, below.)

F. Naming a Custodian or Trustee

You may name one person to manage the property you leave to a young person. You can also name one successor, who will take over if your first choice is unable to serve. If you use the UTMA, these people will be called the custodian and successor custodian. If you use the Quicken WillMaker Plus child's trust or the Quicken WillMaker Plus pot trust, they will be called the trustee and successor trustee.

Choosing someone to manage your children's finances is almost as important a decision as choosing someone to take custody of them after your death—and many people will choose the same person to handle both tasks. Name someone you trust, who is familiar with managing the kind of assets you leave to your children and who shares your attitudes and values about how the money should be spent. (See Section 2, below.)

Parents do not get the job automatically. You may be surprised to learn that the child's other parent probably will not be able to automatically step in and handle property you leave your children in your will. Rather, unless you provide for management in your will, that other parent usually will have to petition the court to be appointed as the property manager and then handle the property under court supervision until the children turn 18. So, if you want your children's other parent to manage the property you are leaving your children, name him or her as the trustee or custodian. Of course, you may wish someone else to manage the property.

Whomever you choose as custodian or trustee, it is essential to get his or her consent first. This will also give you a chance to discuss, in general terms, how you would like the property to be managed to be sure the manager you select agrees with your vision and fully understands the beneficiary's needs.

1. Choosing a Custodian or Trustee

There are a few general principles to follow when choosing a custodian or trustee.

As a general rule, your choice should live in or near to the state where the property will be managed—or at least be willing to travel there if needed.

You need not worry about finding a financial wizard to be your property manager. The custodian or trustee has the power to hire professionals to prepare accountings and tax returns and to give investment advice. Anyone hired for such help may be paid out of the property being managed. The custodian or trustee's main jobs are to manage the property honestly, make basic decisions about how to take care of the assets wisely and sensibly mete out the money to the trust beneficiary.

It is usually preferable to combine the personal care and property management functions for a particular minor child in the hands of one person. Think first who is likely to be caring for the children if you die, and then consider whether that person is also a good choice for property manager. If you must name two different people, try to choose people who get along well; they will have to work together.

If you believe that the person who will be caring for the minor is not the best person to handle the minor's finances, consider another adult who is capable and is willing to serve.

For property you leave to young adults, select an honest person with business savvy to manage the property.

EXAMPLE: Orenthal and Ariadne agree that Ariadne's sister, Penny, should be guardian of their kids should they both die, but that the $100,000 worth of stock the three kids will inherit might better be handled by someone with more business experience and who will be better able to resist the children's urgings to spend the money frivolously. In each of their wills, they name Penny as personal guardian of the children, but also create trusts for the property they are leaving to their children. They name each other as trustees, and Orenthal's mother, Phyllis, who has investment and business knowledge and lots of experience in handling headstrong adolescents, as the alternate trustee, after obtaining her consent. Orenthal and Ariadne also decide that one of their children, who is somewhat immature, should receive his share of the estate—at least the portion not already disbursed for his benefit by the trustee—upon turning 25, and the other two children should get their shares when they turn 21.

2. Selecting an Institution as Custodian or Trustee

If you are using the UTMA, you must name a person as custodian; you cannot name an institution. If you're creating a trust, you can name an institution to serve as trustee, but it is rarely a good idea. Most banks will not accept a trust with less than several hundred thousand dollars' worth of liquid assets.

When banks do agree to take a trust, they charge large management and administrative fees. All trustees are entitled to reasonable compensation for their services—paid from trust assets. But family members or close friends who act as trustees often waive payments or accept far less than banks. If you cannot find an individual you think is suitable for handling your assets and do not have enough property to be managed by a financial institution, you may be better off not creating a trust.

Also, it is common for banks to manage the assets of all trusts worth less than $1 million as part of one large fund, while charging fees as if they were individually managed. Any trustee who invests trust money in a conservatively run mutual fund can normally do at least as well at a fraction of the cost.

G. Choosing an Age to End Management

If you choose a property guardian to manage property received by your minor children outside of your will, that management will end when each child turns 18.

For management under the UTMA, the age at which management terminates is seldom an issue. In all but a few states, the management terminates automatically at age 18 or 21; in some states, it can last until age 25. (See Section D1, above.)

Under the Quicken WillMaker Plus child's trust, you may select any age up to 35 for the management to end. Choosing an age for a particular beneficiary to get whatever trust property has not been spent on the beneficiary's needs will depend on:

- the amount of money or other property involved
- how much control you would like to impose over it
- the beneficiary's likely level of maturity as a young adult (for small children, this may be difficult to predict, but by the time youngsters reach their teens, you should have a pretty good indication), and
- whether the property you leave, such as rental property or a small business, needs sophisticated management that a young beneficiary is unlikely to master.

H. Examples of Property Management

Here are some examples of how the Quicken WillMaker Plus property management options might be selected. The following scenarios are only intended as suggestions. Remember, if you live in South Carolina or Vermont, you cannot create an UTMA custodianship.

EXAMPLE 1: Married, adult children age 25 and older. You want to leave all your property, worth $150,000, to your spouse and name surviving children as alternate beneficiaries. As long as you think the children are all sufficiently mature to handle their shares of the property if your spouse does not survive you, answer no when Quicken WillMaker Plus asks if you wish to set up property management.

EXAMPLE 2: Married, children aged 2, 5 and 9. You want to leave all your property, which is worth $150,000, to your spouse and name your children as alternate beneficiaries. You use the property management feature and select the UTMA option to manage the property if it passes to your children. You name your wife's mother—the same person you have named as personal guardian—as custodian, and name your brother as alternate personal guardian and alternate custodian. The property will be managed by the custodian until the age set by your state's law.

You also name your wife's mother as property guardian if management is needed for property your minor children receive outside of your will.

Later, when your children are older and you have accumulated more property, you may wish to make a new will and switch from the UTMA management approach to a pot trust so that the property can be used to meet the children's needs as required. You are also free to postpone the age at which the children receive the property under this option.

EXAMPLE 3: Single or married; two minor children from a previous marriage and one minor child with your present partner. You want to leave all your property, which is worth $150,000, directly to your children. You can use the UTMA, set up the trust for each child or create a pot trust. You should also name a property guardian to manage any property your minor child might get outside of your will.

Beware of spouse's property rights. If you are married, your spouse may have a right to claim a portion of your property, so it is usually unwise to leave it all to your children unless your spouse agrees with that plan. (See Chapter 5, Section D.)

EXAMPLE 4: Single or married; two adult children from a previous marriage—ages 23 and 27—and one minor child with your present partner. You decide to divide $300,000 equally among the children. To accomplish this, you establish a trust for each child from the previous marriage and put the termination age at 30. You name your current spouse, who gets along well with the children, as trustee and a local trust company as alternate trustee. Because your third child is an unusually mature teenager, you choose the UTMA for this child and select 21 as the age at which this child takes any remaining property outright. You appoint your wife as custodian and your sister as successor custodian.

EXAMPLE 5: Married or single; one daughter, age 32, and three minor grandchildren. You want to leave $50,000 directly to each of the grandchildren. You establish a custodianship under the UTMA for each grandchild and name your daughter as custodian and her husband as successor custodian. ■

Chapter 8

Choosing an Executor

Using Quicken WillMaker Plus, you can name an executor, called a personal representative in some states. After your death, that person will have legal responsibility for safeguarding and handling your property, seeing that debts and taxes are paid and distributing what is left to your beneficiaries as your will directs.

Make your will and records accessible. You can help with the executor's first task: locating your will. Keep the original in a fairly obvious place—such as a desk or file cabinet. And make sure your executor has access to it.

A. Duties of an Executor

Serving as an executor can be fairly easy, or it can require a good deal of time and patience—depending on the amount of property involved and the complexity of the plans for it.

1. The Executor's Job

Your executor will have a number of duties, most of which do not require special expertise and can usually be accomplished without outside help. An executor typically must:

- obtain certified copies of the death certificate
- locate will beneficiaries
- examine and inventory the deceased person's safe deposit boxes
- collect the deceased person's mail
- cancel credit cards and subscriptions
- notify Social Security and other benefit plan administrators of the death

- learn about the deceased person's property—which may involve examining bankbooks, deeds, insurance policies, tax returns and many other records
- get bank accounts released or, in the case of pay-on-death accounts, get them transferred to their new owner, and
- collect any death benefits from life insurance policies, Social Security, veterans benefits and other benefits due from the deceased's union, fraternal society or employer.

In addition to these mundane tasks, the executor will typically have to:

- file papers in court to start the probate process and obtain the necessary authority to act as executor
- handle the probate court process—which involves transferring property and making sure the deceased's final debts and taxes are paid, and
- prepare final income tax forms for the deceased and, if necessary, file estate tax returns for the estate.

For these tasks, it may be necessary to hire an outside professional who will be paid out of the estate's assets—a lawyer to initiate and handle the probate process and an accountant to prepare the necessary tax forms. But in some states, because of simplified court procedures and adequate self-help law materials, even these tasks can be accomplished without outside assistance.

Quicken WillMaker Plus offers help with the task of educating your executor. You have the option of printing out a document titled The Executor's Role, which you can give to the person you name to serve. The document offers guidance on the executor's duties.

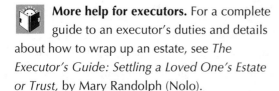 **More help for executors.** For a complete guide to an executor's duties and details about how to wrap up an estate, see *The Executor's Guide: Settling a Loved One's Estate or Trust,* by Mary Randolph (Nolo).

2. Posting a Bond

Sometimes, a probate court asks an executor to post a bond—an insurance policy that protects beneficiaries if the executor is dishonest or incompetent—unless your will expressly waives this requirement. As long as you choose an executor you trust (see Section B1, below), there's no reason your executor should have to go to the trouble of putting up a bond. Furthermore, the cost of the bond—usually about 10% of its face amount—comes out of your estate. If a bond is purchased, your beneficiaries will receive less than they otherwise would.

The will you make with Quicken WillMaker Plus provides that no bond is necessary. If you appoint an executor who lives in another state, however, a few states may require the executor to put up a bond no matter what your will says. (See Section B1a, below.)

3. Getting Paid

The laws of every state provide that an executor may be paid out of the estate. Depending on your state law, this payment may be:

- based on what the court considers reasonable
- a small percentage of the gross or net value of the estate, or
- set according to factors specified in your state's statutes.

When the executor either stands to get a large portion of the estate or is a close family relative, it is common for him or her to do the work without being paid. Some will makers opt to leave their executors a specific bequest of money in appreciation for serving.

However, outside experts will almost always be paid out of the estate. The amount outside experts—including lawyers—are paid is totally under the control of the executor. However, a few states set out maximum fees that may be charged by lawyers and other professionals—usually a percentage of the value of the estate.

Beware of lawyers' fees. Lawyers commonly imply that the maximum fee allowed by statute is the fee that they are required to charge for their services. In fact, lawyers are perfectly free to charge by the hour or to set a flat fee that is unrelated to the size of the estate. One of the most important tasks that your executor can perform is to negotiate a reasonable fee with any lawyer he or she may pick to help probate your estate. Be sure you explain this to your choice for executor.

B. Naming an Executor

Glancing through the list of the executor's duties mentioned above should tip you off about whom you know that might be the best person for the job. The prime characteristics are honesty, skill at organizing and finesse in keeping track of details. For many tasks, such as collecting mail and finding important records and papers, it may be most helpful to name someone who lives nearby or who is familiar with your business matters.

1. Choosing Your Executor

The most important guideline in naming an executor is to choose someone you trust enough to have access to your personal records and finances after your death. Many people choose someone who is also named to get a substantial amount of property under the will. This is sensible, because a person with an interest in how your property is distributed—a spouse, partner, child or close family member—is also likely to do a conscientious job as executor. And he or she will probably also come equipped with knowledge of where your records are kept and an understanding of why you want your property split up as you have directed.

Following are a few more things you may want to consider when making your choice. Whomever you choose, make sure the person you select is willing to do the job. Discuss the possible duties involved with your choice for executor before naming him or her in your will.

a. Naming Someone Who Lives Out of State

As a practical matter, it's wise to name an executor who lives close to you. It will be more difficult for the executor to handle day-to-day matters from a distance. But if the best person for the job lives far away, there's no law against naming that person in your will. Every state allows out-of-state executors to serve, though most states impose special rules on them. The chart below sets out the details.

b. Naming More Than One Person

Some people want to name two or more executors to serve together. Quicken WillMaker Plus allows this option. However, naming two or more executors to share the job is often not wise. Joint executors may act without each other's consent—and if they ever disagree, your estate may be the loser because of lengthy probate delays and court costs.

c. Naming an Institution

While it is almost always best to choose a trusted person for the job, you may not know anyone who is up to the task of winding up your estate—especially if your estate is large and complicated and your beneficiaries are either very old, very young or just inexperienced in financial matters. If so, you can select a professional management firm to act as your executor. (Banks often provide this service.)

If you are considering naming an institution as executor, be sure the one you choose is willing to act. Most will not accept the job unless your estate is fairly large. Also, understand that institutions charge a hefty fee for acting as executor—usually both a percentage of the value of property to be managed and a number of smaller fees for routine services such as buying and selling property.

Restrictions on Out-of-State Executors

Alabama	Nonresident can be appointed executor only if already serving as executor of same estate in another state. (Ala. Code § 43-2-22)
Arkansas	Nonresident executor must appoint an in-state agent to accept legal papers. (Ark. Code Ann. § 28-48-101(b)(6))
Connecticut	Nonresident executor must appoint in-state probate court judge as agent to accept legal papers. (Conn. Gen. Stat. Ann § 52-60)
Delaware	Nonresident executor must appoint county Register of Wills as the agent to accept legal papers. (Del. Code Ann. Tit. 12, § 1506)
District of Columbia	Nonresident executor must publish notices in a newspaper and appoint the probate register as agent to accept legal papers. (D.C. Code Ann. §§ 20-303, 20-343)
Florida	Nonresident can be appointed executor only if he or she is related by blood, marriage or adoption to person making will. (Fla. Stat. Ann. § 733.304)
Illinois	Nonresident executor may be required to post bond, even if will expressly states bond not required. (755 Ill. Comp. Stat. § 5/6-13)
Indiana	Nonresident can serve as executor if resident appointed co-executor and nonresident posts a bond. Nonresident can serve alone if he or she posts a bond, files a written notice of acceptance and appoints an in-state agent to accept legal papers. (Ind. Code Ann. § 29-1-10-1)
Iowa	Nonresident can serve as executor only if resident appointed co-executor, unless court allows nonresident to serve alone. (Iowa Code § 633.64)
Kansas	Nonresident executor must appoint an in-state agent to accept legal papers. (Kan. Stat. Ann. § 59-1706)
Kentucky	Nonresident can be appointed executor only if he or she is related by blood, marriage or adoption to person making will. (Ky. Rev. Stat. Ann. § 395.005)
Maryland	Nonresident executor must publish notices in a newspaper and appoint an in-state agent to accept legal papers. (Md. Code Ann. [Est. & Trusts] §§ 5-105, 5-503)
Massachusetts	Nonresident executor must appoint an in-state agent to accept legal papers. (Mass. Gen. Laws ch. 195, § 8)
Missouri	Nonresident executor must appoint an in-state agent to accept legal papers. (Mo. Rev. Stat. § 473.117)
Nevada	Nonresident can serve as executor only if resident appointed co-executor. (Nev. Rev. Stat. Ann. § 139.010)
North Carolina	Nonresident executor must appoint an in-state agent to accept legal papers. (N.C. Gen. Stat. § 28A-4-2)

Restrictions on Out-of-State Executors, continued

Ohio	Nonresident can be appointed executor only if he or she is related by blood, marriage or adoption to person making will—or if he or she lives in a state that permits nonresidents to serve. (Ohio Rev. Code Ann. § 2109.21)
Oklahoma	Nonresident executor must appoint an in-state agent to accept legal papers. (Okla. Stat. Ann. tit. 58, § 162)
Pennsylvania	Nonresident can serve as executor only with permission of register of wills. Nonresident executor must file an affidavit stating that estate has no known debts in Pennsylvania, and that he or she will not perform any duties prohibited in home state. (20 Pa. Cons. Stat. Ann. §§ 3157, 4101)
Rhode Island	Nonresident executor must be approved by a judge and must appoint an in-state agent to accept legal papers. (R.I. Gen. Laws §§ 33-8-7, 33-18-9)
Tennessee	Nonresident can serve as executor if related by blood or marriage to person making will, or if approved by a judge. Nonresident executor must appoint secretary of state as agent to accept legal papers and may be required to post bond. Nonresident can also serve if resident appointed co-executor. (Tenn. Code Ann. § 35-50-107)
Texas	Nonresident executor must appoint an in-state agent to accept legal papers. (Tex. Prob. Code Ann. § 78)
Vermont	Nonresident executor must appoint an in-state agent to accept legal papers. Nonresident executor can be appointed only with court approval; court must approve nonresident executor upon request of surviving spouse, adult children or parents or guardians of minor children. (Vt. Stat. Ann. tit. 14, § 904)
Virginia	Nonresident executor must post a bond and appoint an in-state agent to accept legal papers. Bond not required if resident appointed co-executor or if value of estate is $15,000 or less. (Va. Code Ann. § 26-59)
Washington	Nonresident executor must post a bond and appoint an in-state agent to accept legal papers. If nonresident is surviving spouse and sole beneficiary of will, or if will expressly states so, bond is not required. (Wash. Rev. Code Ann. §§ 11.28.185, 11.36.010)
West Virginia	Nonresident may serve if clerk of the county commission of the county where the probate is conducted serves as nonresidents' agent. (W. Va. Code Ann. § 44-5-3(c))
Wisconsin	Nonresident executor must appoint an in-state agent to accept legal papers. Nonresident executor can be removed or refused appointment solely on grounds of residency. (Wis. Stat. Ann. § 856.23)
Wyoming	Nonresident executor must appoint an in-state agent to accept legal papers. (Wyo. Stat. § 2-11-301)

2. If You Do Not Name an Executor

If you do not name an executor in your will, the document will still be valid as a will. But your decision will not have been a wise one. It will most often mean that a court will have to scurry and scrounge to come up with a willing relative to serve. If that fails, the court will probably appoint someone to do the job who is likely to be unfamiliar with you, your property and your beneficiaries. People appointed by the court to serve are called administrators.

The laws in many states provide that anyone who is entitled under the will to take over half a person's property has first priority to serve as executor. If no such person is apparent, courts will generally look for someone to serve among the following groups of people, in the following order:

- surviving spouse or registered domestic partner
- children
- grandchildren
- great-grandchildren
- parents
- brothers and sisters
- grandparents
- uncles, aunts, first cousins
- children of deceased spouse
- other next of kin
- relatives of a deceased spouse
- conservator or guardian
- public administrator
- creditors, and
- any other person.

C. Naming an Alternate

In case you name someone to serve as executor who dies before you do or for any other reason cannot take on the responsibilities, you should name an alternate to serve instead.

In choosing an alternate executor, consider the same factors you did in naming your first choice. (See Section B1, above.) ■

Chapter 9

Debts, Expenses and Taxes

Money matters have a way of living on —even after your death. But you can easily guide your survivors through the vexing process of dealing with your debts and expenses by including clear instructions in your will.

In your will, you can:

- forgive debts that others owed you during your lifetime
- designate what property should be used to pay debts you owe at death, and
- designate what property should be used to pay state and federal death taxes owed by your estate or due on the property in it.

Keeping track of your debts, expenses and taxes. At your death, your executor and other survivors may need to learn about the debts you owed and that others owed to you during your life. For help collecting and recording this information, use Quicken WillMaker Plus's "Information for Caregivers and Survivors" form.

A. Forgiving Debts Others Owe You

You can release anyone who owes you a debt from the responsibility of paying it back to your estate after you die. You can cancel any such debt—oral or written. If you do, your forgiveness functions much the same as giving a gift; those who were indebted to you will no longer be legally required to pay the money they owed.

Of course, keep in mind that releasing people or institutions from the debts they owe you may diminish the property that your beneficiaries receive under your will.

Quicken WillMaker Plus prompts you to describe any debt you wish to cancel—including the name of the person who owes it, the approximate date the debt was incurred and the amount you wish to forgive. This information is important so that the debt can be properly identified.

Caution for married people. If you are married and forgiving a debt, first make sure you have the full power to do so. For example, if the debt was incurred while you were married, you may only have the right to forgive half the debt. There is a special need to be cautious about this possibility in community property states. If your debt is a community property debt, you cannot cancel the whole amount due unless your spouse agrees to allow you to cancel his or her share of the debt—and puts that agreement in writing.

Explaining Your Intentions

If you forgive a debt, it is likely to come as a pleasant surprise to those living with the expectations that they must repay it. And you will probably give the gesture considerable thought before including such a direction in your will. While the final document will contain a brief clause stating your intention, you may wish to explain your reasoning beyond this bald statement. If you wish to do so, it is best to write your explanation in a brief letter that you attach to your will. (See Chapter 12, Section B.)

B. Liabilities at Your Death

If you live owing money, chances are you will die owing money. If you do, your executor will be responsible for rounding up your property and making sure all your outstanding debts are satisfied before any of the property is put in the hands of those you have named to get it. The property you own at your death—or your estate—may be liable for several types of debts, expenses and taxes.

1. Debts You Owe

When you leave this credit-happy world, you will likely go out with debts you have not fully paid—personal loans, credit card bills, mortgage loans, income taxes. Whether such debts pass to the beneficiary along with the property, or must be paid out of the estate, depends upon how the debt is characterized. (See Section C, below.)

2. Expenses Incurred After Your Death

There are several expenses incurred after you die —including costs of funeral, burial and probate—which may take your survivors by surprise if you do not plan ahead for paying them.

Funeral and burial expenses, for example, typically cost several thousand dollars. And for those who do not plan ahead, the costs may soar even higher. (See Chapter 24, Section B.) In addition, probate and estate administration fees typically run about 5% to 7% of the value of the property you leave to others in your will. (For a discussion of methods for avoiding probate, see Chapter 13, Section A3.)

3. Estate and Inheritance Taxes

Because of big tax law changes in 2001, estate tax is a concern for fewer and fewer people. The tax is levied on the property you own at death—but a large amount of property is exempt from taxation. (For more on estate tax, see Section E, below.) Unless you specify otherwise in your will, in most states, the taxes will normally be paid proportionately out of the estate's liquid assets. This means that a beneficiary's property will be reduced by the percentage that the property bears to the total liquid assets. Liquid assets include bank accounts, money market accounts and marketable securities. Real estate and tangible personal property such as cars, furniture and antiques are not included. This could cause a problem if, for example, you left your bank account with $50,000 in it to a favorite nephew and your death tax liability—most of which resulted from valuable real property left to another beneficiary—gobbled up all or most of it. (See Section E, below.)

C. Types of Debts

There are two basic kinds of debts with which you need be concerned when making a will—secured and unsecured.

1. Secured Debts

Secured debts are any debts owed on specific property that must be paid before title to that property fully belongs to its owner.

One common type of secured debt occurs when a major asset such as a car, appliance or business is paid for over a period of time. Usually, the lender of credit will retain some measure of legal ownership in the asset—termed a security interest—until it is paid off.

Another common type of secured debt occurs when a lender, as a condition of the loan, takes a security interest in property already owned by the person applying for the money. For instance, most finance companies require their borrowers to agree to pledge "all their personal property" as security for the loan. The legal jargon for this type of security interest is a non-purchase money secured debt—that is, the debt is incurred for a purpose other than purchasing the property that secures repayment.

Other common types of secured debts are mortgages and deeds of trust owed on real estate in exchange for a purchase or equity loan, tax liens and assessments that are owed on real estate and, in some instances, liens or legal claims on personal and real property created as a result of litigation or home repair.

If you are leaving property in your will that is subject to a secured debt, you may be concerned about whether the debt will pass to the beneficiary along with the property, or whether it must be paid by your estate.

a.   Debts on Real Estate

Quicken WillMaker Plus passes all secured debts owed on real estate along with the real estate.

> **EXAMPLE:** Paul owes $50,000 under a deed of trust on his home, signed as a condition of obtaining an equity loan. He leaves the home to his children. The deed of trust is a secured debt on real property and passes to the children along with the property.

> **EXAMPLE:** Sonny and Cati, a married couple, borrow $100,000 from the bank to purchase their home and take out a deed of trust in the bank's favor as security for the loan. They still owe $78,000 and are two years behind in property tax payments. In separate wills, Sonny and Cati leave their ownership share to each other and name their children as alternates to take the home in equal shares. The deed of trust is a purchase money secured debt and, if the children get the property, they will also get the mortgage—and responsibility for paying the past due amount in taxes.

b.   Debts on Personal Property

All debts owed on personal property pass to the beneficiaries of the property.

> **EXAMPLE:** Phil owns a 1999 Ferrari. Although the car is registered in Phil's name, the bank holds legal title pending Phil's payment of the outstanding $75,000 car note. Phil uses Quicken WillMaker Plus to leave the car to his companion Paula. The car note is a secured debt and will pass to Paula with the car.

2.   Unsecured Debts

Unsecured debts are all debts not tied to specific property. Common examples are medical bills, most credit card bills, utility bills and probate fees. Your executor must pay these debts and expenses out of property from your estate. A student loan is another common example of an unsecured debt. However, most student loans can be canceled if the borrower dies before the loan is paid off, so the borrower's estate will owe nothing.

When the Debt Exceeds the Property Value

Because the property is usually worth more than any debt secured by it, a person who takes the property at your death but does not want to owe money can sell the property, pay off the debt and pocket the difference. However, at times, relying on this approach is not satisfactory—especially when it comes to houses.

For example, if you leave your daughter your house with the hope that it will be her home, you will probably not want her to have to sell the house because she cannot meet the mortgage payments. If you think a particular beneficiary will need assistance with paying a debt owed on property, try to leave the necessary money or valuable assets to him or her as well.

D. Paying Debts and Expenses

Quicken WillMaker Plus offers two options for paying debts, including the expenses of probate. You can:

- designate a particular asset or assets to be used or sold to pay debts and expenses, or
- choose not to designate specific assets, which will mean that your executor will pay the debts and expenses as required by the laws of your state.

When You Need Not Worry— And When You Should

Typically, you do not need to leave instructions about debts if any of the following are true:

- Your debts and expenses are likely to be negligible—or to represent only a tiny fraction of a relatively large estate.
- You are leaving all your property to your spouse or specify that it should be shared among a very few beneficiaries, without divvying it up in specific bequests.
- You understand and approve of how your state law deals with debts and expenses.

On the other hand, you may need to be concerned about covering your debts and death taxes when your will-making plan involves dividing up your property among a number of beneficiaries.

And you need to plan more carefully if debts payable by your estate are likely to be large enough to cut significantly into bequests left to individuals and charitable institutions. The danger, of course, is that unless you plan carefully, the people whose bequests are used to pay debts and expenses may be the very people whom you would have preferred to take your property free and clear.

EXAMPLE: Ruth has $40,000 in a money market account and several valuable musical instruments, also worth $40,000. She makes a will leaving the money market account to her daughter and the instruments to her musician son but does not specify how her debts and expenses should be paid. Due to medical bills and an unpaid personal loan from a friend, Ruth dies owing $35,000. After Ruth's death, her executor must follow state law, which first requires that debts be paid out of the residuary estate. But because there is no residuary—all property is used up by specific bequests—a second rule applies that requires that debts be paid out of liquid assets. As a result, the executor pays the $35,000 out of the money market account, leaving the daughter with only $5,000. The son receives the $40,000 worth of musical instruments.

1. Designating Specific Assets

One helpful approach to taking care of debts and expenses is to designate one or more specific assets that your executor must use to pay them. For example, if you designate a savings or money market account to be used for paying off your debts and expenses, and the amount in the account is sufficient to meet these obligations, the other bequests you make in your will won't be affected by your estate's indebtedness.

If you select specific assets to pay your debts and expenses, you'll probably want to select liquid assets over nonliquid assets. Liquid assets are those easily converted into cash at full value: bank and deposit accounts, money market accounts, stocks and bonds. On the other hand, tangible assets such as motor vehicles, planes, jewelry, stamp and coin collections, electronic items and musical instruments must be sold to raise the necessary cash. Hurried sales seldom bring in anywhere near the full value, which means the net worth of your estate will also be reduced.

EXAMPLE: Harry writes mystery books for a living. He has never produced a blockbuster but owns 15 copyrights, which produce royalties of about $70,000 a year. During his life, Harry has traveled widely and collected artifacts from around the world. They have a value of $300,000 if sold carefully to knowledgeable collectors. Harry makes a will leaving his copyrights to his spouse and the artifacts to his children. He also designates that the artifacts should be used to pay his debts and expenses—which total $150,000 at death. Harry's executor, who is not a collector and has little time or inclination to sell the artifacts one by one, sells them in bulk for $140,000—less than half of their true value. To raise the extra $10,000, two of the copyrights are sold, again at less than their true value. As a result, Harry's children receive nothing and his spouse gets less than Harry intended.

Avoid designating property you have left to specific beneficiaries. It is important to review your specific bequests before designating assets to pay debts and expenses. If possible, designate liquid assets that have not been left to specific beneficiaries. Only as a last resort should you earmark a tangible item also left in a specific bequest for first use to pay debts and expenses.

One exception to this general recommendation occurs if you believe you are unlikely to owe much when you die and that the expenses of probate will be low. Then, it makes sense for you to designate a substantial liquid asset left as a specific bequest to also pay debts and expenses.

Covering Your Debts With Insurance

One way to deal with the problem of large debts and small assets is to purchase a life insurance policy in an amount large enough to pay your anticipated debts and expenses and have the proceeds made payable to your estate. You can then specify in your will that these proceeds should be used to pay your debts and expenses—with the rest going to your residuary beneficiary or a beneficiary named in a specific bequest.

But be careful. If large sums are involved, talk with an estate planner or accountant before adopting this sort of plan. Having insurance money paid to your estate subjects that amount to probate. A better alternative may be to provide that estate assets be sold, with the proceeds used to pay the debts. Then have the insurance proceeds made payable directly to your survivors free of probate.

Of course, if the source you specify is insufficient to pay all the bills, your executor will still face the problem of which property to use to make up the difference. For this reason, it is often wise to list several resources and specify the order in which they should be used. Also, make sure that they are worth more than what is likely to be required.

EXAMPLE: Ella, a widow, makes a will that contains the following bequests:

- My house at 1111 Soto Street in Albany, New York, to Hillary Bernette. (The house has an outstanding mortgage of $50,000, for which Hillary will become responsible.)
- My coin collection (appraised at $30,000) to Stanley, Mark and Belinda Bernette.
- My three antique chandeliers to Herbert Perkins.
- The rest of my property to Denise Everread. Although not spelled out in the will, this property consists of a savings account ($26,000), a car ($5,000), a camera ($1,000) and stock ($7,000).

Using Quicken WillMaker Plus, Ella specifies that her savings account and stock be used in the order listed to pay debts and expenses. When Ella dies, she owes $8,000; the expenses of probating her estate total $4,000. Following Ella's instructions, her executor would close the savings account, use $12,000 of it to pay debts and expenses and turn the rest over to Denise along with the stock and camera.

EXAMPLE: Now suppose Ella has only $6,000 in the savings account. When she dies, her executor, following the same instructions, would close the account ($6,000) and sell enough stock to make up the difference ($6,000). The remaining $1,000 worth of stock, the camera and the car would pass to Denise.

⚠ Describe property consistently. If you designate property both as a specific bequest and as a source for paying your debts, be sure to describe it exactly the same in both instances to avoid confusion.

2. Not Specifying Assets

If you do not specify how you want your debts and expenses to be paid, your executor will need to follow your state's laws, and your Quicken WillMaker Plus will instructs him or her to do so.

Some states require that debts and expenses be paid first out of property in your estate that does not pass under your will for some reason—for example, neither your residuary beneficiary nor alternate survive you—and next from the residuary of your estate. In other states, your debts and expenses must first be paid out of liquid assets such as bank accounts and securities, then from tangible personal property and, as a last resort, from real estate.

E. Estate and Inheritance Taxes

Before you concentrate on how you want your estate or inheritance taxes to be paid, consider whether you need to be concerned about these types of taxes at all. Most people do not.

These taxes are imposed on the transfer of property after someone dies. Some people confuse probate-avoidance devices, such as living trusts and joint tenancy, with schemes to save on taxes. But avoiding probate does not reduce these taxes.

Whether or not your estate will be required to pay taxes depends on two factors:
- the value of your taxable estate—that is, your net estate minus any gifts or expenses that are tax-exempt, and
- the laws of the state in which you live.

1. Federal Estate Taxes

Only a fraction of estates end up owing federal estate tax. Primarily, that's because a large amount of property is exempt from the tax, and the exemption is growing steadily bigger. For deaths occurring in 2006, estates smaller than $2 million do not owe estate tax.

The sweeping law changes, however, also make planning for estate taxes quite complicated. If you think your estate might be large enough to owe estate tax, see Chapter 13, which explains the system.

2. State Inheritance and Estate Taxes

State taxes normally do not take a deep enough bite to cause serious concern unless your estate is very large. Still, your executor has an obligation to pay the taxes and will therefore deduct them from each bequest unless you specify differently in your will, as you can do when using Quicken WillMaker Plus. For information about state inheritance and estate taxes, see Chapter 13, Section B.

💼 Getting help with large estates. As you might imagine, financial planning experts have devised many creative ways to plan for paying estate and inheritance taxes. If your estate is large enough to warrant concern about possible federal estate and state inheritance taxes, it is large enough for you to afford a consultation with an accountant, estate planning specialist or lawyer specializing in estates and trusts. (See Chapter 13.)

F. Choosing How to Pay Taxes

Quicken WillMaker Plus offers the following options for paying estate and inheritance taxes. You can:

- pay them from all property you own at death
- designate specific assets, or
- choose not to specify how your taxes will be paid, leaving that matter up to state law.

If the value of your estate is well below the federal and state tax range, and you have no reasonable expectation that your estate will grow much larger before your death, you may want to skip this discussion of your options for paying taxes and choose the option "Don't specify."

If you are a relatively young, healthy person and your estate is only slightly larger than $1.5 million, you may want to adopt one of the Quicken WillMaker Plus tax payment options now and worry about more sophisticated tax planning later. After all, by the time you die, federal and state tax rules may have changed many times.

1. Paying Taxes From All Property You Own

For the purpose of computing estate and inheritance tax liability, your estate consists of all property you legally own at your death, whether it passes under the terms of your will or outside of your will—such as a joint tenancy, living trust, savings bank trust or life insurance policy. Because your estate's tax liability will be computed on the basis of all this property, you may wish to have the beneficiaries of the property share proportionately in the responsibility for paying the taxes.

EXAMPLE: Julie Johanssen, a widow, owns a house (worth $1 million), stocks ($200,000), jewelry ($150,000) and investments as a limited partner in a number of rental properties ($800,000). To avoid probate, Julie puts the house in a living trust for her eldest son, Warren; puts the stocks in a living trust for another son, Alain; and uses her will to leave the jewelry to a daughter, Penelope and the investments to her two surviving brothers, Sean and Ivan. She specifies that all beneficiaries of property in her taxable estate share in paying any estate and inheritance taxes.

When Julie dies, the net worth of her estate, which consists of all the property mentioned, is over the amount of the estate tax exemption in the year of her death, so there is federal estate tax liability.

Each of Julie's beneficiaries will be responsible for paying a portion of this liability. Each portion will be measured by the proportion that beneficiary's inheritance has to the estate as a whole.

2. Designating Specific Assets

As with payment of debts and expenses, it may be a good approach to designate one or more specific property items to satisfy the amount you owe in taxes. Again, if you designate a bank, brokerage or money market account to be used for paying taxes, and the amount in the account is adequate to meet these obligations, the other bequests you make in your will should not be affected.

Of course, if the resource you specify for payment of your estate and inheritance taxes is not sufficient to cover the amount due, your executor will still face the problem of which property will be used to make up the difference. So, again, it is a good idea to list several resources which should be used to pay estate and inheritance taxes in the order listed.

! Guidance for selecting specific assets. If you do choose to select specific assets to be used to pay your taxes, follow the general rules set out in Section D, above.

3. Not Specifying Method of Payment

If you choose this option, your will directs your executor to pay your estate and inheritance taxes as required by the laws of your state. As with your debts and expenses, your state law controls how your executor is to approach this issue if you do not establish your own plan. Some states leave the method of payment up to your executor, while others provide that all beneficiaries must share the tax burden. Depending on your financial and tax situation and the law of your state, more variables set in than can reasonably be covered here. If you are concerned about the possible legal repercussions of choosing this option, consider researching your state's law. (See Chapter 25.) ■

Chapter 10

Make It Legal: Final Steps

Once you have proceeded through all the Quicken WillMaker Plus screens and responded to all the questions the program poses, your will is nearly finished. There are just a few more steps you must take to make it legally effective so that the directions you expressed in it can be carried out after your death.

Note for perfectionists: No accents or umlauts. Quicken WillMaker Plus does not allow you to use special characters, such as accent marks or umlauts. You may be tempted to ink one in if your name, or the name of a beneficiary, carries the mark in question. Don't do it. The fact that the punctuation is missing may be displeasing to you, but it will have no adverse impact on your will's legality or effectiveness. Nor will minor spelling errors, typos or even awkward wording in text that you enter.

A. Checking Your Will

Before you sign your will, take some time to scrutinize it and make sure it accurately expresses your wishes. You can do this either by calling it up on the screen or by printing out a draft copy. (Consult the Users' Manual if you need additional guidance.)

Having an Expert Check Your Will

You may want to have your will checked by an attorney or tax expert. This makes good sense if you are left with nagging questions about the legal implications of your choices, or if you own a great deal of property or have a complicated idea of how you want to leave it. But keep in mind that you are your own best expert on most issues and decisions involved in making a will—what property you own, your relation to family members and friends and your own favorite charities. Also, some attorneys don't support the self-help approach to making a will, so you may have to find one who is cooperative. (See Chapter 25.)

B. Signing and Witnessing Requirements

To be valid, a will must be legally executed. This means that you must sign your will in front of witnesses. These witnesses must sign the will not only in your presence, but also in the presence of all the other witnesses.

Two witnesses are required in every state except Vermont, where three are necessary.

1. Requirements for Witnesses

There are a few legal requirements for witnesses. The witnesses need to be of sound mind. In most states, the witnesses need to be 18 or older. Many states also require that the witnesses not be people who will take property under the will. Thus we require that you not use someone to whom you leave property in your will, even as an alternate or residuary beneficiary, as a witness.

As a matter of common sense, the people you choose to be witnesses should be easily available when you die. While this bit of future history is impossible to foretell with certainty, it is usually best to choose witnesses who are in good health, are younger than you are and likely to remain in your geographic area. However, the witnesses do not have to be residents of your state.

2. The Self-Proving Option

For a will to be accepted by a probate court, the executor must show that the document really is the will of the person it purports to be—a process called proving the will. In the past, all wills were proved either by having one or two witnesses come into court to testify or swear in written, notarized statements called affidavits that they saw you sign your will.

Today, most states allow people to make their wills self-proving—that is, they can be admitted in probate court without the hassle of herding up witnesses to appear in court or sign affidavits. This is accomplished when the person making the will and the witnesses all appear before a notary public and sign an affidavit under oath, verifying that all necessary formalities for execution have been satisfied.

If you live in a state that offers the self-proving option, Quicken WillMaker Plus automatically produces the correct affidavit for your state, with accompanying instructions. For the exception of New Hampshire, the self-proving affidavit is not part of your will, but a separate document. To use it, you and your witnesses must first sign the will as discussed above. Then, you and your witnesses must sign the self-proving affidavit in front of a notary public. This may be done any time after the will is signed but, obviously, it is easiest to do it while all your witnesses are gathered together to watch you sign your will. Most notaries will charge at least a minimal amount for their services—and will require you and your witnesses to present some identification verifying that you are who you claim to be.

Many younger people—who are likely to make a number of wills before they die—decide not to make their wills self-proving, due to the initial trouble of getting a notary at the signing. If you are one of these people, file the uncompleted affidavit and instructions in a safe place in case you change your mind later.

States without self-proving laws. The self-proving option is not available in the District of Columbia, Maryland, Ohio or Vermont. In these states, your executor will be required to prove your will.

Note for California and Indiana readers. In California or Indiana, the self-proving feature does not require a separate affidavit. Instead, the fact that the witnesses sign the will under the oath printed above their signatures is sufficient to have the will admitted into probate, unless a challenge is mounted. There is no need to take further steps to make a California or Indiana will self-proving.

3. Signing Procedure

You need not utter any magic words when signing your will and having it witnessed, but a few legal requirements suggest the best way to proceed:

- Gather all witnesses together in one place.
- Inform your witnesses that the papers you hold in your hand are your last will and testament. This is important, because the laws in many states specifically require that you acknowledge the document as your will before the witnesses sign it. The witnesses need not read your will, however, and there is no need for them to know its contents. If you want to ensure that the contents of the will stay confidential, you may cover all but the signature portion of your will with a separate sheet of paper while the witnesses sign.
- Initial each page of the will at the bottom on the lines provided. The purpose of initialing is to prevent anyone from challenging the will as invalid on the grounds that changes were made to it by someone else.
- Sign the last page on the signature line while the witnesses watch. Use the same form of your name that appears in your Quicken WillMaker Plus will. This should be the form of the name you most commonly use to sign legal documents such as deeds, checks and loan applications. (See Chapter 4, Section A.)
- Ask each of the witnesses to initial the bottom of each page on a line there, then watch as they sign and fill in their addresses on the last page where indicated. Their initials act as evidence if anyone later claims you changed your will without going through the proper legal formalities.

C. Changing Your Quicken WillMaker Plus Will

Once you have signed your will and had it witnessed, it is extremely important that you do not alter it by inserting handwritten or typed additions or changes. Do not even correct misspellings. The laws of most states require that after a will is signed, any additions or changes to it, even clerical ones, must be made by following the same signing and witnessing requirements as for an original will.

Although it is legally possible to make handwritten corrections on your will before you sign it, that is a bad idea since, after your death, it will not be clear to the probate court that you made the corrections before the will was signed. The possibility that the changes were made later may throw the legality of the whole will into question.

If you want to make changes after your will has been signed and witnessed, there are two ways to accomplish it: You can either make a new will or make a formal addition, called a codicil, to the existing one. Either approach requires a new round of signing and witnessing.

One of the great advantages of Quicken WillMaker Plus is that you can conveniently keep current by simply making a new will. This does away with the need to tack on changes to the will in the form of a codicil and involves no need for additional gyrations. Codicils are not a good idea when using Quicken WillMaker Plus because of the possibility of creating a conflict between the codicil and the original will. It is simpler and safer to make a new Quicken WillMaker Plus will, sign it and have it witnessed.

D. Storing Your Will

Once your will is properly signed and witnessed, be sure that your executor can easily locate it at your death. Here are some suggestions:

- Store your printed and witnessed will in an envelope on which you have typed your name and the word "Will."
- Place the envelope in a fireproof metal box, file cabinet or home safe. An alternative is to place the original will in a safe deposit box. But before doing that, learn the bank's policy about access to the box after your death. If, for instance, the safe deposit box is in your name alone, the box can probably be opened only by a person authorized by a court, and then only in the presence of a bank employee. An inventory may even be required if any person enters the box or for state tax purposes. All of this takes time, and in the meantime, your document will be locked away from those who need access to it.

Helping Others Find Your Will

Your will should be easy to locate at your death. You want to spare your survivors the anxiety of having to search for your will when they are already dealing with the grief of losing you. Make sure your executor, and at least one other person you trust, knows where to find your will.

E. Making Copies of Your Will

Some people are tempted to prepare more than one signed and witnessed original of their wills in case one is lost. While it is legal in most states to prepare and sign duplicate originals, it is never a good idea. Common sense tells you why: If you later want to change your will, it can be difficult to locate all the old copies to destroy them.

It can sometimes be a good idea, however, to make several unsigned copies of your current will. Give one to your proposed executor. And, if it is appropriate, give other copies to your spouse, friends or children. In a close family, it can be a relief to everyone to learn your plans for distributing your property. But, obviously, there are many good reasons why you may wish to keep the contents of your will strictly confidential until your death. If so, do not make any copies.

Giving Your Documents File a Good Home

Once you have printed out your will, you should make a copy of it in electronic form. Follow the instructions in the Users' Manual on backing up your documents files. Find a safe, private place to store the CD or floppy disk so that you can use it to restore or update your will if that becomes necessary. Other people should not have access to the computer file without your permission.

As with other unsigned and unwitnessed copies, the copy of your will stored in your computer, or on a CD or floppy disk, does not constitute a valid will. To be valid, a will must be printed out and formally signed and witnessed as discussed above. ■

Chapter 11

Updating Your Will

Your will is an extremely personal document. Information such as your marital status, where you live, the property you own and whether you have children—all are examples of life choices that affect what you include in your will and what laws will be applied to enforce it.

Life wreaks havoc on even the best-laid plans. You may sell one house and buy another. You may divorce. You may have or adopt children. Eventually you will face the grief of losing a loved one. Not all life changes require you to change your will. However, significant ones often do. This chapter tells you when it's necessary to make a new will.

A. When to Make a New Will

The following occurrences signal that it is time for you to make a new will.

1. Marrying or Divorcing

Suppose that after you use Quicken Willmaker to leave all or part of your property to your spouse, you get divorced. Under the law in many states, the divorce automatically cancels the bequest to the former spouse. The alternate beneficiary named for that bequest, or, if there is none, your residuary beneficiary, gets the property. In some states, however, your former spouse would still be entitled to take your property as directed in the will. If you remarry, state legal rules become even more murky.

Rather than deal with all these complexities, follow this simple rule: Make a new will if you marry, divorce or if you are separated and seriously considering divorce.

Beware of state laws on spouse's shares. If you leave your spouse out of your will because you are separated, and you die before you become divorced, it is possible that the spouse could claim a statutory share of your estate. (See Chapter 5, Section E.) Consult a lawyer to find out how the laws of your state apply to this situation. (See Chapter 25.)

2. Getting or Losing Property

If you leave all your property in a lump to one or more people or organizations, there is no need to change your will if you acquire new items of property or get rid of existing ones—those individuals or organizations take all of your property at your death, without regard to what it is.

But if you have made specific bequests of property that you no longer own, it is wise to make a new will. If you leave a specific item—a particular Tiffany lamp, for example—to someone, but you no longer own the item when you die, the person named in your will to receive it may be out of luck. In most states, that person is not entitled to receive another item or money instead. In some states, however, the law presumes that you wanted the beneficiary to have something—and so gives him or her the right to a sum of money equal to the value of the gift. While this may be what you want, it could still disrupt your plan for how you want your property distributed. The legal word for a bequest that fails to make it in this way is ademption. People who do not get to take the property in question are often heard to use an earthier term.

However, in some circumstances, if a specific item has merely changed form, the original beneficiary may still have a claim to it. Examples of this are:

- a promissory note that has been paid and for which the cash is still available, and
- a house that is sold in exchange for a promissory note and deed of trust.

A problem similar to ademption occurs when there is not enough money to go around. For example, if you leave $50,000 each to your spouse and two children, but there is only $90,000 in your estate at your death, the gifts in the will must all be reduced. In legal lingo, this is called an abatement. How property is abated under state law is often problematic.

You can avoid the vexatious legal problems of ademption and abatement if you adjust the type and amount of your bequests to reflect reality—a task that may require both diligence and the commitment to make a new will periodically.

3. Adding or Losing Children

Each time a child is born or legally adopted into your family, the new child should be named in the will—where you are asked to name your children—and provided for according to your wishes. If you do not do this, the child might later challenge your will in court, claiming that he or she was overlooked as an heir and is entitled to a substantial share of your property. (See Chapter 4, Section F.)

If any of your children die before you and leave children, you should name those grandchildren in your will. If they are not mentioned in your will, they might later be legally entitled to claim a share of your estate. (See Chapter 4, Section G.)

4. Moving to a Different State

Quicken Willmaker applies several state-specific laws when it helps you create your will. These laws are especially important in two situations.

- If you have set up one form of management for young beneficiaries and then move to a different state, you may find when making a new will that Quicken Willmaker presents you with different management options. This is because some states have adopted the Uniform Transfers to Minors Act and others have not. If you want to see whether your new state offers different management options, see Chapter 7, Section D.
- If you are married and do not intend to leave all or most of your property to your spouse, review Chapter 5, Section D, which discusses the rules if you move from a community property state to a common law state or vice versa.

5. Losing Beneficiaries

If a beneficiary you have named to receive a significant amount of property dies before you, you should make a new will. It is especially important to do this if you named only one beneficiary for a bequest and did not name an alternate—or if the alternate you named is no longer your first choice to get the property.

6. Losing Guardians or Property Managers

The first choice or alternate named to serve as a personal guardian for your minor children or those you have named to manage their property may move away, become disabled or simply turn out to be someone you consider unsuitable for the job. If so, you will probably want to make a new will naming a different person.

7. Losing an Executor

The executor of your estate is responsible for making sure your will provisions are carried out. If you decide that the executor you originally named is no longer suitable—or if he or she dies before you do—you should make a new will in which you name another person for the job.

8. Losing Witnesses

The witnesses who sign your will are responsible for testifying that the signature on your will is valid and that you appeared capable of making a will when you did so. If two or more of your witnesses become unable to fulfill this function, you may want to make a new will with new witnesses—especially if you have some inkling that anyone is likely to contest your will after you die. But a new will is probably not necessary if you have made your will self-proving. (See Chapter 10, Section B2.)

B. How to Make a New Will

It is easy to make a new will using Quicken Willmaker. In fact, a subsequent swoop through the program will proceed even more quickly than the first time through, since you will know what to expect and will likely be familiar with many of the legal concepts you had to learn at first.

If you review your will and wish to change some of your answers, the program will automatically alert you to specific changes that may signal different laws applying to your situation. These include changes in:

- your marital status
- your state of residence
- the number of children you have, and
- your general approach to will making—from simple to complex, or vice versa.

If you make a new will, even if it only involves a few changes, you must follow the legal requirements for having it signed and witnessed just as if you were starting from scratch. If you choose to make your will self-proving, you must also complete a new affidavit.

In with the new, out with the old. As soon as you print, sign and have your new will witnessed, it will legally replace all wills you have made before it. But to avoid possible confusion, you should physically destroy all other original wills and any copies of them. ■

Chapter 12

Explanatory Letters

n addition to the tasks that you can accomplish in a Quicken WillMaker Plus will, you may also wish to:

- explain why you are giving property to certain beneficiaries and not to others
- explain disparities in bequests
- express positive or negative sentiments about a beneficiary
- express wishes about caring for a pet, or
- leave your loved ones a statement about your personal experiences, values or beliefs.

Quicken WillMaker Plus does not allow you to do these things in your will for one important reason: The program has been written, tested and tested again with painstaking attention to helping you make your own legal and unambiguous will. If you add general information, personal statements or reasons for making or not making a bequest, you risk the possibility of producing a document with conflicting, confusing or possibly even illegal provisions.

Fortunately, there is a way you can have a final say about personal matters without seriously risking your will's legal integrity. You can write a letter to accompany your will expressing your thoughts to those who survive you.

Since what you put in the letter will not have legal effect as part of your will, there is little danger that your expressions will tread upon the time-tested legal language of the will or cause other problems later. In fact, if your will is ambiguous and your statement in the letter sheds some light on your intentions, judges may use the letter to help clarify your will. However, if your statements in the letter fully contradict provisions in your will, you may be guilty of creating interpretation problems after your death. For example, if you cut your daughter out of your will and also state in a letter attached to the will that

she is your favorite child and that is why you are leaving her the family home, you are setting the stage for future confusion.

Keeping these cautions in mind, writing a letter to those who survive you to explain why you wrote your will as you did—and knowing they will read your reasoning at your death—can give you a great deal of peace of mind during life. It may also help explain potential slights and hurt feelings of surviving friends and family members. This chapter offers some guidance on how you can write a clear letter that expresses your wishes without jeopardizing the legality of your will.

A. An Introduction for Your Letter

A formal introduction to the letter you leave can help make it clear that what you write is an expression of your sentiments and not intended as a will—or an addition to or interpretation of your will.

After the introduction, you are free to express your sentiments, keeping in mind that your estate may be held liable for any false, derogatory

statements you make about an individual or organization.

One suggested introduction follows.

To My Executor:

This letter expresses my feelings and reasons for certain decisions made in my will. It is not my will, nor do I intend it to be an interpretation of my will. My will, which I signed, dated and had witnessed on _____, is the sole expression of my intentions concerning all my property and other matters covered in it.

Should anything I say in this letter conflict with, or seem to conflict with, any provision of my will, the will shall be followed.

I request that you give a copy of this letter to each person named in my will to take property, or act as a guardian or custodian, and to anyone else you determine should receive a copy.

B. Expressing Sentiments and Explaining Choices

There is little that a manual such as this can say to guide you in personal expressions of the heart. What follows are some suggestions about topics you might wish to cover.

1. Explaining Why Gifts Were Made

The Quicken WillMaker Plus requirement that you must keep descriptions of property and beneficiaries short and succinct may leave you unsat-

isfied. You may have thought hard and long about why you want a particular person to get particular property—and are constrained in your will to listing your wishes in a few bloodless words. You can remedy that by explaining the whys and wherefores of your will directives in a letter.

EXAMPLE:

[Introduction]

The gift of my fishing boat to my friend Hank is in remembrance of the many companionable days we enjoyed fishing together on the lake. Hank, I hope you're out there for many more years.

EXAMPLE:

[Introduction]

Julie, the reason I have given you the farm is that you love it as much as I do and I know you'll do your best to make sure it stays in the family. But please, if the time comes when personal or family concerns mean that it makes sense to sell it, do so with a light heart—and knowing that it's just what I would have done.

---

2. Explaining Disparities in Gifts

You may also wish to explain your reasons for leaving more property to one person than another. While it is certainly your prerogative to make or not make bequests as you wish, you can also guess that in a number of family situations, unbalanced shares may cause hurt feelings or hostility after your death.

Ideally, you could call those involved together during your life, explaining to them why you plan to leave your property as you do. However, if you wish to keep your property plans private until after you die—or would find such a meeting too painful or otherwise impossible—you can attach a letter of explanation to your will.

EXAMPLE:

[Introduction]

I love all my children equally. The reason I gave a smaller ownership share in the house to Tim than to my other children is that Tim received family funds to purchase his own home, so it is fair that my other two children receive more of my property now.

EXAMPLE:

[Introduction]

I am giving the bulk of my property to my son Jason for one reason: because of his health problems, he needs it more.

Ted and Ellen, I love you just as much, and I am extremely proud of the life choices you have made. But the truth is that you two can manage fine without a boost from me, and Jason cannot.

3. Expressing Positive or Negative Sentiments

Whatever your plans for leaving your property, you may wish to attach a letter to your will in which you clear your mind of some sentiments you formed during life. These may be positive—thanking a loved one for kind acts. Or they may be negative—explaining why you are leaving a person out of your will.

EXAMPLE:

[Introduction]

The reason I left $10,000 to my physician Dr. Buski is not only that she treated me competently over the years but that she was unfailingly gentle and attentive. I always appreciated that she made herself available—day or night—and took the time to explain my ailments and treatments to me.

EXAMPLE:

[Introduction]

I am leaving nothing to my brother Malcolm. I wish him no ill will. But over the years, he has decided to isolate himself from me and the rest of the family and I don't feel I owe him anything.

4. Providing Care for Your Pet

Legally, pets are property. Many pet owners, of course, disagree. They feel a bond with their animals and want to be sure that when they die, their pets will get good care and a good home. The easiest way to do this is to make an arrangement with a friend or family member to take care of your pet. Then, in your will, you leave your pet to that person, along with some money for the expense of your pet's feeding and care.

Make the bequest of your pet and money as a specific bequest in your Quicken WillMaker Plus will. (Remember, you can't leave money or other property directly to your pet in your will.) Then attach a letter to your will explaining your wishes to the new owner and include specific instructions for your pet's care. Of course, make sure you get the prospective owner's welcome approval before making such a bequest.

EXAMPLE:

[Introduction]

I have left my dog Cesna to my neighbor Belinda Mason because she has been a loving friend to him, taking care of him when I was on vacation or unwell. I know that Belinda and her three children will provide a caring and happy home for Cesna when I no longer can.

I request that Belinda continue to take Cesna for his twice yearly check-ups with Dr. Schuler at Madison Valley Pet Hospital and have left her $4,000 to help cover the cost of that care.

Finding a Loving Home for Your Pet

If you're not able to find someone both willing and able to take care of your pet after you die, you're not without options. More and more programs are springing up across the country to help assure people that their pets will have a loving home when they can no longer care for them.

SPCA programs. After the San Francisco SPCA fought, successfully, to save a dog that was to be put to death after its owner died, the organization began a special service to find good homes for the pets of deceased San Francisco SPCA members. The new owners are entitled to free lifetime veterinary care for the pets at the SPCA's hospital. Other SPCAs have created similar programs. Contact local SPCAs and similar organizations in your area for more information.

Veterinary school programs. A number of veterinary schools take in pets whose owners leave substantial endowments to the school. These programs typically provide a home-like atmosphere and lifetime veterinary care for the animals. Here is a list of some schools that currently offer this option:

Indiana
Peace of Mind Program
School of Veterinary Medicine, Purdue University
800-830-0104
www.vet.purdue.edu/devel/giving.html

Kansas
Perpetual Pet Care Program
Kansas State University School of Veterinary Medicine
785-532-4013
www.vet.ksu.edu/depts/development/perppet.htm

Oklahoma
Cohn Family Shelter for Small Animals
Oklahoma State University, College of Veterinary Medicine
405-744-6728
www.cvm.okstate.edu/development/CohnFamilyShelter.htm

Texas
Stevenson Companion Animal Life-Care Center
College of Veterinary Medicine, Texas A&M University
979-845-1188
www.cvm.tamu.edu/petcare

Washington
Perpetual Pet Care Program
Washington State University, College of Veterinary Medicine
509-335-5021
www.vetmed.wsu.edu/depts-prd/pc.asp

5. Describing Personal Experiences and Values

Many people are interested in leaving behind more than just property. If you wish, you can also leave a statement about the experiences, values, and beliefs that have shaped your life. This kind of letter or document is often known as an "ethical will," and it can be of great worth to those who survive you.

While you could legally include an ethical will statement in your regular will — that is, the one you make to leave your property to others — we recommend that you include these sentiments in your explanatory letter or in a separate document. The reasons are the same as those mentioned earlier: It's better to avoid including anything potentially confusing or ambiguous in your legal will.

As long as you don't contradict the provisions of your legal will, your options for expressing yourself are limited only by the time and energy you have for the project. You could do something as simple as use your explanatory letter to set out a concise description of your basic values. Or, if you feel inspired, you may leave something much more detailed for your loved ones. Many survivors are touched to learn about important life stories, memories and events. You might also consider including photographs or other mementos with your letter. If writing things down seems like too much effort, you could use an audio or videotape to talk to those who are closest to you. A little thought will surely yield many creative ways to express yourself to those you care for.

More information about ethical wills. If you want to go beyond writing down some of your experiences and values in your explanatory letter, there is a growing body of websites and literature that can help you explore different ways of making an ethical will. You might begin by visiting www.ethicalwill .com. The site offers some basic free information and sells ethical will-writing kits. ■

Chapter 13

About Living Trusts

A trust is an arrangement under which one person, called the trustee, owns property on behalf of someone else, called the beneficiary. You can create a trust simply by preparing and signing a document called a Declaration of Trust.

The trusts you can make with Quicken WillMaker Plus are called "revocable living trusts." Revocable means you can revoke them at any time. They're called "living" trusts because they're created when you're alive, not at your death like some other kinds of trusts. Sometimes, living trusts are known by their Latin name: *inter vivos* (among the living) trusts.

Quicken WillMaker Plus makes two kinds of revocable living trusts. The first is a basic living trust, which lets your family inherit your property without going through the notoriously slow and expensive probate court process. A second kind of living trust, called an AB trust, both avoids probate and may also let your heirs save thousands of dollars on estate taxes after your death.

A Mini-Glossary of Living Trust Terms

Unfortunately, you can't escape legal lingo entirely when you deal with living trusts. A complete onscreen glossary is always available when you're using Quicken WillMaker Plus. (See the Users' Manual.) But keeping it to a minimum, here's what you need to know:

- The person who sets up the living trust (that's you, or you and your spouse) is called a **grantor**, **trustor** or **settlor**.
- The person who has complete power over the trust property is called the **trustee**. You are the original trustee of your living trust, so you keep total control over property in the trust. If you and your spouse make a trust together, both of you are trustees.
- The property you transfer to the trustee is called, collectively, the trust property

or trust **principal**. (And, of course, there's a Latin version: the trust **corpus**.)

- The person you name to take over as trustee after your death (or, with a shared trust, after the death of both spouses) is called the **successor trustee**. The successor trustee's job is to transfer the trust property to the beneficiaries, following the instructions in the Declaration of Trust. The successor trustee may also manage trust property inherited by young beneficiaries.
- The trust **beneficiaries** inherit the trust property when the grantor dies. With a basic trust, there is just one kind of beneficiary. If you make an AB trust, there are two kinds: the **life beneficiary,** who is always the surviving spouse, and the **final beneficiaries,** who inherit trust property after both spouses have died.

A. The Probate-Avoidance Basic Living Trust

This basic trust is simple to set up, and makes transferring property after your death quick and easy. It does not affect taxes at all.

1. How a Basic Trust Helps Your Family

If you make a basic living trust, you can save your family a great deal of time and money. The big advantage, of course, is that property left through a trust avoids probate. There are other pluses as well.

a. Avoiding Probate

Unless you make a trust or use some other probate-avoidance method (such as owning real estate in joint tenancy or designating a payable-on-death beneficiary for a bank account), your property will probably have to go through probate before the beneficiaries receive it. Generally, property left through a will must go through probate.

In the probate process, the will (if there is one) is proved valid in court, and debts are paid. Then, the remaining property is distributed to the beneficiaries named in the will, or, if there isn't a will, the closest relatives. The cost of probate varies widely from state to state, but attorney, court and other fees can eat up about 5% of your estate (the property you leave at death), leaving that much less to go to the people you want to get it. If the estate is complicated, the fees can be even larger.

The Cost of Probate	
If you leave property worth:	Probate may cost about:
$200,000	$10,000
$500,000	$25,000

At least as bad as the expense of probate is the delay it causes. In many states, probate can take a year or two, during which time the beneficiaries generally get nothing unless the judge allows the immediate family a small "family allowance."

If you own real estate in more than one state, it's usually necessary to have a whole separate probate proceeding in each state. That means the surviving relatives must probably find and hire a lawyer in each state and pay for multiple probate proceedings.

From the family's point of view, probate's headaches are rarely justified. If the estate contains common kinds of property—a house, stocks, bank accounts, a small business, cars—and no relatives are fighting about it, the property merely needs to be handed over to the new owners. In the vast majority of cases, the probate process entails nothing more than tedious paperwork, and the attorney is nothing more than a very highly paid clerk.

b. Avoiding the Need for a Conservatorship or Guardianship

A living trust can be useful if you become incapable, because of physical or mental illness, of taking care of your financial affairs. That's because the person you named to serve as trustee at your death (or, if you made a shared trust, your spouse) takes over management of the trust assets. The person who takes over has authority to manage all property in the trust and to use it for your benefit.

> **EXAMPLE:** Margaret creates a living trust, appointing herself as trustee. The trust states that if she someday can no longer manage her own affairs, her daughter Elizabeth will replace her as trustee.

If there is no living trust and you haven't made other arrangements for someone to take over your finances if you become incapacitated, a court must appoint someone. Typically, the spouse or adult child of the person seeks this authority and is called a conservator or guardian. (See Chapter 22.)

c.   Keeping Your Estate Plan Confidential

When your will is filed with the probate court after you die, it becomes a matter of public record. A living trust, on the other hand, is a private document in most states. Because the living trust document is never filed with a court or other government entity, what you leave to whom remains private. (There is one exception: Records of real estate transfers are always public.)

Some states require that you register your living trust with the local court. But there are no legal consequences or penalties if you don't. (Registration is explained in Chapter 18.)

The only way the terms of a living trust might become public is if—and this is very unlikely—someone files a lawsuit to challenge the trust or collect a court judgment you owe. (See Section F, below.)

⚠ **Special state rules.** In a few states, after a grantor dies, the successor trustee must disclose certain facts about the living trust. For details, see Chapter 21.

2.   How a Basic Trust Works

A basic revocable living trust does, essentially, what a will does: leaves your property to the people you want to inherit it. But because a trustee owns your property, your assets don't have to go through probate at your death.

When you create a revocable living trust, you appoint yourself trustee, with full power to manage trust property. Then you transfer ownership of some or all of your property to yourself as trustee, keeping absolute control over the property held in trust. You can:

- sell, mortgage or give away property held in trust
- put ownership of trust property back in your own name
- add property to the trust
- change the beneficiaries
- name a different successor trustee
- revoke the trust completely.

> **EXAMPLE:** Ashley creates a revocable living trust and names herself as trustee. She transfers her valuable property—a house and some stocks—to herself as trustee. As trustee, she can sell, mortgage or give away the trust property, or take it out of the trust and put it back into her name.

If you and your spouse create a trust together, both spouses must consent to changes, although either of you can revoke the trust entirely.

After you die, the person you named in your trust document to be "successor trustee" takes over. This person transfers the trust property to the relatives, friends or charities you named as the trust beneficiaries. No probate is necessary for property that was held in trust. In most cases, the whole thing can be handled within a few weeks. When the property has all been transferred to the beneficiaries, the living trust ceases to exist. ⸝

If any of your beneficiaries inherit trust property while still young (not yet 35), the successor trustee (or your spouse, if you made a trust together) will follow the instructions you left in the trust document, and either:

- transfer the property inherited by the child to the "custodian" you chose, to manage the property until the child reaches an age specified by your state's law (21 in most states, but up to 25 in a few states), or
- keep the property in a "child's subtrust," using it for the child's benefit, until the child reaches an age you designate.

Both methods are explained in Chapters 15, 16 and 17.

3. Other Ways to Avoid Probate

A living trust isn't the only probate-avoidance method around. Here are some methods you might want to investigate, to use with or instead of a living trust.

a. Payable-on-Death Bank Accounts

Payable-on-death bank accounts offer one of the easiest ways to keep money—even large sums of it—out of probate. All you need to do is fill out a simple form, provided by the bank, naming the person you want to inherit the money in the account at your death.

As long as you are alive, the person you named to inherit the money in a payable-on-death (P.O.D.) account has no rights to it. You can spend the money, name a different beneficiary or close the account. At your death, the beneficiary just goes to the bank, shows proof of the death and of his or her identity and collects whatever funds are in the account. The probate court is never involved.

b. Transfer-on-Death Registration of Securities

Almost every state has adopted a law (the Uniform Transfer-on-Death Securities Registration Act) that lets you name someone to inherit your stocks, bonds or brokerage accounts without probate. It works very much like a payable-on-death bank account. When you register your ownership, either with the stockbroker or the company itself, you make a request to take ownership in what's called "beneficiary form." When the papers that show your ownership are issued, they will also show the name of your beneficiary. After you have registered ownership this way, the beneficiary has no rights to the stock as long as you are alive. You are free to sell it, give it away or name a different beneficiary. But on your death, the beneficiary can claim the securities without probate, simply by providing proof of death and some identification to the broker or transfer agent. (A transfer agent is a business that is authorized by a corporation to transfer ownership of its stock from one person to another.)

c. Transfer-on-Death Deeds for Real Estate

In a handful of states, you can actually prepare a deed now but have it take effect only at your death. These "transfer-on-death" deeds must be prepared, signed, notarized and recorded (filed in the county land records office) just like a regular deed. But unlike a regular deed, you can revoke a transfer-on-death deed. The deed should expressly state that it does not take effect until death.

Check your state's statute for the rules in your state. Several of the statutes provide deed forms. The states that currently authorize transfer-on-death deeds are Arizona, Colorado, Kansas, Missouri, New Mexico and Ohio.

d.   Transfer-on-Death Registration for Vehicles

So far, only California, Connecticut, Kansas, Missouri and Ohio offer car owners the sensible option of naming a beneficiary, right on the certificate of title or title application, to inherit a vehicle. If you do this, the beneficiary you name has no rights as long as you are alive. You are free to sell or give away the car, or name someone else as the beneficiary.

To name a transfer-on-death beneficiary, all you do is apply for a certificate of car ownership (title) in "beneficiary form." The new certificate lists the name of the beneficiary, who will automatically own the vehicle after your death. You can find more information on the website of your state's motor vehicles department.

e.   Retirement Plans

Retirement plans such as IRAs, 401(k)s and Keoghs don't have to go through probate. All you need to do is name a beneficiary to receive the funds at your death, and no probate will be necessary.

f.   Life Insurance

Life insurance proceeds are subject to probate only if the beneficiary named in the policy is your estate. That's done occasionally if the estate will need immediate cash to pay debts and taxes, but it's usually counterproductive.

g.   Joint Tenancy

Joint tenancy is an efficient and practical way to transfer some kinds of property without probate.

Joint tenancy is a way two or more people can hold title to property they own together. All joint owners (called joint tenants) must own equal shares of the property. (Vermont is the only exception; joint owners may own unequal shares.) When one joint owner dies, the surviving owners automatically get complete ownership of the property. This is called the "right of survivorship." The property doesn't go through probate court—there is only some simple paperwork to fill out to transfer the property into the name of the surviving owner.

A joint tenant cannot leave his or her share to anyone other than the surviving joint tenants. So, for example, even if your will leaves your half-interest in joint tenancy property to someone else, the surviving owners will still inherit it.

This rule isn't as ironclad as it may sound. You can, while still alive, break the joint tenancy by transferring your interest in the property to someone else (or, in some states, to yourself, but not as a "joint tenant").

Joint tenancy often works well when couples acquire real estate or other valuable property together. If they take title in joint tenancy, probate is avoided when the first owner dies—though not (unlike a living trust) when the second owner dies.

Joint tenancy is usually a poor estate planning device when an older person, seeking only to avoid probate, puts solely owned property into joint tenancy with someone else. If you make someone else a co-owner, in joint tenancy, of property that you now own yourself, you give up half ownership of the property. The new owner has rights that you can't take back. For example, the new owner can sell or mortgage his or her share. And federal gift tax may be assessed on the transfer.

There can also be serious problems if one joint tenant becomes incapacitated and cannot make decisions. The other owners must get legal authority to sell or mortgage the property. That may mean going to court to get someone (called a conservator or guardian, in most states) appointed to manage the incapacitated person's affairs. (This problem can be partially dealt with if the joint tenant has signed a document called a "durable power of attorney," giving someone authority to manage her affairs if she cannot. See Chapter 22.) With a living trust, if you (the grantor) become incapacitated, the successor trustee (or the other spouse, if you made a trust together) takes over and has full authority to manage the property. No court proceedings are necessary.

For a list of states that have abolished or restricted joint tenancy, see Chapter 5, Section A.

h. Tenancy by the Entirety

"Tenancy by the entirety" is a form of property ownership that is similar to joint tenancy. Not all states offer it, and it is limited to married couples (with two exceptions: in Hawaii to "reciprocal beneficiaries," and in Vermont to couples who go through a civil union).

States That Allow Tenancy by the Entirety		
Alaska*	Kentucky*	Oklahoma
Arkansas	Maryland	Oregon*
Connecticut	Massachusetts	Pennsylvania
Delaware*	Michigan	Rhode Island
Dist. of	Mississippi	Tennessee
Columbia	Missouri	Utah*
Florida*	New Jersey	Vermont
Hawaii	New York*	Virginia
Illinois*	North Carolina	Wyoming
Indiana*	Ohio**	

*Allowed for real estate only

**Only if created before April 4, 1985

Tenancy by the entirety has many of the same advantages and disadvantages of joint tenancy and is most useful in the same kind of situation: when a couple acquires property together. When one owner (spouse) dies, the surviving co-owner (the other spouse) inherits the property. The property doesn't go through probate.

If property is held in tenancy by the entirety, neither spouse can transfer his or her half of the property alone, either while alive or by will or trust. It must go to the surviving spouse. (This is different from joint tenancy; a joint tenant is free to transfer his or her share to someone else during his life.)

> **EXAMPLE:** Fred and Ethel hold title to their house in tenancy by the entirety. If Fred wanted to sell or give away his half-interest in the house, he could not do so without Ethel's signature on the deed.

i. Community Property With Right of Survivorship

In a few states, married couples (and in California, registered domestic partners) can own property together "as community property with right of survivorship." When one spouse dies, the other automatically inherits the property, without probate. The states that offer this option are Alaska, Arizona, California, Nevada and Wisconsin.

j.   Simplified Probate Proceedings

Many states have begun, albeit slowly, to dismantle some of the more onerous parts of probate. They have created categories of property and beneficiaries that don't have to go through a full-blown probate court proceeding. If your family can take advantage of these procedures after your death, you may not need to worry too much about avoiding probate.

Almost every state has some kind of simplified (summary) probate or out-of-court transfer process for one or more of these categories:

Small estates. Most states offer streamlined probate court procedures for small estates; what qualifies as a small estate varies widely from state to state. In many states, even if your total estate is too large to qualify as a small estate, your heirs can still make use of the simplified procedures if the amount that actually goes through probate is under the limit.

Personal property. If the estate is small, many states also let people collect personal property (that's anything but real estate) they've inherited by filling out a sworn statement (affidavit) and giving it to the person who has the property. Typically, the beneficiary must also provide some kind of proof of his or her right to inherit, such as a death certificate and copy of the will.

Property left to the surviving spouse. In some states, if a surviving spouse inherits less than a certain amount of property, no probate is necessary.

Resources. For more about probate avoidance, see *8 Ways to Avoid Probate*, by Mary Randolph (Nolo).

B. The Tax-Saving AB Trust

The federal estate/gift tax is imposed after your death, on property you gave away during your life (though most ordinary gifts are tax-free) and left at your death. Because everyone is entitled to a large estate tax exemption, the tax affects only large estates, and only a small percentage of Americans end up owing it. And because of changes in the law, that number will soon be smaller still.

1. The Future of the Estate and Gift Tax

In 2001, Congress passed legislation repealing the estate tax—but not until 2010. Meanwhile, the exemption amount will go up, and the tax rates will go down, meaning that fewer people than ever will need to worry about estate tax. The exact dates and amounts are shown below.

It's possible that Congress could revive the tax in some form before 2010. In 2011, the estate tax repeal will expire unless Congress votes to renew it.

Congress did not repeal the federal gift tax, although it raised the exemption and lowered the maximum rate. The lifetime gift tax exemption is $1 million, and (unlike the estate tax exemption) will stay there. That means you can make a total of $1 million of taxable gifts before owing any federal gift tax.

How the Estate Tax Will Fade Away			
Year of Death	Unified Estate/Gift Tax Exemption Rate	Gift Tax Exemption	Highest Estate and Gift Tax Rate
2005	$1.5 million	$1 million	47%
2006	$2 million	$1 million	46%
2007	$2 million	$1 million	45%
2008	$2 million	$1 million	45%
2009	$3.5 million	$1 million	45%
2010	Estate tax repealed	$1 million	top individual income tax rate (gift tax only)
2011	$1 million	unless Congress extends repeal	50% unless Congress extends repeal

2. How an AB Trust May Help Your Family

If you're married, estate tax is most likely to be an issue when the second spouse dies. When the first spouse dies, everything left to the survivor, if he or she is a U.S. citizen, passes tax-free. This rule is called the unlimited marital deduction.

Sounds good. But older couples who have a large combined estate and leave everything to each other may be in for a big estate tax bill on the death of the second spouse. The marital deduction really just postpones estate tax until the second spouse dies.

Say, for example, a husband leaves all his property to his wife. At the husband's death, no estate tax is due. But when the widow dies, the marital deduction won't apply—and now her estate may exceed the amount of the federal estate tax exemption. Her estate will have to pay a much larger tax than if the husband had left his property directly to children or other beneficiaries.

An AB trust can eliminate estate tax for couples who together own up to twice as much as the es-tate tax exemption. It works by making the first spouse's estate subject to tax at his death—but not at the second spouse's. That way, each spouse's estate stays under the estate tax threshold; they're never combined for estate tax purposes. Just how the trust does this is explained in the next section.

Same-sex couples. Married same-sex couples have special concerns when it comes to estate tax planning. Under current laws, same-sex marriage is legal in Massachusetts. But the federal government does not now recognize these marriages, which means a surviving same-sex spouse does not inherit property from the deceased spouse free of estate tax.

3. How an AB Trust Works

In a nutshell, an AB trust works like this: The first spouse to die leaves his property to his children, not his spouse. But the children don't get it out-right—it's in trust. And the trust gives the surviv-ing spouse the right to any income from the property, and the right to spend the property it-self for certain purposes, for the rest of her life. Only at the second spouse's death does the property go outright to the kids.

The tax break comes because the surviving spouse never legally owns the trust property, and so the property isn't part of her estate. If the survivor had inherited the property outright, it would have been subject to estate tax at her death.

EXAMPLE: Thomas and Maria, husband and wife, are in their mid-70s, and each has assets worth $1.2 million. Thomas dies in 2006, and Maria two years later. Here's the tax situation, with and without an AB trust:

- **Without an AB trust.** Thomas leaves everything outright to Maria. No estate tax is assessed because of the marital deduction. But the size of Maria's estate rises to $2.4 million. At her death, all property in excess of the exempt amount in 2008, $2 million, is taxed.
- **With an AB trust.** Thomas and Maria establish an AB trust, with the income to go to the survivor for life and the principal to the children at the survivor's death. When Thomas dies, his $1.2 million is not taxed because it's below the exempt amount. The value of Maria's estate remains at $1.2 million. When Maria dies, $2 million can be left to anyone free of estate tax, so there is no estate tax liability on her $1.2 million, which goes to the children. The $1.2 million that Thomas left in trust also goes to the children; it isn't taxed, because it was already taxed at Thomas's death. It isn't part of Maria's estate, because she is not considered the owner.

Unlike a basic revocable living trust, an AB trust controls what happens to property for years after the first spouse's death. If you make one, you must be sure that the surviving spouse will be financially and emotionally comfortable receiving only the income from the money or property placed in trust, with the children (or other persons) as the actual owner of the property.

The surviving spouse is entitled to any income Trust A property produces. More important, the trust document gives the survivor the right to use any amount of the principal of Trust A necessary for his or her "health, education, support and maintenance in accord with his or her accustomed manner of living." This is the broadest standard the IRS allows for an AB trust. (26 CFR 20.2041-1(c)(2).) If the surviving spouse were given broader powers, the IRS would consider her the owner of the property—which would destroy the estate tax advantage of holding the property in trust.

This means that the surviving spouse can, for example, live in a house owned by the irrevocable trust. And if faced with a need to spend trust principal for medical needs or another kind of emergency, she can go ahead.

You can, if you wish, give the surviving spouse the power to decide whether or not to set up a tax-saving "bypass" trust. This option, and how to decide whether or not an AB trust is right for you, are discussed in Chapter 14.

4. Other Ways to Save on Estate Taxes

Here are other tax-saving strategies you may want to use in addition to—or instead of—an AB trust.

Annual tax-exempt gifts. If you don't need all your income and property to live on, making sizeable gifts while you're alive can be a good way to reduce eventual federal estate taxes before that tax is repealed. Currently, only gifts larger than $11,000 made to one person or organization in one calendar year count toward the personal estate tax exemption. You can give smaller gifts tax-free.

> **EXAMPLE:** Allen and Julia give each of their two daughters $22,000 every year for four years. They have transferred $176,000 without becoming liable for gift tax.

Other tax-exempt gifts. Other gifts are exempt regardless of amount, including:

- gifts between spouses who are U.S. citizens (gifts to spouses who are not United States citizens are exempt only up to $114,000 per year)
- gifts paid directly for medical bills or school tuition, and
- gifts to tax-exempt charitable organizations.

Charitable trusts. If you want to make a big contribution to a charitable cause you care about—and at the same time cut your income taxes now and guarantee some income for life—then a charitable trust may be for you. They're not just for the very rich; you can contribute to a "pooled" charitable trust with as little as $5,000.

QTIPs and QDOTs. These trusts, known by their catchy acronyms (easier to say than "Qualified Terminable Interest Property" trust, you have to admit), are mainly used by married couples who have more than $2 million. A QTIP lets couples postpone paying estate tax until the second spouse's death, and also lock in, while both are still alive, who inherits the property at the second spouse's death. A QDOT is useful when a spouse who is not a U.S. citizen stands to inherit a large amount of property.

Life insurance trusts. Although the proceeds of a life insurance policy don't go through probate, they are included in your estate for federal estate tax purposes. You can reduce the tax bill by giving ownership of the policy to a life insurance trust (or to the beneficiary directly) at least three years before your death. But like other estate tax-saving strategies, this one will have to be reassessed in light of the planned estate tax repeal.

State Estate and Inheritance Taxes

Even if your estate isn't big enough to owe federal estate tax, the state may still take a bite.

Estate tax. Until recently, most states didn't impose their own estate tax; instead, they took a share of the federal estate tax paid by large estates. (This is called a "pick-up" or "sop" tax.) But the federal legislation that started the phase-out of the federal estate tax also took away the share of estate tax that states got to keep. To get back some of what they lost, some states are collecting tax from estates that aren't big enough to owe any federal tax. So far, almost half the states have changed their laws so they can keep collecting estate tax.

Inheritance tax. Some states impose a separate tax on a deceased person's property, called an inheritance tax. The tax rate depends on who inherits the property; usually, spouses and other close relatives pay nothing or a low rate.

For each state's rules, see *Plan Your Estate*, by Denis Clifford and Cora Jordan or *The Executor's Guide: How to Settle a Loved One's Estate or Trust*, by Mary Randolph (both published by Nolo).

C. What Living Trusts Cannot Do

As wonderful as living trusts can be, they aren't a complete estate plan by themselves. Here are some things that trusts can't do.

1. Shelter Assets for Purposes of Medicaid Eligibility

You cannot affect your eligibility for Medicaid by holding property in a revocable living trust. Assets held in a living trust are "countable resources" for purposes of Medicaid qualification. Because you have complete control over trust assets, those assets are treated just as if you owned them in your own name.

Resources. *Long-Term Care: How to Plan and Pay for It,* by Joseph Matthews (Nolo), explains Medicaid eligibility and asset protection in detail.

2. Convey Your Wishes About Medical Intervention

A living trust has absolutely nothing to do with conveying your wishes about life support systems and other medical intervention at the end of life. You'll need other documents—an advance directive ("living will") and durable power of attorney—to make your wishes clear and legally binding. (See Chapter 23.)

3. Protect Assets From Creditors

A living trust does not provide any protection from creditors, at least while you're alive. Because you keep the power to transfer the property back to yourself or revoke the trust entirely, if a creditor sues you and wins, and a court issues a judgment against you, the creditor can seize trust property to pay off the judgment.

As a practical matter, a living trust can, however, provide some protection after your death. (See Section E, below.)

D. Using a Back-Up Will

Even though you create a living trust, you will almost certainly need a simple back-up will, too. Like a living trust, a will is a document in which you specify what is to be done with your property when you die. You can make your will with Quicken WillMaker Plus. See Chapter 3.

1. Why Make a Back-Up Will

Having a will is important for several reasons.

First, a will is an essential back-up device for property that you don't get around to transferring to your living trust. For example, if you acquire property shortly before you die, you may not think to transfer ownership of it to your trust—which means that it won't pass under the terms of the trust document. But in your back-up will, you can include a clause that says who should get any property that you haven't specifically left to someone.

If you don't have a will, any property that isn't transferred by your living trust or other probate-avoidance device (such as joint tenancy) will go to your closest relatives, in an order determined by state law. These laws may not distribute property in the way you would have chosen. For example, if you die leaving a spouse and children, all the property that isn't subject to a living trust or will may be divided among your spouse and children. If your children are minors, that means there must be a court proceeding to get a guardian appointed to manage the property for them.

Second, in a will you can name someone to be the personal guardian of your minor child, in case you and the child's other parent die while the child is still under 18. You can't do that in a living trust.

Finally, if you want to leave nothing to your spouse or a child, you must make your wishes clear in a will. (State law may give your spouse or minor child the right to claim some of your estate; see Chapter 15, 16 or 17.)

2. Avoiding Conflicts Between Your Will and Living Trust

When you make both a living trust and a back-up will, pay attention to how the two work together. If your will and your trust document contain conflicting provisions, at the least you will create confusion among your inheritors, and at the worst, bitter disputes—maybe even a lawsuit—among friends and family.

Here are some no-no's:

- Don't leave the same property in your living trust and will, even if it's to the same beneficiary. If you transfer the property to your living trust and name a beneficiary in the trust document, that's all you need to do. Mentioning the property in the will raises the possibility of probate.
- Don't leave the same property to different beneficiaries in your will and your living trust.
- Don't name different people to be executor of your will and successor trustee of your living trust, especially if you think they might quarrel about how your affairs should be handled. There's one important excep-

tion: If you make a trust with your spouse, you may want to name your spouse as executor of your will, but not as successor trustee—the successor trustee takes over only after both spouses have died. (See Chapter 15, 16 or 17.)

3. Pour-Over Wills

Some lawyers advise people who make living trusts to make "pour-over wills" instead of a plain back-up will. A pour-over will takes all the property you haven't gotten around to transferring to your living trust and, at your death, leaves it to the trust.

Pour-over wills (named because everything is "poured over" from the will to your living trust) do not avoid probate. All property that is left through a will—any kind of will—must go through probate. It makes no difference that the beneficiary of the will is a living trust. If the value of the property left through a pour-over will is small, some states exempt it from probate or offer streamlined probate procedures. But the same is true whether or not the will is a pour-over one.

Pour-over wills are not usually a good idea. It's better to simply use a standard back-up will to take care of this property. In the back-up will, you can name the people you want to get the property and skip the unnecessary extra step of pouring the property through the living trust after your death.

A pour-over will actually has a disadvantage that standard wills don't: It forces the living trust to go on for months after your death, because the property left through the will must go through probate before it can be transferred to the trust. Usually, the property left in a living trust can be distributed to the beneficiaries, and the trust ended, within a few weeks after the person's death.

EXAMPLE: Joy transfers her valuable property to her living trust. She also makes a pour-over will, which states that any property she owns at death not specifically left to someone in the will goes to the living trust. When Joy dies, the property left through her will goes to the trust and is distributed to the residuary beneficiary of her living trust, her son Louis. The living trust must be kept going until probate of the will is finished, when property left by the will is poured over into the living trust.

If Joy had simply named Louis as the residuary beneficiary of a plain back-up will, the result would have been the same, but the process would have been simpler. The living trust would have been ended a few weeks after Joy's death. And after probate was finished, Louis would have received whatever property passed through Joy's will.

There is, however, one situation in which you might want to use a pour-over will. If you set up a child's subtrust for a young beneficiary in your living trust, you may want any property that child inherits through your will to go into the subtrust. Otherwise, you would create two trusts for the beneficiary: one in the will and one in your living trust.

EXAMPLE: Jessica makes a living trust and leaves the bulk of her property to her 12-year-old son. She arranges, in the trust document, for any trust property her son inherits before the age of 30 to be kept in a subtrust. Jessica also makes a back-up will, in which she again arranges for a subtrust to be set up if she should die before her son is 30. So if Jessica dies before her son reaches 30, two subtrusts will be set up for him.

If Jessica used a pour-over will, any property her son inherited through the will would go into the subtrust created by her living trust. Only half the paperwork would be necessary.

E. Drawbacks of a Living Trust

A living trust—especially an AB trust—does have unique problems and complications. Most people think the benefits outweigh the drawbacks, but you should be aware of them.

1. Paperwork

Setting up a living trust isn't difficult or expensive, but it requires some paperwork. The first step is to use Quicken WillMaker Plus to create and print out a trust document, which you should sign in front of a notary public. That's no harder than making a will.

There is, however, one more essential step to making a living trust effective: You must make sure that ownership of all the property you listed in the trust document is legally transferred to you as trustee of the trust.

If an item of property doesn't have a title (ownership) document, you can simply list it on a document called an Assignment of Property. (Quicken WillMaker Plus generates this document automatically.) Most books, furniture, electronics, jewelry, appliances, musical instruments and many other kinds of property can be handled this way.

But if an item has a title document—real estate, stocks, mutual funds, bonds, money market accounts or vehicles, for example—you must change the title document to show that the property is held in trust. For example, if you want to put your house into your living trust, you must prepare and sign a new deed, transferring ownership to you as trustee of the trust (or, in Colorado, to the trust itself). (Chapter 19 explains how.)

2. Record Keeping

After a revocable living trust is created, little day-to-day record keeping is required. No separate income tax records or returns are necessary as long as you are both the grantor and the trustee. (IRS Reg. § 1.671-4.) Income from property held in the living trust is reported on your personal income tax return.

You must keep written records whenever you transfer property to or from the trust, which isn't difficult unless you transfer a lot of property in and out of the trust. (Chapter 20 discusses transferring property in and out of your living trust.)

> **EXAMPLE:** Monica and David Fielding put their house in a living trust to avoid probate, but later decide to sell it. In the real estate contract and deed transferring ownership to the new owners, Monica and David sign their names "as trustees of the Monica and David Fielding Revocable Living Trust."

An AB trust requires additional record keeping and paperwork after the first spouse dies. It also usually entails legal fees when, at the first spouse's death, the trust may be split into Trust A and Trust B. (One trust contains the deceased spouse's assets and is irrevocable; the other contains the surviving spouse's assets and is revocable.) Splitting the couple's assets in a way that yields the greatest tax benefits can be a tricky job, requiring the services of a good tax lawyer.

The surviving spouse must then obtain a taxpayer ID number for the irrevocable trust. The surviving spouse must also file an annual trust income tax return, IRS Form 1041. This usually isn't a big deal but, like any tax return, it requires some work.

The surviving spouse must also keep two sets of records, one of income and transactions involving her own property, including property in Trust B, and one for Trust A property. For many AB trusts, all you need is two separate bank or investment accounts. But if complex property holdings are involved, such as shares in a closely held S corporation or depreciated real estate, you'll need a more sophisticated system.

3. Transfer Taxes

In most states, transfers of real estate to revocable living trusts are exempt from transfer taxes that are usually imposed on real estate transfers. But in a few states, transferring real estate to your living trust could trigger a tax. (See Chapter 19.)

4. Difficulty Refinancing Trust Property

Because legal title to trust real estate is held in the name of the trustee, a few banks and title companies may balk if you want to refinance it. They should be sufficiently reassured if you show them a copy of your trust document, which specifically gives you, as trustee, the power to borrow against trust property.

In the unlikely event you can't convince an uncooperative lender to deal with you in your capacity as trustee, you'll have to find another lender (which shouldn't be hard) or transfer the property out of the trust and back into your name. Later, after you refinance, you can transfer it back into the living trust.

5. No Cutoff of Creditors' Claims

Most people don't worry that after their death, creditors will try to collect large debts from property in the estate. In most situations, the surviving relatives simply pay the valid debts, such as outstanding bills, taxes and last illness and funeral expenses. But if you are concerned about the possibility of large claims, you may want to let your property go through probate instead of a living trust.

If your property goes through probate, creditors have only a certain amount of time to file claims against your estate. A creditor who was properly notified of the probate court proceeding cannot file a claim after the period—about six months, in most states—expires.

> **EXAMPLE:** Elaine is a real estate investor with a good-sized portfolio of property. She has many creditors and is sometimes named in lawsuits. It might be to her advantage to have assets go through a probate, which cuts off the claims of creditors who are properly notified of the probate proceeding.

On the other hand, when property isn't probated, creditors still have the right to be paid (if the debt is valid) from the property. There is no formal claim procedure, however. The creditor may not know who inherited the deceased debtor's property, and once the property is found, the creditor may have to file a lawsuit, which may not be worth the time and expense.

If you want to take advantage of probate's creditor cutoff, you must let all your property pass through probate. If not, there's a good chance the creditor could still sue (even after the probate claim cutoff) and try to collect from the property that didn't go through probate and passed instead through your living trust.

F. When Living Trusts Can Fail

Living trusts usually work easily and smoothly to transfer property at death. When they fail, it is usually because the property listed in the trust document was not actually transferred to the trustee's name. If property that has a title document (such as real estate, stocks or vehicles) isn't owned in the trustee's name, the terms of the Declaration of Trust have no effect on it, and it will probably end up going through probate. (How to transfer property into a living trust is explained in Chapter 19.)

Court challenges to living trusts, like challenges to wills, are rare. You don't need to concern yourself with them unless you think a close relative might have an axe to grind after your death.

1. Challenges to the Validity of the Trust

Someone who wanted to challenge the validity of a living trust would have to bring a lawsuit and prove that:

- when the grantor made the trust, he or she was mentally incompetent or unduly influenced by someone, or
- the trust document itself is flawed—for example, the signature is forged.

It's generally considered more difficult to successfully challenge a living trust than a will. That's because your continuing involvement with a living trust after its creation (transferring property in and out of the trust, or making amendments) helps show that you were competent to manage your affairs.

2. Lawsuits From Spouses

Most married people leave much, if not all, of their property to their spouses. But if you don't leave your spouse at least half of your property, your spouse may have the right to go to court and claim some of your property after your death. Some or all of the property you had earmarked for other beneficiaries would go to your spouse.

Be cautious if you're getting divorced. You could also run into trouble from a former spouse if you try to transfer assets in or out of trust while your divorce proceeding is pending. Some states have very specific rules about what you may and may not do during this period.

The rights of spouses vary from state to state. The most important differences are between community property states and non-community property states.

Don't try to cut out your spouse. If you don't plan to leave at least half of the property in your estate to your spouse, you should consult a lawyer experienced in estate planning.

a. Community Property States

Alaska*	Nevada
Arizona	New Mexico
California	Washington
Idaho	Wisconsin
Louisiana	Texas

*If spouses sign a community property agreement.

In these states, the general rule is that spouses together own all property that either acquires during the marriage, except property one spouse acquires by gift or inheritance. Each spouse owns a half-interest in this "community property."

You are free to leave your separate property and your half of the community property to anyone you choose at death. Your spouse—who already owns half of all the community property—has no right to inherit any of it. But if you don't want to leave anything to your spouse, you should make a will and include in it a specific statement to that effect. If you don't, in certain situations your spouse may be able to claim at least some—possibly all—of your half of the community property after your death.

b. Non-Community Property States

Alabama	Missouri
Alaska*	Montana
Arkansas	Nebraska
Colorado	New Hampshire
Connecticut	New Jersey
Delaware	New York
District of Columbia	North Carolina
Florida	North Dakota
Georgia	Ohio
Hawaii	Oklahoma
Illinois	Oregon
Iowa	Pennsylvania
Indiana	Rhode Island
Kansas	South Carolina
Kentucky	South Dakota
Maine	Tennessee
Maryland	Utah
Massachusetts	Vermont
Michigan	Virginia
Minnesota	West Virginia
Mississippi	Wyoming

* Spouses can, however, create community property by signing a community property agreement.

In these states, you cannot disinherit your spouse. A surviving spouse who doesn't receive one-third to one-half of the deceased spouse's property (through a will, living trust or other method) is entitled to insist upon that much. The exact share depends on state law.

Even property given away before death may legally belong to the surviving spouse under these laws. For example, take the case of a man who set up joint bank accounts with his children from a previous marriage. After his death, his widow sued to recover her interest in the accounts. She won; the Kentucky Supreme Court ruled that under Kentucky's "dower" law, a spouse is entitled to a half-interest in the other spouse's personal property (everything but real estate). Her husband had not had the legal right to give away her interest in the money in the accounts. (*Harris v. Rock*, 799 S.W.2d 10 (Ky. 1990).) Most non-community property states have similar laws.

State law may also give your spouse the right to inherit the family residence, or at least use it for his or her life. The Florida constitution, for example, gives a surviving spouse the deceased spouse's residence. (Fla. Const. Art. 10, § 4.) And Minnesota law requires that a homestead (a dwelling owned and occupied by a deceased person at his death) pass to the surviving spouse, regardless of a will provision to the contrary, if the deceased has no descendents. If there are descendents, the homestead goes to the surviving spouse for life and then to the descendents. (Minn. Stat. § 524.2-402.)

3. Lawsuits by a Child

Children usually have no right to inherit anything from their parents. There are two exceptions: laws that give minor children certain rights and laws that protect children who are unintentionally overlooked in a will.

a. Minor Children

State law may give your minor children (less than 18 years old) the right to inherit the family residence. The Florida constitution, for example, prohibits the head of a family from leaving his residence in his will (except to his spouse) if he is survived by a spouse or minor child. (Fla. Const. Art. 10, § 4.)

b. Overlooked Children

State laws protect offspring who appear to have been unintentionally overlooked in a parent's will. As the use of living trusts become more widespread, states may expand protection to children who go unmentioned in living trusts; California has already done so. Even without a statutory change, it's possible that a court could apply these laws to living trusts, reasoning that the trusts are serving the function of wills.

Typically, these laws protect a child born after the parent's will is signed. The law presumes that the parent didn't mean to cut that child out, but simply didn't get around to writing a new will. The child can claim a share (the size depends on state law) of the deceased parent's property, which may include property in a living trust.

If, for whatever reason, you don't want to leave any property to one or more of your children, the easy way to avoid any later misunderstandings or legal claims is to make a will and mention each child in it. You don't have to leave the child any property. (See Chapter 4.)

Overlooked grandchildren. Children have no right to inherit from their grandparents unless their parent has died. In that case, the grandchildren can claim whatever the deceased child would have been legally entitled to. ■

Chapter 14

What Kind of Living Trust Do You Need?

Quicken WillMaker makes two kinds of revocable living trusts: a basic trust, which avoids probate, and an AB trust, which avoids both probate and federal estate tax.

You May Not Need a Living Trust

You may already be convinced that you want to avoid probate or save on estate taxes—but you may not need to be concerned about these goals, at least right now. Or you may be able to accomplish them without a trust. Before you plunge ahead with a trust, read on. You may **not** need a living trust if:

- **You're young and healthy.** Your estate planning goals are probably simple. You want to make sure that in the unlikely event of your early death, your property will go to the people or institutions you want to get it and, if you have young children, that they are well cared for. You can accomplish those goals by writing a will (in which you name a guardian to raise the children) and perhaps buying some life insurance. If you do want to take some probate-avoidance steps now, check out simpler methods, such as payable-on-death bank accounts.

- **You own your big assets jointly with someone else.** If you're married or in a long-term relationship, you probably own many, if not all, of your valuable assets together with your mate. If you hold title in joint tenancy, tenancy by the entirety or (in some states) community property, the property will go to the survivor, without probate, when the first owner dies. You may decide to wait to create a trust, which will avoid probate at the second death, until later.

- **You can name beneficiaries outside of your will for most of your assets.** You don't need a trust to avoid probate for bank or retirement accounts; all you have to do is fill out a form provided by the bank or account custodian, naming the beneficiary. You can do the same thing for stocks and bonds in almost every state.

- **You don't own much.** Small estates (defined differently by each state) don't have to go through regular probate; streamlined procedures are available. And if you're considering an AB trust, keep in mind that currently only large estates owe estate tax. In 2010, the estate tax is scheduled to be repealed.

A. When to Use a Basic Probate-Avoidance Trust

Like a will, a basic revocable living trust lets you leave your property to the people you want to inherit it. The advantage of a living trust is that your assets don't have to go through probate at your death. Consider a living trust if any of the following applies to you:

You're middle-aged or older, or in poor health. As you get older, you'll want to think more about sparing your family the expense and delay of probate.

Simpler probate-avoidance methods aren't available. A living trust is an excellent way to avoid probate for real estate that you own alone and many other miscellaneous assets. But if your money is in bank, brokerage or retirement accounts, it's simpler and equally effective just to name payable-on-death beneficiaries for each account. These methods don't offer all the features of a living trust—most important, you probably won't be able to name an alternate beneficiary. But especially for younger people, that drawback may be outweighed by convenience.

Your estate probably won't qualify for simplified probate. Most states allow certain amounts or types of property to be transferred without probate or by a streamlined court procedure, even if it's left by will. If your estate is eligible for a simple transfer procedure, you may not need to create a trust. Simplified probate is available to estates of just a few thousand dollars in some states, all the way up to $200,000 in Nevada. In some states, if a surviving spouse inherits less than a certain amount of property, no probate is necessary.

 Resources. Every state's approach to handling small estates is listed in *The Executor's Guide: How to Settle a Loved One's Estate or Trust*, by Mary Randolph; *Plan Your Estate*, by Denis Clifford and Cora Jordan; and *8 Ways to Avoid Probate*, by Mary Randolph, all published by Nolo.

You own out-of-state real estate. Using a living trust can let you avoid probate proceedings in that state, saving your family a big headache.

You aren't worried about big creditors' claims. If you own a business that has many creditors, you may want your assets to go through probate, so that creditors' claims are cut off after a certain period. If creditors don't make their claims by the deadline, your inheritors can take your property free of concern that creditors will surface later and attempt to claim a share.

You're concerned about privacy. A will is filed with the probate court after you die and becomes a matter of public record. A living trust, on the other hand, is not, so what you leave to whom remains private. (There is one exception: Records of real estate transfers are always public.)

You don't mind some extra paperwork. Creating a trust document is no harder than making a will. There is, however, one more essential step to making a living trust effective: You must make sure that ownership of all the property you listed in the trust document is legally transferred to you as trustee of the trust.

You're concerned about incapacity. A living trust can be useful if you become incapable, because of injury or illness, of taking care of your financial affairs. With a trust, the person named to serve as trustee after your death can take over management of the trust assets. Without a living trust or other arrangements, a court must appoint someone to take over.

B. When to Use a Regular Tax-Saving AB Trust

A basic living trust does nothing to reduce federal estate tax—for that, you need an AB trust. But should you even be concerned about estate tax? Most people don't need to worry about it; only a tiny fraction—fewer than 2%—of estates owe estate tax, even before the big changes that took effect in 2002. But as explained in Chapter 13, these massive legislative changes have made it difficult for some people to know whether or not they should even try to plan for avoiding estate tax.

Currently, the amount that you can leave that is exempt from estate tax is scheduled to rise steadily until 2010, at which time the estate tax will no longer be imposed at all. But unless Congress extends the estate tax repeal, the tax will pop up again in 2011 (with a $1 million exemption). That raises the possibility that someone who dies on December 31, 2010, will not owe estate tax, but the estate of someone with the same amount of assets who lives until the next day could owe tens of thousands of dollars.

Consider an AB trust only if any of the following apply to you:

You expect to owe estate tax when the second spouse dies. If you and your spouse have combined assets worth more than the amount that is exempt from estate tax, your family may be in for a hefty estate tax bill when the second spouse dies.

But as the exemption amount increases in the next few years, that scenario becomes more and more remote for most people. Unless you expect to leave a very large amount of property at your death, you don't need an AB trust or other estate tax-saving plan.

An AB trust could actually cost your family money if, when you die, there is no estate tax.

That's because the new tax law changes the rules for determining the tax basis of inherited property. Under the current law, the basis of inherited property is the value at the date of death. In most cases, that arrangement is a boon for the person who inherits the property, because the new basis usually is higher, and a higher ("stepped-up") tax basis means less taxable profit when the property is eventually sold.

But if the estate tax is repealed as scheduled (in 2010), not all inherited property will automatically get a stepped-up basis. Instead, the executor of the estate will be able to choose up to $1.3 million of property in the estate to get a stepped-up basis. If the property is in an AB trust instead of the estate, it won't be eligible to get a date-of-death basis. (Property in a basic, revocable trust will qualify for a stepped-up basis.)

If you think your wealth may exceed the amount that is exempt from estate tax, it's a tough call. Whether or not you want to make an AB trust to try to avoid possible eventual tax may depend on two unknowable things: how long you will live and what Congress does in the next few years.

First, you could simply postpone making an AB trust until the future of the estate tax is decided by Congress. If the tax comes back in 2011, you may need an AB trust after all.

Second, you could use Quicken WillMaker Plus to make a "disclaimer" trust. That's an AB trust that gives the surviving spouse the power to decide, after the first spouse dies, whether or not to put the tax-saving features of the AB trust into effect. (More on this in Section C, below.)

Third, you can always make an AB trust and revoke it, if the estate tax exemption reaches a level at which you no longer need to worry about estate taxes. But you can't revoke the whole trust after one spouse dies; part of it becomes irrevocable then. The deceased spouse's share of the trust property will be tied up for the rest of the surviving spouse's life, and there's nothing you can do about it.

Estate Tax Exemptions: On the Rise	
Year of Death	**Estate Tax Exemption**
2005	$1.5 million
2006, 2007, 2008	$2 million
2009	$3.5 million
2010	Estate tax repealed
2011	$1 million unless Congress extends repeal

You're married. The AB trust made by Quicken WillMaker Plus is for married couples only. If, however, you're married to someone of the same sex (currently an option only in Massachusetts), don't use the Quicken WillMaker Plus AB trust. The AB trust is based on the tax law that lets a surviving spouse inherit from the deceased spouse without owing any estate tax. But the federal government does not now recognize same-sex marriages, which means that a surviving same-sex spouse does not get that tax break.

You and your spouse are in your 50s, 60s or older. If one or both of you expects to live many more years, you can leave everything directly to your spouse, who can inherit an unlimited amount without paying tax (as long as the surviving spouse is a U.S. citizen). The survivor would have a long time to use the money and to plan for reducing eventual estate taxes.

You don't mind restricting the surviving spouse's use of trust property. With an AB trust, the surviving spouse does not have unlim-

ited access to the property inherited from the deceased spouse. Although Quicken WillMaker Plus's AB trust gives the survivor as much control as the IRS will allow (and still get the tax break), there are restrictions. The survivor gets only the income from the deceased spouse's half of the property and can spend principal only for health, education, support and maintenance, in accord with his or her accustomed manner of living.

Family members get along well. You should be confident that the surviving spouse and the children (or other final beneficiaries) won't quarrel over management of the trust property. Until the surviving spouse dies, he or she and the children will essentially share ownership of the trust assets. Children hoping to inherit big sums have been known to resent the parent's use of trust property—forgetting that the parents didn't have to set up the trust and took the trouble to do so solely to benefit the children.

You don't mind some hassles and legal fees after the first spouse dies. After one spouse dies, the survivor will need to consult an attorney (or possibly a certified public accountant) to split the trust into Trusts A and B, or to decide whether or not to create the bypass trust (if you chose the disclaimer trust option). And each year, a trust income tax return will have to be filed for the irrevocable bypass trust.

Keep an eye on the estate tax laws. The uncertainty in the current estate tax law has made it almost inevitable that Congress will again take up the matter of estate taxes in the next few years. Otherwise, people simply cannot plan ahead. So, keep up to date as these changes work their way through the political process. If the estate tax really is eliminated, you will almost certainly not want an AB trust.

C. When to Use a Disclaimer AB Trust

Consider adding the disclaimer clause to your AB trust if you're not sure whether or not the estate of the second spouse to die will owe estate tax, and you don't yet want to lock in your choice of an AB trust.

A disclaimer trust works just like a regular AB trust in most ways. The difference is that when the first spouse dies, the surviving spouse isn't forced to split the trust into Trusts A and B. If it looks like creating the irrevocable bypass trust isn't necessary to save on estate taxes (perhaps because the estate tax exemption has gone up and you no longer own enough to be taxed), he or she doesn't have to do it. The surviving spouse can make the decision based on current information—the tax laws and the surviving spouse's resources at the time. Those things are impossible to predict now.

It's good to have this flexibility, especially given the uncertainty in the federal estate tax laws, because splitting an AB trust and maintaining the bypass trust for years takes a fair amount of time and money. A surviving spouse must keep separate records for the assets in the bypass trust and file an annual income tax return for it. If the trust isn't going to save on estate taxes, you don't want to have to go to all that trouble.

If the surviving spouse decides not to split the AB trust, he or she inherits all the trust property (except for items left specifically to other beneficiaries). It stays in the surviving spouse's revocable trust, which requires no special record keeping or tax returns.

If, however, it makes financial sense, the surviving spouse can go ahead and split the AB trust. The spouse decides how much property should go into the irrevocable bypass trust and "disclaims"—turns down—that amount of property. A disclaimer must be made within nine months after the death and is subject to strict legal rules. One important rule is that the spouse cannot benefit from an asset—for example, use the interest generated by a bank account—and then disclaim it.

The bottom line is that whether you make a regular or a disclaimer trust, the surviving spouse will need professional tax advice after the first spouse's death.

EXAMPLE: Steve and his wife Vanita have assets worth almost $3 million—an amount that's subject to estate tax in 2006, when they're doing their planning, but that will no longer be taxed as of 2009, when the estate tax exemption rises to $3.5 million. Because they're not sure if estate tax will be an issue for them, they make an AB trust with a disclaimer clause.

When Steve dies in 2009, it's up to Vanita to decide how much, if anything, to put in the bypass trust. Because of investment downturns, Vanita and Steve's combined assets are worth only about $2 million at Steve's death. Meanwhile the estate tax exemption has jumped to $3.5 million. Vanita talks to a tax lawyer and realizes that she can inherit all the trust property outright, save herself the hassle of creating the irrevocable bypass trust and not owe any estate tax at her death (unless her net worth rises dramatically and unexpectedly).

So she doesn't disclaim any trust property, and as a result it all goes into her revocable survivor's trust. She has complete control over the trust and doesn't need to keep separate records or file tax returns for it.

Don't use a disclaimer trust unless you're both comfortable with giving the surviving spouse complete control over the couple's assets when the first spouse dies—just as if he or she inherited everything outright. This is fine with many couples, who set up AB trusts only for tax savings and will be relieved if the trouble and expense of an AB trust are not necessary. But if you don't want the surviving spouse to control who inherits the trust property at his or her death, you may

want to use a regular AB trust. For example, if you want to be sure that your children from a previous marriage will inherit your share of the trust property, then you would not want a disclaimer trust.

D. If You're Married: One Trust or Two?

If you're married and decide to make a basic probate-avoidance trust, you can make one trust together or make separate trusts. (If you make an AB trust, you must make one shared trust.) Many couples prefer to make one shared trust, because that way they don't have to divide property they own together.

If, however, you and your spouse each own substantial amounts of separate property and want to keep it separate, you may prefer to make individual living trusts. It's increasingly common for couples, especially if they are older and have children from a prior marriage, to sign an agreement (before or during the marriage) to own property separately. Or they may not make a formal agreement, but carefully avoid mixing their property together.

Another reason to make separate trusts is if each spouse wants to keep sole control over his or her own trust property. With a shared trust, either spouse has authority over all trust property while both spouses are alive. (See Chapter 16.)

Your decision may be affected by the marital property laws of your state. This section briefly explains the two systems of marital property laws: community property and non-community property.

Are You Married?

Same-sex couples. Only Massachusetts allows marriage between two people of the same sex. But even if you're a legally married Massachusetts couple, you shouldn't make a shared trust with Quicken WillMaker Plus. That's because the shared trust document uses the language "husband" and "wife," which is not appropriate for a same-sex couple. You can still accomplish all your estate planning goals by making individual trusts—you're free to leave your trust property exactly as you wish (to your spouse or others) and to name your spouse as the successor trustee of your living trust.

If you want a trust document that spells out your relationship with your life partner—whether it's marriage, domestic partnership, civil union or something else—you should see a lawyer.

If you're separated but not yet divorced. See a lawyer before you create a trust or transfer property in or out of one. To protect the rights of each spouse, your state may have very specific rules about what you can and cannot do after separation but before your divorce is final.

Common law marriages. In some states, a couple can become legally married by living together, intending to be married and presenting themselves to the world as a married couple. See Chapter 4, Section E for more information.

1. Community Property States

Alaska*	Nevada
Arizona	New Mexico
California**	Washington
Idaho	Wisconsin
Louisiana	Texas

*If spouses sign a community property agreement.

**Registered domestic partners are also covered by California's community property laws.

In these states, the general rule is that spouses share everything 50-50, so it usually makes sense to make one shared marital trust, especially if you have been married for a number of years.

All property earned or otherwise acquired by either spouse during the marriage, regardless of whose name is on the title slip, is community property. Each spouse owns a one-half interest in it. Property acquired by one spouse by gift or inheritance, however, or before marriage, is not community property; it is the separate property of that spouse.

> **EXAMPLE:** Rob and Cecile live in Nevada, a community property state. They have been married for 20 years. Except for some bonds that Cecile inherited from her parents, virtually all their valuable property—house, stocks, car—is owned together. The money they brought to the marriage in separate bank accounts has long since been mixed with community property, making it community property, too. Rob and Cecile decide to make a shared living trust.

Making two individual living trusts would require splitting ownership of the co-owned assets, which can be a clumsy process. For example, to hold a co-owned house in two separate trusts would require the spouses to sign and record a deed transferring a half-interest in the house to each spouse as trustee. And to transfer household furnishings to separate trusts, spouses would have to allocate each item to a trust—or end up transferring a half-interest in a couch to separate trusts.

There is another advantage to making a shared trust if you and your spouse want to leave significant trust property to each other. With a shared trust, property left by one spouse to the survivor stays in the living trust when the first spouse dies; no transfer is necessary when the first spouse dies. With separate trusts, property left to the surviving spouse must usually be transferred first from the trust to the surviving spouse, and then (to avoid probate) to the surviving spouse's living trust.

If you and your spouse own most of your property together but each of you has some separate property, a shared marital trust is fine. You can transfer all of it to the trust, and each spouse can name beneficiaries (including each other) to receive his or her separate property.

If, however, you and your spouse own most of your property separately, you may want to make individual trusts. Most couples in this situation fit one of these profiles:

- You and your spouse signed an agreement stating that each spouse's earnings and other income are separate, not community property, and you have kept your property separate.
- You are recently married and have little or no community property.
- You each own mostly separate property acquired before your marriage (or by gift or inheritance), which you conscientiously keep from being mixed with community property. Couples who marry later in life and no longer work often fit into this category. Not only is the property they owned before the marriage separate, but federal Social Security benefits and certain retirement plan benefits are also separate, not community, property.

If you and your spouse decide on separate living trusts, each of you will transfer your separately owned property to your individual trust. If you own some property—a house, for example—together, you can each transfer your portion to your trust.

2. Non-Community Property States

Alabama	Missouri
Alaska*	Montana
Arkansas	Nebraska
Colorado	New Hampshire
Connecticut	New Jersey
Delaware	New York
District of Columbia	North Carolina
Florida	North Dakota
Georgia	Ohio
Hawaii	Oklahoma
Illinois	Oregon
Indiana	Pennsylvania
Iowa	Rhode Island
Kansas	South Carolina
Kentucky	South Dakota
Maine	Tennessee
Maryland	Utah
Massachusetts	Vermont
Michigan	Virginia
Minnesota	West Virginia
Mississippi	Wyoming

*Spouses can, however, create community property by signing a community property agreement.

In a non-community property state, it's usually fairly easy for spouses to keep track of who owns what. The spouse whose name is on the title document (deed, brokerage account paper or title slip, for example) owns it. If you own most of your property together, you'll probably want to make a shared trust; if you own things separately, consider individual trusts.

EXAMPLE: Howard and Louisa live in Indiana, a non-community property state. Both have grown children from prior marriages. When they married, they moved into Howard's house. They both have their own bank accounts and investments, and one joint checking account which they own as joint tenants with right of survivorship.

Each makes an individual living trust. Howard, who dies first, leaves his house to Louisa, but most of his other property is left to his children. The funds in the checking account are not included in his living trust but pass to Louisa, also without probate, because the account was held in joint tenancy. Howard's other accounts go to his children, under the pay-on-death arrangement he has with the bank. (Joint tenancy, pay-on-death accounts and other probate-avoidance methods are discussed in Chapter 13.) ■

Chapter 15

Creating an Individual Trust

When you create your living trust document with Quicken WillMaker Plus, you have only a few choices to make. Basically, you must decide:

- what property you want to put in your living trust
- whom you want to receive the trust property at your death (these people or organizations are the beneficiaries of your living trust)
- who is to be the successor trustee—the person you want to distribute trust property at your death, and
- how you should arrange for someone to manage trust property inherited by beneficiaries who are too young to handle it without supervision.

You may already have a good idea of how you want to decide these issues. This chapter discusses the factors you should think about as you make each decision. It is organized the same way as the program is (Parts 1 through 6), so that you can easily refer to it while you're actually making your trust document. It's a good idea, though, to read through this chapter before you sit down at the computer—it will make the whole process clearer and easier.

How an Individual Trust Works: An Overview

Here, in brief, are the important points about how an individual trust works:

Control of trust property. You will be the trustee of your living trust, so you'll have control over the property in the trust.

Amendments or revocation. At any time, you can revoke the trust, add property to it, remove property from it, or modify any term of the trust document.

After your death. After you die, the person named in the trust document as successor trustee takes over. He or she is responsible for distributing trust property to the beneficiaries and managing any trust property left to a young beneficiary in a child's subtrust (explained later).

EXAMPLE: Lenora sets up a basic revocable living trust to avoid probate. In the trust document, she makes herself the trustee and appoints her son Ben as successor trustee, to take over as trustee after her death. She transfers her valuable property—her house, savings accounts and stocks—to the living trust.

The trust document states that Lenora's grandson, Max, is to receive the stocks when she dies. She provides that if Max is not yet 21 when she dies, the stocks will stay in a "child's subtrust," managed by the successor trustee Ben. Everything else goes to her son Ben.

When Lenora dies, Ben becomes trustee. He follows the terms of the trust document and, in his capacity as trustee, distributes all the trust property except the stocks to himself, without probate.

He also manages the stocks inherited by Max, who is 16 at Lenora's death, until his 21st birthday. When all the property in the subtrust is given to Max or spent on his behalf, the subtrust ends.

EXAMPLE: Your birth certificate lists your name as Rose Mary Green. But you've always gone by Mary and always sign documents as Mary McNee, your married name. You would use Mary McNee on your living trust.

Use only one name; don't enter various versions of your name joined by "aka" (also known as).

If you go by more than one name, be sure that the name you use for your living trust is the one that appears on the ownership documents for property you plan to hold in trust. If it isn't, it could cause confusion later, and you should change the name on your ownership documents before you transfer the property to the trust.

EXAMPLE: You use the name William Dix for your trust but own real estate in your former name of William Geicherwitz. You should prepare and sign a new deed, changing the name of the owner to William Dix, before you prepare another deed to transfer the property to yourself as trustee.

Part 1: Your Name

Entering this information is easy: just type in your name. The name you enter will form part of the name of your trust. For example, if you enter "William S. Jorgensen," your trust will be named "The William S. Jorgensen Revocable Living Trust." Your name will also automatically appear as the original trustee of your living trust. (See Part 2, below.)

Enter your name the way it appears on other formal business documents, such as your driver's license or bank accounts. This may or may not be the name on your birth certificate.

Part 2: Trustees

To be legally valid, every trust must have a trustee—a person or institution to manage the property held in trust. When you create a living trust with this program, you are the trustee now. You will name someone else to be the successor trustee, who will take over after you have died.

A. The Original Trustee

You will be the original trustee of your living trust. As trustee, you will have complete control over the property that will be held in the trust.

As a day-to-day, practical matter, it makes little difference that your property is now held in trust. You won't have any special duties as trustee of your trust. You do not even need to file a separate income tax return for the living trust. If the property generates income, just report it on your personal income tax return, as if the trust did not exist.

You have the same freedom to sell, give away or mortgage trust property as you did before you put the property into the living trust. The only difference is that you must now sign documents in your capacity as trustee.

> **EXAMPLE:** Celeste wants to sell a piece of land that is owned in her name as trustee of her living trust. She prepares a deed transferring ownership of the land to the new owner, and signs the deed as "Celeste Tornetti, trustee of the Celeste Tornetti Revocable Living Trust dated February 4, 1994."

You can't name someone else as trustee. In the unlikely event you don't want to be the original trustee of your living trust, you cannot use Quicken WillMaker Plus; you need to see an estate planning lawyer to draw up a more specialized living trust. Naming someone else as trustee has important tax consequences and means you give up control over trust property.

B. The Successor Trustee

You must choose a successor trustee—someone to act as trustee after your death or incapacity. The successor trustee has no power or responsibility while you are alive and capable of managing your affairs.

1. The Successor Trustee's Duties If You Are Incapacitated

If you become physically or mentally incapacitated and unable to manage your affairs, the successor trustee takes over management of the property in your living trust. Before the successor trustee can take over, your incapacity must be documented in writing by a majority of three people you named in the trust document.

You will name, in the trust document, three people who will determine whether or not you're capable of managing your trust if the issue ever comes up. These people do not have to be doctors. Ideally, you will choose people who know you well and can give an unbiased opinion about whether or not you need help taking care of financial and property matters.

If your successor trustee thinks it's time to take over management of the trust, he or she must ask the people you choose to give, in writing, their opinion of whether or not you are capable of managing the trust. (If the successor trustee makes reasonable efforts to contact all of them, but one or more isn't available, the successor trustee may rely on the opinions of the ones who can be reached.) If a majority of them think the successor trustee should take over, he or she is authorized to begin serving as trustee.

In this situation, the successor trustee has authority to use trust property for your health care, support and welfare. The law requires him or her to act honestly and prudently in managing the property. And because you are no longer the trustee, the new trustee must file an income tax return for the trust. At your death, any remaining trust property is distributed to your beneficiaries.

The successor trustee has no power over property not in your living trust, and no authority to make health care decisions for you. For this reason, it's also wise to create documents called durable powers of attorney, giving the successor trustee authority to manage property not held in trust and to make health care decisions. (See Chapters 22 and 23.)

2. The Successor Trustee's Duties After Your Death

After your death, the successor trustee takes over as trustee. His or her primary responsibility is to distribute trust property to the beneficiaries named in your Declaration of Trust. That is usually a straightforward process that can be completed in a few weeks. An outline of the steps the successor trustee needs to take to transfer certain common kinds of property is in Chapter 21.

The successor trustee may, however, have long-term duties if the trust document creates a child's subtrust for trust property inherited by a young beneficiary (this is explained in Part 6, below). If the successor trustee is in charge of managing property over the long term, the trust document produced by Quicken WillMaker Plus gives him or her very broad authority, so that the trustee will be able to do whatever is necessary to respond to the demands of the circumstances. For example, the trustee has the power to invest trust funds in accounts, such as money market accounts, that are not federally insured. The trustee can also spend trust income or property for the health and welfare of the beneficiary.

3. Choosing a Successor Trustee

The person or institution you choose as successor trustee will have a crucial role: to manage your trust property (if you become incapacitated) or distribute it to your beneficiaries (after your death).

Obviously, when you are giving someone this much power and discretion, you should choose someone with good common sense whom you trust completely. If you don't know anyone who fits this description, think twice about establishing a living trust. Most people pick an adult son or daughter, other relative or close friend.

In most situations, the successor trustee will not need extensive experience in financial management; common sense, dependability and complete honesty are usually enough. A successor trustee who may have long-term responsibility over a young beneficiary's trust property needs more management and financial skills than a successor trustee whose only job is to distribute trust property. The successor trustee does have authority, however, under the terms of the trust document, to get any reasonably necessary professional help—from an accountant, lawyer or tax preparer, perhaps—and pay for it out of trust assets.

Usually, it makes sense to name just one person as successor trustee, to avoid any possibility of conflicts. But it's legal and may be desirable to name more than one person. For example, you might name two or more of your children, if you don't expect any disagreements between them and you think one of them might feel hurt and left out if not named.

Having more than one successor trustee is especially likely to cause serious problems if the successor trustees are in charge of the property you have left to a young beneficiary in a child's subtrust. The trustees may have to manage a young beneficiary's property for many years and will have many decisions to make about how to spend the money—greatly increasing the potential for conflict. (Children's subtrusts are discussed in Part 6, below.)

If you appoint cotrustees, you'll have to decide how they'll have authority to act—that is, whether each one can act independently or they must all agree before they can act. Obviously, it's easy to let each act without waiting for formal, written consent from the others. You may, however, prefer to have them all formally agree before taking action on behalf of the trust.

If you name more than one successor trustee, and one of them can't serve, the others will serve. If none of them can serve, the alternate you name (later in this section of the program) will take over.

It's perfectly legal to name a beneficiary of the trust (someone who will receive trust property after your death) as successor trustee. In fact, it's common.

> EXAMPLE: Mildred names her only child, Allison, as both sole beneficiary of her living trust and successor trustee of the living trust. When Mildred dies, Allison uses her authority as trustee to transfer the trust property to herself.

The successor trustee does not have to live in the same state as you do. But if you are choosing between someone local and someone far away, think about how convenient it will be for the person you choose to distribute the living trust property after your death. Someone close by will

probably have an easier job, especially with real estate transfers. But for transfers of property such as securities and bank accounts, it usually won't make much difference where the successor trustee lives.

Institutions as Successor Trustees

Normally, your first choice as successor trustee should be a flesh-and-blood person, not the trust department of a bank or other institution. Institutional trustees charge hefty fees, which come out of the trust property and leave less for your family and friends. And most aren't even interested in "small" living trusts—ones that contain less than several hundred thousand dollars worth of property.

But if there's no close relative or friend you think is capable of serving as your successor trustee, probably your best bet is to consider naming a private trust services company as successor trustee. Typically, their fees are pricey, but as a rule they charge less than a bank, and your affairs will probably receive more personal attention.

For a very large living trust, another possibility is to name a person and an institution as cosuccessor trustees. The bank or trust services company can do most of the paperwork, and the person can keep an eye on things and approve all transactions.

Obviously, before you finalize your living trust, you must check with the person or institution you've chosen to be your successor trustee. You want to be sure your choice is willing to serve.

If you don't, you may well create problems down the line. The person you've chosen may not want to serve, for a variety of reasons. And even if the person would be willing, if he or she doesn't know of his or her responsibilities, transfer of trust property after your death could be delayed.

If you choose an institution, you must check out the minimum size of trust it will accept and the fees it charges for management, and make arrangements for how the institution will take over as trustee at your death.

> ### Avoiding Conflicts With Your Will and Other Documents
>
> Your living trust gives your successor trustee the authority to manage trust property if you become incapacitated. To avoid conflicts, it's a good idea to name your successor to two other posts:
>
> - In your will, appoint your successor trustee to be executor, to be responsible for distributing property that doesn't pass through your living trust.
> - In your durable power of attorney for finances, appoint your successor trustee to be your attorney-in-fact, to have authority to make financial and property management decisions for property (except trust property) if you become incapacitated.

4. Payment of the Successor Trustee

Typically, the successor trustee of a simple probate-avoidance living trust isn't paid. This is because, in most cases, the successor trustee's only job is to distribute the trust property to beneficiaries soon after the grantor's death. Often, the successor trustee inherits most of the trust property.

An exception is a successor trustee who manages the property in a child's subtrust. In that case, the successor trustee is entitled, under the terms of the trust document, to "reasonable compensation." The successor trustee decides what is reasonable and takes it from the trust property left to the young beneficiary.

Allowing the successor trustee to set the amount of the payment can work well, as long as your successor trustee is completely trustworthy. If the young beneficiary feels the trustee's fees are much too high, he or she will have to go to court to challenge them.

5. Naming an Alternate Successor Trustee

Quicken WillMaker Plus asks you to name an alternate, in case your first choice as successor trustee is unable to serve.

If you named more than one successor trustee, the alternate won't become trustee unless none of your original choices can serve.

> EXAMPLE: Caroline names her two children, Eugene and Vanessa, as successor trustees. She names a close friend, Nicole, as alternate successor trustee. When Caroline dies, Vanessa is ill and can't serve as trustee, so Eugene acts as sole successor trustee. If he becomes unable to serve, Nicole would take over.

If no one you named in the trust document can serve, the last trustee to serve has the power to appoint, in writing, another successor trustee. (See Chapter 21.)

> EXAMPLE: To continue the previous example, if Nicole were ill and didn't have the

energy to serve as successor trustee, she could appoint someone else to serve as trustee.

Part 3: Property to Be Put in Trust

Now you're getting to the heart of the program. In this part, you must list each item of property you want to transfer to your living trust. It will take some thought to decide what property to include and how to list it in the trust document. (Later in the program, you will name beneficiaries to receive each item of trust property at your death.)

This is a crucial step: Any property you don't list will not go into your living trust and will not pass under the terms of the trust. It may instead have to go through probate.

Adding property to the trust later. If you mistakenly leave something out or acquire more valuable property after you create your trust, you can add it to your living trust later. Chapter 20 explains how.

⚠ **Listing property in the trust document is not enough.** If an item has a title (ownership) document, such as a deed or title slip, you must change the title document to show that you, as trustee, are the legal owner of the property. If you don't, the trust won't work. *You should transfer ownership as soon as possible after you print out and sign your Declaration of Trust.* Instructions are in Chapter 19.

A. Inventory Your Valuable Property

The first step is to take inventory—write down the valuable items of property you own. The categories listed below should jog your memory.

Valuable Property	
Animals	Real estate
Antiques	–Agricultural land
Appliances	–Boat/marina dock
Art	space
Books	–Co-op
Business interests	–Condo
–Sole proprietorship	–Duplex
–Partnership	–House
–Corporation	–Mobile home
–Limited liability co.	–Rental property
Business property*	–Time-share
Cameras & photo	–Undeveloped land
equipment	–Vacation house
Cash accounts	Retirement accounts**
–Certificates of deposit	Royalties
–Checking	Securities
–Money market funds	–Bonds
–Savings	–Commodities
China, crystal, silver	–Mutual funds
Coins, stamps	–Stocks
Collectibles	–U.S. bills, notes
Computers	and bonds
Copyrights, patents,	Tools
trademarks	Vehicles
Electronic equipment	–Bicycles
Furniture	–Cars
Furs	–Motorcycles
Jewelry	–Motorhomes/RVs
Limited partnership	–Planes
Precious metals	–Boats

*If you own a sole proprietorship
**Can't be held in trust (see Section B, below)

Even if you plan to leave everything to your spouse or children, you must make a list. That's because every item (or group of items, in some circumstances) must be specifically described and listed in the trust document.

When you list your property in the program, you can group items, if you're leaving them all to one beneficiary. For example, if you want to leave all your books to your best friend, there's no need to describe each one individually—unless your collection includes some particularly valuable or important books that you want to make extra sure get to the beneficiary.

After you've made an inventory, the next section will help you decide which items you want to hold in trust so they don't have to go through probate after your death.

Getting organized. While you're taking stock of all your valuable property, it might be a good time to go a step further and gather the information your family will need at your death. For help collecting this information, use Quicken WillMaker Plus's "Information for Caregivers and Survivors" form.

If you're married or in a domestic partnership. If you are married but are making an individual trust, remember that you can transfer to the trust only the property you own. To be sure you understand what you own and what your spouse owns, see Chapter 16, Part 3. Similarly, if you and your same-sex partners have registered your relationship with the state, be sure you know how state law affects your rights. In California, for example, registered domestic partners are covered by state community property laws.

B. Decide What Property to Hold in Trust

Now that you've got a list of what you own, you're ready to decide what items you want to hold in trust to avoid probate fees. Think about including:

- houses and other real estate
- jewelry, antiques, furs and valuable furniture
- stock in a closely held corporation
- stock, bond and other security accounts held by brokerages
- small business interests
- patents and copyrights
- precious metals
- valuable works of art
- valuable collections of stamps, coins or other objects.

You don't need to put everything you own into a living trust to save money on probate. For some assets, you may decide to use other probate-avoidance devices instead of a living trust. (See Chapter 13.)

1. Real Estate

The most valuable thing most people own is their real estate: their house, condominium or land. Many people create a living trust just to make sure a house doesn't go through probate. You can probably save your family substantial probate costs by transferring your real estate through a living trust.

If you own the property with someone else, however, you may not want to transfer your real estate to an individual living trust. (See Section 8, below.)

Co-op apartments. If you own shares in a co-op corporation that owns your apartment, you'll have to hold your shares in trust. Some corporations are reluctant to let a trustee own shares;

check the co-op corporation's rules to see if the transfer is allowed.

2. Small Business Interests

The delay, expense and court intrusion of probate can be especially detrimental to an ongoing small business. Using your living trust to transfer business interests to beneficiaries quickly after your death is almost essential if you want the beneficiaries to be able to keep the business running.

If you want to control the long-term management of your business, however, a revocable living trust is not the right vehicle. See an estate planning lawyer to draft a different kind of trust, with provisions tailored to your situation.

Different kinds of business organizations present different issues when you want to hold your interest in trust:

Sole proprietorships. If you operate your business as a sole proprietorship, with all business assets held in your own name, you can simply transfer your business property to yourself as trustee. You should also transfer the business's name itself: that transfers the customer goodwill associated with the name.

Partnership interests. If you operate your business as a partnership with other people, you can probably transfer your partnership share to yourself as trustee. If there is a partnership certificate, it must be changed.

Some partnership agreements require the people who inherit a deceased partner's share of the business to offer that share to the other partners before taking it. But that happens after death, so it shouldn't affect your ability to transfer the property through a living trust.

It's not common, but a partnership agreement may limit or forbid holding your interest in trust.

If yours does, you and your partners may want to see a lawyer before you make any changes.

Solely owned corporations. If you own all the stock of a corporation, you should have no difficulty transferring it to yourself as trustee.

Closely held corporations. A closely held corporation is a corporation that doesn't sell shares to the public. All its shares are owned by a few people who are usually actively involved in running the business. Normally, you can use a living trust to transfer shares in a closely held corporation by listing the stock in the trust document and then having the stock certificates reissued in your name as trustee.

You'll want to check the corporation's bylaws and articles of incorporation to be sure that you will still have voting rights in your capacity as trustee of the living trust; usually, this is not a problem. If it is, you and the other shareholders should be able to amend the corporation's bylaws to allow it.

There may, however, be restrictions that affect the transfer of shares. Check the corporation's bylaws and articles of incorporation, as well as any separate shareholders' agreements. One fairly common rule is that surviving shareholders (or the corporation) have the right to buy the shares of a deceased shareholder. In that case, you can still use a living trust to transfer the shares, but the people who inherit them may have to sell them.

Limited liability companies. If your small business is an LLC, you'll need the consent of a majority or all of the other owners (check your operating agreement) before you can transfer your interest to yourself as trustee. That shouldn't be a problem; they'll just want to know that you, as trustee of your own trust, will have authority to vote on LLC decisions. Another way to address this concern would be to transfer your economic interest in the LLC, but not your right to vote.

3. Bank Accounts

It's not difficult to transfer bank accounts to your living trust. But you may well decide that you don't need to. That's because you can directly designate a beneficiary for the funds in a bank account. If you do, you don't need to transfer those accounts to a living trust just to avoid probate. Their contents won't go through probate in the first place.

This option can be especially useful for personal checking accounts, which you may not want to transfer to your living trust—it can be difficult to cash checks that say the account is owned by a revocable living trust.

A living trust, however, offers one advantage that most pay-on-death arrangements do not: You can name an alternate beneficiary to receive the account if your first choice isn't alive at the time of your death. Pay-on-death accounts are discussed in Chapter 13.

4. Vehicles and Property That Is Often Sold

Some kinds of property are cumbersome to keep in a living trust. It's not a legal problem, just a practical one. Two common examples are:

- **Cars or other vehicles you use.** Having registration and insurance in your name as trustee could be confusing, and some insurance companies might balk. If you have valuable antique autos, or a mobile home that is permanently attached to land and considered real estate under your state's law, however, you may want to go ahead and hold them in trust. You should be able to find an insurance company that will cooperate.
- **Property you buy or sell frequently.** If you don't expect to own the property at

your death, there's no compelling reason to hold it in trust. (Remember, the probate process you want to avoid doesn't happen until after your death.) On the other hand, if you're buying property, it's no more trouble to acquire it in your name as trustee.

Other arrangements for property not in your living trust. If you choose not to put valuable items in your living trust, you can probably make arrangements to have them avoid probate in some other way. (See Chapter 13.)

5. Life Insurance

If you own a life insurance policy at your death, the insurance company will give the proceeds to the named beneficiary, without probate. (The proceeds are, however, considered part of your estate for federal estate tax purposes.)

If you have named a minor or young adult as the beneficiary, you may want to name your living trust instead. Then, in the trust document, you name the child as beneficiary of any insurance proceeds paid to the trust and arrange for an adult to manage the policy proceeds if the beneficiary is still young when you die. If you don't arrange for management of the money, and the beneficiary is still a minor (under 18) when you die, a court will have to appoint a financial guardian after your death. (Young beneficiaries are discussed in Part 6, below.)

Passing the proceeds of a life insurance policy through your living trust is a bit more complicated than leaving other property this way. You must take two steps:

1. Name the living trust as the beneficiary of your life insurance policy. (Your insurance agent will have a form that lets you change the beneficiary of the policy.)

2. When you list property items in the living trust document, list the proceeds of the policy, not the policy itself. (Section C, below, contains sample descriptions.)

6. Securities

If you buy and sell stocks regularly, you may not want to go to the trouble of acquiring and selling them using your authority as trustee of the trust.

Fortunately, there's an easier way to do it: hold your stocks in a brokerage account that is owned in your name as trustee. All securities in the account are then held in trust, which means that you can use your living trust to leave all the contents of the account to a specific beneficiary. If you want to leave stock to different beneficiaries, you can either establish more than one brokerage account or leave one account to more than one beneficiary to own together.

Stock in closely held corporations. See Section 2, above.

An Alternative: Transfer-on-Death Registration

Most states now allow ownership of securities to be registered in a "transfer-on-death" form. You can designate someone to receive the securities, including mutual funds and brokerage accounts, after your death. No probate will be necessary. Ask your broker about the forms you need to fill out to name a beneficiary for your securities.

The only states that do not yet allow transfer-on-death securities registration are New York, North Carolina and Texas. If you live in one of these states, ask a knowledgeable broker to let you know when your state jumps on the bandwagon.

7. Cash

It's common for people to want to leave cash gifts to beneficiaries—for example, to leave $5,000 to a relative, friend or charity. Don't, however, just type in "$5,000 cash" when you list the property you want to transfer to the living trust. There's no way to hold cash in trust unless its source is identified.

You can, however, easily accomplish your goal by transferring ownership of a cash account—a savings or money market account, for example—to yourself as trustee of your trust. You can then name a beneficiary to receive the contents of the account. So if you want to leave $5,000 to cousin Fred, all you have to do is put the money in a bank or money market account, transfer it to your living trust and name Fred, in the trust document, as the beneficiary of the account.

If you don't want to set up a separate account to leave a modest amount of cash to a beneficiary, think about buying a savings bond and leaving it to the beneficiary or leaving one larger account to several beneficiaries.

EXAMPLE: Michael would like to leave some modest cash gifts to his two grown nephews, Warren and Brian, whom he's always been fond of. He puts $5,000 into a money market account and then transfers the account into his living trust. In his trust document, he names Warren and Brian as beneficiaries of the account. After Michael's death, the two nephews will inherit the account together, and each will be entitled to half of the funds.

8. Co-Owned Property

If you co-own property with someone, you can hold your share of the property in trust. But whether or not you will want to depends on how you hold title to the property.

If you do decide to transfer just your interest in co-owned property to your living trust, you don't need to specify that your share is one half or some other fraction. For example, if you and your sister own a house together, you need only list "the house at 7989 Lafayette Court, Boston, MA." Your trust document will simply state that you have transferred all your interest in that property to the trust.

If you are married and want to transfer only your share of property you own together with your spouse, see Chapter 16, Part 3.

a.   Property held in joint tenancy

Property owned in joint tenancy does not go through probate until the last surviving owner dies. When one co-owner (joint tenant) dies, his or her share goes directly to the surviving co-owners, without probate. So if avoiding probate is your only concern, you don't need to transfer joint tenancy property to your living trust. A living trust does, however, offer more flexibility than joint tenancy.

Beneficiaries. If you transfer your share of joint tenancy property to a living trust, the joint tenancy is destroyed. You can leave your share of

the property to anyone you choose—it won't automatically go to the surviving co-owners.

Simultaneous death. Joint tenancy doesn't avoid probate if the joint owners die simultaneously. If that happens, each co-owner's interest in the property is passed to the beneficiaries named in the residuary clauses of their wills. If there's no will, the property passes to the closest relatives, under state law.

If you hold the property in your living trust, you can name an alternate beneficiary to receive your share of the property. You're assured that probate will be avoided even in the (statistically very unlikely) event of simultaneous death.

b.   Property held in tenancy by the entirety

"Tenancy by the entirety" is, basically, a kind of joint tenancy that's only for married couples (and, in Hawaii and Vermont, for same-sex couples who have registered with the state). It is allowed in the states listed in Chapter 13.

You cannot hold your half-interest in tenancy by the entirety property in an individual living trust. Neither spouse can transfer his or her half of the property alone, either while alive or by will or trust. (This is different from joint tenancy; a joint tenant is free to transfer his or her share to someone else during his life.)

c.   Community property

Alaska*	Nevada
Arizona	New Mexico
California	Washington
Idaho	Wisconsin
Louisiana	Texas

*If spouses sign a community property agreement.

Community property is another form of ownership that's only for married couples, in the states listed above. If you and your spouse together own community property, you should probably create a shared living trust. See Chapter 14.

9. Retirement Plans

Individual retirement accounts cannot be held in trust. Instead, avoid probate by naming a beneficiary to inherit whatever's left in your retirement account at your death. The plan administrator or account holder can provide forms on which to designate your beneficiary.

You can name a living trust as a beneficiary, but there's rarely a reason to. Under current IRS rules, money left to a trust must be distributed based on the life expectancy of the trust beneficiary.

 Resources. *IRAs, 401(k)s & Other Retirement Plans: Taking Your Money Out,* by Twila Slesnick and John C. Suttle (Nolo), explains the options of those who inherit money in a retirement account.

10. Other Valuable Property

Other valuable items—everything from jewelry and antiques to boats and airplanes—can also be placed in trust.

C. How to Describe Trust Property

When Quicken WillMaker Plus asks you to list the property you want to hold in your trust, describe each item clearly enough so that the successor trustee can identify the property and transfer it to the right person. No magic legal words are required.

Think about whom the property will ultimately go to. If you're leaving everything to one person, or just a few, there's less need to go into great detail. But if there will be a number of trust beneficiaries, and objects could be confused, be more specific about each one. When in doubt, err on the side of including more information.

> ### Rules for Entering Descriptions of Trust Property
>
> - Don't use "my" in a description. Don't, for example, enter "my books" or "my stereo system." That's because once the property is in the living trust it doesn't belong to you anymore—it belongs to the trust.
> - Don't begin a description with a capital letter (unless it must begin with a proper name, like "Steinway"). That's because the descriptions will be inserted into a sentence in the trust document, and it would look odd to see a capital letter in the middle of a sentence.
> - Don't end a description with a period. Again, this is because the descriptions will be inserted into a sentence in the trust document.

If the property you're describing is valuable—expensive jewelry or artworks, for example—describe it in detail, much as you would if you were listing it on an insurance policy.

Here are some sample descriptions:

Real estate

- "the house at 321 Glen St., Omaha, NE"
- "the house at 4444 Casey Road, Fandon, Illinois and the 20-acre parcel on which it is located"

Usually, the street address is enough. It's not necessary to use the "legal description" found on the deed, which gives a subdivision plat number or a metes-and-bounds description. But if the property has no street address—for example, if it is undeveloped land out in the country—you will need to carefully copy the full legal description, word for word, from the deed.

If you own a house and several adjacent lots, it's a good idea to indicate that you are transferring the entire parcel to your living trust by describing the land as well as the house.

If you own the property with someone else and are transferring only your share, you don't need to specify the share you own. Just describe the property. The trust document will show that you are transferring all your interest in the property, whatever share that is, to the living trust.

Bank accounts

- "Savings Account No. 9384-387, Arlington Bank, Arlington, MN"
- "Money Market Account 47-223 at Charles Schwab & Co., Inc., San Francisco, CA"

Household items

- "all the furniture normally kept in the house at 44123 Derby Ave., Ross, KY"
- "the antique brass bed in the master bedroom in the house at 33 Walker Ave., Fort Lee, New Jersey"
- "all furniture and household items normally kept in the house at 869 Hopkins St., Great Falls, Montana"

Sole proprietorship business property

- "Mulligan's Fish Market"
- "Fourth Street Records and CDs"
- "all accounts receivable of the business known as Garcia's Restaurant, 988 17th St., Atlanta, GA"
- "all food preparation and storage equipment, including refrigerator, freezer, hand mixers and slicer used at Garcia's Restaurant, 988 17th St., Atlanta, GA"

As explained in Section B, above, you should both list the name of the business and separately list items of business property.

Partnership interest

- "Don and Dan's Bait Shop Partnership owned by the grantor before being held in this living trust"

Because a partnership is a legal entity that can own property, you don't need to list items of property owned by the partnership.

Shares in a closely held corporation

- "The stock of ABC Hardware, Inc."

Shares in a solely owned corporation

- "all shares in the XYZ Corporation"
- "all stock in Fern's Olde Antique Shoppe, Inc., 23 Turnbridge Court, Danbury, Connecticut"

Securities

- "all securities in account No. 3999-34-33 at Smith Brokerage, 33 Lowell Place, New York, NY"
- "200 shares of General Industries, Inc. stock"
- "Good Investment Co. mutual fund account No. 888-09-09"

Life insurance proceeds

- "the proceeds of Acme Co. Life Insurance Policy #9992A"

Miscellaneous items

- "Macintosh computer (serial number 129311) with keyboard (serial number 165895)"
- "the medical textbooks in the office at 1702 Parker Towers, San Francisco, CA"
- "the stamp collection usually kept at 321 Glen St., Omaha, NE"
- "the collection of European stamps, including [describe particularly valuable stamps], usually kept at 440 Loma Prieta Blvd., #450, San Jose, CA"
- "the Martin D-35 acoustic guitar, serial number 477597"
- "the signed 1960 Ernie Banks baseball card kept in safe deposit box 234, First National Bank of Augusta, Augusta, IL"
- "the Baldwin upright piano kept at 985 Dawson Court, South Brenly, Massachusetts"

Part 4: Beneficiaries of Trust Property

Once you've entered a list of the property you're going to hold in trust, the next step is to say whom you want to inherit that property. Quicken WillMaker Plus lets you name a beneficiary for each item of trust property separately or name one beneficiary to receive everything.

The beneficiaries you name in your trust document are not entitled to anything while you are alive. You can amend your trust document and change the beneficiaries any time you wish.

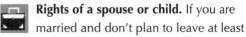 **Rights of a spouse or child.** If you are married and don't plan to leave at least half of what you own to your spouse, consult a lawyer experienced in estate planning. State law may entitle your spouse to claim some of the property in your living trust.

In most circumstances, you don't have to leave anything to your children. But if you want to disinherit a child, you should make a back-up will and specifically mention the child in it. (See Chapter 4.)

A. How Do You Want Your Property Distributed?

Quicken WillMaker Plus asks you first whether you want to leave all your trust property to one beneficiary (or more than one, to share it all) or leave different items to different beneficiaries.

The simplest approach is to leave all your trust property to one person or to one or more persons to share. If you choose that option, all you have to do is name each beneficiary and then name an alternate beneficiary for each, who will inherit the trust property if a primary beneficiary does not survive you by five days. (Alternates are discussed in Section C, below.)

If you choose to leave different items to different beneficiaries, you will be shown a list of all the property items you listed earlier. You can then name beneficiaries for them.

1. Minors or Young Adults

You can name minors (children under 18) to inherit trust property. If a beneficiary you name is a minor or a young adult who can't yet manage property without adult help, you can arrange for an adult to manage the trust property for the beneficiary. Quicken WillMaker Plus lets you do this after you have named all your beneficiaries. (See Part 6, below.)

2. Your Successor Trustee

It's very common, and perfectly legal, to make the person you named to be successor trustee (the person who will distribute trust property after your death) a beneficiary as well.

> **EXAMPLE:** Nora names her son Liam as successor trustee of her living trust. She also names him as sole beneficiary of her trust property. When Nora dies, Liam, acting as trustee, will transfer ownership of the trust property to himself.

3. Naming More Than One Beneficiary to Share Property

You can name more than one beneficiary to share any item of trust property. Simply list their names in the box on the screen. Type the names one per line; don't join the names with an "and." (See the Users' Manual for examples.)

Always use the beneficiaries' actual names; don't use collective terms such as "my children." It's not always clear who is included in such descriptions. And there can be serious confusion if one of the people originally included as a group member dies before you do.

Obviously, if you name cobeneficiaries for a piece of property that can't be physically divided—a cabin, for example—give some thought to whether or not the beneficiaries are likely to get along. If they are incompatible, disagreements could arise over taking care of property or deciding whether or not to sell it. If they can't settle their differences, any co-owner could go to court

and demand a partition—a court-ordered division and sale—of the property.

Cobeneficiaries will share the property equally unless you state otherwise. We'll ask you, after you enter the names, whether or not you want an item of trust property to be shared equally by the beneficiaries.

> **EXAMPLE:** Georgia wants to leave her house to her two children, Ross and Ryan, but wants Ross to have a 75% share of it. She enters their names and then, on a later screen, enters their interests, in fractions: 3/4 for Ross and 1/4 for Ryan.
>
> When the children inherit the property, they own it together. But Ross will be liable for 75% of the taxes and upkeep cost, and entitled to 75% of any income the house produces. If they sell it, Ross will be entitled to 75% of the proceeds.

4. Beneficiaries for Your Share of Co-Owned Trust Property

If you own property together with someone else, you will name beneficiaries for your share of the property. At your death, only your interest in the property will go to the beneficiary you name.

As with naming cobeneficiaries (Section 3, above), pay attention to who will end up as co-owners of the property after your death. If, for example, you and your brother own a house together, and you leave your share to your daughter—who detests her uncle—problems are likely.

B. Entering Beneficiaries' Names

When you enter a beneficiary's name, use the name by which the beneficiary is known for purposes such as a bank account or driver's license.

Generally, if the name you use clearly and unambiguously identifies the person, it is sufficient.

If you name an institution (charitable or not) to inherit trust property, enter its complete name. It may be commonly known by a shortened version, which could cause confusion if there are similarly named organizations. Call to ask if you're unsure. (An institution that stands to inherit some of your money will be more than happy to help you.) Also be sure to specify if you want a branch or part of a national organization to receive your gift—for example, a local chapter of the Sierra Club.

C. Alternate Beneficiaries

Quicken WillMaker Plus allows you to name an alternate for every person you name as a primary beneficiary. The alternate will get the property left to the primary beneficiary if your first choice does not live for more than 120 hours (five days) after your death. This "survivorship" period ensures that if you and a primary beneficiary die simultaneously or almost so, the property will go to the alternate beneficiary you chose, not to the primary beneficiary's heirs.

> EXAMPLE: Laura leaves all her trust property to her sister Jean, and names her daughter as alternate beneficiary. Laura and Jean are seriously injured in a car accident; Jean dies a day after Laura does. Because Jean did not survive Laura by at least five days, the trust property she would have inherited from Laura goes to Laura's daughter instead.
>
> If there had been no survivorship requirement, at Laura's death the trust property would have gone to Jean; when she died a day later, it would have gone to her heirs.

You don't have to name an alternate for a charitable (or other) institution you name as a beneficiary. If the institution is well established, it is probably safe to assume that it will still exist at your death.

With other beneficiaries, however, there is always the chance that the primary beneficiary may not survive you. If you don't name an alternate, the property that beneficiary would have received will be distributed to the person or institution you name, in the next part of the program, as your "residuary beneficiary." (See Part 5, below.)

You can name more than one person or institution as alternate beneficiaries. If you do, they will share the property equally.

> EXAMPLE: Sherry transfers her half-interest in a house to her living trust. She names her brother, the co-owner, as beneficiary. As alternate beneficiaries, she names her three children, Sean, Colleen and Tim.
>
> Sherry's brother dies shortly before she does, leaving his half of the house to Sherry. At Sherry's death, the house goes to the three children equally. All three own equal shares in all of it.

Part 5: Residuary Beneficiaries

Unless you leave all your trust property to one person (or a group of people to share), you must name a residuary beneficiary for your living trust. The person or organization you name will receive:

- any trust property for which both the primary and alternate beneficiaries you named die before you do
- any trust property that you didn't leave to a named beneficiary (this could include property you transfer to the trust later and don't name a beneficiary for)

- any property you leave to your living trust through your will (such a will is called a pour-over will)
- any property that you actually transferred to yourself as trustee but didn't list in the trust document.

Often, the residuary beneficiary of a living trust doesn't inherit anything from the trust. Usually, naming a residuary beneficiary is just a back-up measure, to guard against the extremely small chance that both a primary and alternate trust beneficiary do not survive you.

Part 6: Property Management for Young Beneficiaries

If any of your beneficiaries (including alternate and residuary beneficiaries) might inherit trust property before they are ready to manage it without an adult's help, you should arrange for someone else to manage it for them for a while. There are several ways to go about it:

- **Leave the property to an adult to use for the child.** Many people don't leave property directly to a child. Instead, they leave it to the child's parent or to the person they expect to have care and custody of the child if neither parent is available. There's no formal legal arrangement, but they trust the adult to use the property for the child's benefit.
- **Name a custodian under a law called the Uniform Transfers to Minors Act (UTMA).** In almost every state, you can name a "custodian" to manage property you leave a child until the child reaches 18 or 21, depending on state law (up to 25 in a few states). If you don't need management to last beyond that age, a custodianship is preferable.

- **Create a child's subtrust.** You can use Quicken WillMaker Plus to establish a "child's subtrust" in your living trust. If you do, your successor trustee will manage the property you left the child and dole it out for education, health and other needs. The subtrust ends at whatever age you designate (up to 35), and any remaining property is turned over to the child outright.

Subtrusts and custodianships are explained below.

! Children with special needs. These property management options are not designed to provide long-term property management for a child with serious disabilities. You should see a lawyer and make arrangements geared to your particular situation.

A. Should You Arrange for Management?

It's up to you whether or not to make arrangements, in the trust document, to have someone manage trust property if it is inherited by young beneficiaries.

The consequences of forgoing management for trust property inherited by a young beneficiary depend on whether the beneficiary is over or under age 18 at your death.

1. Children Under 18 Years Old

Minors—children under 18—cannot, legally, own or manage significant amounts of property. An adult must be in charge if the minor acquires more than a few thousand dollars' worth of property. (The exact amount depends on state law.)

If your minor beneficiaries won't inherit anything of great value—if you're leaving them objects that have more sentimental than monetary value—you don't need to arrange for an adult to manage the property.

But if a beneficiary inherits valuable trust property while still a minor, and you have not arranged for the property to be managed by an adult, a court-appointed guardian may have to manage the property.

There is one other option: In most states, the successor trustee can appoint a custodian for property inherited by a minor. If the value of property exceeds a certain amount—$10,000 in most states—a court must approve the appointment. And the custodianship must end at 18 in most states—earlier than many parents may choose. So it's still better to name a custodian yourself.

Contrary to what you might expect, a child's parent does not automatically have legal authority to manage any property the child inherits. So even if one or both of the beneficiary's parents are alive, they may have to ask the court to grant them that authority, and will be subject to the court's supervision. If neither parent is alive, there may be no obvious person for the court to appoint as property guardian. In that case, it may be even more important for you to name someone in your living trust.

2. Young Adults 18 to 35 Years Old

If a living trust beneficiary is 18 or older when he or she inherits trust property, you do not need, legally, to have anyone manage the property on the beneficiary's behalf. And if you don't make any arrangements, the beneficiary will get the property with no strings attached. But you can arrange for property management to last until a beneficiary turns any age up to 35.

There is no legal requirement that management for a trust beneficiary's property must end at 35,

but we think 35 is a reasonable cutoff. If you don't want to give a beneficiary free rein over trust property by the time he or she reaches 35, you probably need to see a lawyer and tailor a plan to the beneficiary's needs.

B. Which Is Best: Subtrust or Custodianship?

Using Quicken WillMaker Plus, you can create either a child's subtrust or a custodianship under the Uniform Transfer to Minors Act (if it's available in your state). Both are safe, efficient ways of managing trust property that a young person inherits. Under either system, the person in charge of the young beneficiary's property has the same responsibility to use the property for the beneficiary's support, education and health.

The most significant difference is that a child's subtrust can last longer than a custodianship, which must end at age 18 to 21 in most states (up to 25 in a few). For that reason, a child's subtrust is a good choice when a child could inherit a large amount of property.

Because an UTMA custodianship is much easier to administer, it is usually preferable if the beneficiary will inherit no more than about $50,000 worth of trust property ($100,000 or more if the child is quite young). That amount is likely to be used up for living and education expenses by the time the beneficiary is 18 to 21, so there's no need to create a subtrust that can continue beyond that age.

A custodianship has other advantages as well:

- Handling a beneficiary's property is easier with a custodianship than with a trust. A custodian's powers are written into state law, and most institutions, such as banks and insurance companies, are familiar with the rules. Trusts, on the other hand, vary in their terms. So before a bank lets a trustee act on behalf of a beneficiary, it may demand to see and analyze a copy of the Declaration of Trust.

- You can name whomever you wish to be a custodian, and you can name different custodians for different beneficiaries. So if you want to arrange custodianships for grandchildren, for example, you could name each child's parent as custodian. A child's subtrust is not quite so flexible: The successor trustee will be the trustee of all children's subtrusts created for your young beneficiaries.

- If the property in a subtrust earns income, and that income isn't distributed quickly to the beneficiary, the trust will have to pay tax on it. The federal tax rate on such retained income may be higher than it would be if the young beneficiary were taxed on it. The trustee may well need to hire experts to help with trust accounting and tax returns.

States That Have Adopted the Uniform Transfers to Minors Act

State	Age at Which Minor Gets Property	State	Age at Which Minor Gets Property
Alabama	21	Missouri	21
Alaska	18 to 25	Montana	21
Arizona	21	Nebraska	21
Arkansas	18 to 21	Nevada	18 to 25
California	18 to 25	New Hampshire	21
Colorado	21	New Jersey	18 to 21
Connecticut	21	New Mexico	21
Delaware	21	New York	21
District of Columbia	18 to 21	North Carolina	18 to 21
Florida	21	North Dakota	21
Georgia	21	Ohio	18 to 21
Hawaii	21	Oklahoma	18 to 21
Idaho	21	Oregon	21 to 25
Illinois	21	Pennsylvania	21 to 25
Indiana	21	Rhode Island	21
Iowa	21	South Dakota	18
Kansas	21	Tennessee	21 to 25
Kentucky	18	Texas	21
Maine	18 to 21	Utah	21
Maryland	21	Virginia	18 to 21
Massachusetts	21	Washington	21
Michigan	18 to 21	West Virginia	21
Minnesota	21	Wisconsin	21
Mississippi	21	Wyoming	21

C. Custodianships

A custodianship is the preferable alternative for many people. Here's how it works.

1. How a Custodianship Works

In the trust document, you name someone to serve as custodian for a particular beneficiary. That person manages any trust property the young beneficiary inherits until the beneficiary reaches the age at which state law says the custodianship must end. (See table in Section B, above.)

> **EXAMPLE:** In her living trust, Sandra leaves 100 shares of General Motors stock to her niece, Jennifer. She names Hazel, Jennifer's mother, as custodian under the Illinois Uniform Transfers to Minors Act.
>
> After Sandra's death, her successor trustee gives the stock to the custodian, Hazel. She will manage it for Jennifer until Jennifer turns 21, the age Illinois law says she must be given the property outright.

In some states, you can specify—within limits—at what age the custodianship will end. If your state allows this, we'll ask you to enter an age at which you want the custodianship to end.

> **EXAMPLE:** If Sandra, in the previous example, lived in New Jersey, the state's law would allow her to choose any age from 18 to 21 for the custodianship to end.

2. The Custodian's Responsibilities

A custodian has roughly the same responsibility as the trustee of a child's subtrust: to manage the beneficiary's property wisely and honestly. The custodian's authority and duties are set out by state law (the Uniform Transfers to Minors Act, as enacted by your state). No court directly supervises the custodian.

The custodian must:

- Manage the property until the beneficiary reaches the age at which, by law, he or she gets the property outright. If the child is a minor at your death, this can be a number of years.
- Use the property or income to pay for expenses such as the young beneficiary's support, education and health care.
- Keep the property separate from his or her own property.
- Keep separate records of transactions. The custodian does not have to file a separate income tax return; income from the property can be reported on the young beneficiary's return. (By comparison, the trustee of a child's subtrust must file a separate tax return for the subtrust.)

A custodian who needs to hire an accountant, tax lawyer or other expert can use the property to pay a reasonable amount for the help.

If state law allows it, the custodian is entitled to reasonable compensation and reimbursement for reasonable expenses. The payment, if any is taken, comes from the custodial property.

3. Choosing a Custodian

You can name a different custodian for each young beneficiary, if you wish.

In most cases, you should name the person who will have physical custody of the minor child. That's almost always one of the child's parents. If the beneficiary is your child, name the child's other parent unless you have serious reservations about that person's ability to handle the property for the child.

Only one person can be named as custodian for one beneficiary. You can, however, name an alternate custodian to take over if your first choice is unable to serve.

D. Children's Subtrusts

Quicken WillMaker Plus allows you to set up a separate "child's subtrust" for each young beneficiary.

1. How a Child's Subtrust Works

In your trust document, you state the age at which the beneficiary should receive trust property outright. If at your death the beneficiary is younger than the age you specified, a subtrust will be created for that beneficiary. (If the beneficiary is older, he or she gets the trust property with no strings attached, and no subtrust is created.) Each beneficiary gets a separate child's subtrust.

Quicken WillMaker Plus is set up so that the successor trustee will serve as trustee of any children's subtrusts. If you want different people to manage property inherited by different beneficiaries, you may want to use a custodianship instead of a child's subtrust. (To appoint someone else to be trustee of a child's subtrust, the trust document would have to be changed significantly; see a lawyer.)

Whatever trust property the beneficiary is entitled to receive upon your death will go into the child's subtrust, if the child is still under the age set for termination of the subtrust. The trustee will manage the subtrust property and use it as necessary for the beneficiary's health, education and support. After your death, the subtrust cannot be revoked or amended. Until then, you are free to change your mind about having a subtrust set up for a particular beneficiary.

The child's subtrust will end when the beneficiary reaches the age you designated in your Declaration of Trust. This can be any age up to and including 35. The trustee will then give the beneficiary what remains of the subtrust property.

EXAMPLE: In his trust document, Stanley names his 14-year-old son Michael as beneficiary of $100,000 worth of stock. He specifies that any stock Michael becomes entitled to when Stanley dies should be kept in a subtrust until Michael is 25, subject to the trustee's right to spend it on Michael's behalf.

Stanley dies when Michael is 19. The stock goes into a subtrust for him, managed by the successor trustee of Stanley's living trust. The trustee uses the stock (or the income it produces) to pay for Michael's education and support. Michael receives what's left of the stock when he turns 25.

EXAMPLE: Victoria creates a living trust and leaves her trust property to her daughters, who are 22 and 25. She specifies that any trust property they inherit should stay in children's subtrusts until each daughter reaches 30. Victoria names her sister, Antoinette, as successor trustee.

Victoria dies in a car accident when one daughter is 28 and the other is 31. The 28-year-old's half of the trust property stays in a subtrust, managed by Antoinette, until she turns 30. The 31-year-old gets her half outright; no subtrust is created for her.

2. The Trustee's Duties

The subtrust trustee must:

- manage and invest subtrust property until the beneficiary reaches the age set out in the trust document—which can take years
- keep the beneficiary (or the beneficiary's guardian, if the beneficiary is a minor) reasonably well informed about how the assets are being invested
- use subtrust property or income to pay for expenses such as the beneficiary's support, education and health care, and
- keep separate records of subtrust transactions and file income tax returns for the subtrust.

The trustee's powers and responsibilities are spelled out in the trust document. If the subtrust trustee needs to hire an accountant, tax lawyer or other expert, he or she can use subtrust assets to pay a reasonable amount for the help.

The trust document also provides that the trustee of a subtrust is entitled to reasonable compensation for his or her work as trustee. The trustee decides what is a reasonable amount; the compensation is paid from the subtrust assets.

For more on the trustee's responsibilities, see Chapter 21.

Declaration of Trust

Part 1. Trust Name

This revocable living trust shall be known as the Judith M. Avery Revocable Living Trust.

Part 2. Declaration of Trust

Judith M. Avery, called the grantor, declares that she has transferred and delivered to the trustee all her interest in the property described in Schedule A attached to this Declaration of Trust. All of that property is called the "trust property." The trustee hereby acknowledges receipt of the trust property and agrees to hold the trust property in trust, according to this Declaration of Trust.

The grantor may add property to the trust.

Part 3. Terminology

The term "this Declaration of Trust" includes any provisions added by valid amendment.

Part 4. Amendment and Revocation

A. Amendment or Revocation by Grantor

The grantor may amend or revoke this trust at any time, without notifying any beneficiary. An amendment must be made in writing and signed by the grantor. Revocation may be in writing or any manner allowed by law.

B. Amendment or Revocation by Other Person

The power to revoke or amend this trust is personal to the grantor. A conservator, guardian or other person shall not exercise it on behalf of the grantor, unless the grantor specifically grants a power to revoke or amend this trust in a Durable Power of Attorney.

Part 5. Payments From Trust During Grantor's Lifetime

The trustee shall pay to or use for the benefit of the grantor as much of the net income and principal of the trust property as the grantor requests. Income shall be paid to the grantor at least annually. Income accruing in or paid to trust accounts shall be deemed to have been paid to the grantor.

Part 6. Trustees

A. Trustee

Judith M. Avery shall be the trustee of this trust.

B. Trustee's Responsibilities

The trustee in office shall serve as trustee of all trusts created under this Declaration of Trust, including children's subtrusts.

C. Terminology

In this Declaration of Trust, the term "trustee" includes successor trustees or alternate successor trustees serving as trustee of this trust. The singular "trustee" also includes the plural.

D. Successor Trustee

Upon the death or incapacity of Judith M. Avery, the trustee of this trust and of any children's subtrusts created by it shall be Robert S. Avery and Anne Avery Puckett. Each successor trustee has full and independent authority to act for and represent the trust. If Robert S. Avery and Anne Avery Puckett are unable or unwilling to serve as successor trustee, David R. Puckett shall serve as trustee.

E. Resignation of Trustee

Any trustee in office may resign at any time by signing a notice of resignation. The resignation must be delivered to the person or institution who is either named in this Declaration of Trust, or appointed by the trustee under Section F of this Part, to next serve as the trustee.

F. Power to Appoint Successor Trustee

If no one named in this Declaration of Trust as a successor trustee or alternate successor trustee is willing or able to serve as trustee, the last acting trustee may appoint a successor trustee and may require the posting of a reasonable bond, to be paid for from the trust property. The appointment must be made in writing, signed by the trustee and notarized.

G. Bond

No bond shall be required for any trustee named in this Declaration of Trust.

H. Compensation

No trustee shall receive any compensation for serving as trustee, unless the trustee serves as a trustee of a child's subtrust created by this Declaration of Trust.

I. Liability of Trustee

With respect to the exercise or non-exercise of discretionary powers granted by this Declaration of Trust, the trustee shall not be liable for actions taken in good faith. Such actions shall be binding on all persons interested in the trust property.

Part 7. Trustee's Management Powers and Duties

A. Powers Under State Law

The trustee shall have all authority and powers allowed or conferred on a trustee under Illinois law, subject to the trustee's fiduciary duty to the grantors and the beneficiaries.

B. Specified Powers

The trustee's powers include, but are not limited to:

1. The power to sell trust property, and to borrow money and to encumber trust property, including trust real estate, by mortgage, deed of trust or other method.

2. The power to manage trust real estate as if the trustee were the absolute owner of it, including the power to lease (even if the lease term may extend beyond the period of any trust) or grant options to lease the property, to make repairs or alterations and to insure against loss.

3. The power to sell or grant options for the sale or exchange of any trust property, including stocks, bonds, debentures and any other form of security or security account, at public or private sale for cash or on credit.

4. The power to invest trust property in every kind of property and every kind of investment, including but not limited to bonds, debentures, notes, mortgages, stock options, futures and stocks, and including buying on margin.

5. The power to receive additional property from any source and add it to any trust created by this Declaration of Trust.

6. The power to employ and pay reasonable fees to accountants, lawyers or investment experts for information or advice relating to the trust.

7. The power to deposit and hold trust funds in both interest-bearing and non-interest-bearing accounts.

8. The power to deposit funds in bank or other accounts uninsured by FDIC coverage.

9. The power to enter into electronic fund transfer or safe deposit arrangements with financial institutions.

10. The power to continue any business of the grantor.

11. The power to institute or defend legal actions concerning this trust or the grantor's affairs.

12. The power to execute any documents necessary to administer any trust created by this Declaration of Trust.

13. The power to diversify investments, including authority to decide that some or all of the trust property need not produce income.

Part 8. Incapacity of Grantor

If the grantor becomes physically or mentally incapacitated, whether or not a court has declared the grantor incompetent or in need of a conservator or guardian, the successor trustee named in Part 6 shall be trustee.

The determination of the grantor's capacity to manage this trust shall be made by those of the people listed here who are reasonably available when the successor trustee (or any of them, if two or more are named to serve together) requests their opinion. These people are: Leah Corval, Amy Peterson and Jeffrey Mosley. If a majority of them state, in writing, that in their opinion the grantor is no longer reasonably capable of serving as trustee, the successor trustee shall serve as trustee.

In that event, the trustee shall manage the trust property. The trustee shall use any amount of trust income or trust property necessary for the grantor's proper health care, support, maintenance, comfort and welfare, in accordance with the grantor's accustomed manner of living. Any income not spent for the benefit of the grantor shall be accumulated and added to the trust property. Income shall be paid to the grantor at least annually. Income accruing in or paid to trust accounts shall be deemed to have been paid to the grantor.

The successor trustee shall manage the trust until the grantor is again able to manage her affairs.

Part 9. Death of a Grantor

When the grantor dies, this trust shall become irrevocable. It may not be amended or altered except as provided for by this Declaration of Trust. It may be terminated only by the distributions authorized by this Declaration of Trust.

The trustee may pay out of trust property such amounts as necessary for payment of the grantor's debts, estate taxes and expenses of the grantor's last illness and funeral.

Part 10. Beneficiaries

At the death of the grantor, the trustee shall distribute the trust property as follows:

1. Robert S. Avery shall be given all Judith M. Avery's interest in 200 shares of General Industries stock. If Robert S. Avery does not survive Judith M. Avery, that property shall be given to Cheryl Avery.

2. Anne Avery Puckett shall be given all Judith M. Avery's interest in Account No. 3999-34-3 at Smith Brokerage, 33 Lowell Street, New York, NY. If Anne Avery Puckett does not survive Judith M. Avery, that property shall be given to David R. Puckett.

3. David R. Puckett shall be given all Judith M. Avery's interest in two $100 United States Savings Bonds kept in safe deposit box no. 3551 at First Union Bank, Crystal Lake, Illinois.

4. Anne Avery Puckett and Robert S. Avery shall be given all Judith M. Avery's interest in house at 88823 Lakeview Dr., Crystal Lake, Illinois and all household furnishings in the house at 88823 Lakeview Dr., Crystal Lake, Illinois in equal shares. If Anne Avery Puckett does not survive Judith M. Avery, his or her interest in this property shall be given to David R. Puckett. If Robert S. Avery does not survive Judith M. Avery, his or her interest in this property shall be given to Cheryl Avery.

5. Anne Avery Puckett and David R. Puckett shall be given Judith M. Avery's interest in the trust property not otherwise specifically and validly disposed of by this Part as follows:

Anne Avery Puckett shall receive a 1/3 share.

David R. Puckett shall receive a 2/3 share.

If either of these beneficiaries does not survive Judith M. Avery, the interest of the deceased beneficiary shall be given to the beneficiary who survives Judith M. Avery.

All distributions are subject to any provision in this Declaration of Trust that creates a child's subtrust or a custodianship under the Uniform Transfers to Minors Act.

A beneficiary must survive the grantor for 120 hours to receive property under this Declaration of Trust. As used in this Declaration of Trust, to survive means to be alive or in existence as an organization.

All personal and real property left through this trust shall pass subject to any encumbrances or liens placed on the property as security for the repayment of a loan or debt.

If property is left to two or more beneficiaries to share, they shall share it equally unless this Declaration of Trust provides otherwise. If any of them does not survive the grantor, the others shall take that beneficiary's share, to share equally, unless this Declaration of Trust provides otherwise.

Part 11. Custodianships Under the Uniform Transfers to Minors Act

1. Any property to which David R. Puckett becomes entitled under Part 10 of this Declaration of Trust shall be given to Anne Avery Puckett, as custodian for David R. Puckett under the Illinois Uniform Transfers to Minors Act, until David R. Puckett reaches the age of 21. If Anne Avery Puckett is unable or ceases to serve as custodian, Anthony B. Puckett shall serve as custodian.

Part 12. Grantor's Right to Homestead Tax Exemption

If the grantor's principal residence is held in trust, grantor has the right to possess and occupy it for life, rent-free and without charge except for taxes, insurance, maintenance and related costs and expenses. This right is intended to give grantor a beneficial interest in the property and to ensure that grantor does not lose eligibility for a state homestead tax exemption for which she otherwise qualifies.

Part 13. Severability of Clauses

If any provision of this Declaration of Trust is ruled unenforceable, the remaining provisions shall stay in effect.

Certification of Grantor

I certify that I have read this Declaration of Trust and that it correctly states the terms and conditions under which the trust property is to be held, managed and disposed of by the trustee, and I approve the Declaration of Trust.

_____ Dated: _____

Judith M. Avery, Grantor and Trustee

Certification of Acknowledgment of Notary Public

State of _____

County of _____

On _____, before me, _____, a notary public for said state, personally appeared Judith M. Avery, personally known to me (or proved to me on the basis of satisfactory evidence) to be the person whose name is subscribed to the within instrument, and acknowledged to me that she executed the same in her authorized capacity and that by her signature on the instrument the person, or the entity upon behalf of which the person acted, executed the instrument.

Witness my hand and official seal.

_____

NOTARY PUBLIC for the State of _____

My commission expires _____.

Schedule A
Share Property Placed in Trust

1. 200 shares of General Industries stock.

2. Account No. 3999-34-3 at Smith Brokerage, 33 Lowell Street, New York, NY.

3. Two $100 United States Savings Bonds kept in safe deposit box no. 3551 at First Union Bank, Crystal Lake, Illinois.

4. House at 88823 Lakeview Dr., Crystal Lake, Illinois.

5. All household furnishings in the house at 88823 Lakeview Dr., Crystal Lake, Illinois.

Chapter 16

Creating a Shared Marital Trust

When you create your living trust document with Quicken WillMaker Plus, you must decide:

- what property you want to put in your living trust
- whom you want to receive trust property at your death (these people or organizations are the beneficiaries of your living trust)
- who is to be the successor trustee—the person or institution who, after both spouses have died, will distribute the surviving spouse's trust property, and
- how you should arrange for someone to manage trust property inherited by beneficiaries who are too young to handle it without supervision.

You may already have a good idea of how you want to decide these issues. This chapter discusses the factors you should think about as you make each decision. It is organized the same way as the program is (Parts 1 through 6), so that you can easily refer to it while you're actually making your trust document. It's a good idea, though, to read through this chapter before you sit down at the computer—it will make the whole process clearer and easier.

Checklist for Creating a Valid Living Trust

✔ Prepare the trust document with Quicken Willmaker Plus.

✔ Print out the trust document and sign it in front of a notary public.

✔ Transfer ownership of the property listed in the trust document into your names, as trustees.

✔ Update your trust document when needed.

How a Shared Marital Trust Works: An Overview

Here, in brief, are the important points about how a shared trust works:

Control of trust property. You and your spouse will both be trustees of your living trust, so you'll both have control over the property in the trust. Either spouse can act on behalf of the trust—sell or give away trust property, for example. (As a practical matter, the consent of both spouses may be necessary—see Part 3, below.)

Amendments or revocation. Either spouse can revoke the trust or add separately owned property to it at any time. Both spouses, however, must consent to change any terms of the trust document—who gets what property, or who is named as successor trustee, for example.

This way either spouse can, by revoking the trust, return the situation to exactly what it was before the trust was formed. (Co-owned property is returned to both spouses, and separately owned property to the owner-spouse.) But while both spouses are living, neither can alone change what they've decided on in the trust—who should get what property when each spouse dies.

Death of the first spouse. When the first spouse dies, the shared living trust is automatically split into two trusts:

- Trust #1 contains the deceased spouse's share of trust property, except any trust property left to the surviving spouse.
- Trust #2 contains the surviving spouse's share, including any trust property left by the deceased spouse to the survivor.

The surviving spouse is sole trustee of both trusts. The survivor must distribute the deceased spouse's property (what's in Trust #1) exactly as he or she instructed in the trust document, with no modifications. The surviving spouse is also responsible for managing any Trust #1 property left to a young beneficiary in a child's subtrust (explained later in the chapter). When all the property in Trust #1 is distributed to the beneficiaries, Trust #1 ceases to exist.

Continuation of the living trust. Trust #2 (the survivor's) goes on as before, with the addition of any trust property the survivor inherited from the deceased spouse. The surviving spouse is free to change the trust document as he or she wishes. For example, the surviving spouse might name someone else as successor trustee or name a new beneficiary for property that was to have gone to the deceased spouse.

Death of the second spouse. When the second spouse dies, the person named in the trust document as successor trustee takes over. He or she is responsible for distributing trust property to the beneficiaries and managing any trust property left to a young beneficiary in a child's subtrust (explained later).

> **EXAMPLE:** Harry and Maude, a married couple, set up a shared revocable living trust to avoid probate. In the trust document, they make themselves cotrustees and appoint their niece Emily as successor trustee, to take over as trustee after they have both died. They transfer much of their co-owned property—their house, savings accounts and stocks—to themselves as trustees. Maude also puts some of her family heirlooms, which are her separate property, in the trust.
>
> The trust document states that Maude's brother is to receive the heirlooms when she dies; everything else goes to Harry. Harry leaves all his trust property to Maude.
>
> Maude dies first. The trust splits into Trust #1, which contains Maude's heirlooms, and Trust #2, which contains everything else: Harry's trust property and the trust property he inherits from Maude. Harry becomes the sole trustee of both trusts.
>
> Following the terms of the trust document, Harry distributes Maude's heirlooms (Trust #1) to her brother, without probate. When the property is distributed, Trust #1 ceases to exist. Harry doesn't have to do anything with the trust property Maude left him; it's already in Trust #2.
>
> After Maude's death, Harry decides to make a couple of changes in his living trust document. He names his nephew, Burt, as successor trustee. And he names his 12-year-old granddaughter, Cecile, to receive some trust property. In the trust document, he provides that if Cecile is not yet 25 when he dies, the trust property she inherits will stay in a child's subtrust, managed by the successor trustee, Burt.
>
> When Harry dies, Burt becomes trustee and distributes the trust property following Harry's instructions in the trust document. He also manages the property inherited by Cecile, who is 21 at Harry's death, until her 25th birthday. When all the property is given to Harry's beneficiaries, the trust ends.

Part 1: Your Names

This part is easy: Just enter your names. The names you enter will form part of the name of your trust. For example, if you enter "William S. Jorgensen" and "Helga M. Jorgensen," your trust will be named "The William S. Jorgensen and Helga M. Jorgensen Revocable Living Trust." Your names will also appear as the original trustees of your living trust. (See Part 3, below.)

Enter your name the way it appears on other formal business documents, such as your driver's license or bank accounts. This may or may not be the name on your birth certificate.

If you go by more than one name, use only one; don't enter various versions of your name joined by "aka" (also known as). Be sure that the name you use is the one that appears on the ownership documents for property you plan to hold in trust. If it isn't, it could cause confusion later, and you should change the name on your ownership documents before you transfer the property to yourself as trustee.

> **EXAMPLE:** You use the name William Dix for your trust, but own real estate in your former name of William Geicherwitz. You should prepare and sign a new deed, changing the name of the owner to William Dix, before you prepare another deed to transfer the property to your living trust.

Part 2: Trustees

To be legally valid, every living trust must have a trustee—someone to manage the property held in trust. When you create a revocable living trust with this program, you and your spouse are the trustees while you are alive. You'll name someone else to be the successor trustee, to take over after both you and your spouse have died.

A. The Original Trustees

You and your spouse will be the original trustees of your living trust. That way, both spouses have control over trust property, and taxation doesn't get complicated.

You can't name someone else as trustee. In the unlikely event you and your spouse don't want to be the trustees or want only one of you to be trustee, you cannot use Quicken WillMaker Plus. See an estate planning lawyer.

As a day-to-day, practical matter, it makes little difference that your property is now held in trust. You won't have any special duties as trustees of your trust. You do not even need to file a separate income tax return for the living trust. If the property generates income, just report it on your personal income tax return, as if the trust did not exist.

You have the same freedom to sell, give away or mortgage trust property as you did before you put the property into the living trust. The only difference is that you must now sign documents in your capacities as trustees.

> **EXAMPLE:** Celeste and Robert want to sell a piece of land that is owned in the name of their living trust. They prepare a deed transferring ownership of the land from the trust to the new owner, and sign the deed as "Celeste Tornetti and Robert Tornetti, trustees of the Celeste Tornetti and Robert Tornetti Revocable Living Trust dated February 4, 2001."

It's important to realize that once the property is held in trust, either trustee (spouse) has authority over it. That means that either spouse can sell or give away any of the trust property—including any property that was co-owned or was the separate property of the other spouse before it was transferred to the trust. In practice, however, both spouses will probably have to consent to transfer real estate out of the living trust. Especially in community property states, buyers and title insurance companies usually insist on both spouses' signatures on transfer documents.

If you don't want to give your spouse legal authority over your separately owned property, it's best to make separate living trusts. (See Chapter 14.)

B. The Trustee After One Spouse's Death or Incapacity

When one spouse dies or becomes incapacitated and unable to manage his or her affairs, the other becomes sole trustee.

You will name, in the trust document, three people who will determine whether or not you are able to manage the trust, if the question ever comes up. These people do not have to be doctors. Ideally, you will choose people who know you well and can give an unbiased opinion about whether or not you need help taking care of financial and property matters.

If one spouse asks them to, the people you choose must state, in writing, their opinion of whether or not the other spouse is capable of managing the trust. (If one or more isn't available, a spouse may rely on the opinions of the ones he or she can reach.) If a majority of them think the other spouse should act as sole trustee, he or she is authorized to do so.

The other spouse, as sole trustee, takes over management of trust property. That's the extent of his or her authority; he or she has no power over property not held in trust, and no authority to make health care decisions for the incapacitated spouse. For this reason, it's also wise for each spouse to create documents called durable powers of attorney, giving the other spouse authority to manage property not owned in the name of the trust and to make health care decisions. (See Chapters 22 and 23.)

After one spouse's death, the surviving spouse, as trustee, is responsible for distributing trust property of the deceased spouse that is not left to the surviving spouse. The surviving spouse must follow the deceased spouse's wishes as they are set out in the trust document. The surviving spouse has no legal power to modify the deceased spouse's intentions in any way. (See Chapter 21.)

Usually, the process takes only a few weeks. The surviving spouse may, however, have long-term duties if the trust document creates a child's subtrust for trust property inherited by a young beneficiary. It falls to the surviving spouse to manage trust property left to a young beneficiary in this way, possibly for many years (this is explained in Part 6, below).

C. The Successor Trustee

You and your spouse must also choose a successor trustee—someone to act as trustee after both of you have died or become incapacitated. The successor trustee has no power or responsibility if at least one spouse is alive and capable of managing the trust.

1. The Successor Trustee's Duties After Both Spouses' Deaths

After both spouses have died, the successor trustee named in the trust document takes over as trustee. The successor trustee's primary responsibility is to distribute trust property to the beneficiaries named in the trust document. That is usually a straightforward process that can be completed in a few weeks. (How to transfer certain common kinds of property is explained in Chapter 21.)

The successor trustee may, however, have long-term duties if the trust document creates a "child's subtrust" for trust property inherited by a young beneficiary (this is explained in Part 6 below). The trust document gives the successor trustee very broad authority, so that the trustee will be able to do whatever is necessary to respond to the demands of the circumstances. For example, the trustee has the power to invest trust funds in accounts, such as money market accounts, that are not federally insured. The trustee is also free to spend trust income or property for the health and welfare of the beneficiary.

2. The Successor Trustee's Duties If Either Spouse Is Incapacitated

The successor trustee will take over as trustee before both spouses have died if both spouses are unable to manage their affairs. A spouse's incapacity is determined by the three people named in the trust document for this purpose. (See Section B, above.) In this situation, the successor trustee has broad authority to manage the property in the living trust and use it for both spouses' health care, support and welfare. The law requires him or her to act honestly and prudently. And because the grantors are no longer the trustees, the new trustee must file an annual income tax return for the trust.

3. Choosing a Successor Trustee

The person or institution you choose as successor trustee will have a crucial role: to distribute trust property to your beneficiaries after you and your spouse have died. And if you and your spouse become incapacitated, the successor will manage trust property on your behalf; if you leave prop-

erty to a young beneficiary in trust, the successor will manage that property until the beneficiary is old enough to handle it alone.

Obviously, when you are giving someone this much power and discretion, you should choose someone with good common sense whom you trust completely. If you don't know anyone who fits this description, think twice about establishing a living trust. Most people pick an adult son or daughter, other relative or close friend.

Keep in mind that the successor trustee does not take over until both spouses have died (or become incapacitated). That means that after one spouse's death, the surviving spouse will probably have plenty of time to amend the trust document and name a different successor trustee if he or she wishes.

In most situations, the successor trustee will not need extensive experience in financial management; common sense, dependability and complete honesty are usually enough. A successor trustee who may have long-term responsibility over a young beneficiary's trust property needs more management and financial skills than a successor trustee whose only job is to distribute trust property. The successor trustee does have authority, however, under the terms of the trust document, to get any reasonably necessary professional help—from an accountant, lawyer or tax preparer, perhaps—and pay for it out of trust assets.

Usually, it makes sense to name just one person as successor trustee, to avoid any possibility of conflicts. But it's legal and may be desirable to name more than one person. For example, you might name two or more of your children, if you don't expect any disagreements between them and you think one of them might feel hurt and left out if not named.

Having more than one successor trustee is especially likely to cause serious problems if the successor trustees are in charge of the property you have left to a young beneficiary in a child's subtrust. The trustees may have to manage a young beneficiary's property for many years and will have many decisions to make about how to spend the money—greatly increasing the potential for conflict. (Children's subtrusts are discussed in Part 6, below.)

If you appoint cotrustees, you'll have to decide how they'll have authority to act—that is, whether each one can act independently or they must all agree before they can act. Obviously, it's easy to let each act without waiting for formal, written consent from the others. You may, however, prefer to have them all formally agree before taking action on behalf of the trust.

If you name more than one successor trustee, and one of them can't serve, the others will serve. If none of them can serve, the alternate you name (in the next section of the program) will take over.

It's perfectly legal to name a beneficiary of the trust (someone who will inherit trust property) as successor trustee. In fact, it's common.

EXAMPLE: Mildred and James name their only child, Allison, to be successor trustee of their living trust. They name each other as trust beneficiaries, and Allison as alternate beneficiary. When James dies, his share of the trust property goes to Mildred. When Mildred dies, Allison uses her authority as trustee to transfer the remaining trust property to herself, the beneficiary.

Institutions as Successor Trustees

Normally, your first choice as successor trustee should be a flesh-and-blood person, not the trust department of a bank or other institution. Institutional trustees charge hefty fees, which come out of the trust property and leave less for your family and friends. And most aren't interested in "small" living trusts—ones that contain less than several hundred thousand dollars' worth of property.

But if there's no close relative or friend you think is capable of serving as your successor trustee, probably your best bet is to consider naming a private trust services company as successor trustee. Typically, their fees are pricey, but as a rule they charge less than a bank, and your affairs will probably receive more personal attention.

For a very large living trust, another possibility is to name a person and an institution as cosuccessor trustees. The bank or trust services company can do most of the paperwork, and the person can keep an eye on things and approve all transactions.

The successor trustee does not have to live in the same state as you do. But if you are choosing between someone local and someone far away, think about how convenient it will be for the person you choose to distribute the living trust property after your death. Someone close by will probably have an easier job, especially with real estate transfers. But for transfers of property such as securities and bank accounts, it usually won't make much difference where the successor trustee lives.

Obviously, before you and your spouse finalize your living trust, you should check with the person you've chosen to be your successor trustee. You want to be sure your choice is willing to serve. If you don't, you may well create problems down the line. The person you've chosen may not want to serve, for a variety of reasons. And even if the person would be willing, if he or she doesn't know of his or her responsibilities, transfer of trust property after your death could be delayed.

If you choose an institution, you must check out the minimum size of trust it will accept and the fees it charges for management and make arrangements for how the institution will take over as trustee at the second spouse's death.

Avoiding Conflicts With Your Will and Other Documents

Your living trust gives your spouse the authority to manage trust property if you become incapacitated. To avoid conflicts, you should also give your spouse authority to make other decisions if you can't:

- In your will, appoint your spouse to be executor, to be responsible for distributing property left through your will.
- In your Durable Power of Attorney for Finances, appoint your spouse to be your "attorney-in-fact," to have authority to make decisions about property not held in trust if you become incapacitated.

If you do choose different people to be your attorney-in-fact and successor trustee, each will have a role if you become incapacitated. The successor trustee will be in charge of all trust property, and the attorney-in-fact will have authority over property not held in trust.

4. Payment of the Successor Trustee

Typically, the successor trustee of a simple probate-avoidance living trust isn't paid. This is because, in most cases, the successor trustee's only job is to distribute the trust property to beneficiaries soon after the grantor's death—and often, the successor trustee inherits most of the trust property anyway.

An exception is a successor trustee who manages the property in a child's subtrust. In that case, the successor trustee is entitled, under the terms of the trust document, to "reasonable compensation." The successor trustee decides what is reasonable and takes it from the trust property left to the young beneficiary.

Allowing the successor trustee to set the amount of the payment can work well, as long as your successor trustee is completely trustworthy. If the young beneficiary feels the trustee's fees are much too high, he or she will have to go to court to challenge them.

5. Naming an Alternate Successor Trustee

We'll ask you to name an alternate successor trustee, in case your first choice is unable to serve.

If you name two or more successor trustees, the alternate won't become trustee unless none of your original choices can serve.

EXAMPLE: Caroline and Oscar name their two grown children, Eugene and Vanessa, as successor trustees. They name a close friend, Nicole, as alternate successor trustee. After Caroline and Oscar have died, Vanessa is ill and can't serve as trustee. Eugene acts as sole successor trustee. If he were unable to serve or had died, Nicole would take over.

If no one you named in the trust document can serve, the last trustee to serve has the power to appoint, in writing, another successor trustee. (See Chapter 21.)

> **EXAMPLE:** To continue the previous example, if Nicole were ill and didn't have the energy to serve as successor trustee, she could appoint someone else to serve as trustee.

Part 3: Property to Be Put in Trust

In this part of the program, you and your spouse must list each item of property—both jointly owned and separately owned—you want to transfer to your living trust. It will take some thought to decide what property to include and how to list it in the trust document. (Later in the program, you will name beneficiaries to receive each item of trust property at your death.)

This is a crucial step. Any property you don't list will not go into your living trust and will not pass under the terms of the trust. It may instead have to go through probate.

Adding property to the trust later. If you mistakenly leave something out or acquire more valuable property after you create your trust, you will be able to add it to your living trust. Chapter 20 explains how.

! **Listing property in the trust document is not enough.** If an item has a title (ownership) document, such as a deed or title slip, you must change the title document to show that you, as trustee, are the legal owner of the property. If you don't, the trust won't work. *You should transfer ownership as soon as possible after you print out and sign your Declaration of Trust.* Instructions are in Chapter 19.

A. Inventory Your Valuable Property

Before you begin to list your property in the program, sort out what you have and who owns it: you, your spouse or both of you. You need to label each item this way because each spouse names beneficiaries for his or her share of the trust property separately.

After you've made an inventory, the next section will help you decide which items you want to hold in trust so they don't have to go through probate after your death.

1. Take Inventory

First, get out a pencil or your word processor and list all the valuable items of property you own. The categories below should jog your memory.

Even if you plan to leave everything to your spouse or children, you should make a list. That's because every item (or group of items, in some circumstances) must be specifically described and listed in the trust document.

When you list your property in the program, you can group items if you're leaving them all to one beneficiary. For example, if you want to leave all your books to your daughter, there's no need to describe each one individually—unless your collection includes some particularly valuable or important books that you want to make extra sure get to the beneficiary.

Getting organized. While you're taking stock of all your valuable property, it might be a good time to go a step further and gather the information your family will need at your death. For help collecting this information, use Quicken WillMaker Plus's "Information for Caregivers and Survivors" form.

Valuable Property	
Animals	Real estate
Antiques	–Agricultural land
Appliances	–Boat/marina dock
Art	space
Books	–Co-op
Business interests	–Condo
–Sole proprietorship	–Duplex
–Partnership	–House
–Corporation	–Mobile home
–Limited liability co.	–Rental property
Business property*	–Time-share
Cameras & photo	–Undeveloped land
equipment	–Vacation house
Cash accounts	Retirement accounts**
–Certificates of deposit	Royalties
–Checking	Securities
–Money market funds	–Bonds
–Savings	–Commodities
China, crystal, silver	–Mutual funds
Coins, stamps	–Stocks
Collectibles	–U.S. bills, notes
Computers	and bonds
Copyrights, patents,	Tools
trademarks	Vehicles
Electronic equipment	–Bicycles
Furniture	–Cars
Furs	–Motorcycles
Jewelry	–Motorhomes/RVs
Limited partnership	–Planes
Precious metals	–Boats

*If you own a sole proprietorship
**Can't be held in trust (see Section B, below)

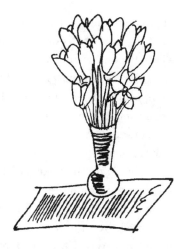

2. Who Owns It?

You'll need to label each item as "his, hers or ours" when you enter it in the program. This is because only your share of the trust property is distributed at your death.

For many couples, especially if they've been married a long time, nearly everything is owned together. But if you haven't been married long or have been married before, you may own a sizeable amount of property separately. If you're unsure about who owns what, read this section, which explains the ownership rules for your state.

a. Community Property States

Alaska*	Nevada
Arizona	New Mexico
California**	Texas
Idaho	Washington
Louisiana	Wisconsin

*If spouses sign a community property agreement.

**Registered domestic partners are also covered by California's community property laws.

If you live in a community property state and you aren't sure who owns what, don't rely on whose name is on the title document. For example, if while you were married you bought a house with money you earned, your spouse legally owns a share of that property—even if only your name is on the deed.

Generally, any property that either spouse earns or acquires during the marriage (before permanent separation) is community property. Both spouses (the "community") own it together, and each spouse can leave his or her half-interest through a will or living trust. The main exception to this shared ownership rule is that property one spouse acquires by gift or inheritance belongs to that spouse alone. Property acquired before marriage also belongs to each spouse separately.

Even separate property may, however, turn into community property if it is mixed ("commingled") with community property. For example, if you deposit separate property funds into a joint bank account and then make more deposits and withdrawals, making it impossible to tell what part of the account is separate money, it's all considered community property.

Survivorship Community Property

In Alaska, Arizona, California, Nevada and Wisconsin, couples can hold title to community property in a way that entails a right of survivorship. When property is held this way, after the first spouse dies, the survivor automatically owns all the property, without probate. So if you have survivorship community property, you don't need to put it into a living trust to avoid probate.

b. Non-Community Property States

Alabama	Missouri
Alaska*	Montana
Arkansas	Nebraska
Colorado	New Hampshire
Connecticut	New Jersey
Delaware	New York
District of Columbia	North Carolina
Florida	North Dakota
Georgia	Ohio
Hawaii	Oklahoma
Illinois	Oregon
Indiana	Pennsylvania
Iowa	Rhode Island
Kansas	South Carolina
Kentucky	South Dakota
Maine	Tennessee
Maryland	Utah
Massachusetts	Vermont
Michigan	Virginia
Minnesota	West Virginia
Mississippi	Wyoming

*Spouses can, however, create community property by signing a community property agreement.

In these states, it is usually fairly simple to figure out who owns what. If the property has a title document—for example, a deed to real estate or a car title slip—then the spouse whose name is on the title is the owner. If the property doesn't have a title document, it belongs to the spouse who paid for it or received it as a gift. (It's possible, though, that if there were a dispute, a judge could determine, based on the circumstances, that a spouse whose name is not on the title document might own an interest in the property.)

If the trust is revoked, the property will be returned to each spouse based on the same ownership rights they had before the property was held in trust.

B. Decide What Property to Hold in Trust

Now that you've got a list of what you and your spouse own, you're ready to decide what items you want to hold in trust to avoid probate fees. Think about including:

- houses and other real estate
- jewelry, antiques, furs and valuable furniture
- stock in a closely held corporation
- stock, bond and other security accounts held by brokerages
- small business interests
- money market and bank accounts
- patents and copyrights
- precious metals
- valuable works of art
- valuable collections of stamps, coins or other objects.

You don't need to put everything you own into a living trust to save money on probate. For some assets, you may decide to use other probate-avoidance devices instead of a living trust. And at least some of the property left to a surviving spouse can probably be transferred without a full-blown probate court proceeding. (See Chapter 13.)

1. Real Estate

The most valuable thing most people own is their real estate: their house, condominium or land. You and your spouse can probably save your family substantial probate costs by transferring your real estate through a living trust.

In some situations, however, you and your spouse may not want to hold your real estate in living trust. See:

- Section 8, Property Held in Joint Tenancy
- Section 9, States That Allow Tenancy by the Entirety
- Section 10, Community Property States

If You're Not Sure How You Hold Title

If you own real estate with someone else but aren't sure how the title is held, look at the deed. It should say how title is held: in joint tenancy, tenancy in common, community property (in community property states) or tenancy by the entirety. In a community property state, if the deed says the property is owned "as husband and wife," that means community property.

If you or your spouse own real estate with someone else, you can transfer just your interest in it to your living trust. You won't need to specify that your share is one-half or some other fraction. For example, if you and your sister own a house together, you need only list "the house at 7989 Lafayette Court, Boston, MA." Your trust document will state that you have transferred all your interest in that property to the trust. The share of the property owned by your sister, obviously, is not included.

Co-op apartments. If you own shares in a co-op corporation that owns your apartment, you'll have to hold your shares in trust. Some corporations are reluctant to let a trustee own shares; check the co-op corporation's rules to see whether the transfer is allowed.

2. Small Business Interests

The delay, expense and court intrusion of probate can be especially detrimental to an ongoing small business. Using your living trust to transfer business interests to beneficiaries quickly after your death is almost essential if you want the beneficiaries to be able to keep the business running.

If you want to control the long-term management of your business, however, a revocable living trust is not the right vehicle. See an estate planning lawyer to draft a different kind of trust, with provisions tailored to your situation.

Different kinds of business organizations present different issues when you want to hold your interest in trust:

Sole proprietorships. If you operate your business as a sole proprietorship, with all business assets held in your own name, you can simply transfer your business property to yourself as trustee. You should also transfer the business's name itself: that transfers the customer goodwill associated with the name.

Partnership interests. If you operate your business as a partnership with other people, you can probably transfer your partnership share to yourself as trustee. If there is a partnership certificate, it must be changed.

Some partnership agreements require the people who inherit a deceased partner's share of the business to offer that share to the other partners before taking it. But that happens after death, so it shouldn't affect your ability to transfer the property through a living trust.

It's not common, but a partnership agreement may limit or forbid holding your interest in trust. If yours does, you and your partners may want to see a lawyer before you make any changes.

Solely owned corporations. If you own all the stock of a corporation, you should have no difficulty transferring it to yourself as trustee.

Closely held corporations. A closely held corporation is a corporation that doesn't sell shares to the public. All its shares are owned by a few people who are usually actively involved in running the business. Normally, you can use a living trust to transfer shares in a closely held corporation by listing the stock in the trust document and then having the stock certificates reissued in your name as trustee.

You'll want to check the corporation's bylaws and articles of incorporation to be sure that you will still have voting rights in your capacity as trustee of the living trust; usually, this is not a problem. If it is, you and the other shareholders should be able to amend the corporation's bylaws to allow it.

There may, however, be restrictions that affect the transfer of shares. Check the corporation's bylaws and articles of incorporation, as well as any separate shareholders' agreements. One fairly common rule is that surviving shareholders (or the corporation) have the right to buy the shares of a deceased shareholder. In that case, you can still use a living trust to transfer the shares, but the people who inherit them may have to sell them.

Limited liability companies. If your small business is an LLC, you'll need the consent of a majority or all of the other owners (check your operating agreement) before you can transfer your interest to yourself as trustee. This shouldn't be a problem; they'll just want to know that you, as trustee of your own trust, will have authority to vote on LLC decisions. Another way to address this concern would be to transfer your economic interest in the LLC, but not your right to vote.

3. Bank Accounts

It's not difficult to transfer bank accounts to your living trust. But you may well decide that you don't need to. That's because you can directly designate a beneficiary for the funds in a bank account. If you do, you don't need to transfer those accounts to a living trust just to avoid probate. Their contents won't go through probate in the first place.

This option can be especially useful for personal checking accounts, which you may not want to transfer to your living trust—it can be difficult to cash checks on accounts owned in a trustee's name.

A living trust, however, offers one advantage that most pay-on-death arrangements do not: You can name an alternate beneficiary to receive the account if your first choice isn't alive at your death. Pay-on-death accounts are discussed in Chapter 13.

Jointly owned accounts. If you want to hold a joint account in your living trust, things are more complicated, and you may just want to name a payable-on-death beneficiary for the account instead. The reason is that almost all joint accounts have what's called the "right of survivorship," which means that when one owner dies, the survivor automatically owns all the money in the account. A provision in a will or living trust can't override that. So no matter what your living trust says, the share of the first spouse to die will go to the survivor; the money in the account will go to a trust beneficiary only when the second spouse dies.

> **EXAMPLE:** Joan and Alex have a joint savings account. They go to the bank and change the registration card on the account to read "Joan and Alex Crookshank, trustees of the Joan and Alex Crookshank Revocable Living Trust dated August 23, 2000." In the trust document, Alex leaves his half of the account to his friend Max. Joan leaves hers to her daughter Linda. Alex dies first. The account is now owned by Joan, and when she dies, all the funds will go to Linda. Max won't inherit anything.

4. Vehicles and Property That Is Often Sold

Some kinds of property are cumbersome to keep in a living trust. It's not a legal problem, just a practical one. Two common examples are:

- **Cars or other vehicles you use.** Having registration and insurance in your name as trustee could be confusing, and some insurance companies might balk. If you have valuable antique autos, or a mobile home that is permanently attached to land and considered real estate under your state's law, however, you may want to go ahead and hold them in trust. You should be able to find an insurance company that will cooperate.
- **Property you buy or sell frequently.** If you don't expect to own the property at your death, there's no compelling reason to hold it in trust. (Remember, the probate process you want to avoid doesn't happen until after your death.) On the other hand, if you're buying property, it's no more trouble to acquire it in your name as trustee.

Other arrangements for property not in your living trust. If you choose not to put valuable items in your living trust, you can probably make arrangements to have them avoid probate in some other way. (See Chapter 13.)

5. Life Insurance

If you own a life insurance policy at your death, the insurance company will give the proceeds to the named beneficiary, without probate. (The proceeds are, however, considered part of your estate for federal estate tax purposes.)

If you have named a minor or young adult as the beneficiary, you may want to name your living trust instead. Then, in the trust document, you name the child as beneficiary of any insurance proceeds paid to the trust and arrange for an adult to manage the policy proceeds if the beneficiary is still young when you die. If you don't arrange for management of the money, and the beneficiary is still a minor (under 18) when you die, a court will have to appoint a financial guardian after your death. (Young beneficiaries are discussed in Part 6, below.)

Passing the proceeds of a life insurance policy through your living trust is a bit more complicated than leaving other property this way. You must take two steps:

1. Name the living trust as the beneficiary of your life insurance policy. (Your insurance agent will have a form that lets you change the beneficiary of the policy.)
2. When you list property items in the living trust document, list the proceeds of the policy, not the policy itself. (Section C, below, contains sample descriptions.)

6. Securities

If you buy and sell stocks regularly, you may not want to go to the trouble of acquiring and selling them using your authority as trustee of the trust.

Fortunately, there's an easier way to do it: Hold your stocks in a brokerage account that is owned in your name as trustee. All securities in the account are then held in trust, which means that you can use your living trust to leave all the contents of the account to a specific beneficiary. If you want to leave stock to different beneficiaries, you can either establish more than one brokerage account or leave one account to more than one beneficiary to own together.

> ### An Alternative: Transfer-on-Death Registration
>
> Most states now allow ownership of securities to be registered in a "transfer-on-death" form. You can designate someone to receive the securities, including mutual funds and brokerage accounts, after your death. No probate will be necessary. Ask your broker about the forms you need to fill out to name a beneficiary for your securities.
>
> Only New York, North Carolina and Texas do not allow transfer-on-death securities registration.

Stock in closely held corporations. See Section 2, above.

7. Cash

It's common for people to want to leave cash gifts to beneficiaries—for example, to leave $5,000 to a relative, friend or charity. Don't, however, just type in "$5,000 cash" when you list the property you want to hold in trust. There's no way to own cash as a trustee, unless that cash is specifically identified.

The way to identify the cash is to transfer ownership of a cash account—a savings or money market account, for example—to yourself as trustee. You can then name a beneficiary to receive the contents of the account. So if you want to leave $5,000 to cousin Fred, all you have to do is put the money in a bank or money market account, transfer it to yourself as trustee and name Fred, in the trust document, as the beneficiary of the account.

If you don't want to set up a separate account to leave a modest amount of cash to a beneficiary, think about buying a savings bond and leaving it to the beneficiary or leaving one larger account to several beneficiaries.

> **EXAMPLE:** Michael would like to leave some modest cash gifts to his two grown nephews, Warren and Brian, whom he's always been fond of. He puts $5,000 into a money market account and then transfers the account to himself as trustee. In his trust document, he names Warren and Brian as beneficiaries of the account. After Michael's death, the two nephews will inherit the account together, and each will be entitled to half of the funds.

Remember, too, that you can simply name a payable-on-death beneficiary for a bank account and avoid probate that way. (See Section 3, above.)

8. Property Held in Joint Tenancy

Property owned in joint tenancy does not go through probate until the last surviving owner dies. When one co-owner (joint tenant) dies, his or her share goes directly to the surviving co-owners, without probate. So if avoiding probate is your only concern, you and your spouse don't need to transfer your joint tenancy property to your living trust.

Joint tenancy doesn't avoid probate, however, if the joint owners die simultaneously—there is no survivor to inherit the other's share. If spouses die at the same time, each spouse's half-interest in the joint tenancy property is passed to the ben-

eficiaries named in the residuary clauses of their wills. If a spouse didn't make a will, the property passes to the closest relatives under the state "intestate succession" law.

If you're concerned about what would happen to the property in the (statistically very unlikely) event that you and your spouse died simultaneously, you have two choices.

- You can name a beneficiary, who would inherit the property in the event of simultaneous death, in your back-up will. If the property passes under your will, however, it will probably go through probate.
- You can hold the property in your living trust, and each spouse can name the other as primary beneficiary and name an alternate beneficiary to receive his or her share of the property in case of simultaneous death. It's a bit more paperwork, but you're assured that probate will be avoided even in the event of simultaneous death.

There's another reason to use a living trust for joint tenancy property: if you want to leave your share of the property to someone besides the other joint tenant(s). Joint tenancy property automatically goes to the surviving co-owners when one co-owner dies. But if you transfer joint tenancy property to a living trust, the joint tenancy is destroyed, and you can leave your share to anyone you please.

9. Property Held in Tenancy by the Entirety

You and your spouse may hold title to property in "tenancy by the entirety"—basically, a kind of joint tenancy that's only for married couples (and in Hawaii and Vermont, same-sex couples that have registered with the state). Not all states have this form of ownership; see Chapter 13, Section A, for a list.

Like joint tenancy, tenancy by the entirety property does not go through probate when one spouse dies; it automatically goes to the surviving spouse. So if avoiding probate is your only concern, you and your spouse don't need to transfer your tenancy by the entirety property to your living trust. Also like joint tenancy property, tenancy by the entirety property doesn't avoid probate if the spouses die simultaneously. If you're concerned about that possibility, you have two choices: Name a beneficiary in your back-up will, or hold the property in trust. These options are discussed in Section 8, just above.

10. Community Property States

Alaska*	Nevada
Arizona	New Mexico
California	Texas
Idaho	Washington
Louisiana	Wisconsin

*If spouses sign a community property agreement.

If you and your spouse own significant community property, and you want to leave it to each other, you may not want to transfer it to your living trust. Your options depend on what state you live in.

Alaska, Arizona, California, Nevada or Wisconsin. In these states, you may want to take advantage of an option that lets you avoid probate completely for community property. You can add the right of survivorship to your community property so that when one spouse dies, the other automatically owns it.

California also allows community property that isn't held with an express right of survivorship to pass outside of probate, via two different

procedures. For real estate, the spouse simply files a one-page affidavit (sworn statement) with the county recorder's office. The affidavit states that he or she is entitled to full ownership of the property. For other property, the spouse requests a Spousal Property Order from the probate court, which then authorizes the transfer into the surviving spouse's name.

Idaho offers a simple probate procedure when the surviving spouse is the only beneficiary. The survivor files a petition with the probate court, and the court issues an order stating that he or she now owns everything.

Washington offers no probate shortcuts for community property. It goes through probate just like everything else.

New Mexico allows a surviving spouse to take title to a home held in community property without probate. But there are several limitations: It's allowed only after a six-month waiting period, only if probate isn't necessary for any other assets and only if all debts and taxes have been paid.

In any state, community property does not avoid probate when the second spouse dies. To avoid probate then, the property must be left via a living trust or other probate-avoidance device.

Community property also doesn't avoid probate if both spouses die simultaneously. If you're concerned about that possibility, you can hold the property in trust, and each spouse can name the other as primary beneficiary and name an alternate beneficiary to receive his or her share of the property in case of simultaneous death. It's a bit more paperwork, but you're assured that probate will be avoided even in the event of simultaneous death.

What Happens to Community Property Put in a Living Trust

Community property (owned by both spouses equally) held in your living trust will stay community property. Separately owned property (property of only one spouse) will remain the separate property of the spouse. That means that community property held in trust is still eligible for the favorable tax treatment given community property at one spouse's death. (Both halves of community property left to the surviving spouse get a "stepped-up basis" for income tax purposes if the value of the property has increased.)

If either spouse revokes the living trust, ownership of the property will go back to the spouses as it was before the property was held in trust. Community property goes back to both spouses equally, and separate property goes to the spouse who owned it.

11. Retirement Plans

Individual retirement accounts cannot be held in trust. Instead, avoid probate by naming a beneficiary to inherit whatever's left in your retirement account at your death. The plan administrator or account holder can provide forms on which to designate your beneficiary.

Because retirement account funds don't go through probate (as long as you name a beneficiary other than your estate), there is usually no reason to name your trust as the beneficiary. If you do name a revocable living trust as the beneficiary of your retirement account, then (under current IRS rules) after your death required minimum distributions will be based on the life expectancy of the trust beneficiary.

 Resources. *IRAs, 401(k)s & Other Retirement Plans: Taking Your Money Out,* by Twila Slesnick and John C. Suttle (Nolo), explains the options of those who inherit money in a retirement account.

12. Other Valuable Property

Other valuable items—everything from jewelry and antiques to boats and airplanes—can also be placed in trust.

C. How to Describe Trust Property

When we ask you to list the property you want to hold in trust, describe each item clearly enough so that the surviving spouse or successor trustee can identify the property and transfer it to the right person. No magic legal words are required.

Think about whom the property will ultimately go to. If you're leaving everything to one person, or just a few, there's less need to go into great detail. But if there will be a number of trust beneficiaries, and objects could be confused, be more specific about each one. When in doubt, err on the side of including more information; describe particularly valuable items in detail, much as you would if you were listing them on an insurance policy.

Rules for Entering Descriptions of Trust Property

- Don't use "my" in a description. Don't, for example, enter "my books" or "my stereo system." That's because once the property is in the living trust, it doesn't belong to you anymore—it belongs to the trust.
- Don't begin a description with a capital letter (unless it must begin with a proper name, like "Steinway"). That's because the descriptions will be inserted into a sentence in the trust document, and it would look odd to see a capital letter in the middle of a sentence.
- Don't end a description with a period. Again, this is because the descriptions will be inserted into a sentence in the trust document.

Here are some sample descriptions:

Real estate

- "the house at 321 Glen St., Omaha, NE"
- "the house at 4444 Casey Road, Fandon, Illinois and the 20-acre parcel on which it is located"

Usually, the street address is enough. It's not necessary to use the "legal description" found on the deed, which gives a subdivision plat number or a metes-and-bounds description. But if the property has no street address—for example, if it is undeveloped land out in the country—you will need to carefully copy the full legal description, word for word, from the deed.

If you own a house and several adjacent lots, it's a good idea to indicate that you are transfer-ring the entire parcel to your living trust by describing the land as well as the house.

If you own the property with someone else and are transferring only your share, you don't need to specify the share you own. Just describe the property. The trust document will show that you are transferring all your interest in the property, whatever share that is, to the living trust.

Bank accounts

- "Savings Account No. 9384-387, Arlington Bank, Arlington, MN"
- "Money Market Account 47-223 at Charles Schwab & Co., Inc., San Francisco, CA"

Household items

- "all the furniture normally kept in the house at 44123 Derby Ave., Ross, KY"
- "the antique brass bed in the master bedroom in the house at 33 Walker Ave., Fort Lee, New Jersey"
- "all furniture and household items normally kept in the house at 869 Hopkins St., Great Falls, Montana"

Sole proprietorship business property

- "Mulligan's Fish Market"
- "Fourth Street Records and CDs"
- "all accounts receivable of the business known as Garcia's Restaurant, 988 17th St., Atlanta, GA"
- "all food preparation and storage equipment, including refrigerator, freezer, hand mixers and slicer, used at Garcia's Restaurant, 988 17th St., Atlanta, GA"

As explained in Section B, above, you should both list the name of the business and separately list items of business property.

Partnership interest

- "Don and Dan's Bait Shop Partnership owned by the grantor before being held in this living trust"

Because a partnership is a legal entity that can own property, you don't need to list items of property owned by the partnership.

Shares in a closely held corporation

- "The stock of ABC Hardware, Inc."

Shares in a solely owned corporation

- "all shares in the XYZ Corporation"
- "all stock in Fern's Olde Antique Shoppe, Inc., 23 Turnbridge Court, Danbury, Connecticut"

Securities

- "all securities in account No. 3999-34-33 at Smith Brokerage, 33 Lowell Place, New York, NY"
- "200 shares of General Industries, Inc. stock"
- "Good Investment Co. mutual fund account No. 888-09-09"

Life insurance proceeds

- "the proceeds of Acme Co. Life Insurance Policy #9992A"

Miscellaneous items

- "Macintosh computer (serial number 129311) with keyboard (serial number 165895)"
- "the medical textbooks in the office at 1702 Parker Towers, San Francisco, CA"
- "the stamp collection usually kept at 321 Glen St., Omaha, NE"
- "the collection of European stamps, including [describe particularly valuable stamps], usually kept at 440 Loma Prieta Blvd., #450, San Jose, CA"
- "the Martin D-35 acoustic guitar, serial number 477597"
- "the signed 1960 Ernie Banks baseball card kept in safe deposit box 234, First National Bank of Augusta, Augusta, IL"
- "the Baldwin upright piano kept at 985 Dawson Court, South Brenly, Massachusetts"

Part 4: Beneficiaries of Trust Property

Once you've entered a list of the property you're going to hold in trust, the next step is to say whom you want to inherit that property. In the trust document, you and your spouse must each name beneficiaries—the family, friends or organizations who will receive your share of the trust property.

Each spouse names beneficiaries separately, because each one's trust property is distributed when that spouse dies. When the first spouse dies, his or her trust property will be distributed to the beneficiaries he or she named. If it is left to the other spouse, it stays in the trust. When the second spouse dies, the rest of the property in the trust is distributed to his or her beneficiaries.

EXAMPLE: Roger and Marilyn Foster create a shared living trust. Each puts co-owned and separately owned property in the trust. When Roger dies, Marilyn takes over as sole trustee and distributes Roger's trust property to the beneficiaries he named in the trust document. Her property, including the trust property she inherits from Roger, stays in the living trust.

The beneficiaries you name in your trust document are not entitled to any trust property while both spouses are alive. You can amend your trust document and change the beneficiaries any time you wish.

Rights of a spouse or child. If you are married and don't plan to leave at least half of what you own to your spouse, consult a lawyer experienced in estate planning. State law may entitle your spouse to claim some of the property in your living trust. In most circumstances, you don't have to leave anything to your children. But if you want to disinherit a child, you should make a back-up will and specifically mention the child in it. (See Chapter 4.)

A. How Do You Want Your Property Distributed?

We'll ask you first whether you want to leave all your trust property to one beneficiary (or more than one, to share it all) or leave different items to different beneficiaries.

Many couples want to leave all trust property to the survivor. If you choose that option, we'll insert your spouse's name (entered earlier) as beneficiary of all your trust property. All you have to do is name an alternate beneficiary, who will inherit your trust property if your spouse does not survive you by five days. (Alternates are discussed in Section D, below.)

If you choose to leave different items to different beneficiaries, you will be shown a list of all the property items you listed earlier. You can then name beneficiaries (including your spouse, if you wish) for them.

1. Your Spouse

It's common for spouses to leave each other all or a substantial portion of the property in their shared marital trust. In a shared trust, if one spouse leaves the other trust property, it stays in the living trust when the first spouse dies.

EXAMPLE: Max and Joan make a shared basic living trust. Each leaves all his or her trust property to the other. Max dies first. All his interest in trust property stays in what is now Joan's living trust. Joan has the right to amend the trust document to name beneficiaries for the trust property that is now hers. (See Chapter 21.)

2. Children From Prior Marriages

If you or your spouse have children from a prior marriage, you may well want to leave them property in your living trust. A common way to do this is to leave the children specific items—real estate, life insurance policy proceeds, bank accounts or whatever—and leave everything else to your spouse.

A more complicated way of ensuring that both your current spouse and children from an earlier marriage are taken care of is to create an AB trust. It gives the surviving spouse the right to use income from (or live in) certain property for his or her life; then the property goes to the children. (See Chapter 14.)

3. Minors or Young Adults

You can name minors (children under 18) to inherit trust property. If a beneficiary you name is a minor or a young adult who can't yet manage property without help, you can arrange for an adult to manage the trust property for the beneficiary. (See Part 6, below.)

4. Your Successor Trustee

It's very common and perfectly legal to make the person you named to be successor trustee (the person who will distribute trust property after the second spouse dies) a beneficiary as well.

> **EXAMPLE:** Nora and Sean name their son Liam as successor trustee of their living trust. Each spouse names the other as sole beneficiary of his or her trust property, and both name Liam as alternate beneficiary. When Nora dies, her trust property goes to Sean and stays in the trust. After Sean's death, Liam, acting as trustee, will transfer ownership of the trust property to himself.

5. Naming More Than One Beneficiary to Share Property

You can name more than one beneficiary to share any item of trust property. Simply list their names in the box on the screen. Type the names one per line; don't join the names with an "and." (See the Users' Manual for examples.)

Always use the beneficiaries' actual names; don't use collective terms such as "my children." It's not always clear who is included in such descriptions. And there can be serious confusion if one of the people originally included as a group member dies before you do.

Obviously, if you name cobeneficiaries for a piece of property that can't be physically divided—a cabin, for example—give some thought to whether or not the beneficiaries are likely to get along. If they are incompatible, disagreements could arise over taking care of property or deciding whether or not to sell it. If they can't settle their differences, any co-owner could go to court and demand a partition—a court-ordered division and sale—of the property.

Cobeneficiaries will share the property equally unless you state otherwise. We'll ask you, after you enter the names, whether or not you want an item of trust property to be shared equally among the beneficiaries.

> **EXAMPLE:** Georgia wants to leave her house to her two children, Ross and Ryan, but wants Ross to have a 75% share of it. She enters their names and then, on a later screen, enters their interests, in fractions: 3/4 for Ross and 1/4 for Ryan.
>
> When the children inherit the property, they own it together. But Ross will be liable for 75% of the taxes and upkeep cost, and entitled to 75% of any income the house produces. If they sell it, Ross will be entitled to 75% of the proceeds.

B. Entering Beneficiaries' Names

When you enter a beneficiary's name, use the name by which the beneficiary is known for purposes such as a bank account or driver's license. Generally, if the name you use clearly and unambiguously identifies the person, it is sufficient.

If you name an institution (charitable or not) to inherit trust property, enter its complete name. It may be commonly known by a shortened version, which could cause confusion if there are similarly named organizations. Call to ask if you're unsure. (An institution that stands to inherit some of your money will be more than happy to help you.) Also be sure to specify if you want a branch of a national organization to receive your gift—for example, a local chapter of the Sierra Club.

C. Beneficiaries for Co-Owned Trust Property

As you name your beneficiaries, remember that when it comes to property you and your spouse co-own, you're naming people to receive only your share. When one spouse dies, only his or her interest in the co-owned property will go to the named beneficiary.

> **EXAMPLE:** Marcia and Perry transfer all the property they own together into their living trust. Marcia names Perry as the beneficiary of all her interest in the trust property. Perry names Marcia to inherit all of his half except his half-interest in their vacation cabin, which he leaves to his son from a previous marriage, Eric. If Perry dies first, Perry's half-interest in the cabin will go to Eric, who will co-own it with Marcia.

D. Alternate Beneficiaries

You can name an alternate beneficiary for every person you name as a primary beneficiary. The alternate will get the property left to the primary beneficiary if your first choice does not live for more than 120 hours (five days) after your death. This "survivorship" period ensures that if you and a primary beneficiary die simultaneously or almost so, the property will go to the alternate beneficiary you chose, not to the primary beneficiary's heirs.

> **EXAMPLE:** Laura and her husband Juan-Carlos make a shared living trust. Laura leaves all her trust property to Juan-Carlos and names her daughter from a previous marriage as alternate beneficiary. Laura and Juan-Carlos are seriously injured in a car accident; Juan-Carlos dies a day after Laura does. Because Juan-Carlos did not survive Laura by at least five days, the trust property he would have inherited from Laura goes to Laura's daughter instead.

If there had been no survivorship requirement, the trust property would have gone to Juan-Carlos; when he died a day later, it would have gone to the beneficiaries he had named.

You don't have to name an alternate for a charitable (or other) institution you name as a beneficiary. If the institution is well established, it is probably safe to assume that it will still exist at your death.

If you don't name an alternate, and the primary beneficiary does not survive you, the property that beneficiary would have received will be distributed to the person or institution you name, in the next part of the program, as your "residuary beneficiary." (See Part 5, below.) One exception to this rule: If you name cobeneficiaries and don't name alternates for them, the surviving cobeneficiaries will inherit a deceased beneficiary's share.

You can name more than one person or institution as alternate beneficiaries. If you do, they will share the property equally.

> **EXAMPLE:** Sherry names her husband as beneficiary of her interest in their house, which they hold in trust. As alternate beneficiaries, she names their three children, Sean, Colleen and Tim.
>
> Sherry's husband dies before she does, leaving his half of the house to Sherry. Under the terms of the trust document, it stays in the living trust. At Sherry's death, the house goes to the three children equally. All three own equal shares in all of it.

Part 5: Residuary Beneficiaries

Unless you leave all your trust property to one beneficiary (or a group of beneficiaries to share), each spouse must name a residuary beneficiary. The person or organization you name will receive:

- any trust property for which both the primary and alternate beneficiaries you named die before you do
- any trust property that you didn't leave to a named beneficiary (this could include property you transfer to the trust later and don't name a beneficiary for, and trust property that was owned by your spouse, which he or she left you)
- any property you leave to your living trust through your will (such a will is called a pour-over will)
- any property that you actually transferred to yourself as trustee but didn't list in the trust document.

Often, the residuary beneficiary of a living trust doesn't inherit anything from the trust. Usually, naming a residuary beneficiary is just a back-up measure, to guard against the extremely small chance that both a primary and alternate trust beneficiary do not survive you.

Part 6: Property Management for Young Beneficiaries

If any of the beneficiaries (including alternate and residuary beneficiaries) named by either spouse might inherit trust property before they are ready to manage it without an adult's help, that spouse should arrange for someone to manage it for them for a while. There are several ways to go about it:

- **Leave the property to an adult to use for the child.** Many people don't leave property directly to a child. Instead, they leave it to the child's parent or to the person they ex-

pect to have care and custody of the child if neither parent is available. There's no formal legal arrangement, but they trust the adult to use the property for the child's benefit.

- **Name a custodian under a law called the Uniform Transfers to Minors Act (UTMA).** In almost every state, you can name a "custodian" to manage property you leave a child until the child reaches 18 or 21, depending on state law (up to 25 in a few states). If you don't need management to last beyond that age, a custodianship is preferable.
- **Create a child's subtrust.** You can use Quicken WillMaker Plus to establish a "child's subtrust" in your living trust. If you do, your surviving spouse (or the successor trustee, after both spouses' death) will manage the property you left the child and dole it out for education, health and other needs. The subtrust ends at whatever age you designate (up to 35), and any remaining property is turned over to the child outright.

Subtrusts and custodianships are explained below.

Children with special needs. These property management options are not designed to provide long-term property management for a child with serious disabilities. You should see a lawyer and make arrangements geared to your particular situation.

A. Should You Arrange for Management?

Each spouse chooses whether or not to arrange to have someone manage trust property if it is inherited by young beneficiaries.

The consequences of forgoing management for trust property inherited by a young beneficiary depend on whether the beneficiary is over or under age 18 at your death.

1. Children Under 18 Years Old

Minors—children under 18—cannot, legally, own or manage significant amounts of property. An adult must be in charge if the minor acquires more than a few thousand dollars' worth of property. (The exact amount depends on state law.)

If your minor beneficiaries won't inherit anything of great value—if you're leaving them objects that have more sentimental than monetary value—you don't need to arrange for an adult to manage the property.

But if a beneficiary inherits valuable trust property while still a minor, and you have not arranged for the property to be managed by an adult, a court-appointed guardian may have to manage the property. Contrary to what you might expect, a child's parent does not automatically have legal authority to manage any property the child inherits. So even if one or both of the beneficiary's parents are alive, they will have to ask the court to grant them that authority and will be subject to the court's supervision. If neither parent is alive, there may be no obvious person for the court to appoint as property guardian. In that case, it may be even more important for you to name someone in your living trust.

There is one other option: In most states, the successor trustee can name a custodian to manage property inherited by a minor. If the value of the property exceeds a certain amount—$10,000 in most states—a court must approve the appointment. And the custodianship must end at 18 in most states—earlier than many parents may

choose. So it's still better to name a custodian yourself.

2. Young Adults 18 to 35 Years Old

If a living trust beneficiary is 18 or older when he or she inherits trust property, you do not need, legally, to have anyone manage the property on the beneficiary's behalf. And if you don't make any arrangements, the beneficiary will get the property with no strings attached. But you can arrange for property management to last until a beneficiary turns any age up to 35.

There is no legal requirement that management for a trust beneficiary's property must end at 35, but we think 35 is a reasonable cutoff. If you don't want to let a beneficiary get his or her hands on trust property by the time he or she reaches 35, you probably need to see a lawyer and tailor a plan to the beneficiary's needs.

B. Which Is Best: Subtrust or Custodianship?

Using Quicken WillMaker Plus, you can create either a child's subtrust or a custodianship under the Uniform Transfer to Minors Act (if it's available in your state). Both are safe, efficient ways of managing trust property that a young person inherits. Under either system, the person in charge of the young beneficiary's property has the same responsibility to use the property for the beneficiary's support, education and health.

The most significant difference is that a child's subtrust can last longer than a custodianship, which must end at age 18 to 21 (25 in a few states) in most states. (Each state's rule is set out in Chapter 15, Part 6.) For that reason, a child's subtrust is a good choice when a child could inherit a large amount of property.

Because an UTMA custodianship is much easier to administer, it is usually preferable if the beneficiary will inherit no more than about $50,000 worth of trust property ($100,000 or more if the child is quite young). That amount is likely to be used up for living and education expenses by the time the beneficiary is 18 to 21, so there's no need to create a subtrust that can continue beyond that age.

A custodianship has other advantages as well:

- Handling a beneficiary's property is much easier with a custodianship than with a trust. A custodian's powers are written into state law, and most institutions, such as banks and insurance companies, are familiar with the rules. Trusts, on the other hand, vary in their terms. So before a bank lets a trustee act on behalf of a beneficiary, it may demand to see and analyze a copy of the Declaration of Trust.

- You can name whomever you wish to be a custodian, and you can name different custodians for different beneficiaries. So if you want to arrange custodianships for grandchildren, for example, you could name each child's parent as custodian. A child's subtrust is not quite so flexible: The surviving spouse, or the successor trustee if you are the second spouse to die, will be the trustee of all children's subtrusts created for your young beneficiaries.

- If the property in a subtrust earns income, and that income isn't distributed quickly to the beneficiary, the trust will have to pay tax on it. The federal tax rate on such retained income may be higher than it would be if the young beneficiary were taxed on it. The trustee may well need to hire experts to help with trust accounting and tax returns.

C. Custodianships

A custodianship is the preferable alternative for many people. Here's how it works.

1. How a Custodianship Works

In the trust document, you name someone to serve as custodian for a particular beneficiary. That person manages any trust property the young beneficiary inherits from that spouse until the beneficiary reaches the age at which state law says the custodianship must end. (See table in Chapter 15, Part 6.)

> **EXAMPLE:** Sandra and Don make a living trust. Sandra leaves 100 shares of General Motors stock to her niece, Jennifer Frankel. She names Hazel Frankel, Jennifer's mother, as custodian under the Illinois Uniform Transfers to Minors Act.
>
> After Sandra's death, Don, as trustee, turns the stock over to the custodian, Hazel. She will manage it for Jennifer until Jennifer turns 21, the age Illinois law says she must be given the property outright.

In some states, you can specify—within limits—at what age the custodianship will end. If your state allows this, the program will ask you to enter an age at which you want the custodianship to end.

> **EXAMPLE:** If Sandra, in the previous example, lived in New Jersey, the state's law would allow her to choose any age from 18 to 21 for the custodianship to end.

2. The Custodian's Responsibilities

A custodian has roughly the same responsibility as the trustee of a child's subtrust: to manage the beneficiary's property wisely and honestly. The custodian's authority and duties are set out by a law called the Uniform Transfers to Minors Act, as enacted by your state. No court directly supervises the custodian.

The custodian must:

- manage the property until the beneficiary reaches the age at which, by law, he or she gets the property outright. If the child is a minor at your death, this can be a number of years
- use the property or income to pay for expenses such as the young beneficiary's support, education and health care
- keep the property separate from his or her own property, and
- keep separate records of transactions. The custodian does not have to file a separate income tax return; income from the property can be reported on the young beneficiary's return. (By comparison, the trustee of a child's subtrust must file a separate tax return for the subtrust.)

A custodian who needs to hire an accountant, tax lawyer or other expert can use the property to pay a reasonable amount for the help.

If state law allows it, the custodian is entitled to reasonable compensation and reimbursement for reasonable expenses. The payment, if any is taken, comes from the custodial property.

3. Choosing a Custodian

You can name a different custodian for each young beneficiary, if you wish.

In most cases, you should name the person who will have physical custody of the minor child. That's almost always one of the child's parents. If the beneficiary is your child, name the child's other parent unless you have serious reser-

vations about that person's ability to handle the property for the child.

Only one person can be named as custodian for one beneficiary. You can, however, name an alternate custodian to take over if your first choice is unable to serve.

D. Children's Subtrusts

Quicken WillMaker Plus allows you to set up a separate child's subtrust for each young beneficiary.

1. How a Child's Subtrust Works

In your trust document, you state the age at which the beneficiary should receive trust property outright. If at your death the beneficiary hasn't reached that age, a subtrust will be created for that beneficiary. (If the beneficiary is older, he or she gets the trust property with no strings attached, and no subtrust is created.) Each beneficiary gets a separate child's subtrust.

Quicken WillMaker Plus is set up so that the surviving spouse, or the successor trustee after both spouses die, will serve as trustee of all children's subtrusts. If you want different people to manage property inherited by different beneficiaries, you may want to use a custodianship instead of a child's subtrust. (To appoint someone else to be trustee of a child's subtrust, the trust document would have to be changed significantly; see a lawyer.)

Whatever trust property the beneficiary is entitled to receive upon one spouse's death will go into the child's subtrust, if the child is still under the age set for termination of the subtrust. The trustee will manage the subtrust property and use it as necessary for the beneficiary's health, education and support. After the spouse's death, the subtrust cannot be revoked or amended. Until then, that spouse is free to change his or her mind about having a subtrust set up for a particular beneficiary.

The child's subtrust will end when the beneficiary reaches the age designated by the spouse in the Declaration of Trust. This can be any age up to and including 35. The trustee will then give the beneficiary what remains of the subtrust property.

EXAMPLE: In the trust document that Stanley makes with his wife Natalie, he names his 14-year-old son Michael as beneficiary of $100,000 worth of stock. He specifies that any stock Michael becomes entitled to when Stanley dies should be kept in a subtrust until Michael is 25, subject to the trustee's right to spend it on Michael's behalf.

Stanley dies when Michael is 19. The stock goes into a subtrust for him, managed by Natalie. She uses the stock (and the income it produces) to pay for Michael's education and support. Michael receives what's left of the stock when he turns 25.

EXAMPLE: Roger and Victoria create a living trust and leave their trust property to the other. They name their daughters, who are 22 and 25, as alternate beneficiaries, and arrange for any trust property they inherit to stay in children's subtrusts until each daughter reaches 30. They name Victoria's sister, Antoinette, as successor trustee.

Roger and Victoria die in a car accident when one daughter is 28 and the other is 31. The 28-year-old's half of the trust property stays in a subtrust, managed by Antoinette, until she turns 30. The 31-year-old gets her half outright; no subtrust is created for her.

2. The Subtrust Trustee's Duties

The subtrust trustee must:

- keep the beneficiary (or the beneficiary's guardian, if the beneficiary is a minor) reasonably well informed about how the assets are being invested
- manage and invest subtrust property until the beneficiary reaches the age set out in the trust document—which can take years
- keep the beneficiary (or the beneficiary's guardian, if the beneficiary is a minor) reasonably well informed about how trust assets are being invested
- use subtrust property or income to pay for expenses such as the beneficiary's support, education and health care, and
- keep separate records of subtrust transactions and file income tax returns for the subtrust.

The trustee's powers and responsibilities are spelled out in the trust document. If the subtrust trustee needs to hire an accountant, tax lawyer or other expert, he or she can use subtrust assets to pay a reasonable amount for the help.

The trust document also provides that the trustee of a subtrust is entitled to reasonable compensation for his or her work as trustee. The trustee decides what is a reasonable amount; the compensation is paid from the subtrust assets.

For more on the trustee's responsibilities, see Chapter 21.

Declaration of Trust

Part 1. Trust Name

This revocable living trust shall be known as the William C. Carey and Leslie M. Carey Revocable Living Trust.

Part 2. Declaration of Trust

William C. Carey and Leslie M. Carey, called the grantors, declare that they have transferred and delivered to the trustees all their interest in the property described in Schedules A, B and C attached to this Declaration of Trust. All of that property is called the "trust property." The trustees hereby acknowledge receipt of the trust property and agree to hold the trust property in trust, according to this Declaration of Trust.

Either grantor may add property to the trust.

Part 3. Terminology

The term "this Declaration of Trust" includes any provisions added by valid amendment.

Part 4. Character of Trust Property

While both grantors are alive, property held in this trust shall retain its original character as community or separate property, as the case may be.

If the trust is revoked, the trustee shall distribute the trust property listed on Schedule A to the grantors as their community property. The trust property listed in Schedule B shall be distributed to Leslie M. Carey as her separate property, and the trust property listed in Schedule C shall be distributed to William C. Carey as his separate property.

Part 5. Amendment and Revocation

A. Revocation by Grantor

Either grantor may revoke this trust at any time, without notifying any beneficiary. Revocation may be made in writing or any manner allowed by law.

B. Amendment by Grantors

While both grantors are alive, this Declaration of Trust may be amended only by both of them acting together. All amendments must be in writing and signed by both grantors.

C. Amendment or Revocation by Other Person

The power to revoke or amend this trust is personal to the grantors. A conservator, guardian or other person shall not exercise it on behalf of either grantor, unless a grantor specifically grants a power to revoke or amend this trust in a Durable Power of Attorney.

Part 6. Payment From Trust During Grantors' Lifetimes

The trustees shall pay to or use for the benefit of the grantors as much of the net income and principal of the trust property as the grantors request. Income shall be paid to the grantors at least annually. Income accruing in or paid to trust accounts shall be deemed to have been paid to the grantor.

Part 7. Trustees

A. Original Trustees

William C. Carey and Leslie M. Carey are the trustees of this trust. Either alone may act for or represent the trust in any transaction.

B. Trustee at Death of Original Trustee

Upon the death of William C. Carey or Leslie M. Carey, the surviving trustee shall serve as sole trustee.

C. Trustee's Responsibilities

The trustee in office shall serve as trustee of all trusts created under this Declaration of Trust, including children's subtrusts.

D. Terminology

In this Declaration of Trust, the term "trustee" includes successor trustees or alternate successor trustees serving as trustee of this trust. The singular "trustee" also includes the plural.

E. Successor Trustee

Upon the death or incapacity of the surviving spouse, or the incapacity of both spouses, Jeffrey R. Carey shall serve as trustee. If Jeffrey R. Carey is unable or unwilling to serve as successor trustee, Susan DiFlorio shall serve as trustee.

F. Resignation of Trustee

Any trustee in office may resign at any time by signing a notice of resignation. The resignation must be delivered to the person or institution who is either named in this Declaration of Trust, or appointed by the trustee under Section G of this Part, to next serve as the trustee.

G. Power to Appoint Successor Trustee

If no one named in this Declaration of Trust as a successor trustee or alternate successor trustee is willing or able to serve as trustee, the last acting trustee may appoint a successor trustee and may require the posting of a reasonable bond, to be paid for from the trust property. The appointment must be made in writing, signed by the trustee and notarized.

H. Bond

No bond shall be required for any trustee named in this Declaration of Trust.

I. Compensation

No trustee shall receive any compensation for serving as trustee, unless the trustee serves as a trustee of a child's subtrust created by this Declaration of Trust.

J. Liability of Trustee

With respect to the exercise or non-exercise of discretionary powers granted by this Declaration of Trust, the trustee shall not be liable for actions taken in good faith. Such actions shall be binding on all persons interested in the trust property.

Part 8. Trustee's Management Powers and Duties

A. Powers Under State Law

The trustee shall have all authority and powers allowed or conferred on a trustee under California law, subject to the trustee's fiduciary duty to the grantors and the beneficiaries.

B. Specified Powers

The trustee's powers include, but are not limited to:

1. The power to sell trust property, and to borrow money and to encumber trust property, including trust real estate, by mortgage, deed of trust or other method.

2. The power to manage trust real estate as if the trustee were the absolute owner of it, including the power to lease (even if the lease term may extend beyond the period of any trust) or grant options to lease the property, to make repairs or alterations and to insure against loss.

3. The power to sell or grant options for the sale or exchange of any trust property, including stocks, bonds, debentures and any other form of security or security account, at public or private sale for cash or on credit.

4. The power to invest trust property in every kind of property and every kind of investment, including but not limited to bonds, debentures, notes, mortgages, stock options, futures and stocks, and including buying on margin.

5. The power to receive additional property from any source and add it to any trust created by this Declaration of Trust.

6. The power to employ and pay reasonable fees to accountants, lawyers or investment experts for information or advice relating to the trust.

7. The power to deposit and hold trust funds in both interest-bearing and non-interest-bearing accounts.

8. The power to deposit funds in bank or other accounts uninsured by FDIC coverage.

9. The power to enter into electronic fund transfer or safe deposit arrangements with financial institutions.

10. The power to continue any business of either grantor.

11. The power to institute or defend legal actions concerning this trust or the grantors' affairs.

12. The power to execute any documents necessary to administer any trust created by this Declaration of Trust.

13. The power to diversify investments, including authority to decide that some or all of the trust property need not produce income.

Part 9. Incapacity of Grantors

If William C. Carey or Leslie M. Carey becomes physically or mentally incapacitated, whether or not a court has declared the grantor incompetent or in need of a conservator or guardian, the other spouse shall be sole trustee until the incapacitated grantor is again able to manage his or her affairs.

If both spouses become incapacitated, the successor trustee named in Part 7 of this Declaration of Trust shall serve as trustee.

The determination of a grantor's capacity to manage this trust shall be made by those of the people listed here who are reasonably available when the other grantor requests their opinion. These people are: Leah Corval, Amy Peterson and Jeffrey Mosley. If a majority of them state, in writing, that in their opinion one grantor is no longer reasonably capable of serving as trustee, the other grantor shall serve as trustee.

The trustee shall manage the trust property and use any amount of trust income or trust principal necessary for the proper health care, support, maintenance, comfort and welfare of both grantors, in accordance with their accustomed manner of living. Income shall be paid to the grantors at least annually. Income accruing in or paid to trust accounts shall be deemed to have been paid to the grantor.

Declaration of Trust—Page 4 of 9

Part 10. Death of a Grantor

The first grantor to die shall be called the "deceased spouse." The other grantor shall be called the "surviving spouse."

Upon the deceased spouse's death, the trustee shall divide the property of the William C. Carey and Leslie M. Carey Revocable Living Trust listed on Schedules A, B and C into two separate trusts, Trust #1 and Trust #2. The trustee shall serve as trustee of Trust #1 and Trust #2.

Trust #1 shall contain all the property of the William C. Carey and Leslie M. Carey Revocable Living Trust owned by the deceased spouse before it was held in trust, plus accumulated income, except trust property left by the terms of this trust to the surviving spouse. Trust #1 shall become irrevocable at the death of the deceased spouse. The trustee shall distribute the property in Trust #1 to the beneficiaries named in Part 11 of this Declaration of Trust.

Trust #2 shall contain all the property of the William C. Carey and Leslie M. Carey Revocable Living Trust owned by the surviving spouse before it was held in trust, plus accumulated income, and any trust property left by the deceased spouse to the surviving spouse. It shall remain revocable until the death of the surviving spouse.

The trustee may pay out of trust property such amounts as necessary for payment of debts, estate taxes and expenses of the last illness and funeral of the deceased or surviving spouse.

Part 11. Beneficiaries

A. Husband's Beneficiaries

At the death of William C. Carey, the trustee shall distribute the trust property listed on Schedule C, plus accumulated interest; the share of the property on Schedule A owned by William C. Carey before it was transferred to the trustee, plus accumulated interest; and if William C. Carey is the second spouse to die, any property listed on Schedule B left to him by the deceased spouse, plus accumulated interest; as follows:

1. Leslie M. Carey shall be given all William C. Carey's interest in all the furniture in the house at 3320 Windmill Road, Auburn, California, the condominium at 19903 Forest Way, #43, Wawona, California and the house at 3320 Windmill Road, Auburn, California. If Leslie M. Carey does not survive William C. Carey, that property shall be given to Claudia A. Carey.

2. Jonathan Goldfarb shall be given all William C. Carey's interest in account no. 3301-A94 at International Brokers, San Francisco, California. If Jonathan Goldfarb does not survive William C. Carey, that property shall be given to Melissa Goldfarb.

3. Claudia A. Carey shall be given all William C. Carey's interest in the trust property not otherwise specifically and validly disposed of by this Part. If Claudia A. Carey does not survive William C. Carey, that property shall be given to the Nature Conservancy and Mills College, in equal shares.

B. Wife's Beneficiaries

At the death of Leslie M. Carey, the trustee shall distribute the trust property listed on Schedule B, plus accumulated interest; the share of the property on Schedule A owned by Leslie M. Carey before it was transferred to the trustee, plus accumulated interest; and if Leslie M. Carey is the second spouse to die, any property listed on Schedule C left to her by the deceased spouse, plus accumulated interest; as follows:

1. William C. Carey shall be given all Leslie M. Carey's interest in the trust property. If William C. Carey does not survive Leslie M. Carey, that property shall be given to Claudia A. Carey.

2. Claudia A. Carey shall be given all Leslie M. Carey's interest in the trust property not otherwise specifically and validly disposed of by this Part.

C. Property Left to the Surviving Spouse

Any trust property left by the deceased spouse to the surviving spouse shall remain in the surviving spouse's revocable trust, Trust #2.

D. Terms of Property Distribution

All distributions are subject to any provision in this Declaration of Trust that creates a child's subtrust or a custodianship under the Uniform Transfers to Minors Act.

A beneficiary must survive the grantor for 120 hours to receive property under this Declaration of Trust. As used in this Declaration of Trust, to survive means to be alive or in existence as an organization.

All personal and real property left through this trust shall pass subject to any encumbrances or liens placed on the property as security for the repayment of a loan or debt.

If property is left to two or more beneficiaries to share, they shall share it equally unless this Declaration of Trust provides otherwise. If any of them does not survive the grantor, the others shall take that beneficiary's share, to share equally, unless this Declaration of Trust provides otherwise.

Declaration of Trust—Page 6 of 9

Part 12. Children's Subtrusts

A. Beneficiaries for Whom Subtrusts May Be Created

1. If Claudia A. Carey becomes entitled to any trust property under Part 11.B before reaching the age of 29, that trust property shall be kept in a separate child's subtrust, under the provisions of this Part, until Claudia A. Carey reaches the age of 29. The subtrust shall be known as the "William C. Carey and Leslie M. Carey Revocable Living Trust, Claudia A. Carey Subtrust."

2. If Claudia A. Carey becomes entitled to any trust property under Part 11.A before reaching the age of 29, that trust property shall be kept in a separate child's subtrust, under the provisions of this Part, until Claudia A. Carey reaches the age of 29. The subtrust shall be known as the "William C. Carey and Leslie M. Carey Revocable Living Trust, Claudia A. Carey Subtrust."

B. Powers of Subtrust Trustee

The trustee may distribute as much of the net income or principal of the child's subtrust as the trustee deems necessary for the beneficiary's health, support, maintenance or education. Education includes, but is not limited to, college, graduate, postgraduate and vocational studies, and reasonably related living expenses.

In deciding whether or not to make a distribution, the trustee may take into account the beneficiary's other income, resources and sources of support. Any subtrust income not distributed by the trustee shall be accumulated and added to the principal of the subtrust.

The trustee is not required to make any accounting or report to the subtrust beneficiary.

C. Assignment of Subtrust Assets

The interests of the beneficiary of a child's subtrust shall not be transferable by voluntary or involuntary assignment or by operation of law before receipt by the beneficiary. They shall be free from the claims of creditors and from attachments, execution, bankruptcy or other legal process to the fullest extent permitted by law.

D. Compensation of Trustee

Any trustee of a child's subtrust created under this Declaration of Trust is entitled to reasonable compensation, without court approval, out of the subtrust assets for ordinary and extraordinary services, and for all services in connection with the termination of any subtrust.

E. Termination of Subtrust

A child's subtrust shall end when any of the following events occurs:

1. The beneficiary reaches the age specified in Section A of this Part. If the subtrust ends for this reason, the remaining principal and accumulated income of the subtrust shall be given outright to the beneficiary.

2. The beneficiary dies. If the subtrust ends for this reason, the subtrust property shall pass to the beneficiary's heirs.

3. The trustee distributes all subtrust property under the provisions of this Declaration of Trust.

Part 13. Homestead Rights

If the grantors' principal residence is held in this trust, grantors have the right to possess and occupy it for life, rent-free and without charge, except for taxes, insurance, maintenance and related costs and expenses. This right is intended to give grantors a beneficial interest in the property and to ensure that the grantors, or either of them, do not lose eligibility for a state homestead tax exemption for which either grantor otherwise qualifies.

Part 14. Severability of Clauses

If any provision of this Declaration of Trust is ruled unenforceable, the remaining provisions shall stay in effect.

Certification of Grantors

We certify that we have read this Declaration of Trust and that it correctly states the terms and conditions under which the trust property is to be held, managed and disposed of by the trustees, and we approve the Declaration of Trust.

_____ Dated: _____
William C. Carey, Grantor and Trustee

_____ Dated: _____
Leslie M. Carey, Grantor and Trustee

Certificate of Acknowledgment of Notary Public

State of _____

County of _____

On _____, before me, _____ a notary public for said state, personally appeared William C. Carey and Leslie M. Carey, personally known to me (or proved to me on the basis of satisfactory evidence) to be the persons whose names are subscribed to the within instrument, and acknowledged to me that they executed the same in their authorized capacities and that by their signatures on the instrument the persons, or the entity upon behalf of which the persons acted, executed the instrument.

Witness my hand and official seal.

_____

NOTARY PUBLIC for the State of _____

My commission expires _____.

Schedule A

SHARED PROPERTY PLACED IN TRUST

1. All the furniture in the house at 3320 Windmill Road, Auburn, California.

2. The condominium at 19903 Forest Way, #43, Wawona, California.

3. The house at 3320 Windmill Road, Auburn, California.

Schedule B

WIFE'S SEPARATE PROPERTY PLACED IN TRUST

1. Scudder International Fund Account 993-222-1.

2. The 4-volume American stamp collection kept at 3320 Windmill Road, Auburn, California.

Schedule C

HUSBAND'S SEPARATE PROPERTY PLACED IN TRUST

1. Account no. 3301-A94 at International Brokers, San Francisco, California.

Declaration of Trust—Page 9 of 9

Creating an AB Trust

When you create your AB living trust document with Quicken WillMaker Plus, you must decide:

- whether you want to make a "disclaimer" AB trust, which gives the surviving spouse the option of not splitting the AB trust when the first spouse dies (in case by that time the AB trust isn't necessary to save on estate taxes)
- what property you want to hold in trust
- whether or not you would like to leave some items of trust property at your death to someone other than your spouse
- whom you want to be the final beneficiaries (the people who will inherit trust property after both spouses have died)
- who is to be the successor trustee (the person or institution who, after both spouses have died, will distribute the trust property), and
- how you should arrange for someone to manage trust property inherited by beneficiaries who are too young to handle it without supervision.

This chapter discusses the factors you should think about as you make each decision. It is organized the same way as the program is (Parts 1 through 6), so that you can easily refer to it while you're actually making your trust document. It's

a good idea, though, to read through this chapter before you sit down at the computer—it will make the whole process clearer and easier.

Checklist for Creating a Valid AB Living Trust

✔ Prepare the trust document with Quicken WillMaker Plus.

✔ Print out the trust document and sign it in front of a notary public.

✔ Transfer ownership of the property listed in the trust document into your names as trustees.

✔ When one spouse dies, get expert help to split the trust into Trust A and Trust B (or to decide whether or not to split the trust, if you used the "disclaimer trust" option).

✔ Update your trust document when needed.

How an AB Trust Works: An Overview

Here, in brief, are the important points about an AB trust:

Control of trust property. You and your spouse will both be trustees of your living trust, so you'll both have control over the property held in trust. Either spouse can act on behalf of the trust—sell or give away trust property, for example. (As a practical matter, the consent of both spouses may be necessary—see Part 2, below.)

Amendments or revocation. Both spouses must consent to change any terms of the trust document—for example, who is named as successor trustee or final beneficiary.

Either spouse can, however, revoke the trust. This way either spouse can return the situation to exactly what it was before the trust was formed. (Co-owned property is returned to both spouses, and separately owned property to the owner-spouse.)

Death of the first spouse. What happens after the death of the first spouse depends on what kind of AB trust you made. If you made a regular AB trust, without the "disclaimer" option, then the AB trust must be split into two trusts. The surviving spouse will want to hire expert help to decide exactly how assets should be divided.

- **Trust A, the bypass trust.** This trust contains the deceased spouse's share of trust assets, except any items of trust property left directly to someone other than the surviving spouse. This trust is now irrevocable; its terms cannot be changed. The surviving spouse has the right to use Trust A property but does not own it outright.
- **Trust B, the survivor's trust.** This trust contains the surviving spouse's share of trust property. The surviving spouse has complete control over and ownership of Trust B property. The survivor can also amend the trust document—for example, to name a new final beneficiary for Trust B property.

The surviving spouse is sole trustee of both trusts, and both will exist until the second spouse dies.

If you chose the "disclaimer trust" option, the surviving spouse must decide whether or not to create the bypass trust. If no bypass trust is created, the surviving spouse receives all trust property in the survivor's trust.

Death of the second spouse. When the second spouse dies, the person named in the trust document as successor trustee takes over and distributes the trust property to the final beneficiaries. The successor trustee also manages any trust property left to a young beneficiary in a child's subtrust (explained later).

EXAMPLE: William and Kay, a married couple, set up an AB living trust. In the trust document, they name their two grown children, Emily and Brendan, as final beneficiaries. They appoint Emily as successor trustee, to take over as trustee after they have both died. They decide to transfer much of their co-owned property—their house and some valuable furniture and art—to their names as trustees of the trust. Kay also puts some family heirlooms, which are her separate property, in the trust.

Kay provides, in the trust document, that her brother is to receive the heirlooms when she dies; everything else goes to William, in trust, and then to the children. William leaves all his trust property to Kay, in trust, and then to the children.

Kay dies first. William, as sole trustee, gives the heirlooms to Kay's brother, as the trust document instructs. He then splits the trust into Trust A and Trust B, each of which contains half of the couple's co-owned property. To accomplish this split, William enlists the help of an experienced estate planning attorney, who explains the tax consequences of dividing the property in different ways.

After Kay's death, William decides to make a change in his living trust document. In an amendment to the trust document, he names his 12-year-old granddaughter, Cecile, to inherit some of his trust property. He states that if Cecile is not yet 25 when he dies, the trust property she inherits will stay in a child's subtrust, managed by the successor trustee.

When William dies, Emily becomes trustee and distributes the trust property following the instructions in the trust document. She also manages the property inherited by Cecile, who is 21 at William's death, until her 25th birthday. When all the property is given to the beneficiaries, the trust ends.

Part 1: Your Names

This part is easy; just enter your names. The names you enter will determine the name of your trust. For example, if you enter "William S. Jorgensen" and "Helga M. Jorgensen," your trust will be named "The William S. Jorgensen and Helga M. Jorgensen AB Revocable Living Trust." Your names will also appear as the original trustees of your living trust. (See Part 2, below.)

Enter your name the way it appears on other formal business documents, such as your driver's license or bank accounts. This may or may not be the name on your birth certificate.

If you go by more than one name, use only one; don't enter various versions of your name joined by "aka" (also known as). Be sure that the name you use is the one that appears on the ownership documents for property you plan to hold in trust. If it isn't, it could cause confusion later, and you should change the name on your ownership documents before you transfer the property to yourselves as trustees.

EXAMPLE: You use the name William Dix for your trust but own real estate in your former name of William Geicherwitz. You should prepare and sign a new deed, changing the name of the owner to William Dix, before you prepare another deed to transfer the property to yourself as trustee.

Part 2: Trustees

To be legally valid, every living trust must have a trustee—someone to manage the property held in trust. When you create a revocable living trust with this program, you and your spouse are the trustees while you are alive. You'll name someone else to be the successor trustee, to distribute trust property to the final beneficiaries after both you and your spouse have died.

A. Your Duties as Trustees

You and your spouse will be the original trustees of your living trust. That way, both of you have control over trust property, and taxation doesn't get complicated.

You can't name someone else as trustee. In the unlikely event you and your spouse don't want to be the trustees or want only one of you to be trustee, you cannot use Quicken WillMaker Plus. See an estate planning lawyer.

1. While Both Spouses Are Alive and Well

As trustees, both of you will have complete control over the property that is held in trust.

As a day-to-day, practical matter, it makes little difference that your property is held in trust. You won't have any special duties as trustees of your trust. You do not even need to file a separate income tax return for the living trust. If trust property generates income, just report it on your personal income tax return, as if the trust did not exist.

You have the same freedom to sell, give away or mortgage trust property as you did before you put the property in trust. The only difference is that if you and your spouse must sign documents relating to the property, you do so in your capacity as trustees.

> **EXAMPLE:** Celeste and Robert want to sell a piece of land that they hold in their AB trust. They prepare a deed transferring ownership of the land to the new owner and sign the deed as "Celeste Tornetti and Robert Tornetti, trustees of the Celeste Tornetti and Robert Tornetti AB Living Trust dated February 4, 20xx."

It's important to realize that once the property is held in trust, either trustee (spouse) has authority over it. That means that either spouse can sell or give away any of the trust property—including any property that was co-owned or was the separate property of the other spouse before it was transferred to the trust. In practice, however, both spouses will probably have to consent to transfer real estate out of the living trust. Especially in community property states, buyers and title insurance companies usually insist on both spouses' signatures on transfer documents.

2. If One Spouse Becomes Incapacitated

If one spouse becomes incapacitated and unable to manage his or her affairs, the other becomes sole trustee. (If the other spouse has already died, the successor trustee takes over; see Section B, below.) You will name, in the trust document, three people who will determine whether or not you are able to manage the trust, if the question ever comes up. These people do not have to be doctors. Ideally, you will choose people who know you well and can give an unbiased opinion about whether or not you need help taking care of financial and property matters.

If one spouse asks them to, the people you choose must state, in writing, their opinion of whether or not the other spouse is capable of managing the trust. (If one or more isn't available, a spouse may rely on the opinions of the ones he or she can reach.) If a majority of them think the other spouse should act as sole trustee, he or she is authorized to do so.

The survivor has no power over property not held in the living trust, and no authority to make health care decisions for the incapacitated spouse. For this reason, it's also wise for each spouse to create documents called durable powers of attorney, giving the other spouse authority over more than trust property. (See Chapters 22 and 23.)

3. After One Spouse's Death

After one spouse dies, the surviving spouse is sole trustee. The survivor's first task is to oversee the division of the trust into two trusts, Trust A (the deceased spouse's trust) and Trust B (the survivor's). If the trust document contains the "disclaimer" clause, the surviving spouse has the option of not splitting the trust, and to instead inherit all trust property. Either way, the surviving spouse will need expert tax advice before acting. (See Chapter 21.)

Once the trust is split, it's up to the survivor to manage the deceased spouse's trust property, which is now in Trust A. The trust made by Quicken WillMaker Plus gives the surviving spouse the broadest possible authority allowed by IRS rules. (See Chapter 21.)

The survivor has two other possible duties:

- Distributing trust property to other beneficiaries. If the deceased spouse left items of trust property directly to any beneficiaries, the surviving spouse must distribute them, following the terms of the trust document. The surviving spouse has no legal power to modify the deceased spouse's intentions in any way. (See Chapter 21.) Usually, the process takes only a few weeks.
- Managing property left to a young person. If the deceased spouse left trust property to a young beneficiary and directed that it should stay in trust, the surviving spouse will be in charge of the property. This job will last until the beneficiary is old enough, under the terms of the trust, to receive the trust property outright. (See Part 6, below.)

B. The Successor Trustee

You and your spouse must choose a successor trustee—someone to act as trustee after both of you have died or can no longer manage your affairs. The successor trustee has no power or responsibility if at least one spouse is alive and capable of managing the trust.

1. The Successor Trustee's Duties After Both Spouses' Deaths

After both spouses have died, the successor trustee takes over as trustee of Trust A and Trust B. The successor trustee's job is to distribute trust property to the final beneficiaries. That is usually a straightforward process that can be completed in a few weeks. (How to transfer certain common kinds of property is explained in Chapter 21.)

The successor trustee may also have long-term duties, if the trust document creates a "child's subtrust" for trust property inherited by a young beneficiary (this is explained in Part 6, below). The trust document gives the successor trustee very broad authority, so that the trustee will be able to respond to the demands of the circumstances. For example, the trustee may invest trust funds in accounts, such as money market accounts, that are not federally insured. The trustee may also spend trust income or property for the beneficiary's health and welfare.

2. The Successor Trustee's Duties If One Spouse Is Incapacitated

The successor trustee will take over as trustee before both spouses have died only if neither spouse is able to manage the trust. The determination of the spouses' capacity to manage the trust will be made by the three people named to do so in the trust document. (See Section A, above.)

In this situation, the successor trustee has broad authority to manage the property in the living trust and use it for both spouses' health care, support and welfare. The law requires him or her to act honestly and prudently. And because the grantors are no longer the trustees, the new trustee must file an annual income tax return for the trust.

3. Choosing a Successor Trustee

The person or institution you choose as successor trustee will have a crucial role: to distribute trust property to your beneficiaries after you and your spouse have died. And if you and your spouse become incapacitated, the successor will manage trust property on your behalf; if you leave property to a young beneficiary in trust, the successor will manage that property until the beneficiary is old enough to handle it alone.

Obviously, when you are giving someone this much power and discretion, you should choose someone with good common sense whom you trust completely. If you don't know anyone who fits this description, think twice about establishing a living trust. Most people pick an adult son or daughter, other relative or close friend.

In most situations, the successor trustee will not need extensive experience in financial management; common sense, dependability and complete honesty are usually enough. A successor trustee who may have long-term responsibility over a young beneficiary's trust property needs more management and financial skills than a successor trustee whose only job is to distribute trust property. The successor trustee does have authority, however, under the terms of the trust document, to get any reasonably necessary professional help—from an accountant, lawyer or tax preparer, perhaps—and pay for it out of trust assets.

Usually, it makes sense to name just one person as successor trustee, to avoid any possibility of conflicts. But it's legal and may be desirable to name more than one person. For example, you might name two or more of your children, if you don't expect any disagreements between them

and you think one of them might feel hurt and left out if not named.

Having more than one successor trustee is especially likely to cause serious problems if you leave property to a young beneficiary in a child's subtrust. The trustees may have to manage a young beneficiary's property for many years and will have many decisions to make about how to spend the money—greatly increasing the potential for conflict. (Children's subtrusts are discussed in Part 6, below.)

If you name more than one successor trustee, and one of them can't serve, the others will serve. If none of them can serve, the alternate you name (in the next section of the program) will take over.

It's perfectly legal to name a beneficiary of the trust (someone who will inherit trust property) as successor trustee. In fact, it's common.

EXAMPLE: Mildred and James name their only child, Allison, to be both final beneficiary and successor trustee of their AB living trust. When James dies, Mildred manages both Trust A and Trust B. When Mildred dies, Allison uses her authority as trustee to transfer the property in both Trust A and Trust B to herself, the final beneficiary.

Institutions as Successor Trustees

Normally, your first choice as successor trustee should be a flesh-and-blood person, not the trust department of a bank or other institution. Institutional trustees charge hefty fees, which come out of the trust property and leave less for your beneficiaries. And most aren't even interested in small living trusts—ones that contain less than several hundred thousand dollars' worth of property.

But if there's no close relative or friend you think is capable of serving as your successor trustee, probably your best bet is to consider naming a private trust services company as successor trustee. Typically, their fees are pricey but less than a bank's, and your affairs will probably receive more personal attention.

For a very large living trust, another possibility is to name a person and an institution as cosuccessor trustees. The bank or trust services company can do most of the paperwork, and the person can keep an eye on things and approve all transactions.

The successor trustee does not have to live in the same state as you do. But if you are choosing between someone local and someone far away, think about how convenient it will be for the person you choose to distribute the living trust property after your death. Someone close by will probably have an easier job, especially with real estate transfers. But for transfers of property such as securities and bank accounts, it usually won't make much difference where the successor trustee lives.

Obviously, before you and your spouse finalize your trust, you must check with the person you've chosen to be your successor trustee. You want to be sure your choice is willing to serve. If you don't, you may well create problems down the line. The person you've chosen may not want to serve, for a variety of reasons. And even if the person would be willing, if he or she doesn't know of his or her responsibilities, transfer of trust property after your death could be delayed.

If you choose an institution, you must check out the minimum size of trust it will accept and the fees it charges for management and make arrangements for how the institution will take over as trustee at the second spouse's death.

Avoiding Conflicts With Your Will and Other Documents

Your AB living trust gives your spouse the authority to manage trust property if you become incapacitated. To avoid conflicts, you should also give your spouse authority to make other decisions if you can't:

- In your will, appoint your spouse to be executor, to be responsible for distributing property left through your will.
- In your durable power of attorney for finances, appoint your spouse to be your "attorney-in-fact," to have authority to make decisions about property not held in trust if you become incapacitated.

If you do choose different people to be your attorney-in-fact and successor trustee, each will have a role if you become incapacitated. The successor trustee will be in charge of all trust property, and the attorney-in-fact will have authority over property not held in trust.

4. Payment of the Successor Trustee

Typically, the successor trustee of an AB trust isn't paid. This is because, in most cases, the successor trustee's only job is to distribute the trust property to the final beneficiaries—and often, the successor trustee inherits the property anyway.

An exception is a successor trustee who manages the property in a child's subtrust. In that case, the successor trustee is entitled, under the terms of the trust document, to "reasonable compensation." The successor trustee decides what is reasonable and takes it from the trust property left to the young beneficiary.

Allowing the successor trustee to set the amount of the payment can work well, as long as your successor trustee is completely trustworthy. If the young beneficiary feels the trustee's fees are much too high, he or she will have to go to court to challenge them.

5. Naming an Alternate Successor Trustee

We'll ask you to name an alternate successor trustee, in case your first choice is unable to serve.

If you name two or more successor trustees, the alternate won't become trustee unless none of your original choices can serve.

> EXAMPLE: Caroline and Oscar name their two grown children, Eugene and Vanessa, as successor trustees. They name a close friend, Nicole, as alternate successor trustee. After Caroline and Oscar have died, Vanessa is ill and can't serve as trustee. Eugene acts as sole successor trustee. If he were also unable to serve, Nicole would take over.

If no one you named in the trust document can serve, the last trustee to serve has the power to appoint, in writing, another successor trustee. (See Chapter 21.)

> EXAMPLE: To continue the previous example, if Nicole were ill and didn't have the energy to serve as successor trustee, she could appoint someone else to serve as trustee.

Part 3: Property to Be Put in Trust

In this part of the program, you and your spouse must list each item of property—both jointly owned and separately owned—you want to hold in trust. It will take some thought to decide what property to include and how to list it in the trust document.

This is a crucial step. Any property you don't list will not go into your living trust and will not pass under the terms of the trust. It may instead have to go through probate.

Adding property to the trust later. If you mistakenly leave something out or acquire more valuable property after you create your trust, you will be able to add it to your living trust. Chapter 20 explains how.

Listing property in the trust document is not enough. If an item has a title (ownership) document, such as a deed or title slip, you must change the title document to show that you, as trustee, are the legal owner of the property. If you don't, the trust won't work. *You should transfer ownership as soon as possible after you print out and sign your Declaration of Trust.* Instructions are in Chapter 19.

A. Taking Inventory of Your Valuable Property

Before you begin to list your property in the program, sort out what you have. First, get out a pencil or your word processor and list all the valuable items of property you own. The categories below should jog your memory.

Making a list helps for two reasons. First, when you make your trust document, you'll have to list and describe every item (or group of items, in some circumstances) anyway. You can group items together if it will be clear what you mean and you don't feel a need to specifically describe any item in the group. For example, if you want to leave all your books through your trust, there's no need to describe each one individually—unless your collection includes some particularly valuable or important books that you want to make extra sure get to the beneficiary.

Second, listing your assets this way will help you get an idea of their total monetary value. If either of you owns assets worth more than the federal estate tax exempt amount, an AB trust won't completely shelter your estate from federal estate tax. You may want to explore other ways of lessening the tax burden.

For purposes of estimating your net worth, you don't need precise figures—so don't run out and get appraisals. After all, your assets and their value will undoubtedly change before your death. You just need a ballpark estimate.

Getting organized. While you're taking stock of all your valuable property, it might be a good time to go a step further and gather the information your family will need at your death. For help collecting this information, use Quicken WillMaker Plus's "Information for Caregivers and Survivors" form.

Valuable Property	
Animals	Real estate
Antiques	–Agricultural land
Appliances	–Boat/marina dock
Art	space
Books	–Co-op
Business interests	–Condo
–Sole proprietorship	–Duplex
–Partnership	–House
–Corporation	–Mobile home
–Limited liability co.	–Rental property
Business property*	–Time-share
Cameras & photo	–Undeveloped land
equipment	–Vacation house
Cash accounts	Retirement accounts**
–Certificates of deposit	Royalties
–Checking	Securities
–Money market funds	–Bonds
–Savings	–Commodities
China, crystal, silver	–Mutual funds
Coins, stamps	–Stocks
Collectibles	–U.S. bills, notes
Computers	and bonds
Copyrights, patents,	Tools
trademarks	Vehicles
Electronic equipment	–Bicycles
Furniture	–Cars
Furs	–Motorcycles
Jewelry	–Motorhomes/RVs
Limited partnership	–Planes
Precious metals	–Boats

*If you own a sole proprietorship
**Can't be held in trust (see Section B, below)

B. Who Owns What?

You'll need to label each item as "his, hers or ours" when you enter it in the program. This is because when the first spouse dies, you need to know what property should be divided between Trust A and Trust B. And you might want to leave some of your separate property items to someone other than your spouse.

For many couples, especially if they've been married a long time, nearly everything is owned together. But if you haven't been married long, or have been married before, you may own a sizeable amount of property separately. If you're unsure about who owns what, read this section, which explains the ownership rules of your state.

1. Community Property States

Alaska*	Nevada
Arizona	New Mexico
California**	Texas
Idaho	Washington
Louisiana	Wisconsin

*If spouses sign a community property agreement.

**Registered domestic partners are also covered by California's community property laws.

If you live in a community property state and you aren't sure who owns what, don't rely on whose name is on the title document. For example, if while you were married you bought a house with money you earned, your spouse legally owns a share of that property—even if only your name is on the deed.

Generally, any property that either spouse earns or acquires during the marriage (before permanent separation) is community property. Both spouses (the "community") own it together. The main exception to this rule is that property one spouse acquires by gift or inheritance, or acquired before the marriage, belongs to that spouse alone.

Even separate property may, however, turn into community property if it is mixed ("commingled") with community property. For example, if you deposit separate property funds into a joint bank account and then make more deposits and withdrawals, making it impossible to tell what part of the account is separate money, it's all considered community property.

2. Non-Community Property States

Alabama	Missouri
Alaska*	Montana
Arkansas	Nebraska
Colorado	New Hampshire
Connecticut	New Jersey
Delaware	New York
District of Columbia	North Carolina
Florida	North Dakota
Georgia	Ohio
Hawaii	Oklahoma
Illinois	Oregon
Indiana	Pennsylvania
Iowa	Rhode Island
Kansas	South Carolina
Kentucky	South Dakota
Maine	Tennessee
Maryland	Utah
Massachusetts	Vermont
Michigan	Virginia
Minnesota	West Virginia
Mississippi	Wyoming

* Spouses can, however, create community property by signing a community property agreement.

In these states, it is usually fairly simple to figure out who owns what. If the property has a title document—for example, a deed to real estate or a car title slip—then the spouse whose name is on the title is the owner. If the property doesn't have a title document, it belongs to the spouse who paid for it or received it as a gift. (It's possible, though, that if there were a dispute, a judge could determine, based on the circumstances, that a spouse whose name is not on the title document might own an interest in the property.)

If the trust is revoked, the property will be returned to each spouse based on the same ownership rights they had before the property was held in trust.

C. How Much Property to Put in Your AB Trust

Now that you've got a list of what you and your spouse own, you're ready to decide what items you want to hold in trust. You need to think about two issues: the total value of property you want to hold in trust, and what kinds of property are best suited to an AB trust. This section discusses "how much"; the next one discusses "which assets."

1. How Much the AB Trust Can Shelter

If you make an AB trust with Quicken WillMaker Plus, you and your spouse can shelter from estate tax twice the amount of the federal estate tax exemption. That amount depends on the year of the first spouse's death, as shown below.

The Estate Tax Exemption	
Year of Death	Estate Tax Exemption
2005	$1.5 million
2006, 2007, 2008	$2 million
2009	$3.5 million
2010	Estate tax repealed
2011	$1 million unless Congress extends repeal

EXAMPLE: Maureen and Lester have a net worth of $2 million, shared equally. They create an AB trust together. Lester dies in 2005, when he can leave up to $1.5 million free of estate tax. His $1 million worth of trust property passes to the bypass trust (Trust A). His estate doesn't owe any tax because the amount he leaves is below the federal estate tax exemption for that year.

When Maureen dies later in 2005, her property (let's say its value has remained at $1 million, though of course it could have gone up or down) is now subject to tax. But because it is also under the estate tax exemption for that year, no tax is due.

a. The Regular AB Trust

If you don't expect your half of your combined estate to exceed the estate tax exemption, you can safely put everything in your AB trust. No estate tax will be due.

If, however, either spouse has an estate that exceeds the federal estate tax exemption in the year of death, and you create a regular AB trust (without a "disclaimer" clause, as discussed below), the estate will owe federal estate tax. This is true even if the total combined value of the couple's estates is less than the amount that could be sheltered by an AB trust.

EXAMPLE: Lidia and Mark create an AB trust, and Lidia dies in 2005. At her death, her share of the trust property is worth $1.8 million—more than the $1.5 million that can pass tax-free in 2005. Her estate owes federal estate tax. When Mark dies in 2008, his estate is valued at $1.8 million, too. But in 2008, an estate of that size doesn't owe any tax.

Obviously, none of us knows when we're going to die. So for purposes of estate planning (only!), you may want to take the most pessimistic route possible and assume that the bypass trust will become operational—that is, a spouse will die—in the year you create the trust. So if you're doing your trust planning in 2005, you know that your AB trust will shelter up to $3 million from estate tax. If both you and your spouse live until at least 2006, however, your trust could shelter up to $4 million. And if you live until 2010, you won't owe estate tax no matter how much you leave. After that, it all depends on Congress.

b.   The Disclaimer AB Trust

Another way to deal with the uncertainty is to make a "disclaimer" trust, as discussed in Chapter 14. Including the disclaimer clause in your Quicken WillMaker Plus trust allows the surviving spouse to decide, after the first spouse dies, how much trust property (if any) should go into the bypass trust. The spouse can "disclaim" property he or she would otherwise inherit, sending that property (under the terms of the trust document) into the bypass trust.

The only limit is that the spouse cannot transfer more than the amount of the current estate tax exemption—which means that the bypass trust won't ever be large enough to be subject to estate tax.

EXAMPLE: Charlotte and her husband Winston make a disclaimer trust. They leave everything to each other and name their children as the final beneficiaries.

When Winston dies in 2008, the couple's trust property is worth $2.5 million. The federal estate tax exemption for that year is $2 million.

After talking with a tax expert, Charlotte decides to split the AB trust into Trust A, the bypass trust, and Trust B, her survivor's trust. She further decides she wants $1 million to go into the bypass trust. That will leave $1.5 million under her complete control. She figures that even if she invests wisely and increases the value of her holdings, estate tax still won't be due at her death.

To put this plan into effect, Charlotte's lawyer draws up a disclaimer—a document in which Charlotte gives up (disclaims) $1 million of the trust property. Under the terms of the trust document, the property goes into Trust A, the bypass trust. Charlotte will have the right to use the income it produces and to spend the principal itself for certain purposes allowed by law. At her death it will go to the couple's children.

Watch out for state estate taxes. Because of recent changes in federal and state tax laws, estate taxes imposed by states are becoming of greater concern to many people. It may no longer be enough just to plan to avoid federal estate taxes.

Before 2005, if an estate was big enough to pay federal estate tax, the state would claim a share of the money. This tax was called a pick-up or sponge tax. It didn't actually increase the tax paid; the state was merely entitled, by federal law, to take a certain percentage of the federal tax due. But states no longer get a share of federal estate taxes. To make up for this loss of revenue, some states have enacted their own estate taxes, which are no longer connected to the federal system. Estates may have to pay state tax even if they aren't large enough to pay federal estate tax.

This is true even if you use an AB trust. If you leave an amount of property that might exceed your state's threshold for state estate tax, you may owe state tax even though your estate doesn't exceed the threshold for federal estate tax.

EXAMPLE: Roy and his wife Ann, who are Rhode Island residents, make an AB trust. At Roy's death, his share of the couple's property is $800,000. That amount goes in Trust B, the deceased spouse's trust. Because Roy's estate is under the federal estate tax threshold, it does not owe federal estate tax. It will, however, owe Rhode Island estate tax, because that state no longer just imposes a pick-up estate tax; it currently taxes estates of $675,000 or more.

In most cases, the state tax amount will not be huge. But if you're concerned about it, see a tax lawyer in your state (and, if you own real estate elsewhere, in that state, too) who can bring you up to date on this rapidly changing area of the law.

2. What to Do If One Spouse Owns More Than the Estate Tax Exemption

If your individual estate may exceed the estate tax exemption, you need to think about how much of your property you want to leave to your AB trust. For example, if you and your spouse have shared property worth $4 million, and your share is

worth $3 million, if you leave it all to your Trust A, part of it will be subject to estate tax if you die before 2009.

There are several strategies to deal with this issue:

- Use a disclaimer trust, as discussed above in Section 1b.
- Use an AB trust with a "formula" clause. This clause directs that only property worth up to the amount of the estate tax exemption in the year of death be put into Trust A, the bypass trust. It's especially desirable if it seems likely that one spouse will long outlive the other; the survivor will have many years to use the money and take measures to reduce eventual estate taxes. (Quicken WillMaker Plus does not make a formula trust.)
- Leave some of your property (whatever exceeds the exempt amount) directly to your spouse, who won't pay tax on it because of the marital deduction.
- Leave some of your property (whatever exceeds the exempt amount) in a QTIP or QDOT trust; this lets you defer tax until the death of the second spouse and control who inherits it after the surviving spouse dies. (Quicken WillMaker Plus does not make QTIP or QDOT trusts.)
- If one spouse's estate is much larger than the other's, equalize the size of the estates by transferring some property to the spouse with less property. This may bring the other spouse's estate below the estate tax exemption, or at least reduce the amount of tax owed.
- Leave all your property to the bypass trust, fully expecting that some estate tax may be due at your death. If you don't expect the second spouse to live much longer than the first spouse, this may actually save money on taxes, by making each spouse's estate closer in value.

• Reduce the size of your estate by making tax-free gifts of some of your property while you're alive.

 If you need more. As you can see, there's no one solution that's right for everyone, especially in light of the estate tax law uncertainty. If you own more property than an AB trust can currently shelter, see a lawyer to discuss which strategy is right for you.

D. What Kinds of Property to Hold in Trust

Think about including:
- houses and other real estate
- jewelry, antiques, furs and valuable furniture
- stock in a closely held corporation
- stock, bond and other security accounts held by brokerages
- small business interests
- money market and bank accounts
- patents and copyrights
- precious metals
- valuable works of art
- valuable collections of stamps, coins or other objects.

1. Real Estate

The most valuable thing most people own is their real estate: their house, condominium or land. You'll probably want to hold your real estate in your AB trust.

If you or your spouse owns real estate with someone else, you can transfer just your interest in it to your living trust. You won't need to specify that your share is one-half or some other fraction. For example, if you and your sister own a house together, you need only list "the house at 7989 Lafayette Court, Boston, MA." Your trust document will state that you have transferred all your interest in that property to the trust. The share of the property owned by your sister, obviously, is not included.

Co-op apartments. If you own shares in a co-op corporation that owns your apartment, you'll have to hold your shares in trust. Some corporations are reluctant to let a trustee own shares; check the co-op corporation's rules to see whether the transfer is allowed.

2. Small Business Interests

The delay, expense and court intrusion of probate can be especially detrimental to an ongoing small business. And if a business is a major asset, you'll want to include it in your trust to avoid estate tax.

 If you want to control the long-term management of your business. If you want to control the long-term management of your business, however, a revocable living trust is not the right vehicle. See an estate planning lawyer to draft a different kind of trust, with provisions tailored to your situation.

Different kinds of business organizations present different issues when you want to hold your interest in your living trust:

Sole proprietorships. If you (or you and your spouse) operate your business as a sole proprietorship, with all business assets held in your own name, you can simply transfer your business property to yourselves as trustees. You should also transfer the business's name itself; that transfers the customer goodwill associated with the name.

Partnership interests. If you operate your business as a partnership with other people, you can probably transfer your partnership share to your living trust. If there is a partnership certificate, it must be changed.

Some partnership agreements require the people who inherit a deceased partner's share of the business to offer that share to the other partners before taking it. But that happens after death, so it shouldn't affect your ability to transfer the property through a living trust.

It's not common, but a partnership agreement may limit or forbid holding your interest in a living trust. If yours does, you and your partners may want to see a lawyer before you make any changes.

Solely owned corporations. If you own all the stock of a corporation, you should have no difficulty transferring it to you and your spouse as trustees.

Closely held corporations. A closely held corporation is a corporation that doesn't sell shares to the public. All its shares are owned by a few people who are usually actively involved in running the business. Normally, you can use a living trust to transfer shares in a closely held corporation by listing the stock in the trust document and then having the stock certificates reissued in the trustees' names.

You'll want to check the corporation's bylaws and articles of incorporation to be sure you will still have voting rights in your capacity as trustee of the living trust; usually, this is not a problem. If it is, you and the other shareholders should be able to amend the corporation's bylaws to allow it.

There may, however, be restrictions that affect the transfer of shares. Check the corporation's bylaws and articles of incorporation, as well as any separate shareholders' agreements. One fairly common rule is that surviving shareholders (or the corporation) have the right to buy the shares of a deceased shareholder. In that case, you can still use a living trust to transfer the shares, but the people who inherit them may have to sell them.

Limited liability companies. If your small business is an LLC, you'll need the consent of a majority or all of the other owners (check your operating agreement) before you can transfer your interest to yourself as trustee. Getting the other owners to agree shouldn't be a problem; they'll just want to know that you, as trustee of your own trust, will have authority to vote on LLC decisions. Another way to address this concern would be to transfer your economic interest in the LLC, but not your right to vote.

3. Bank Accounts

It's not difficult to transfer bank accounts to your living trust.

You may not, however, want to hold your personal checking accounts in a living trust—it can be difficult to cash checks on accounts owned in a trustee's name.

Jointly owned accounts. If you want to hold a joint account in your living trust, things are more complicated, and you may just want to name a payable-on-death beneficiary for the account instead. The reason is that almost all joint accounts have what's called the "right of survivorship," which means that when one owner dies, the survivor automatically owns all the money in the account. A provision in a will or living trust can't override that. So no matter what your living trust says, the share of the first spouse to die will go to the survivor; the money in the account will go to a trust beneficiary only when the second spouse dies.

EXAMPLE: Joan and Alex have a joint savings account. They go to the bank and change the registration card on the account to read "Joan and Alex Crookshank, trustees of the Joan and

Alex Crookshank AB Revocable Living Trust dated August 23, 20xx." In the trust document, Alex leaves his half of the account to his friend Max. Alex dies first. The account is now owned by Joan; Max won't inherit anything.

4. Vehicles and Property That Is Often Sold

Some kinds of property are cumbersome to keep in a living trust. It's not a legal problem, just a practical one. Two common examples are:

- **Cars or other vehicles you use.** Having registration and insurance in the your name as trustee could be confusing, and some insurance companies might balk. If you have valuable antique autos, or a mobile home that is permanently attached to land and considered real estate under your state's law, however, you may want to go ahead and hold them in trust. You should be able to find an insurance company that will cooperate.
- **Property you buy or sell frequently.** If you don't expect to own the property at your death, there's no compelling reason to hold it in trust. (Remember, probate and taxes aren't issues until after your death.) On the other hand, if you're buying property, it's no more trouble to acquire it in your name as trustee.

5. Life Insurance

If you own a life insurance policy at your death, the insurance company will give the proceeds to the named beneficiary without probate. The proceeds are, however, considered part of your estate for federal estate tax purposes.

If you have named a minor or young adult as the beneficiary of an insurance policy, you may want to name your living trust instead. Then, in the trust document, you name the child as beneficiary of any insurance proceeds paid to the trust and arrange for an adult to manage the policy proceeds if the beneficiary is still young when you die. If you don't arrange for management of the money, and the beneficiary is still a minor (under 18) when you die, a court will have to appoint a financial guardian after your death. (Young beneficiaries are discussed in Part 6, below.)

Passing the proceeds of a life insurance policy through your living trust is a bit more complicated than leaving other property this way. You must take two steps:

1. Name the living trust as the beneficiary of your life insurance policy. (Your insurance agent will have a form that lets you change the beneficiary of the policy.)
2. When you list property items in the living trust document, list the proceeds of the policy, not the policy itself. (Section E, below, contains sample descriptions.)

6. Securities

If you buy and sell stocks regularly, you may not want to go to the trouble of acquiring and selling them using your authority as trustees of the trust. Fortunately, there's an easier way to do it: Hold your stocks in a brokerage account that you own as trustees. All securities in the account are then held in your trust. In most states, you can also register securities in "beneficiary" form so that they avoid probate, without holding them in trust.

Stock in closely held corporations. See Section 2, above. In most states, you can also register securities in "beneficiary" form so they avoid probate without holding them in trust.

7. Cash

If you want to leave a few cash gifts to beneficiaries—for example, $5,000 to a relative, friend or charity—in addition to leaving the bulk of your property to your spouse, you can do so. You can't, however, just list "$5,000 cash" in your trust document—you must identify exactly where that cash is coming from. The way to do it is to hold a cash account (a savings or money market account, for example) in your trust and name a beneficiary to receive the contents of the account. So to leave $5,000 to cousin Fred, all you have to do is put the money in a bank or money market account, transfer it to yourself as trustee and name Fred, in the trust document, as the beneficiary of the account.

Especially if the amounts involved are small, it may be simpler, however, to just name a payable-on-death beneficiary for a bank account. (See Chapter 13.)

8. Community Property

Alaska*	Nevada
Arizona	New Mexico
California**	Texas
Idaho	Washington
Louisiana	Wisconsin

*If spouses sign a community property agreement.

**Registered domestic partners are also covered by California's community property laws.

Community property (owned by both spouses equally) held in your living trust will stay community property. Separately owned property (property of only one spouse) will remain the separate property of the spouse. That means that community property held in trust is still eligible for the favorable tax treatment given community property at one spouse's death. (Both halves of community property left to the surviving spouse get a date-of-death tax basis for income tax purposes, if the value of the property has gone up.)

If either spouse revokes the living trust, ownership of the property will go back to the spouses as it was before the property was held in the living trust. Community property goes back to both spouses equally, and separate property goes to the spouse who owned it.

9. Retirement Plans

Individual retirement accounts cannot be held in trust.

You can name a living trust as a beneficiary, but it's usually not a good idea. Under current IRS rules, money left to a trust is distributed based on the life expectancy of the trust beneficiary.

 Resources. *IRAs, 401(k)s & Other Retirement Plans: Taking Your Money Out,* by Twila Slesnick and John C. Suttle (Nolo), explains the options of those who inherit money in a retirement account.

10. Other Valuable Property

Other valuable items—everything from jewelry and antiques to boats and airplanes—can also be placed in trust.

E. How to Describe Trust Property

When we ask you to list the property you want to hold in your trust, describe each item clearly enough so that it will get to the right person after your death. Most or all of your trust property will go for the use of your spouse, in Trust A. If, however, you're going to leave an item as a specific gift, just make sure your surviving spouse (or successor trustee, if you're the second spouse to die) can identify the property and transfer it to the beneficiary. No magic legal words are required.

Think about whom the property will ultimately go to. If you're leaving everything to one person, or just a few, there's less need to go into great detail. But if there will be a number of trust beneficiaries and objects could be confused, be more specific about each one. When in doubt, err on the side of including more information; describe particularly valuable items much as you would if you were listing them on an insurance policy.

Rules for Entering Descriptions of Trust Property

- Don't use "my" in a description. Don't, for example, enter "my books" or "my stereo system." That's because once the property is in the living trust, it doesn't belong to you anymore—it belongs to the trust.
- Don't begin a description with a capital letter (unless it must begin with a proper name, like "Steinway"). That's because the descriptions will be inserted into a sentence in the trust document, and it would look odd to see a capital letter in the middle of a sentence.
- Don't end a description with a period. Again, this is because the descriptions will be inserted into a sentence in the trust document.

Here are some sample descriptions:

Real estate

- "the house at 321 Glen St., Omaha, NE"
- "the house at 4444 Casey Road, Fandon, Illinois and the 20-acre parcel on which it is located"

Usually, the street address is enough. It's not necessary to use the "legal description" found on the deed, which gives a subdivision plat number or a metes-and-bounds description. But if the property has no street address—for example, if it is undeveloped land out in the country—you will need to carefully copy the full legal description, word for word, from the deed.

If you own a house and several adjacent lots, it's a good idea to indicate that you are transferring the entire parcel to your living trust by describing the land as well as the house.

If you own the property with someone else and are transferring only your share, you don't need to specify the share you own. Just describe the property. The trust document will show that you are transferring all your interest in the property, whatever share that is, to the living trust.

Bank accounts

- "Savings Account No. 9384-387, Arlington Bank, Arlington, MN"
- "Money Market Account 47-223 at Charles Schwab & Co., Inc., San Francisco, CA"

Household items

- "all the furniture normally kept in the house at 44123 Derby Ave., Ross, KY"
- "the antique brass bed in the master bedroom in the house at 33 Walker Ave., Fort Lee, New Jersey"

- "all furniture and household items normally kept in the house at 869 Hopkins St., Great Falls, Montana"

Sole proprietorship business property

- "Mulligan's Fish Market"
- "Fourth Street Records and CDs"
- "all accounts receivable of the business known as Garcia's Restaurant, 988 17th St., Atlanta, GA"
- "all food preparation and storage equipment, including refrigerator, freezer, hand mixers and slicer used at Garcia's Restaurant, 988 17th St., Atlanta, GA"

As explained in Section D, above, you should both list the name of the business and separately list items of business property.

Partnership interest

- "the Don and Dan's Bait Shop Partnership owned by the grantor before being held in this living trust"

Because a partnership is a legal entity that can own property, you don't need to list items of property owned by the partnership.

Shares in a closely held corporation

- "The stock of ABC Hardware, Inc."

Shares in a solely owned corporation

- "all shares in the XYZ Corporation"
- "all stock in Fern's Olde Antique Shoppe, Inc., 23 Turnbridge Court, Danbury, Connecticut"

Securities

- "all securities in account No. 3999-34-33 at Smith Brokerage, 33 Lowell Place, New York, NY"
- "200 shares of General Industries, Inc. stock"

- "Good Investment Co. mutual fund account No. 888-09-09"

Life insurance proceeds

- "the proceeds of Acme Co. Life Insurance Policy #9992A"

Miscellaneous items

- "Macintosh computer (serial number 129311) with keyboard (serial number 165895)"
- "the medical textbooks in the office at 1702 Parker Towers, San Francisco, CA"
- "the stamp collection usually kept at 321 Glen St., Omaha, NE"
- "the collection of European stamps, including [describe particularly valuable stamps], usually kept at 440 Loma Prieta Blvd., #450, San Jose, CA"
- "the Martin D-35 acoustic guitar, serial number 477597"
- "the signed 1960 Ernie Banks baseball card kept in safe deposit box 234, First National Bank of Augusta, Augusta, IL"
- "the Baldwin upright piano kept at 985 Dawson Court, South Brenly, Massachusetts"

Part 4: Specific Beneficiaries

Once you've entered a list of the property you're going to hold in trust, the next step is to say whom you want to inherit it. With an AB trust, this is pretty simple, because each spouse leaves all or the bulk of his or her trust property to the other, in Trust A. (This is true whether or not you use the disclaimer trust option.) So all each spouse has to do is name:

- beneficiaries for any specific gifts—items you don't want to leave to the surviving spouse in Trust A, and

• the final beneficiaries, who inherit all the trust property after both spouses have died. (See Part 5, below.)

EXAMPLE: Roger and Marilyn create an AB trust. Each puts co-owned and separately owned property in the trust. They name their three children as final beneficiaries. When Roger dies, Marilyn takes over as sole trustee and splits the AB trust into Trust A (the irrevocable bypass trust) and Trust B (her ongoing revocable trust). When Marilyn dies, the successor trustee distributes the property to the children.

The beneficiaries you name in your trust document are not entitled to any trust property while both spouses are alive. You can amend your trust document and change the beneficiaries until your death.

⚠️ **Children's rights to inherit.** In most circumstances, you don't have to leave anything to your children. But if you want to disinherit a child, it's a good idea to make a will and specifically mention the child in it. (See Chapter 4.)

A. Choosing Specific Beneficiaries

We'll ask you first whether you want make any specific gifts or just leave all trust property in Trust A for your spouse (and, eventually, the final beneficiaries). Just skip this part if you want to leave everything to your spouse in the bypass trust. If you choose to make some specific gifts, we'll show you a list of all the items you listed earlier. You can choose any number of them and name beneficiaries (including your spouse, if you wish) for them.

If you leave your spouse a specific gift, it will stay in his or her revocable living trust—not in Trust A, the irrevocable bypass trust—if you are the first to die.

EXAMPLE: Max and Joan make an AB trust. Max wants Joan to have some property outright, with no restrictions, so he leaves some items to her directly as specific gifts. Max dies first. The specific gifts go into Trust B, Joan's revocable living trust. (See Chapter 21.)

As you name your specific beneficiaries, remember that when it comes to property you and your spouse co-own, you're naming people to receive only your share. Only your interest in the co-owned property will go to the beneficiary.

EXAMPLE: Marcia and Perry transfer all the property they own together into their living trust. Perry leaves his half-interest in the couple's vacation cabin to his son from a previous marriage, Eric. When Perry dies, his half-interest in the cabin will go to Eric, who will co-own it with Marcia.

B. Alternate Beneficiaries

You can name an alternate beneficiary for every person you name as a specific beneficiary. The alternate will get the property left to the primary beneficiary if your first choice does not live for more than 120 hours (five days) after your death. This survivorship period ensures that if you and a primary beneficiary die simultaneously or almost so, the property will go to the alternate beneficiary you chose, not to the primary beneficiary's heirs.

You don't have to name an alternate for a charitable (or other) institution you name as a beneficiary. If the institution is well established, it is probably safe to assume that it will still exist at your death.

You can name more than one person or institution as alternate beneficiaries. If you do, they will share equally any property they inherit.

C. Common Concerns

Here are some issues that may come up when you name beneficiaries.

1. Naming Minors or Young Adults

You can name minors (children under 18) to inherit trust property. If a beneficiary you name is a minor or a young adult who can't yet manage property without help, you can arrange for an adult to manage the trust property for the beneficiary. (See Part 6, below.)

2. Naming Your Successor Trustee as a Beneficiary

It's very common, and perfectly legal, to make the person you named to be successor trustee (the person who will distribute trust property after the second spouse dies) a beneficiary as well.

> **EXAMPLE:** Nora and Sean name their son Liam as successor trustee of their AB trust. They name Liam and his sister Meg as final beneficiaries. After Nora and Sean have both died, Liam, acting as trustee, will transfer ownership of the trust property to himself and Meg.

3. Naming More Than One Beneficiary to Share Property

You can name more than one beneficiary to share any item of trust property. Obviously, give some thought to whether or not the beneficiaries are likely to get along. If they are incompatible, disagreements could arise over taking care of property or deciding whether or not to sell it.

Cobeneficiaries will share property equally unless you state otherwise. We'll ask you, after you enter their names, whether or not you want them to get equal shares.

> **EXAMPLE:** Georgia wants to leave her house to her two children, Ross and Ryan, but wants Ross to have a 75% share of it. She enters their names and then, on a later screen, enters their interests, in fractions: 3/4 for Ross and 1/4 for Ryan.
>
> When the children inherit the property, they own it together. But Ross will be liable for 75% of the taxes and upkeep cost and entitled to 75% of any income the house produces. If they sell it, Ross will be entitled to 75% of the proceeds.

D. Entering Beneficiaries' Names

When you enter a beneficiary's name, use the name by which the beneficiary is known for purposes such as a bank account or driver's license. Generally, if the name you use clearly and unambiguously identifies the person, it is sufficient.

If you name an institution (charitable or not) to inherit trust property, enter its complete name. It may be commonly known by a shortened version, which could cause confusion if there are similarly named organizations. Call to ask if you're unsure. (An institution that stands to inherit some of your money will be more than happy to help you.) Also be sure to specify if you want a specific branch of a national organization to receive your gift—for example, a local chapter of the Sierra Club.

Cobeneficiaries. Simply enter their names in the box on the screen. Type the names one per line.

Always use the beneficiaries' actual names; don't use collective terms such as "my children." It's not always clear who is included in such descriptions. And there can be serious confusion if one of the group dies before you do.

Part 5: Final Beneficiaries

Final beneficiaries are the people or organizations that inherit trust property after both spouses have died.

A. How It Works

Each spouse names final beneficiaries separately, although in most cases they name the same people. If they do name the same people, then the final beneficiaries inherit trust property after the second spouse dies.

> **EXAMPLE:** Peggy and Michael make their AB trust, naming their two children as final beneficiaries. The children won't inherit anything until after Peggy and Michael have both died; then they will inherit the property in Trusts A and B.

You and your spouse, however, can name different final beneficiaries. That's because each of you chooses final beneficiaries for your share of the trust property. For example, if you have children from a previous marriage, you may want to name them as your final beneficiaries, while your spouse names someone else.

> **EXAMPLE:** Peggy and Basil both have children from previous marriages. When they

make their AB trust, each names his own children as final beneficiaries. Basil dies first; his share of the trust property goes into Trust A, the bypass trust, for Peggy to use until her death. Peggy's share goes into Trust B, which she owns outright. When Peggy dies five years later, her children get the Trust B property, and Basil's children inherit the Trust A property.

Things may work a little differently if you choose to include the disclaimer option in your trust document, essentially making the bypass trust optional.

If the spouses name the same final beneficiaries, nothing changes. After both spouses have died, those final beneficiaries will inherit all the trust property, whether or not the surviving spouse decided to create the bypass trust.

If the spouses name different final beneficiaries, however, they can't be sure what trust property the final beneficiaries of the first spouse to die will inherit. Those beneficiaries might not inherit anything from the trust. That's because the surviving spouse decides how much trust property, if any, goes into the bypass trust. If the surviving spouse decides that a bypass trust isn't necessary to save on estate taxes, it won't be created, and there will be nothing for the final beneficiaries of that trust to inherit when the second spouse dies.

> **EXAMPLE:** Clarisse and Harold make a disclaimer trust. Clarisse names her daughter from a previous marriage as her final beneficiary, and Harold names his son from his previous marriage.
>
> When Harold dies, the estate tax exemption has risen so high that his widow Clarisse decides there's no tax reason to split the AB

trust and create the irrevocable bypass trust. So, under the terms of the trust, she does nothing and inherits all the trust property. When she dies, the property goes to her final beneficiary, her daughter. Harold's son inherits no trust property.

This isn't a problem unless the spouses name different final beneficiaries and both want to be sure that their own final beneficiaries will inherit. In that situation, a disclaimer trust isn't a good idea.

B. Choosing Final Beneficiaries

Most couples name their children as their final beneficiaries, but you can name anyone you wish. (If for some reason you don't want to leave anything to a child, you should make a will and specifically mention the child in it. See Chapter 13.)

Here are some other common choices.

1. The Successor Trustee

It's fine to name someone as both your successor trustee and a final beneficiary.

2. Charities

You can name a charity as a final beneficiary, but doing so raises some issues you should think about.

Problems may arise only if your estate owes federal estate tax at your death—that is, your estate exceeds the amount of the estate tax threshold in the year in which you die. Because gifts made to charities are not subject to estate tax, any tax due will be taken out of the amounts left to other, noncharitable final beneficiaries. They may end up getting less than you intended.

 If you think your estate may run into this problem, see an estate planning lawyer. You may want to customize your trust document to include a provision stating that taxes are to be paid from the charity's share. This way, the other beneficiaries will get their entire shares, and the charity will get what's left.

3. More Than One Final Beneficiary

You can name more than one final beneficiary. If you do, you can specify what share of your trust property you want each one to inherit. You cannot, however, specify who gets what particular items; they will share all the property.

Always use the beneficiaries' actual names, not terms such as "my children." It's not always clear who is included in such groups. And there can be serious confusion if one of the group dies before you do.

4. Minors or Young Adults

If a final beneficiary is a minor or a young adult, you can arrange for someone to manage the trust property for the beneficiary. (See Part 6, below.)

C. Final Beneficiaries' Rights

Choose your final beneficiaries carefully. After one spouse has died, final beneficiaries have certain legal rights even before they inherit trust property. If they believe the surviving spouse is spending bypass trust assets wastefully or in violation of the terms of the trust document, they could go to court. They could ask a judge to order the surviving spouse to manage the trust assets differently, or even to appoint a different person as trustee. Such conflicts are rare—but you should be confident that your final beneficiaries understand that you are going to the trouble of setting up an AB trust to benefit them, that doing so is a generous act on your part and that they should defer to the surviving spouse's decisions about the use of bypass trust property.

You may require the surviving spouse to give final beneficiaries copies of the annual trust income tax return, however. We'll ask you whether or not you want to require this.

D. If You Change Your Mind

After the first spouse dies, his or her final beneficiaries can't be changed. But if you are the surviving spouse, you can change the beneficiaries of your own revocable trust. (See Chapter 21.)

Part 6: Property Management for Young Beneficiaries

If any of the beneficiaries (including alternates) named by either spouse might inherit trust property before they are ready to manage it without an adult's help, you should arrange for someone to manage it for them for a while.

A. Your Options

There are several ways to arrange for an adult to manage property inherited by a young person:

- **Leave the property to an adult to use for the child.** Many people don't leave property directly to a child. Instead, they leave it to the child's parent or to the person they expect to have care and custody of the child if neither parent is available. There's no formal legal arrangement, but they feel confident that the adult will use the property for the child's benefit.
- **Name a "custodian" under the Uniform Transfers to Minors Act (UTMA).** In almost all states, you can name a custodian to manage property you leave a child until the child reaches 18 or 21, depending on state law (up to 25 in several states). If you don't need management to last beyond that age, a custodianship is probably the way to go.
- **Create a child's subtrust.** You can use Quicken WillMaker Plus to establish a child's subtrust in your living trust. If you do, your surviving spouse (or the successor trustee, after both spouses' death) will manage the property left to the child and dole it out for education, health and other needs. The subtrust ends at whatever age you designate, up to 35, and then any remaining property is turned over to the child outright.

Subtrusts and custodianships are explained below.

 Children with special needs. These property management options are not designed to provide long-term property management for a child with serious disabilities. You should see a lawyer and make arrangements geared to your particular situation.

B. Should You Arrange for Management?

Each spouse chooses whether or not to arrange to have someone manage trust property that's inherited by young beneficiaries.

The consequences of forgoing management for trust property inherited by a young beneficiary depend on whether the beneficiary is over or under age 18 at your death.

1. Children Under 18 Years Old

Minors—children under 18—cannot, legally, own or manage significant amounts of property. An adult must be in charge if the minor acquires more than a few thousand dollars' worth of property. (The exact amount depends on state law.)

If your minor beneficiaries will inherit objects that have more sentimental than monetary value, you don't need to arrange for an adult to manage the property.

But if a beneficiary inherits valuable trust property while still a minor, and you have not arranged for the property to be managed by an adult, a court-appointed guardian may have to manage the property. Contrary to what you might expect, a child's parent does not automatically have legal authority to manage any property the child inherits. So even if one or both of the beneficiary's parents are alive, they will have to ask the court to grant them that authority and will be subject to the court's supervision. If neither parent is alive, there may be no obvious person for the court to appoint as property guardian. In that case, it may be even more important for you to name someone in your living trust.

There is one other option: In most states, the successor trustee can name a custodian to manage property inherited by a minor. If the value of property exceeds a certain amount—$10,000 in most states—a court must approve the appointment. And the custodianship must end at 18 in most states—earlier than many parents may choose. So it's still better to name a custodian yourself.

2. Young Adults 18 to 35 Years Old

If a living trust beneficiary is 18 or older when he or she inherits trust property, you do not need, legally, to have anyone manage the property on the beneficiary's behalf. And if you don't make any arrangements, the beneficiary will get the property with no strings attached. But you can arrange for property management to last until a beneficiary turns any age up to 35.

There is no legal requirement that management for a trust beneficiary's property must end at 35, but we think 35 is a reasonable cutoff. If you don't want to give a beneficiary free rein over trust property by the time he or she reaches 35, you probably need to see a lawyer and tailor a plan to the beneficiary's needs.

C. Which Is Best: Subtrust or Custodianship?

Using Quicken WillMaker Plus, you can create either a child's subtrust or a custodianship under the Uniform Transfer to Minors Act (if it's available in your state). Both are safe, efficient ways of managing trust property that a young person inherits. Under either system, the person in charge of the young beneficiary's property has the responsibility to use the property for the beneficiary's support, education and health.

The most significant difference is that a child's subtrust can last longer than a custodianship, which must end at age 18 to 21 in most states (up to 25 in several states). For that reason, a child's subtrust is a good choice when a child could inherit a large amount of property.

Because an UTMA custodianship is much easier to administer, it is usually preferable if the beneficiary will inherit no more than about $50,000 worth of trust property ($100,000 or more if the child is quite young). That amount is likely to be used up for living and education expenses by the time the beneficiary is 21, so there's no need to create a subtrust that can continue beyond that age.

A custodianship has other advantages as well:

- Handling a beneficiary's property can be easier with a custodianship than with a trust. A custodian's powers are written into state law, and most institutions, such as banks and insurance companies, are familiar with the rules. Trusts, on the other hand, vary in their terms. So before a bank lets a trustee act on behalf of a beneficiary, it may demand to see and analyze a copy of the Declaration of Trust.

- You can name whomever you wish to be a custodian, and you can name different custodians for different beneficiaries. So if you want to arrange custodianships for grandchildren, for example, you could name each child's parent as custodian. A child's subtrust is not quite so flexible: The surviving spouse, or the successor trustee if you are the second spouse to die, will be the trustee of all children's subtrusts created for your young beneficiaries.

- If the property in a subtrust earns income, and that income isn't distributed quickly to the beneficiary, the trust will have to pay tax on it. The federal tax rate on such retained income may be higher than it would be if the young beneficiary were taxed on it. The trustee may well need to hire experts to help with trust accounting and tax returns.

D. Custodianships

A custodianship is the preferable alternative for many people. Here's how it works.

1. How a Custodianship Works

In the trust document, you name someone to serve as custodian for a particular beneficiary. That person manages any trust property the young beneficiary inherits from that spouse until the beneficiary reaches the age at which state law says the custodianship must end. (See the table in Chapter 15, Part 6.)

EXAMPLE: Sandra and Don make an AB trust. Sandra leaves, as a specific gift, 100 shares of General Motors stock to her niece, Jennifer Frankel. She names Hazel Frankel, Jennifer's mother, as custodian under the Illinois Uniform Transfers to Minors Act.

After Sandra's death, Don, as trustee, turns the stock over to the custodian, Hazel. She will manage it for Jennifer until Jennifer turns 21, the age Illinois law says she must be given the property outright.

In some states, you can specify—within limits—at what age the custodianship will end. If your state allows this, we'll ask you to enter an age at which you want the custodianship to end.

EXAMPLE: If Sandra, in the previous example, lived in Nevada, state law would allow her to choose any age from 18 to 25 for the custodianship to end.

2. The Custodian's Responsibilities

A custodian has roughly the same responsibility as the trustee of a child's subtrust: to manage the beneficiary's property wisely and honestly. The custodian's authority and duties are set out by a law called the Uniform Transfers to Minors Act, as enacted by your state. No court directly supervises the custodian.

The custodian must:

- Manage the property until the beneficiary reaches the age at which, by law, he or she gets the property outright. If the child is a minor at your death, this can be a number of years.
- Use the property or income to pay for expenses such as the young beneficiary's support, education and health care.
- Keep the property separate from his or her own property.
- Keep separate records of transactions. The custodian does not have to file a separate income tax return; income from the property can be reported on the young beneficiary's return. (By comparison, the trustee of a child's subtrust must file a separate tax return for the subtrust.)

A custodian who needs to hire an accountant, tax lawyer or other expert can use the property to pay a reasonable amount for the help.

If state law allows it, the custodian is entitled to reasonable compensation and reimbursement for reasonable expenses. The payment, if any is taken, comes from the custodial property.

3. Choosing a Custodian

You can name a different custodian for each young beneficiary, if you wish.

In most cases, you should name the person who will have physical custody of the minor child. That's almost always one of the child's parents. If the beneficiary is your child, name the child's other parent unless you have serious reservations about that person's ability to handle the property for the child.

Only one person can be named as custodian for one beneficiary. You can, however, name an alternate custodian to take over if your first choice is unable to serve.

E. Children's Subtrusts

Quicken WillMaker Plus allows you to set up a separate child's subtrust for each young beneficiary.

1. How a Child's Subtrust Works

In your trust document, you state the age at which the beneficiary should receive trust property outright. If at your death the beneficiary hasn't reached that age, a subtrust will be created for that beneficiary. (If the beneficiary is older, he or she gets the trust property with no strings attached, and no subtrust is created.) Each beneficiary gets a separate child's subtrust.

Quicken WillMaker Plus is set up so that the surviving spouse, or the successor trustee after both spouses die, will serve as trustee of all children's subtrusts. If you want different people to manage property inherited by different beneficiaries, you may want to use a custodianship instead of a child's subtrust. (To appoint someone else to be trustee of a child's subtrust, the trust document would have to be changed significantly; see a lawyer.)

Whatever trust property the beneficiary is entitled to receive will go into the child's subtrust, if the child is still under the age set for termination of the subtrust. The trustee will manage the subtrust property and use it as necessary for the beneficiary's health, education and support. After the spouse's death, the subtrust cannot be revoked or amended. Until then, that spouse is free to change his or her mind about having a subtrust set up for a particular beneficiary.

The child's subtrust will end when the beneficiary reaches the age designated by the spouse in the Declaration of Trust. This can be any age up to and including 35. The trustee will then give the beneficiary what remains of the subtrust property.

EXAMPLE: In the AB trust that Oliver makes with his wife Natalie, Oliver leaves a specific gift, $100,000 worth of stock, to his 14-year-old grandson Michael. He specifies that the stock should be kept in a subtrust until Michael is 25, subject to the right of the trustee (Natalie) to spend it on his behalf.

Oliver dies when Michael is 19. The stock goes into a subtrust for him, managed by Natalie. She uses the stock (and the income it produces) to pay for Michael's education and support. Michael receives what's left of the stock when he turns 25.

EXAMPLE: Herb and Laura create an AB trust and leave all their trust property to the other. They name their daughters, who are 22 and 25, as final beneficiaries and arrange for any trust property they inherit to stay in subtrusts until each daughter reaches 30. They name Laura's sister, Antoinette, as successor trustee.

Herb and Laura die in a car accident when one daughter is 28 and the other is 31. The 28-year-old's half of the trust property stays in a subtrust, managed by Antoinette, until

she turns 30. The 31-year-old gets her half outright; no subtrust is created for her.

2. The Subtrust Trustee's Duties

The subtrust trustee must:

- manage and invest subtrust property until the beneficiary reaches the age set out in the trust document—which can take years
- keep the beneficiary (or the beneficiary's guardian if the beneficiary is a minor) reasonably well informed about how trust assets are being invested
- use subtrust property or income to pay for expenses such as the beneficiary's support, education and health care, and
- keep separate records of subtrust transactions and file annual income tax returns for the subtrust.

The trustee's powers and responsibilities are spelled out in the trust document. If the subtrust trustee needs to hire an accountant, tax lawyer or other expert, he or she can use subtrust assets to pay a reasonable amount for the help.

The trust document also provides that the trustee of a subtrust is entitled to reasonable compensation for his or her work as trustee. The trustee decides what is a reasonable amount; the compensation is paid from the subtrust assets.

For more on the trustee's responsibilities, see Chapter 21.

Declaration of Trust

Part 1. Trust Name

This trust shall be known as the Jorge Ruiz and Adriana Ruiz AB Living Trust.

Part 2. Declaration of Trust

Jorge Ruiz and Adriana Ruiz, called the grantors, declare that they have set aside and hold in this trust all their interest in the property described in the attached Schedules A, B and C. All of that property is called the "trust property."

The trustees acknowledge receipt of the trust property and agree to hold it in trust, according to this Declaration of Trust.

The trust property shall be used for the benefit of the trust beneficiaries and shall be administered and distributed by the trustees in accordance with this Declaration of Trust.

The term "this Declaration of Trust" includes any provisions added by valid amendment.

Part 3. Character of Trust Property

While both grantors are alive, property transferred to this trust shall retain its original character as community or separate property, as the case may be. If the trust is revoked, the trustee shall distribute the trust property to the grantors based on the same ownership rights they had before the property was held in trust.

Part 4. Adding Property to the Trust

Either grantor, or both, may add property to this trust at any time.

Part 5. Grantors' Rights

A. Payments From Trust During Grantors' Lifetimes

The trustees shall pay to or use for the benefit of the grantors as much of the net income and principal of the trust property as the grantors request. Income shall be paid to the grantors at least annually. Income accruing in or paid to trust accounts shall be deemed to have been paid to the grantors.

B. Rights Retained by Grantors

As long as both grantors are alive, both retain all rights to income, profits and control of the trust property listed on Schedule A.

Declaration of Trust—Page 1 of 12

As long as Jorge Ruiz is alive, he retains all rights to income, profits and control of any property listed on Schedule C.

As long as Adriana Ruiz is alive, she retains all rights to income, profits and control of any property listed on Schedule B.

Part 6. Amendment and Revocation

A. Revocation by Grantor

As long as both grantors are alive, either one may revoke this trust at any time, without notifying any beneficiary. Revocation may be in writing or any manner allowed by law.

B. Amendment by Grantor

While both grantors are alive, this Declaration of Trust may be amended only by both of them acting together. All amendments must be in writing and signed by both grantors.

After the death of one grantor, the surviving spouse can amend his or her revocable living trust, Trust B, The Surviving Spouse's Trust, as defined in Part 14.

C. Amendment or Revocation by Other Person

The power to revoke or amend this trust is personal to the grantors. A conservator, guardian or other person may not exercise it on behalf of either grantor unless the grantor specifically grants the power to revoke or amend this trust in a Durable Power of Attorney.

Part 7. Homestead Rights

If the grantors' principal residence is held in this trust, grantors have the right to possess and occupy it for life, rent-free and without charge, except for taxes, insurance, maintenance and related costs and expenses. This right is intended to give grantors a beneficial interest in the property and to ensure that the grantors, or either of them, do not lose eligibility for a state homestead tax exemption for which either grantor otherwise qualifies.

Part 8. Trustees

A. Original Trustees

Jorge Ruiz and Adriana Ruiz are the trustees of this trust and any other trust or child's subtrust created under this Declaration of Trust. Either original trustee alone may act for and represent the trust in any transaction.

B. Trustee at Death of Original Trustee

When one original trustee dies, the other shall serve as sole trustee.

C. Successor Trustee at Death of Both Original Trustees

When both original trustees have died, Robert Ruiz shall serve as trustee. If Robert Ruiz is unable or unwilling to serve as successor trustee, Ana Portillo shall serve as trustee.

D. Trustee's Responsibility

The trustee in office shall serve as trustee of all trusts, including any child's subtrust, created under this Declaration of Trust.

E. Terminology

The term "trustee" includes successor trustees or alternate successor trustees serving as trustee of this trust. The singular "trustee" also includes the plural.

F. Resignation of Trustee

Any trustee in office may resign at any time by signing a notice of resignation. The resignation must be delivered to the person or institution who is either named in this Declaration of Trust, or appointed by the trustee under Section G of this Part, to next serve as the trustee.

G. Power to Appoint Successor Trustee

If no one named in this Declaration of Trust to serve as trustee is willing and able to serve as trustee, the last acting trustee may appoint a successor trustee and may require the posting of a reasonable bond, to be paid for with the trust property. The appointment must be made in writing, signed by the trustee and notarized.

H. Bond

No bond shall be required of any trustee named in this Declaration of Trust.

I. Compensation

No trustee shall receive compensation for serving as trustee, unless the trustee serves as a trustee of Trust A, the Bypass Trust, or of a child's subtrust created by this Declaration of Trust.

J. Liability of Trustee

With respect to the exercise or non-exercise of discretionary powers granted by this Declaration of Trust, the trustee shall not be liable for actions taken in good faith. Such actions shall be binding on all persons interested in the trust property.

Part 9. Trustee's Powers and Duties

A. Power Under State Law

To carry out the provisions of this Declaration of Trust, the trustee shall have all authority and power allowed or conferred under Texas law, subject to the trustee's fiduciary duty to the grantors and the beneficiaries.

B. Specified Powers

The trustee's powers include, but are not limited to:

1. The power to sell trust property, and to borrow money and to encumber trust property, including trust real estate, by mortgage, deed of trust or other method.

2. The power to manage trust real estate as if the trustee were the absolute owner of it, including the power to sell, lease (even if the lease term may extend beyond the period of any trust) or grant options to lease the property, to make repairs or alterations and to insure against loss.

3. The power to sell or grant options for the sale or exchange of any trust property, including stocks, bonds, debentures and any other form of security or security account, at public or private sale for cash or on credit.

4. The power to invest trust property in every kind of property and every kind of investment, including but not limited to bonds, debentures, notes, mortgages, stock options, futures and stocks, and including buying on margin.

5. The power to receive additional property from any source and add to any trust created by this Declaration of Trust.

6. The power to employ and pay reasonable fees to accountants, lawyers, investment experts or other professionals for information or advice relating to the trust.

7. The power to deposit and hold trust funds in both interest-bearing and non-interest-bearing accounts.

8. The power to deposit funds in bank or other accounts uninsured by FDIC coverage.

9. The power to enter into electronic fund transfer or safe deposit arrangements with financial institutions.

10. The power to continue any business of either grantor.

11. The power to institute or defend legal actions concerning this trust or the grantors' affairs.

12. The power to execute any documents necessary to administer any trust created by this Declaration of Trust.

13. The power to diversify investments, including authority to decide that some or all of the trust property need not produce income.

Declaration of Trust—Page 4 of 12

Part 10. Incapacity of Grantors

A. Incapacity of One Grantor

While both grantors are alive, if one of them becomes physically or mentally incapacitated, as stated in writing by a licensed physician, whether or not a court has declared the grantor incompetent or in need of a conservator or guardian, the other grantor shall serve as sole trustee until the incapacitated grantor dies or until a licensed physician states in writing that the formerly incapacitated grantor is no longer incapacitated.

B. Incapacity of Both Grantors

If both grantors become physically or mentally incapacitated, the successor trustee named in Part 8 shall serve as trustee.

The determination of the grantors' capacity to manage this trust shall be made by those of the people listed here who are reasonably available when the successor trustee (or any of them, if two or more are named to serve together) requests their opinion. These people are: Leah Corval, Amy Peterson and Jeffrey Mosley. If a majority of them state, in writing, that in their opinion the grantors are no longer reasonably capable of serving as trustee, the successor trustee shall serve as trustee.

The successor trustee shall pay trust income at least annually to, or for the benefit of, the grantors. Income accruing in or paid to trust accounts shall be deemed to have been paid to the grantors. The trustee may also spend any amount of trust principal necessary, in the trustee's discretion, for the health, education, support, comfort, welfare and maintenance of the grantors, in accordance with their accustomed standard of living, until at least one grantor is no longer incapacitated.

C. Incapacity of Surviving Spouse

If, after the death of one spouse, the surviving spouse becomes physically or mentally incapacitated, the successor trustee shall serve as trustee of Trust A and Trust B and of any other trusts created by this Declaration of Trust. The successor trustee shall serve as trustee until the surviving spouse is no longer incapacitated.

The determination of the surviving spouse's capacity to manage the trust shall be made by those of the people listed here who are reasonably available when the successor trustee (or any of them, if two or more are named to serve together) requests their opinion. These people are: Leah Corval, Amy Peterson and Jeffrey Mosley. If a majority of them state, in writing, that in their opinion the surviving spouse is no longer reasonably capable of serving as trustee, the successor trustee shall serve as trustee.

The trustee shall pay income from Trust B at least annually to, or for the benefit of, the surviving spouse. The trustee may also spend any amount of Trust B principal necessary, in the successor trustee's discretion, for the proper health, education, support, comfort, welfare and maintenance of the surviving spouse, in accordance with his or her accustomed standard of living.

Any income not spent for the benefit of the surviving spouse shall be accumulated and added to Trust B.

Part 11. Beneficiaries

A. Wife's Beneficiaries

At the death of Adriana Ruiz, the trustee shall distribute her share of the trust property listed on Schedule A and any separate property listed on Schedule B as specified in this section.

If Adriana Ruiz is the first grantor to die, her trust property shall be transferred to and administered as part of Trust A, The Bypass Trust, as defined in Part 13. If she is the second grantor to die, her trust property shall be given to her final beneficiaries, named in Part 13.

B. Husband's Beneficiaries

At the death of Jorge Ruiz, the trustee shall distribute his share of the trust property listed on Schedule A and any separate property listed on Schedule C as specified in this section.

Robert Ruiz shall be given all Jorge Ruiz's interest in the cabin at 2210 Cedar Road, Kerrville, Texas. If Robert Ruiz does not survive Jorge Ruiz, that property shall be given to Jaime Ruiz.

All Jorge Ruiz's interest in 500 shares of Applied Dynamics stock shall be given in equal shares to Alicia Ruiz and Teresa Ruiz.

If Jorge Ruiz is the first grantor to die, his remaining trust property shall be transferred to and administered as part of Trust A, The Bypass Trust, as defined in Part 13. If he is the second grantor to die, his remaining trust property shall be given to his final beneficiaries, named in Part 13.

Part 12. Division of Trust Property Into Trust A and Trust B

At the death of the first grantor to die, the trustee shall divide the property held in the Jorge Ruiz and Adriana Ruiz AB Living Trust between two separate trusts, known as Trust A, the Bypass Trust, and Trust B, the Surviving Spouse's Trust. The trustee does not need to physically segregate the trust assets to divide them between Trust A and Trust B. The trustee shall exclusively determine what records, documents and actions are required to establish and maintain Trust A and Trust B.

Declaration of Trust—Page 6 of 12

A. Trust A Property

After the trustee makes any specific gifts of the deceased spouse provided for in Part 11, the trustee shall place all remaining trust property of the deceased spouse in a trust known as Trust A, the Bypass Trust. The "trust property of the deceased spouse" is all property of this trust owned by the deceased spouse at the time it was transferred to the trustees, plus accumulated income, appreciation in value and the like attributable to the ownership interest of the deceased spouse, and his or her share of all property acquired in the trustees' names.

B. Trust B Property

The trustee shall place all trust property of the surviving spouse in a trust known as Trust B, The Surviving Spouse's Trust. The "trust property of the surviving spouse" is all property of this trust owned by the surviving spouse at the time it was transferred to the trustees, plus accumulated income, appreciation in value and the like attributable to the ownership interest of the surviving spouse, and his or her share of all property acquired in the trustees' names.

Part 13. Terms of Trust A, The Bypass Trust

All property held in Trust A shall be administered as follows:

A. Revocation

Trust A is irrevocable.

B. Life Beneficiary

The surviving spouse is the life beneficiary of Trust A.

C. Payments From Trust A

The trustee shall pay to or spend for the benefit of the surviving spouse the net income of Trust A at least quarterly. Income accruing in or paid to trust accounts shall be deemed to have been paid to the surviving spouse. The trustee shall also pay to or spend for the benefit of the surviving spouse any sums from the principal of Trust A necessary for the surviving spouse's health, education, support and maintenance, in accordance with his or her accustomed manner of living.

D. Trustee's Responsibilities and Compensation

The trustee has the rights and responsibilities set out in Part 8.

The trustee is entitled, without court approval, to reasonable compensation from the assets of Trust A for services rendered managing Trust A. The trustee is not required to make any accounting or report to trust beneficiaries.

E. Final Beneficiaries

At the death of the life beneficiary, the trustee shall distribute the property of Trust A, the Bypass Trust, to the final beneficiary of the deceased spouse.

Adriana Ruiz's final beneficiary is Jaime Ruiz. If Jaime Ruiz does not survive the life beneficiary, his interest shall be given to the American Cancer Society.

Jorge Ruiz's final beneficiary is Jaime Ruiz.

Part 14. Terms of Trust B, the Surviving Spouse's Trust

A. Surviving Spouse's Rights

During his or her life, the surviving spouse retains all rights to all income, profits and control of the property in Trust B.

B. Amendment and Revocation

The surviving spouse may amend or revoke Trust B at any time during his or her lifetime, without notifying any beneficiary. Trust B becomes irrevocable at the death of the surviving spouse.

C. Beneficiaries

At the death of the surviving spouse, the trustee shall make any specific gifts of the surviving spouse provided for in Part 11, and then distribute all remaining property of Trust B to the surviving spouse's final beneficiaries, named in Part 13. All these gifts are subject to any provision in this Declaration of Trust that creates a child's subtrust or creates a custodianship under the Uniform Transfers to Minors Act.

Part 15. Terms of Property Distribution

All distributions are subject to any provision in this Declaration of Trust that creates a child's subtrust or a custodianship under the Uniform Transfers to Minors Act.

A beneficiary must survive the grantor for 120 hours to receive property under this Declaration of Trust. As used in this Declaration of Trust, to survive means to be alive or in existence as an organization.

All personal and real property left through this trust shall pass subject to any encumbrances or liens placed on the property as security for the repayment of a loan or debt.

If property is left to two or more beneficiaries to share, they shall share it equally unless this Declaration of Trust provides otherwise. If any of them does not survive the grantor, the others shall take that beneficiary's share, to share equally, unless this Declaration of Trust provides otherwise.

Part 16. Simultaneous Death

If both grantors die simultaneously, or under such circumstances as to render it difficult or impossible to determine who predeceased the other, for purposes of this living trust it shall be conclusively presumed that both died at the same moment, and neither survived the other. The trustee shall make any specific gifts provided for in Part 11, and then distribute all remaining property to each spouse's final beneficiaries, named in Part 13.

Part 17. Payment of Grantors' Debts and Taxes

The trustee may pay out of trust property such amounts as necessary for payment of debts, estate taxes and expenses of the last illness and funeral of either spouse.

Part 18. General Administrative Provisions

A. Controlling Law

The validity of this trust and construction of its provisions shall be governed by the laws of Texas.

B. Severability of Clauses

If any provision of this Declaration of Trust is ruled unenforceable, the remaining provisions shall nevertheless remain in effect.

Part 19. Children's Subtrusts

A. Subtrust Beneficiaries and Age Limits

If Jaime Ruiz becomes entitled to any trust property under the terms of this trust before reaching the age of 29, that trust property shall be kept in a separate subtrust, under the provisions of this Part. The subtrust shall end when Jaime Ruiz reaches the age of 29. The subtrust shall be known as the "Jorge Ruiz and Adriana Ruiz AB Living Trust, Jaime Ruiz Subtrust."

If Jaime Ruiz becomes entitled to any trust property under the terms of this trust before reaching the age of 29, that trust property shall be kept in a separate subtrust, under the provisions of this Part. The subtrust shall end when Jaime Ruiz reaches the age of 29. The subtrust shall be known as the "Jorge Ruiz and Adriana Ruiz AB Living Trust, Jaime Ruiz Subtrust."

B. Powers and Duties of Subtrust Trustee

The trustee may distribute as much of the net income or principal of the child's subtrust as the trustee deems necessary for the beneficiary's health, support, maintenance or education. Education includes, but is not limited to, elementary, high school, college, graduate, postgraduate and vocational studies, and reasonably related living expenses.

In deciding whether or not to make a distribution to the beneficiary, the trustee may take into account the beneficiary's other income, resources and sources of support.

Any subtrust income that is not distributed by the trustee shall be accumulated and added to the principal of the subtrust.

The trustee is not required to make any accounting or report to the subtrust beneficiary.

C. Assignment of Subtrust Assets

The interests of the beneficiary are not transferable by voluntary or involuntary assignment or by operation of law before actual receipt by the beneficiary. These interests shall be free from the claims of creditors and from attachments, execution, bankruptcy or other legal process to the fullest extent permitted by law.

D. Compensation of Trustee

Any trustee of a child's subtrust created under this Declaration of Trust is entitled to reasonable compensation, without court approval, out of the subtrust assets for ordinary and extraordinary services, and for all services in connection with the termination of any subtrust.

E. Termination of Subtrust

A child's subtrust shall end when any of the following events occurs:

1. The beneficiary reaches the age specified in Section A of this Part. If the subtrust ends for this reason, the remaining principal and accumulated income of the subtrust shall be given outright to the beneficiary.

2. The beneficiary dies. If the subtrust ends for this reason, the subtrust property shall pass to the beneficiary's heirs.

3. The trustee distributes all subtrust property under the provisions of this Declaration of Trust.

Certification by Grantors

We certify that we have read this Declaration of Trust and that it correctly states the terms and conditions under which the trust property is to be held, managed and disposed of by the trustees, and we approve the Declaration of Trust.

_____   Dated:_____

Jorge Ruiz, Grantor and Trustee

_____   Dated:_____

Adriana Ruiz, Grantor and Trustee

Certificate of Acknowledgment of Notary Public

State of _____

County of _____

On _____ , before me, _____ , a notary public for said state, personally appeared Jorge Ruiz and Adriana Ruiz, personally known to me (or proved to me on the basis of satisfactory evidence) to be the persons whose names are subscribed to the within instrument, and acknowledged to me that they executed the same in their authorized capacities and that by their signatures on the instrument the persons, or the entity upon behalf of which the persons acted, executed the instrument.

Witness my hand and official seal.

_____

NOTARY PUBLIC for the State of _____

My commission expires _____.

_____

_____

SCHEDULE A

SHARED PROPERTY PLACED IN TRUST

1. The house at 13410 Encino St., El Paso, Texas.

2. The furnishings in the house at 13410 Encino St., El Paso, Texas.

3. T. Rowe Price brokerage account 42-1014-A5.

_____

_____

SCHEDULE B

WIFE'S SEPARATE PROPERTY PLACED IN TRUST

All Adriana Ruiz's interest in the following property:

1. The collection of 19th century dollhouses and dollhouse furnishings.

_____

SCHEDULE C

HUSBAND'S SEPARATE PROPERTY PLACED IN TRUST

All Jorge Ruiz's interest in the following property:

1. The cabin at 2210 Cedar Road, Kerrville, Texas.

2. 500 shares of Applied Dynamics stock.

Chapter 18

Signing, Storing and Registering Your Trust

You don't yet have a valid living trust when you've completed the program and printed out your living trust document. Here's what to do next.

A. Before You Sign

When you've printed out the trust document, take plenty of time to read it. Carefully. Make sure it says what you want it to say. Check to be sure you have:

- included all property you want to leave through the trust
- clearly and accurately identified all property (double check any account or serial numbers, for example)
- included all beneficiaries to whom you want to leave property
- spelled beneficiaries' names correctly and consistently, and
- made adequate arrangements for management of trust property that young beneficiaries might inherit.

If you want to make changes, go back to the part of the program you need to change, enter the new data and print out another trust document. (If you need help, see the Users' Manual.)

B. Consulting a Lawyer

Although in most instances it isn't necessary, you may also want to have an experienced estate planning lawyer look over the trust document before you sign it. We recommend that you see a lawyer if:

- you're unsure about the legal effect of anything in the trust document, or
- you want to make changes, even if they seem insignificant, to the trust document.

The cost of paying an estate planning attorney to review the trust document should be reasonable, especially compared to the cost of having an attorney do the whole thing from scratch. (Chapter 25 discusses how to find a lawyer and get the most help for your legal fees.)

A word of caution: Be aware that a lawyer who has a set way of doing things may disparage your efforts and try to sell you expensive services you don't need. Before you sign up, be sure that the work is really necessary and justifies the expense.

C. Signing Your Trust Document in Front of a Notary

To create a valid living trust, you must sign the trust document. A living trust document, unlike a will, does not need to be signed in front of witnesses. (In Florida, two witnesses are customary but not required; if you want witnesses, they can sign the Florida witness statement that automatically prints out with the trust document.) But you do need to sign your living trust document in front of a notary public for your state. If you and your spouse create a living trust together, both of you need to sign the trust document in front of the notary. If anyone challenges the authenticity of your signature after your death, the notarization will serve as evidence that it is genuine. And some institutions (stock brokerage houses, for example) may require that the signature be notarized before they will transfer assets into your name as trustee.

You can usually find a notary public at a bank, title or escrow company, real estate brokerage or library. Or check the Yellow Pages under "Notaries Public."

Getting a signature notarized is quite simple. You show some evidence of your identity, and then the notary watches you sign the trust document and signs and dates it, too. The notary also stamps a notarial seal on the document.

Your living trust document includes, at the end of the document, lines for your signature and a place for the notarization. The notarization form should be valid in most places, but if the notary public for your state wants to modify it, that's fine; some states require slightly different wording.

D. Making Copies

You will probably need copies of the trust document to transfer certain kinds of property (stocks, for example) to yourself in your capacity as trustee. (The details are in Chapter 19.) If a broker, bank or other institution wants to see your trust document, use a photocopy of the original trust document—the one you signed and had notarized. Do not just print out and sign another copy. Each copy you actually sign becomes, legally, an original trust document. Later, if you amend or revoke your living trust, you don't want lots of duplicate original trust documents floating around.

You should give a copy of the trust document to anyone you named to be a custodian of trust property inherited by a young beneficiary. The custodian may need it to show his or her authority to manage the property on behalf of the beneficiary.

It's not usually advisable to give copies of the trust document to beneficiaries. The problem is that if you later revoke or amend the trust but don't collect all the old copies, outdated copies of your trust document will still exist.

States That Provide for Registration of Living Trusts		
Alaska	Hawaii	Michigan
Colorado**	Idaho	Missouri*
Florida*	Maine	Nebraska*
		North Dakota

*Not mandatory.

**Registration of a revocable living trust not required until the grantor's death; no registration required if all trust property is distributed to the beneficiaries then.

E. Registering the Trust

Some states require that the trustee of a trust register the trust with the local court. But there are no legal consequences or penalties if you don't.

Registration of a living trust doesn't give the court any power over the administration of the trust, unless there's a dispute. Registration serves to give the court jurisdiction over any disputes involving the trust—for example, if after your death a beneficiary wants to object to the way your successor trustee distributed the trust property. But if you don't register your trust, the result is the same: the court still has jurisdiction if a disgruntled relative or creditor files suit. (The only exception is that if a court demands that a trustee register a trust, and the trustee refuses, the trustee can be removed.)

To register a revocable living trust, the trustee must file a statement with the court where the trustee resides or keeps trust records. The statement must include:

- the name and address of the trustee
- an acknowledgment of the trusteeship
- the name(s) of the grantor(s)
- the name(s) of the original trustee(s), and
- the date of the trust document.

A trust can be registered in only one state at a time.

F. Storing the Trust Document

Store your living trust document, the software CD and the manual where you keep important papers such as your will or durable power of attorney. A fireproof box in your home or office is fine. If you want to be extra careful, a safe deposit box is a good choice.

Make sure your successor trustee (or spouse, if you made a trust together) knows where the original trust document is and can get hold of it soon after your death. The new trustee will need it to carry out your instructions on how to manage and distribute trust property. The new trustee will also need the information in Chapter 21 to carry out his or her duties.

Copies of your trust document stored on your computer are not valid living trusts. The trust document must be printed out and signed to create a trust. ■

Chapter 19

Transferring Property to the Trust

After you sign your living trust document, you have a valid living trust. But the trust is of absolutely no use to you until the property you listed in the trust document is actually transferred into your name as trustee (or, in Colorado, to the name of the trust itself). Lawyers call this "funding" the trust.

Funding your living trust is crucial. It takes some time and paperwork, but it's not difficult. You should be able to do it yourself, without a lawyer. This chapter shows you how.

Promptly transfer property to the trust. Failing to transfer property to the trustee's name is the most common and serious mistake people make when creating a living trust. If you don't get around to preparing and signing the transfer documents, the trust document will have no effect on what happens to your property after your death. Instead, the property will pass through your will, if you have one (you should—see Chapter 13). If you don't have a will, the property will go to certain close relatives, according to state law. Either way, your probate- and tax-avoidance goals will not be met.

A. Making a Certification or Abstract of Trust

When you go to transfer property in or out of your living trust, a bank or other institution may ask to see the trust document. The institution wants to know that the trust exists and that you really have the authority you say you do.

If you don't want to show your trust document, in most cases you can use a shorter version of it, called a certification, certificate, abstract or memorandum of trust (different states use different names). This document gives institutions the information they need but lets you keep some key provisions private. Notably, you don't have to disclose the names of the beneficiaries to whom you're leaving trust property. A certification is almost universally accepted in place of an entire trust document.

Recently, many states have passed laws stating that if a certification of trust includes certain information, institutions must accept it in lieu of the entire trust document. California law, for example, states that someone who refuses to accept a valid certification and demands to see the whole trust document may be liable for any monetary loss suffered by the trust grantor.

With Quicken WillMaker Plus, you can make a certification that meets the requirements of many states (for example, California). Even if it doesn't contain everything your state's form does, it will still be acceptable in a great many cases. However, an institution may insist that you use the form that has been approved by your state legislature. The states that have their own forms, and the statutes that set out the requirements, are listed below. You can look up your state's law if you need to; see Chapter 25 for tips. In addition, institutions such as banks and title companies may have their own forms, which they would prefer you to use.

Whenever you want to create a certification, you can use Quicken WillMaker Plus to print out a new one. The only additional information you need to give is the date the trust document was signed, along with your current address.

You should sign the certification in front of a notary public. If you and your spouse made the trust together, you both need to sign the certification. Either spouse can make a certification after the other has died.

A sample is shown below.

States With Their Own Certification Rules

These states have enacted statutes setting out the contents for a certification of trust. If your certification meets the state requirements, institutions must accept it or be liable to you for your losses.

If you want to look up your state's statute, go to the Legal Research Center at www.nolo.com/statute/state.cfm. You can also find them in a law library.

State	Statute sections on certification of trust
California	Cal. Prob. Code § 18100.5
Idaho	Idaho Code § 68-115
Iowa	Iowa Code § 633.4604
Michigan	Mich. Comp. Laws Ann. § 565.432
Minnesota	Minn. Stat. § 501B.56
Mississippi	Miss. Code Ann. § 91-9-7
Nevada	Nev. Rev. Stat. § 164.410
Ohio	Ohio Rev. Code § 5301.01
Oklahoma	Okla. Stat. tit. 60, § 175.6
Oregon	Or. Rev. Stat. § 128.236
Rhode Island	R.I. Gen. Laws § 34-4-27
South Dakota	S.D. Cod. Laws Ann. § 55-4-42
West Virginia	W. Va. Code § 36-1-4a

Certification of Trust

The trustees of the William C. Carey and Leslie M. Carey Revocable Living Trust declare as follows:

Existence and Name of Trust/Grantor

William C. Carey and Leslie M. Carey, called the grantors, created a revocable living trust, known as the William C. Carey and Leslie M. Carey Revocable Living Trust, by Declaration of Trust dated May 1, 2001. This trust has not been revoked, modified or amended in such a way that would contradict what is stated in this Certification of Trust and remains in full force and effect.

Grantors' address is:
3320 Windmill Road
Auburn, California 95603

Amendment or Revocation by Grantor

The grantors may amend or revoke the William C. Carey and Leslie M. Carey Revocable Living Trust at any time, without notifying any beneficiary. The power to revoke or amend the trust is personal to the grantors. A conservator, guardian or other person shall not exercise it on behalf of the grantors, unless the grantors specifically grant a power to revoke or amend the trust in a Durable Power of Attorney.

Title to Trust Assets

Title to trust assets should be taken in the name of William C. Carey and Leslie M. Carey, trustees of the William C. Carey and Leslie M. Carey Revocable Living Trust, dated May 1, 2001.

Trustees

William C. Carey and Leslie M. Carey are the currently acting trustees of the trust.

The trustees in office shall serve as trustees of all trusts created under this Declaration of Trust, including children's subtrusts.

Trustee's Management Powers and Duties

Powers Under State Law

The trustees shall have all authority and powers allowed or conferred on a trustee under California law, subject to the trustees' fiduciary duty to the grantors and the beneficiaries.

Specified Powers

The trustees' powers shall also include:

1. The power to sell trust property, and to borrow money and to encumber trust property, including trust real estate, by mortgage, deed of trust or other method.

2. The power to manage trust real estate as if the trustee were the absolute owner of it, including the power to sell, lease (even if the lease term may extend beyond the period of any trust) or grant options to lease the property, to make repairs or alterations and to insure against loss.

3. The power to sell or grant options for the sale or exchange of any trust property, including stocks, bonds, debentures and any other form of security or security account, at public or private sale for cash or on credit.

4. The power to invest trust property in every kind of property and every kind of investment, including but not limited to bonds, debentures, notes, mortgages, stock options, futures and stocks, and including buying on margin.

5. The power to receive additional property from any source and add to any trust created by this Declaration of Trust.

6. The power to employ and pay reasonable fees to accountants, lawyers, investment experts or other professionals for information or advice relating to the trust.

7. The power to deposit and hold trust funds in both interest-bearing and non-interest-bearing accounts.

8. The power to deposit funds in bank or other accounts uninsured by FDIC coverage.

9. The power to enter into electronic fund transfer or safe deposit arrangements with financial institutions.

10. The power to continue any business of either grantor.

11. The power to institute or defend legal actions concerning this trust or the grantors' affairs.

12. The power to execute any documents necessary to administer any trust created by this Declaration of Trust.

13. The power to diversify investments, including authority to decide that some or all of the trust property need not produce income.

This Certification of Trust is being signed by all currently acting trustees.

_____ Dated: _____

William C. Carey, Grantor and Trustee

_____ Dated: _____

Leslie M. Carey, Grantor and Trustee

Certificate of Acknowledgment of Notary Public

State of California

County of _____

On _____, _____ before me, _____, a notary public in and for said state, personally appeared William C. Carey and Leslie M. Carey, personally known to me (or proved on the basis of satisfactory evidence) to be the persons whose names are subscribed to the within Declaration of Trust, and acknowledged to me that they executed the same in their authorized capacities and that by their signatures on the instrument the persons, or the entity upon which the persons acted, executed the Declaration of Trust.

Witness my hand and official seal.

_____

NOTARY PUBLIC for the State of _____

My commission expires _____

B. Property Without Title Documents

If an item doesn't have an official title document, you can hold it in trust very easily, with a document called an Assignment of Property. Quicken WillMaker Plus automatically assembles this document; you can print it out when you print the trust document itself.

The Assignment of Property lists every item of trust property that you've indicated doesn't have a title document, plus ones you weren't sure about. It simply says that you're transferring all those items to you (or you and your spouse) as the trustees of your trust. All you need to do is sign it and keep it with your trust document.

Examples of Items Without Title Documents		
Appliances	Computers	Stereos
Artworks	Dishes	Tools
Books	Furniture	
Clothing	Jewelry	

Remember that the Assignment of Property works only for items that do not have their own specific title documents. If an item has a title document—for example, the deed to a house or the title slip to a car—you'll need to create a new one. The rest of this chapter explains how.

C. Real Estate

To transfer real estate (also called real property) into your trust, you must prepare and sign a new deed, transferring ownership. You can fill out a new deed yourself; it's not difficult.

Co-op apartments. If you own a co-op apartment, you can't use a deed to transfer your shares in the co-op. You will have to check the co-op corporation's rules to see if the transfer is allowed. Some co-ops resist such transfers because they are afraid a trustee isn't a proper shareholder in the corporation. You can probably overcome any resistance you encounter by reminding the powers that be that for all practical purposes, you and the trust are the same—you have the same tax identification number, for example.

1. Preparing the Deed

First, get a deed form. In many places, you can find blank deed forms in stationery or office supply stores. If you can't find what you need there, try a local law library; look for books on "real property" that have deed forms you can photocopy. You can use a "quitclaim" or "grant" deed form. (If you use a grant deed, you are promising the new owner (the trustee) that you have good title to the property. If you use a quitclaim deed, you are promising only to transfer whatever interest you own in the property. The distinction isn't important when you control the trust.)

 Resources. If you're in California, you can find deed forms and instructions for filling them out in *Deeds for California Real Estate*, by Mary Randolph (Nolo). Much of the information in the book is valid in other states as well, but it's best to use a deed form that's in common use in your area.

Deed forms vary somewhat, but they all require the same basic information. Type in:

- The current owners' names. If you are the sole owner, or if you and someone else co-own the property and you are transferring just your share, only your name goes here. If you and your spouse own the property together and are transferring it to a shared trust, type in both of your names. Use exactly the same form of your name as is used on the deed that transferred the property to you and you used in your living trust document.

- The new owner's name. Fill in your name(s) as trustee(s) exactly as it appears in the first paragraph of your trust document, and the date you signed the trust document in front of a notary public.

⚠ Transferring Colorado real estate. Colorado law makes it advantageous to hold real estate under the name of the trust itself, not the trustee. So if you hold Colorado real estate in trust, the new owner's name should be, for example, "The Jonathan L. Geery Living Trust, dated November 15, 20xx." (Colo. Rev. Stat. § 38-30-108.5.)

- The "legal description" of the property. Copy the description exactly as it appears on the previous deed.

If you co-own the property with someone and are transferring only your share, you must also state, with the legal description, that you are transferring only that share (a one-half interest, for example) or that you are transferring "all your interest in" the property.

EXAMPLE: Amanda, who owns a house with her sister, wants to transfer her half of the property to her living trust. When she fills out a new deed, she can insert either "a one-half interest in" or "all my interest in" before the legal description of the real estate.

After everything is filled in, sign and date the deed in front of a notary public for the state in which the property is located. Everyone you listed as a current owner, who is transferring his or her interest in the property to the trustee, must sign the deed.

2. Recording the Deed

After the deed is signed, you need to "record" it—that is, put a copy of the notarized deed on file in the county office that keeps local property records. In most places, the land records office is called the County Recorder's Office, Land Registry Office or County Clerk's office.

Just take the original, signed deed to the land records office. For a small fee, a clerk will make a copy and put it in the public records. You'll get your original back, stamped with a reference number to show where the copy can be found in the public records.

3. Transfer Taxes

In most places, you will not have to pay a state or local transfer tax when you transfer real estate to yourself as trustee. Most real estate transfer taxes are based on the sale price of the property and do not apply when no money changes hands. Others specifically exempt transfers where the real owners don't change—as is the case when you transfer property to yourself as trustee of a revocable living trust.

Before you record your deed, you can get information on transfer tax from the county tax assessor, county recorder or state tax officials. Many counties now make this information available online; check your county's website.

4. Insurance

After you have transferred ownership of real estate, call your insurance agent to report the change. The company will change its records on the policy, but the change shouldn't affect your coverage or the cost of the policy.

5. Due-on-Sale Mortgage Clauses

Many mortgages contain a clause that allows the bank to call ("accelerate") the loan—that is, demand that you pay the whole thing off immediately—if you transfer the mortgaged property. Fortunately, in most instances lenders are forbidden by federal law to invoke a due-on-sale clause when property is transferred into a living trust. The lender can't call the loan if the borrower is a trust beneficiary and the transfer is "unrelated to occupancy" of the premises. (Garn-St. Germain Depository Institutions Act of 1982 (96 Stat. 1505).)

California Property Taxes

In California, increases in real estate taxes are limited by constitutional amendment (Proposition 13). The assessed value of the property can't go up more than 2% annually until a piece of property is sold. When the property is sold, however, the house is taxed on its market value. Transferring real property to yourself as trustee of your own revocable living trust—or back to yourself—does not trigger a reassessment for property tax purposes. (Cal. Rev. & Tax Code § 62(d).)

You may, however, have to file a form called a Preliminary Change of Title Report with the county tax assessor. Call the assessor to find out.

D. Bank Accounts and Safe Deposit Boxes

It should be simple to reregister ownership of a bank account as trustee of your living trust or open a new account in the trustee's name. Just ask the bank what paperwork you need to submit.

The bank will be concerned with the authority granted to the trustees to act on behalf of the trust. Depending on the kind of account, the bank may want to know if the trustees have the power to borrow money, put funds in a non-interest-bearing account or engage in electronic transfers. (The trust document created by Quicken WillMaker Plus includes all these powers.)

To verify your authority, the bank may want to see a copy of your trust document or have you fill out its own form, often called a Trust Certification.

If you want to transfer title to a safe deposit box, you'll have to reregister its ownership, too. The bank will have a form for you to fill out.

Credit Unions

If you want to transfer a credit union account to your living trust, you cannot simply change the name on the account. Because credit unions are membership organizations, the trust must qualify as a member of the credit union. Most credit unions accept living trusts as members. Ask your credit union for instructions.

E. Vehicles

Most people don't hold vehicles in trust, for reasons discussed in Part 3 of Chapters 15, 16 and 17.

But if you want to hold a vehicle in trust, you must fill out a change of ownership document and have title to the vehicle reissued in the trustee's name. The title certificate to your vehicle may contain instructions. If you have questions, call your state's motor vehicles agency or check its website.

You need special forms to transfer some vehicles to your name as trustee, including:

- **Airplanes.** The Federal Aviation Administration, which registers all aircraft, has forms for you to use. For information about its Civil Aviation Registry, check out the FAA's website at www.faa.gov.
- **Large boats.** The Coast Guard has its own forms. (See www.uscg.mil.)

F. Securities

How you transfer stocks, bonds and other securities to your living trust depends on whether you hold your stocks in a brokerage account or separately.

1. Brokerage Accounts

If you hold your stocks, bonds or other securities in a brokerage account, either change the account to your name as trustee or open a new account in that name. Simply contact your broker and ask for instructions. The brokerage company will probably have a straightforward form that you can fill out, giving information about the trustees and their authority.

If not, you will probably need to send the broker:

- a copy of the trust document or a "certification of trust" (see Section A, above), and
- a letter instructing the holder to transfer the brokerage account to (or open a new account in) your name as trustee.

After you've submitted your request, get written confirmation that the account's ownership has in fact been changed.

With some brokerage houses, you may run into a slight glitch. Here's what happens: When you go to transfer your account into your name as trustee, the brokerage house assigns it a new account number. Suddenly your property schedule, where you listed the account, has the wrong account number on it.

What to do? Just amend your property schedule to show the new account number. (See Chapter 21.) Then replace the old schedule with the new one, and you're all set.

2. Stock Certificates

If you have the stock certificates or bonds in your possession—most people don't—you must get new certificates issued, showing that you hold the shares in trust. Ask your broker for help. If the broker is unwilling or unable to help, write to the "transfer agent" of the corporation that issued the stock. You can get the address from your broker or the investor relations office of the corporation. The transfer agent will give you simple instructions.

You will probably have to send in:

- your certificates or bonds
- a form called a "stock or bond power," which you must fill out and sign, and
- a copy of the trust document or a certification of trust.

The stock or bond power may be printed on the back of the certificates; if not, you can probably find a copy at an office supply store. Send these documents to the transfer agent with a letter requesting that the certificates be reissued in your name as trustee of the living trust.

Stock in closely held corporations. See Section H, below.

3. Government Securities

To transfer government securities—for example, Treasury bills or U.S. bonds—have your broker contact the issuing government agency, or do it yourself.

G. Mutual Fund Accounts

Ask the company that issues the mutual fund what it requires for you to reregister ownership of your mutual fund account in your living trust's name. Most will send you an easy-to-use form to fill out. In addition, it will usually want a copy of your trust document or a certification of trust. (See Section A, above.)

H. Business Interests

How you transfer small business interests to your living trust depends on the way the business is owned.

1. Sole Proprietorships

First, list the business, by name, as an item of property in the trust document. That transfers the name and whatever customer goodwill goes with it.

Because you own the business assets in your own name (a sole proprietorship, unlike a corporation, is not an entity that can own property), you transfer them as you would any other valuable property. (See the Valuable Property Inventory in Chapter 15.)

If you have a registered trademark or service mark, you must reregister ownership in the living trust's name.

 Resources. *Trademark: Legal Care for Your Business & Product Name*, by Stephen Elias (Nolo), contains sample forms for reregistering trademarks.

2. Solely Owned Corporations

If you own all the stock of a corporation, you shouldn't have any problem transferring it to yourself as trustee of your living trust. Follow these four steps:

Step 1: Fill out the stock transfer section on the back of the certificate.

Step 2: Mark the certificate "cancelled" and place it in your corporate records book.

Step 3: Reissue a new certificate in your name as trustee.

Step 4: Show the cancellation of the old certificate and the issuance of the new certificate on the stock ledger pages in your corporate records book.

3. Closely Held Corporations

Normally, you can transfer your shares in a closely held corporation to your living trust by following corporate bylaws and having the stock certificates reissued in the living trust's name. But first, check the corporation's bylaws and articles of incorporation, as well as any separate shareholders' agreements, to see if there are any restrictions on such transfers. If an agreement limits or forbids transfers, it will have to be changed before you can hold your shares in trust.

Special rules for S corps. If you own shares in an S corporation, you cannot hold them in trust unless the trust is "qualified" under IRS rules. Consult a tax adviser.

4. Partnership Interests

To transfer a partnership interest, you must notify your business partners and modify the partnership agreement to show that your partnership interest is now held in trust. If there is a partnership certificate, it must also be changed.

Occasionally a partnership agreement limits or forbids transfers to a trustee. If so, you and your partners may want to see a lawyer before you make any changes.

5. Limited Liability Companies

You should get the consent of all of the other owners before you can transfer your interest to yourself as trustee. (Even if your operating agreement requires the consent of only a majority of the other owners, it's a good idea to have everyone's consent, just to head off any difficulties.) Getting the other owners to agree shouldn't be a problem; they'll just want to know that you, as trustee of your own trust, will have authority to vote on LLC decisions.

To make the transfer, you'll need a document transferring your interest. You can use the "Approval of Transfer of Membership" form in *Your Limited Liability Company: An Operating Manual*, by Anthony Mancuso (Nolo).

I. Limited Partnerships

Limited partnerships are a form of investment, governed by securities laws. Contact the partnership's general partner to find out what paperwork is necessary to hold your interest in trust.

J. Copyrights

If you want to hold your interest in a copyright in trust, you should list the copyright in the trust document and then sign and file, with the U.S. Copyright Office, a document transferring all your rights in the copyright to yourself as trustee. Sample transfer forms are in *The Copyright Handbook*, by Stephen Fishman (Nolo).

K. Patents

If you own a patent and want to hold it in trust, you should prepare a document called an "assignment" and record it with the Patent and Trademark Office in Washington, DC. There is a small fee for recording. Sample assignment forms and instructions are in *Patent It Yourself*, by David Pressman, and *Inventor's Guide to Law, Business & Taxes*, by Stephen Fishman (both published by Nolo).

L. Property That Names the Trust as Beneficiary

You can name your living trust as beneficiary of a life insurance policy, individual retirement account (IRA) or Keogh account. You don't (can't, in the case of retirement accounts) transfer the policy or account itself to the trust. You are the owner. The living trust is the beneficiary, which will receive the proceeds at your death. ■

Chapter 20

Living With Your Living Trust

As a day-to-day, practical matter, it makes little difference that your property is now held in your revocable living trust. You have no special paperwork to prepare, forms to file or other duties to perform as the trustee of your own trust. But you may need to change your trust to reflect changed circumstances in your life. This chapter explains how.

A. What to Do If …

This section tells you how to proceed if you run into any of these common situations, listed above.

1. Trust Property Earns Income

No separate income tax records or returns are necessary as long as you are the trustee of your own living trust. (I.R.S. Reg. § 1.671-4.) Income from property in the trust must be reported on your personal income tax return.

However, if a trust is ongoing after a grantor dies—for example, a child's subtrust or a bypass trust created after an AB trust grantor dies—you may need to file a trust tax return. See Chapter 21.

2. You Sell or Give Away Trust Property

You have complete control over the property you hold in the living trust. If you want to sell or give away any of it, simply go ahead, using your authority as trustee. You (or you and your spouse, if you made a trust together) just sign ownership or transfer documents (the deed, bill of sale or other document) in your capacity as trustee of the living trust.

> EXAMPLE: Mel holds his house in his living trust. When he sells it, he signs the new deed as "Melvin Owens, trustee of the Melvin Owens Revocable Living Trust dated June 8, 20xx."

If you and your spouse made a trust together, either of you has authority over trust property. That means that either spouse can sell or give away any of the trust property—including the property that was co-owned or was the separate property of the other spouse before it was transferred to the trust. In practice, however, both spouses will probably have to consent to transfer real estate out of the living trust. Especially in community property states, buyers and title insurance companies usually insist on both spouses' signatures on transfer documents.

If for any reason you want to take property out of the trust but keep ownership of it, you can transfer it to yourself. The process is, essentially, the reverse of the process you followed to transfer the property to the trust. (See Chapter 19.)

> EXAMPLE: Janice wants to take her house out of her living trust but keep ownership in her own name. She makes the deed out from "Janice Yamaguchi, trustee of the Janice Yamaguchi Revocable Living Trust dated November 6, 20xx" to "Janice Yamaguchi."

If you take property out of the trust, you will also need to make some changes to your trust document:

- Modify the property schedule of your trust document to reflect the change. If you don't, the schedule will still show that the property is owned by the trust, and the discrepancy could be confusing to the people who carry out your wishes after your death.
- If the property doesn't have a title document, create and print out an Assignment of Property form, showing that you've transferred the item back to you as an individual.
- If you named a specific beneficiary to receive the item, delete that trust provision, using a trust amendment.

Section B, below, shows how to make these changes using Quicken WillMaker Plus.

EXAMPLE: Wendy and Brian made a basic living trust several years ago. Wendy transferred a valuable antique dresser, which she inherited from her father before she was married, to the living trust. It's listed on Schedule B of the trust document as her separate property. The trust document provides that the dresser will go to her son at her death. But she's changed her mind and wants her daughter to have the dresser right now.

After Wendy gives the dresser to her daughter, she uses Quicken WillMaker Plus to prepare and print out three documents. First, she prepares a new Schedule B, deleting the dresser from the list of property, and replaces the old Schedule B attached to the trust document. Second, she prepares an Assignment of Property, showing that she's transferred the dresser from herself as trustee to herself. Third, she prepares a trust amendment, stating that the paragraph that left the dresser to her son is deleted from the trust document. After she signs the amendment in front of a notary public, her trust document reflects her wishes.

3. You Add Valuable Property to the Trust

If you add property to your living trust, you may need to amend the trust document (as well as the property schedule) to name a beneficiary to inherit the property. (See Section B, below.)

4. You Change Your Mind About a Beneficiary or Trustee

You may simply change your mind about whom you want to inherit trust property, or whom you want to serve as your successor trustee. To change these or other terms of your living trust, you'll need to make a trust amendment. (See Section B, below.)

5. You Marry or Have a Child

If you get married or have a child, you'll almost certainly want to amend your trust document to provide for your new spouse or offspring. (Your spouse or child may be entitled, under state law, to some of your property; see Chapter 13.)

6. You Get Divorced

If you divorce, you should revoke your living trust. In several states, provisions of a living trust that affect a spouse are automatically revoked by divorce, but you shouldn't rely on these laws. Better to have it in writing.

7. You Move to Another State

Your living trust is still valid if you prepare it in one state and then move to another. You may, however, need to take some actions after your move:

- Your new state may require you to register your living trust document with the local court. (See Chapter 18.)
- You may want to amend the trust document if the new state's laws differ on matters such as marital property rights or property management for young trust beneficiaries.

a. Your New State Has Different Marital Property Laws

If you and your spouse move to another state, in most cases, the move does not change who owns what. But everything you and your spouse acquire in the new state is subject to that state's laws regarding ownership.

> **EXAMPLE:** Leah and Ben move from Texas, a community property state, to Illinois, a non-community property state. In Texas, money either earned from working belonged to both spouses equally, which means that the car Leah bought with her salary is jointly owned by Leah and Ben. That doesn't change when they move to Illinois. After they move, however, each spouse's salary is his or her separate property.

If, however, you move from a non-community property state to a community property state, the move may change which spouse owns what. California, Idaho, Washington and Wisconsin have rules that treat certain property you bring with you as if you had acquired it in the community property state. Here's the general rule: If the property would have been community property had you acquired it in the new state, it is treated like community property at death or divorce. (The legal term for such property is "quasi-community property" or, in Wisconsin, "deferred marital property.") This means that each spouse owns half of this property and can leave only that share at death. One important exception: These rules usually don't apply to real estate.

> **EXAMPLE:** Carlo and Sylvia, a married couple, move from New York to California. Their car, bought in New York with Carlo's earnings and registered in his name, is quasi-community property—which means that once Carlo and Sylvia settle in California, the car would be considered to belong to both of them if they divorce or one of them dies.

Obviously, this can be a very complicated subject. The good news is that you need be con-cerned about this issue only if all of these three things are true:

- You move to California, Idaho, Washington or Wisconsin from a non-community property state.
- You are concerned that because of the move, trust property that was formerly owned by only one spouse might now be considered to be owned by both.
- In the trust document, you did not leave at least a half-interest in that property to your spouse.

In this situation, you have two options:

- Make a trust amendment, changing ownership of the property from separate property to community property. If you made a basic trust, have both spouses name beneficiaries for the property. If you made an AB trust, it will probably be going to the surviving spouse anyway.
- See a lawyer who's knowledgeable about your new state's law. If the property you're concerned about is valuable—a large amount of stock, for example—the cost of an expert will be well worth the peace of mind you get.

b. The New State Has Different Rules About Property Management for Young Beneficiaries

Your state's law determines the choices you have when it comes to arranging for someone to manage property left to young beneficiaries. In all states, you can use Quicken WillMaker Plus to create a "child's subtrust" for any beneficiary who might inherit trust property before he or she is 35. But state law determines whether or not you have another option: appointing someone to be the "custodian" of trust property inherited by a young beneficiary. (See Chapter 15, 16 or 17, Part 6.)

Only South Carolina and Vermont do not allow custodianships. If you move from either of those states, you may want to create a trust amendment, changing your trust document to let you create a custodianship.

If you move after you have already created a custodianship, the custodianship will still be valid. You can, however, create a trust amendment that deletes the old custodianship clause and adds a new one that conforms to your new state's law.

c. Your New State Gives Spouses or Children Different Rights

Different states entitle surviving spouses (and in some unusual circumstances, children) to claim different shares of a deceased spouse's estate. (See Chapter 13.) If you haven't left much property to your spouse or child and are concerned that either might challenge your estate plan after your death, you'll want to know what your new state's laws say. You may want to amend your trust document or other parts of your estate plan.

 See an estate planning lawyer. If you haven't left at least half of your property to your spouse, we recommend that you see an estate planning lawyer.

8. Your Spouse Dies

If you and your spouse made a shared living trust, when one spouse dies the other will probably inherit some, if not all, of the deceased spouse's trust property outright.

a. Basic Living Trust

The surviving spouse may need to amend his or her trust to name beneficiaries for property inherited from the deceased spouse. (See Chapter 21.) The survivor may also want to amend the trust document if he or she left property to the now-deceased spouse. (See Section 9, just below.)

b. AB Trust

With an AB trust, the deceased spouse's property goes into Trust A, the bypass trust. The spouse has certain rights over bypass trust property but doesn't own it outright. The final beneficiaries of that property are already set (they were named by the deceased spouse) and can't be changed.

There is, however, work for the survivor, who must see to it that the trust assets are split into Trust A (the bypass trust, the irrevocable trust that contains the deceased spouse's trust property) and Trust B (the revocable trust that contains the survivor's trust property). If the trust contains the disclaimer clause, then the surviving spouse must decide whether to split the property into Trust A and Trust B and, if so, how much property should go into Trust A. That process is explained in Chapter 21.

9. A Major Beneficiary Dies

You may need to amend your trust document if a major beneficiary dies.

a. Basic Trust

If you made a basic trust and left much or all of your trust property to one person, and that person dies before you do, you may well want to amend your trust document. If you named an alternate beneficiary for the deceased beneficiary, there's not an urgent need to amend the trust document; the alternate will inherit the property. But amending it makes sense, so that you can name another alternate beneficiary.

EXAMPLE: Marty and Frank make a basic living trust together. Marty leaves all her trust property to Frank, but he dies before she does. Because she named her daughter Stephanie as alternate beneficiary for her husband, she has already planned for the possibility of Frank's death. But it still makes sense for her to amend her trust document, to name an alternate beneficiary for Stephanie.

Remember that your trust document has another back-up device built into it: the residuary beneficiary. If both the primary and alternate beneficiaries die before you do, the residuary beneficiary will inherit the trust property.

b. AB Trust

If you made an AB trust with your spouse, then your spouse is your main beneficiary. If, however, you left a few items of trust property to others, and one of those beneficiaries dies before you do, you may want to amend your trust document to name a new beneficiary for the property. Also, if the final beneficiary (or one of them) dies, you and your spouse may want to amend the trust to name a new beneficiary.

After one spouse has died, the survivor can amend his or her trust (Trust B) to name a new final beneficiary. The final beneficiary of Trust A, the bypass trust, can't be changed.

10. You Want to Make Extensive Revisions

If you want to make extensive revisions to the terms of the trust document, you should revoke it and start fresh with a new trust document. If you don't, you risk creating inconsistencies and confusion.

11. Your Estate Tax Situation Changes

If you've made an AB trust, keep an eye on the law and on your net worth. Because the estate tax exemption is scheduled to rise rapidly in the next few years (see Chapter 13), you may find that you don't need a tax-saving AB trust after all. If both spouses are still alive, you can revoke your AB trust and create a basic probate-avoidance trust instead. That will save you paperwork, money (because you would need to hire an expert to help you with the AB trust when the first spouse died) and hassle (because an AB trust ties up the property of the first spouse to die).

If, however, you made a disclaimer trust, you don't need to revoke it even if you are no longer concerned about estate taxes. That's because when the first spouse dies, the surviving spouse has the power to decide not to split the AB trust to create the irrevocable bypass trust.

You might find, though, that your wealth increases much more rapidly than you expected— perhaps because of a surprise inheritance or business success. If your newfound wealth might mean an estate tax bill after your death, you might want to look into creating an AB trust. (Chapter 14 explains when an AB trust makes sense.)

Keep an eye on the estate tax laws. The uncertainty in the estate tax legislation passed in 2001 has made it almost inevitable that Congress will again take up the matter of estate taxes in the next few years. So keep up to date as these changes work their way through the political process. If the estate tax really is permanently eliminated, or the exemption amount is fixed so high that you don't need to worry about estate tax, you will almost certainly not want an AB trust.

B. Amending Your Living Trust Document

Quicken WillMaker Plus makes it easy for you to amend certain provisions of your trust document. By using the program to create and print out a trust amendment or a new property schedule, you can change:

- beneficiaries
- successor trustees
- custodians (people who will manage trust property inherited by young beneficiaries)
- property in the trust.

You don't need to (and the program won't let you) create a trust amendment until you've printed out and signed a trust document. Before that point, you can go back to any part of Quicken WillMaker Plus and change any of the information you've entered. After you've printed a trust document, when you start the program again, we'll ask you whether or not you've signed it, creating a valid trust. If you have, you will not be allowed to make changes to that original trust document. Instead, you'll automatically go to the amendment part of Quicken WillMaker Plus. (See the Users' Manual.)

If you do create and print out an amendment, you should sign it in front of a notary public and attach it to the signed original trust document. Then give a copy to anyone who already has a copy of the original trust document.

Every time you make a trust amendment and sign it, the amendment becomes legally part of your trust document. To change it, you must make another trust amendment.

Do not change the trust document except with the amendment module of Quicken WillMaker Plus. Any other changes could create serious problems for your beneficiaries or even invalidate your trust.

1. Who Can Amend Your Trust Document

Who can amend the terms of a living trust document depends on whether you created an individual living trust or a shared one with your spouse.

Someone Acting on Your Behalf

The trust document created by Quicken WillMaker Plus cannot be amended or revoked by someone acting on your behalf, unless you give that authority in another document.

That means someone who is appointed by a court to handle your affairs (a conservator or guardian) or someone you have given authority to act for you in a document called a power of attorney (your "attorney-in-fact") cannot amend the trust document absent specific authorization. If you want to give your attorney-in-fact authority to amend your living trust, you must specifically grant this authority in your power of attorney. (See Chapter 22.)

a. Individual Living Trust

If you created an individual living trust, you can amend the trust document at any time.

b. Shared Basic Living Trust

If you made a trust with your spouse, while both of you are alive, you both must agree to amend any provision of the trust document—for example, to change a beneficiary, a successor trustee or the property management set up for a young beneficiary.

After one spouse dies, the shared living trust is split into two trusts, one of which can no longer be amended. (This is explained in Chapter 21.) Basically, the surviving spouse is free to amend the terms of the trust document that deal with his or her property but can't change what happens to the deceased spouse's trust property. As a practical matter, the surviving spouse would have little reason to change the deceased spouse's trust, because that trust should be terminated shortly after the first spouse's death.

c. AB Trust

While both spouses are alive, both must agree to amend any provision of the living trust document—for example, to change a final beneficiary, a successor trustee or the property management set up for a young beneficiary.

After one spouse dies, the AB trust is split into two trusts, and the couple's jointly owned property is divided between them. (This is explained in Chapter 21.) Trust A, the bypass trust, cannot be amended. The surviving spouse can amend the terms of the trust document that deal with Trust B, the surviving spouse's trust—for example, to change the final beneficiary for Trust B property.

If the couple made a disclaimer trust, however, the surviving spouse may decide not to create the bypass trust at the first spouse's death. In that case, the trust is treated just like a basic marital trust. (See Chapter 14.)

2. Adding or Deleting Property

If you acquire valuable items of property after you create your living trust, you should promptly add them to the trust. You may also want to remove some items.

a. Basic Trust, or AB Trust If Both Spouses Are Still Alive

For a basic trust, or an AB trust when both spouses are still alive, there are four steps to take:

Step 1: Use the amendment module of Quicken WillMaker Plus to create a revised Property Schedule A, B or C of your trust document, adding new items or deleting old ones. (See the Users' Manual.) If you made an individual trust, you have only one schedule, Schedule A. If you and your spouse made a trust together, Schedule A lists your co-owned property, Schedule B lists the wife's property and Schedule C lists the husband's property.

Step 2: Print out the new schedule and replace the old one on your signed original trust document. That's all you have to do; schedules don't have to be signed.

Step 3: If you added property, transfer ownership of the property to yourself as trustee. You'll need to change the property's title document or, if the item doesn't have a title document, use the Assignment of Property form, showing that you are holding the item in trust. (See Chapter 19.) If you removed an item, transfer it out of the trust, either by changing its title document (a deed, for example) or using an Assignment of Property that transfers it from you as trustee to you as individual.

Step 4: If you need to name a beneficiary for property you've added, create a trust amendment. (See Section 4, below.) You won't need to create a trust amendment if you left all your trust property to one person, if you want the new property to go to the residuary beneficiary of a basic trust or if you made an AB trust and want the property to go to your spouse.

EXAMPLE: Rose and her husband Michael created a trust several years ago. Now they're buying a house and take title as "Rose Morris and Michael Morris, Trustees of the Rose Morris and Michael Morris Revocable Living Trust dated January 13, 1997." They then prepare a revised Schedule A (which lists co-owned property) of their trust document, print it out and replace the old Schedule A.

Because their trust document leaves all their property to each other, they do not need to prepare a trust amendment.

b. AB Trust If One Spouse Has Died

After one spouse has died, and the trust has been split into Trusts A and B, you cannot use Quicken WillMaker Plus to add or remove property from either Trust A (the bypass trust) or Trust B (the survivor's trust). Trust A cannot be changed in any way after one spouse dies.

Trust B cannot be changed with this program because the original property schedules, prepared when you created the trust, are no longer accurate or meaningful. They show only what was in the combined AB trust, and which spouse owned it originally.

When one spouse died, you should have had new property schedules prepared, showing which property is now held in the new Trust A and new Trust B. If you want to add or delete any property from your Trust B, you'll need to modify this new Trust B property schedule. You may also want to amend the provision in the trust document that stated to whom you were leaving the property.

If you want to add or delete property, see the lawyer who helped you divide the trust property into Trust A and Trust B and draw up your new property schedules.

3. Changing a Successor Trustee

If something happens to the person you chose to serve as successor trustee after your death, you may want to change your trust document.

a. Basic Trust, or AB Trust If Both Spouses Are Still Alive

You can use Quicken WillMaker Plus to amend your trust document if you change your mind about whom you want to serve as:

- successor trustee (the person who handles the trust, and any children's subtrusts, after your death or after the surviving spouse's death if a shared trust was created), or
- alternate successor trustee (the person who takes over as trustee if your first choice can't serve).

All you need to do is enter the name of the new successor trustee (or more than one) and then name an alternate. A sample amendment is shown below.

Amendment to the Judith M. Avery Revocable Living Trust

Under the power reserved to the grantor by Part 4 of the Declaration of Trust creating the Judith M. Avery Revocable Living Trust dated May 1, 20xx, the grantor amends the Declaration of Trust as follows:

The following is deleted from Part 6.D of the trust document:

Upon the death or incapacity of Judith M. Avery, the trustee of this trust and of any children's subtrusts created by it shall be Robert S. Avery and Anne Avery Puckett. Each successor trustee has full and independent authority to act for and represent the trust. If Robert S. Avery and Anne Avery Puckett are unable or unwilling to serve as successor trustee, David R. Puckett shall serve as trustee.

The following is added to Part 6.D of the trust document:

Upon the death or incapacity of Judith M. Avery, the trustee of this trust and of any children's subtrusts created by it shall be Andrea Puckett. If Andrea Puckett is unable or unwilling to serve as successor trustee, Susan Puckett McGuire shall serve as trustee.

_____ Dated: _____

Judith M. Avery, Grantor and Trustee

Certificate of Acknowledgment of Notary Public

State of _____

County of _____

On _____, before me, _____, a notary public for said state, personally appeared Judith M. Avery, personally known to me (or proved to me on the basis of satisfactory evidence) to be the person whose name is subscribed to the within instrument, and acknowledged to me that she executed the same in her authorized capacity and that by her signature on the instrument the person, or the entity upon behalf of which the person acted, executed the instrument.

Witness my hand and official seal.

_____

NOTARY PUBLIC for the State of _____

My commission expires _____

b. AB Trust If One Spouse Has Died

If you made an AB trust and one spouse has died, you can change the successor trustee of Trust B, the surviving spouse's trust. You cannot change the successor trustee of Trust A, the bypass trust.

We urge you, however, not to change the successor trustee of your trust unless absolutely necessary. If you name someone new, it means that at your death, different people will be in charge of distributing the property in Trust A and Trust B—a potentially very confusing situation.

If you and your spouse both created a subtrust for a young beneficiary, the successor trustee named by the deceased spouse will be in charge of the subtrust, even if you change your successor trustee. That is to forestall the tangled situation of having two subtrusts, with different trustees, for the same young beneficiary.

> **EXAMPLE:** Joe and Sue make an AB trust. Both name the same final beneficiaries: their son Jeff and their granddaughter Emily, whose mother (Joe and Sue's daughter) has died. Both say that Emily's money should go into a subtrust till she's 25. They name Jeff as their successor trustee.

> Joe dies. Sue has a falling out with Jeff and doesn't want him as successor trustee anymore. She makes an amendment changing the successor trustee of her trust (Trust B) to her sister, Maggie. When Sue dies, Jeff will be trustee of Trust A, the bypass trust, and of Emily's subtrust. Maggie will be trustee of Sue's Trust B.

4. Adding a Beneficiary

If you've added property to the trust by amending a property schedule (Section 1, above), and you want to name a beneficiary to receive the property, you should use the amendment module of Quicken WillMaker Plus to create a trust amendment. Two samples are shown below.

Remember, if you made an AB trust and want the property to go to your spouse in trust, you don't need to add an amendment.

Amendment to the Judith M. Avery Revocable Living Trust

Under the power reserved to the grantor by Part 4 of the Declaration of Trust creating the Judith M. Avery Revocable Living Trust dated May 1, 20xx, the grantor amends the Declaration of Trust as follows:

The following is added to Part 10 of the trust document:

6. Rosemary Warkowsky shall be given all Judith M. Avery's interest in the first edition of Roughing It, by Mark Twain. If Rosemary Warkowsky does not survive Judith M. Avery, that property shall be given to Kasimira Warkowsky.

_____ Dated: _____
Judith M. Avery, Grantor and Trustee

Certificate of Acknowledgment of Notary Public

State of _____

County of _____

On _____, before me, _____, a notary public for said state, personally appeared Judith M. Avery, personally known to me (or proved to me on the basis of satisfactory evidence) to be the person whose name is subscribed to the within instrument, and acknowledged to me that she executed the same in her authorized capacity and that by her signature on the instrument the person, or the entity upon behalf of which the person acted, executed the instrument.

Witness my hand and official seal.

_____

NOTARY PUBLIC for the State of _____

My commission expires _____

Amendment to the Judith M. Avery Revocable Living Trust—Page 1 of 1

Amendment to the Jorge Ruiz and Adriana Ruiz AB Living Trust

Under the power reserved to the grantors by Part 6 of the Declaration of Trust creating the Jorge Ruiz and Adriana Ruiz AB Trust dated May 2, 20xx, the grantors amend the Declaration of Trust as follows:

The following is deleted from Part 11.A of the trust document:

If Adriana Ruiz is the first grantor to die, her trust property shall be transferred to and administered as part of Trust A, The Bypass Trust, as defined in Part 13. If she is the second spouse to die, her trust property shall be given to her final beneficiaries, named in Part 13.

The following is added to Part 11.A of the trust document:

Ana Portillo shall be given all Adriana Ruiz's interest in the condominium at 550-A Sierra Vista, Sedona, Arizona. If Ana Portillo does not survive Adriana Ruiz, that property shall be given to Lucia Portillo.

The following is added to Part 11.A of the trust document:

If Adriana Ruiz is the first grantor to die, her remaining trust property shall be transferred to and administered as part of Trust A, The Bypass Trust, as defined in Part 13. If she is the second spouse to die, her remaining trust property shall be given to her final beneficiaries, named in Part 13.

_____ Dated: _____
Jorge Ruiz, Grantor and Trustee

_____ Dated: _____
Adriana Ruiz, Grantor and Trustee

Certificate of Acknowledgment of Notary Public

State of _____

County of _____

On _____, before me, _____, a notary public for said state, personally appeared Jorge Ruiz and Adriana Ruiz, personally known to me (or proved to me on the basis of satisfactory evidence) to be the persons whose names are subscribed to the within instrument, and acknowledged to me that they executed the same in their authorized capacities and that by their signatures on the instrument the persons, or the entity upon behalf of which the persons acted, executed the instrument.

Amendment to the Jorge Ruiz and Adriana Ruiz AB Living Trust

Witness my hand and official seal.

_____

NOTARY PUBLIC for the State of _____

My commission expires _____.

Amendment to the Jorge Ruiz and Adriana Ruiz AB Living Trust—Page 2 of 2

---

5. Changing a Beneficiary

You may change your mind about leaving certain trust property to a beneficiary you named in the trust document, or a beneficiary may die before you do. If so, you'll need to prepare a trust amendment.

> **EXAMPLE:** Jim and Toni created their basic living trust three years ago and named Jim's sister Eileen as beneficiary of some stock that Jim transferred to the trust. But since then Jim and his sister have had a falling out. He wants to amend the trust document to leave the stock to his son, Aaron.

All Jim and Toni need to do is use Quicken WillMaker Plus to prepare an amendment. The amendment deletes the paragraph in the Declaration of Trust that left the stock to Eileen. It also adds a paragraph leaving the stock to Aaron and stating that if Aaron doesn't survive Jim, the stock should go to his nephew David.

(If they eliminated the gift to Eileen but didn't name a new beneficiary for the property, it would go the residuary beneficiary of the trust.)

A sample amendment is shown below.

Amendment to the William C. Carey and Leslie M. Carey Revocable Living Trust

Under the power reserved to the grantors by Part 5 of the Declaration of Trust creating the William C. Carey and Leslie M. Carey Revocable Living Trust dated May 1, 20xx, the grantors amend the Declaration of Trust as follows:

The following is deleted from Part 11.A of the trust document:

2. Jonathan Goldfarb shall be given all William C. Carey's interest in account no. 3301-A94 at International Brokers, San Francisco, California. If Jonathan Goldfarb does not survive William C. Carey, that property shall be given to Melissa Goldfarb.

The following is added to Part 11.A of the trust document:

4. Daniel Zeller shall be given all William C. Carey's interest in account no. 3301-A94 at International Brokers, San Francisco, California. If Daniel Zeller does not survive William C. Carey, that property shall be given to Ingrid Zeller.

_____ Dated: _____

William C. Carey, Grantor and Trustee

_____ Dated: _____

Leslie M. Carey, Grantor and Trustee

Certificate of Acknowledgment of Notary Public

State of _____

County of _____

On _____, before me, _____, a notary public for said state, personally appeared William C. Carey and Leslie M. Carey, personally known to me (or proved to me on the basis of satisfactory evidence) to be the persons whose names are subscribed to the within instrument, and acknowledged to me that they executed the same in their authorized capacities and that by their signatures on the instrument the persons, or the entity upon behalf of which the persons acted, executed the instrument.

Amendment to the William C. Carey and Leslie M. Carey Revocable Living Trust

Witness my hand and official seal.

_____

NOTARY PUBLIC for the State of _____

My commission expires _____.

Amendment to the William C. Carey and Leslie M. Carey Revocable Living Trust—Page 2 of 2

---

6. Changing Property Management for a Young Beneficiary

You can make any number of changes to your trust document if you want to arrange for someone to manage trust property inherited by a young beneficiary. You can:

- Add a child's subtrust to your trust document, whether or not your original trust document created any subtrusts.
- Change the age at which a subtrust ends. (A sample amendment is shown below.)

- Add a child's custodianship to your trust document, whether or not your original trust document created any custodianships, if your state's law allows custodianships. (See Part 6 of Chapter 15, 16 or 17.) (A sample amendment is shown below.)
- Change the custodian or alternate custodian you named earlier. (A sample amendment is shown below.)
- Change the age at which the custodianship ends, if your state law allows it. Be sure to read the restrictions on your choices in Chapter 15, 16 or 17.

Amendment to the William C. Carey and Leslie M. Carey Revocable Living Trust

Under the power reserved to the grantors by Part 5 of the Declaration of Trust creating the William C. Carey and Leslie M. Carey Revocable Living Trust dated May 1, 20xx, the grantors amend the Declaration of Trust as follows:

The following is deleted from Part 12.A of the trust document:

1. If Claudia A. Carey becomes entitled to any trust property under Part 11.B before reaching the age of 29, that trust property shall be kept in a separate child's subtrust, under the provisions of this Part, until Claudia A. Carey reaches the age of 29. The subtrust shall be known as the "William C. Carey and Leslie M. Carey Revocable Living Trust, Claudia A. Carey Subtrust."

The following is added to Part 12.A of the trust:

1. If Claudia A. Carey becomes entitled to any trust property under Part 11.B before reaching the age of 33, that trust property shall be kept in a separate child's subtrust, under the provisions of this Part, until Claudia A. Carey reaches the age of 33. The subtrust shall be known as the "William C. Carey and Leslie M. Carey Revocable Living Trust, Claudia A. Carey Subtrust."

_____ Dated: _____

William C. Carey, Grantor and Trustee

_____ Dated: _____

Leslie M. Carey, Grantor and Trustee

Certificate of Acknowledgment of Notary Public

State of _____

County of _____

On _____, before me, _____, a notary public for said state, personally appeared William C. Carey and Leslie M. Carey, personally known to me (or proved to me on the basis of satisfactory evidence) to be the persons whose names are subscribed to the within instrument, and acknowledged to me that they executed the same in their authorized capacities and that by their signatures on the instrument the persons, or the entity upon behalf of which the persons acted, executed the instrument.

Witness my hand and official seal.

_____

NOTARY PUBLIC for the State of _____

My commission expires _____.

Amendment to the William C. Carey and Leslie M. Carey Revocable Living Trust—Page 1 of 1

Amendment to the Judith M. Avery Revocable Living Trust

Under the power reserved to the grantor by Part 4 of the Declaration of Trust creating the Judith M. Avery Revocable Living Trust dated May 1, 20xx, the grantor amends the Declaration of Trust as follows:

The following is added to Part 11 of the trust document:

2. Any property to which Cheryl Avery becomes entitled under Part 10 of this Declaration of Trust shall be given to Ramona V. Marcus, as custodian for Cheryl Avery under the Illinois Uniform Transfers to Minors Act, until Cheryl Avery reaches the age of 21. If Ramona V. Marcus is unable or ceases to serve as custodian, Henry Luce Marcus shall serve as custodian.

_____ Dated: _____

Judith M. Avery, Grantor and Trustee

Certificate of Acknowledgment of Notary Public

State of _____

County of _____

On _____, before me, _____, a notary public for said state, personally appeared Judith M. Avery, personally known to me (or proved to me on the basis of satisfactory evidence) to be the person whose name is subscribed to the within instrument, and acknowledged to me that she executed the same in her authorized capacity and that by her signature on the instrument the person, or the entity upon behalf of which the person acted, executed the instrument.

Witness my hand and official seal.

_____

NOTARY PUBLIC for the State of _____

My commission expires _____.

C. Revoking Your Living Trust

If you're like most people, amending your living trust will take care of your changing circumstances over the years, and you will never need to revoke your trust. But there are, of course, a few exceptions to that rule.

You can revoke your living trust at any time. Revoking a living trust (unlike revoking a will) requires some work: You must transfer ownership of all the trust property out of your name as trustee.

1. Who Can Revoke Your Trust

If you created an individual living trust, you can revoke it at any time.

Either spouse can revoke a shared basic trust or AB trust, wiping out all terms of the trust. The trust property is returned to each spouse according to how they owned it before transferring it to the trust.

> EXAMPLE: Yvonne and Andre make a basic probate-avoidance living trust together. Each transfers separately owned property to the trust. They also transfer ownership of their house, which they own together, to the trust. Later Yvonne, anticipating a divorce, revokes the living trust. She transfers the property she owned back to herself, and the property her husband owned back to him. The co-owned property goes back to both of them.

The trust document cannot be revoked by someone acting on your behalf unless you have specifically granted that authority. (See Section B1, above.) If you made a trust with your spouse, and you are the survivor, you can revoke only your revocable trust. So if you made a basic trust, you can revoke Trust #2; if you made an AB trust, you can revoke Trust B.

2. How to Revoke Your Trust

To revoke your living trust, follow these steps:

Step 1: Transfer ownership of trust property from yourself as trustee back to yourself. Basically, you must reverse the process you followed when you transferred ownership of the property to yourself as trustee. (See Chapter 19.) You can make the transfer because of your authority as trustee of the trust.

Step 2: Use Quicken WillMaker Plus to prepare a document called a Revocation of Trust. After you've printed your trust document, when you start the program again, it will ask you whether or not you've signed the trust document, creating a legally valid trust. If you have, the program will take you to a screen that lets you choose "Revoke Trust."

Step 3: Print out the Revocation of Trust and sign it in front of a notary public.

Step 4: If you registered your trust with the local court (a procedure authorized in certain states; see Chapter 18), notify the court that the trust has been terminated.

A sample is shown below.

Revocation of the Jorge Ruiz and Adriana Ruiz AB Living Trust

We, Jorge Ruiz and Adriana Ruiz, hereby revoke the Jorge Ruiz and Adriana Ruiz AB Living Trust, created by Declaration of Trust signed May 2, 20xx, according to the power reserved to the grantors by Part 6 of the Declaration of Trust.

All property held in the trust shall be returned to the grantors.

_____ Dated: _____

Jorge Ruiz, Grantor and Trustee

_____ Dated: _____

Adriana Ruiz, Grantor and Trustee

Certificate of Acknowledgment of Notary Public

State of _____

County of _____

On _____, before me, _____, a notary public for said state, personally appeared Jorge Ruiz and Adriana Ruiz, personally known to me (or proved to me on the basis of satisfactory evidence) to be the persons whose names are subscribed to the within instrument, and acknowledged to me that they executed the same in their authorized capacities and that by their signatures on the instrument the persons, or the entity upon behalf of which the persons acted, executed the instrument.

Witness my hand and official seal.

_____

NOTARY PUBLIC for the State of _____

My commission expires _____.

Chapter 21

After a Grantor Dies

Themer benefit of a revocable living trust doesn't come until after the grantor's death, when trust property is transferred to beneficiaries without probate or shifted into an irrevocable, tax-saving trust. The all-important responsibility of handling that transfer falls to your surviving spouse if you made a trust together, or your successor trustee if you made an individual living trust. This chapter outlines the responsibilities of the person who is in charge of a trust after a grantor dies, so you can understand what the successor trustee will have to do.

More information for trustees. Your successor trustee can find much more extensive information, when it's necessary, in these two Nolo books: *How to Probate an Estate in California*, by Julia Nissley, and *The Executor's Guide: How to Settle a Loved One's Estate or Trust*, by Mary Randolph.

A. What Happens When a Grantor Dies: An Overview

The process works differently depending on whether you made an individual living trust or a shared trust with your spouse.

Special Duty for Ohio Trustees

If your trust holds any real estate, Ohio imposes special requirements on the trustee. (Ohio Rev. Code § 5302.171.) When a successor trustee takes over following the death of a grantor (or if an alternate successor trustee takes over from the first successor trustee), the new trustee must file an affidavit (sworn statement) in the county where the real estate is located. The affidavit must be filed with the county auditor and county recorder. It must contain:

- the names and addresses of all the trustees
- a reference to the deed that transferred the real estate to the trustee, and
- a legal description of the property.

The affidavit isn't necessary if the trustee has already filed a "memorandum of trust" (Ohio Rev. Code § 5301.255) with the county recorder.

1. Individual Trust

When the grantor, who is also the trustee, dies, the successor trustee named in the Declaration of Trust takes over as trustee. The new trustee is responsible for distributing the trust property to the beneficiaries named in the trust document.

The trust continues to exist only as long as it takes the successor trustee to distribute trust property to the beneficiaries. In many cases, a living trust can be wound up in only a few weeks after a grantor's death.

The successor trustee is also in charge of managing any property left to a young beneficiary in a child's subtrust. A subtrust will exist until the beneficiary is old enough to get the property outright (at the age specified in the trust document), so if there's a subtrust the successor trustee may have years of work ahead. (See Section K, below.)

If trust property inherited by a young beneficiary is to be managed by a custodian under the Uniform Transfers to Minors Act, the person named as custodian will be responsible for that property. That person may or may not be the successor trustee. (See Section L, below.)

The Successor Trustee's Duties

- Notify beneficiaries that the trust exists, if necessary.
- Get an appraisal of valuable trust property.
- Prepare an Affidavit of Assumption of Duties.
- Distribute trust property to beneficiaries named in the trust document.
- Manage trust property left in a child's subtrust, if any.
- File tax returns, if necessary. (This is the responsibility of the executor of the estate, if there was a will.)

2. Basic Marital Trust

When a married couple creates a basic probate-avoidance living trust with Quicken WillMaker Plus, both spouses are the original trustees. When the first spouse dies, the surviving spouse becomes sole trustee.

The trust itself is automatically split into two trusts:

- Trust #1 contains the deceased spouse's share of trust property, excluding any trust property left to the surviving spouse. Its terms cannot be changed, and it cannot be revoked.
- Trust #2 contains the surviving spouse's share, including any of the deceased spouse's share of the trust property that is left to the surviving spouse. (The Declaration of Trust provides that trust property left to the survivor does not go to the surviving spouse outright but instead stays in the living trust. If it did not contain such a provision, the property would have to be transferred from the living trust to the spouse and then, if the surviving spouse wanted it to avoid probate, back to the living trust again.) The surviving spouse is still free to revoke Trust #2 or amend its terms.

The survivor is sole trustee of Trust #1, Trust #2 and any children's subtrusts set up for the deceased spouse's young beneficiaries. (See Section K, below.)

It's the surviving spouse's job to distribute the property in Trust #1 to the beneficiaries the deceased spouse named in the trust document. If, as is common, much of the trust property is left to the surviving spouse, that spouse will have little to do—the trust property he or she inherits is already in the living trust and does not need to be transferred. (Section H, below, has more about transferring property to the surviving spouse.)

Trust #2 goes on as before, as a revocable living trust. It contains only the surviving spouse's property, and the surviving spouse is free to change any terms of the trust.

When the second spouse dies, the successor trustee named in the trust document takes over as trustee. The process of winding up the living trust is the same as that for an individual trust (See Section 1, above.)

EXAMPLE: Harry and Maude, a married couple, set up a basic revocable living trust. They appoint Maude's cousin Emily as successor trustee, to take over as trustee after they have both died. They transfer ownership of much of their co-owned property—their house, savings accounts and stocks—to the trust. Maude also puts some family heirlooms, which are her separate property, in the living trust.

In the trust document, Maude leaves her heirlooms to her younger sister. She leaves her half of the trust property she and Harry own together to Harry.

When Maude dies, Harry becomes the sole trustee. Following the terms of the trust document, he distributes Maude's heirlooms (Trust #1) to her sister, without probate. Maude's half of the property they had owned together stays in the trust (Trust #2); no transfer is necessary. After Maude's death, Harry decides to amend the trust document to name his nephew, Burt, as successor trustee instead of Maude's cousin Emily.

When Harry dies, Burt becomes trustee and distributes the trust property following Harry's instructions in the trust document. When he has given all the property to Harry's beneficiaries, the trust ends.

The Surviving Spouse's Duties

- Get an appraisal of valuable trust property.
- Prepare an Affidavit of Assumption of Duties.
- Distribute the deceased spouse's share of the trust property to beneficiaries named in the trust document.
- Manage property left in a child's subtrust, if any.
- File tax returns, if necessary. (This is the executor's responsibility, if a will named someone else as executor of the estate.)

3. AB Trust

When a married couple creates an AB living trust with Quicken WillMaker Plus, both spouses are the original trustees. When the first spouse dies, the surviving spouse becomes sole trustee.

What happens next depends on how the trust was structured.

If the trust document contains the "disclaimer trust" option, then the surviving spouse must decide whether or not to create Trust A, the bypass trust. If the survivor concludes that it's worthwhile to create the trust, she must disclaim (turn down) trust assets she would otherwise inherit. The disclaimed property goes into the bypass trust.

If there is no disclaimer clause in the trust document, then the survivor must see that the AB trust is split into two trusts:

- Trust A, the Bypass Trust, contains half (by value) of the couple's shared trust property, and the deceased spouse's separately owned property. This trust's terms cannot be changed, and it cannot be revoked.

- Trust B is the surviving spouse's trust. It includes the rest of the couple's shared trust property, any trust property the deceased spouse left directly to the surviving spouse and the survivor's separately owned property, if any. (Your Declaration of Trust provides that trust property left to the survivor does not go to the surviving spouse outright but instead stays in the survivor's revocable trust.) The surviving spouse is free to revoke it or amend its terms.

Section F, below, explains the process of creating Trusts A and B.

The survivor is sole trustee of Trust A, Trust B and any children's subtrusts set up for the deceased spouse's young beneficiaries.

When the second spouse dies, the successor trustee named in the trust document takes over as trustee of Trusts A and B. The process of winding up the trusts is the same as that for an individual trust (See Section 1, above.)

> EXAMPLE: Gary and his wife Beth set up an AB living trust, naming their daughter Emily as successor trustee and final beneficiary. They transfer ownership of much of their co-owned property—their house, bank accounts and stocks—to the trust. Beth also puts some family heirlooms, which are her separate property, in the trust.
>
> In the trust document, Beth leaves her heirlooms to her younger sister. She leaves her half of the trust property she and Gary own together to Gary, in trust.
>
> When Beth dies, Gary becomes the sole trustee. Following the terms of the trust document, he distributes Beth's heirlooms to her sister, without probate. He also sees to it that half of the trust property they had owned together goes into Trust A, and the other half into Trust B.

When Gary dies, Emily becomes trustee and distributes the property in Trusts A and B to herself. When it has all been transferred to her, Trusts A and B cease to exist.

The Surviving Spouse's Duties

- Notify beneficiaries that the trust exists, if necessary.
- Get an appraisal of valuable trust property.
- Prepare an Affidavit of Assumption of Duties.
- Distribute any specific gifts of trust property made by the deceased spouse to beneficiaries named in the trust document.
- Manage property left in a child's subtrust, if any.
- Get expert help to divide trust property into Trust A (bypass trust) and Trust B (survivor's trust) or, if it's a disclaimer trust, to decide whether or not to create Trust A and how much property to put into it.
- Get federal tax ID number for Trust A and file annual income tax returns.
- File tax returns, if necessary. (This is the executor's responsibility, if a will named someone else as executor of the estate.)

B. Who Serves as Trustee

With a basic marital trust or an AB trust, when one spouse dies, the surviving spouse serves as trustee. With an individual trust, or when the surviving spouse dies, the successor trustee is in charge.

Who Serves as Trustee			
	Individual Trust	**Basic Marital Trust**	**AB Trust**
When first grantor dies	Successor trustee(s)	Surviving spouse	Surviving spouse
When second grantor dies	N/A	Successor trustee(s)	Successor trustee(s)
If successor trustee can't serve	Alternate successor trustee(s)	Alternate successor trustee(s)	Alternate successor trustee(s)

1. More Than One Successor Trustee

If more than one person is named in the trust document as successor trustee, they all serve together. The trust document may require them all to agree before taking any action with regard to the living trust property, or it may allow them to act independently.

If one of the trustees cannot serve, the others remain as trustees. The person named as alternate successor trustee does not take over unless all the people named as successor trustees cannot serve.

2. If a Trustee Resigns

A trustee can resign at any time by preparing and signing a letter of resignation. The ex-trustee should deliver the notice to the person who is next in line to serve as trustee (see table above).

If no one named in the trust document can serve, the last acting trustee can appoint someone else to take over. The appointment must be in writing, signed and notarized.

3. Removing a Trustee

Very rarely, a beneficiary becomes seriously unhappy with the way a trustee handles trust property. For example, the beneficiary of a child's subtrust might complain that the trustee isn't spending enough of the trust property on the beneficiary's education. If the dispute can't be worked out, the beneficiary can file a lawsuit to try to force the removal of the trustee.

C. Getting an Appraisal

Whoever serves as trustee when a grantor dies should promptly get written appraisals of the market value of all significant trust assets. It's important for at least two reasons:

- Whoever inherits property gets a new tax basis in that property: the market value at the date of death. The new owner needs to know what that market value is to correctly figure tax liability later, when the property is eventually sold.

- If the executor or trustee needs to file a federal estate tax return (see Chapter 17), there is a choice of valuing the assets either as of the date of death or six months later. Getting a reliable estimate soon after the death means there will be something to compare it to later.

How to Get Common Kinds of Property Appraised	
Real estate	Ask two local brokers or hire an appraiser.
Stocks and bonds	Look in the newspaper (or on the Web) for the price on the date of death.
Valuable jewelry, collections or art	Get an appraisal by an expert in the field.

D. Preparing an Affidavit of Assumption of Duties

The successor trustee may be asked to show proof that he or she actually has authority to act on behalf of the trust. This is especially likely for transactions involving real estate.

It may be enough for the trustee to show both the trust document and the grantor's death certificate. Another way is to prepare a sworn statement (affidavit) setting out the facts that give the trustee authority, and to record (file in the public records) this document in the county land records office.

In most states, there isn't any set form for this kind of statement, but it should include:

- the name of the trust
- the date the trust was signed, and
- the name of the successor trustee.

The trustee should sign the statement in front of a notary public and attach a certified copy of the death certificate. Certified copies of the death certificate are available from the county or state vital records office; in many places, you can order them online.

E. Notifying Beneficiaries

Trustees must always keep trust beneficiaries informed about administration of the trust. This rule is intended to make sure that the beneficiaries have enough information to enforce their legal rights—for example, to make sure that trust assets aren't being mismanaged.

With a simple probate-avoidance trust, there is usually not much need for communication with beneficiaries. (The successor trustee may be, in fact, the only beneficiary.) The trust exists only long enough for the trustee to gather and distribute the assets. The trustee does not have to invest trust assets or decide how much money beneficiaries receive—issues that can complicate other trustee-beneficiary relationships.

With an AB trust, there is a greater need to keep final beneficiaries informed about trust administration. What these beneficiaries will inherit from the trust is directly affected by the trustee's actions.

1. General Rules

If the successor trustee thinks beneficiaries of the trust don't know about it, he or she should promptly notify them when the grantor dies. A simple letter, telling the beneficiary that the trust has become irrevocable because of the grantor's death, and that the successor trustee is now in charge of trust assets and will distribute them as soon as is practical, will do in most states.

2. Special State Requirements

Some states—currently, California, Kansas, New Mexico, Tennessee and Wyoming, but the list may be different by the time your trust becomes irrevocable—have very specific rules about how and when the successor trustee must notify beneficiaries about the existence of the trust. The notice must include certain information and be formatted in a certain way.

Help for California trustees. *How to Probate an Estate in California*, by Julia Nissley (Nolo), contains a form successor trustees can use to give the required notice.

These rules may change. By the time your trust becomes irrevocable, it's likely that more states will have adopted specific notice requirements. A successor trustee should always check current state law and may want to consult a lawyer.

F. Splitting the Trust Into Trusts A and B (AB Trust Only)

Dividing the assets of the trust when one spouse dies is the most complicated part of using an AB trust. The uncertainty surrounding the estate tax makes these decisions even thornier. The surviving spouse will need to get expert help from an experienced estate planning attorney to reap the greatest tax benefits.

1. Deciding Whether or Not to Split the Trust

If you chose to make a disclaimer AB trust, then the threshold question for the surviving spouse is whether or not to split the AB trust and create the tax-saving bypass trust. The trust document, remember, says that if the spouse decides that dividing the trust is too much trouble and not worth the tax savings, then everything can just stay in the survivor's trust.

EXAMPLE: Judith and Colin make an AB trust and include the disclaimer provision. They both live many years longer. When Colin dies, tax laws have changed, and the estate tax exemption is so high that Judith no longer has to worry about a big estate tax bill at her death. So to save herself the hassle and expense of creating and managing the irrevocable bypass trust, she exercises her authority under the trust document and does not split the AB trust. As a result, all the trust property stays in Judith's revocable survivor's trust.

The surviving spouse does, however, have the option of splitting the AB trust and treating it just like a regular AB trust.

EXAMPLE: Gwen and Michael also make a disclaimer trust. But when Gwen dies, Michael concludes that unless he acts, his estate could be liable for a big estate tax bill at his death. So he decides to go ahead and split the AB trust, creating the irrevocable bypass trust and the revocable survivor's trust. After consulting an estate planning lawyer, he decides to disclaim about a third of the trust property, which under the terms of the trust document means that property goes into the bypass trust. The rest goes into his survivor's trust.

2. Deciding How to Split the Assets

The goal is to divide the couple's jointly owned trust assets in a way that Trust A and Trust B each contain half of the total value of those assets. The assets can be divided in any way, as long as each trust (Trust A, the bypass trust, and Trust B, the survivor's) holds assets of equal value. Every item does not have to be divided 50-50. For example, if the trust contained stock worth

$200,000, all of it could be put into Trust A, if other co-owned trust property of equal value were allocated to Trust B.

There are several factors to consider when deciding what property goes in which trust. One is the likelihood that the asset will increase in value. For example, say a surviving spouse puts the couple's $400,000 house in Trust A, because she think it could well be worth $600,000 by the time of her death. If that happens, the increase in value won't be subject to estate tax. (That's because, remember, the house was subject to tax at the first spouse's death.) But if real estate values are expected to sink, she might be better off putting stocks in Trust A—or, since nobody knows what's going to happen, to hedge her bets and split ownership of the house and the stocks between Trust A and Trust B.

Another factor that affects a family residence is the chance that the surviving spouse will want to sell it. An individual owner who sells his or her house gets a big (currently $250,000) exemption from capital gains tax; a trust does not. So if the house is held in the bypass trust, more capital gains tax may be owed if the house is sold.

See an expert. As you can see, this gets complicated fast. It's well worth the cost to consult an expert with good real-world experience.

3. Preparing the Paperwork

The surviving spouse does not need to create a new trust document to create Trusts A and B. But some other documents are required:

- New property schedules, listing what's in Trust A and Trust B.

- For property with title documents (real estate or stocks, for example), new title documents showing that property is now owned by the trustee of "The John Donaldson and Corrine Donaldson AB Revocable Trust, Trust A." The surviving spouse signs these documents, in her capacity as trustee of both trusts.

- For property without title documents, a new Assignment of Property, showing that these items are held in Trust A or Trust B.

G. The Surviving Spouse's Duties and Rights (AB Trust Only)

Once the AB trust has been divided into Trust A and Trust B, the surviving spouse has new responsibilities as trustee of Trust A. That trust is now very different from the couple's original living trust: it is irrevocable, and it exists as a separate taxable entity.

The surviving spouse, as trustee of Trust A, must:

- Get a federal taxpayer ID number from the IRS for the trust.
- Manage the property prudently.
- Keep separate, clear tax records of all transactions involving Trust A property.
- File federal (Form 1041) and state income tax returns for Trust A every year.

If the spouse needs help from an accountant, tax preparer or lawyer, the trust authorizes her to pay for it from trust assets.

If the grantors required it in the trust document, the trustee must give the final beneficiaries a copy of the trust's federal income tax return each year. The trustee also has a responsibility to keep the final beneficiaries reasonably well in-formed about management of the trust assets. (See Section E, above.)

The trustee owes a duty of complete honesty and responsibility to the final beneficiaries; this is called a "fiduciary duty." As trustee, the survivor must act in the best interest of those beneficiaries—but the trust document also authorizes the survivor to use trust assets for her own benefit, as discussed in Chapter 13.

The trustee is entitled, without court approval, to reasonable compensation from the assets of Trust A for serving as trustee. Usually the surviving spouse doesn't take compensation. But if the spouse becomes incapacitated, and the successor trustee takes over, the successor may want to take some trust money as compensation for the time and effort spent looking after the trust.

H. Transferring Property to the Surviving Spouse (Basic Trust Only)

If you make a basic marital trust with your spouse, and one spouse leaves property to the other, the survivor who inherits that property doesn't need to take any steps to transfer it to her trust (Trust #2). Under the terms of the trust document, the property stays in her revocable living trust.

The surviving spouse may, however, want to amend the trust document to name beneficiaries for the property.

> EXAMPLE: Edith and Jacques create a basic shared living trust. They transfer their house, which they own together, into the trust and name each other as beneficiaries. Edith names her son as alternate beneficiary.

When Jacques dies, Edith inherits his half-interest in the house. Because of the way the trust document is worded, she doesn't have to change the trust document to name a beneficiary for this half-interest in the house. Both halves will go to her son at her death. She may, however, want to amend the trust to make her son the primary beneficiary and name someone else to be alternate beneficiary.

For instructions on how to make a trust amendment, see Chapter 20.

I. Transferring Property to Beneficiaries

Whoever serves as trustee after a grantor dies (see Section B, above) must transfer property to beneficiaries in these situations:

- **Individual trust.** All trust property must be transferred.
- **Basic marital trust, when one spouse dies.** The surviving spouse must transfer the deceased spouse's trust property.
- **Basic marital trust, when both spouses have died.** The successor trustee must transfer the trust property of the second spouse to die.
- **AB trust, when one spouse dies.** The surviving spouse must transfer any property specifically left to beneficiaries and not left in Trust A, the irrevocable trust.
- **AB trust, when both spouses have died.** The successor trustee must transfer the property in Trusts A and B to the final beneficiaries.

The procedure for transferring trust property to the beneficiaries who inherit it depends on the kind of property the trustee is dealing with. Generally, a copy of the grantor's death certificate (both grantors', if the trust property was originally co-owned) and a copy of the trust document are necessary. In some cases, the trustee will need to prepare some other paperwork.

Specific requirements for transferring property vary slightly from place to place, and the trustee may have to make inquiries to banks, stock brokerages and other institutions about current procedures, but here are the general rules. A trustee who runs into difficulties has the authority to get help—from a lawyer, accountant or other expert—and pay for it from trust assets.

 Resources. *How to Probate an Estate in California*, by Julia Nissley (Nolo), contains instructions on transferring the property of a deceased California resident, including living trust property.

1. Property Without Title Documents

For trust property that doesn't have a title document—furniture, for example—the task of the trustee is quite simple. The trustee must promptly distribute the property to the beneficiaries named in the trust. If the trustee thinks it's a good idea, have the recipient sign a receipt.

2. Property With Title Documents

If an item of trust property has a title document that shows ownership in the name of the original trustee, the trustee must prepare and sign a new title document transferring ownership to the beneficiary. Usually, the trustee will need a copy of

the trust document and of the trust grantor's death certificate if the property is in someone else's possession.

Basically, the process of transferring trust property to beneficiaries is the reverse of transferring it into the trust in the first place. (That process is explained in Chapter 19.) For example, if you transfer real estate to your trust, you need a deed; to transfer it back out again, your successor trustee will also need a deed. If the trustee is dealing with a third party—for example, a brokerage company—it can help with the transaction or at least tell the successor trustee what documents are required.

If a vehicle was owned by the trust, the trustee should contact the state department of motor vehicles to get the forms required to transfer it to the beneficiary.

J. Preparing and Filing Tax Returns

Final personal tax returns and, if necessary, state or federal estate tax returns must be filed. Doing so is the responsibility of the executor named in the decedent's will. Usually, the same person is both executor and trustee.

A federal estate tax return must be filed if the decedent's gross estate was large enough. (See Chapter 13.) It's a complicated document, due nine months after the decedent's death, and will require expert help. Again, the trustee is entitled to pay for professional help out of the trust assets.

K. Administering a Child's Subtrust

If, in the trust document, the deceased grantor set up a child's subtrust, the trustee will have to manage that property until the beneficiary is old enough to receive it. A child's subtrust comes into being only if the beneficiary has not yet reached the age the grantor specified.

EXAMPLE: Carl sets up a living trust and names his two young children as beneficiaries. He specifies that if the children are younger than 30 when he dies, the property they are to receive from the trust should be kept in a separate children's subtrust for each child.

When Carl dies, one child is 30; the other is 25. The 30-year-old will receive her trust property with no strings attached. But a child's subtrust will be created for the 25-year-old. Carl's successor trustee is responsible for managing the property and turning it over to the child when he turns 30.

The trustee must:

- Invest subtrust property prudently. The trustee must always act honestly and in the best interests of the beneficiary. For example, the trustee must not make risky investments with subtrust property.
- Keep beneficiaries informed about the administration of the trust. (State law may require specific notices.)
- Use the income from subtrust property, or the subtrust property itself, to pay for the beneficiary's needs. The living trust document created with Quicken WillMaker Plus gives the trustee broad authority to use subtrust assets for the beneficiary's health, support, maintenance or education.

- File an annual trust income tax return. The subtrust may also have to pay estimated income taxes.
- Give the remaining subtrust property to the beneficiary when he or she reaches the age designated in the trust document.

The trustee can use subtrust assets to get professional assistance if necessary. For example, the trustee might want to pay a tax preparer for help with the subtrust's income tax return or consult a financial planner for investment advice.

The trust document also provides that the trustee of a subtrust is entitled to reasonable compensation for his or her work as trustee. The trustee decides what is a reasonable amount; the compensation is paid from the subtrust assets. A beneficiary who disagrees with the trustee's decisions about payment—or other decisions about management or distribution of the subtrust property—must go to court to challenge the trustee's decisions.

L. Administering a Custodianship

Someone who is appointed, in the trust document, to be the custodian of trust property inherited by a young beneficiary has about the same management responsibilities as the trustee of a child's subtrust. (See Section K, above.) The specifics are set out in the Uniform Transfers to Minors Act, as adopted by the particular state's legislature.

A custodian, however, does not have to file a separate income tax return. Any income from the property is reported on the beneficiary's own return. ■

Durable Powers of Attorney for Finances

Many people fear that they may some-day become seriously ill and unable to handle their own financial affairs—that they might be unable to pay bills, make bank deposits, watch over investments or collect insurance and government benefits. As you grow older or face the possibility of an incapacitating illness, it's wise to plan for such a contingency. Fortunately, there's a simple way to do so: preparing a durable power of attorney for finances.

A durable power of attorney for finances is an inexpensive, reliable legal document. In it, you name someone who will make your financial decisions if you become unable to do so yourself. If you ever do become incapacitated, the durable power of attorney will likely appear as a minor miracle to those who are close to you.

The perils of forging a signature. If someone becomes incapacitated, panicky family members may consider just faking the signatures necessary to carry on routine financial matters. It may seem perfectly acceptable to sign Aunt Amanda's name to a check if the money is used to pay her phone bill.

But this is forgery—and it's a crime. The law is strict in this area to guard against dishonest family members who might loot a relative's assets.

Forging a signature on checks, bills of sale, tax returns or other financial documents may work for a while, but it will probably be discovered eventually. And then the court proceeding everyone was trying to avoid will be necessary—and a judge will not be eager to put a proven liar in charge of a relative's finances.

Important Terms

- **Principal.** The person who creates and signs the power of attorney document, authorizing someone else to act for him or her. If you make a durable power of attorney for finances, you are the principal.
- **Attorney-in-Fact.** The person who is authorized to act for the principal. In many states, the attorney-in-fact is also referred to as an agent of the principal.
- **Alternate Attorney-in-Fact.** The person who takes over as attorney-in-fact if your first choice cannot or will not serve. Also called successor attorney-in-fact.
- **Durable Power of Attorney.** A power of attorney that will remain in effect even if the principal becomes incapacitated, or will take effect only if the principal becomes incapacitated. This is the kind of power of attorney you make with Quicken WillMaker Plus.
- **Incapacitated.** Unable to handle one's own financial matters or health care decisions. Also called disabled or incompetent in some states. Usually, a physician makes the determination.

Keeping track of information for your attorney-in-fact. The attorney-in-fact you name may need to know a vast number of details about your property and how you deal with it. With Quicken WillMaker Plus you can make an "Information for Caregivers and Survivors" form to help with this task. With this document, you can provide a comprehensive guide of the details of your life—ranging from information about your property and your financial accounts, to the names and addresses of people you want contacted in the event of your illness—to the person who will care for you in the event of your incapacity. To find out more, click on the Document List button and select Information for Caregivers and Survivors from the list.

A. What Quicken WillMaker Plus Can Do

Quicken WillMaker Plus allows you to create your own durable power of attorney for finances. Using Quicken WillMaker Plus, you can:

- name the person who will handle your financial matters; this person is called your attorney-in-fact
- appoint someone to replace your attorney-in-fact if he or she cannot serve, and
- state exactly how much authority you want your attorney-in-fact to have over your finances.

In addition to your durable power of attorney for finances, Quicken WillMaker Plus prints out a number of related documents. The first of these is an information sheet for you to give to your attorney-in-fact, explaining what his or her responsibilities will be. There are also several forms designed to make your attorney-in-fact's job easier—including forms for delegating tasks to others and resigning from the job if that becomes necessary. Finally, Quicken WillMaker Plus produces a form that you can use to revoke your durable power of attorney if you change your mind. Each document is explained in this chapter.

How a Durable Power of Attorney Fits Into an Estate Plan

A durable power of attorney for finances serves an important purpose by arranging for the management of your finances and avoiding the need for a conservatorship. But it is only part of an estate plan—that is, a plan for distributing your property and taking care of your family at your death. (See Chapter 1.)

You need other documents to accomplish other goals. Quicken WillMaker Plus allows you to create a basic estate plan using the following documents:

- your will (see Chapters 2 through 12)
- a living trust (see Chapters 13 through 21)
- your health care documents (see Chapter 23)
- your durable power of attorney for finances, and
- a document specifying what you would like in terms of final arrangements—that is, body disposition, memorial services and organ donation (see Chapter 24).

B. What This Document Can Do

Almost everyone with property or an income can benefit from a durable power of attorney for finances. It's particularly important, however, to have a durable power of attorney if you fear that health problems may make it impossible for you to handle your financial matters.

The main reason to make a durable power of attorney for finances is to avoid court proceedings if you become incapacitated. If you don't have a durable power of attorney, your relatives or other loved ones will have to ask a judge to name someone to manage your financial affairs.

These proceedings are commonly known as conservatorship proceedings. Depending on where you live, the person appointed to manage your finances is called a conservator, guardian of the estate, committee or curator.

Avoiding Conservatorship Proceedings

Conservatorship proceedings can be complicated, expensive and even embarrassing. Your loved ones must ask the court to rule that you cannot take care of your own affairs—a public airing of a very private matter. Court proceedings are matters of public record; in some places, a notice may even be published in a local newspaper. If relatives fight over who is to be the conservator, the proceedings will surely become even more disagreeable, sometimes downright nasty. And all of this causes costs to mount up, especially if lawyers must be hired.

If a judge decides to appoint a conservator, there is no guarantee that the person who gets the job will be the person you would have chosen. A judge may ask you to express a preference for conservator—and will strongly consider what you say—but even this will not ensure that your choice will serve. To increase the chances that your wishes will be followed, you can use the durable power of attorney you make with Quicken WillMaker Plus to name your attorney-in-fact as conservator, if a court must ever appoint one. (See Section K, below.)

If you don't name a conservator in your power of attorney document, state law generally provides a priority list for who should be appointed. For example, a number of states make the person's spouse the first choice as conservator, followed by an adult child, parent and brother or sister. In many states, the law allows the court to appoint whoever it determines will act in your best interests.

The appointment of a conservator is usually just the beginning of court proceedings. Often the conservator must:

- post a bond—a kind of insurance policy that pays if the conservator steals or misuses property
- prepare detailed financial reports—or hire a lawyer or accountant to prepare them and periodically file them with the court, and
- get court approval for certain transactions, such as selling real estate or making slightly risky investments.

All of this, of course, costs money—your money.

A conservatorship isn't necessarily permanent, but it may be ended only by the court.

You can probably avoid the troubles of a conservatorship if you take the time to create a durable power of attorney for finances now. When you make a durable power of attorney, you give your attorney-in-fact full legal authority to handle your financial affairs. A conservatorship proceeding would be necessary only if no one were willing to serve as attorney-in-fact, the attorney-in-fact wanted guidance from a court or a close relative thought the attorney-in-fact wasn't acting in your best interests.

1. If You Are Married

If you are married, don't assume that your spouse will automatically be able to manage all of your finances if you cannot do so.

Your spouse does have some authority over property you own together—for example, your spouse may pay bills from a joint bank account or sell stock in a joint brokerage account. There are significant limits, however, on your spouse's right to sell property that both of you own. For example, in most states, both spouses must agree to the sale of co-owned real estate or cars. Because an incapacitated spouse can't consent to such a sale, the other spouse's hands are tied.

And when it comes to property that belongs only to you, your spouse has no legal authority. You must use a durable power of attorney to give your spouse authority over your property.

EXAMPLE: New York residents Michael and Carrie have been married for 47 years. Their major assets are a home and stock. They own the home in both their names as joint tenants. The stock was bought only in Michael's name, and the couple has never transferred it into shared ownership. Michael becomes incapacitated and requires expensive medical treatment. Legally, Carrie cannot sell the stock to pay for medical costs.

EXAMPLE: Janice's husband, Hal, is incapacitated and living in a nearby nursing home. Janice wants to raise money by selling Hal's old car, which he can no longer drive, but she can't because the title is in Hal's name.

2. If You Have a Living Trust

A central purpose of a revocable living trust is to avoid probate. (See Chapter 13.) But the trust can also be useful if you become incapable of taking care of your financial affairs. That's because the person who will distribute trust property after your death—called the successor trustee—can also, in most cases, take over management of the trust property if you become incapacitated.

But few people transfer all their property to a living trust, and the successor trustee has no authority over property that the trust doesn't own. So although a living trust may be helpful, it is not a complete substitute for a durable power of attorney for finances.

The two documents work well together, however, especially if you name the same trusted person to be your attorney-in-fact and the successor trustee of your living trust. That person will have authority to manage property both in and out of your living trust. You can also give your attorney-in-fact the power to transfer items of your property into your living trust. (See Section H8, below.)

EXAMPLE: Consuela, a widow, owns all the stock of a prosperous clothing manufacturing corporation. To avoid probate, she transfers the stock into a living trust, naming her brother, Rodolfo, as successor trustee. If Consuela becomes incapacitated, Rodolfo will become acting trustee and manage the stock in the trust for Consuela's benefit.

Consuela also prepares a durable power of attorney for finances and names Rodolfo as her attorney-in-fact. That gives him authority over assets she does not transfer to the trust—for example, her bank accounts and car. In her durable power of attorney, she also gives Rodolfo the power to transfer property into her living trust, if he feels that's in her best interest.

3. If You Own Joint Tenancy Property

Joint tenancy is a way that two or more people can own property together. The most notable feature of joint tenancy is that when one owner dies, the other owners automatically get the deceased person's share of the property. But if you become incapacitated, the other owners have very limited authority over your share of the joint tenancy property.

For example, if you and someone else own a bank account in joint tenancy, and one of you becomes incapacitated, the other owner is legally entitled to use the funds. The healthy joint tenant can take care of the financial needs of the incapacitated person simply by paying bills from the joint account. But the other account owner has no legal right to endorse checks made out to the incapacitated person. In practice, it might be possible—if not technically legal—to get an incapacitated person's checks into a joint account by stamping them "For Deposit Only," but that's not the easiest way to handle things.

Matters get more complicated with other kinds of joint tenancy property. Real estate is a good example. If one owner becomes incapacitated, the other has no legal authority to sell or refinance the incapacitated owner's share.

In a durable power of attorney, you can give your attorney-in-fact authority over property you own in joint tenancy—including real estate and bank accounts.

C. What This Document Cannot Do

The expense and intrusion of a conservatorship are rarely desirable. In a few situations, however, special concerns justify the process. For example, you may not know anyone who could handle the job of managing your finances—or you may expect disgruntled family members to cause trouble for the person you choose as your attorney-in-fact. In these situations, it's probably better not to make a durable power of attorney for finances. In some other situations, a document other than a durable power of attorney for finances will better meet your needs.

1. Provide Court Supervision of Your Finances

If you can't think of someone you trust enough to appoint as your attorney-in-fact, with broad authority over your property and finances—and who is willing to take on the responsibility— don't create a durable power of attorney. A conservatorship, with the safeguard of court supervision, may be worth the extra cost and trouble for this purpose.

2. Protect Against Family Fights

A durable power of attorney is a powerful legal document. Once you've finalized yours, anyone who wants to challenge your plans for financial management will face an uphill battle in court. But if you expect that family members will challenge your document or make continual trouble for your attorney-in-fact, a conservatorship may be preferable. Your relatives may still fight, but at least the court will be there to keep an eye on your welfare and your property.

Help if your family is feisty. If you expect family fights and feel uncomfortable making a durable power of attorney for finances, you may want to talk with a knowledgeable lawyer. He or she can help you weigh your concerns and options, and decide whether a durable power of attorney is the best option for you. (See Chapter 25.)

3. Authorize Health Care Decisions

A durable power of attorney for finances does not give your attorney-in-fact legal authority to make health care decisions for you. To make sure that your wishes for health care are known and followed, you should use Quicken WillMaker Plus to create a health care directive. (See Chapter 23.)

4. Authorize Decisions About Marriage, Adoption, Voting, Wills

You cannot authorize your attorney-in-fact to marry, adopt, vote in public elections or make a will on your behalf. These acts are considered too personal to delegate to someone else.

5. Give Powers Delegated to Others

If you've already given someone legal authority to manage some or all of your property, you cannot delegate that authority to your attorney-in-fact.

For example, if you become incapacitated, your attorney-in-fact will not be able to:

- control property in a living trust you created giving the successor trustee power over that property, or
- manage your interest in a partnership business if you have a signed agreement giving your partners authority to do so.

6. Create, Modify or Revoke a Trust

Quicken WillMaker Plus's power of attorney form doesn't allow you to give your attorney-in-fact permission to create, modify or revoke a trust on your behalf—with one exception. If you've already set up a revocable living trust, you may give your attorney-in-fact the power to transfer property to that trust.

D. About Your Attorney-in-Fact

This section explains more about the responsibilities the person you name as attorney-in-fact will have toward you and your property.

1. Possible Powers

Commonly, people give an attorney-in-fact broad power over their finances. But it's up to you. Using Quicken WillMaker Plus, you can give your attorney-in-fact authority to do some or all of the following:

- use your assets to pay your everyday expenses and those of your family
- handle transactions with banks and other financial institutions
- buy, sell, maintain, pay taxes on and mortgage real estate and other property
- file and pay your taxes
- manage your retirement accounts
- collect benefits from Social Security, Medicare or other government programs or civil or military service
- invest your money in stocks, bonds and mutual funds
- buy and sell insurance policies and annuities for you
- operate your small business

- claim or disclaim property you get from others
- make gifts of your assets to organizations and individuals that you choose
- transfer property to a living trust you've already set up, and
- hire someone to represent you in court.

(These powers are discussed in detail in Section H, below.)

Quicken WillMaker Plus allows you to tailor your durable power of attorney for finances to fit your needs by choosing which powers you grant and placing certain conditions and restrictions upon the attorney-in-fact. For example, you can give your attorney-in-fact authority over your real estate, with the express restriction that your house may not be sold.

2. Legal Responsibilities

The attorney-in-fact you appoint in your durable power of attorney is a fiduciary—someone who holds a position of trust and must act in your best interests. The law requires your attorney-in-fact to:

- handle your property honestly and prudently
- avoid conflicts of interest
- keep your property completely separate from his or her own, and
- keep adequate records.

These standards do not present problems in most simple situations. For example, if you just want your attorney-in-fact to sign for your pension check, deposit it in your bank account and pay for your basic needs, there is little possibility of uncertainty or dispute.

Sometimes, however, these rules impose unnecessary hardships on an attorney-in-fact. For example, your property may already be mixed with that of your attorney-in-fact, and it may make

good sense for that to continue. Quicken WillMaker Plus allows you to insert clauses in your power of attorney document that permit your attorney-in-fact to deviate from some of the rules above, so that the attorney-in-fact's freedom isn't unnecessarily fettered. (See Section I, below.)

3. Liability for Mistakes

Your attorney-in-fact must be careful with your money and other property. State laws require an attorney-in-fact to act as a prudent person would under the circumstances. That means the primary goal is not to lose your money.

The attorney-in-fact may, however, make careful investment moves on your behalf. For example, if your money is in a low-interest bank account, the attorney-in-fact might invest the money in government bonds, which pay higher interest but are still very safe.

Because most people choose a spouse, close relative or friend to be attorney-in-fact, your Quicken WillMaker Plus power of attorney makes your attorney-in-fact liable only for losses resulting from intentional wrongdoing or extreme carelessness—not for a well-meaning decision that turns out badly.

4. Record Keeping Responsibilities

Your attorney-in-fact is legally required to keep accurate and separate records for all transactions made on your behalf. Good records are particularly important if the attorney-in-fact ever wants to resign and turn the responsibility over to another person.

Record keeping isn't an onerous requirement. The attorney-in-fact must simply be able to show where and how your money has been spent. In most instances, it's enough to have a balanced checkbook and receipts for bills paid and claims made. And because the attorney-in-fact will probably file tax returns on your behalf, income and expense records may be necessary.

EXAMPLE: Keiji appoints Kathryn, his niece, to serve as his attorney-in-fact. Keiji receives income from his savings, two IRAs, Social Security and stock dividends. Kathryn must keep records of the income for bank and tax purposes.

You and your prospective attorney-in-fact should discuss and agree on what record keeping is appropriate. The attorney-in-fact may also want to review your current records now to make sure they're in order. If you don't have clear records, the attorney-in-fact may have to spend a lot of time sorting things out later.

As part of managing your finances, the attorney-in-fact may hire a bookkeeper, accountant or other financial adviser and pay for the services from your property.

Getting help with organizing. If, like many people, you keep records in haphazardly labeled shoe boxes and file folders, this may be a good time to get organized. For help getting organized, use Quicken WillMaker Plus's "Information for Caregivers and Survivors" form.

When Court Supervision May Be Required

An attorney-in-fact is not directly supervised by a court; that's the whole point of naming one. The attorney-in-fact is not required to file reports with any courts or government agencies.

But a court may become involved if someone close to you fears that the attorney-in-fact is acting dishonestly or not in your best interests. It's rare, but close relatives or friends may ask a court to order the attorney-in-fact to take certain actions. Or they may ask the court to terminate the power of attorney and appoint a conservator to look after your affairs. If a conservator is appointed for you, the attorney-in-fact will have to account to the conservator—or the conservator may revoke your durable power of attorney altogether. (See Section P, below.) As mentioned above, you can use your durable power of attorney for finances to name your attorney-in-fact as your first choice for conservator. (See Section K, below.)

Some states have statutes that set out specific procedures for such court actions. For example, a California statute authorizes any interested person, including relatives and friends of the principal, to ask a court to resolve questions relating to the durable power of attorney. Tennessee law provides that the next of kin can petition a court to require an attorney-in-fact to post a bond—something like an insurance policy, generally issued by a surety company.

Even if your state does not have a statute specifically authorizing court actions, someone interested in your welfare and upset with the attorney-in-fact could still go to court and ask for a conservator to be appointed.

E. The Basics of Your Durable Power of Attorney

You can create a valid power of attorney if you are at least 18 years old and of sound mind. This mental competency requirement isn't hard to meet. Generally, you must understand what a durable power of attorney for finances is and does—and you must understand that you are making one.

To make your durable power of attorney with Quicken WillMaker Plus, you must enter some basic identifying information about yourself. This section explains the questions the program poses, in the order they appear.

1. Your Name

If you have already used Quicken WillMaker Plus to prepare your will, living trust, health care directives or final arrangements, your name will automatically appear on the screen that requests this information.

If it does not, enter your name the way it appears on formal business documents, such as your driver's license, bank accounts or real estate deeds. This may or may not be the name that appears on your birth certificate.

If you have used different names in important documents, you can list all of them on the screen, separated by aka, which stands for "also known as." Be sure to enter all names in which you hold bank accounts, stocks, bonds, real estate and other property. This will make it far easier for your attorney-in-fact to get his or her job done.

If you use more than one name and you're up for some extra work, you may also consider settling on one name for your Quicken WillMaker Plus document, and then changing your other

documents to conform. That will clean up your records and save your attorney-in-fact some trouble later on. To change your name on official documents and records—for example, bank accounts, deeds or Social Security records—you'll have to contact the appropriate government office or financial institution to find out what documentation they'll need.

2. Your Social Security Number

Quicken WillMaker Plus asks you to enter your nine-digit Social Security number. Although you are not legally required to disclose the number, it can be a good idea to provide it. Your attorney-in-fact—and the people and institutions whom he or she deals with on your behalf—will need the number to obtain your financial information and take care of your affairs.

That said, if you don't want to include your Social Security number in your durable power of attorney, you don't have to. You may, for example, prefer not to provide your Social Security number if you know that you will file your document with the local land records office. (See Section L4, below.) This will keep the number out of the public records. If you don't include your Social Security number in your power of attorney, be very sure that your attorney-in-fact knows what the number is.

3. Your Gender

Quicken WillMaker Plus asks whether you are male or female so that your durable power of attorney document will include the correct gender pronoun instead of the awkward "he or she" and "his or her."

4. Your Address

Enter the complete address of your residence. If during the course of the year you live in more than one state, use the address in the state where you vote, register vehicles, own valuable property, have bank accounts or run a business. If you've already made your will, health care directives or a living trust, be consistent: Use the same address for every document.

F. When Your Document Takes Effect

Your durable power of attorney for finances is effective as soon as you sign it. This means that your attorney-in-fact can start acting on your behalf whenever you choose. If you need someone to help you keep an eye on your finances, you may want your attorney-in-fact to start acting for you right away. On the other hand, you may prefer that your attorney-in-fact use the document only if you are unable to handle matters yourself, either because you are temporarily ill or injured or because of long-term incapacity.

If you want your attorney-in-fact to use the document only if you become incapacitated and unable to take care of your finances, be sure to clearly convey those wishes to the person you name. If you don't trust that your attorney-in-fact will refrain from using the document unless and until you are incapacitated, consider naming someone else to represent you.

Discussing Your Wishes

Set aside time to talk with your attorney-in-fact about when he or she should start taking care of financial tasks for you. You can agree with your attorney-in-fact that he or she should not exercise any authority under the document unless you become completely unable to take care of yourself and your property — or unless you otherwise direct him or her to do so. With respect to exercising authority under the document, your attorney-in-fact is legally required to follow your wishes.

If you become dissatisfied with your attorney-in-fact's actions, and you are still of sound mind, you can revoke the durable power of attorney and end your attorney-in-fact's power to act for you.

Springing powers of attorney. You may have heard of "springing" powers of attorney—that is, documents that become effective only if you are incapacitated. Many people like the idea of these documents, because no one can take action regarding your finances until at least one doctor certifies that you're not well enough to manage them yourself. Unfortunately, there are many inconveniences involved in making a springing document and getting it accepted. Because of the hassles involved, most experts advise that you make an immediately effective power of attorney document. If you feel strongly that you want a springing document instead, consult an attorney.

G. Choosing Your Attorney-in-Fact

Next, Quicken WillMaker Plus asks you to name your attorney-in-fact. This is the most important decision you must make when you create a durable power of attorney.

Depending on the powers you grant, the attorney-in-fact may have tremendous power over your property. You need to choose someone you trust completely. Fortunately, most of us know at least one such person—usually a spouse, relative or close friend. If there's no one you trust completely with this authority, a durable power of attorney isn't for you.

Remember that you can't count on anyone to keep an eye on the attorney-in-fact once he or she takes over your finances. If your attorney-in-fact handles your affairs carelessly or dishonestly, the only recourse would be a lawsuit—usually not a satisfactory approach. Lawsuits are burdensome and expensive, and would entangle your loved ones in all the legal red tape a power of attorney is designed to avoid. And there's no guarantee that money an incompetent attorney-in-fact lost would ever be recovered. This reality is not intended to frighten you needlessly, but simply to underscore the need to make a careful choice about who will represent you.

Any competent adult can serve as your attorney-in-fact; the person most definitely doesn't have to be a lawyer. But don't appoint someone without first discussing it with that person and making sure he or she accepts this serious responsibility. If you don't, you may well cause problems down the line. The person you've chosen may not want to serve, for a variety of reasons. And even if the person would be willing, if he or she doesn't know of his or her responsibilities, confusion and delay are inevitable if you become incapacitated.

Getting help. Quicken WillMaker Plus prints out an information sheet you can give to your attorney-in-fact explaining the responsibilities of the job. You can use this document to help you remember the main issues when talking with your attorney-in-fact about his or her duties.

In most situations, the attorney-in-fact does not need extensive experience in financial management; common sense, dependability and complete honesty are enough. Your attorney-in-fact can get any reasonably necessary professional help—from an accountant, lawyer or tax preparer, perhaps—and pay for it out of your assets.

Sometimes it's tough to know whom to choose. Perhaps your mate is ill or wouldn't be a good choice for other reasons. Or you may not know anyone that you feel entirely comfortable asking to take over your financial affairs. Or, if you have an active, complex investment portfolio or own a business, you might decide that your attorney-in-fact needs business skills, knowledge or management abilities beyond those of the people closest to you.

If you're not sure whom your attorney-in-fact should be, read the rest of this section and discuss the issue with those close to you. If you can't come up with a family member or close friend to name, you may want to consider asking your lawyer, business partner or banker to serve as attorney-in-fact. If you really know and trust the person, it may be a good option for you. Keep in mind that it's better not to make a durable power of attorney than to entrust your affairs to someone in whom you don't have complete confidence.

Poor Choices for Attorney-in-Fact

Here are some suggestions on whom to avoid when you're choosing an attorney-in-fact:

- To carry out duties and responsibilities properly and promptly, it's usually best that the attorney-in-fact live nearby. Although overnight mail, faxes, email and other technological wonders have made it easier to conduct business long-distance, it's still best for your attorney-in-fact to be close at hand—or at least willing to travel and spend time handling your affairs when needed. After all, this is the person who will be responsible for day-to-day details of your finances: opening your mail, paying bills, looking after property and so on. Of course, many families are spread across the country these days. If there's only one person you trust enough to name as attorney-in-fact, and he or she lives far away, you may have to settle for the less than ideal situation.

- Don't name an institution, such as a bank, as attorney-in-fact. It isn't legal in some states, and it's definitely not desirable. Serving as attorney-in-fact is a personal responsibility, and there should be personal connection and trust between you and your attorney-in-fact. If the person you trust most happens to be your banker, appoint that person, not the bank.

! Avoiding family conflict. If there are long-standing feuds among family members, they may object to your choice of attorney-in-fact or the extent of the authority delegated. If you foresee any such conflicts, it's wise to try to defuse them in advance. A discussion with the people who are leery of the power of attorney might help. If you still feel uncomfortable after talking things over, you may want to discuss the troubles with a knowledgeable lawyer. A lawyer can review your estate planning documents and might help you feel reassured that your plans will be carried out as you wish.

1. If You Are Married

If you're married, you'll probably want to name your spouse as your attorney-in-fact unless there is a compelling reason not to do so. There are powerful legal and practical reasons, in addition to the emotional ones, for appointing your spouse. The main one is that naming anyone else creates the risk of conflicts between the attorney-in-fact and your spouse over how to manage property that belongs to both spouses.

> **EXAMPLE:** Henry and Amelia, a married couple, each create a durable power of attorney for finances. Henry names Amelia as his attorney-in-fact, but Amelia names her sister Anna. Later, Amelia becomes unable to manage her financial affairs, and Anna takes over as her attorney-in-fact. Soon Anna and Henry are arguing bitterly over what should be done with the house and investments that Henry and Amelia own together. If they can't resolve their differences, Henry or Anna may have to go to court and ask a judge to determine what is in Amelia's best interests.

However, if your spouse is ill, quite elderly or simply not equipped to manage your financial affairs, you may have to name someone else as attorney-in-fact. The wisest course is for you and your spouse to agree on whom the attorney-in-fact should be, perhaps one of your grown children.

> ⚠ **Divorce may not end your spouse's authority.** If your spouse is your attorney-in-fact, that designation does not automatically end if you get divorced, except in Alabama, California, Colorado, Illinois, Indiana, Kansas, Minnesota, Missouri, Ohio, Pennsylvania, Texas, Washington and Wisconsin. In any state, after a divorce you should revoke the power of attorney and create a new one, naming someone else as your new attorney-in-fact.

2. If You Have a Living Trust

If you have created a revocable living trust to avoid probate or minimize estate taxes, the successor trustee you named in the trust document will have power over the trust property if you become incapacitated. If you and your spouse made a living trust together, the trust document almost certainly gives your spouse authority over trust property if you become incapacitated. (See Section B2, above, and Chapter 13.)

Creating a durable power of attorney for finances doesn't change any of this. Your attorney-in-fact will not have authority over property in your living trust. To avoid conflicts, it is usually best to have the same person managing both trust property and nontrust property if you become incapacitated. So, normally, you'll name the same person as successor trustee and as your attorney-in-fact.

EXAMPLE: Carlos, a widower, prepares a revocable living trust to avoid probate and a durable power of attorney for finances in case he becomes incapacitated. He names his son, Jeffrey, as successor trustee of the living trust and attorney-in-fact under the durable power of attorney.

Several years later Carlos has a stroke and is temporarily unable to handle his everyday finances. Jeffrey steps in to deposit his father's pension checks and pay monthly bills, using his authority as attorney-in-fact. As successor trustee, he also has legal authority over the property Carlos transferred to his living trust, including Carlos's house.

3. Appointing More Than One Person

In general, it's a bad idea to name more than one attorney-in-fact, because conflicts between them could disrupt the handling of your finances. Also, some banks and other financial institutions prefer to deal with a single attorney-in-fact.

Still, it is legal to name more than one person—and Quicken WillMaker Plus allows you to name up to three people to serve together. But if you're tempted to name more than one person simply so that no one feels hurt or left out, think again. It may be better to pick one person for the job and explain your reasoning to the others now. If you name more than one person and they don't get along, they may wind up resolving their disputes in court. The result might be more bad feelings than if you had just picked one person to be attorney-in-fact, and explained your choice, in the first place.

a. Making Decisions

If you name more than one attorney-in-fact, you'll have to grapple with the question of how they should make decisions. You can require co-agents to carry out their duties in one of two ways:

- they must all reach agreement before they take any action on your behalf, or
- they may make decisions independent of one another.

Both methods have strengths and pitfalls, and there's no hard-and-fast rule on which is better. Choose the approach that feels most comfortable to you.

Requiring your attorneys-in-fact to act jointly ensures that decisions are made carefully and with the knowledge of everyone involved, but co-ordinating multiple decision makers can be burdensome and time-consuming. On the other hand, allowing your attorneys-in-fact to act separately makes it easy to get things done, but allowing two or three people to make independent decisions about your finances can lead to poor record keeping and general confusion. For example, your attorneys-in-fact may independently take money out of your bank accounts or buy and sell stock without full knowledge of what the others are doing to manage your investments.

b. If There Is a Disagreement

If your attorneys-in-fact get into a dispute that interferes with their ability to represent you properly, they may need help working things out. Getting help could mean submitting the dispute to mediation or arbitration—or going to court to have a judge decide what's best. Your attorneys-in-fact can decide how they want to handle the matter, keeping in mind that their foremost responsibility is to act in your best interest. The downside of all this is not just that there could be confusion and delays in handling your finances, but that you'll probably be the one to pay the costs of settling the dispute. All these are reasons to name just one attorney-in-fact.

c. If One or More Cannot Serve

If you name more than one attorney-in-fact, and one of them can't serve, the others will continue to serve. If none of them can serve, an alternate can take over.

 If you want to name more than three people. The best approach is usually to choose just one attorney-in-fact. But Quicken WillMaker Plus allows you to name up to three people to serve together. Asking two or three people to manage your finances may prove unwieldy enough—counting on more than three to coordinate their actions on your behalf would be a logistical nightmare. If you want to name more than three attorneys-in-fact, talk with a lawyer.

4. Naming Alternates

It's a good idea to name someone to take over as your attorney-in-fact in case your first choice can't serve or needs to resign. Quicken WillMaker Plus allows you to name up to two alternate attorneys-in-fact, officially called successors. Your first alternate would take over if your initial choice can't serve. The second alternate would take the job only if your first and second choices can't keep it.

When naming alternates, use the same criteria that you used to make your first choice for attorney-in-fact. Your alternates should be every bit as trustworthy and competent. If you don't know anyone you trust well enough to name as a first or second alternate, skip the matter altogether.

Someone who is asked to serve as an alternate attorney-in-fact may be worried about possible liability for the acts of the original attorney-in-fact. To protect against this, the Quicken WillMaker Plus power of attorney form states that a successor attorney-in-fact is not liable for any acts of a prior attorney-in-fact.

You can also authorize your attorney-in-fact to appoint someone to serve if all those you named cannot. You do this by giving your attorney-in-fact permission to delegate tasks to others. (See Section I2, below.) Allowing your attorney-in-fact to delegate his or her job to someone else eliminates the risk that the position might become vacant because of the original attorney-in-fact's disability or resignation. If this occurs, and you haven't named a successor or none of your successors are available, your durable power of attorney would be useless. There would have to be a conservatorship proceeding to find someone to manage your finances.

If You Name More Than One Attorney-in-Fact

If you name more than one attorney-in-fact, the person you name as a first alternate will take over only if all of your attorneys-in-fact must give up the job. If any number of your first choices can continue to serve, they may do so alone, without the addition of your alternate.

If you name a second alternate, that person will take over only in the extremely unlikely event that all of your named attorneys-in-fact and your first alternate cannot serve.

H. Specific Financial Powers

Using Quicken WillMaker Plus, you can give your attorney-in-fact up to 14 specific financial powers. The powers may put an enormous amount of control over your finances into the hands of your attorney-in-fact, and it's important that you understand exactly what each power authorizes your attorney-in-fact to do. To that end, Quicken WillMaker Plus walks you through each power, one at a time, asking whether you want to grant it or not.

If you grant all the powers, your attorney-in-fact will be able to handle your investments, real estate, banking and other financial tasks. The attorney-in-fact can use your assets to pay your debts and expenses—including home maintenance, taxes, insurance premiums, wage claims, medical care, child support, alimony and your personal allowance. The attorney-in-fact can sign deeds, make gifts, pay school expenses, and endorse and deposit checks.

As you go through the list of powers, you may find yourself feeling concerned about how much power you're putting in someone else's hands. These feelings are not unusual, as the lists of actions your attorney-in-fact can take are long, exhaustive and perhaps a bit overwhelming. As reassurance, keep in mind your attorney-in-fact's overriding legal duty to act carefully—and always with your best interests at heart. (See Section D2, above.) If you still find yourself feeling uncomfortable, take some time to reflect on your choice of attorney-in-fact; be sure you've chosen the best person for the job.

Each of the financial powers is explained here. They are numbered as they appear in the Quicken WillMaker Plus program.

1. Real Estate Transactions

This power puts the attorney-in-fact in charge of any real estate you own. Your attorney-in-fact must, for example, use your assets to pay your mortgage and taxes and arrange for necessary repairs and maintenance to your home. Most important, the attorney-in-fact may sell, mortgage, partition or lease your real estate.

The attorney-in-fact may also take any other action connected to real estate. For example, your attorney-in-fact may:

- buy or lease real estate for you
- refinance your mortgage to get a better interest rate
- pay off legal claims on your property
- buy insurance for your property
- build, remodel or remove structures on your property
- grant easements over your property, and
- bring or defend lawsuits over real estate.

Restricting the Sale of Your Home

Losing your home, especially if you've lived there many years, can be a disturbing prospect. Some people feel quite strongly that the attorney-in-fact should not sell their home—no matter what happens. If you want to grant the real estate power but forbid your attorney-in-fact from selling or mortgaging your home, Quicken WillMaker Plus allows you to include that restriction.

But think carefully before you tie the hands of your attorney-in-fact in this way. You certainly don't want to lose your home—but a financial emergency may make it necessary. You should probably trust the person you name as your attorney-in-fact to use discretion to make the decision based on your best interests—particularly if you have named your spouse or other co-owner of your home to serve as your attorney-in-fact.

2. Personal Property Transactions

Personal property here means physical items of property—for example, cars, furniture, jewelry, computers and stereo equipment. It does not include real estate or intangible kinds of property such as stocks or bank notes.

If you grant this power, your attorney-in-fact can buy, sell, rent or exchange personal property on your behalf. Your attorney-in-fact can also insure, use, move, store, repair or pawn your personal things. Again, all actions must be taken in your best interest.

EXAMPLE: Paul names his wife, Gloria, as his attorney-in-fact for financial matters. When he later goes into a nursing home, his old car, which he can no longer use, becomes an expense Gloria cannot afford. As Paul's attorney-in-fact, she has legal authority to sell the car.

3. Stock, Bond, Commodity and Option Transactions

This power gives your attorney-in-fact the power to manage your securities—including stocks, bonds, mutual funds, certificates of deposit, commodities and call and put options. Your attorney-in-fact can buy or sell securities on your behalf, accept or transfer certificates or other evidence of ownership and exercise voting rights.

Brokers may use different forms. Many brokerage houses have their own durable power of attorney forms. If yours does, it's a good idea to use it in addition to your Quicken WillMaker Plus power of attorney. Using your broker's form will make things easier for your attorney-in-fact, because your broker will have no need to investigate your power of attorney and quibble over its terms. The broker will already have its form on file and will understand exactly what your attorney-in-fact is authorized to do.

4. Banking and Other Financial Institution Transactions

One of the most common reasons for making a durable power of attorney is to arrange for someone to handle banking transactions. If you give your attorney-in-fact authority to handle your bank accounts, your bills can be paid, and pension or other checks can be deposited in your accounts even if you can no longer take care of these matters yourself.

EXAMPLE: Virginia, who is in her 70s, is admitted to the hospital for emergency surgery. She's too weak to even think about paying her bills or depositing her Social Security check—and, anyway, she can't get to the bank. Fortunately, she earlier created a durable power of attorney for finances, naming her niece Marianne as her attorney-in-fact. Marianne can deposit Virginia's check and sign checks to pay the bills that come while Virginia is in the hospital.

Your attorney-in-fact may open and close accounts with banks, savings and loans, credit unions or other financial institutions on your behalf. The attorney-in-fact may write checks on these accounts, endorse checks you receive and receive account statements. The attorney-in-fact also has access to your safe deposit box, to withdraw or add to its contents.

In most states, the attorney-in-fact may also borrow money on your behalf and pledge your assets as security for the loan.

Financial institutions may use different forms. Many banks and other financial institutions have their own durable power of attorney forms. Even though granting Quicken WillMaker Plus's banking power will give your attorney-in-fact authority to act on your behalf at any financial institution, it's a good idea to use the financial institution's form in addition to your Quicken WillMaker Plus form. Using the form that your financial institution is most familiar with will make it easier for your attorney-in-fact to get things done.

Signing Checks and Other Documents

Many people wonder how the attorney-in-fact signs checks and other documents on behalf of the principal. Exact procedures vary depending on both local custom and the procedures of a particular financial institution or government agency. In some places, after establishing authority with a particular institution or agency, the attorney-in-fact will sign his or her own name to checks and documents, followed by "POA" or other language such as "under power of attorney dated June 15, 2003." In other locations, the attorney-in-fact will first sign your name and then his or her own name, followed by the "POA" designation.

5. Business Operating Transactions

This power gives your attorney-in-fact authority to act for you in operating a business that you own yourself or that you run as a partnership, limited liability company or corporation. Subject to the terms of a partnership agreement, operating agreement or corporate rules set out in the bylaws and shareholders' agreements, your attorney-in-fact may:

- sell or liquidate the business
- merge with another company
- prepare, sign and file reports, information and returns with government agencies
- pay business taxes
- enforce the terms of any partnership agreement in court, and
- exercise any power or option you have under a partnership agreement.

If your business is a sole proprietorship, the attorney-in-fact may also:

- hire and fire employees
- move the business
- change the nature of the business or its methods of operation, including selling, marketing, accounting and advertising
- change the name of the business
- change the form of the business's organization—that is, enter into a partnership agreement or incorporate the business
- continue or renegotiate the business's contracts
- enter contracts with lawyers, accountants or others, and
- collect and spend money on behalf of the business.

If you're a sole proprietor, a durable power of attorney is a very useful way to let someone else run the business if you become unable to do so. No court proceedings are required for the attorney-in-fact to take over if you become incapacitated, so there should be no disruption of your business. Be sure to work out a business plan with the person you plan to appoint as your attorney-in-fact; explain what you want for your business and how you expect it to be managed.

Check your existing agreements. If you operate your business with other people as a partnership, limited liability company or closely held corporation, your business agreement should cover what happens if a partner or shareholder becomes incapacitated. Typically, the other business owners can operate the business during the incapacitated person's absence or even buy out his or her share. A durable power of attorney will not affect these rules you already have in place.

EXAMPLE: Mike wants his wife, Nancy, to be his attorney-in-fact to manage his finances if he becomes incapacitated. Mike, a house painter, runs the M-J Painting Co. with his equal partner, Jack. Their agreement provides that if one partner becomes incapacitated, the other has exclusive authority to operate the business.

If Jack and Nancy have conflicts over money, however, there could be some problems. Mike, Jack and Nancy should think through the arrangement carefully and may want to consult a lawyer. Whatever they decide on should be spelled out in detail in the partnership agreement. They may also want to create a customized durable power of attorney, with the lawyer's help, that sets out the details of the business arrangements.

6. Insurance and Annuity Transactions

This power allows your attorney-in-fact to buy, borrow against, cash in or cancel insurance policies or annuity contracts for you and your spouse, children and other dependent family members. The attorney-in-fact's authority extends to all your policies and contracts, whether they name you or someone else as the beneficiary—that is, the person who will receive any proceeds of the policy when you die.

The one exception to this rule covers insurance policies you own with your spouse. Under these policies, your spouse must consent to any transaction that affects the policy. So if your attorney-in-fact is not your spouse, he or she will have to obtain your spouse's permission before taking action. Especially in community property states, even policies that are in one spouse's name may in fact be owned by both spouses. (See Chapter 5, Section D, above.) If you have questions about who owns your insurance policies, consult a lawyer. (See Chapter 25.)

If you already have an insurance policy or annuity contract, your attorney-in-fact can keep paying the premiums or cancel it—whichever he or she decides is in your best interests.

Your attorney-in-fact is also permitted to change and name the beneficiaries of your insurance policies or annuity contracts. This is a broad power, and it's a good idea to discuss your wishes about it with your attorney-in-fact. If you don't want your attorney-in-fact to change your beneficiary designations, make that clear. If you have strong feelings about whom the designated beneficiary of any new policies should be, you can discuss that as well.

There is one important limitation on your attorney-in-fact's ability to designate beneficiaries. Your attorney-in-fact cannot name himself or herself as beneficiary on a renewal, extension or substitute for an existing policy unless he or she was already the beneficiary before you signed the power of attorney.

7. Estate, Trust and Other Beneficiary Transactions

This power authorizes your attorney-in-fact to act on your behalf to claim or disclaim property you get from any other source. For example, if you were entitled to money from a trust fund, your attorney-in-fact could go to the trustee—the person in charge of the trust—and press your claim on your behalf. Or, if you didn't really need the money and it would cause your eventual estate tax bill to increase, your attorney-in-fact could turn down the cash.

Disclaiming property—saying that you don't want it—can be a good idea if taking it would increase the size of your estate and generate a big estate tax bill at your death. (See Chapter 13.)

8. Transferring Property to Your Living Trust

A revocable living trust is a legal structure you create by preparing and signing a document that specifies who will receive certain property at your death. Living trusts are designed to avoid probate, though some may also help you save on estate taxes or set up long-term property management. (See Chapter 13.)

If you've already set up a living trust, this power gives your attorney-in-fact the authority to transfer items of your property to that trust. But your attorney-in-fact can transfer property into your living trust only if you've given him or her authority over that type of property elsewhere in your document. For example, if you want your attorney-in-fact to be able to transfer real estate into the living trust, you must also grant the real estate power. And if you want your attorney-in-fact to transfer bank accounts to your living trust, you must also grant transactions power.

9. Legal Actions

This provision allows your attorney-in-fact to act for you in all matters that involve courts or government agencies. For example, your attorney-in-fact can bring or settle a lawsuit on your behalf. He or she can also accept court papers intended for you and hire an attorney to represent you in court, if necessary. Unless your attorney-in-fact is a lawyer, he or she may not actually represent you in court but must hire someone to do so. If you

lose a lawsuit, the attorney-in-fact can use your assets to pay the winner whatever you owe.

10. Personal and Family Care

This is an important power. It gives the attorney-in-fact the authority to use your assets to pay your everyday expenses and those of your family. The attorney-in-fact can spend your money for your family's food; shelter; education; cars; medical and dental care; membership dues for churches, clubs or other organizations; vacations; and travel. The attorney-in-fact is allowed to spend as much as it takes to maintain the standard of living to which you, your spouse, children and anyone else you usually support are accustomed.

If you regularly take care of others—for example, you are the primary caretaker for a disabled sibling or parent—your attorney-in-fact can use your assets to continue to help those people.

11. Government Benefits

This power allows your attorney-in-fact to apply for and collect any benefits you may be entitled to from Social Security, Medicare, Medicaid or other government programs, or civil or military service. To collect most government benefits, your attorney-in-fact must send the government office a copy of the durable power of attorney to prove his or her authority. Social Security is an exception, however. (See below.)

Social Security Checks

To collect your Social Security benefits, your attorney-in-fact will have to take the power of attorney document to a local Social Security office. A representative will interview the attorney-in-fact and establish him or her as your "representative payee"—that is, someone entitled to receive your Social Security checks for you.

If you're creating a power of attorney that's effective immediately, you can save your attorney-in-fact some work by simply contacting the Social Security Administration and naming your attorney-in-fact as your representative payee. However, that means your attorney-in-fact will start receiving your Social Security checks right away, and you may not want that. If it's not yet time for the attorney-in-fact to take control under an immediately effective document, or if you're creating a springing power of attorney, you're better off granting the government benefits power and letting the attorney-in-fact deal with the Social Security Administration when the time comes.

In addition to granting the government benefits power, you might also consider having your Social Security check deposited directly into a bank account where your attorney-in-fact will have access to the funds without the hassles of dealing with the SSA. You can set up a direct deposit arrangement at any time, as long as you are of sound mind.

To appoint a representative payee or arrange for direct deposit of your benefits, contact the SSA at 800-772-1213.

12. Retirement Plan Transactions

This power gives your attorney-in-fact authority over retirement plans such as IRAs and Keogh plans. The attorney-in-fact may select payment options and designate beneficiaries—the people who will take any money left in the fund at your death. He or she can also change current beneficiary designations, make voluntary contributions to your plan, change the way the funds are invested and roll over plan benefits into other retirement plans. The attorney-in-fact may also perform any other actions authorized by the plan, including borrowing from it.

This power is powerful. The power to change the beneficiaries of your retirement funds is a drastic one. Talk with your attorney-in-fact to be sure he or she understands your wishes with respect to this power.

13. Tax Matters

This provision gives your attorney-in-fact authority to act for you in all state, local and federal tax matters. The attorney-in-fact can prepare and file tax returns and other documents, pay tax due, contest tax bills and collect refunds. To file a tax return on your behalf, the attorney-in-fact must include a copy of the power of attorney with the return. The attorney-in-fact is also authorized to receive confidential information about you from the IRS.

14. Making Gifts

This last financial power allows your attorney-in-fact to make gifts of your property. You may already know that you want your attorney-in-fact to be able to give away your property under some circumstances. On the other hand, allowing your attorney-in-fact to make gifts might feel like giving up too much control.

a. Reasons to Allow Gifts

There are many reasons why you might want to permit your attorney-in-fact to make gifts of your property. Here are a few of the most common.

Estate tax savings. If you have substantial assets and are concerned about your eventual estate tax liability, you may be planning to reduce estate taxes by giving away some of your property while you are still alive. If you have set up this sort of gift-giving plan, you'll probably want to authorize your attorney-in-fact to continue it.

Other gift-giving plans. There are lots of reasons to give gifts that have nothing to do with estate planning and avoiding taxes. You may, for example, want to donate regularly to your church or a favorite charity. Or perhaps you've made a commitment to help a family member with college or starting up a business.

Family emergencies. All of us are occasionally caught off guard by unexpected financial troubles. You may want your attorney-in-fact to be able to help out if a loved one faces such an emergency.

b. Possible Gift Tax Consequences

If your attorney-in-fact gives away more than a certain amount—currently $11,000—to any one person or organization in one calendar year, a federal gift tax return will probably have to be filed.

Several kinds of gifts, however, are not taxable regardless of amount: gifts to your spouse, gifts that directly pay for medical expenses or tuition and gifts to tax-exempt charities. Gift tax may eventually have to be paid, but unless you make hundreds of thousands of dollars' worth of taxable gifts during your life, no tax will actually be due until after your death. Because your attorney-in-fact is required to act in your best interest, making large gifts could put him or her in a bind. On one hand, your attorney-in-fact may feel that you would want to make a sizable gift—even if it's a taxable one—to a particular person or organization. On the other hand, if you have a large estate that is likely to owe estate tax at your death, he or she won't want to increase your eventual tax liability.

For this reason, if you do permit your attorney-in-fact to make gifts, it's particularly important that you explain, ahead of time, what you intend and whether you have any limits.

More information about estate taxes. If you want to learn more about estate and gift taxes, read Chapter 13, Section B. For help beyond this book, see *Plan Your Estate*, by Denis Clifford and Cora Jordan (Nolo). It's a detailed guide to estate planning, including all major methods of reducing or avoiding estate and gift taxes. If you still have questions, talk with a knowledgeable attorney.

c.   Gifts to the Attorney-in-Fact

First, you must decide whether you want to allow your attorney-in-fact to make gifts to himself or herself. Because this raises some unique issues, you must consider it separately from the question of gifts to other people.

If you want to allow gifts to your attorney-in-fact, you must place an annual limit on them. This is because of a tricky legal rule called a general power of appointment. If your attorney-in-fact has an unlimited power to give your property to himself or herself, and he or she dies before you do, the attorney-in-fact could become the legal owner of all your property. In this case, your attorney-in-fact would be subject to taxes based not only his or her own assets, but on yours as well.

To avoid this problem, you must limit the amount of money your attorney-in-fact may accept in any given year. To avoid trouble with gift taxes, you may want to let the current gift tax threshold be your guide and set the limit at $11,000 or less. Whatever amount you choose, be sure it's far less than what you're worth. If you set the limit too high, you may inadvertently create a general power of appointment—and increase the chances that your attorney-in-fact will use too much of your property for his or her own purposes.

Gifts to the Alternate Attorney-in-Fact

You may want to allow your primary attorney-in-fact to receive gifts of your property, but not your alternate attorney-in-fact. Quicken WillMaker Plus allows you to include this restriction in your power of attorney document. If you allow gifts to your first choice attorney-in-fact, and you've also named an alternate attorney-in-fact, the program will ask you whether or not your alternate is allowed to receive gifts of your property.

If you wish to allow your alternate to make gifts to himself or herself, that's fine, too. If you do allow gifts to your alternate, the annual gift limit will be the same as the amount you set for your first choice attorney-in-fact.

d.   Gifts to Others

After you've decided whether you want to allow gifts to your attorney-in-fact, Quicken WillMaker Plus asks you about gifts to other people and organizations. If you're comfortable giving your attorney-in-fact broad authority, you can allow gifts to anyone your attorney-in-fact chooses. Or, you can specify the people and organizations to whom your attorney-in-fact may give your property.

If you give your attorney-in-fact broad authority to make gifts, be sure to discuss your intentions. Your attorney-in-fact should have a sound understanding of your plans for giving gifts—including the recipients you have in mind, under what circumstances gifts should be made and in what amounts.

Forgiving Loans

When you give your attorney-in-fact the power to make gifts, you also give the power to forgive or cancel debts others owe you. If anyone owes you money and you've authorized your attorney-in-fact to make gifts to them, be sure you let your attorney-in-fact know which debts you want to be paid and which may be forgiven.

If you've authorized gifts to your attorney-in-fact and he or she owes you money, your attorney-in-fact can forgive those debts, too. But for these debts, your attorney-in-fact can't cancel amounts worth more than his or her maximum gift amount in any calendar year. For example, your son, whom you've named as attorney-in-fact, owes you $20,000. You've placed the annual gift limit at $7,000. He can forgive his debt to you at the rate of $7,000 per year.

Remember that any gifts your attorney-in-fact makes must be in your best interest or according to your explicit instructions. For example, your attorney-in-fact may make annual gifts to each of your three children to reduce your estate tax liability. Or, he or she may make periodic gifts to your niece because you promised to help her with college costs. Your attorney-in-fact should follow the guidelines you have set out in the power of attorney document.

Talk With Your Attorney-in-Fact

It's critically important that you talk with your attorney-in-fact, not just to be sure he or she is willing to take on the job of handling your finances, but to be sure he or she understands what that job entails. Sit down and discuss the list of powers you grant, being especially careful to cover those areas where your attorney-in-fact might exercise a lot of personal discretion.

Now is the time to clarify any special needs or concerns that you have. For example, if there are certain items of personal property you'd never want your attorney-in-fact to sell, note them down and let your attorney-in-fact know how you feel. Or, if you are allowing your attorney-in-fact to make gifts to help out family members or other loved ones who need help, talk frankly about whom you'd feel comfortable helping, as well as when and to what extent.

There is one caveat here: While it is wise to let your attorney-in-fact know what your wishes are, it's generally a bad idea to create a lot of complicated restrictions for him or her. There is no way to know what the future will bring—and, ideally, your attorney-in-fact will have enough flexibility to take whatever actions he or she deems necessary to take care of you. It is important to let your attorney-in-fact know what you want, but also to trust him or her enough to make the right decisions when the time comes.

I. Additional Duties and Responsibilities

After you've named your attorney-in-fact and decided which financial powers to grant, you have just a few more choices to make about how your attorney-in-fact will carry out his or her duties. These last few questions include:

- whether you want your attorney-in-fact to make periodic reports to anyone about your finances
- whether you want to allow your attorney-in-fact to delegate tasks to others
- whether your attorney-in-fact may benefit financially from actions taken on your behalf
- whether the attorney-in-fact must keep his or her property separate from yours, and
- whether you want to pay your attorney-in-fact.

1. Periodic Reports

Quicken WillMaker Plus lets you require the attorney-in-fact to issue reports to people you name. Unless you require it, your attorney-in-fact doesn't have to report to anyone about your finances. In most cases, that arrangement is fine.

But in some circumstances, you may want to require reports. For example, if the attorney-in-fact is in charge of your business, investors may need to receive periodic financial statements, audited or reviewed by an accountant. Or perhaps you want to defuse a potentially explosive personal conflict by reassuring suspicious family members that they'll receive regular reports about your finances. Quicken WillMaker Plus allows you to require quarterly or semi-annual reports to people that you name.

EXAMPLE: Theodore, who is ill, appoints his son, Jason, as his attorney-in-fact for finances. Theodore's two other children, Nancy and Ed, live out of state and aren't on the best of terms with Jason.

To prevent conflict between his children over Jason's handling of Theodore's finances, Theodore decides to require Jason to give Nancy and Ed semi-annual reports of all financial transactions he engages in as attorney-in-fact.

Special requirements for attorneys-in-fact in Utah. If you live in Utah, your attorney-in-fact will have additional reporting responsibilities. These involve what the state calls "interested persons"—that is, anyone who may inherit property under your will or, if you don't make a will, according to state law.

Here's what your attorney-in-fact must do:

- If you become incapacitated, your attorney-in-fact must notify all interested persons that he or she is your attorney-in-fact and provide them with his or her address. The attorney-in-fact has 30 days from the date of your incapacity to do this. However, since it is usually difficult to pin down the particular date on which someone becomes incapacitated, it is perhaps wiser for the attorney-in-fact to notify people within a month of first taking action under the power of attorney document.
- If any interested person requests it, your attorney-in-fact must provide a copy of the durable power of attorney.
- If any interested person requests it, your attorney-in-fact must provide an annual accounting of the assets to which the durable power of attorney applies, unless

you specify that reports are not required, as Quicken WillMaker Plus permits you to do.

- Your attorney-in-fact must notify all interested persons when you die.
- If your attorney-in-fact turns over the job to an alternate, the new attorney-in-fact has ten days to notify inheritors of the change. The new attorney-in-fact must comply with all the reporting requirements listed above.

There are a couple of things you can do to help your attorney-in-fact comply with these requirements. First, give the attorney-in-fact the "Information for the Attorney-in-Fact" that prints out with your power of attorney document. It explains these reporting rules. Second, if you've made a will, give your attorney-in-fact a list of all the people to whom you are leaving property. It's not necessary to disclose exactly what you're leaving to each person, but without a simple list of names, your attorney-in-fact will have no sure way of knowing who needs to be contacted under the law.

This Utah law is unusual because it places such strict reporting requirements on the attorney-in-fact. Because the law is new and somewhat extreme, it may change again soon. Before taking action under the power of attorney document, your attorney-in-fact may want to look at the Utah statutes to find the current requirements. The law is contained in Sections 75-5-501(2) and (3) of the Utah Code, which can easily be found online. (See Nolo's Legal Research Center at www.nolo.com/statute/state.cfm.)

About Reports

The idea of making your attorney-in-fact accountable to people may appeal to you. But before you enter a long list of names of people to whom your attorney-in-fact must make reports, ask yourself whether or not these reports are truly necessary.

One of the most important reasons for making a durable power of attorney is to give control of your finances to someone you trust completely, bypassing the court system. One big advantage of this tactic is that you spare your attorney-in-fact the hassle and expense of preparing reports and accountings for a court.

If you want someone to keep tabs on your attorney-in-fact, think again about whether you truly trust the person you've named.

The Quicken WillMaker Plus power of attorney document requires that all reports include income received by you and expenses incurred. If you want other details included, be certain your attorney-in-fact knows what they are.

Unless the timing of reports is governed by a business agreement or other legally binding document, you are free to require quarterly or semi-annual reports. Weigh the need for the reports against the inconvenience to your attorney-in-fact and the expense of preparing the reports. If you have a very anxious relative, for example, you may want to authorize quarterly reports. Making these reports could be less hassle for your attorney-in-fact than dealing with constant interference from your family members. If the situation is not so tense, semi-annual reports will probably do fine.

2. Delegating Powers

If your attorney-in-fact resigns from the job, the alternate you named will take over. But if there is no alternate available, or if your attorney-in-fact is only temporarily unavailable, the attorney-in-fact will need to find another person to do the job.

If you allow it, your attorney-in-fact can turn over all or part of his or her duties to someone else in this situation. This reassignment of duties is called delegation.

If you allow your attorney-in-fact to delegate tasks, he or she is free to turn over any or all of the job to a competent third person. This person may step in temporarily or permanently, depending on the situation.

EXAMPLE: Caroline names her son, Eugene, as her attorney-in-fact for finances, effective immediately. She names a close friend, Nicole, as alternate attorney-in-fact. A year later, Eugene goes on vacation for three weeks, so he delegates his authority over Caroline's bank accounts to Nicole until he returns.

EXAMPLE: Anthony names his wife, Rosa, as his attorney-in-fact; his son Michael is the alternate attorney-in-fact. When Rosa declines to serve because of her own poor health, Michael takes over but soon finds that other responsibilities make it impossible to continue. He delegates all his authority to his sister, Theresa.

Quicken WillMaker Plus prints out a form that your attorney-in-fact can use to delegate authority to someone else. The new representative will use the signed form, along with your power of attorney document, to act on your behalf.

If You Named More Than One Attorney-in-Fact

Delegation becomes more complicated if you've named more than one attorney-in-fact.

Attorneys-in-Fact Who Must Act Jointly

If you require your attorneys-in-fact to act together in all that they do, it's a good idea to give them the power to delegate responsibilities. This is to avoid trouble in the event that one or more of your attorneys-in-fact becomes unable to act on your behalf. If this happens, the unavailable attorney-in-fact can use the Quicken WillMaker Plus delegation form to give his or her authority to the remaining attorneys-in-fact, temporarily or permanently. Your remaining attorneys-in-fact can use the delegation form to prove that they are permitted to act alone. If you don't grant the delegation power, an attorney-in-fact who will be unavailable will have to execute an affidavit—a sworn, notarized statement—that he or she cannot act for you. (If one of your attorneys-in-fact permanently resigns, he or she can sign a resignation form; the remaining attorneys-in-fact can use that form to prove their authority.)

In the unlikely event that all of your attorneys-in-fact will be temporarily unavailable, they can get together to choose a person to take over.

Attorneys-in-Fact Who May Act Separately

If you've authorized your attorneys-in-fact to act independently, allowing them to delegate tasks is probably not necessary or wise. The main reason for allowing delegation is to ensure that someone will always be on hand to take care of your finances. In your situation, if just one of your attorneys-in-fact is temporarily unable to act on your behalf, the others may simply act alone, without any special documents or fuss. And you can name up to two alternate attorneys-in-fact to take over if all of your attorneys-in-fact must step down. (See Section G4, above.)

Allowing delegation in your situation could, in fact, create much unnecessary confusion. Because your attorneys-in-fact may act independently, they could each delegate tasks to individuals that they choose—without consulting each other. When it comes to your finances, it's better not to open the door to that sort of chaos.

3. Exceptions to Legal Responsibilities

As discussed, your attorney-in-fact must always act in your best interests, must act honestly and prudently when managing your property and must keep good records. However, you may want to allow your attorney-in-fact to deviate from some standard legal duties, including:

- avoiding conflicts of interest, and
- keeping your property completely separate from his or her own.

a. Conflicts of Interest

In most states, an attorney-in-fact has no right to engage in activities from which he or she personally stands to benefit. Such activities, which create conflicts of interest between the principal and attorney-in-fact, are called self-dealing. The attorney-in-fact's motive is irrelevant. If the transaction is challenged in court, it is presumed fraudulent until the attorney-in-fact proves otherwise.

EXAMPLE: David is the attorney-in-fact for his elderly mother, Irene. After Irene's failing eyesight makes it impossible for her to drive, David decides to buy her car from her. He looks up the car's fair market value to make sure he is paying a fair amount, writes a check and deposits it in Irene's bank account.

This transaction is forbidden, even though David isn't cheating Irene, unless Irene's power of attorney specifically allows David to benefit from his management of her property and finances.

The ban on self-dealing is intended to protect you; after all, the attorney-in-fact is supposed to be acting on your behalf. It's quite sensible, however, to give the attorney-in-fact permission to self-deal if he or she is your spouse, a close family member, a business partner or another person whose finances are already intertwined with yours. Quicken WillMaker Plus allows you to grant this permission in your power of attorney document.

EXAMPLE: Maurice wants Alice, his best friend, to serve as his attorney-in-fact. They have been involved in many real estate transactions together—including several current projects. Maurice doesn't want to risk disrupting these projects or curtailing Alice's ability to do business, so he specifically states in his durable power of attorney that Alice may benefit from transactions she undertakes on Maurice's behalf as his attorney-in-fact.

Making Gifts

When you grant financial powers to your attorney-in-fact, you may allow him or her to receive gifts of your property. (See Section H14, above.) If you explicitly grant the gift-making power in your document, receiving permitted gifts is not considered a conflict of interest. In other words, it's perfectly fine to forbid your attorney-in-fact from using your power of attorney document for personal benefit while also allowing him or her to receive some of your property as a gift.

b. Mixing Funds

An attorney-in-fact is never allowed to mix or commingle your funds with his or her own unless the power of attorney specifically authorizes it. You will probably want to grant that authority if you appoint your spouse, mate or immediate family member as attorney-in-fact, and your finances are already thoroughly mixed together in joint bank or security accounts.

EXAMPLE: Jim and Eduardo have been living together for 25 years. They have a joint checking account and share all basic living expenses. Each names the other as his attorney-in-fact. To avoid any possible problems, Jim and Eduardo both include, in their powers of attorney, specific provisions that allow commingling of funds.

J. Paying Your Attorney-in-Fact

Quicken WillMaker Plus asks you whether or not you want to pay your attorney-in-fact. If you do, you can specify your payment arrangement.

In family situations, an attorney-in-fact is normally not paid if the duties won't be complicated or burdensome. If your property and finances are extensive, however, and the attorney-in-fact is likely to devote significant time and effort managing them, it seems fair to offer compensation for the work. Discuss and resolve this issue with the proposed attorney-in-fact before you finalize your document.

If you decide to pay your attorney-in-fact something for managing your financial affairs, Quicken WillMaker Plus allows you to set your own rate—for example, $10,000 per year, $10 per hour or some other figure on which you agree. Or, if you don't want to decide on an amount right now, you can allow your attorney-in-fact to determine a reasonable wage when he or she takes over. No single strategy works best for everyone. Choose the approach—and the amount—that feels right to you.

EXAMPLE: Frederick is quite wealthy. He owns and operates a successful chain of convenience stores in a large city. He also owns a house, several pieces of investment property and a wide array of stocks. When he is diagnosed with a life-threatening illness, he creates a durable power of attorney for finances appointing his close friend Barbara as his attorney-in-fact. Because he expects Barbara to watch over his business as well as tend to his other financial affairs, he feels it's appropriate to pay her for her services. Frederick and Barbara settle on a rate of $15,000 per year for her services.

EXAMPLE: Martin creates a durable power of attorney naming his brother, Andrew, as attorney-in-fact. Martin owns a complex investment portfolio, and the brothers agree that Andrew should be paid if he has to manage Martin's finances. They consider an hourly wage but decide not to be that specific now. In his durable power of attorney, Martin states that Andrew may pay himself "reasonable" fees for his services.

If You Named More Than One Attorney-in-Fact

If you named more than one attorney-in-fact and you want to pay them, the amount you enter—for example, $5,000 per year or $12 per hour—applies to each one. If you want to allow your attorneys-in-fact to determine a reasonable amount for their services, each is allowed to set his or her own fee.

K. Nominating a Conservator or Guardian

It is possible, though highly unlikely, that a court proceeding could be brought to invalidate or overrule your durable power of attorney for finances. (See Section Q2, below.) If your document is invalidated for any reason, a judge will appoint someone to manage your finances. This person is usually called a "guardian of your estate" or "conservator of your estate."

You can use Quicken WillMaker Plus to nominate your attorney-in-fact to serve as your financial guardian or conservator, if a court must appoint someone to that position. The court will follow your recommendation unless there is a compelling reason not to do so—for example, if someone has proved that your attorney-in-fact is mishandling your money. (Again, this type of outcome is very rare.)

If you do not nominate your attorney-in-fact to serve as the guardian or conservator of your estate, your power of attorney document will not mention the issue at all. In this case, the court would appoint a guardian or conservator by determining what would be in your best interests, but would do so without input from you.

L. Making It Legal

After you've done the hard work of putting together a durable power of attorney, you must carry out some simple tasks to make sure the document is legally valid and will be accepted by the people with whom your attorney-in-fact may have to deal. This section explains what to do.

Before You Sign

Before you finalize your power of attorney, you may want to show it to the banks, brokers, insurers and other financial institutions you expect your attorney-in-fact to deal with on your behalf.

Discussing your plans with people at these institutions before it is final—and giving them a copy of the durable power of attorney, after you sign it, if you wish—can make your attorney-in-fact's job easier. An institution may require that you include specific language in your durable power of attorney, authorizing the attorney-in-fact to do certain things on your behalf. You may have to go along if you want cooperation later. If you don't want to change your durable power of attorney, find another bank that will accept the document as it is.

1. Signing and Notarizing

A durable power of attorney is a serious document, and to make it effective you must observe certain formalities when you sign the document.

In all states but California, you must sign your durable power of attorney in the presence of a notary public for your state. (In California, you may choose whether to have your document notarized or witnessed. See "For California Residents: Making the Choice," below.) In many states, notarization is required by law to make the durable power of attorney valid. But even where law doesn't require it, custom usually does. A durable power of attorney that isn't notarized may not be accepted by people with whom your attorney-in-fact tries to deal.

The notary public watches you sign the durable power of attorney and then signs it, too, and stamps it with an official seal. The notary will want proof of your identity, such as a driver's license that bears your photo and signature. The notary's fee is usually inexpensive—$5 to $10 in most places.

Finding a notary public shouldn't be a problem; many advertise in the Yellow Pages. Or check with your bank, which may provide notarizations as a service to customers. Real estate offices and title companies also have notaries.

If you are gravely ill, you'll need to find a notary who will come to your home or hospital room. To arrange it, call around to notaries listed in the Yellow Pages. Expect to pay a reasonable extra fee for a house call.

2. Witnessing

Most states don't require the durable power of attorney to be signed in front of witnesses. (See "States That Require Witnesses," below.) Nevertheless, it doesn't hurt to have a witness or two watch you sign, and sign the document themselves. Witnesses' signatures may make the power of attorney more acceptable to lawyers, banks, insurance companies and other entities the attorney-in-fact may have to deal with. Part of the reason is probably that some other legal documents with which people are more familiar—including wills and health care directives—must be witnessed to be legally valid.

Witnesses can serve another function, too. If you're worried that someone may challenge your capacity to execute a valid durable power of attorney later, it's prudent to have witnesses. If necessary, they can testify that in their judgment you knew what you were doing when you signed the document.

The witnesses must be present when you sign the document in front of the notary. Witnesses must be mentally competent adults, preferably ones who live nearby and will be easily available if necessary. (See "States That Require Witnesses," below.) The person who will serve as attorney-in-fact should not be a witness. In most states, the attorney-in-fact does not have to sign the durable power of attorney document. (See below.)

For California Residents: Making the Choice

If you live in California, your durable power of attorney is valid if you have it notarized *or* if you sign it in front of two witnesses. Some people feel most comfortable using both methods together, but you are legally required to choose only one. Quicken WillMaker Plus lets you indicate how you want to finalize your document.

When choosing a method, there's one important consideration to keep in mind. If your power of attorney grants your attorney-in-fact authority over your real estate, you should absolutely have your document notarized. This is because you will have to put a copy of your document on file in the county recorder's office (see Section 4, below)—and in order to record your document, it must be notarized.

States That Require Witnesses

State	No. of Witnesses	Other Requirements
Arizona	1	Witness may not be your attorney-in-fact, the spouse or child of your attorney-in-fact or the notary public who acknowledges your document.
Arkansas	2	The attorney-in-fact may not be a witness.
California	2	Witnesses are required only if your document is not notarized. The attorney-in-fact may not be a witness.
Connecticut	2	The attorney-in-fact may not be a witness.
District of Columbia	2	Witnesses are necessary only if your power of attorney is to be recorded. (See Section 4, below.) The attorney-in-fact may not be a witness.
Florida	2	The attorney-in-fact may not be a witness.
Georgia	2	The attorney-in-fact may not be a witness. In addition, one of your witnesses may not be your spouse or blood relative.
Illinois	1	The attorney-in-fact may not be a witness.
Michigan	2	Witnesses are necessary only if your power of attorney is to be recorded. (See Section 4, below.) The attorney-in-fact may not be a witness.
Oklahoma	2	Witnesses may not be your attorney-in-fact, or anyone who is related by blood or marriage to you or your attorney-in-fact.
Pennsylvania	2	Witnesses are necessary only if the power of attorney is finalized with a mark (rather than a signature) or if it is signed by another person on behalf of and at the direction of the principal. Witnesses may not be your attorney-in-fact or the person who signs the document for you, if you can't sign it yourself.
South Carolina	2	The attorney-in-fact may not be a witness.
Vermont	1	Witness may not be your attorney-in-fact, or the notary public who acknowledges your document.
Wisconsin	2	Witnesses may not be your attorney-in-fact, or anyone related by blood or marriage, or anyone entitled to a portion of your estate under your will.

3. Obtaining the Attorney-in-Fact's Signature

In the vast majority of states, the attorney-in-fact does not have to agree in writing to accept the job of handling your finances. The exceptions to this rule are California, Georgia, New Hampshire, Pennsylvania, Vermont and Wisconsin.

a. California

In California, your attorney-in-fact must date and sign the durable power of attorney before taking action under the document. Ask the attorney-in-fact to read the "Notice to Person Accepting the Appointment as Attorney-in-Fact" at the beginning of the form. If your attorney-in-fact will begin using the power of attorney right away, he or she should date and sign the designated blanks at the end of the notice. If you've asked your attorney-in-fact not to use the document unless or until you become incapacitated, there's no need to obtain the signature now. Your attorney-in-fact can sign later, if it's ever necessary.

b.   Georgia

In Georgia, your attorney-in-fact must sign the durable power of attorney document and complete an "Acceptance of Appointment" form. The acceptance form states that the attorney-in-fact understands the legal responsibilities involved in serving as an attorney-in-fact and agrees to carry out the duties to the best of his or her ability.

First, have your attorney-in-fact read and sign the acceptance form that prints out along with your power of attorney document. (After signing, the attorney-in-fact should attach the acceptance form to the original, finalized power of attorney document.) Then, ask the attorney-in-fact to sign the designated blank at the end of the power of attorney document itself, after your own signature.

If you've asked your attorney-in-fact not to use the document unless or until you become incapacitated, you don't have to obtain the attorney-in-fact's signatures right away. Keep the acceptance form together with the original power of attorney document. Your attorney-in-fact can complete it and sign the power of attorney later, if it ever becomes necessary to use the document.

c.   New Hampshire and Pennsylvania

In New Hampshire or Pennsylvania, your attorney in fact must complete and sign an acknowledgment form. This simple form ensures that your attorney-in-fact understands the legal responsibilities involved in acting on your behalf. When you print out your durable power of attorney, it will be accompanied by an acknowledgment form for your attorney-in-fact to sign.

If your attorney-in-fact will begin using the power of attorney right away, give the acknowledgment form to him or her along with the finalized, original power of attorney document. Your attorney-in-fact must complete the form and attach it to the power of attorney before taking action under the document.

If you've asked your attorney-in-fact not to use the power of attorney unless or until you become incapacitated, keep the acknowledgment form together with the original power of attorney document. Your attorney-in-fact can complete it later, if it ever becomes necessary to use the power of attorney.

d.   Wisconsin and Vermont

If you live in Wisconsin or Vermont, your attorney-in-fact must sign the power of attorney before taking action under the document. If your attorney-in-fact will begin using the power of attorney right away, ask him or her to print and then sign his or her full name in the designated blanks at the end of the form. If you've asked your attorney-in-fact not to use the document unless or until you become incapacitated, there's no need to obtain the attorney-in-fact's signature now. He or she can sign the document later, if it's ever necessary.

4.   Recording

You may need to put a copy of your durable power of attorney on file in the land records office of the counties where you own real estate, called the county recorder's or land registry office in most states. This is called recording, or registering in some states.

a. Mandatory Recording

Just two states, North Carolina and South Carolina, require you to record a power of attorney for it to be durable—that is, for it to remain in effect if you become incapacitated.

In other states, you must record the power of attorney if it gives your attorney-in-fact authority over your real estate. Essentially, this means you must record the document if you granted the real estate power. In this case, if you don't record the document, your attorney-in-fact won't be able to sell, mortgage or transfer your real estate.

Recording makes it clear to all interested parties that the attorney-in-fact has power over the property. County land records are checked whenever real estate changes hands or is mortgaged; if your attorney-in-fact attempts to sell or mortgage your real estate, there must be something in the records that proves he or she has authority to do so.

There is no time limit on when you must record a durable power of attorney. So if you've created a document that won't be used unless and until you become incapacitated, you may not want to record it immediately. Your attorney-in-fact can always record the document later, if he or she ever needs to use it.

Even if recording is not legally required, you can do so anyway; officials in some financial institutions may be reassured later on by seeing that you took that step.

Note for North Carolina Readers

In your state, a durable power of attorney must be:
- recorded with the Register of Deeds, and
- filed with the clerk of the Superior Court within 30 days after recording, unless the durable power of attorney waives the requirement that the attorney-in-fact file inventories and accountings with the court. Your Quicken WillMaker Plus power of attorney form waives this filing requirement.

Note for Illinois, Kentucky and Minnesota Readers

If you live in Illinois, Kentucky or Minnesota, when you review your power of attorney document, you'll notice a "preparation statement" at the very end of it. The preparation statement is a simple listing of the name and address of the person who prepared the document. Quicken WillMaker Plus adds this statement because, in these three states, you cannot record your document without it.

In most cases, the name of the principal and the name of the person who prepared the document will be the same: your own. Occasionally, however, someone may use Quicken WillMaker Plus to prepare a form for another person—an ailing relative, for example. In that case, the name and address of the person who stepped in to help should appear in the preparation statement.

b. Where to Record

In most states, each county has its own office for a recorder or registry of deeds. If you're recording to give the attorney-in-fact authority over real estate, take the durable power of attorney to the office in the county where the real estate is located. If you want your attorney-in-fact to have authority over more than one parcel of real estate, record the power of attorney in each county where you own property. If you're recording for any other reason, take the document to the office in the county where you live.

c. How to Record

Recording a document shouldn't be complicated, though some counties can be quite fussy about their rules (See below.) You may even be able to record your by mail, but it's safer to go in person. Typically, the clerk makes a copy for the public records. It will be assigned a reference number, often in terms of books and pages—for example, "Book 14, Page 1932 of the Contra Costa County, California records." In most places, it costs just a few dollars per page to record a document.

Check your county's recording procedures before you finalize your document. Some counties will ask you to meet very particular requirements before they will put your power of attorney on file. Or, if you don't adhere to their rules, they will charge you an extra fee for filing the document.

For example, in some counties you may be required to file an original document, rather than a photocopy, with the land records office. In this case, you'll need to make a second original, being sure to have it signed, notarized and witnessed (if necessary), just like the first.

And some counties require a margin of a certain number of inches at the top of the first page of a power of attorney. This is where they put the filing stamp when you record the document. Local customs vary widely here; some counties will accept a standard one-inch margin while others ask for a margin of two, three or even four inches. When you make your document, Quicken WillMaker Plus lets you set the correct number of inches for the top margin of the first page.

To avoid hassles and extra expenses, you should call the land record's office before you finalize your power of attorney to make sure you're prepared to meet any special requirements for putting it on file.

M. What to Do With the Signed Document

Your attorney-in-fact will need the original power of attorney document, signed and notarized, to act on your behalf. So, if you want your attorney-in-fact to start using the document right away, give the original document to the attorney-in-fact.

If you named more than one attorney-in-fact, give the original document to one of them. Between them, they will have to work out the best way to prove their authority. For example, they may decide to visit some financial institutions or government offices together to establish themselves as your attorneys-in-fact. Or they may need to take turns with the document. Some agencies, such as the IRS, will accept a copy of the document, rather than the original: Such flexible policies make things easier on multiple attorneys-in-fact who need to share the original document.

What to Do With the Additional Documents

Quicken WillMaker Plus prints out several additional documents along with your durable power of attorney form. These are discussed throughout the chapter, but here is a quick summary of these documents and what you should do with them.

Information for an Attorney-in-Fact

This sheet is intended to help your attorney-in-fact understand the job. It discusses the attorney-in-fact's duties and responsibilities, including the duty to manage your property honestly and prudently and to keep accurate records. You should give a copy to the person you name in your document and take some time to talk together about the responsibilities involved. (See Section D, above.)

Delegation of Authority

If you allow your attorney-in-fact to delegate tasks to others, he or she may want to use Quicken WillMaker Plus's "Delegation of Authority" form. Give a copy to your attorney-in-fact. Or, if your power of attorney won't be used right away, keep the form with your power of attorney document so your attorney-in-fact will have easy access to it later. (See Section I2, above.)

Resignation of Attorney-in-Fact

Your attorney-in-fact can use the Resignation of Attorney-in-Fact form to resign from the job. He or she should fill out the form and send it to the alternate attorney-in-fact. If you name more than one attorney-in-fact, the one who resigns may send the form to the others. Give a copy of this form to your attorney-in-fact along with your power of attorney document. Or, if your power of attorney won't be used right awy, keep the forms together in a safe place known by your attorney-in-fact; he or she can obtain them if it becomes necessary.

Notice of Revocation of Durable Power of Attorney

If you ever want to revoke your power of attorney, prepare and sign a Notice of Revocation. Keep a copy of this form on file in case you need it later. (See Section P3, below.)

Notice of Revocation of Recorded Power of Attorney

If you record your power of attorney, then change your mind and want to cancel the document, you must also record a Notice of Revocation. To do this, you can use Quicken WillMaker Plus's "Notice of Revocation of Recorded Power of Attorney" form. Keep a blank copy on file for future use. (See Section P3, below.)

If the durable power of attorney won't be used unless and until you are incapacitated, keep the notarized, signed original. Store it in a safe, convenient place to which the attorney-in-fact has quick access. A fireproof box in your home or office is fine.

A safe deposit box isn't the best place to store a durable power of attorney, unless the attorney-in-fact is a cotenant with access to the box. It's better to keep the document wherever you file other important legal papers. Make sure that the attorney-in-fact knows where it is.

N. Making and Distributing Copies

If you wish, you can give copies of your durable power to the people your attorney-in-fact will need to deal with—in banks or government offices, for example. If the durable power is in their records, it may eliminate hassles for your attorney-in-fact later because they will be familiar with the document and expecting your attorney-in-fact to take action under it.

If your power of attorney won't be used unless and until you become incapacitated, however, it may seem premature to contact people and institutions about a document that may never go into effect. It's up to you.

Be sure to keep a list of everyone to whom you give a copy. If you later revoke your durable power of attorney, notify each institution of the revocation. (See Section P3, below.)

O. Keeping Your Document Up to Date

If you make a power of attorney that your attorney-in-fact won't use unless and until you become incapacitated, it's a good idea to revoke it and create a new one every five to seven years, especially if your circumstances have changed significantly. A durable power of attorney never expires, but if the document was signed many years before it is used, the attorney-in-fact may have more difficulty getting banks, insurance companies or people in government agencies to accept it.

If You Move to Another State

If you move to another state, it's best to revoke your old durable power of attorney as described below and create a new one, complying with all regulations of your new state. This is true even though your old power of attorney may be acceptable under your new state's laws.

If you don't make a new document, your attorney-in-fact may run into problems that are more practical than legal. For example, the document may need to be recorded with the local land records office in the new state. If the document does not meet certain requirements, the recorder's office in the new state may not accept it. Making a new document will ensure that things will go smoothly for your attorney-in-fact.

P. Revoking Your Durable Power of Attorney

After you make a power of attorney, you can revoke it at any time, as long as you are of sound mind. But to make the revocation legally effective, you must carefully follow all the procedures set out in this section.

1. Who Can Revoke

Only you, or someone a court appoints to act for you, can revoke your power of attorney.

a. When You Can Revoke

You can revoke your durable power of attorney as long as you are of sound mind and physically able to do so. The sound mind requirement is not difficult to satisfy. If someone challenged the revocation, a court would look only at whether or not you understood the consequences of signing the revocation. (The competency requirement is the same as that required to create a valid power of attorney in the first place; see Section R1, below.)

> **If you and your attorney-in-fact can't agree.** An attorney-in-fact who refuses to accept a revocation can create serious problems. If you get into such a dispute with your attorney-in-fact, consult a lawyer. (See Chapter 25.)

b. If a Conservator or Guardian Is Appointed

If your attorney-in-fact is satisfactorily handling your financial affairs while you can't, it's very unlikely that a court will need to appoint a conservator for you. (See Section B, above.) And if it does become necessary, you can use your document to name your attorney-in-fact to the post. (See Section K, above.)

If, however, you or a family member objected to the attorney-in-fact's actions, a court might appoint someone else as conservator. In a few states, appointment of a conservator automatically revokes a durable power of attorney. In that case, the conservator would become solely responsible for your property and financial matters.

In many states, the conservator would have the legal authority to revoke your durable power of attorney. Someone appointed to take physical care of you—usually called a guardian or guardian of the person—not your property, may also, depending on state law, have the power to revoke a financial power of attorney. (See "Right of Conservator or Guardian to Revoke Power of Attorney," below.)

Right of Conservator or Guardian to Revoke Power of Attorney

State	Who May Revoke	State	Who May Revoke
Alabama	Curator or guardian of the estate can revoke power of attorney	Georgia	Power of attorney automatically revoked if guardian of the property or receiver appointed
Alaska	Conservator can revoke power of attorney	Hawaii	Conservator can revoke power of attorney
Arizona	Conservator can revoke power of attorney	Idaho	Conservator or guardian of the estate can revoke power of attorney
Arkansas	Conservator or guardian of the estate can revoke power of attorney	Illinois	Guardian can revoke power of attorney only if ordered by court
California	Conservator or guardian of the estate can revoke power of attorney only if authorized by court	Indiana	Guardian can revoke power of attorney only if ordered by court
		Iowa	Conservator can revoke power of attorney
Colorado	Conservator can revoke power of attorney	Kansas	Conservator or guardian of the estate can revoke power of attorney
Connecticut	Power of attorney automatically revoked if conservator of the estate appointed	Kentucky	Power of attorney automatically revoked if fiduciary appointed
		Maine	Conservator or guardian of the estate can revoke power of attorney
Delaware	Power of attorney revoked to the extent that the attorney-in-fact's powers are specifically granted to the guardian of the person or of the estate; guardian can revoke power of attorney only if authorized by court	Maryland	Guardian can revoke power of attorney
		Massachusetts	Conservator or guardian of the estate can revoke power of attorney
		Michigan	Conservator or guardian of the estate can revoke power of attorney
District of Columbia	Conservator or guardian of the estate can revoke power of attorney	Minnesota	Conservator or guardian can revoke power of attorney
		Mississippi	Conservator or guardian of the estate can revoke power of attorney
Florida	Power of attorney automatically suspended if a guardianship proceeding begun; revoked if guardian appointed	Missouri	Conservator, guardian or legal representative can revoke power of attorney only with court approval

Right of Conservator or Guardian to Revoke Power of Attorney, continued

State	Who May Revoke	State	Who May Revoke
Montana	Conservator can revoke power of attorney	South Carolina	Attorney-in-fact's powers revoked as to matters within scope of the guardianship or conservatorship, unless the power of attorney provides otherwise
Nebraska	Conservator or guardian of the estate can revoke power of attorney		
Nevada	Guardian can revoke power of attorney	South Dakota	Guardian or conservator can revoke power of attorney only with court approval
New Hampshire	Guardian or conservator can revoke power of attorney		
		Tennessee	Conservator or guardian of the estate can revoke power of attorney
New Jersey	Conservator or guardian of the estate can revoke power of attorney only with court approval		
		Texas	Power of attorney automatically revoked when permanent guardian of the estate appointed
New Mexico	Conservator can revoke power of attorney only if authorized by court		
		Utah	Conservator can revoke power of attorney only if ordered by court
New York	Committee or guardian can revoke power of attorney		
		Vermont	If a guardian is appointed, court can terminate or restrict power of attorney if court finds that to do so is in the best interests of the principal
North Carolina	Conservator, guardian of the estate or guardian of the person can revoke power of attorney		
North Dakota	Conservator or guardian of the estate can revoke power of attorney		
		Virginia	Conservator, guardian, or committee can revoke power of attorney only if authorized by court
Ohio	Guardian can revoke power of attorney		
Oklahoma	Conservator or guardian of the estate can revoke power of attorney	Washington	Guardian can revoke power of attorney
		West Virginia	Conservator or guardian of the estate can revoke power of attorney
Oregon	Conservator can revoke power of attorney		
Pennsylvania	Guardian of the estate can revoke power of attorney	Wisconsin	Conservator or guardian of the estate can revoke power of attorney, unless court rules otherwise
Rhode Island	Conservator or guardian can revoke power of attorney		
		Wyoming	Conservator can revoke power of attorney

2. When to Revoke

If you've prepared a power of attorney that won't be used unless you're incapacitated, years may elapse between the time you sign the durable power of attorney and when it is put to use. During that interval—or even after your attorney-in-fact starts using the document, as long as you are mentally competent—you may decide you need to revoke the durable power of attorney. Here are the most common situations in which you should revoke a power of attorney and start over.

a. Changing the Terms

There is no accepted way to amend a power of attorney. If you want to change or amend a durable power of attorney, the safe course is to revoke the existing document and prepare a new one. Don't go back and modify your old document with pen, typewriter or correction fluid—you could throw doubt on the authenticity of the whole thing.

> EXAMPLE: Tom signed a durable power of attorney several years ago. Now he is in declining health and wants to add to the authority he gave his attorney-in-fact, Sarah, giving her the power to sell Tom's real estate if necessary. Tom should revoke his old durable power of attorney and create a new one, granting the additional authority.

Similarly, you should revoke your durable power of attorney if you change your mind about your choice of attorney-in-fact. If you create a durable power of attorney that won't be used until later, the person you named to be your attorney-in-fact may become unavailable before he or she is needed. Or you may simply change your mind. If that's the case, you can revoke the durable power of attorney before it is ever used.

b. Moving to Another State

If you move to a different state, your attorney-in-fact may run into some trouble getting others to accept the validity of a power of attorney signed in your old state. (See Section O, above.) It's best to revoke your power of attorney and prepare a new one.

c. Losing the Document

If you lose your signed power of attorney document, it's wise to formally revoke it, destroy any copies and create a new one. Very few people are likely to accept your attorney-in-fact's authority if they can't look at the document granting the authority. By officially revoking the lost version, you reduce chances that the old power of attorney might someday resurface and confuse matters.

d. Marrying or Divorcing

If you get married after signing a durable power of attorney, you'll probably want to designate your new spouse to be your attorney-in-fact, if he or she wasn't the person you named originally.

If you name your spouse as your attorney-in-fact and later divorce, you will probably want to revoke the power of attorney and create a new one, naming someone else as the attorney-in-fact.

In a number of states (see Section G1, above), the designation is automatically ended if you divorce the attorney-in-fact. In that case, any alternate you named would serve as attorney-in-fact. You still may want to create a new power of attorney—one that doesn't mention your former spouse and lets you name another alternate attorney-in-fact.

3. Revoking Your Document

There are two ways to revoke your power of attorney. You can:

- prepare and sign a document called a Notice of Revocation, or
- destroy all existing copies of the document.

The first method is always preferable, because it creates proof that you really revoked the power of attorney.

Some states may allow you to revoke your power of attorney simply by preparing a new one. It's still advisable, however, to prepare a separate Notice of Revocation and notify everyone who needs to know about the revocation.

a. Preparing a Notice of Revocation

The purpose of a Notice of Revocation is to notify the attorney-in-fact and others that you have revoked the durable power of attorney.

Quicken WillMaker Plus prints out two kinds of Notice of Revocation forms for you to use. If you didn't record your durable power of attorney in the county land records office (see Section L4, above), choose the Notice of Revocation for an unrecorded document. If you did record the original durable power of attorney, you must also record the revocation; choose the Notice of Revocation for a recorded document.

b. Signing and Notarizing the Document

You must sign and date the Notice of Revocation. It need not be witnessed, but witnessing may be a prudent idea—especially if you have reason to believe that someone might later raise questions regarding your mental competence to execute the revocation. If you want witnesses' signatures, Quicken WillMaker Plus offers that option.

Choose the appropriate revocation document and indicate that you will have it witnessed.

Sign the Notice of Revocation in front of a notary public. (For more on notarization, see Section L1, above.)

c. Recording the Document

If you recorded the original durable power of attorney at your local recorder of deeds office, you must also record the revocation. (See Section L4, above.)

But even if the original durable power of attorney was not recorded, you can record a revocation if you fear that the former attorney-in-fact might try to act without authorization. If the revocation is part of the public records, people who check those records in dealing with the real estate later will know that the former attorney-in-fact is no longer authorized to act on your behalf.

Note for North Carolina Readers

When you register the revocation in the Register of Deeds Office, it must be accompanied by a document showing that a copy of the revocation notice has been delivered to—or served on—the former attorney-in-fact. This document is called a proof of service.

The revocation must be served on the attorney-in-fact by the county sheriff or someone else authorized by law to serve legal papers.

d. Notifying Others

It's not enough to sign a revocation, or even to record it, for it to take effect; there's one more crucial step. You must notify the former attorney-in-fact and all institutions and people who have dealt or might deal with the former attorney-in-fact. Each of them must receive a copy of the Notice of Revocation.

If you don't give this written notification, people or institutions who don't know the durable power of attorney has been revoked might still enter into transactions with the former attorney-in-fact. If they do this in good faith, they are legally protected. You may well be held legally liable for the acts of your attorney-in-fact, even though you have revoked his or her authority. In other words, once you create a durable power of attorney, the legal burden is on you to be sure everyone knows you have revoked it.

> **EXAMPLE:** Before Michael undergoes a serious operation, he makes a durable power of attorney. After his convalescence, Michael revokes the power of attorney in writing. He sends a copy of the revocation to Colette, his attorney-in-fact, but neglects to send a copy to his bank. Colette, fraudulently acting as Michael's attorney-in-fact, removes money from Michael's accounts and spends it. The bank isn't responsible to Michael for his loss.

Who Needs to Know?

When you're ready to send out revocation notices, try to think of everyone with whom the attorney-in-fact has had, or may have, dealings. These may include:

- banks
- mortgage companies
- title companies
- stockbrokers
- insurance companies
- Social Security offices
- Medicare or Medicaid offices
- military or civil service offices
- IRS
- pension fund administrators
- post offices
- hospitals
- doctors
- schools
- relatives
- business partners
- landlords
- lawyers
- accountants
- real estate agents, and
- maintenance and repair people.

Q. When the Power of Attorney Ends

A durable power of attorney for finances is valid until you revoke it, you die or there is no one to serve as your attorney-in-fact. A court can also invalidate a power of attorney, but that happens very rarely.

1. Revocation

As long as you are mentally competent, you can revoke a power of attorney for finances at any time, whether or not it has taken effect. All you need to do is fill out a simple form, sign it in front of a notary public, and give copies to the attorney-in-fact and to people or institutions with whom the attorney-in-fact has been dealing. (See Section P, above.) You can use Quicken WillMaker Plus to print out a revocation form.

> **EXAMPLE:** Susan prepares a durable power of attorney naming her closest friend, Tina, as her attorney-in-fact. Three years later, they have a bitter fight. Susan prepares a one-page document that revokes the durable power of attorney and gives Tina a copy. She destroys the old document and then prepares a new one, naming her sister Joan as her attorney-in-fact.

2. Invalidation

Even if you sign a durable power of attorney for finances, if you become incapacitated there is a remote possibility that a disgruntled relative could ask a court to appoint a conservator to manage your financial affairs. (See Section B, above.)

It's rare, but a power of attorney could be ruled invalid if a judge concludes that you were not mentally competent when you signed the durable power of attorney, or that you were the victim of fraud or undue influence. The power of attorney could also be invalidated for a technical error, such as the failure to sign your document in front of witnesses if your state requires it. If that happens, the judge could appoint a conservator to take over management of your property.

In most states, if a court appoints a conservator, the attorney-in-fact becomes accountable to the conservator—not just to you—and the conservator has the power to revoke your durable power of attorney if he or she doesn't approve of the way your attorney-in-fact is handling your affairs. In a few states, however, your durable power of attorney is automatically revoked, and the conservator assumes responsibility for your finances and property. (See Section P1, above.)

3. Divorce

In a handful of states (see Section G1, above), if your spouse is your attorney-in-fact and you divorce, your ex-spouse's authority is immediately terminated. If you named an alternate attorney-in-fact in your power of attorney, that person takes over as attorney-in-fact. If you didn't name an alternate, your power of attorney ends.

In any state, however, others may question the validity of a document created before a divorce that names the ex-spouse as attorney-in-fact. For this reason, if you get divorced you should revoke your durable power of attorney and make a new one.

R. Possible Challenges to Your Document

A common fear is that your durable power of attorney for finances will not be accepted by those around you. While rare, challenges are sometimes raised by people who feel you were not of sound mind when you signed the document or who fear that the document is not legally valid.

1. Your Mental State

You must be of sound mind when you create your durable power of attorney for finances. When you sign the document, no one makes a determination about your mental state. The issue will come up only if someone goes to court and challenges the durable power of attorney, claiming that you weren't mentally competent when you signed it. That kind of lawsuit is very rare.

Even in the highly unlikely event of a court hearing, the competency requirement is not difficult to satisfy. If you understood what you were doing when you signed your durable power of attorney, that's enough. To make this determination, a judge would probably question any witnesses who watched you sign the document and others who knew you well at the time. There would be no general inquiry into your life. It wouldn't matter, for example, that you were occasionally forgetful or absentminded around the time when you signed your power of attorney document.

4. No Attorney-in-Fact Is Available

A durable power of attorney must end if there's no one to serve as the attorney-in-fact. To avoid this, Quicken WillMaker Plus lets you name up to two alternate attorneys-in-fact, so someone will be available to serve if your first choice can't do the task. (See Section G4, above.)

For a bit of extra insurance, you can also allow the alternate attorney-in-fact to delegate his or her duties to someone else. (See Section I2, above.)

5. Death

A durable power of attorney ends when the principal dies. In most states, however, if the attorney-in-fact doesn't know of your death and continues to act on your behalf, his or her actions are still valid.

If you want your attorney-in-fact to have any authority over winding up your affairs after your death, grant that authority in your will—and in your living trust, if you make one. (See Chapter 8 for information about executors; see Chapter 13, for more on living trusts.)

Heading Off Problems

If you think someone is likely to go to court and challenge the legitimacy of your durable power of attorney or claim that you were coerced into signing it, you can take several steps to head off problems:

- **See a lawyer.** An experienced estate planning lawyer can answer questions about your durable power of attorney and about your other estate planning documents as well. For example, you may also be expecting challenges to your will, a trust or health care wishes. You can talk with a lawyer about all of these issues. The point is to have the lawyer put your fears to rest by answering your questions and reviewing or modifying your documents. He or she can help to ensure that your estate plan will hold up under the challenges of your stubborn relatives. Your attorney can also testify about your mental competency, should the need arise.

- **Sign your document in front of witnesses.** You can sign your document in front of witnesses, even if your state does not require it. (See Section L2, above.) After watching you sign, the witnesses themselves sign a statement that you appeared to know what you were signing and that you signed voluntarily. If someone later challenges your competency, these witness statements will be strong evidence that you were of sound mind at the time you signed your document.

- **Get a doctor's statement.** You may also want to get a doctor's statement around the time you sign your durable power of attorney. The doctor should write, date and sign a short statement saying that he or she has seen you recently and believes you to be mentally competent. You can attach this statement to your power of attorney document. Then, if necessary, your attorney-in-fact can produce the statement as evidence that you were of sound mind when you signed your power of attorney.

- **Make a videotape.** You can also videotape a statement of your intent to make and sign the durable power of attorney. Be warned, however, that using a videotape may work against you. The person challenging your power of attorney will want to use any visible quirks of behavior or language as evidence that you were not in fact competent when you made your document. If you do make a videotape, keep it with your power of attorney document.

2. The Document's Validity

It's reasonable for someone to want to make sure that your durable power of attorney is still valid and hasn't been changed or revoked. To reassure other people, your attorney-in-fact can show that person the power of attorney document. To lay any fears to rest, it clearly states that any person who receives a copy of the document may accept it without the risk of legal liability—unless he or she knows that the document has been revoked.

Laws in most states also protect people who rely on apparently valid powers of attorney. For example, many states have laws stating that a written, signed power of attorney is presumed valid, and a third party may rely on it.

As a last resort, the attorney-in-fact can sign a sworn statement or affidavit in front of a notary public, stating that as far as he or she knows, the durable power of attorney has not been revoked and that you are still alive. Most states have laws that make such a statement conclusive proof that the durable power of attorney is in fact still valid.

3. The Powers Granted

Any other person who relies on a durable power of attorney must be sure that the attorney-in-fact has the power he or she claims to have. That means the person must examine the document, to see what power it grants.

The Quicken WillMaker Plus power of attorney document is very specific about the attorney-in-fact's powers. For example, if you give your attorney-in-fact authority over your banking transactions, the document expressly states that the attorney-in-fact is empowered to write checks on your behalf. Your attorney-in-fact can point to the paragraph that grants that authority, so a doubting bank official can read it in black and white.

An attorney-in-fact who runs into resistance should seek, politely but insistently, someone higher up in the bureaucracy. ■

Chapter 23

Health Care Directives

You have the legal right to direct your own medical care. Every state provides standard methods and documents you can use to express your health care wishes in advance and to appoint a person to speak for you if you can no longer communicate. Quicken WillMaker Plus helps you create these documents.

A. What Quicken WillMaker Plus Can Do

Using Quicken WillMaker Plus, you can create a document that clearly expresses your preferences for your medical care if you become unable to communicate your wishes. Prompted by the questions and information in the program, you can specify what care you want provided or withheld if you are diagnosed to have a terminal illness or to be permanently unconscious. A few states allow you to address your wishes for medical care in other situations as well. (See Section H, below.)

You can use Quicken WillMaker Plus to create a document that will:

- specify whether or not you want your life prolonged with medical treatments and procedures
- identify specific medical treatments and procedures that you want provided or withheld, and
- appoint someone to see to it that your wishes are carried out.

Quicken WillMaker Plus also prints out a letter directed to your health care provider. This letter helps emphasize your choices and summarizes them so that they are clear to all who glance through your medical file.

If you are currently under a doctor's care, or you are preparing your health care directives in anticipation of a hospitalization or other extensive medical treatment, it is a good idea to use the letter as a starting point for discussing your wishes with those involved in providing your care. The more you do to make your thoughts known and communicate them clearly to medical personnel involved in your care, the more likely they will be followed.

See also Section Q, below.

Keeping track of your health care information. While Quicken WillMaker Plus's health care directive allows you to give explicit instructions of your wishes about the kind of medical care you want to receive, it's wise to keep track of other medical information as well.

With Quicken WillMaker Plus you can make an "Information for Caregivers and Survivors" form to help with this task. With this document, you can provide a comprehensive guide to the details of your life, including the names and contact information of your health care providers and information about your medical insurance coverage, to the persons who will care for you in the event of your incapacity. To find out more, click on the Document List button and select Information for Caregivers and Survivors from the list.

B. Legal History

Many assume that an individual's right to direct his or her own health care is a long-cherished legal principle. In fact, the first legal battles over patients' rights were fought during the last three decades. Not coincidentally, those battles coincided with dramatic advances in medical technology and equipment.

The first legal wranglings over health care were couched in terms of the Right to Die—cases that tested the bounds of what medical treatment can be administered in the face of a patient's desire to die naturally, free from artificial, life-prolonging machinery. Over time, the Right to Die movement became a much broader movement, in which supporters agitated for patients' rights to demand as well as reject medical treatment.

1. Court Decisions

The first time the public became aware of the right to direct medical care as a social issue was during the hard-fought legal battles over the life and death of Karen Ann Quinlan. The 22-year-old Quinlan was admitted to a New Jersey hospital after experiencing severe breathing difficulties. She lost and never regained consciousness. Severely brain damaged, she remained unresponsive, emaciated and in a fetal position—kept technically alive by round-the-clock nursing care, antibiotics, a respirator, a catheter and a feeding tube.

Doctors pronounced that there was no hope of Quinlan's recovery but balked at her parents' repeated requests to remove the equipment attached to her, claiming that would clash with "medical practices, standards and traditions." Quinlan's family members persisted, claiming the extensive medical procedures ran counter to what the patient would have wanted. After several expensive, time-consuming and personally wrenching appeals, the New Jersey Supreme Court held that the patient's constitutional right to privacy mandated that her family could enforce her right to refuse treatment on her behalf. (*Matter of Quinlan*, 355 A.2d 647 (1976).)

The 1976 *Quinlan* decision galvanized individuals who previously felt powerless up against the medical establishment. From 1976 through 1988, over 60 cases were filed nationwide, claiming that doctors should be legally bound to follow their patients' wishes for their own medical treatment.

In 1990, the U.S. Supreme Court was asked to decide whether the U.S. Constitution grants individuals the right to have life-sustaining treatment withheld or withdrawn. The case arose when Nancy Cruzan, 30, was admitted to a Missouri hospital after suffering severe injuries in a car accident. Cruzan was diagnosed as permanently brain damaged and in a coma or persistent vegetative state. There was no hope of recovery. Her parents unsuccessfully pleaded with hospital officials to discontinue Cruzan's artificial food and water, which would eventually cause her death.

In a court challenge to the hospital's position, the parents pointed to evidence of Cruzan's own wishes—conversations in which she told friends that if she were sick or injured, she "would not wish to continue her life unless she could live at least halfway normally." The Supreme Court held that everyone retains a constitutional right to control his or her own medical care. It held that "clear and convincing" evidence of an individual's wishes about medical care should be followed—even if they conflict directly with the wishes of close family members. (*Cruzan v. Director, Missouri Dept. of Health*, 497 U.S. 261 (1990).)

2. State Legislation

In the wake of court decisions carving out individuals' rights to direct their own health care, people penned the first living wills—usually simply worded requests that a person "be allowed to die with dignity." These missives met with mixed reaction in the medical community.

Some doctors welcomed the living wills as legal permission to honor their patients' preferences for specific kinds of medical care, free from the threat of lawsuits charging them with negligence or even as criminal accomplices in a patient's suicide. Other doctors, unsure about whether to enforce the directives—most of which directed that life support be withheld or withdrawn—sought advice from lawyers. Most of the lawyers worked on the hospital staffs—and most cautiously advised that the documents could be ignored if the doctor thought that was "in the patient's best interest."

Waves of activism in the late '60s and early '70s led to catalytic consumer lobbying efforts for legal recognition of individuals' rights to direct their medical care. In 1976, California became the first state to pass a law allowing individuals to write health care directives—documents informing doctors of the specific kind of medical care they want provided, withheld or withdrawn. Today, nearly every state has a law allowing some sort of directive.

3. Federal Law

A federal law called the Patient Self-Determination Act has done much to increase the use and awareness of health care directives. The law mandates that all facilities that receive Medicare or Medicaid must discuss health care directives with newly admitted patients. Because of this law, when admitted to nearly any hospital, you should be given a written explanation of your state's law on health care directives and an explanation of the hospital's policies on enforcing them. The Patient Self-Determination Act also directs health care facilities to record patients' health care directives as part of their medical records.

C. Putting Your Wishes in Writing

You will have the most thorough assurance that your preferences for medical care will be followed if you complete:

- specific written instructions—usually called a declaration or living will—that describes the medical care you want if you can no longer express your wishes, and
- a written authorization—usually called a health care proxy or a durable power of attorney for health care—that names another person to supervise your wishes.

In a number of states, the instructions and authorization are combined in a single document. The program will assemble the documents according to the laws of your state. Using Quicken WillMaker Plus, you can make both a directive and a proxy.

1. Health Care Directives

In a health care directive—whether known as a living will, a directive to physicians or a declaration—a person can set out wishes about what life-prolonging treatment should be withheld or provided if he or she becomes unable to communicate those wishes.

Because health care directives sprang from the Right to Die movement, many people tend to think of them as documents for ordering the withholding or withdrawal of life-prolonging procedures. However, these documents should more correctly be viewed as a way to direct doctors to provide you with whatever type of medical care you want, within reality and reason. For example, some people want to reinforce that they would like to receive all medical treatment that is available—and a health care directive is the proper place to specify that.

A doctor who receives a properly signed and witnessed or notarized directive is under the duty either to honor its instructions or to make sure the patient is transferred to the care of another doctor who will honor them. In the early confusion about health care directives, people were concerned that doctors who followed them would risk being prosecuted for aiding in a suicide. Every law on health care directives now exempts from prosecution doctors who follow their dictates. And in fact, many laws now impose penalties on doctors who refuse to follow them.

You Control Your Health Care If You Are Able

Most people know it is a good idea to complete a health care directive. But some run smack into a psychological roadblock. They are worried that they may experience a change of heart or mind later—and that they will receive more or less medical care than they would want in a particular situation.

If you are one of these fretful souls, it may help to keep two soothing axioms in mind.

First, the directions set out in your written health care directive will only be followed if you later become unable to communicate your wishes about the treatment. If, for example, you indicate in a health care directive that you do not wish to have water provided, health care providers will not deny you a glass of water as long as you are able to communicate your wishes for one.

Second, you can change or revoke your written health care wishes at any time in the future. If you find that your document no longer accurately expresses your wishes for your medical care, you can easily draw up and finalize a new one to meet your needs. (See Section M, below.)

2. Who Can Make a Health Care Directive

In most states, you must be 18 years old to make a valid document directing your health care; a few states allow parents to make health care directives for their minor children.

Every state law requires that the person making a health care directive must be legally competent—that is, able to understand what the document means, what it contains and how it works. People with mental disabilities who cannot understand the contents of a health care document cannot make one that will be valid. People with physical disabilities may make valid health care documents; they can direct another to sign for them if they are unable to do so.

While the laws of every state require you to be of sound mind to create a directive, many states allow you to revoke your directive regardless of your mental state. This can lead to an odd situation where, if your mind is slipping, you may be able to revoke your directive but not be able to create a new one if you have second thoughts. There's not much you can do about this legal wrinkle, but you should be aware of it. The logic behind it is that, when it comes to terminating life support, your current wishes should hold sway over something you wrote long ago, so long as you are coherent enough to make your wishes known. If you have appointed an agent, however, you must be of sound mind to revoke their authority—just one of many good reasons to appoint someone you completely trust. (See Section P, below.)

3. Naming Someone to Make Sure Your Wishes Are Followed

Using Quicken WillMaker Plus, you can create a document authorizing a representative you name to make sure care providers honor the wishes you set out in your health care directive. This document is usually called a durable power of attorney for health care or health care proxy. The person you name will be referred to as your agent, proxy or attorney-in-fact. Note that your agent's powers under this document are limited to enforcing the wishes you have expressed in your instructions.

It does not authorize your agent to make decisions about other aspects of your health care. (See Section J, below.)

If you do name a health care representative, Quicken WillMaker Plus will provide users in most states with a separate document containing that authorization. In a few states, the health care directive and the document appointing a health care representative will be combined in one document.

If you choose not to name a proxy. Even if you do not know anyone you trust to name as your health care proxy or agent, it is still important to complete and finalize a directive recording your wishes. That way, your doctors will still be bound to follow your wishes.

4. What Happens If You Have No Documents

State laws differ on what happens if you have not completed either a formal document such as a health care directive to express your wishes or a durable power of attorney to appoint someone to make health care decisions on your behalf. In some states, the doctors who attend you may use their own discretion in deciding what kind of medical care you will receive. In other states, the law dictates who will be consulted as your "surrogate" to make decisions for you. Generally these laws designate your spouse and immediate relatives as your surrogate. A scant few states allow a "close friend" to act as surrogate.

Whether required by law or not, if there is a question about whether surgery or some other serious procedure is authorized, doctors will usually turn for guidance to a close relative—spouse, parent, child. Friends and unmarried partners, although they may be most familiar with your wishes for your medical treatment, are rarely consulted, or—worse still—are sometimes purposefully left out of the decision making process.

Problems arise where partners and family members disagree about what treatment is proper. The most common result is that emotions run high as family members and loved ones take sides, with both camps claiming they want what is best for the patient. And, more recently, religious organizations have begun to finance court challenges against the practice of removing artificial feeding from patients who are permanently unconscious. In the most complicated scenarios, these battles over medical care wind up in court, where a judge, who usually has little medical knowledge and no familiarity with you, is called upon to decide the future of your treatment. Such battles—which are costly, time-consuming and painful to those involved—are unnecessary if you have the care and foresight to use a formal document to express your wishes for your health care.

5. The Documents You Produce Using Quicken WillMaker Plus

State legislatures often jealously covet their power to control the specifics of what makes a document legal in their own state. And nowhere is this more evident than in the area of health care directives, where each state may impose its own requirements regarding the form of the document, whether it must be notarized, what can be included and even on the definitions of terminal illness and permanent unconsciousness.

The health care document you produce using Quicken WillMaker Plus enables you to set out clear and effective directions for your medical care. If your state law requires you to use a specific form, your document will be in that format. However, in some instances, the directions that

Quicken WillMaker Plus produces as a result of your choices may go beyond what is addressed by your state law. For example, your state's law may be silent on whether individuals can direct their own health care if they become permanently unconscious, or your state's law may specifically restrict you from removing life support if you are pregnant. However, if you indicate that you want to address these issues when using Quicken WillMaker Plus, you can.

The reason that Quicken WillMaker Plus lets you go beyond your state's law is that state strictures on your right to direct your own health care contradict what the U.S. Supreme Court held in the *Cruzan* case: that the Constitution guarantees every individual this right. The Court also ruled that if an individual has left "clear and convincing evidence" of his or her wishes for medical care, those wishes should be followed. While the Court intimated that evidence of conversations about health care wishes might pass legal muster as an indication of a person's wishes, detailed written instructions are even better evidence of this intent.

The document you print using Quicken WillMaker Plus reflects your actual wishes rather than the constrictions of your state's law. If your choices are beyond or contrary to what your state law allows, your health care directive will call special attention to the fact. And it will state that the specific directions in the document you produce should be respected and followed in keeping with your constitutional right to direct your own health care.

On the off-chance that anyone later challenges your health care directive in a court because it goes beyond your state law, there is an additional legal failsafe. Your document contains a paragraph that allows the rest of your health care directive to be enforced as written even if any one of the directions you leave is found to be legally invalid.

Table of State Restrictions

In the following states, the options offered in Quicken WillMaker Plus do not exceed any state-imposed restrictions: Arizona, California, Florida, Hawaii, Maine, Maryland, Massachusetts, Missouri, New Jersey, New Mexico, New York, Oregon, Tennessee, Virginia and West Virginia.

If you live in some other state, the choices you make in Quicken WillMaker Plus may exceed what is authorized in your state. Check the chart below shows to see which restrictions your state imposes.

What each restriction means:

Food and water. State law does not authorize a patient to refuse artificially administered food and water. (See Section G, below.)

Permanent unconsciousness. State law does not specifically authorize a person to specify what health care they should receive if they end up in a permanently unconscious state. (See Section H2, below.)

Pregnancy. State law does not allow a woman to refuse life support if she is pregnant. Some states impose this restriction only if the fetus could be brought to term without hurting the mother. (See Section L, below.)

State	Restrictions	State	Restrictions
Alabama	Pregnancy	Missouri	Permanent unconsciousness, Pregnancy
Alaska	Pregnancy		
Arizona	No relevant restrictions	Montana	Permanent unconsciousness, Pregnancy
Arkansas	Pregnancy		
California	No restrictions	Nebraska	Pregnancy
Colorado	Pregnancy, Permanent unconsciousness	Nevada	Pregnancy
		New Hampshire	Pregnancy
Connecticut	Pregnancy		
Delaware	Pregnancy	North Dakota	Permanent unconsciousness, Pregnancy
District of Columbia	Permanent unconsciousness		
		Ohio	Pregnancy
Georgia	Pregnancy	Oklahoma	Pregnancy
Idaho	Pregnancy	Pennsylvania	Pregnancy
Illinois	Food and water, Pregnancy	Rhode Island	Permanent unconsciousness, Pregnancy
Indiana	Permanent unconsciousness, Pregnancy		
		South Carolina	Pregnancy
Iowa	Pregnancy	South Dakota	Pregnancy
Kansas	Pregnancy, Permanent unconsciousness	Texas	Pregnancy
		Utah	Pregnancy
Kentucky	Pregnancy	Vermont	Permanent unconsciousness
Michigan	Pregnancy	Washington	Pregnancy
Mississippi	No relevant restrictions	Wisconsin	Pregnancy
		Wyoming	Pregnancy

D. Identifying Whom the Document Is For

The initial screens in this portion of Quicken WillMaker Plus ask you to provide some basic identifying information about whom the document is for and what state's laws should be applied.

1. Your Name

If you have already used Quicken WillMaker Plus to prepare a will, living trust , durable power of attorney for finances, or final arrangements document, your name should automatically appear on the screen that requests this information. Otherwise, enter your name in the same form that you use on other formal documents, such as your driver's license or bank accounts. This may or may not be the name that appears on your birth certificate. If you customarily use more than one name for business purposes, list all of them in your Quicken WillMaker Plus answer, separated by aka, which stands for "also known as."

There is room for you to list several names. But use your common sense. For purposes of your health care directive, your name is needed to identify you and to match you with your medical records. Be sure to include the name you have used on other medical documents such as prior hospital or doctor records.

2. Your Gender

Many states have restrictions or special considerations that may apply to health care directives of women who are pregnant. If you are a woman using Quicken WillMaker Plus, it may be necessary for you to answer a few more questions to address this possibility. (See Section L, below.)

Quicken WillMaker Plus also uses information about your gender to make your documents and instructions grammatically elegant.

Some states ask for more. A few states, including Oregon, ask you to provide even more complete biographical information, including your birthdate. The health care document you print will contain this information, too. The reason for including it is to better match you with your directive.

3. Your State

You are asked to specify the state of your legal residence, sometimes called a domicile. This is the state where you make your home now and for the indefinite future. This information is important, because Quicken WillMaker Plus assembles and produces a health care directive that is specifically geared to the laws of the state you select.

If you divide up the year living in two or more states, you may not be sure which state is your legal residence. To decide, choose the state where you are the most rooted—that is, the state in which you:

- are registered to vote
- register your motor vehicles
- own valuable property—especially property with a title document, such as a house or car
- have checking, savings and other investment accounts, and
- maintain a business.

If You Move or Spend Time in More Than One State

Some people assume that once they have completed health care directives, those documents will be valid in every other state to which they may roam. Others worry that they may need to complete directives in all states in which they vacation or customarily spend time. The truth depends, somewhat confusingly, on what states are involved. However, as a general rule, people are safe in doing it in their own state, even if their documents need to be used in another state.

State	Rule for recognizing directives from other state	State	Rule for recognizing directives from other state
Alabama	Invalid to the extent it exceeds what Alabama law allows	Kansas	Must comply with laws of original state
Alaska	Must comply with laws of original state	Kentucky	No law on the subject
Arizona	Invalid to the extent it exceeds what Arizona law allows	Maine	Must comply with original state's laws or Maine law
Arkansas	Must comply with original state's laws or Arkansas law	Maryland	Invalid to the extent it exceeds what Maryland law allows
California	Must comply with original state's laws or California law	Massachusetts	Must comply with laws of original state
Colorado	Must comply with laws of original state	Michigan	No law on the subject
Connecticut	Must comply with original state's laws or Connecticut law	Minnesota	Must comply with original state's laws or Minnesota law
Delaware	Must comply with original state's laws or Delaware law	Mississippi	Must comply with original state's laws and substantially comply with Mississippi law
District of Columbia	No law on the subject	Missouri	No law on the subject
Florida	Must comply with original state's laws or Delaware law	Montana	Must comply with original state's laws and substantially comply with Montana law
Georgia	Invalid to the extent it exceeds what Georgia law allows	Nebraska	Must comply with original state's laws or Nebraska law
Hawaii	Must comply with original state's laws and substantially comply with Hawaii law	Nevada	Must comply with original state's laws or Nevada law
Idaho	No law on the subject	New Hampshire	Invalid to the extent it exceeds what New Hampshire law allows
Illinois	Must comply with original state's laws or Illinois law	New Jersey	Must comply with original state's laws or New Jersey law
Indiana	Must comply with original state's laws or Indiana law	New Mexico	Must comply with laws of original state
Iowa	Invalid to the extent it exceeds what Iowa law allows	New York	Must comply with laws of original state

If You Move or Spend Time in More Than One State	
State	**Rule for recognizing directives from other state**
North Carolina	No law on the subject
North Dakota	Must comply with original state's laws or North Dakota law
Ohio	Must comply with original state's laws or Ohio law
Oklahoma	Invalid to the extent it exceeds what Oklahoma law allows
Oregon	Must comply with original state's laws or Oregon law
Pennsylvania	No law on the subject
Rhode Island	Must comply with laws of original state
South Carolina	No law on the subject
South Dakota	Must comply with laws of original state
Tennessee	Must comply with original state's laws or Tennessee law
Texas	Invalid to the extent it exceeds what Texas law allows
Utah	Must comply with laws of original state
Vermont	Must comply with laws of original state
Virginia	Must comply with original state's laws or Virginia law
Washington	Invalid to the extent it exceeds what Washington law allows
West Virginia	Must comply with original state's laws or West Virginia law
Wisconsin	Invalid to the extent it exceeds what Wisconsin law allows
Wyoming	No law on the subject

4. Your Address

Health care directives in some states require that you fill in your address on them. If your state requires this information, use the address of your residence—the place you live most of the year. Your address is just one additional piece of information that will help ensure that you are properly matched with your written directions for health care.

E. Life-Prolonging Medical Care

Health care directives in most states ask for your preferences about life-prolonging treatments or procedures. Many people who attempt to fill in the blanks on their state forms unaided by Quicken WillMaker Plus or some sound medical advice are confounded by the question.

This section of the manual briefly discusses medical procedures that are most often deemed "life-prolonging." Ponderous as it seems, most people should at least read quickly through the definitions below so that they understand what the term life-prolonging means from a medical perspective. However, if you are firmly resolved to direct that all procedures be provided—or that all procedures be withheld—you will not need to deal with these definitions while preparing your health care directive, and you can skip directly to Section I, below.

Bear in mind that the types of medical procedures that are available will change over time. Technological advances mean that currently unfathomable procedures and treatments will become available and treatments that are now common will become obsolete. Also, the treatments that are available vary drastically with region, depending on the sophistication and funding levels of local medical facilities.

While putting together your health care directive, the best that you can do is to become familiar with the kinds of medical procedures that are most commonly administered to patients who are seriously ill. The best that the Quicken WillMaker Plus program can do is to provide you with clear definitions. Both of these feats will help you to produce the health care document that most accurately reflects your wishes.

It Does Not Get More Personal Than This

For many people, the desire to direct what kind of medical care they want to receive is driven by a very specific event—watching a loved one die, having an unsatisfactory brush with the medical establishment, preparing for serious surgery.

Your ultimate decisions are likely to be influenced by many complicating factors: your medical history, your knowledge of other people's experiences with life-prolonging medical procedures or your religious beliefs. If you are having great difficulty in deciding about your preferences for medical care, take a few moments to figure out what's getting in your way. If you are unsure about the meaning or specifics of a particular medical treatment, turn to a doctor you trust for a more complete explanation. If the impediment is fear of sickness or death, talk over your feelings with family members and friends. (See Section Q, below.)

---

1. Blood and Blood Products

Blood is composed of a pale yellow fluid called plasma. Within the plasma, red blood cells (erythrocytes), white blood cells (leukocytes), platelets and a variety of chemicals including hormones, proteins, carbohydrates and fats are suspended.

Partial or full blood transfusions may be recommended to combat diseases that impair the blood system, to foster healing after a blood loss or to replenish blood lost through surgery, disease or injury.

2. Cardio-Pulmonary Resuscitation (CPR)

Cardio-pulmonary resuscitation (CPR) is used when a person's heart or breathing has stopped. CPR includes applying physical pressure and using mouth-to-mouth resuscitation. Electrical shocks are also used if available. CPR is often accompanied by intravenous drugs used to normalize body systems. A final step in CPR is often attaching the patient to a respirator.

In an Emergency: DNR Orders

In addition to the health care documents produced by Quicken WillMaker Plus, you may want to secure a Do Not Resuscitate order, or DNR order. A DNR order documents the wish that you not be administered cardio-pulmonary resuscitation (CPR) and will alert emergency medical personnel to this wish. DNR orders were first used in hospital settings to alert hospital staff that CPR should be withheld from a patient, but now they are frequently used in situations where a person might require emergency care while outside of the hospital.

You may want to consider a DNR order if you:

- have a terminal illness
- have an increased risk for cardiac or respiratory arrest, or
- have strong feelings against the use of CPR under any circumstances.

In most states, any adult may secure a DNR order. But some states, such as South Carolina and Utah, allow you to create an order only if you have been diagnosed as having a terminal illness.

Because emergency response teams must act quickly in a medical crisis, they often do not have the time to determine whether you have a valid health care directive explaining treatments you want provided or withheld. If they do not know your wishes, they must provide you with all possible life-saving measures. But if emergency care providers see that you have a valid DNR order—which is often made apparent by an easily identifiable bracelet, anklet or necklace—they will not administer CPR.

If you ask to have CPR withheld, you will not be provided with:

- chest compression
- electric shock treatments to the chest
- tubes placed in the airway to assist breathing
- artificial ventilation, or
- cardiac drugs.

If you want to secure a DNR order, or if you would like to find out more about DNR orders, talk with a doctor. A doctor's signature is required to make the DNR valid—and in most states, he or she will obtain and complete the necessary paperwork. If the doctor does not have the form or other information you need, call the Health Department for your state and ask to speak with someone in the Division of Emergency Medical Services.

If you obtain a DNR order, discuss your decision with your family or other caretakers. They should know where your form is located—and whom to call if you require emergency treatment. Even if you are wearing identification, such as a bracelet or necklace, keep your form in an obvious place. You might consider keeping it by your bedside, on the front of your refrigerator, in your wallet or in your suitcase if you are traveling. If your DNR order is not apparent and immediately available, or if it has been altered in any way, CPR will most likely be performed.

3. Diagnostic Tests

Diagnostic tests are commonly used to evaluate urine, blood and other body fluids and to check on all bodily functions. Diagnostic tests can include X-rays and more sophisticated tests of brainwaves or other internal body systems. Some diagnostic tests—including surgery—can be expensive and invasive, producing pain and other side effects.

4. Dialysis

A dialysis machine is used to clean and add essential substances to the blood—through tubes placed in blood vessels or into the abdomen—when kidneys do not function properly. The entire cleansing process takes three or more hours and is performed on most dialysis patients from two to three times a week. With the portability of dialysis machines, it is often possible to have the procedure performed at home rather than in a hospital or other advanced care facility.

5. Drugs

The most common and most controversial drugs given to seriously ill or comatose patients are antibiotics—administered by mouth, through a feeding tube or by injection. Antibiotics are used to arrest and squelch infectious diseases. Patients in very weakened conditions may not respond even to massive doses of antibiotics.

Many health care providers argue that infectious diseases can actually be a benefit to those in advanced stages of an illness, since they may render a patient unconscious, and presumably not in pain, or help to speed up the dying process. Others contend that if an antibiotic can eliminate symptoms of an illness, it is almost always the proper medical treatment.

Drugs may also be used to eliminate or alleviate pain. If, within your health care directive, you state that you do not want drugs to prolong your life, they will still be administered for pain control. (See Section F, below.)

6. Respirator

A mechanical respirator or a ventilator assists or takes over breathing for a patient by pumping air in and out of the lungs. These machines dispense a regulated amount of air into the lungs at a set rate—and periodically purge the lungs. Patients are connected to respirators either by a tube that goes through the mouth and throat into the lung or attaches directly through the lung surgically.

Respirators are often used to stabilize patients who are suffering from an acute trauma or breathing crisis. Once a patient has been attached to a respirator, most doctors will buck against removing the machinery unless there is clear written direction that this is what the patient would want.

7. Surgery

Surgical procedures such as amputation are often used to stem the spread of life-threatening infections or to keep vital organs functioning. Major surgery such as a heart bypass is also typically performed on patients who are terminally ill or comatose. You might want to consider the cost, time spent recovering from the invasive surgery and ultimate prognosis when deciding whether to include surgery in your final medical treatment.

F. Comfort Care (Palliative Care)

If you want death to occur naturally—without life-prolonging intervention—it does not mean you must forgo treatment to alleviate pain or keep you comfortable. In fact, the health care directive you make with Quicken WillMaker Plus will state that you wish to receive any care that is necessary to keep you pain-free. This type of care, sometimes known as "comfort care," is now more commonly called "palliative care." Rather than focusing on a cure or prolonging life, palliative care emphasizes quality of life and dignity by helping a patient to remain comfortable and free from pain until life ends naturally. For example, hospice programs provide palliative care to individuals in the final stages of terminal illness and support services to the family.

Studies have shown that palliative care services are greatly appreciated by the family and friends of dying patients. Numerous organizations promote public awareness of palliative care options, and information about treatment options is widely available on the Internet. (See below.) However, despite the wide recognition of the benefits of palliative care, a major nationwide study in 2002 revealed that relatively few people take advantage of this option. Most hospitals do not have integrated palliative care plans among their treatment options. Very few doctors understand it well and it is still not emphasized in medical training. As a result, many people die in hospital intensive care units, sometimes in severe pain, with no knowledge that palliative care was an option. You may wish to spend some time educating yourself about palliative care so that you can discuss your wishes with your health care proxy (see Section I, below) and your treatment providers.

 Resources. Here are some resources that can help you understand your options when it comes to palliative care:

Websites

www.growthhouse.org. A nationwide clearinghouse of palliative care information and resources.

www.pbs.org/wnet/onourownterms. *On Our Own Terms* is a website created in conjunction with a Bill Moyers/PBS documentary on end-of-life treatment. The site features interviews with professionals, patients and loved ones sharing insights and perspectives on making these difficult choices.

Books

Numerous books have been written in the past ten years about the dying process. Here are a few that feature informative discussions of the issue of pain control at the end of life:

Handbook for Mortals: Caring for the Dying Patient, by Joanne Lynn, M.D., and Joan Harrold, M.D. (Oxford University Press)

Caring for Patients at the End of Life: Facing an Uncertain Future Together, by Timothy E. Quill (Oxford University Press)

The Needs of the Dying: A Guide for Bringing Hope, Comfort, and Love to Life's Final Chapter, by David Kessler (Quill).

G. Artificially Administered Food and Water

If you are close to death from a terminal condition or are permanently unconscious and cannot communicate to others your preferences for your own health care, it is also likely that you will not be able to voluntarily take in water or food through your mouth. The medical solution to this is to provide you with food and water—as a mix of nutrients and fluids—through tubes inserted in a vein, into your stomach through your nose or directly into your stomach through a surgical incision, depending on your condition.

Intravenous (IV) feeding, where fluids are introduced through a vein in an arm or a leg, is a short-term procedure. Tube feeding through the nose (nasogastric tube), stomach (gastrostomy tube), intestines (jejunostomy tube) or largest vein, the vena cava (total parenteral nutrition), can be carried on indefinitely.

Permanently unconscious patients can sometimes live for years with artificial feeding and hydration without regaining consciousness. If food and water are removed, death will occur in a relatively short time due to dehydration, rather than starvation. Such a course of action is generally combined with a plan of medication to keep the patient comfortable.

Quicken WillMaker Plus allows you to choose whether you want artificially administered food and water withheld or provided. This decision is difficult for many people. Keep in mind that as long as you are able to communicate your wishes, by whatever means, you will not be denied food and water if you want it.

 Resources. The following resources may help you make choices about artificially administered food and water:

Hard Choices for Loving People: CPR, Artificial Feeding, Comfort Care and the Patient With a Life-Threatening Illness, by Hank Dunn (A & A Publishers), is a well-written resource that features a good discussion of the issues surrounding artificial nutrition and hydration, exploring the vari-

ous medical, religious and philosophical views on the subject. You can download the entire text of the book for free from www.hardchoices.com.

"Assisted Oral Feeding and Tube Feeding," a paper published by the Alzheimer's Association, is available at www.alz.org/Resources/ FactSheets/FSOralfeeding.pdf. This pamphlet discusses various medical studies on the benefits and risks of tube feeding of dementia patients who have lost the ability to swallow.

"Policy Concerns: Tube Feeding in Elderly Demented Patients," published by The Center for Gerontology and Health Care Research, is available at www.chcr.brown.edu/dying/policy feedtube.htm. This 2002 report features state-by-state statistics on the prevalence of tube feeding in nursing homes. These statistics show that large numbers of nursing home patients receive tube feeding, despite the growing consensus that it may be of little benefit to most patients. The study emphasizes the need for individuals to create advance medical directives that address this issue.

H. Directing Health Care for Different Situations

Despite drastic technological advances in medicine, much about physical symptoms and effects remains uncharted. For example, medical experts disagree over whether comatose patients can feel pain and over whether some treatments are universally effective.

People who have strong feelings about what medical care they want to receive are usually guided by personal experience rather than a greater knowledge of current medical capabilities or future advances. For example, if you have watched a parent suffer a prolonged death while hooked to a respirator, you may opt not to have a respirator as part of your medical care. If a friend who was diagnosed as terminally ill was much improved by a newly developed antibiotic, you may adamantly demand that drugs be administered to you, no matter what the medical prognosis.

Quicken WillMaker Plus allows you to specify that you should receive different kinds of medical care when you are permanently unconscious and when you are diagnosed to be close to death from a terminal condition. This flexibility is built in to accommodate health care wishes stemming from personal preference and experience, while balancing the unknowns of medicine.

For example, medical personnel usually give those diagnosed to be terminally ill a short time to live—less than six months or so. Some people feel that the best medical care under such a prognosis would be to have as much pain and suffering alleviated as possible through drugs and IVs, without any heroic medical maneuvers, such as invasive surgery or additional painful diagnostic tests.

However, patients often prove doctors wrong. Those diagnosed to die of a terminal illness within a few months sometimes stabilize or improve and live on for many years. If you opt to direct that no life-prolonging treatments be provided, you gamble that your condition will not improve—a gamble you must weigh against your own definitions of life.

Permanently unconscious patients can be kept alive for many years with some mechanical assistance to keep breathing, circulation and other vital bodily functions operating. While chances are statistically miniscule that these patients will ever regain consciousness, in these cases there is a chance that the diagnoses were incorrect in the first place. (See Section 2, below.)

There is no general rule, no strict legal guidance, to offer on this topic. People fashioning documents to direct their health care will likely be guided by their own very personal definitions of quality of life. Some hold out hope for the possibility of some medical cure for their condition—and direct that all possible medical treatments be administered to them if they become permanently unconscious. Others feel strongly that life without consciousness would completely lack meaning—and direct that all medical procedures, including food and water, be discontinued. And still others walk the middle ground, opting to be kept alive by food and water, but not by other life-sustaining measures.

If you are having a difficult time making this choice, you may get good guidance by discussing the matter with a doctor you trust, or with another experienced health care worker. There are also resources on the Internet that discuss the medical, spiritual and philosophical aspects of this decision (see below).

Where to Go For More Help

The growing awareness of health care directives is coupled with a growing number of resources you can turn to if you need help completing your directive or have specific questions about it.

A local senior center may be a good place to go for help. Many of them have trained health care staff on hand who are willing to discuss health care options.

The patient representative or social worker at a local hospital may also be a good person to contact for help. And if you have a regular physician, by all means discuss your concerns with him or her.

Local special interest groups and clinics may help you fill out your directive—particularly organizations set up to meet the needs of the severely ill, such as AIDS or cancer groups. Check your telephone book for a local listing—or call one of the group's hotlines for more information or a possible referral. In addition, the Internet site www.growthhouse.org has an extensive listing of local resources.

There are also a number of seminars offered. Beware of groups that offer such seminars for a hefty fee, however. Hospitals and senior centers often provide them free of charge.

1. Close to Death From a Terminal Condition

Generally, a terminal condition is any disease or injury from which doctors believe there is no chance of recovery and from which death is likely to occur within a short time—such as the final stages of cancer.

State laws on health care directives define terminal condition slightly differently, but commonly refer to it as "incurable," or "hopeless." Many state laws explain in addition that a patient who is terminally ill will die unless artificially supported through life-sustaining procedures.

Most states require that one or two physicians verify that the patient has a terminal condition before the documents directing health care will go into effect. In some states, this verification must be in writing.

2. Permanently Unconscious

Permanent unconsciousness may be caused by various medical conditions, head traumas or other body injuries.

While permanently unconscious people appear to go through sleep cycles and to respond to some noises and physical stimulation, medical experts disagree about whether a permanently unconscious person is capable of experiencing pain or discomfort. Most permanently unconscious people do not require mechanical assistance with breathing or circulation but must be provided food and water—usually through tubes inserted in the veins or stomach—if the condition persists.

Generally, people who lose consciousness either recover consciousness within a short time (often a matter of hours, days or sometimes weeks) or enter a permanent coma or a persistent vegetative state in which it is extremely unlikely that they will ever regain consciousness. They may be kept alive for many months or even years. Medical personnel usually declare that a person who remains in a persistent vegetative state for many months without change has passed into a terminal condition.

Once a condition of unconsciousness is diagnosed as permanent, the chances of recovery are statistically extremely low. But medical technology (respirators and tube feeding and hydration) can typically keep an unconscious person alive indefinitely—48 years in one case. Consequently, the only way to allow a permanently unconscious person to die naturally may be to discontinue tube feeding and hydration.

To complicate matters, the external symptoms of permanent unconsciousness are somewhat subjective and can be misdiagnosed or the subject of dispute. The recent, highly publicized case of Terri Schiavo involved a Florida woman kept alive by feeding tubes for more than ten years. While most medical experts declared her to be unconscious of her surroundings, at least one doctor offered the opinion that her responses to stimuli were not just reflexive, but were, in fact, evidence that she was conscious of her environment.

Other factors, such as overmedication, can cause an unresponsive, unconscious condition that may abate once the treatment is halted or changed. To guard against misdiagnosis, many states require two physicians, at least one of whom is an expert on such conditions, to declare a patient permanently unconscious before any stated wishes are carried out.

In cases such as these, the person you appoint as your health care representative can play a crucial role, to make sure that diagnoses are not made in haste or that second opinions can be sought if there is reason to doubt the initial diagnosis. (See Section I, below.)

3. Other Medical Conditions

A few states allow patients to request withdrawal of life support in conditions where death may not be "imminent" but where the medical condition is nonetheless irreversible. If your state's official form addresses a condition like this, Quicken WillMaker Plus allows you to choose the kind of treatment you want.

Texas users will be asked to specify their care in an "irreversible" condition, while Florida and Maryland residents will be asked about care if they are in an "end-stage condition," including cases of end-stage Alzheimer's or dementia.

Oregon's official form allows patients to request removal of support in cases of advanced illness (same as end-stage condition) or in cases of "extraordinary suffering." Quicken WillMaker Plus allows Oregon residents to express treatment wishes for these other conditions.

I. Choosing a Health Care Proxy

By taking the time and making the effort to draw up your health care documents, you have already done much to assure that your wishes will be followed. The next desirable step is to discuss those wishes with a doctor if you have one—and with patient administrators if you anticipate being admitted to a hospital. In most cases, medical personnel and relatives faced with difficult decisions about continuing or discontinuing another's medical care are relieved and delighted to take direction from the person by following the health care documents.

If your health care wishes are different from what your doctors or close relatives want for you, however, problems may arise. That's why it's always wise to name someone—usually called a health care proxy, agent or attorney-in-fact—to be sure that the wishes you have expressed are followed as closely as possible. Your agent will be on hand to ensure that medical personnel know of your wishes and to see that they are enforced, even if it means arguing with doctors or going to court.

1. Guidance in Choosing a Proxy

The person you name as your health care proxy should be someone you trust—and someone with whom you feel confident discussing your wishes. While your proxy need not agree with your wishes for your medical care, you should believe that he or she respects your right to get the kind of medical care you want.

The person you appoint to oversee your health care wishes could be a spouse or partner, relative or close friend. Keep in mind your proxy may have to fight to assert your wishes in the face of a medical establishment that is hard to budge from its position—and against the wishes of family members who may be driven by their own beliefs and interests, rather than yours. If you foresee the possibility of a conflict in enforcing your wishes, be sure to choose a proxy who is strong-willed and assertive.

While you need not name someone who lives in the same state as you do, proximity may be one factor you consider. If you languish long with a protracted illness, the reality is that the person you name may be called upon to spend weeks or months near your bedside, making sure medical personnel abide by your wishes for your medical treatment.

Do not choose medical personnel. Do not name as your proxy either your doctor or an employee of a hospital or nursing home where you are receiving treatment. In fact, the laws in many states prevent you from naming such a person. In a few instances, this legal constraint may frustrate your wishes. For example, you may wish to name your spouse or partner as your representative, but if he or she also works as a hospital employee, that alone may bar you from naming him or her in some states. If the laws in your state ban your first choice, you may have to name another person to serve instead. (See the listing below for more on your state's law on health care proxy restrictions.)

2. State Requirements for Proxies

A number of states have strict bans against allowing some people to serve as your health care proxy. Attending physicians and other health care providers are those commonly banned from serving. Some states presume that the motivations of such people may be clouded by self-interest. For example, an attending physician may be motivated to provide every medical procedure available—to try every heroic or experimental treatment—even if that flies in the face of a patient's wishes.

Consult the listing below for the specifics of your state's law on proxy requirements and restrictions before you select a proxy.

State Proxy Requirements

Alabama

Your health care representative may not be:

- your treating health care provider
- an employee of your treating health care provider, unless the employee is related to you.

Alaska

Your health care representative may not be an owner, operator, or employee of the health care institution at which you are receiving care, unless related to you by blood, marriage, or adoption.

Arizona

Your health care representative must be at least 18 years old.

Arkansas

Your health care representative must be at least 18 years old.

California

Your health care representative may not be:

- your treating health care provider
- an employee of your treating health care provider, unless the employee is related to you or you and the employee both work for your treating health care provider
- an operator of a community care facility
- an employee of the operator of the community care facility, unless the employee is related to you or you and the employee both work at the community care facility
- an operator of a residential care facility for the elderly, or
- an employee of the operator of the residential care facility for the elderly, unless the employee is related to you or you and the employee both work at the residential care facility.

Colorado

Your health care representative must be at least 21 years old.

Connecticut

If, when you appoint your health care representative, you are a patient or a resident of, or have applied for admission to, a hospital, home for the aged, rest home with nursing supervision or chronic and convalescent nursing home, your health care representative may not be:

- an operator, unless the operator is related to you by blood, marriage or adoption
- an administrator, unless the administrator is related to you by blood, marriage or adoption, or
- an employee, unless the employee is related to you by blood, marriage or adoption.

In any case, your health care representative may not be:

- under the age of 18
- a witness to the document appointing him or her as your health care representative
- your attending physician, or
- an employee of a government agency which is financially responsible for your medical care—unless that person is related to you by blood, marriage or adoption.

Delaware

Your health care representative may not be an owner, operator or employee of a long-term health care institution where you are receiving care, unless he or she is related to you by blood, marriage or adoption.

District of Columbia

Your health care representative may not be your health care provider.

State Proxy Requirements

Florida

Your health care representative may not be a witness to the document naming your health care representative.

Georgia

Your health care representative may not be your health care provider if your health care provider is directly or indirectly involved in the medical treatment given to you under your durable power of attorney for health care.

Hawaii

Your health care representative may not be an owner, operator or employee of your treating health care provider, unless the person is related to you by blood, marriage or adoption.

Idaho

Your health care representative may not be:

- your treating health care provider
- an employee of your health care provider, unless the employee is related to you
- an operator of a community care facility, or
- an employee of an operator of a community care facility, unless the employee is related to you.

Illinois

Your health care representative may not be:

- your health care provider, or
- your attending physician.

Indiana

No requirements.

Iowa

Your health care representative may not be:

- your health care provider, or
- an employee of your health care provider, unless these individuals are related to you by blood, marriage or adoption—limited to parents, children, siblings, grandchildren, grandparents, uncles, aunts, nephews, nieces and great-grandchildren.

Kansas

Your health care representative may not be:

- your treating health care provider
- an employee of your treating health care provider, or
- an employee, owner, director or officer of a health care facility.

These restrictions do not apply, however, if the representative is:

- related to you by blood, marriage or adoption, or
- a member of the same community of people to which you belong who have vowed to lead a religious life and who conduct or assist in conducting religious services and actually and regularly engage in religious, charitable or educational activities or the performance of health care services.

Kentucky

Your health care representative may not be an employee, owner, director or officer of a health care facility where you are a resident or patient, unless they are:

- related to you more closely than first cousins, once removed, or
- a member of the same religious order.

State Proxy Requirements

Maine

Your health care representative may not be an owner, operator or employee of a residential long-term health care institution in which you are receiving care, unless he or she is related to you by blood, marriage or adoption.

Maryland

Your health care representative may not be an owner, operator or employee of a health care facility where you are receiving treatment unless he or she would qualify as your surrogate decisionmaker under Maryland law. This restriction includes your spouse, parent, child, sibling, guardian, close friend or relative.

Massachusetts

Your health care representative may not be an operator, administrator or employee of a facility where you are a patient or resident or have applied for admission, unless the operator, administrator or employee is related to you by blood, marriage or adoption.

Michigan

Your health care representative must be at least 18 years old.

Minnesota

Your health care representative may not be your treating health care provider or an employee of your treating health care provider, unless he or she is related to you by blood, marriage, registered domestic partnership or adoption.

Mississippi

Your health care representative may not be an owner, operator or employee of a residential long-term care facility where you are receiving treatment, unless related to you by blood, marriage or adoption. This restriction does not apply, however, if you are a patient in a state-operated facility who has no spouse, adult child, parent or adult sibling available to act as your representative.

Missouri

Your health care representative may not be:

- your attending physician
- an employee of your attending physician, or
- an owner, operator or employee of the health care facility where you live, unless:
  ✓ you and your health care representative are related as parents, children, siblings, grandparent or grandchildren, or
  ✓ you and your health care representative are members of the same community of people who have vowed to lead a religious life and who conduct or assist in conducting religious services and actually and regularly engage in religious, charitable or educational activities or the performance of health care services.

Montana

Your health care representative must be at least 18 years old.

Nebraska

Your health care representative may not be:

- under the age of 19, unless he or she is married
- a witness to your durable power of attorney for health care
- your attending physician
- an employee of your attending physician, unless the employee is related to you by blood, marriage or adoption

State Proxy Requirements

- a person unrelated to you by blood, marriage or adoption who is an owner, operator or employee of a health care provider of which you are a patient or resident, or
- a person unrelated to you by blood, marriage or adoption who is presently serving as a health care representative for ten or more people.

Nevada

Your health care representative may not be:

- your health care provider
- an employee of your health care provider
- an operator of a health care facility, or
- an employee of a health care facility, unless he or she is your spouse, legal guardian or next of kin.

New Hampshire

Your health care representative may not be:

- your health care provider
- an employee of your health care provider, unless the employee is related to you
- your residential care provider, or
- an employee of your residential care provider, unless the employee is related to you.

New Jersey

Your health care representative may not be:

- under the age of 18, or
- an operator, administrator or employee of a health care institution in which you are a patient or resident, unless the operator, administrator or employee is related to you by blood, marriage or adoption, or, in the case of a physician, is not your attending physician.

New Mexico

Your health care representative may not be an owner, operator or employee of a health care facility at which you are receiving care—unless related to you by blood, marriage or adoption.

New York

Your health care representative may not be:

- under the age of 18, unless he or she is the parent of a child, or married
- your attending physician
- presently appointed health care representative for ten or more other people, unless he or she is your spouse, child, parent, brother, sister or grandparent
- an operator administrator or employee of a hospital if, at the time of the appointment, you are a patient or resident of, or have applied for admission to, such hospital. This restriction shall not apply to:
  - ✓ an operator, administrator or employee of a hospital who is related to you by blood, marriage or adoption, or
  - ✓ a physician, who is not your attending physician, except that no physician affiliated with a mental hygiene facility or a psychiatric unit of a general hospital may serve as agent for you if you are living in or being treated by such facility or unit unless the physician is related to you by blood, marriage or adoption.

North Carolina

Your health care agent may not be:

- under the age of 18, or
- providing health care to you for compensation.

State Proxy Requirements

North Dakota

Your health care representative may not be:

- your treating health care provider
- an employee of your treating health care provider, unless the employee is related to you
- an operator of a long-term care facility, or
- an employee of an operator of a long-term care facility, unless the employee is related to you.

Ohio

Your health care representative may not be:

- under the age of 18
- your attending physician
- an administrator of any nursing home in which you are receiving care
- an employee or agent of your attending physician, or
- an employee or agent of any health care facility in which you are being treated.

These restrictions do not apply, however, if your representative is 18 years of age or older and a member of the same religious order as you—or is related to you by blood, marriage or adoption.

Oklahoma

Your health care representative must be at least 18 years old.

Oregon

Your health care representative may not be:

- under the age of 18
- your attending physician or an employee of your attending physician, unless the physician or employee is related to you by blood, marriage or adoption, or
- an owner, operator or employee of a health care facility in which you are

patient or resident, unless related to you by blood, marriage or adoption—or appointed before you were admitted to the facility.

Pennsylvania

No requirements.

Rhode Island

Your health care representative may not be:

- your treating health care provider
- an employee of your treating health care provider, unless the employee is related to you
- an operator of a community care facility, or
- an employee of an operator of a community care facility, unless the employee is related to you.

South Carolina

Your health care representative may not be:

- under the age of 18
- your health care provider at the time you execute your health care power of attorney, unless he or she is related to you
- a spouse or employee of your health care provider, unless he or she is related to you, or
- an employee of the nursing care facility where you live, unless he or she is related to you.

South Dakota

No requirements.

Tennessee

Your health care representative may not be:

- your treating health care provider
- an employee of your treating health care provider, unless he or she is related to you by blood, marriage or adoption

State Proxy Requirements

- an operator of a health care institution
- an employee of an operator of a health care institution, unless he or she is related to you by blood, marriage or adoption, or
- your conservator, unless you are represented by an attorney who signs a specific statement—required by Tennessee Code § 36-6-203(c).

Texas

Your health care representative may not be:

- your health care provider
- an employee of your health care provider, unless the employee is related to you
- your residential care provider, or
- an employee of your residential care provider, unless the employee is related to you.

Utah

Your health care representative must be at least 18 years old.

Vermont

Your health care representative may not be:

- your health care provider
- an owner, operator, employee, agent, or contractor of a residential care facility, health care facility, or correctional facility in which you reside, unless related to you by blood, marriage, civil union or adoption.

Virginia

Your health care representative must be at least 18 years old.

Washington

Your health care representative may not be:

- any of your physicians
- your physicians' employees
- owners, administrators or employees of the health care facility where you live or receive care.

These restrictions do not apply, however, if your representative is your spouse, adult child or sibling.

West Virginia

Your health care representative may not be:

- your treating health care provider
- an employee of your treating health care provider, unless he or she is related to you
- an operator of a health care facility serving you, or
- an employee of an operator of a health care facility, unless he or she is related to you.

Wisconsin

Your health care representative may not be:

- your health care provider or the spouse or employee of your health care provider unless he or she is related to you, or
- an employee or spouse of an employee of the health care facility in which you are a patient, unless he or she is related to you.

Wyoming

Your health care representative may not be an owner, operator or employee of a residential or community care facility where you are receiving care, unless he or she is related to you by blood, marriage or adoption.

3. Choosing an Alternate

Do not choose as an alternate someone who may be disqualified by state law from serving in your state. (See Section I2, above.)

A Bad Idea:
Naming More Than One Representative

Name only one person as your representative, even if you know of two or more people who are suitable candidates and who agree to undertake the job together. There may be problems, brought on by passing time and human nature, with naming people to share the job. In the critical time during which your representatives will be overseeing your wishes, they could disagree or suffer a change of heart, rendering them ineffective as lobbyists on your behalf.

If you know of two people you would like to name as your representatives, it is better to name only one person for the job—and name the other as an alternate to take over in case your first choice is unable to act when needed.

---

4. If You Do Not Name a Representative

Naming a health care representative is an optional part of making out your directives for your health care. If you do not know of anyone you trust to oversee your medical care, skip this part of the program. It is better not to name anyone than to name someone who is not comfortable with the directions you leave—or who is not likely to assert your wishes strongly.

Medical personnel are still technically bound to follow your written wishes for your health care—or to find someone who will care for you in the way you have directed. It is far better to put your wishes for final health care in writing than to let the lack of a representative stand in the way. If you do not name a health care proxy, redouble your efforts to discuss your wishes for medical care with a doctor or patient representative likely to be involved in providing that care.

J. Your Representative's Powers

The document you produce with Quicken WillMaker Plus gives the person you name the limited authority to supervise and enforce your written wishes for the type of medical care you wish to receive.

The power of attorney that prints out specifically gives the person you name as your health care proxy the authority to:

- review your medical records
- grant releases to medical personnel
- take any legal action necessary to ensure your wishes are followed
- hire and fire medical personnel such as homecare providers and attending physicians, and
- visit you in a hospital or other health care facility.

This should allow your proxy to do everything needed to make sure your health care wishes are carried out as written—and if they are not, to get you transferred to another facility or to the care of another doctor who will enforce them.

1. Possible Additional Powers

Be aware that most states allow you to prepare durable powers of attorney for health care that delegate much broader authority than the one produced for you by the Quicken WillMaker Plus program. Such powers of attorney may authorize your representative to make health care decisions for you even if you are not terminally ill or permanently unconscious, but, for example, you have an ongoing medical condition such as Alzheimer's disease that renders you incompetent. This type of document is beyond the scope of Quicken WillMaker Plus.

2. Durable Powers of Attorney for Finances

Another type of durable power of attorney—called a durable power of attorney for finances—can be used to give a person you trust the legal authority to handle your financial matters if you become unable to do so. People who are facing illness, injury or old age are particularly good candidates for this type of document.

If you need a durable power of attorney for finances, you can use Quicken WillMaker Plus to produce one. See Chapter 22.

3. Why Separate Documents Are Required

Although the Quicken WillMaker Plus program does not provide for the option, some state laws allow people to draw up a single durable power of attorney in which one person is named to oversee both health care and financial matters. While this sounds like a logical and simple solution to planning for possible incapacity, it is usually not a good idea, for a number of reasons:

- Most forms for durable powers of attorney that combine medical and financial matters do not allow you to include many specific details about how you would like to direct either your medical care or your finances.
- Each of these types of durable power of attorney will be used for a very different purpose and must be presented to different people and organizations—often at different times.
- If you use two separate documents, you do not have to show your medical wishes to people who are concerned only with your finances—and vice versa.
- It is essential for the documents delegating authority for your health care and finances to be kept current to reflect your changing wishes, adjustments in your money matters—even advances in medical technology. Having a single document that controls both finances and health care makes it unwieldy to update any of your wishes.

K. When Your Documents Take Effect

Your health care directive takes effect when all of the following occur:

- You are diagnosed to be close to death from a terminal condition or to be permanently unconscious—or to have one of the other conditions in which your state allows directives to be effective.
- You cannot communicate your own wishes for your medical care—orally, in writing or through gestures.
- Medical personnel attending you are notified of your written directions for your medical care.

In most instances, you can ensure that your directive becomes part of your medical record when you are admitted to a hospital or other care facility. But to ensure that your wishes will be followed if your need for care arises unexpectedly or while you are out of your home state or country, it is best to give copies of your completed documents to several people. (See Section N, below.)

L. How Pregnancy May Affect Your Directive

There is one limited situation in which a patient's specific directions about health care might be challenged or ignored: when the patient is pregnant. Many states specifically restrict the effect of health care documents if a woman is pregnant, stating that wishes that life support be withdrawn or removed will not be honored.

These state restrictions have rankled many supporters of women's rights and have become legally suspect since the U.S. Supreme Court set out and reaffirmed that the Constitution protects women's right to choose whether or not to bear children. In 1973, the Court in the case of *Roe v. Wade* (401 U.S. 113) overturned a restrictive Texas anti-abortion law, with a tersely delineated holding. The Court held that:

- during the first trimester of pregnancy, states may not intervene to regulate pregnancy
- during the second trimester, states may set up restrictions only to protect a woman's health, and
- during the third trimester, or at the point of viability, when a fetus "presumably has the capability of meaningful life outside the mother's womb," states can intervene to protect it.

Several states fashioning or refining their health care directives took a cue from this holding. They wrote into their legislation the condition that a health care directive will not take effect "if your doctors believe the fetus can be brought to term while you are receiving life-sustaining procedures."

Other state attempts to control choices about health care before a fetus is viable would most certainly be held unconstitutional. However, it is good to be aware of the restrictions that may exist in your state for pregnant women's health care directives. (See "State Laws on Pregnancy and Health Care Directives," below.)

1. Choices When Using Quicken WillMaker Plus

Quicken WillMaker Plus allows all women for whom pregnancy may be possible to specify that their health care directions:

- be given no effect during the course of a pregnancy, or
- be carried out as written.

If you specify that your health care directives be given no effect, your health care providers will have the discretion to decide what care is appropriate. They are most likely to administer whatever life-prolonging procedures are available—particularly if the fetus is at least four or five months old and potentially viable and unharmed by your condition.

If you choose that your health care directions be carried out as written if you are pregnant, beware that you may meet some resistance from the medical establishment. This is particularly true if you have directed that life-prolonging treatment, comfort care or food and water should be withheld. And you are more apt to run into resistance the more advanced your pregnancy becomes. If you are into the second trimester—fourth through sixth months—doctors are likely to administer all medical care they deem necessary to keep you and the fetus alive.

By the third trimester of a pregnancy—seventh through ninth months—it may be practically impossible to overcome a state's proscription against withholding life-prolonging medical care. And doctors who balk at enforcing your contrary wishes have some legal support for ignoring you and administering all available care. Since the *Roe* decision discussed above, they can argue that while individuals may have the right to direct their own health care, they have no right to direct that care for another living being—arguably, a fetus six months old or older.

If you are pregnant or anticipate becoming pregnant and have strong feelings about overcoming your state's strictures—that is, you live in a state that renders your directive completely ineffective if you are pregnant, but you wish to have it enforced—it is especially important for you to name a proxy to lobby on your behalf. Discuss your wishes and alert your proxy to any differences between your wishes and your state law. It would also be wise to write a brief explanation of your thoughts and understanding on this specific issue and attach it to your health care directive. (See Section Q, below.)

2. State Laws

Check the summary below for the specific provisions in your state law that may affect your wishes if you are pregnant when your health care document is enforced. To refresh your memory, Quicken WillMaker Plus will also include a synopsis of your state law on the instructions that print out with your documents.

State Laws on Pregnancy and Health Care Directives

"No Effect" means that the law in your state does not allow your document directing health care to take effect when you are pregnant.

"To Term" means that the law in your state will not allow your document directing health care to take effect if you are pregnant and your doctors believe the fetus could be brought to term while you are receiving life-sustaining treatment.

"No Statute" means that your state does not have any law about prohibiting withdrawal of life support if you are pregnant.

Alabama	No Effect
Alaska	To Term
Arizona	You may indicate whether or not you want your health care directions to be carried out in the event of your pregnancy.
Arkansas	To Term
California	No Statute
Colorado	To Term
Connecticut	No Effect
Delaware	To Term
District of Columbia	No Statute
Florida	If you are pregnant, life-prolonging procedures will be provided unless you have expressly indicated that your health care surrogate may authorize that life-prolonging procedures may be withheld if you are pregnant, or if your health care surrogate obtains court approval for withholding life-prolonging procedures.
Georgia	If you are pregnant, life-sustaining procedures will be provided unless the fetus could not develop to the point of live birth and you expressly indicate that you want your health care instructions to be carried out.
Hawaii	No Statute
Idaho	No Effect
Illinois	To Term
Indiana	No Effect
Iowa	To Term
Kansas	No Effect
Kentucky	No Effect
Maine	No Statute
Maryland	You may indicate whether or not you want your health care directions to be carried out in the event of your pregnancy.
Massachusetts	No Statute
Michigan	Your health care representative cannot make any medical decision to withhold or withdraw treatment that would result in your death if you are pregnant.
Minnesota	You may indicate whether or not you want your health care directives to be carried out in the event of your pregnancy.

State Laws on Pregnancy and Health Care Directives, continued

Mississippi	No Statute
Missouri	No Effect
Montana	To Term
Nebraska	To Term
Nevada	To Term
New Hampshire	No Effect
New Jersey	If you are pregnant when diagnosed to be terminally ill and near death or permanently unconscious, your express wishes as to your care during pregnancy, if written in your advance directive, will be carried out.
New Mexico	No Statute
New York	No Statute
North Carolina	No Statute
North Dakota	If you are pregnant, life-sustaining procedures will be provided unless those procedures will not permit the fetus to develop to the point of live birth, or your doctor concludes that prolonging your life would cause you physical harm or severe pain, or would prolong severe pain that cannot be alleviated by medication.
Ohio	To Term
Oklahoma	No Effect
Oregon	No Statute
Pennsylvania	If you are pregnant, life-sustaining procedures will be provided unless the fetus could not develop to the point of live birth with continued application of those life-sustaining procedures, or your doctors conclude that prolonging your life would cause you unreasonable pain or prolong severe pain that cannot be alleviated by medication.
Rhode Island	No Effect
South Carolina	No Effect
South Dakota	If you are pregnant, life-sustaining procedures will be provided unless the fetus could not develop to the point of live birth with continued application of those life-sustaining procedures, or your doctors conclude that prolonging your life would cause you unreasonable pain or prolong severe pain that cannot be alleviated by medication.
Tennessee	To Term
Texas	No Effect
Utah	No Effect
Vermont	No Statute
Virginia	To Term
Washington	No Effect
West Virginia	No Statute
Wisconsin	No Effect
Wyoming	No Statute

M. Making It Legal: Final Steps

By proceeding through this portion of the Quicken WillMaker Plus program and answering all the questions you can about your future health care, you have put the hard parts behind you. You have overcome the forces of procrastination and death-avoidance to assert your right to keep control over your own health care.

However, there are still a few technical requirements with which you must comply before the documents that print out will be considered legally valid and binding. Quicken WillMaker Plus provides detailed, state-specific instructions that will print out with each of your documents. But first, review the documents and make sure they are accurate.

1. Signing Your Documents

Every state law requires that you sign your documents—or direct another person to sign them for you—as a way of verifying that you understand them and that they contain your true wishes.

But do not sign them immediately. Every state law also has a requirement that you sign your documents in the presence of witnesses or a notary public—sometimes both. The purpose of this additional formality is so that there is at least one other person who can attest that you were of sound mind and of legal age when you made the documents. (See Section C2, above.)

2. Having Your Documents Witnessed and Notarized

In most states, you must have your document witnessed. In some states, you may have your documents notarized instead of witnessed. In others, you will be required to have both witnesses and a notary sign your document. The chart below lists the witnessing and notarizing requirements for your state. Note that a few states have different requirements for your document directing your health care and your document naming a proxy.

Witnessing. Many states require that two witnesses see you sign your health care documents and that they verify in writing that you appeared to be of sound mind and signed the documents without anyone else influencing your decision.

Each state's qualifications for these witnesses are slightly different. In many states, for example, a spouse, another close relative or any person who would inherit property from you is not allowed to act as a witness for the document directing health care. And many states prohibit your attending physician from being a witness.

The purpose of the laws restricting who can witness your documents is to avoid any appearance or possibility that another person was acting against your wishes in encouraging specific medical care. States that prevent witnesses who are close relatives or who may take property under your will, for example, justify their restrictions by noting that these people may be subject to ulterior influences. Some people, anxious to hold on to any sign of life, may urge that all possible medical treatments be administered, no matter what little hope they offer for a cure. Others, driven by fears of bankruptcy or dreams of riches, may encourage that no additional treatment be administered. Either course may not be what an individual patient would want.

If your state has restrictions on who may serve as witnesses to your health care documents, those restrictions are listed in the chart below and will also be noted on your documents, just before the witness signature lines.

Notarizing. A notary public is an individual who is certified to verify signatures on documents. You can locate one by looking in the telephone book; most banks, insurance and title companies also have a notary on staff. Most will charge a small fee for notarizing your documents.

The chart below, as well as the instructions accompanying your documents, will tell you if your state requires that your documents be notarized.

If you do go to a notary, bring with you some identification that will help prove that you are who you say you are.

Glossary of Witnessing Terms

If you have read the requirements for witnesses in your state, you may find some unfamiliar words. This section provides brief definitions of the terms that most commonly occur.

Beneficiary. Any person who is entitled to receive property belonging to a deceased person.

Beneficiary of a will. Any person or organization named in a will to receive property, either as a first choice or if the first choice as beneficiary does not survive the person making the will.

Claim against the estate. Any right that a person has to receive property from a person's estate. This may arise under a will or living trust, from a contract or because of a legal liability that the deceased owes to the person.

Devisee. A person who has been named to receive property in a will.

Heir at law. Any person who qualifies to inherit property from a person on the basis of his or her relationship with that person. Usually,

heirs at law are spouses, children, parents, brothers and sisters. However, if none of these people exist, an heir at law might be a niece, a nephew or even a distant cousin.

Inherit by operation of law. When a person dies owning property that has not been distributed in a will or by some other legal device such as a living trust, the property will be distributed according to the laws of the state where the person died—that is, by operation of law. These laws—commonly referred to as the "laws of intestate succession"—usually cause the property to be distributed first to a spouse and children and then to parents, brothers and sisters.

Known devisee. Any person who either is entitled to inherit property from a person under the state's law or who has been named to inherit the property in a will or living trust.

Presumptive heir. Any person who either is entitled to inherit property from a person under the state's law or who has been named to inherit the property in a will or living trust.

State Witnessing and Notarizing Requirements

Alabama

Single document: Advance Directive for Health Care

Two witnesses are required. Neither of your witnesses may be:

- under the age of 19
- your health care representative
- the person who signed your advance directive for you, if you were unable to sign it yourself
- related to you by blood, marriage or adoption
- entitled to any portion of your estate by operation of law or under your will, or
- directly financially responsible for your medical care.

Alaska

Health Care Directive

Must either be signed by two adult witnesses or notarized.

If you choose to have the document witnessed, neither of your witnesses may be:

- your health care representative
- a health care provider employed at the health care institution or health care facility where you are receiving health care
- an employee of the health care provider who is providing health care to you, or
- an employee of the health care institution or health care facility where you are receiving health care.

In addition, at least one of your witnesses must not be related to you by blood, marriage or adoption — and must not be entitled to any part of your estate under a will or codicil (amendment to a will).

Document Appointing Health Care Representative

Must either be signed by two adult witnesses or notarized.

If you choose to have the document witnessed, neither of your witnesses may be:

- your health care representative
- a health care provider employed at the health care institution or health care facility where you are receiving health care
- an employee of the health care provider who is providing health care to you, or
- an employee of the health care institution or health care facility where you are receiving health care.

In addition, at least one of your witnesses must not be related to you by blood, marriage or adoption — and must not be entitled to any part of your estate under a will or codicil (amendment to a will).

Arizona

Health Care Directive

Document Appointing Health Care Representative

Both documents must be signed by one witness or notarized.

If you choose to have the document witnessed, your witness may not be:

- your health care representative
- any person involved in providing your health care
- related to you by blood, marriage or adoption, or
- entitled to any part of your estate by operation of law or under your will.

State Witnessing and Notarizing Requirements, Continued

Arkansas

Health Care Directive

Document Appointing Health Care Representative

Both documents must be signed by two witnesses who are at least 18 years old.

California

Single document: Advance Directive for Health Care

Must either be signed by two witnesses or notarized.

If you choose to have the document witnessed, neither of your witnesses may be:

- your health care representative
- your health care provider
- an employee of your health care provider
- the operator of a community care facility
- an employee of a community care facility
- the operator of a residential care facility for the elderly, or
- an employee of a residential care facility for the elderly.

In addition, one of your witnesses must not be related to you by blood, marriage or adoption—and must not be entitled to any part of your estate by operation of law or under your will.

Finally, if you are in a skilled nursing facility, the document must also be witnessed by a patient advocate or ombudsman. (This requirement applies whether the document is witnessed or notarized.)

Colorado

Health Care Directive

Document Appointing Health Care Representative

Both documents must be signed by two witnesses and may also be notarized.

If you choose to have the document witnessed, neither of your witnesses may be:

- your attending physician
- any other physician
- an employee of your attending physician
- an employee of a health care facility where you are a patient
- a person with a claim against your estate, or
- a person entitled to any part of your estate by operation of law or under your will.

In addition, if you are a patient or resident of a health care facility, the witnesses cannot be patients of that facility.

Connecticut

Health Care Directive

Must be signed by two witnesses.

Document Appointing Health Care Representative

Must be signed by two witnesses who are both at least 18 years old. Neither of your witnesses may be your health care representative.

If you are a resident in a facility operated or licensed by the Department of Mental Health and Addiction Services, at least one of the witnesses must not be affiliated with the facility, and at least one witness shall be a physician or clinical psychologist with specialized training in treating mental illness.

If you are a resident in a facility operated or licensed by the Department of Mental Retar-

State Witnessing and Notarizing Requirements, Continued

dation, at least one of the witnesses must not be affiliated with the facility, and at least one witness shall be a physician or clinical psychologist with specialized training in developmental disabilities.

Delaware

Health Care Directive

Document Appointing Health Care Representative

Both documents must be signed by two witnesses. Neither of your witnesses may be:

- under the age of 18
- related to you by blood, marriage or adoption
- a person with a controlling interest in, or an owner, operator or employee of, a health care institution in which you are a patient or resident
- a person directly financially responsible for your medical care
- a person with a claim against your estate, or
- a person entitled to any part of your estate by operation of law or under your will.

District of Columbia

Health Care Directive

Must be signed by two witnesses. Neither of your witnesses may be:

- under the age of 18
- related to you by blood or marriage
- your attending physician
- an employee of your attending physician
- an employee of a health care facility where you are a patient
- the person who signed your Declaration for you, if you were unable to sign it yourself

- a person entitled to any part of your estate by operation of law or under your will, or
- a person directly financially responsible for your medical care.

If you are a patient in a skilled care facility, one witness must be a patient advocate or ombudsman.

Document Appointing Health Care Representative

Must be signed by two witnesses. Neither of your witnesses may be:

- under the age of 18
- your health care representative
- your health care provider, or
- an employee of your health care provider.

In addition, one of your witnesses must not be related to you by blood, marriage or adoption and must not be entitled to any part of your estate by operation of law or under your will.

Florida

Health Care Directive

Must be signed by two witnesses, one of whom must not be related to you by blood or marriage.

Document Appointing Health Care Representative

Must be signed by two witnesses, both of whom must be at least 18 years old. Neither witness may be your health care representative. In addition, one of your witnesses must not be related to you by blood or marriage.

Georgia

Health Care Directive

Must be signed by two witnesses. Neither of your witnesses may be:

- under the age of 18

State Witnessing and Notarizing Requirements, Continued

- related to you by blood or marriage
- your attending physician
- an employee of your attending physician
- an employee of a hospital or skilled nursing facility where you are a patient
- a person who is directly financially responsible for your medical care
- a person with a claim against your estate, or
- a person entitled to any part of your estate by operation of law or under your will.

If you are a patient in a hospital, the chief of staff, a physician or other designated member of the hospital staff must also witness your document.

If you are a patient in a skilled nursing facility, the medical director or a physician must witness your document.

Document Appointing Health Care Representative

Must be signed by two witnesses, both of whom must be at least 18 years old.

If you are a patient in a hospital or skilled nursing facility, your attending physician must also witness your document.

Hawaii

Single document: Advance Directive for Health Care

Must be signed by two witnesses or notarized. If you choose to have the document witnessed, neither of your witnesses may be:

- a health care provider
- an employee of a health care provider facility, or
- your health care proxy.

In addition, at least one of your witnesses must be neither:

- related to you by blood, marriage or adoption, nor
- entitled to any portion of your estate by current will or by operation of law.

Idaho

Health Care Directive

Document Appointing Health Care Representative

Idaho law does not require that your documents be witnessed or notarized. However, witnesses are recommended to avoid concerns that the document was forged, that you were forced to sign it, or that it does not represent your wishes. If you choose to have your documents witnessed, we suggest that your witnesses be at least 18 years old and that your health care representative not act as a witness.

Illinois

Health Care Directive

Must be signed by two witnesses. Neither of your witnesses may be:

- under the age of 18
- the person who signed your declaration for you, if you were unable to sign it yourself
- a person entitled to any part of your estate by operation of law or under your will, or

State Witnessing and Notarizing Requirements, Continued

- a person directly financially responsible for your medical care.

Document Appointing Health Care Representative

Must be signed by one witness who is at least 18 years old.

Indiana

Health Care Directive

Must be signed by two witnesses. Neither of your witnesses may be:

- under the age of 18
- your parent, spouse or child
- a person entitled to any part of your estate
- a person directly financially responsible for your medical care, or
- the person who signed your declaration for you, if you were unable to sign it yourself.

Document Appointing Health Care Representative

Must be notarized.

Iowa

Health Care Directive

Document Appointing Health Care Representative

Both documents must follow the same requirements:

Must be signed by two witnesses or notarized.

If you choose to have the document witnessed, neither of your witnesses may be:

- under the age of 18
- your health care representative
- your health care provider, or
- an employee of your health care provider.

In addition, one of your witnesses must not be related to you by blood, marriage or adoption within the third degree of consanguinity (parents, children, siblings, grandchildren, grandparents, uncles, aunts, nephews, nieces and great-grandchildren).

Kansas

Health Care Directive

Must be signed by two witnesses or notarized. Neither of your witnesses may be:

- under the age of 18
- the person who signed your declaration for you, if you were unable to sign it yourself
- related to you by blood or marriage
- entitled to any part of your estate by operation of law or under your will, or
- directly financially responsible for your health care.

Health Care Directive

Must be signed by two witnesses or notarized.

If you choose to have the document witnessed, neither of your witnesses may be:

- under the age of 18
- your health care representative
- related to you by blood, marriage or adoption
- entitled to any part of your estate by operation of law or under your will, or
- directly financially responsible for your health care.

Kentucky

Single document: Living Will Directive

Must be signed by two witnesses or notarized.

If you choose to have the document witnessed, neither of your witnesses may be:

- related to you by blood
- your beneficiary by operation of Kentucky law

State Witnessing and Notarizing Requirements, Continued

- your attending physician
- an employee of a health care facility where you are a patient, unless the employee serves as a notary public, or
- directly financially responsible for your health care.

Maine

Advance Health Care Directive

Document Appointing Health Care Representative

Both documents must be signed by two witnesses.

Maryland

Health Care Directive

Document Appointing Health Care Representative

Both documents must be signed by two witnesses, neither of whom may be your health care representative.

One of your witnesses must not be entitled to any part of your estate or any financial benefit by reason of your death.

Massachusetts

Health Care Directive

Document Appointing Health Care Representative

Both documents must be signed by two witnesses. Neither of your witnesses may be:

- under the age of 18, or
- your health care representative.

Michigan

Health Care Directive

Must be signed by two witnesses.

Document Appointing Health Care Representative

Must be signed by two witnesses. Neither of your witnesses may be:

- under the age of 18
- your health care representative
- your spouse, parent, child, grandchild or sibling
- your health care provider
- an employee of your life or health insurance provider
- an employee of a health care facility where you are a patient
- an employee of a home for the aged where you live, or
- your presumptive heir or known devisee.

Minnesota

Single document: Health Care Directive

Must be signed by two witnesses or notarized.

Neither your witnesses not the notary may be your health care representative or alternate health care representative.

If you choose to have the document witnessed, at least one of the witnesses may not be a health care provider or employee of a provider directly attending to you.

If you choose to have the document notarized, the notary may be an employee of a health care provider in which you receive care.

Mississippi

Health Care Directive

Document Appointing Health Care Representative

Both documents must be signed by two witnesses or notarized.

State Witnessing and Notarizing Requirements, Continued

If you choose to have the document witnessed, neither of your witnesses may be:

- under the age of 18
- your health care representative
- a health care provider, or
- an employee of a health care provider or facility.

In addition, one witness must not be related to you by blood, marriage or adoption, and must not be entitled to any part of your estate by operation of law or under your will.

Missouri

Health Care Directive

Must be signed by two witnesses. Neither of your witnesses may be:

- under the age of 18, or
- the person who signed your declaration for you, if you were unable to sign it yourself.

Document Appointing Health Care Representative

Must be notarized.

Montana

Health Care Directive

Document Appointing Health Care Representative

Both documents must be signed by two witnesses.

Nebraska

Health Care Directive

Must be signed by two witnesses or notarized.

If you choose to have the document witnessed, neither of your witnesses may be:

- under the age of 18, or

- an employee of your life or health insurance provider.

In addition, one witness may not be a director or employee of your treating health care provider.

Document Appointing Health Care Representative

Must be signed by two witnesses or notarized. If you choose to have the document witnessed, neither of your witnesses may be:

- your health care representative
- your attending physician
- your spouse, parent, child, grandchild or sibling
- your presumptive heir or known devisee, or
- an employee of your life or health insurance provider.

In addition, one of your witnesses must not be an administrator or employee of your health care provider.

Nevada

Health Care Directive

Must be signed by two witnesses.

Document Appointing Health Care Representative

Must be signed by two witnesses or notarized. If you choose to have the document witnessed, neither of your witnesses may be:

- under the age of 18
- your health care representative
- a health care provider
- an employee of a health care provider
- the operator of a health care facility, or
- an employee of the operator of a health care facility.

State Witnessing and Notarizing Requirements, Continued

In addition, one of your witnesses must not be related to you by blood, marriage or adoption and must not be entitled to any part of your estate by operation of law or under your will.

New Hampshire

Health Care Directive

Must be signed by two witnesses and notarized. Neither of your witnesses may be:

- your spouse
- your heir at law
- your attending physician
- any person acting under the direction or control of the attending physician, or
- a person with a claim against your estate.

If you are a resident of a health care facility or a patient in a hospital, no more than one witness may be the health care provider or the provider's employee.

Document Appointing Health Care Representative

Must be signed by two witnesses. Neither of the witnesses may be:

- under the age of 18
- your health care representative
- your spouse
- your heir at law, or
- a person entitled to any part of your estate by operation of law or under your will.

In addition, if you are a resident of a health care facility or a patient in a hospital, no more than one witness may be the health care provider or the provider's employee.

New Jersey

Health Care Directive

Must be signed by two witnesses or notarized.

If you choose to have the document witnessed, neither of your witnesses may be:

- under the age of 18, or
- your health care representative.

Document Appointing Health Care Representative

Must be signed by two witnesses, both of whom are at least 18 years old, or notarized.

New Mexico

Health Care Directive

Document Appointing Health Care Representative

Both documents must be signed by two witnesses.

New York

Health Care Directive

Document Appointing Health Care Representative

Both must be signed by two witnesses. Neither of your witnesses may be:

- under the age of 18
- your health care representative, or
- the person who signed the declaration for you, if you were unable to sign it for yourself.

North Carolina

Health Care Directive

Must be signed by two witnesses and notarized. Neither of your witnesses may be:

- related to you by blood or marriage
- your attending physician or mental health treatment provider
- an employee of your attending physician
- an employee of a health care facility where you are a patient

State Witnessing and Notarizing Requirements, Continued

- an employee of a nursing or group home where you reside
- a person entitled to any part of your estate by operation of law or under your will, or
- a person with a claim against you.

Document Appointing Health Care Representative

Must be signed by two witnesses and notarized. Neither of your witnesses may be:

- under the age of 18
- related to you by blood or marriage
- your attending physician or mental health treatment provider
- an employee of your attending physician
- an employee of a health care facility that is treating you
- an employee of a nursing or group home where you reside
- a person entitled to any part of your estate by operation of law or under your will, or
- a person with a claim against you.

North Dakota

Health Care Directive

Document Appointing Health Care Representative

Each document must be signed by two witnesses or notarized. Neither the witnesses or the notary may be:

- under the age of 18

- your spouse or another person related to you by blood, marriage or adoption
- your health care representative
- a person entitled to any part of your estate upon your death, or
- a person with a claim against your estate.

Ohio

Health Care Directive

Must be signed by two witnesses or notarized.

If you choose to have the document notarized, neither of your witnesses may be:

- under the age of 18
- related to you by blood, marriage or adoption
- your attending physician
- an administrator of a nursing home where you receive care, or
- the person who signed your declaration, if you were unable to sign it yourself.

Document Appointing Health Care Representative

Must be signed by two witnesses or notarized.

If you choose to have the document notarized, neither of your witnesses may be:

- under the age of 18
- related to you by blood, marriage or adoption
- your health care representative
- your attending physician, or
- an administrator of a nursing home where you receive care.

State Witnessing and Notarizing Requirements, Continued

Oklahoma

Single document: Advance Directive for Health Care

Must be signed by two witnesses. Neither of your witnesses may be:

- under the age of 18
- a person with an interest in your estate, or
- a person named to inherit property in your will or other estate planning document.

Oregon

Single document: Advance Directive for Health Care

Must be signed by two witnesses.

Neither of your witnesses may be:

- your health care representative, or
- your attending physician.

One witness may not be:

- related to you by blood, marriage or adoption
- an owner, operator or employee of a health care facility where you are a resident, or
- a person entitled to any part of your estate upon your death.

If you are a patient in a long-term care facility, one witness must be an individual designated by the facility, having the qualifications specified by the Department of Human Resources.

Pennsylvania

Health Care Directive

Must be signed by two witnesses. Neither of your witnesses may be:

- under the age of 18, or
- the person who signed your declaration for you, if you were unable to sign it yourself.

Document Appointing Health Care Representative

Must be signed by two witnesses, both of whom are at least 18 years old.

Rhode Island

Health Care Directive

Must be signed by two witnesses. Your witnesses may not be related to you by blood or marriage.

Document Appointing Health Care Representative

Must be signed by two witnesses. Neither of your witnesses may be:

- under the age of 18
- your health care representative
- a health care provider
- an employee of a health care provider
- the operator of a community care facility, or
- an employee of an operator of a community care facility.

In addition, one of your witnesses must not be related to you by blood, marriage or adoption and must not be entitled to any part of your estate by operation of law or under your will.

State Witnessing and Notarizing Requirements, Continued

South Carolina

Single document: Directive

Must be signed by two witnesses and notarized. Neither of your witnesses may be:

- related to you by blood, marriage or adoption
- your attending physician
- an employee of your attending physician
- a person directly financially responsible for your medical care
- a person entitled to any part of your estate by operation of law or under your will
- a beneficiary of your life insurance policy, or
- a person who has a claim against your estate.

No more than one of your witnesses may be an employee of a health care facility where you are a patient. If you are in a hospital or nursing care facility when you sign your declaration, at least one of your witnesses must be an ombudsman designated by the state.

South Dakota

Health Care Directive

Must be signed by two witnesses, both of whom are at least 18 years old, and may also be notarized, although notarization is optional.

Document Appointing Health Care Representative

Must be signed by two witnesses, both of whom are at least 18 years old.

Tennessee

Health Care Directive

Must be signed by two witnesses and may also be notarized, although notarization is optional. Neither of your witnesses may be:

- related to you by blood or marriage
- your attending physician
- an employee of your attending physician
- an employee of a health care facility where you are a patient
- a person with a claim against your estate, or
- a person entitled to any part of your estate by operation of law or under your will.

Document Appointing Health Care Representative

Must be signed by two witnesses and notarized. Neither of your witnesses may be:

- your health care representative
- a health care provider
- an employee of a health care provider
- the operator of a health care institution
- an employee of a health care institution, or
- a person entitled to any part of your estate.

In addition, at least one of your witnesses must not be related to you by blood, marriage or adoption.

Texas

Health Care Directive

Must be signed by two witnesses. At least one of your witnesses may not be:

State Witnessing and Notarizing Requirements, Continued

- your health care representative
- related to you by blood or marriage
- your attending physician
- an employee of your attending physician
- a person with a claim against your estate, or
- a person entitled to any part of your estate upon your death.

Your witnesses may be employees of a health care facility where you are a patient only if they are not involved in providing direct care to you and not involved in the financial affairs of the facility.

Document Appointing Health Care Representative

Must be signed by two witnesses. At least one of your witnesses may not be:

- your health care representative
- related to you by blood or marriage
- your attending physician
- an employee of your attending physician
- a person with a claim against your estate, or
- a person entitled to any part of your estate upon your death.

Your witnesses may be employees of a health care facility where you are a patient only if they are not involved in providing direct care to you and not involved in the financial affairs of the facility.

Utah

Health Care Directive

Must be signed by two witnesses. Neither of your witnesses may be:

- under the age of 18
- the person who signed your directive for you, if you were unable to sign it yourself
- related to you by blood or marriage
- a person entitled to any part of your estate by operation of law or under your will
- a person directly financially responsible for your medical care, or
- an agent of a health care facility where you are a patient.

Document Appointing Health Care Representative

Must be notarized.

Vermont

Health Care Directive

Document Appointing Health Care Representative

Each document must be signed by two witnesses. Neither of your witnesses may be:

- your health care representative, or
- your spouse, reciprocal beneficiary, parent, sibling, child or grandchild.

If you are a patient in a hospital, nursing home or residential care facility, an ombudsman, clergy member, attorney or other designated person must explain the nature of each document and sign it.

State Witnessing and Notarizing Requirements, Continued

Virginia

Health Care Directive

Document Appointing Health Care Representative

Each document must be signed by two witnesses over the age of 18.

Washington

Health Care Directive

Must be signed by two witnesses. Neither of your witnesses may be:

- related to you by blood or marriage
- your attending physician
- an employee of your attending physician
- an employee of a health care facility where you are a patient
- a person entitled to any part of your estate by operation of law or under your will, or
- a person with a claim against your estate.

Document Appointing Health Care Representative

Must be signed by two witnesses or notarized.

West Virginia

Health Care Directive

Document Appointing Health Care Representative

Both documents must meet the same requirements:

Must be signed by two witnesses and notarized.

Neither of your witnesses may be:

- under the age of 18
- your health care representative or successor representative

- the person who signed your document, if you were unable to sign it yourself
- related to you by blood or marriage
- your attending physician
- a person directly financially responsible for your medical care, or
- a person entitled to any part of your estate by operation of law or under your will.

Wisconsin

Health Care Directive

Must be signed by two witnesses. Neither of your witnesses may be:

- related to you by blood, marriage or adoption
- your health care provider
- an employee of your health care provider, other than a chaplain or a social worker
- an employee of an inpatient health care facility where you are a patient, other than a chaplain or a social worker
- a person directly financially responsible for your medical care
- a person who has a claim against your estate, or
- a person entitled to any part of your estate by operation of law or under your will.

Document Appointing Health Care Representative

Must be signed by two witnesses. Neither of your witnesses may be:

- under the age of 18
- your health care representative
- related to you by blood, marriage or adoption
- your health care provider

- an employee of your health care provider, other than a chaplain or a social worker
- an employee of an inpatient health care facility where you are a patient, other than a chaplain or a social worker
- a person directly financially responsible for your medical care, or
- a person with a claim against your estate.

Wyoming

Health Care Directive

Document Appointing Health Care Representative

Each document must be signed by two witnesses or notarized.

If you choose to have the document witnessed, neither of your witnesses may be:

- your health care representative
- a treating health care provider
- an employee of a treating health care provider
- the operator of a community care facility
- the employee of an operator of a community care facility
- the operator of a residential care facility, or
- the employee of a residential care facility.

N. Making and Distributing Copies

Ideally, you should make an effort to make your wishes for your future health care widely known. Keep a copy of your health care directive, and give other copies to:

- any physician with whom you now consult regularly
- the proxy you named in your directive
- the office of the hospital or other care facility in which you are likely to receive treatment
- the patient representative of your HMO or insurance plan
- close relatives, particularly immediate family members—a spouse, children, siblings, and
- trusted friends.

Some people are hesitant to discuss the particulars of their medical care with other people, feeling that it is an intensely private issue. However, in the case of health care directives, you must weigh this yen for privacy against the need for the documents to be effective. Your carefully reasoned medical directive will simply be wasted words unless you make sure it gets into the hands of the people who need to know about it.

At a minimum, give copies of your signed and completed health care directive to the doctors or medical facility most likely to be treating you and to any proxy you have named.

Keep your documents together. If you have named a health care representative or proxy, he or she will need to have a copy of your health care directive to learn the specific details of your medical care directions. And hospital personnel will need to see a copy of the durable power of attorney for health care that authorizes your agent to supervise your wishes, to get copies of your medical records and to hire and fire medical personnel.

O. Keeping Your Documents Up to Date

Review your health care documents occasionally—at least once a year—to make sure they still accurately reflect your wishes for your medical care. Advances in technology and changes in health are two changes in course that prompt many people to change their minds about the kind of health care they want.

In addition, you should consider making new documents if any of the following occur:

- You move to another state. (See Section D3, above, for more information on this point.)
- You made and finalized a health care directive many years ago, because your state's law controlling them has probably changed substantially.
- The proxy or representative you named to supervise your wishes becomes unable to do so.

P. Revoking Your Documents

If you have a change of heart and want to revoke or cancel your health care directive, you can do so at any time.

1. Legal Requirements

In most states, a health care directive can be revoked with very little formality. Indeed, many state laws say the document may be revoked "at any time in any manner" and "regardless of mental state." (Your state's specific revocation procedures will be included in the instructions that print out with your document.) This points to an important distinction: Although you must be of sound mind to make a living will, in most states, you do not have to be of sound mind to revoke one.

This can create a "Catch 22" situation: If you revoke your document while of unsound mind, your state's law will prohibit you from later changing your mind and making another one, unless you again return to a condition of sound mind. This could become an issue for people who become increasingly disoriented as they approach death. The rule appears to be designed to err on the side of keeping people alive (potentially against their wishes), rather than the other way around. The logic here is that that a person's current wishes, regardless of mental state, should take precedence over a prior stated wish.

It's Okay to Ask for Water

Because many state laws allow a living will to be revoked by "any act," some are concerned that requesting a drink of water may revoke their request that artificially administered hydration be withheld. But this is not so. A request to withhold artificial feeding or hydration does not mean that all food and water must be denied. In fact, it is common to administer ice chips or small sips of water to dying patients to satisfy thirst.

2. Notifying Your Doctor and Loved Ones of Your Revocation

Your revocation is not effective unless and until your health care providers are made aware of it. If health care providers are unaware of your revocation, they cannot be held legally liable for following your written wishes. Accordingly, if you have given copies of your wishes to your health care provider or loved ones, be sure they know you have revoked them. Have all people who have copies of your documents return them to you to be destroyed.

Although no state requires you to use a written document to revoke your health care directive, Quicken WillMaker Plus provides one you can use to inform others of your revocation and to add to your medical records.

A New Document Trumps an Old One

If there is more than one health care directive, the statements in the most recent one win if there is any discrepancy between the two. Technically, there is no need to formally revoke an earlier document. However, confusion may arise if an old document still exists—for example, it covers issues on which the newer document is silent. For this reason, you should do all you can to make sure your old document is clearly revoked and destroyed. And of course you should make sure that your new document is properly signed and witnessed and/or notarized, that you give it to your doctor and your health care agent and that it is placed in your medical records.

Q. Expressing Additional Concerns

Quicken WillMaker Plus produces a health care directive that is a straightforward and unambiguous expression of wishes about medical care. For most people, this provides the best framework and the most effective way to convey their thoughts to the medical establishment that will ultimately provide the care.

But for some people, medical directives—no matter how specifically they address wishes about respirators and surgery—do not reach the heart of their concerns: money available for care, dying with dignity, quality of life, the well-being of those who care for them. These more worldly worries may be a far stronger pull than possible differences in the medical care they might receive if stricken by a coma or terminal illness. For them, their wishes sound simple, and the pieces of paper that make up health care directives seem unfulfilling.

Your true concerns may reflect a number of motivations and fears. For example, you may feel strongly that you would not want:

- to have a spouse become bankrupt spending money on your medical care
- to have your life prolonged by medical intervention if you become unable to live at home, or
- to have life-saving surgery performed if you were never able to walk or talk again.

These are all valid human concerns that do not fit neatly on the lines of your medical directives.

After using Quicken WillMaker Plus, review your health care directive to make sure it is the best possible expression of your tangible wishes for medical care. If you feel frustrated that your documents do not address a vital concern you have, there are several additional steps you can take.

1. Talking With Doctors

There is no substitute for talking over your medical care wishes with the doctors who will be likely to provide your care. Unfortunately, this task is made more difficult by reality. Few people have the luxury of cultivating a meaningful relationship with any individual doctor. Soaring costs of medical care and cutbacks in insurance coverage have made many people miserly about making medical appointments. And many now depend for medical care on monolithic medical centers, in which it is sheer happenstance if you see the same health care provider more than once. Most of us die in the hands of medical personnel who are strangers to us.

However, if you do have a regular doctor, or if you are approaching surgery or some other drastic medical event and have been assigned to a specialist, talk over your directive with him or her. If you have other, more subjective concerns about your medical condition, such as the effects of certain treatments or the probability of carrying on certain life activities, discuss those, too.

2. Talking With Family Members and Friends

It is also best to discuss your health care directives and other medical care concerns with family members and close friends who are likely to oversee or witness your care. Unfortunately, this urging, too, is sometimes frustrated by reality. Families these days are often flung far across the map. And even those who remain geographically close often stray from the Ozzie and Harriet ideal of family harmony.

Still, those who make the effort to discuss the hard topic of what kind of medical care they want if incapacitated usually find the effort worth the price. Not only do those involved get peace of mind in knowing true wishes, the knowledge can often be a bridge to closer relationships. If the topic seems too difficult to broach, consider using a relevant book or magazine article, television show or film as a catalyst for discussion.

3. Writing a Letter Expressing Other Wishes

If your health care directive does not directly address specific concerns that you have, you can write your thoughts in a letter that you attach to your documents. Because it's not uncommon for such thoughts to change over time, you can update this letter as the need arises. Again, it's best to talk over your concerns and wishes with your doctors and loved ones, if possible. Your letter may help underscore your wishes and emphasize to others that your feelings are important to you.

4. Common Issues to Discuss or Write Down

Here are some common concerns that may not be addressed in detail in your health care documents:

a. Enduring Pain vs. Prolonging Life

If you specify in your health care directive that you want all possible treatments to extend your life, you might want to consider how much pain and discomfort you are willing to endure in the effort. This is a fuzzy standard and may be difficult to apply precisely. However, discussing the issue may help decision makers determine which way you might lean if you were presented with a specific treatment decision that is not discussed in your Quicken WillMaker Plus document.

b. Putting Time Limits on Life-Prolonging Treatment

Some people feel that they would like to have every effort made to keep them alive for a while, but not indefinitely. Perhaps you would like to have doctors discontinue life-prolonging treatment only if your condition does not improve after a specific period of time—three to six months, for example. There are two things to consider in making such a request:

First, keep in mind that a request to have life support removed is not triggered until your doctors declare you to be "close to death" or "permanently" unconscious. Until then, efforts to keep you alive will continue in earnest. As such, requesting life-prolonging treatment for an additional amount of time is necessary only if you want your care to extend beyond the triggering event stated in your document—that is, when doctors have declared you to be "close to death"

from a terminal condition or have determined that your unconsciousness will be "permanent."

Second, wishes conditioned on medical improvement can be difficult to interpret because they require a subjective judgment and a firm hand to impose time limits on treatment. As such, they do not fit easily within conventional health care directives; official state living will forms do not offer such choices.

If, despite these concerns, you would like to add these kinds of conditions to your wishes, your best bet is to give complete discretion to your proxy and discuss your desires with him or her thoroughly. The documents created by Quicken WillMaker Plus do not grant unlimited discretion to your proxy. (See Section J, above.) If you would like to pursue this option you may need to see an experienced lawyer to help craft a specialized durable power of attorney for health care, in which you name another person to enforce your specific directions. (See Chapter 25.)

If you know no one to name as a health care proxy, but you want to specify time limits on the medical treatments and procedures that may be administered to you, a conventional directive may not be your best route. In such cases, it may be best to discuss your thoughts with medical personnel and write down your thoughts in a letter or other informal document.

c. Dying at Home Rather Than in a Hospital or Nursing Home

Some find it important to spend their final days in their own home, surrounded by loved ones, rather than in a hospital intensive care unit or nursing home. Palliative care providers are experienced in helping you and your loved ones carry out such wishes and can typically assist those who are caring for you at home as death approaches. If this is something you feel strongly about, discuss it with your doctor and ask (or have your health care agent ask) whether palliative care or hospice services are available, and whether they can be administered in your home.

d.   Spiritual and Philosophical Concerns

A statement of your overall philosophy or religious beliefs on matters of medical treatment and dying can help your care providers apply your perspective to situations and choices that your health care directive does not specifically address.

e.   Requests for Music, Readings and Loved Ones for Your Final Days

Perhaps you would like some favorite music played, or have favorite stories, poems or passages read aloud during your final days, when you may be too weak to speak for yourself. This kind of wish is also appropriate for a separate letter and discussion with your doctor and loved ones. ■

Chapter 24

Final Arrangements

Most people avoid the subject of death —and are especially uncomfortable thinking about their own mortality. You, too, may be tempted to leave the details of your final arrangements for what happens after your death to those who survive you.

But, as discussed in this chapter, there are two good reasons not to do this: care and cost.

A. Making Final Arrangements in Advance

Anyone who has lost a loved one knows how agonizing it can be to decide what he or she would have wanted as a commemoration. And most people have attended funerals or other after-death services that seem uniquely unsuited to the person who has died.

Letting your survivors know what kind of disposition and ceremonies you envision saves them the pain of making such decisions at what is likely to be a difficult time for them. Many family members and friends also find that an open discussion of preferences for final arrangements is a grand relief—especially if a person is elderly or in poor health and death is likely to occur soon.

Planning some of these details in advance, and doing wise comparison shopping, can also help save money. For many people, after-death goods and services are the third most costly expense— just after a home and a car.

Without some direction, your survivors are most likely to choose the most expensive goods and services available, to assuage their own feelings of guilt or grief or perhaps due to coercion by funeral industry providers. The best way to prevent this from happening is to leave a written instruction of your preferences with as much detail as you are able to give.

A Will Is Not the Way

Many people think of a will as the proper document in which to specify final instructions for whether they want to be buried or cremated and whether they wish to have any ceremonies held after they die. A will is a singularly poor place to express your death and burial preferences. It will probably will not be located and read until several weeks after you die—long after the time such final arrangements must occur.

1. The Legal Effect of Your Document

In most cases, your arrangements will be carried out as written.

If a dispute arises among your loved ones—for example, between your partner or spouse and other relatives—the funeral industry personnel involved are usually bound to follow any written instructions you left. The greatest sticking points arise when the deceased person has not provided in advance for payment of the arrangements. Court battles over preferences for body or funeral ceremonies almost never arise, primarily because of the lack of time and the prohibitive cost of litigation.

Attaching a Letter of Explanation

The document you produce using Quicken WillMaker Plus will set out what you want to occur after your death. Your instructions may be as sparse or as detailed as you wish.

In addition to the specifics of body disposition and ceremonies, you may want to explain your choices or leave some final message to your survivors. An excellent way to do this is to write a letter and attach it to the Final Arrangements document that Quicken WillMaker Plus produces. (See Chapter 12, Section B.)

2. What Happens If There Is No Document

If you die without leaving written instructions about your preferences, state law determines who has the right to control how your remains will be disposed of. In most states, the right—and the liability for paying for the reasonable costs of a disposition—is with the following people, in order:

- spouse
- child or children
- parent or parents
- the next of kin, and
- the public administrator, who is appointed by a court.

Most disputes arise where more than one person—three children, for example—is in charge, and they disagree over a fundamental decision, such as whether the body of a parent should be buried or cremated. As mentioned, such disputes can be avoided if you are willing to put your wishes in writing.

If You Have Already Made Some Final Arrangements

If you have already made arrangements for burial or cremation, you may wonder whether it is necessary to use this portion of the Quicken WillMaker Plus program. It is probably wise to do so. It will take only a few minutes—and the program may direct your attention to issues that you did not address in your previous arrangements.

In addition, Quicken WillMaker Plus produces a document that allows you to organize your thoughts and directions for your final disposition. This may be essential for your survivors, who want to see that your wishes are carried out as written. Also, the program prompts you to describe two very common types of arrangements that you may have made:

- donation of one or more organs, and
- donation of your body to a medical institution.

Setting out these arrangements in writing will help assure that the donations are carried out.

B. The Basics of Your Final Arrangements

This portion of the Quicken WillMaker Plus program allows you to state your preferences on the following specific issues:

- the name of the mortuary or other institution that will handle your burial or cremation
- whether you wish to be embalmed
- the type of casket or container in which you will be buried or cremated, including

whether you want it present at any after-death ceremony

- the details of any ceremony you want before the burial or cremation, including specific clothing and jewelry in which you want your body to be attired
- who your pallbearers will be
- how your body will be transported to the cemetery and gravesite
- where your remains will be buried, stored or scattered
- the details of any ceremony you want to accompany your burial, interment or scattering
- the details of any marker you want to show where your remains are buried or interred
- any epitaph you wish placed on your burial marker, and
- the details of any ceremony you want held after you are buried or cremated.

Provide only as many details as you choose. If you have a very simple plan, many of the questions posed to you will not be relevant. Or you may simply be undecided about some aspects of the instructions you wish to leave.

So respond only to those questions you wish to answer. While it behooves you to be as specific as you can in your instructions, the document produced can be as sketchy or complete as you wish. If there is an issue you do not wish to address, simply skip the questions that pertain to it. If you wish, you can always complete a more detailed document after you have mulled over the topic that gave you pause.

C. Help With Your Final Arrangements

There are a number of places you can turn to for help in planning your final arrangements.

1. Mortuaries

Most mortuaries or funeral homes are equipped to handle many of the details related to disposing of a person's remains. These include:

- collecting the body from the place of death
- storing the body until it is buried or cremated
- making burial arrangements with a cemetery
- conducting ceremonies related to the burial
- preparing the body for burial, and
- arranging to have the body transported for burial.

2. Memorial or Funeral Societies

Choosing the institution to handle your burial is probably the most important final arrangement that you can make, from an economic standpoint. For this reason, many people join memorial or funeral societies, which help them find local mortuaries that will deal honestly with their survivors and charge prices that accurately reflect the value of their services.

Society members are generally free to choose whatever final arrangement they wish. Most societies, however, emphasize simple, dignified arrangements over the costly, elaborate services often promoted by the funeral industry.

While the services offered by each society differ, most societies distribute literature and information on options and legal controls on final arrangements.

Members receive a prearrangement form upon joining, which allows them to plan for the goods and services they want and to get them for a predetermined cost. Many societies also serve as watchdogs—making sure that individuals get and pay for only the services they have specified.

The cost for joining these organizations is low —usually from $20 to $40 for a lifetime membership, although some societies charge a small renewal fee periodically.

To find a funeral or memorial society nearest you, look in the Yellow Pages of your telephone book under Funeral Information & Advisory Services, or contact the Funeral Consumers Alliance, 800-765-0107, www.funerals.org, for additional information.

Survivors Caring for the Dead

There is a trend in America for people to care for their own dead, from preparing to burying the deceased person—doing an end-run around all funeral industry personnel.

Despite a monied funeral industry lobby, most states do allow individuals to act completely on their own. But those who do so must be armed with information on what is and what is not allowed. For example, most states have laws that regulate the depth of a site for a body burial. In addition, the laws in several states specifically require that a funeral director must handle the disposition of a deceased person.

If you are considering directing that a family member or friend handle your disposition independently, consult a local funeral or memorial society for information on what restrictions may apply. Contact the Funeral Consumers Alliance, 800-765-0107, for additional information.

In addition, a book entitled *Caring for the Dead: Your Final Act of Love,* by Lisa Carlson (Upper Access Press, Vermont), includes a state synopsis of relevant statutes and a discussion of other concerns for those who wish to bury their own dead.

3. Finding a Mortuary on Your Own

If you are not a member of a funeral or memorial society, then it is important that you find the institution that best meets your needs in terms of style, proximity and cost.

This has become somewhat easier than it used to be, since the Federal Trade Commission (FTC) passed regulations to stem the tide of abuses by the funeral industry. Under the FTC Funeral Rule, those who provide death goods and services must give price lists to consumers who visit a funeral home—and must disclose prices and other information to those who ask for it over the phone.

The law also enables consumers to select and purchase only the goods and services they want, and clamps down on untoward practices such as false or unclear advertising.

However, there is a loophole. Under the law, mortuaries are free to tack on a charge nebulously labeled Professional Services or Overhead. If the cost of such services seems out of line with what is being promised, consumers should negotiate to lower it. Charges for other common mortuary services, such as limousine and chapel services, may also be negotiable.

Beware of Prepayment Plans

Shopping around for the most suitable and affordable funeral goods and services is a wise consumer idea. However, be extremely cautious about paying in advance (or prepaying) for them.

While there are a number of legal controls on how the funeral industry can handle and invest funds earmarked for future services, there are many reported abuses of mismanaged and stolen funds. A great many other abuses go unreported by family members too embarrassed or too grief-stricken to complain.

There are additional pitfalls. When mortuaries go out of business, the consumer who has prepaid may be left without a refund and without recourse. Also, many individuals who move to a new locale during their lifetimes are dismayed to find that their prepayment funds are nonrefundable—or that there is a substantial financial penalty for withdrawing or transferring them. In addition, money paid now may not cover inflated costs of the future—meaning that survivors will be left to cover the substantially inflated costs.

If you are interested in setting aside a fund of money to pay for your final arrangements, a more prudent approach may be to contact a bank or savings institution to set up a payable-on-death account earmarked to pay for your final arrangements. Most financial institutions will do so for free. The funds are easily transferred or withdrawn if need be, and you have complete control over the money during your life.

D. Body and Organ Donations

In response to increased need nationwide, more people opt to donate their bodies or organs for medical research or transplant after they die.

A number of states have attempted to make it easier to put these wishes in effect by adding body and organ donations to their health care directives. (See Chapter 23.) However, enforcement of these provisions is still erratic. Often, the directives are not available in the exigency of the moment. It is still best to arrange for body and organ donations by following the steps discussed here.

1. Whole Body Donations

Most medical schools need donations of whole bodies for research and instruction, and shortages may be especially acute at osteopathic and chiropractic schools. The reason they are called whole body donations is that the donation will be rejected if any of the organs have been removed from the body.

After using a donated body for study or instruction, a medical institution will usually cremate it and bury or scatter the cremains in a specified plot. However, the remains or cremains can be returned to family members for burial—usually within a year or two. Those who want the body or cremains returned to a friend or family members for the final disposition should specify this when arranging for the donation.

No medical institution is allowed to buy a body, but there is usually little or no expense to the survivors when a body is donated. When a death occurs, most medical schools pay to transport the body, as well as pay for any final disposition. Ask the nearest medical institution that accepts body donations whether it has specific arrangements for transporting and disposing of bodies to avoid any unexpected charges.

Arrangements for whole body donations must usually be made while you are alive, although some medical schools will accept a cadaver through arrangements made after death with the written permission of the next of kin.

The best place to contact to arrange a whole body donation is the nearest medical school. If you live in a state with no medical school or one that has very strict requirements for whole body donations, you may find out more about your body donation options from the National Anatomical Service, 800-727-0700.

Your Donation May Be Rejected

Even if you have arranged in advance to donate your body to a medical institution, the institution may reject the donation if any of the following are true:

- You have also donated one or more of your organs and these are taken at your death.
- The institution's current supply exceeds its demand and there are no facilities for storage.
- You die during surgery.
- Your body is unsuitable for study because it is extremely obese, or your death was due to any of a number of diseases that render it unacceptable to the institution.

---

2. Organ Donations

As medical technology has made successful organ and tissue transplants cheaper, easier and safer, organs and tissues are in great demand.

Among the organs and tissues now commonly being transplanted are:

- corneas
- hearts
- livers
- kidneys
- tendons, ligaments, connective tissue
- skin
- pancreas, and
- lungs.

Tissues and corneas can be taken from almost anyone and are often used for research and study. However, there are far greater problems with donating major organs such as hearts and livers. For example, while there are tens of thousands of people now on waiting lists to receive kidneys, only about 1% of all people who die are suitable kidney donors.

It does not cost you or your family anything to donate an organ.

3. How to Arrange for Organ Donations

The principal method for donating organs is by indicating your intent to do so on a donor card. Once signed, this card identifies you to medical personnel as a potential organ donor.

You can get a donor card or form from most hospitals, the county or state office of the National Kidney Foundation or a community eye bank. In most states, you can also obtain an organ donation card from the local Department of

Motor Vehicles. Depending on where you live, you can check a box, affix a stamp or seal, or attach a separate card to your license, indicating your wish to donate one or more organs.

Even if you have not signed a card or other document indicating your intent to donate your organs, your next of kin can approve a donation at your death. And, conversely, even if you have indicated an intent to donate your organs, an objection by your next of kin will often defeat your intention; medical personnel will usually not proceed in the face of an objection from relatives. The best safeguard is to discuss your wishes with close friends and relatives, emphasizing your strong feelings about donating organs.

When Organs Are Removed

Major organs for transplantation must be taken from a donor who was in reasonably good health—and must be removed while the donor's heart is still beating. In reality, nearly all suitable donors of major organs are short-term patients who have been hospitalized and who have received artificial respiration.

Some people fear that agreeing to donate an organ will mean that they run the risk of being declared dead prematurely while eager doctors rush to remove their organs.

There is a strong safeguard against this possibility. Before any organ is removed from a donor, two doctors who are not involved in the transplantation must declare that the patient is "irretrievably deceased"—with an ultimate diagnosis of being brain-dead. From that time on, the cadaver must be maintained on a respirator to keep blood flowing through the organ.

Tell other people about your wishes.

For organ donations to be successful, several people must know about the arrangement before you die. These people include your doctors, personnel at the hospital or other health care facility where you die and the people whom your doctors or the institution are likely to contact if there are any questions about the donation. These might be your spouse, other close relatives or the people you have named to supervise your health care in a durable power of attorney or other document.

4. Consent for Organ Donations

Many states allow coroners to remove some or all organs, body parts or tissues without explicit authorization (either in the form of a donation card signed by the deceased or permission from the next of kin) so long as certain conditions are met. In practice, these laws are not likely to come into play unless the death is sudden, family members cannot be reached and medical personnel can't find evidence of the person's wishes (such as a donor card attached to a license). If you make your wishes known, doctors will not have to fall back on these laws.

The consent provisions of these organ donation laws fall generally into two categories: (1) laws that presume consent for the removal of tissues—generally corneas and/or the pituitary gland—so long as there is no known objection to organ donation, and (2) laws that require the coroner to make "reasonable efforts" to obtain authorization (either getting permission from the next of kin or confirming that the deceased has signed an organ donation form) before certain organs can be removed. In contrast to the first set of presumed consent laws, the "reasonable efforts" laws usually allow removal of any body part. In addition to these consent provisions, there are other conditions that typically must be met before organs can be removed under either the presumed consent or reasonable efforts laws:

- there must be a request for the organ by a qualified recipient
- the removal must not interfere with a pending investigation or autopsy of the body, and
- the removal must not alter the deceased's facial appearance.

About one-third of the states have no presumed consent laws; in those states, removal of organs for donation is not permitted in the absence of explicit consent.

E. Burial or Cremation

When using Quicken WillMaker Plus, you are asked to decide whether:

- your body is to be buried in the ground or other place, or
- your body is to be cremated and whether the remains, called cremains, should be buried, stored or scattered.

You should make this choice even if you have arranged to have some organs or your entire body donated to a medical institution. Keep in mind that if one or more of your organs is accepted for donation, the rest of your body must be disposed of or buried. And even if you have arranged to have your entire body donated, there is the possibility the donation may be rejected because of the condition of your body or simply because it is not needed. And, finally, after the medical institution has finished using the body for teaching or research, it must be disposed of or

buried—usually, between one to two years after it is accepted for donation.

Whether you choose cremation or burial, your choice will likely be guided by a number of personal preferences, which may include religion, community custom, family tradition and cost.

1. Body Burial

While cremation is gaining popularity as an option, most bodies in the United States are buried. Contrary to popular misconception, embalming prior to burial is not usually required by law. (See Section F, below.)

However, body burials customarily involve a number of other concerns, including:

- getting and processing the death certificate
- transporting the body
- opening and closing a grave
- burial vaults, required by most cemeteries, and
- a casket.

Each of these concerns comes with a price tag, and funeral industry personnel will charge additional handling and service charges.

2. Cremation

When a body is cremated, it is heated intensely—1,800 degrees Fahrenheit or higher—in an ovenlike device called a retort, until it is reduced to several pounds of ash and some fragments of bones, called cremains. The entire process usually takes from two to three hours.

The cremains can then be placed in an urn or other container to be buried, stored or scattered. The cost of cremation varies widely but usually runs from $500 to $1,000—substantially less than embalming and full body burial. The costs differ depending on your locale.

However, a number of other charges may be added for:

- getting and processing the death certificate
- a certificate releasing the body for cremation, issued by a medical examiner or coroner in some locales
- transporting the body
- disposing of the cremains
- a casket or container, and
- additional handling and service charges paid to funeral industry personnel.

In addition, most cremation facilities require that a pacemaker must be removed before a body is cremated, since the devices can explode and damage the cremation chamber—and there is usually a charge for the removal.

Cremation Witnesses

In recent years, some mortuaries and crematoriums have been disciplined for mixing the remains of the bodies they cremate, in violation of state laws.

While this may not bother some people, others are horrified at the thought of having their remains mixed with those of other people or animals and want to do everything possible to prevent this. One way is to appoint someone to witness the cremation, which forces the mortuary or crematorium to be scrupulous about not mixing cremains and bodies.

Not all mortuaries and crematoriums cooperate. If the mortuary or crematorium you have selected does not allow witnesses—and witnesses are what you want—select a different institution.

F. Embalming

Embalming is a process in which the blood is drained and replacement fluids are pumped into the body to temporarily retard its disintegration. While it has now become a common procedure, embalming is rarely necessary; refrigeration serves the same purpose.

Originally considered barbaric and paganistic, embalming first gained popularity during the Civil War, when bodies of the war dead were transported over long distances. When the war ended, embalming was promoted, mostly by those who performed the service, as a hygienic means of briefly preserving the body.

1. When Embalming Is Required

There is a popular misconception that embalming is always required by law after death. In fact, it is legally required only in some states and only in a few instances, such as:

- when a body will be transported by plane or train from one country or state to another
- where there is a relatively long time—usually a week or more—between the death and burial or cremation, and
- in some cases, where the death occurred because of a communicable disease.

2. If Your Body Is Not Embalmed

If you choose not to be embalmed, that should have no effect on your final arrangements. Your body will be refrigerated until the time of burial, and, if you choose, you can have a funeral or other service with an open casket.

The only effect of not being embalmed will be that if you opt to be buried, your body will begin to decompose within days instead of weeks.

3. Cost

The cost of embalming ranges from about $200 to $700, depending on your location and on the individual setting the rate.

Refrigeration is usually much less costly, involving a daily charge of about $10 to $30. Some facilities provide refrigeration free of charge.

G. Caskets

The container in which your body will be buried is called a casket or coffin. This item has been subject to more controversy in recent years than any other aspect of the funeral industry, because it traditionally carries the biggest mark-up of all funeral goods and services.

Anyone who has been asked to choose a casket for a deceased loved one knows the complex feelings that this choice engenders—often a mix of pride and guilt tempered by the reality of affordability. The sales personnel are well aware of their customers' vulnerabilities, and some do their best to sell the most expensive models. Lower-priced caskets are often displayed in the dingy, out-of-the-way corners of a funeral home's showroom.

Most funeral establishments now also carry caskets that may be rented and lined with inexpensive liners during viewing of the body instead of purchased for use. However, these too, are generally relegated to far-off, poorly lit corners—or the funeral director may fail to mention this option to grieving family members.

The High Cost of Caskets

Those in the funeral industry mark up the cost of caskets substantially, pricing them from hundreds to many thousands of dollars. The price differentials are usually based on the type of material used for the lining and exterior of the container and the type of hardware used for the handles and clasps. They range from $500 or less for a simple wooden casket to $35,000 or more for an elaborate engraved container with goldleaf decorations.

Most state laws require that caskets displayed in a showroom for potential purchase must be tagged with prices, a description of their composition and identifying model numbers. If an establishment uses a catalog to show the caskets it offers for sale or order, the same information must be included there. These laws allow individuals who have decided on a particular type or model of casket

to comparison shop for the best price. Be skeptical of sales representations that the law requires special devices on a casket such as a sealer or liner. If you feel that you're up against an expensive sell, ask the salesperson to give you the citation to the law that specifies what he's trying to sell you—and check out the law yourself. (See Chapter 25.)

Finally, while they are rare, there are some independent casketmakers or artisans who specialize in making low-cost or uniquely styled caskets. To locate an independent casketmaker, check www.funerals.org (it contains a list of carpenters and woodworkers who build coffins) or the Yellow Pages of your telephone book under Funeral Information & Advisory Services or a similar heading. Your local funeral or memorial society may also provide guidance.

H. Ceremonies

Death often involves at least one ceremony and sometimes more. The most common is the funeral, which occurs just prior to burial—although smaller informal ceremonies, often called wakes or visitations, are also commonly held the night before burial occurs. The details of a funeral or wake can vary enormously, depending on community custom and the religious, cultural and personal backgrounds of the deceased and the survivors.

1. Pre-Burial Ceremonies

There are two good reasons to describe your wishes for a ceremony to be held before your body is buried. The first is that the ceremony is an indirect final way for your survivors—your friends and family members—to say goodbye to you, to comfort one another and to continue the grieving process.

The second is that the more details you arrange while you are alive, the fewer decisions will be left for your survivors at a time when decisions are likely to be hard for them to make.

Some concerns you may wish to address when planning a pre-burial ceremony are:

- where the ceremony should be held
- who should be invited
- whether clergy should be invited to participate, along with specific names of clergy you would like
- any specific music you would like played, along with the names of the musicians or singers you would like to perform it
- preferences for a eulogy, and the name of the person or people you would like to speak
- whether you want your body to be present in a casket at the ceremony and, if so, whether you would like the casket open or closed

- any specific clothing or jewelry in which you wish your body to be attired, and
- whether you want to direct survivors to send flowers or memorial donations.

Making the Choice

Most people will want at least one ceremony held after they die but before they are buried, even if it is simple and informal. However, there may be reasons why a pre-burial ceremony is not appropriate. One may be that you live far from most of your friends and family members, and they would have to drop everything and attend a pre-burial ceremony at a great personal cost. Many people opt not to have a funeral but instead prefer a memorial ceremony, usually held days or weeks after the burial, that is more accessible to more people.

2. Pre-Cremation Ceremonies

A funeral, wake or visitation can be held before cremation occurs.

While people who choose cremation over body burial are often predisposed to direct that any ceremonies held be low on frills, you are free to direct a ceremony to be as simple or as elaborate as you like.

Some concerns you may wish to address when planning a pre-cremation ceremony are:

- where the ceremony should be held
- who should be invited
- whether clergy should be invited to participate, along with specific names of clergy you would like

- any specific music you would like played, along with the names of the musicians or singers you would like to perform it
- preferences for a eulogy, and the name of the person or people you would like to speak
- whether you want your cremains present at the ceremony, either in a casket or other container, or whether you would like a picture displayed instead, and
- whether you want to direct survivors to send flowers or memorial donations.

3. Informal Get-Togethers

Some people prefer an unstructured gathering of friends and family, held before their bodies are buried or cremated, usually in an informal setting such as a home or perhaps a favorite restaurant or club. This is a common choice for people who have not adhered to a specific religion during their lifetimes—and for those who are not strongly tied to family or community traditions.

There are few common elements to more informal after-death ceremonies, which range from the somber to the zany. These ceremonies are most dependent upon the whims and wishes of the deceased person. If you want some sort of informal ceremony held after your death, at a minimum, you may wish to consider:

- where the ceremony should be held
- who should be invited
- any specific music you would like played, along with the names of the musicians or singers you would like to perform it
- preferences for a eulogy, and the name of the person or people you would like to speak, and
- whether you want to direct survivors to send flowers or memorial donations.

There are a great number of additional details you can specify, of course. Some people have directed the survivors who attend to wear bright-colored clothing, bring their favorite pets or read a favorite poem.

4. Funerals

A traditional funeral is a brief ceremony, most often held in a funeral home chapel or a church. The body is usually present, either in an open or a closed casket. Beyond that, there are no absolutes or requirements about what constitutes a funeral. If the deceased person adhered to a particular religion, funerals often include a brief mass, blessing or prayer service.

In some traditions, only family members attend the funeral, while friends and the general public are invited to attend other scheduled ceremonies. In other locales and traditions, this is reversed, and the funeral is the less private event.

Some concerns you may wish to address when planning a funeral are:

- where the ceremony should be held
- who should be invited
- whether clergy should be invited to participate, along with specific names of clergy you would like
- any specific music you would like played, along with the names of the musicians or singers you would like to perform it
- preferences for a eulogy, and the name of the person or people you would like to speak
- whether you want your body or cremains present at the ceremony, either in a casket or other container, or whether you would like a picture displayed instead, and
- whether you want to direct survivors to send flowers or memorial donations.

a. Pallbearers

In some funeral ceremonies, the casket is carried to and from the place where the ceremony is held—and sometimes again carried from a transportation vehicle to a burial site. The people who carry the casket are termed pallbearers. If you envision a ceremony in which your casket will be carried, you can name here people you would wish to serve as pallbearers.

The number of pallbearers usually ranges from four to eight, but you can name as many or as few as you wish while assembling your document using Quicken WillMaker Plus.

b. Transportation to Grave

You may have a preference about the type of vehicle that will carry your body to the cemetery and gravesite from the place where the funeral ceremony is held. This might be a horse-drawn carriage, a favorite antique car or a stretch limousine.

If you have selected a mortuary to handle some of your arrangements, it may have only one type of vehicle available. If the vehicle customarily provided is not what you would want for yourself, check to be sure the mortuary will allow you to provide your own—and be sure that it will not add its transportation charge to your costs. If this is an important issue for you, check with the mortuary you selected earlier and, if its arrangements about transportation are not satisfactory, shop for another mortuary.

5. Graveside Ceremonies

In addition to or instead of holding a ceremony prior to burial, it is common to hold a brief ceremony at the gravesite at which a religious leader or relative or family friend says a few prayers or words of farewell.

If this is something you want, and you have an idea of who should be there, who should speak and what they should say, describe those details.

6. Memorial Ceremonies

A memorial ceremony is a ceremony held to commemorate someone who has died. It usually takes place some time after burial or cremation, so the body is not usually present. Memorial ceremonies may be held anywhere—a mortuary, a religious building, a home, outside or even a restaurant.

Memorial ceremonies are more often the choice of those who wish to have an economic, simple commemoration. While funeral directors, grief counselors or clergy members may be involved in memorial ceremonies, they are not the people to consult for objective advice. Many will advocate that traditional funerals—traditionally more costly and less personalized—are most effective in helping survivors through the mourning process. The truth is that most survivors are likely to take the greatest comfort in attending a ceremony that reflects the wishes and personality of the deceased person.

I. Final Disposition of Your Body

Your directions for the final disposition of your body will turn on your initial choice between burial and cremation.

1. Body Burial

If you have a decided upon a cemetery in which you wish to be buried, record that information. If you have purchased a gravesite in advance, describe it—and attach any pertinent documents to the Final Arrangements document that will print out when you are finished using this portion of Quicken WillMaker Plus.

If you have not purchased a gravesite, but you have a preference as to the part of the cemetery you want to be buried in, state that preference here. There is no guarantee that it will be available to you when you die, but your survivors will know what you had in mind.

2. Scattering Cremains

Many people wish to have their cremated remains, or cremains, scattered over some area that has special significance for them—a garden, a lookout point or the ocean.

Laws and restrictions on the disposition of cremains vary from state to state. In California, for example, cremains may be scattered at sea after being removed from their container; however, a verified statement must be filed nearest the point where the scattering occurred. Also, in California, cremains may be buried but may not be scattered on land.

To find out your state's laws on scattering cremains, check with a local cremation facility, or look up your state's statute online or at the local law library. (See Chapter 25.)

A Caveat on Scattering Services

Most people opt to have family members or friends conduct the scattering in private, in their own time and style.

However, there are some commercial firms that arrange to transport and scatter cremains over land or sea. Beware when dealing with such groups. While several masquerade as nonprofit groups by appending the term Society to their names and charging a membership fee, they are in the business for profit.

If you do decide to hire one of these services, make sure you understand its pricing structures in advance. Also, attach a copy of any written agreement you may enter to the Final Arrangements that print out when you are finished using this portion of Quicken WillMaker Plus.

Contact your local funeral or memorial society—or contact the Funeral Consumers Alliance (800-765-0107, www.funerals.org) for additional information.

3. Placing Cremains in a Container

Crematories usually arrange to return cremains to a family member or friends in a small, inexpensive plastic or cardboard container. The cremains may then be shipped, buried or placed in a niche above ground in a columbarium.

Some people opt to purchase a special container, usually called an urn, in which to store or bury cremains. There are no legal controls on the size, shape or type of urn that may be used, although a number of columbariums and cemeteries impose restrictions due to space if the cremains will be interred or buried.

Urns may be purchased from funeral homes, usually at a substantial mark-up. A small number of artists now also craft low-cost or specialized urns for cremains. Look in the Yellow Pages under Funeral Information and Services or a similar heading, search online or contact the local funeral or memorial society for more information on alternative containers.

4. Burying Cremains

Cremains can be buried in the ground. While there are some legal controls in some states on where the burial may take place—such as that they must be buried a specified distance from a residence—most of these controls are part of local zoning ordinances.

If you wish to have a family member or friend bury your cremains independently, it is a good idea to first check local zoning ordinances to see whether burial is permitted on the site you have chosen. Cremains can also be buried in a cemetery, either in a special urn garden or in a plot. It is not necessary to place the cremains in an urn before burial, although some places may require a plot liner to prevent the earth from sinking over time.

J. Markers and Headstones

It has become an American tradition—and a requirement in many cemeteries and columbariums—that a marker or headstone be placed to indicate where the remains of the deceased have been placed.

1. Crypt Markers

If you have chosen to have your cremains placed in a crypt or drawer in a columbarium, you may wish to have a marker identifying where they are. Depending on the location, you may be restricted to a marker of a certain type or size—for example, a plaque of specific dimensions and of a specific style.

2. Cemetery Markers

A cemetery marker often consists of an upright block of stone with words engraved on it. Some tend toward the elaborate, including sculptures and detailed etchings. However, many cemeteries require that all grave markers be flush with the ground to facilitate mowing surrounding vegetation or impose other restrictions according to either aesthetic or land quality controls.

If you have identified a cemetery where you wish to be buried, check to see whether it has any restrictions on burial markers. Then, within those constraints, identify the marker you want for your grave.

K. Epitaphs

Perhaps the most entertaining aspect of making final arrangements is choosing the words that you wish to appear on your burial marker. These words are known as your epitaph. Your epitaph can be extremely simple, stating only the years you were born and died—or it can reflect your personality by including a witty saying, favorite phrase or poem.

L. Choosing Someone to Oversee Your Wishes

If you have definite ideas about who should carry out your wishes as you have stated them, name the person. And make sure that he or she has a copy of the document that sets out your wishes and agrees to carry them out as you express them.

It is always a good idea to pick an alternate person to carry out your wishes, in case your first choice is unable or unwilling to perform this role when the time comes.

If you do not name anyone, it is likely that your closest relatives will become responsible.

The Importance of Attaching Other Documents

Many people make burial or cremation arrangements while they are still alive, through a local funeral or memorial society or directly with funeral industry providers. These arrangements may consist of:

- buying a burial plot
- contracting for a specific or similar type of casket, or
- indicating that cremation or burial is preferred.

If you have made any such arrangements, find the documents that spell them out and attach copies to the Final Arrangements document you create using Quicken WillMaker Plus. ■

If You Need More Help

You probably won't need a lawyer's help to make a will, a living trust or any of the other Quicken WillMaker Plus legal documents. But you may come up with questions about your particular situation that should be answered by an expert. This is especially likely if you have a very large estate, must plan for an incapacitated minor or have to deal with the assets of a good-sized small business. We highlight these and other "red flags" throughout the manual and program.

A. Learning More

If you've read most of this manual and started making your own will, living trust, health care directive, durable power of attorney or other document, you may know more about estate planning than a fair number of lawyers do. If you have questions that these materials don't address, you may want to consult some other self-help books or websites before you consult a pricey expert. It's often worth the money to pay a good lawyer for advice about your specific situation; it's rarely worth it to pay by the hour for education. Reading some background information before hiring a lawyer is usually the best approach.

Here are some places to get more in-depth information about estate planning:

- **Plan Your Estate**, by Denis Clifford and Cora Jordan (Nolo). This book explains how to draw up a complete estate plan making use of a will, living trust and other devices. It introduces more complex estate planning strategies, including various types of tax-saving trusts for the very wealthy.
- **8 Ways to Avoid Probate**, by Mary Randolph (Nolo). If you're interested in

learning more about some of the probate-avoidance techniques discussed in this manual, check out this book.

B. What Kind of Expert Do You Need?

If you have questions, the first thing to decide is what type of expert you should seek. Questions about estate taxes may be better (and less expensively) answered by an experienced accountant than a lawyer. Or if you're wondering what type of life insurance to buy, you may be better off talking to a financial planner.

Consult a lawyer if you have specific questions about a provision of your will, living trust or other estate planning device. Also see a lawyer if you want to get into more sophisticated estate planning—for instance, if you want to establish a charitable trust or a long-term trust for a disabled child.

C. Different Ways to Get Legal Advice From a Lawyer

Although many consumers (and some lawyers) haven't realized it yet, the way lawyers and their customers structure their relationships is changing very fast. In what is now a very competitive market—due in part to the Internet—many lawyers are offering piecemeal services, tailored to just what a customer wants. You no longer have to walk into a lawyer's office, turn over your legal problems and wait for an answer (and a bill). Instead, you can often buy what you need, whether it's a bit of advice, a particular document, some research, or regular coaching as you handle a probate court proceeding on your own.

1. Advice by Phone

You can now buy a single chunk of advice from a lawyer, just like you bought Quicken WillMaker Plus—and for about the same price. For approximately $40 to $50, you can buy a phone call with a lawyer licensed in your state. You can talk as long as you want about a single matter.

This "Ask an Attorney" service is offered by ARAG, a large provider of prepaid legal insurance. ARAG has put together a network of law firms in all 50 states; these lawyers take questions phoned in by members of prepaid insurance plans (mostly employees of big companies that offer legal insurance as a benefit) and from individuals who pay by credit card.

The attorneys who staff the phones are screened (they must be licensed and in good standing with their state bar association) and monitored by ARAG. They are also forbidden from offering to sell you more services—which means that they have no incentive to recommend more lawyer's services than you need. Finally, there's a money-back guarantee if you're not satisfied. To use this service, visit www.aragdirect.com and click on "Ask an Attorney."

2. Group Legal Plans

Some unions, employers and consumer action organizations offer group legal plans to their members or employees, who can obtain legal assistance free or for low rates. If you are a member of such a plan, check with it first. Your problem may be covered free of charge. If it is, and you are satisfied that the lawyer you are referred to is knowledgeable in estate planning, this route is probably a good choice.

Some plans, however, give you only a slight reduction in a lawyer's fee. In that case, you may be referred to a lawyer whose main virtue is the willingness to reduce fees in exchange for a high volume of referrals.

3. Prepaid Legal Insurance

For basic advice, you may want to consider joining a prepaid legal plan that offers advice, by phone or in person, at no extra charge. (Some of these plans throw in a free simple will, too.) Your initial membership and monthly fee may be reasonable, compared to the cost of hiring a lawyer by the hour, but there's no guarantee that the lawyers available through these plans are of the best caliber.

Many prepaid insurance providers have websites that detail the terms of the plans they offer, so you can do some comparison shopping online. You may also be able to find a list of companies licensed to offer legal insurance in your state from your state's Consumer Affairs agency; call the agency or check out your state's website.

Lawyers sign up for these programs primarily to get new clients—not for the fees the insurance company pays them. As part of your coverage, you also get discounted rates. These aspects of the arrangement mean the lawyers have an incentive to complicate, rather than simplify, your problem. So if a plan lawyer recommends an expensive legal procedure, get a second opinion.

D. Finding a Lawyer

Finding a competent lawyer who charges a reasonable fee and respects your efforts to prepare your own estate planning documents may not be easy. First of all, look for a lawyer who specializes in estate planning. Most general practice lawyers are simply not sufficiently educated in this field to competently address complicated problems. Here are some more suggestions.

1. Businesspeople and Friends

Anyone who owns a small business probably has a relationship with a lawyer. Ask around to find someone you know who is a satisfied client. If that lawyer does not handle estate planning, he or she will likely know someone who does. And because of the continuing relationship with your friend, the lawyer has an incentive to recommend someone who is competent.

Also ask people you know in any social or other organization in which you are involved. They may well know of a good lawyer whose attitudes are similar to yours. Senior citizens' centers and other groups that advise and assist older people may have a list of local lawyers who specialize in wills and estate planning and are well regarded.

Chain Law Firms

Law firms with lots of small offices across the country, such as Jacoby & Meyers, trumpet their low initial consultation fees. It's true that a basic consultation is cheap; anything beyond that isn't. Generally, the rates are about the same as those charged by other lawyers in general practice.

The trick is to quickly extract the information you need and resist attempts to convince you that you need more services. If the lawyer you talk to is experienced in estate planning, however, and you're comfortable with the person and the service, it may be worthwhile. Unfortunately, most of these offices have extremely high turnover, so you may see a different lawyer every time you visit.

2. Attorney Referral Services

A lawyer referral service will give you the name of an attorney who practices in your area. Usually, you can get a referral to an attorney who claims to specialize in estate planning and will give you an initial consultation for a low fee.

Most county bar associations have referral services. In some states, independent referral services, run by or for groups of lawyers, also operate.

Unfortunately, few referral services screen the attorneys they list, which means those who participate may not be the most experienced or competent. Often, the lawyers who sign up with referral services are just starting out and need clients. It may be possible to find a skilled estate planning specialist through a referral service, but be sure to take the time to check out the credentials and experience of the person to whom you're referred.

Living Trust Seminars

Newspapers, radio and TV are full of ads for free "seminars" on living trusts. Usually, these events are nothing more than elaborate pitches for paying a lawyer $1,000 to $1,500 to write a living trust. Is it worth it? Probably not.

For a relatively small estate, Quicken WillMaker Plus will probably be all you need. For more complicated estate planning, you will almost surely get better, less expensive and more personal advice from a local estate planning specialist.

3. The West Legal Directory

This huge directory, which you can find online at http://lawyers.findlaw.com, lists most lawyers in the United States—over 700,000 of them. You can look for a lawyer by location and legal practice category; there's a good chance you'll find more than one in your city who can help you with estate planning matters. As with any listing of lawyers or referral service, however, you should be careful to investigate the credentials and experience of any lawyer you contact. FindLaw's West Legal Directory provides help with this, offering a number of articles on choosing a lawyer, including guidelines for interviewing any lawyer you might want to hire.

In addition to the West Directory, there are other large legal directories available in print or online. If you're comfortable on the Internet, you can simply type "lawyer directory" into a search engine such as Google; this will yield a list of the major legal directories available online. You can also visit a law library and ask the reference librarian to point you to these guides.

4. The Internet

There are lots of websites that try to match lawyers and potential clients. You may be able to search, for example, for lawyers who list estate planning as a practice area and are located in or close to your zip code. It's almost impossible to generalize about these websites—some list ridiculously few attorneys, while others have extensive lists. Lawyers may pay fees, low or high, to get their names listed; screening may be rigorous or nonexistent.

In general, it's still best to get personal recommendations for lawyers and then use the Internet to find out more about them. Many law firms and individual lawyers have their own websites. Estate planning attorneys may publish articles on wills, trusts and related topics; these may give you a good idea of the lawyer's personality and philosophy.

E. Working With a Lawyer

Before you talk to a lawyer, decide what kind of help you really need. Do you want someone to advise you on a complete estate plan, or just to review the documents you prepare to make sure they look all right? If you don't clearly tell the lawyer what you want, you may find yourself agreeing to turn over all your estate planning work.

One good strategy is to do some background research and write down your questions as specifically as you can. If the lawyer doesn't give you clear, concise answers, try someone else. If the lawyer acts wise but says little except to ask that the problem be placed in his or her hands—with a substantial fee, of course—watch out. You're either dealing with someone who doesn't know the answer and won't admit it (common) or someone who finds it impossible to let go of the "me expert, you plebeian" philosophy (even more common).

Lawyer fees usually range from $100 to $350 or more per hour. But price is not always related to quality. It depends on the area of the country you live in, but generally, fees of $150 to $200 per hour are reasonable in urban areas. In rural areas and smaller cities, $100 to $150 is more like it. The fee of an experienced specialist may be 10 to 30% higher than that of a general practitioner, but the specialist will probably produce results more efficiently and save you money in the long run.

Be sure you settle your fee arrangement—preferably in writing—at the start of your relationship. In addition to the hourly fee, you should get a clear, written commitment from the lawyer about how many hours your problem should take to handle.

Resources. For more information about working with lawyers and holding down legal fees, see Nolo's website at www.nolo.com.

F. Doing Your Own Legal Research

There is often a viable alternative to hiring a lawyer to resolve legal questions that affect your estate planning documents: You can do your own legal research. Doing your own legal research can provide some real benefits for those willing to learn how to do it. Not only will you save some money, you will gain a sense of mastery over an area of law, generating confidence that will stand you in good stead should you have other legal problems.

Fortunately, researching wills, living trusts and related estate planning issues is an area generally well suited to doing your own legal research. Most problems do not involve massive or abstruse legal questions. Often you need only check the statutes of your state to find one particular provision.

Resources. Nolo's website, www.nolo.com, offers a section on estate planning that covers a range of topics including living trusts and estate and gift taxes. You can also find links to state and federal statutes from the site.

Legal Research: How to Find and Understand the Law, by Stephen Elias and Susan Levenkind (Nolo), gives instructions and examples explaining how to conduct legal research.

1. Finding Statutes in a Law Library

You can always find state statutes at a law library or, usually, at the main branch of a public library. Depending on the state, statutes are compiled in books called statutes, revised statutes, annotated statutes, codes or compiled laws. For example, the Vermont statutes are found in a series called *Vermont Statutes Annotated*, while Michigan's laws are found in two separate sets of books: *Michigan Statutes* or an alternate series called *Michigan Compiled Laws*. (The term "annotated" means that the statutes are accompanied by information about their history and court decisions that have interpreted them.) The reference librarian can point you toward the books you need.

After you've found the books, check the index for provisions dealing with the specific subject that concerns you—for example, wills, revocable living trusts or powers of attorney. Generally, you will find what you want in the volume of statutes dealing with your state's basic civil or probate laws. Statutes are numbered sequentially, so once you get the correct number in the index, it will be easy to find the statute you need.

Once you find a law in the statute books, it's important to look at the update pamphlet in the back of the book (called the "pocket part") to make sure your statute hasn't changed or been repealed. Pocket parts are published only once per year, so brand-new laws often have not yet made it to the pocket part. Law libraries subscribe to services and periodicals that update the statute books on a more frequent basis than the pocket parts. You can ask a law librarian to help you find the materials you need.

Finally, you may find summaries of relevant court cases immediately following the statute. (These are the "annotations" mentioned just above.) If so, you'll want to skim them. If a summary looks like it might help answer your question, read the full court case cited there. (Ask the librarian for help finding the case, or turn to the legal research resource listed above.)

2. Finding Statutes Online

All states have made their statutes available on the Internet. You can find them by visiting the legal research area of Nolo's website at www.nolo.com/statute/state.cfm. Choose your state to search or browse the statutes.

In addition, almost every state maintains its own website for pending and recently enacted legislation. If you hear about a proposed or new law and you want to look it up, you can use your state's website to find not only the most current version of a bill, but also its history. To find your state's website, open your browser and type in www.state.[your state's postal code].us. Your state's postal code is the two-letter abbreviation you use for mailing addresses. For example, NY is the postal code for New York, so to find New York's state website, type www.state.ny.us. When you open your state's home page, look for links under "government." All states have separate links to their legislatures, and they offer many different ways to look up bills and laws. You can also find any state's legislature through the National Conference of State Legislatures at www.ncsl.org. ■

Users' Manual

Table of Contents

Part 1: Introduction

Welcome to Quicken WillMaker Plus 2006.

With Quicken WillMaker Plus, you and the members of your immediate family can create legal documents yourselves. This product is the work of a team of people dedicated to making the law accessible to everyone. We've made every effort to make the program and manual thorough, accurate and easy to use. It has been refined through hundreds of hours of testing and use by nonlawyers to ensure that you don't need a law degree to understand the information we present.

Quicken WillMaker Plus has two manuals:
- a Users' Manual, and
- a Legal Manual.

The Users' Manual, which you are reading, is available in printed form and in electronic format as part of the program's Help system. It provides general information on how to use the program, regardless of which document you want to create.

The Legal Manual, which is available as part of the program's Help system but not in printed form, describes each document that Quicken WillMaker Plus creates and explains what each document is used for.

The printed version of this manual contains an additional section called "Introduction to Quicken WillMaker Plus." It provides an introduction to making documents and samples of the program's major forms.

A. How Quicken WillMaker Plus Works

Making documents with Quicken WillMaker Plus is like being interviewed. Quicken WillMaker Plus helps you prepare legal forms by asking you questions and providing the information you need to make informed choices. But it is important to realize that the program is not a lawyer in a box. That's why Quicken WillMaker Plus provides a thorough discussion of legal and practical issues that you should consider before making your choices.

After you've answered all the questions needed to complete a document (we call this a "document interview"), Quicken WillMaker Plus combines your answers with appropriate legal language and displays the completed document on the screen. You can review the document, and, if you want to make any changes, you can revisit any part of the interview to revise your answers. When you're sure the document is accurate, you print and sign it, following the signing instructions that accompany every document. (If you wish, you can, of course, check your results with a lawyer.) Once you've signed your document, following the appropriate formalities, the document becomes legally binding.

Using Quicken WillMaker Plus you can produce any document in one evening, but we encourage you to relax and take your time. Remember, Quicken WillMaker Plus doesn't charge by the hour. These are important decisions you are making. Take the time to read the legal help that appears on each screen to make sure you fully understand the implications of each question.

If you don't want to complete an interview all in one sitting, you can stop any time you like or go back to prior questions. When you return to a document interview, you can easily pick up where you left off.

Who Can Use Quicken WillMaker Plus?

The Quicken WillMaker Plus license permits you and members of your immediate family to make their own Quicken WillMaker Plus documents with this copy of Quicken WillMaker Plus.

B. Compatibility With Previous Versions

The information in this section is of interest to past users of Nolo software. If you are new to Quicken WillMaker Plus and are not upgrading from one of the programs listed here, you can skip this section.

- Quicken WillMaker Plus 2005 and 2004
- Quicken Lawyer 2003 Personal and Wills
- Quicken Lawyer 2003
- Quicken Lawyer 2002 Personal Deluxe and Wills
- WillMaker 8 or WillMaker Deluxe
- Living Trust Maker
- Quicken Family Lawyer.

Quicken WillMaker Plus 2006 is an update of older Nolo and Quicken will-writing programs. If you are updating from an older version, see the chart on the next page to determine whether your older program is compatible with the 2006 edition.

If you open your 2005, 2004 or 2003 version documents file (*.pfl) in Quicken WillMaker Plus, all your data will be converted. For details on opening and converting files created with compatible previous versions, see Part 3, Section A2.

C. System Requirements

To install and run Quicken WillMaker Plus, you'll need to meet these minimum requirements:

- **Computer.** Pentium 133 (Pentium II 300 recommended)
- **Operating System.** Windows 98/2000/Me/XP
- **Memory.** 32 MB RAM (64 MB RAM recommended)
- **Hard Disk Space.** 18 MB (23 MB to install)
- **Monitor.** Super VGA (800 x 600) with 256 colors (16-bit color recommended)
- **CD-ROM Drive.** 2x speed
- **Internet Connection.** 14.4 Kbps modem required to access online features (56 Kbps or higher recommended)
- **Printer.** Any printer supported by Windows 98/2000/Me/XP
- **Software.** Microsoft Internet Explorer 5.0 or higher; Adobe Acrobat Reader (optional).

D. Typeface Conventions

The rest of this manual provides instructions on menus, buttons and keys. To make these instructions easier to follow, we use the following typeface conventions:

- KEYS that you are supposed to press are in SMALL CAPS.
- Key combinations are written like ALT+F4, which means "hold down the ALT key while pressing the F4 key."
- Names of buttons and icons are in bold type, such as **Next** and **Back**.
- Names of **Menus** and **Menu Commands** are in bold type, such as **New Documents File** from the **File** menu.

Is ...	... compatible with Quicken WillMaker Plus 2006?
Quicken WillMaker Plus 2005	Yes. All your data is converted when you open your documents file (*.pfl) in Quicken WillMaker Plus 2006.
Quicken WillMaker Plus 2004	Yes. All your data is converted when you open your documents file (*.pfl) in Quicken WillMaker Plus 2006.
Quicken Lawyer 2003 Personal and Wills	Yes. All your data is converted when you open your portfolio file (*.pfl) in Quicken WillMaker Plus 2006.
Quicken Lawyer 2002 Personal Deluxe and Wills	Yes. All your data is converted when you open your portfolio file (*.pfl) in Quicken WillMaker Plus 2006.
WillMaker Deluxe and WillMaker 8	Yes. All your data is converted when you open your portfolio file (*.ww8) in Quicken WillMaker Plus 2006.
Living Trust Maker 2	No. You will not be able to open your Living Trust Maker 2 data files (*.trs) using Quicken WillMaker Plus. If you want to maintain any trust created with Living Trust Maker 2, you should keep Living Trust Maker 2 installed on your computer and amend your trust document using that program, not Quicken WillMaker Plus. Similarly, if you want to revoke a trust created with Living Trust Maker 2, you need to do so using that program, not Quicken WillMaker Plus. After you have revoked a trust document created with Living Trust Maker 2, you can use Quicken WillMaker Plus to create a new living trust.
Quicken Family Lawyer	No. You cannot use data or files from Quicken Family Lawyer in Quicken WillMaker Plus 2006. However, Quicken WillMaker Plus will not interfere with Quicken Family Lawyer program or data files, so you can keep both programs installed on your computer.

• Names of specific Quicken WillMaker Plus screens are in quotation marks, such as the "Congratulations" screen.

E. Register Your Copy

Registered owners of Nolo products receive a variety of services and benefits, including technical support. But, to provide these services, we need to know who you are. Please take the time now to register your copy by opening Quicken WillMaker Plus's **Online** menu and choosing **Online Registration**.

Troubleshooting Tip

If you are having problems connecting to the Internet using Quicken WillMaker Plus's Web links, open your Web browser as you normally would, then choose **Online Registration** from the **Online** menu. Keep the browser open throughout your Quicken WillMaker Plus session.

F. Customer Service

Nolo Customer Service representatives can answer questions on product availability, prices, software upgrades, product features, customer registration, policies, procedures and other nontechnical topics. Here's how to reach us:

Phone: 800-728-3555

Hours: 7:00 a.m. to 7:00 p.m. Pacific Time, Monday through Friday

Email: cs@nolo.com

1. Change of Address

If you move, please send a letter with both your old and new addresses to:

Customer Service
Nolo
950 Parker Street
Berkeley, CA 94710-9867
ATTN: CHANGE OF ADDRESS

2. Defective or Damaged Products

If you are a registered user and your disc is damaged or defective, we'll replace it free of charge. Send the defective disc and a brief explanation to:

Customer Service
Nolo
950 Parker Street
Berkeley, CA 94710-9867
ATTN: REPLACEMENT DISC

G. Technical Support

Nolo offers technical support for Quicken WillMaker Plus to registered users only. If you haven't yet done so, please register your copy.

Website: www.nolo.com/support/software.cfm

Email: support@nolo.com

Phone: 510-549-4660

Hours: 9:00 a.m. to 5:00 p.m. Pacific Time, Monday through Friday

If you have technical questions or problems operating this program, read Part 8 before contacting the Nolo Technical Support Department.

Part 2: Getting Started

In this part, we provide the basic information on how to install, start, update and quit the program.

A. Installing Quicken WillMaker Plus

You must have a CD-ROM drive to install Quicken WillMaker Plus.

You will need approximately 23 MB of free space on your hard disk to install Quicken WillMaker Plus for Windows and its accompanying help files.

1. Start your computer.
2. Insert the Quicken WillMaker Plus disc into your CD-ROM drive.
3. Follow the instructions that appear on the "Welcome to Quicken WillMaker Plus Installation" screen. (If the "Welcome to Quicken WillMaker Plus Installation" screen does not open automatically, see Part 8, Section A.)

Some users may need to restart Windows after installation is complete. If this is necessary in your case, the program will prompt you to do so.

Useful Information

The **Quicken WillMaker Plus 2006** program folder, which is created upon installation, contains useful information that you should read before you start the program. To view this information:

1. Click the **Start** button in the Windows taskbar.
2. Point to **Programs** (Windows 98, 2000 or Me) or **All Programs** (Windows XP) to open the **Programs** folder.
3. Point to **Quicken WillMaker Plus 2006** to open the application folder.
4. Click **Troubleshooting** to see information that didn't make it into this manual.
5. Click **What's New** to see information for **Quicken WillMaker Plus 2005** users.

B. Starting Quicken WillMaker Plus

Once you've installed Quicken WillMaker Plus on your hard disk, you're ready to start the program.

1. Click the **Start** button in the Windows taskbar.
2. Point to **Programs** (Windows 98, 2000 or Me) or **All Programs** (Windows XP) to open the **Programs** folder.
3. Point to **Quicken WillMaker Plus 2006** to open the **Quicken WillMaker Plus** application folder.
4. Click **Quicken WillMaker Plus 2006**.

The program will start and you should see the opening screen shown below.

If You've Created Documents Using an Older Version of Quicken WillMaker

If you've created a documents file (*.pfl) using an older version of Quicken WillMaker, the program automatically detects your most recently used documents file and asks if you'd like to open it.

If you click **Yes**, you'll go to the program's first introductory screen. The name of the documents file you just opened appears in the title bar. When you arrive at the '"Documents List" screen after clicking through the Introduction, all the files you've created with your older version of Quicken WillMaker are listed. You can continue working on a document you've created or start a new one.

If you'd rather work with a brand-new file, click **No** when you're asked if you'd like to open the documents file you've previously created.

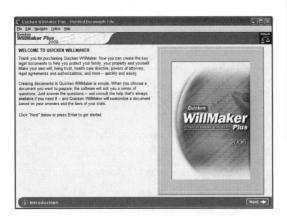

The first time you use the program, you'll go through a series of introductory screens. Though you may be tempted to breeze through them and immediately begin creating your first document, we recommend that you read them all and familiarize yourself with the program and its features. You can go back to the introduction at any time by opening the **Navigate** menu and selecting **Go to Introduction**.

Which Documents Are Right for You?

In the introduction section of Quicken WillMaker Plus, you'll see the "Which Estate Planning Documents Do You Need?" screen with a button labeled **Learn More**. If you click that button, you'll be able to select from a list of life situations that may apply to you. After you choose the situations that reflect your circumstances, the program will suggest several documents and explain why they may be useful to you. The life situations include:

- You're Young and Without Dependents
- You're Paired Up, But Not Married
- You Have Young Children
- You're Middle-Aged and Financially Comfortable
- You're Elderly or Ill.

At your request, the program adds the suggested documents item will be added to your "Document List" (discussed in Part 3, Section B).

You may also want to read:

- Part 3 of the Users' Manual to learn how to work with Quicken WillMaker Plus documents files, and
- Part 5 of the Users' Manual when you're ready to start making documents.

C. Updating Quicken WillMaker Plus From the Internet

We keep this program as up-to-date as possible. Nevertheless, laws can—and do—change. When we need to add new legal information or if a user reports a problem with the program, we update it. And, because software boxes can sit on shelves for a while, you may not have the most recent version of Quicken WillMaker Plus.

To ensure that you're using the current, up-dated version of this program, run Web Update after you install Quicken WillMaker Plus. You'll see a screen in the introduction that explains how to run Web Update.

We also recommend that you run periodic up-dates. To run periodic updates:

1. Open your Internet connection as you would normally. (If you do not have an Internet connection, you will not be able to use Web Update.)
2. Open Quicken WillMaker Plus's **Online** menu and select **Web Update**.
3. Follow the directions that appear onscreen.

Web Update will determine if you have the most recent version of Quicken WillMaker Plus. If it detects an old version of any file installed on your computer, it will download and install the newer file from the Web. When this download process is complete, Quicken WillMaker Plus will restart. This update process can take a few minutes, so please be patient.

Each time you start the program, it automatically checks for Web Updates, provided you have an open Internet connection. If you prefer not to have these checks done automatically, you can turn off this feature by following these steps:

1. Open the **Edit** menu and choose **Preferences**.
2. Click Automatically check for updates when the program starts to clear the checkbox.
3. Click **OK**.

For more on using the **Preferences** menu, see Appendix 1.

If you have problems using Web Update, see Part 8, Section E.

D. Quitting the Program

To quit Quicken WillMaker Plus:

- choose **Exit** from the **File** menu, or
- press ALT+F4.

If you've made any changes since the last time you saved your documents file, these changes will be automatically saved if the Automatically Save Changes feature is on. (See Part 3, Section A3.) If you try to quit when Automatically Save Changes is turned off, you'll be asked whether you want to save your changes before exiting. ■

Part 3: Working With Quicken WillMaker Plus Documents Files

All of the data you enter to create Quicken WillMaker Plus documents is stored on your hard disk in a file we call a "documents file." This part of the manual explains how to create and work with Quicken WillMaker Plus documents files.

A. Creating and Using Documents Files

When you go through the Quicken WillMaker Plus introduction screens, you will be asked to create your first documents file—the file that contains all the documents you create with Quicken WillMaker Plus.

You create your documents file by entering your name when you get to the screen shown below.

Type in your name, then click **Next** or press ENTER. If the Automatically Save Changes option

is on (see Section 3, below), you'll then see a standard Save File dialog box. If the Automatically Save Changes option is off, you won't see the Save File dialog box until you choose **Save** or **Exit** from the **File** menu.

Unless you specify otherwise, the documents file will be named "Documents of [*the name you just entered*]."

Click **Save** in the dialog box to create the documents file and save it to your **My Documents** folder. If you want to, you can save it to a different location. The documents file name now appears in the title bar of the Quicken WillMaker Plus program window with the file extension ".pfl" added.

In addition to your documents file, an identical "backup" copy is created. Each time you save data to your documents file, the same data is automatically saved to its backup. Backup files are stored in

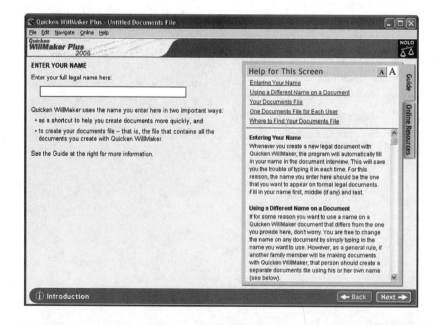

the **Nolo Documents Backup** subfolder of your **My Documents** folder. For more on opening a backup documents file, see Section 2, below.

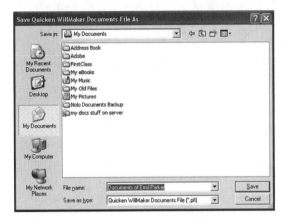

If you need to create more than one documents file, see Section 1, below.

If you are upgrading to Quicken WillMaker Plus 2006 from an older version of the program, see Section 2, below.

1. Creating Additional Documents Files

You can create as many Quicken WillMaker Plus documents files as you want. However, Quicken WillMaker Plus and its manual are copyrighted, and the licensing agreement prohibits you from preparing wills or other documents for people outside your immediate family or for commercial or nonprofit purposes. If you are interested in licensing Quicken WillMaker Plus for commercial or nonprofit purposes, call Nolo at 510-549-1976.

To make a will or any other document for another person in your immediate family, including your spouse, domestic partner, children or parents, you should make a new documents file.

To create a new documents file, choose **New Documents File** from the **File** menu. You will then view a few introductory screens, including the one where you are asked to enter your name, as described above.

2. Opening and Converting Previously Created Documents Files

You can open documents files that you created previously with this program, as well as:

- documents files created with Quicken WillMaker 2005 and 2004, Quicken Lawyer 2003 Personal and Quicken Lawyer 2003 Wills, and
- portfolio files created with Quicken Lawyer 2002 Personal Deluxe, Quicken Lawyer 2002 Wills, Nolo's WillMaker 8 or Valusoft's WillMaker Deluxe.

To open a documents file or portfolio that you created previously:

1. Choose **Open Documents File...** from the **File** menu. You'll then see a standard Open File dialog. You'll need to use this dialog box to locate the file you want to open (in most cases, in the **My Documents** folder).
2. Select the file you want to open by clicking on it (Quicken WillMaker Plus and Quicken Lawyer documents files have a .pfl extension.)
3. Click **Open**.

When a pre-2006 file is opened, you'll see a message confirming that it was created by an older version of the program. Your data is automatically converted into a new Quicken WillMaker Plus 2006 documents file, with the file extension .pfl.

Opening Recently Used Files

If you have created more than one documents file, there's an easy way to get to the file you want to use. Open the **File** menu and select **Recent Files** to see a submenu of recently used documents files. Just click the one you want to use.

Be aware that if you moved a document file to a location that's different from where it was last saved by Quicken WillMaker Plus, you will not be able to open it using the **Recent Files** command. Instead, you'll need to open the **File** menu and select **Open Documents File**.

Opening Backup Documents Files

To protect you from inadvertently overwriting your backups, you will not be able to open a backup documents file stored in the backup folder. If there's a problem with your "real" documents file—and you therefore need to use the backup—you must first copy the backup from the backup folder. If necessary, use the Windows Find or Search feature to find the **Nolo Documents Backup** folder and the backup file you want to copy.

As with all important computer files, it's a good idea to save a copy of your Quicken WillMaker Plus documents files on a floppy disk, recordable CD or other external medium, stored in a safe and secure place, in case something happens to the files on your hard disk. You should safely store a copy of the Quicken WillMaker installation CD as well, in case you ever need to reinstall the program.

Changing the Default Backup Directory

By default, backup files are stored in the **Nolo Document Backups** subfolder of your **My Documents** folder. If you want to back up to a different location, open the **Edit** menu and choose **Preferences**. There, you can change the backup directory.

3. Saving Your Data

There are two ways to save the data you enter into your documents file as you work on it:

- automatically, or
- manually.

To automatically save your file and any changes made to it, leave the **Automatically save changes** command in the Preferences dialog box turned on. To view the Preferences dialog box, open the **Edit** menu and select **Preferences...**.

When you start up Quicken WillMaker Plus for the first time, this feature is on—so if you open the Preferences dialog box you'll see a checkmark next to this command. You can turn off **Automatically save changes** by clicking it; when turned off, the checkmark no longer appears. We strongly suggest you leave this feature turned on.

If **Automatically save changes** is turned off, choose **Save** from the **File** menu to manually save your file and any changes made to it.

Each time you save data (whether manually or automatically) to your documents file, the same data is saved to its backup file as well.

4. Protecting Your Documents File With a Password

To make sure no one else can gain access to your documents file, you can lock it by assigning a password. To lock a documents file, choose **Lock Documents File** from the **File** menu, and enter the password you want to use and a hint to help you remember it. Note that your password is case-sensitive, so you need to be aware of exactly how you enter the password.

! Remember your password. Once locked, your documents file cannot be opened without first entering the correct password. It is your responsibility to remember the password and a hint to help you remember it, so take care choosing your password and hint. While you can later unlock your file (by choosing **Unlock Documents File** from the **File** menu) or change its password (by choosing **Change Documents File Password** from the **File** menu), you can only do so while the file is open.

B. The Documents in Your Documents File

A few screens after you have created your documents file, you will see a screen that lists all the documents you can create using the program. You can use this screen to:

- create a new document (see below if you are using the program for the first time, or Part 5, Section C1, for more details)
- continue working on a document you've already created (see Part 5, Section C2), and
- revise, print, review or export a document you've already completed (see Part 7).

To return to the document selection screen at any time, click the **Document List** icon or choose **Go to Document List** from the **Navigate** menu.

The first time you run the program and see this screen, the drop-down Document List will say "Make a Selection." You can select from the following options:

- **All Documents.** All the documents that you can create using this program.
- **Documents You've Created.** All the documents you have already created. The first time you see the Document List, no documents are listed in this category.
- **Estate Planning.** See the Legal Manual, Chapter 1, Section A. To view the Legal Manual, click on the **Legal Manual** icon in the navigation bar or open Quicken WillMaker Plus's **Help** menu.
- **Executors.** See the Legal Manual, Chapter 1, Section B. To view the Legal Manual, click on the **Legal Manual** icon in the navigation bar or open the **Help** menu.
- **Home and Family.** See the Legal Manual, Chapter 1, Section C. To view the Legal Manual, click on the **Legal Manual** icon in the navigation bar or open the **Help** menu.
- **Personal Finance and Consumer.** See the Legal Manual, Chapter 1, Section D. To view the Legal Manual, click on the **Legal Manual** icon in the navigation bar or open the **Help** menu.
- **Suggested Documents.** The documents that the program recommends you create, based on your answers to the optional screens in the program's introduction. (If you skipped this part of the introduction, this category will not be created for you.) To learn more about which documents are right for you, see Part 2, Section B.

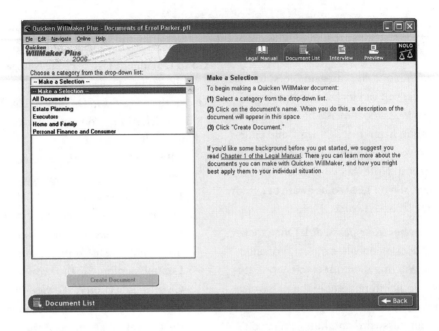

Switching Between Document Interviews

You can switch to a different document interview even if you haven't finished the interview for the document you're working on. When you leave an interview to switch to another, the information you entered is saved so that, when you return at a later time, you can pick up right where you left off.

To switch to another document, (1) click the **Document List** icon, (2) select the document you want to work on and (3) click **Open Document** or **Create Document**. ◼

Part 4: Getting Help From Quicken WillMaker Plus

Quicken WillMaker Plus's Help system offers the following kinds of assistance:

- the Guide, visible on the right side of every Quicken WillMaker Plus interview screen, with legal and practical guidance for the particular screen you are viewing (see Section A)
- a Help file, available from the **Help** menu, containing both this Users' Manual and the Quicken WillMaker Legal Manual (see Section B)
- a glossary of key legal and estate planning terms (see Section C), and
- links to helpful resources and information on the Internet (see Section D).

In this part of the manual, you'll learn about how to get help from all these sources.

A. The Guide Tab

The Guide that appears on the right side of every Quicken WillMaker Plus interview screen is your source for learning about the legal and practical considerations behind each interview question. As you move to each new interview screen, the Guide text changes to provide specific help for the screen you're currently viewing. The Guide is already open when you first come to an interview screen. If necessary, use the scroll bar to read an entire topic.

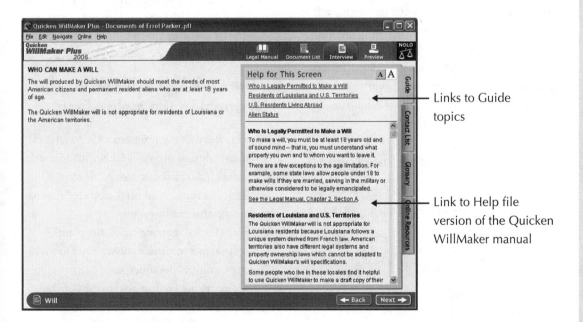

Links to Guide topics

Link to Help file version of the Quicken WillMaker manual

- To learn about the **Contact List** tab, see Part 5, Sections E3 and F.

- To learn about the **Glossary** tab, see Section C, below.

- To learn about the **Online Resources** tab, see Section D, below.

The Guide has hypertext links to related topics in an electronic version of the Quicken WillMaker Plus Manual. (See Section B, below.) To view a related section of the manual, just click on its hypertext link. This will open the Quicken WillMaker Plus Manual in its own window.

The Guide also contains links to helpful websites and resources on the Internet. Links to websites are preceded by a small "globe" icon: 🌐. When you click a Guide link to a website, you'll see it in a separate browser window. Quicken WillMaker Plus remains open, behind your Web browser. You can return to the Quick WillMaker Plus program screen you clicked from by closing or minimizing your browser, using your Windows taskbar or pressing ALT+TAB.

1. Changing Font Size of the Guide

To change the font size of the text in the Guide, click one of the two **A** icons in the upper right of the Guide:

Help for This Screen   A | A

- To show the font in a smaller size, click the icon with the smaller **A**.
- To return the font to a larger size, click the icon with the larger **A**.

The change of font size will take effect immediately.

2. Printing Help Topics in the Guide

To print out the Guide topic you are viewing:

1. Choose **Print Guide Topic** from the **File** menu.
2. You'll then see a standard Print dialog box.
3. Click **OK** to send the topic to your printer.

3. Copying Text From the Guide

You can also copy text from the Guide and paste it into an email or word processing document.

1. Use your mouse to select the text you want to copy.
2. Copy it to your Clipboard by pressing CTRL+C.
3. Use your mouse to point and click to where you want to make the insertion, and paste it in by pressing CTRL+V.

B. The Quicken WillMaker Manual in the Help Menu

Also included in the program's Help system is an online version of the WillMaker Plus Manual. This manual is divided into two sections:

- Users' Manual, based on the printed manual you are now reading, and
- Legal Manual, containing all the plain-English legal information you need to make your own legal documents.

The online manual is displayed in the Quicken WillMaker Plus Manual window, separate from the main Quicken WillMaker Plus program window.

1. Accessing the Manuals

There are several ways to view the manuals from the main Quicken WillMaker Plus program window.

To view the Legal Manual:
- on any screen, you can open the **Help** menu and select **Quicken WillMaker Legal Manual**
- on any screen after the Introduction, click the **Legal Manual** icon (above the Guide), or
- if you see an underlined link to the Legal Manual in the Guide, click it.

To view the Users' Manual:
- on any screen, you can open the **Help** menu and select **Quicken WillMaker Users' Manual**, or
- if you see an underlined link to the Users' Manual in the Guide, click it.

Users' Manual in PDF Format

We've included a version of the Users' Manual in Adobe Acrobat PDF format. This version has the same formatting found in the printed manual (included if you bought a boxed copy of the program). To view the PDF version, you must have Adobe Acrobat Reader installed on your computer. (You can download Adobe Reader for free from www.adobe.com.)

To view the Users' Manual in Adobe Acrobat Reader:

1. Click the **Start** button on your Windows taskbar.
2. Open the **Programs** folder.
3. Open the **Quicken WillMaker Plus 2006** program folder.
4. Click the **Users' Manual** icon.

2. Using the Online Quicken WillMaker Manual

When you open one of the manuals, it appears in its own window on top of the main Quicken WillMaker Plus program window. These are the elements of the Quicken WillMaker Manual window.

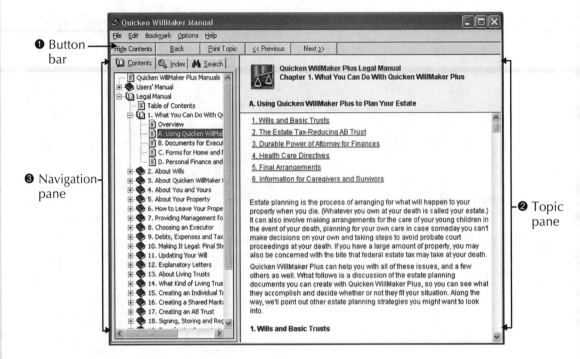

① Button bar

③ Navigation-pane

② Topic pane

① Button bar

The button bar at the top of the Quicken WillMaker Manual window contains the following buttons:

- **Show/Hide Contents.** Toggles the navigation pane, which provides access to the **Contents**, **Index** and **Search** tabs.
- **Back.** Takes you through the manual topics you have already viewed, in the reverse order in which you viewed them.
- **Print Topic.** Prints the manual topic you're currently viewing. (See Section 3, below.)
- **<< Previous.** Takes you to the previous topic in the current chapter. If you're viewing the first topic in the current chapter, it takes you to the last topic in the previous chapter.
- **Next >>.** Takes you to the next topic in the current chapter. If you're viewing the last topic in the current chapter, it takes you to the first topic in the next chapter.

② Topic pane

This is where the text of the manual is displayed. If necessary, use the scroll bar to view the entire topic. The area under the button bar tells you the book and chapter, as well as the name of the topic you're viewing. Many topics include underlined hypertext links to related topics and websites.

When you open the manual, you'll see only the topic pane.

③ Navigation pane

The navigation pane contains three tabs:

- **Contents.** Uses book/chapter/page structure to help you find a particular topic, and keeps track of what you're viewing in the topic pane.
- **Index.** Provides access to a master index of all subjects in both the Users' Manual and the Legal Manual.

• **Search.** Provides a full-text search of every page in both manuals.

When you open the manual, you will see only the topic pane. To see the navigation pane, click **Show Contents** in the button bar.

3. Printing From a Manual

To print out the single topic you're viewing, click the **Print Topic** button in the Quicken WillMaker Manual window's button bar.

You can also print out a complete chapter, or even a complete manual. To print an entire chapter or book:

1. Locate and open the Quicken WillMaker Plus folder in your **Programs Files** folder.
2. Double click the file "qwphelp.hlp." This opens the "Help Topics: Quicken WillMaker Plus Manual" window.
3. Select the manual or chapter you want to print by clicking on it. (If you're printing a chapter, you'll need to open a manual to select a chapter.)
4. Click the **Print** button. This will open a Windows Print dialog box.
5. Click the **Print** button.

Tip: Use the method above only for the Legal Manual. If you want to print the Users' Manual, we recommend you print the PDF version using Adobe Reader. (See Section 1, above.)

C. The Glossary Tab

While answering document interview questions or reading a Help topic, you may encounter a legal or estate planning term you're not familiar with. If this happens, you can look up the term in the glossary.

To look up the definition of a term you're not familiar with:

1. Click on the **Glossary** tab on the right side of the screen. At the top, you'll see all the letters of the alphabet, underlined. Directly below are all the glossary terms, underlined and in alphabetical order. This is the Glossary Index.
2. Click the letter that corresponds to the first letter of the word you want to learn about. You'll then see a list of all glossary terms that begin with that letter.
3. Scroll down to find the term you're interested in. Then, click it to see its definition.

Many of the definitions have underlined terms in them. Underlining indicates that those terms are also defined in the glossary.

• To view the definition of an underlined term, click on it.
• To return to the definition you were viewing before, click the underlined Glossary Index link at the top of the glossary, then repeat Steps 2 and 3.

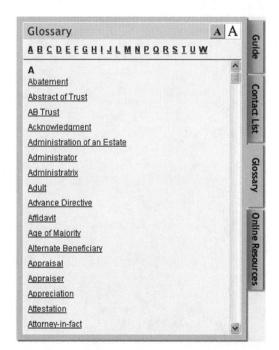

D. The Online Resources Tab

Use the **Online Resources** tab to find information, features and offers on the Internet. Click a link to view its Web page in a separate browser window. ■

Part 5: Creating Documents: The Quicken WillMaker Plus Interview

Quicken WillMaker Plus interviews you to get the information it needs to correctly generate your documents. In this part of the manual, we discuss how to create your documents using Quicken WillMaker Plus's interviews.

Each of the documents you can create has its own interview. (Chapter 1 of the online Legal Manual contains information about what kinds of documents you can create; Section B, below, discusses some technical issues involved with using this program to create different types of documents.) You can start or stop an interview at any time, or switch between interviews by clicking the **Document List** icon. However, we suggest that you work on one interview at a time to avoid confusion.

To take full advantage of Quicken WillMaker Plus:

- Take the time to read each question carefully, and read the Guide (on the right side of each interview screen) before you answer that screen's questions.
- If you need additional legal help, refer to the Legal Manual. (Relevant portions of the Legal Manual can be accessed through hyperlinks in the Guide. To access the full table of contents of the Legal Manual, choose **Quicken WillMaker Legal Manual** from the **Help** menu.)

A. The "Document Interview" Screen

To create a document, you'll answer a series of questions on Quicken WillMaker Plus's document interview screens.

1. The Five Elements of a Typical Interview Screen

Although no two interview screens are identical, most have the five elements described below.

❶ Interview text

Here is where you find information on what you're about to do and answer interview questions.

❷ Navigation bar icons

The navigation bar, which appears above the Guide in the upper right of every program screen, contains the following icons:

- **Legal Manual.** Use this icon to open the section of the Help file that contains all the legal and practical information you need to create your own legal documents. (See Part 4, Section B.)
- **Document List.** Use this icon to view the screen where you choose which document you want to work with. (See Part 3, Section B.)
- **Interview.** Use this icon to start the interview for a document selected on the "Document List" screen, or to return to the interview if you are previewing it on the "Print Preview" screen.

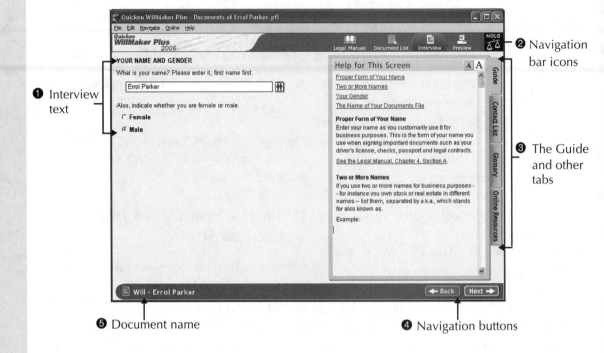

❶ Interview text

❷ Navigation bar icons

❸ The Guide and other tabs

❺ Document name

❹ Navigation buttons

• **Preview.** Use this icon to preview and print your final document. This icon is available only when you're viewing the "Congratulations" screen or the checklist of a completed document, or when a completed document is selected on the "Document List" screen.

The navigation bar icons also help you keep track of where you are in the process of using the program. For example, if you're viewing a document interview screen, the **Interview** icon is highlighted.

❸ The Guide and other tabs

This area, on the right side of every interview screen, provides legal information, practical tips and links to additional helpful resources. It is divided into four sections or tabs:

• **Guide.** Contains context-sensitive legal information you should read before leaving a screen or answering an interview question. (See Part 4, Section A.)

• **Contact List.** Contains all the names you've used in your document interviews. Names can be selected from the list and dropped into a name field of any interview question. (See Sections E3 and F, below.)

• **Glossary.** Contains definitions of important estate planning and legal terms. (See Part 4, Section C.)

• **Online Resources.** Contains links to helpful features and offers on the Internet.

To view one of these sections, just click on its tab. Note that all four tabs are not available on every interview screen.

❹ Navigation buttons

The **Back** and **Next** buttons move you forward and backward through the interview.

❺ Document name

This tells you the type of document you are currently working on (will, pet care agreement and so on) and its subject (the person writing the will, the pet to be cared for and so on).

2. Using Your Keyboard to Move Around an Interview Screen

To move from one object on the screen to another using your keyboard, press the TAB key until the keyboard focus moves to that object.

- If the focus is in a text-entry box, option button or list, use your keyboard to answer the question. (See Sections E and F, below.)
- If the focus is on the **Back** or **Next** button, press the ENTER key or the SPACEBAR to trigger the selected button. (See Section D, below.)

Note: You cannot use the TAB key to move the focus to the tabs on the right. You can, however, use your keyboard to move the focus to the tabs by using the keyboard shortcuts described in Appendix 2.

Using Default Buttons From Your Keyboard

If you see a highlighted button when you first visit a screen, this means it is the default button. To activate the default button, you can click it or press ENTER. For example, on the screen in which you choose your state, if the **Next** button is highlighted, press ENTER to move to the next screen.

If you prefer navigating with your keyboard, you can go to the next screen by choosing **Next** from the **Navigate** menu.

To use your keyboard to activate a button that is not the default button, press TAB until the button you want is highlighted, then press ENTER.

For a full list of keyboard shortcuts:
- choose **Keyboard Shortcuts** from the **Help** menu, or
- see Appendix 2 in this manual.

B. Special Characteristics of Estate Planning Document Interviews

With Quicken WillMaker Plus, you can create customized versions of more than 40 different documents. (See Chapter 1 of the Legal Manual for a discussion of all the forms and documents in this program. To view the Legal Manual, click on the **Legal Manual** icon in the navigation bar or open Quicken WillMaker Plus's **Help** menu.)

Because we've included such a wide variety of forms, it's natural that they should have significant differences. In other words, not all documents are created equal. Some documents are longer and more complex than others. While some require little prior knowledge or preparation to complete (for example, an authorization to let someone use your car), others require a bit of study and research on your part (for example, the living trust document).

At times these differences show up in the document interviews. In particular, the following estate planning documents have special characteristics you need to know about:

- will
- living trust (basic)
- living trust (AB)
- health care directive
- durable power of attorney for finances
- final arrangements form, and
- information for caregivers and survivors form.

For the documents listed above, you must go through several introductory, explanatory screens before you can start entering information. We also strongly recommend that you read all the Guide screens and Legal Manual topics for these documents in order to educate yourself about the tasks at hand and to help you make informed decisions while creating your documents. For the remaining documents, you can pretty much hit the ground running, answering the simpler interview questions without requiring extensive Guide help. For more on the Guide and online Legal Manual, see Part 4.

All of the documents listed above are discussed in Chapter 1, Section A, of the Legal Manual. To view the Legal Manual, click on the **Legal Manual** icon in the navigation bar or open the **Help** menu.

1. Interview Checklists

The interviews used to create the estate planning documents listed above contain checklists that divide the interview into sequential parts and help you keep track of where you are in the interview process. The other documents do not use checklists—their interviews are just a series of screens that must be completed in order. For more on interview checklists see Section D2, below.

2. Creating Duplicate and Multiple Documents in a Single Documents File

There's no limit to the number of documents of each type you can have in a single documents file. For non-estate planning forms and documents (that is, the forms and documents except those listed above), you can even create new versions of documents by duplicating and revising ones you've made previously. (See Section C3, below.)

Keep Just One of Each Estate Planning Document in a Documents File

Each documents file should contain no more than one version of each of the following estate planning documents:

- will
- living trust (basic)
- living trust (AB)
- health care directive (living will)
- durable power of attorney for finances, and
- final arrangements.

If more than one user is using the program to create estate planning documents (for example, you and your spouse each want to create your own will or health care directive), each should have a unique documents file. (See Part 3, Section A, on how to create additional documents files.)

If you want to change or revise an estate planning document you've already created—except a living trust (see below)—don't just create a new one in the same documents file as the original. It's better to:

- change or revise the original (see Part 7, Section C), or
- delete the original before creating a new one (see Section C1, below).

Living Trusts Are Different

Unlike the other Quicken WillMaker Plus estate planning documents, you cannot simply revise or delete a trust document that you have printed and signed. Also, if you're married, both spouses can choose to create one marital trust document together. For a detailed discussion on how to use the program to create living trusts, see Part 6.

C. Using the Document List to Select a Document

In this section, we discuss how to use Quicken WillMaker Plus's Document List to:

- create a new document
- open a document you've already created, or
- create a new document by duplicating one you've already created.

1. Creating a New Document

To create a new document:

1. Go to the "Document List" screen. If you're not already there, click the **Document List** icon in the navigation bar.
2. Use the drop-down menu to select a document category. If you don't know which category to select, choose "All Documents."
3. Select the document you want to make by clicking on it. As you select a document, a general description of that type of document is displayed to the right of the Document List.
4. Click the **Create Document** button below the document list.

Modifying an existing document. To modify a document you've already created, see Section 3, below.

Now your document interview begins. For information on answering document interview questions, see Section E, below.

2. Opening a Document You've Already Created

As you create your documents, they are automatically added to the Document List.

When Is a Document "Created"?

After you create your documents file (Part 3, Section A), you can create an unlimited number of documents that are stored in it. (Remember, as discussed in Section B, above, that you should create only one version of the key estate planning documents per documents file.)

In Quicken WillMaker Plus, a document is created only after you enter and save some information in a document interview.

So, if you merely select a document and read an introductory interview screen without answering a question and saving your answer, you have not yet "created" that document.

To open a document that you've already created:

1. Go to the "Document List" screen. If you're not already there, click the **Document List** icon in the navigation bar.
2. Use the drop-down menu to select "Documents You've Created."

3. Select the document you want to open by clicking on it. The documents you've created are listed in blue with the name of the document's subject (or author). When you select a document you've already created, the creation date is displayed below the Document List.
4. Click the **Open Document** button below the Document List.
   - *If you selected a document that uses a checklist,* you'll see the checklist for that document. (Checklists are discussed in Section D2, below.)
   - *If you selected a document that does not use a checklist,* you'll see the next interview screen for that document (that is, the screen where you left off).

3. Creating New Versions of Documents You've Already Created

If you haven't already completed a document. You can skip this section if you haven't created any documents yet.

This section explains how to create additional documents after you've already completed one of that type. For example, you created a temporary guardianship authorization for your daughter two months ago and now want to create a similar authorization for your son.

As discussed in Section B2, above, we recommend that you do not have more than one will, living trust, durable power of attorney for finances, health care directive or final arrangements document in your documents file. You therefore should not create additional versions of those documents using the methods described below.

With the remaining forms and documents, however, there's no limit to the number of documents of each type you can have in the same documents file. You have two options for creating an additional document of the same type as one you've created previously:

- create a new document from scratch, or
- reuse information you entered when you previously created a document of this type.

In most cases, you'll want to choose the second option. If this applies to you, skip ahead to Subsection b, below.

> EXAMPLE: You created a temporary guardianship authorization for your daughter two months ago and now want to create a similar document for your son. Much of the information in the two documents—for example, your personal contact information—will be the same. To save yourself the trouble of entering all that information from scratch, you can reuse information you entered for your daughter's authorization.

a. Creating a New Document From Scratch

In most cases, you will not want to choose this option, because you won't be able to make use of relevant information you entered in an earlier document interview.

Here's how to create a new document from scratch:

1. Go to the "Document List" screen. If you're not already there, click the **Document List** icon. (See Part 3, Section B.) At that screen,

you'll see a list of all documents you've already created. If that list is not displayed, use the drop-down menu to select "Documents You've Created."

2. Select the document you want to create. If you want to create a new document from scratch, make sure you select the document name and not the previously created document.

3. Click the **Create Document** button below the document list.

You'll then begin a new interview for that document.

b. Creating a New Document Using Information From a Previously Created Document

In most cases, you'll want to choose this option and make use of relevant personal information you entered in an earlier document interview, rather than start the interview from scratch. As discussed above, this method will not work with the key estate planning documents: will, living trust, durable power of attorney for finances, health care directive and final arrangements.

Here's how to create an additional document reusing personal information you entered previously:

1. Go to the "Document List" screen. If you're not already there, click the **Document List** icon. (See Part 3, Section B.) At that screen, you'll see a list of all documents you've already created. If that list is not displayed, use the drop-down menu to select "Documents You've Created."

2. The documents you've created are listed in blue, with the name of the document's subject (or author). When you select a document you've already created, its creation

date and status—in progress or completed—is displayed below the Document List. Select the document you want to use as the basis for a new document by clicking on it.

3. Open the **Edit** menu and select **Duplicate Document**. (If you select a will, health care directive, durable power of attorney for finances, final arrangements or living trust document, the **Edit** menu's **Duplicate Document** command will be unavailable.)

4. This will create a new listing for the duplicated document in the Document List, just below the one you selected in Step 2. Select that newly duplicated document. Notice that the creation date (below the Document List) is today's date.

5. Click the **Open Document** button.

The program then takes you to the first interview screen for that document. Each interview screen contains the same answers as the document that you duplicated.

Carefully review each interview screen's questions and your answers, changing your answers to suit the new document you are creating. To continue our example, if you are duplicating a temporary guardianship authorization for your daughter to make one for your son, you will at the minimum need to change some of the data on the "Information About Your Child" screen, such as the child's name and date of birth.

When the interview is over and you've entered all the required information, you'll see the "Congratulations" screen. From there you can print out your document. (For more on printing your documents, see Part 7.)

D. Navigating Through a Document Interview

Each document interview takes you through a series of screens that explain the legal and practical issues pertaining to the document and then ask you questions.

- To move through the interview from screen to screen, click **Next**.
- To backtrack one screen at a time, click **Back**.
- To switch to a different document interview, click the **Document List** icon in the navigation bar in the upper right of the interview screen.

1. If You Can't Go Farther

Some information requested by the program is optional, and you can go on to the next screen without giving an answer. However, at certain points, you must answer a question before you can continue to the next screen. In such cases, if you try to go farther without answering, an alert will pop up stating that you must give an answer.

If you are unable to or don't want to answer yet, you can:

- answer as best you can now, and return to it later to change it
- switch to another document by clicking the **Document List** icon, or
- quit the program and return to the interview later. (When you return to the document, the interview will pick up where it left off.)

Generally it's a good idea to take the time to answer questions correctly the first time, because often the questions you are asked later in the interview are determined by the answers you've given earlier.

Going Backwards

If you need to backtrack though the interview, you can go back only one screen at a time. When you return to a screen where you made a choice or entered data, your answer is displayed.

Because the program does not record your answer until you click **Next**, if you change or enter an answer and then click **Back**, you are warned that your answer or change will not be saved. If you want to save your answer, you must click **Next** to move one screen forward. Then you can back up to previous screens if you need to.

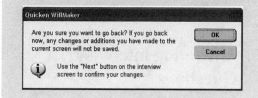

steps (or parts) involved in creating your document. Each document that uses a checklist has a different number of parts. In addition, the number of parts for a specific document can vary depending on your previous answers.

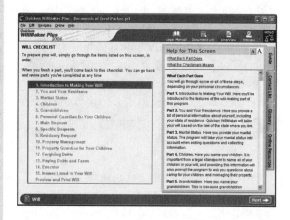

You must go through each part in order. To work on a part, select it and click **Next**. After you complete that part, the program returns you to the checklist.

The final listed item is **Preview and Print**, which can be selected only after all the previous parts have been completed.

2. Using Interview Checklists to Track Your Progress

Not all documents use checklists. Only the following document interviews use checklists: will, health care directive, durable power of attorney for finances, final arrangements form, information for caregivers and survivors form and living trust. If you're interested in creating any other type of document, you can skip this section.

After you select the kind of estate planning document you want to make, you'll come to its checklist. The checklist divides the interview into

a. Why Some Parts Are Dimmed

As you complete a document, you will notice that some parts of the checklist are dimmed.

Parts you haven't come to yet. You must complete the interview in the proper order. The parts are numbered sequentially, so those that come after the one you're currently working on are dimmed. The listed parts become available for selection one by one, as you complete each interview part. After you have entered all the information needed to create your document, completing each part on the checklist as it becomes available, you can preview or print out your document. (See Part 7.)

> ### The Information for Caregivers and Survivors Form Is Different
>
> Unlike the other document interviews that have checklists, the caregivers and survivors form interview does not need to be completed sequentially. Although you must go through the introductory section first, you can then enter information into the other parts in any order you choose.

Parts that don't apply because of choices you've previously made. In some interviews, you will find that your checklist skips a part, and that the part that is skipped is dimmed. This is because, based on your previous answers, you do not need to do that part of the interview.

> EXAMPLE: In Part 4 of the will interview, Stanley Glick enters the information that he has no children. As a result, he does not need to complete Part 6—the section where you can name a personal guardian for your children—which will now always remain dimmed.

b.   What the Checkmarks Mean

A checkmark appears next to each part that you've completed—that is, you've entered all the required information. If you begin an interview part but leave without completing it, that part will not be checked when you return to the checklist. You will not be able to start the next part before completing the unfinished one.

c.   Returning to a Part of the Interview

You can return to any part of the interview you have already been through to review your answers, even if you have not completed all parts of the entire interview. As you go through the screens again, the answers you entered previously are visible.

d.   Printing Your Completed Document

When you've completed a document interview, **Preview and Print**, the final item on the checklist, will be available. If you select this button and click **Next**, you'll come to the "Congratulations" screen. From there you can preview, print or export your document. For more on previewing, printing and exporting your documents, see Part 7.

E.   Answering Interview Questions

Quicken WillMaker Plus asks questions in a variety of ways. Some questions are multiple choice—that is, you choose your answer from several options. Others require you to type in an answer. And some questions require you to create a list or add information to items that already appear in a list.

This section explains, in general terms, how to answer these different question formats. Instructions on how to answer specific questions are found on each interview screen.

The program does not record (or save) your answer until you click **Next**. So, if you change or enter an answer and then click **Back**, you are warned that your answer or change will not be saved.

If you have already answered an interview
question but want to change your answer,
click the **Back** button until you see the question that you want.

After you change your answer, click **Next**
to confirm your new answer and move forward.

You can also review and change answers
at the end of the interview, as described in
Part 7, Section C.

1. Multiple Choice Questions

If a question requires you to select your answer
from several choices, it can take the form of
option buttons (radio buttons), a list or check
boxes.

Option buttons (radio buttons). To choose an
answer with an option (or radio) button, click on
the button. If an option is already selected when
you first come to the screen, make sure it's the
answer you want to give. If not, change it by
clicking on a different button. You can also make
a selection by using the ARROW keys on your keyboard.

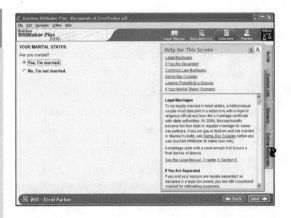

Pick lists. On the screen where you select your
state, make your choice by clicking your state in
the list. Use the scroll bar or ARROW keys to see
the entire list. You can also type the first letter of
what you want. This will move the selection bar to
the first list item that begins with that letter. Then,
use the ARROW keys, if necessary, to select the list
item you want.

Check boxes. A few interview screens have check
boxes you use to choose from one or more listed
options. Clicking on a check box marks the box

with a ✓, or clears the ✓ if it is already checked. You can press the TAB key to select a check box item, and then press the SPACEBAR to mark the item with a ✓ (or clear it).

Remember that clicking another check box does not automatically deselect a previous choice. You must select or deselect each choice one at a time.

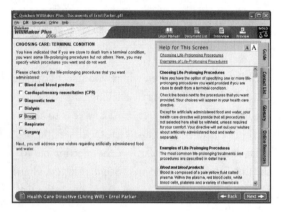

Drop-down lists. Some interview screens have drop-down lists to help you select from a set of options. Click the arrow to the right of the list, then use the scroll bar or ARROW keys to see the entire list.

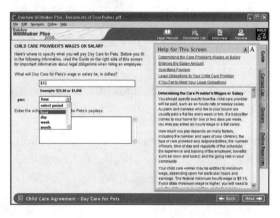

2. Fill-in-the-Blank Questions

Some screens require you to type in information —such as a name, address, fraction, date or description of an item of property. At these screens, the box where you enter the requested information has a blinking cursor in it. If the cursor is not blinking in the box, click in the box to put the cursor there. You can also use the TAB key to move the cursor into a text-entry box. To enter your answer, just start typing. If you're asked for a date, click the "calendar" icon to the right of the date field to select the month, day, and year.

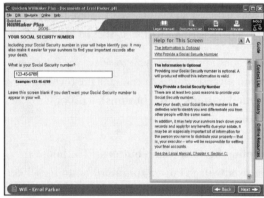

Note: Some screens may appear to have a text-entry box which is actually a list. You can't type directly into such a list. If you see a button called **Add to List** on the same screen, you know that the box is a list—not a fill-in-the-blank text box. See Section 4, below, for instructions on using lists.

Entering Multiple Names in a Multiline Text Box
If your answer can contain more than one name, you need to enter each name on a separate line. To start a new line for an additional name, make sure your cursor is in the text-entry box and press ENTER. (On most screens *without* multiline text

boxes, pressing ENTER will trigger the default navigation button.)

To insert multiple names that have already been entered into your document file, use the **Contact List** icon. (See Section 3b, below.) Each interview screen that lets you enter multiple names includes instructions on how to do so.

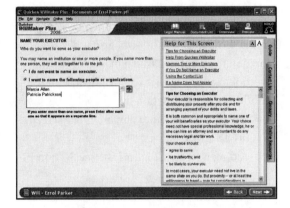

3. Special Considerations for Entering Names

Throughout the interviews, you are asked to type in names of family members, friends you want to inherit your property and so on.

The program keeps track of every name you enter and stores it in the Contact List. Using this list, the program checks your answers for logical inconsistencies and alerts you if a name entered in one place can't be used there based on answers you've given earlier.

To enable Quicken WillMaker Plus to perform its error checking correctly, certain rules shoud be followed.

a. Basic Rules for Entering Names

- Use full names, first name first.
- Be consistent—use the same exact name for a person or organization throughout the document interview. For example, don't use a full name (or title) in one answer and a nickname (or abbreviation) in another. The program will assume they are different and will add both to the Contact List. If you have entered the same name using different capitalization, you are asked which capitalization is correct.
- Carefully check the spelling of all names before you leave the screen. The program assumes different spellings are different people and adds both names to the Contact List. Misspelled names can be corrected by choosing **Manage Contact List...** from the **Edit** menu. (See Section F, below, for more information.)
- As you type in a name, Quicken WillMaker Plus automatically checks the Contact List for similar names. When it finds a match based on the letters you've already typed, it automatically completes the rest of the name. It does not always guess correctly, however, especially if the Contact List contains more than one person with the same first name.
- If a name is filled in automatically after you've typed in a few characters, carefully check that it's the name you want to enter. If it isn't, continue typing the correct name.
- To turn off the "automatic completion" feature, open the **Edit** menu and select **Preferences....**
- Enter only one name per line. To begin a new line for an additional name, follow the onscreen instructions.

• Whenever possible, use the Contact List to paste in names that you've entered previously, as described below.

b. Entering Names From the Contact List

Any name in your Contact List can be pasted into a name field, so you won't need to retype it. (See Section F, below, for details.)

There are several ways to paste a name from the Contact List.

Using the Contact List Icon

This method can be used whenever you see the **Contact List** icon, shown below, next to a name field.

1. Click the **Contact List** icon. This opens a menu listing all the names you've previously entered in every document in your documents file.
2. Select the name you want to paste by clicking it. That name is pasted into the name field.

Using the Contact List Tab

1. Click on the **Contact List** tab on the right side of the screen. You'll see a list of all names you've entered during your document interviews. (**Note:** Names you've just added on the current screen do not appear on the list until you click **Next** and move to the next interview screen.)
2. Select the name you want to paste by clicking it. The mouse pointer will change to show that the name has been copied from the list.
3. Move the pointer to the field you want the name to go in.

4. Click anywhere in the field to paste the name there.

Automatically Inserting Additional Information

If you have already entered additional information for a person or organization—such as birth date, address or phone number—that information is automatically inserted into the relevant interview fields whenever you enter the person's or organization's name in any document interview. This is because all this information is already stored in the Contact List database. Automatic insertion occurs whether you originally entered the additional information by:

• typing it directly into any interview screen (as described above)
• adding it to the Contact List (see Section F1, below), or
• importing Contact List data from another documents file (see Section F2, below).

> ⚠ **Revising information that is automatically inserted.** Be aware that, if you revise any information after it is automatically inserted from the Contact List, it gets changed not only in the document you're working on, but in every Quicken WillMaker Plus document in which that information is used.

4. Using Lists

Document interviews occasionally require you to enter your answers in a list. For example, you may be asked to list the names of your children or grandchildren. Other times, you'll see a list that was compiled based on previous answers. For example, the "List of Names" screen at the end of the will interview includes every name you've entered in that interview. You may be prompted to add to a list or to select a listed item and enter additional information about that selection.

This section explains in general terms how to use the different kinds of lists found in the program. Each list screen contains more detailed instructions on how to use its particular list.

a. Using Buttons in General

When you first see some list screens, the list may be empty and look like an empty box. The default button is **Add to List…**.

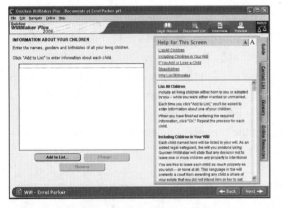

After clicking this button, you're asked to answer one or more questions in a pop-up dialog box. For example, after clicking Add to List… on the "Your Children's Names and Birthdates" screen, you're asked to enter the child's name, gender and date of birth.

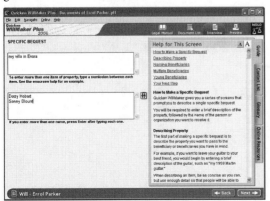

After you've entered the required information, click **OK** to close the dialog box and return to the list, which now includes the name you just entered. You can then use the other buttons on this screen to:

- add a new item to the list
- change an existing item, or
- remove an existing item from the list.

To change any part of your answer or remove a listed name entirely, first select it by clicking it and then click the appropriate button. If the **Change** or **Remove** button is dimmed and unavailable, it's because you haven't yet made a selection from the list. If the list is large, use the scroll bar or the UP and DOWN ARROW keys to see the entire list.

b. Lists for Entering More Information

At certain points in the will interview, you'll be asked to enter more information about names that you have already entered. The names appear in a list box.

To add the requested information for a specific name, you must:

1. Select the name from the list by clicking it.
2. Click the appropriate button that lets you add the requested information. (Each screen will have its own instructions for this.) This will open a corresponding dialog box.
3. Add the requested information in the dialog box and click **OK**.

When you return to the list, it will indicate in some manner that the data was entered. Different lists use different indicators depending on the situation. You'll need to repeat this process for each listed name for which you want to add information.

EXAMPLE: In your will, you name your nieces Dotty Hobart and Sonny Blount to receive your villa in Evora. You are next asked whether you want them to share the property in equal or unequal proportions. If you select unequal shares, you'll see a list of the beneficiaries named (Dotty and Sonny) for that property, and you will be asked to specify a share for each of them.

To do this, (1) select Dotty's name from the list by clicking on it; (2) click the **Specify Share** button to open the Beneficiary's Share dialog box; (3) type in the fractional share (⅔); and (4) click **OK** to close the dialog box and return to the list of beneficiaries. Next to Dotty's name is "⅔," indicating the share that was entered. Repeat this process for Sonny, entering her share as ⅓. When both shares have been specified, click **Next** to continue the interview.

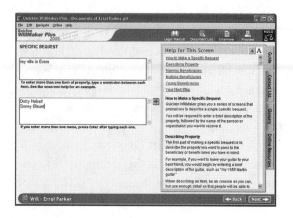

Each time you finish entering the required information, you return to the bequest list, which now includes all the bequests you have made, numbered in the order entered. To help you keep track of what you've given to whom, you can view bequests by property or beneficiary by clicking the **Property** or **Beneficiary** button below the bequest list.

c. Lists of Specific Bequests or Gifts

In the will interview, you have the option of making specific bequests of property. For each bequest, you are asked a series of questions on several different screens. When a bequest is complete, you're returned to a screen that lists the bequests you've made so far. From here you can add more bequests; if you do, you'll be asked the same series of questions for each additional bequest.

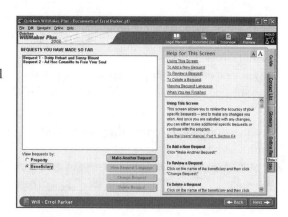

Use the other buttons on this screen to:
- make another bequest
- view how the complete bequest will be worded in your will
- change the information contained in an existing bequest, or
- delete the bequest.

To make a new bequest, simply click the **Make Another Bequest** button. You'll repeat the series of screens you used to make your first bequest.

To change, delete or view a bequest, you must first select a bequest from the list, then click the appropriate button.

When you've finished making all the specific bequests you want to make, click **Next**.

EXAMPLE: Your first bequest is to leave your Barbie doll collection to your niece Gloria Sadowski. You proceed through a series of screens in which you describe the property ("my Barbie collection"), enter Gloria's name and name who should get it if Gloria does not survive you.

When you have finished, "Bequest 1" is added to the bequest list. You can view the bequest by property (Bequest 1—my Barbie collection) or by beneficiary (Bequest 1—Gloria Sadowski). To view this bequest as it will appear in your will, select it, then click **View Bequest Language**.

To make another bequest, click the **Make Another Bequest** button to cycle through the questions again. When you're finished making specific bequests, click **Next** and continue on to the next part of the interview.

Specific Gifts in Your Living Trust

As in the will document, you also have the option of making gifts of individual items of property to specific people or organizations in the living trust interview. In the living trust interview, however, you are asked to first list all the property you want to "hold" in the trust before you specify beneficiaries. (For more on making gifts in your trust documents, see Part 4 of Chapters 15, 16 and 17 of the Legal Manual. To view the Legal Manual, click on the **Legal Manual** icon in the navigation bar or open the **Help** menu.)

F. Adding to and Revising the Contact List

As discussed in Section E3, above, the Contact List allows you to enter previously entered names without typing. In this section you'll learn how to:
- add names directly to the Contact List, one at a time
- enter additional information about each name
- modify existing Contact List entries
- import batches of names from other documents files, and
- print out names and information stored in the Contact List.

1. Adding Names Directly to the Contact List

The program automatically adds names of people and organizations to your documents file's Contact List any time you enter a name during a document interview. Whenever you click **Next** to go to the next screen, the program (1) checks the Contact List to see if you've entered any names that weren't already in the list, and (2) if so, adds those names to the list.

You can also add names to the Contact List at any time by choosing **Manage Contact List…** from the **Edit** menu. You can do this in order to:

- enter all the names you intend to use ahead of time, so you can easily paste them from the Contact List later, or
- add information about a person or organization, such as an address and phone number. This information can be automatically inserted into other Quicken WillMaker Plus documents. (See Section E3, above.)

When you choose the **Manage Contact List…** command, the Manage Contact List dialog box appears.

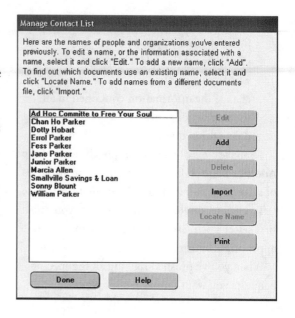

Manage Contact List

Here are the names of people and organizations you've entered previously. To edit a name, or the information associated with a name, select it and click "Edit." To add a new name, click "Add". To find out which documents use an existing name, select it and click "Locate Name." To add names from a different documents file, click "Import."

Ad Hoc Committe to Free Your Soul
Chan Ho Parker
Dotty Hobart
Errol Parker
Fess Parker
Jane Parker
Junior Parker
Marcia Allen
Smallville Savings & Loan
Sonny Blount
William Parker

Edit
Add
Delete
Import
Locate Name
Print

Done   Help

- To add a new name to the list, click **Add**. Another dialog box will appear in which you can enter the name as well as other information (address, gender, phone numbers) for this name.
- To change the information associated with an already-listed name, or to enter missing contact information in any field, select the name and click **Edit**. Another dialog box will appear in which you can add or revise information (address, gender, phone numbers) for this name. To change the spelling of the name, you must click the **Edit Name** button.

Note: You can also add information about any person or organization using the **Contact List** tab. Just double click on a name to open the dialog box for adding or changing information associated with that name.

- To remove a name that isn't actively used in any of your Quicken WillMaker Plus documents, select the name and click **Delete**. There is no "undo" for this feature, so use it carefully.
- To import names from other Quicken WillMaker Plus documents files, click **Import**. (For more on importing Contact List data, see Section 2, below.)
- To view help on using this dialog box, click **Help**.
- To close this dialog box, click **Done**.

2. Importing Contact List Data From Another Documents File

The end user license agreement allows other members of your family to use the program to create their own documents. They do this by creating their own documents files. (See Part 3, Section A1.)

Because spouses and other family members have relatives and friends in common, we've designed the program so that Contact List data can be imported from one documents file into another.

To import names from another Quicken WillMaker Plus documents file:

1. Choose **Manage Contact List...** from the **Edit** menu. This opens the Manage Contact List dialog box.
2. Click **Import**. You'll then see the "Select the file you want to import names from:" dialog box.

3. Locate and select the Quicken WillMaker Plus documents file you want to import name data from. (Documents files have the .pfl file extension.)
4. Click **Open**.
5. At the prompt that tells you how many names you've imported, click **OK**.

When you import names, only those names *not* already in your documents file are added.

3. Revising Information in the Contact List

To change the information associated with an already-listed name or enter missing contact information into any field, choose **Manage Contact List...** from the **Edit** menu. This opens the Manage Contact list dialog box. Select the name you want to revise information about and click **Change**. Another dialog box will appear in which you can enter other information (address, gender, phone numbers) for this name. To change the spelling of the name, you must click the **Edit Name** button.

While the Manage Contact List dialog box is open, you can:

- remove any names that aren't actively used in any of your Quicken WillMaker Plus documents by clicking **Delete** (there is no undo for this feature, so use it carefully)
- import names from documents files created by Quicken WillMaker Plus and other compatible programs by clicking **Import** (see Section 2, above), or
- view help on using this dialog box by clicking **Help**.

To close the Manage Contact List dialog box, click **Done**.

Revising Information Using the Contact List Tab

You can also add extra information about any person or organization by using the **Contact List** tab. Just double click on a name to open the dialog box for adding or changing information associated with that name. If you change information that was already entered in your documents file, the change will appear in all documents in which that information is used.

4. Locating a Name in Your Documents

To locate every document in your documents file in which a particular name is used, choose **Manage Contact List...** from the **Edit** menu. This opens the Manage Contact List dialog box. Select the name you want to locate and click **Locate Name**. You'll then see a dialog box listing each document in your documents file that contains the selected name.

5. Printing the Contact List

If you'd like to print out all the names and information in the Contact List for your documents file, here's how:

1. Go to any document interview screen and click on the **Contact List** tab.
2. Choose **Print Contact List** from the **File** menu. You'll then see a standard Print dialog box.
3. Click **OK** to send the list to your printer.

G. When You Complete an Interview

When you've completed a document interview, the program has all the information it needs to assemble and print your document. What happens next depends on whether the interview you have completed uses a checklist to divide the interview into numbered parts. (Checklists are discussed in Section D2, above.)

- If the document interview uses a checklist, **Preview and Print** (the last item in the checklist) will now be available. Select **Preview and Print** and click **Next** to view the "Congratulations" screen.
- If the document interview does not use a checklist, you'll go directly to the "Congratulations" screen.

For more information about the "Congratulations" screen, and how to view, print and export your document, see Part 7.

Opening a Completed Document

If you open a document you've already completed (as described in Section C2, above), you'll either go directly to the "Congratulations" screen or to that document's checklist (if the selected document uses a checklist in its interview).

The exception is the living trust document. If you open a completed trust document that you've already printed out, you'll see some screens that require you to answer a few questions about whether and when you signed the document. This is explained in detail in Part 6, Section C.

Part 6: Creating a Living Trust

Because of the nature of living trusts, creating a trust document using Quicken WillMaker Plus is a little different from creating other Quicken WillMaker Plus documents. (If you haven't done so already, we strongly suggest that you read Chapters 13 and 14 of the Legal Manual *before* you begin working on your living trust document. To view the Legal Manual, just click on the **Legal Manual** icon in the navigation bar or open the **Help** menu.) Correspondingly, there are some aspects of the living trust document interview that are different as well. In this part of the manual, we highlight some special issues involved with using the program to create a living trust.

A. Choosing the Type of Trust You Want to Create

Your first step is to select the type of living trust you want to make. You do this on the "Document List" screen. (See Part 5, Section C, on creating documents.) You can choose from two kinds of living trusts:

- a basic trust, or
- an AB trust.

If you need help in deciding which type of trust to create, read Chapter 14 of the Legal Manual. To view the Legal Manual, just click on the **Legal Manual** icon in the navigation bar or open the **Help** menu.

After you make your selection, you'll begin the document interview. As discussed in Part 5, Section B, the living trust is one of the estate planning documents that uses a checklist to guide you through its interview.

B. Issues in the Living Trust Interview

Here are some issues that you may come across during the document interview for creating and revising your living trust documents.

1. Both Spouses Must Enter Information

To create a basic shared trust or an AB trust for a married couple, both spouses must enter the required information separately. That's why Parts 4-6 of the interview checklist for the living trust for married couples have separate items assigned to the husband and the wife. For example, Part 4 has separate items for both the Beneficiaries of the Wife's Trust (4a) and Beneficiaries of the Husband's Trust (4b):

- Although the wife's items (4a, 5a and 6a) are listed before the corresponding husband's items (4b, 5b and 6b), the wife is not required to enter her information before her spouse does. When you come to any of the checklist parts that have separate items for both spouses, you can select the husband's or the wife's item in the order you prefer.
- Nor are both spouses required to complete both their respective items before either can go on to the next part of the interview. For example, after the wife completes Part 4a (Beneficiaries of the Wife's Trust), Part 5a (Wife's Residuary Beneficiaries) will be available for selection whether or not the husband has completed Part 4b (Beneficiaries of the Husband's Trust).

- However, both spouses must complete all items before the completed document can be displayed and printed. (For more on printing documents, see Part 7.)

2. Changing Your State

As with many Quicken WillMaker Plus documents—especially the will, durable power of attorney for finances and health care directives—changing your state has important legal ramifications. While laws that govern living trusts, and property ownership in particular, vary from state to state, your living trust remains valid if you prepare it in one state and then move to another. For information on how moving to a different state affects your living trust, see the Legal Manual, Chapter 20, Section A7.

At the beginning of the trust interview, you are asked to select the state where you reside. If for some reason you later want to change your selection, you will not be able to do so by returning to the screen where you initially made it.

- **If you haven't yet signed your document,** you'll need to delete your in-progress trust document and start a new one. Because the trust has not yet taken effect, doing this won't cause any legal problems for you.

- **If you have already signed your document,** the only way to change your state is by revoking your living trust and creating a new one.

3. Putting Property Into the Trust

After entering information about you, your spouse (if applicable) and your trustee(s), you'll come to Part 3 of the living trust document interview, where you list all the property you plan to transfer into your living trust. For each item of property you list, you'll be asked to:

- describe it
- indicate which spouse owns it or if it's jointly owned, and
- state whether or not there is a title document for it.

The property you enter here will appear in a document called a "property schedule," which you must attach to your trust document. In an individual trust, this document is called Schedule A. In a shared basic trust or AB trust, there are three schedules, labeled A, B and C—one for co-owned property and one for each spouse's solely owned property. The program keeps track of all the property you enter and adds it to the appropriate property schedule.

⚠️ **Property ownership laws for married couples are tricky.** Some items you may think are owned separately by one spouse may, in fact, be owned jointly by both spouses—especially if you live in a community property state. (See Part 3 of Chapter 15, 16 or 17 of the Legal Manual. To view the Legal Manual, click on the **Legal Manual** icon in the navigation bar or open the **Help** menu.)

After you've listed all the property you want to transfer, you'll come to the part of the interview where you choose beneficiaries for the listed trust property—that is, who will receive the property after you pass away.

4. Changing Property Ownership After Naming a Beneficiary

If you are a married couple making a shared trust, and have named different beneficiaries for different items in Part 4, be careful about re-entering Part 3 to change property ownership.

To see what will happen if you change the designation of who owns an item of property, see the table below.

If you do change any ownership designations in Part 3, return to Part 4 and review all the gifts you previously entered.

Effects of Changing Property Ownership		
If the property was ...	**and is now ...**	**then ...**
Co-owned	Wife's	The property item will be deleted from any gifts entered by Husband.
Co-owned	Husband's	The property item will be deleted from any gifts entered by Wife.
Husband's	Wife's	The property item will be deleted from any gifts entered by Husband. Wife should reenter Part 4 and designate beneficiaries for the property.
Wife's	Husband's	The property item will be deleted from any gifts entered by Wife. Husband should reenter Part 4 and designate beneficiaries for the property.
Wife's	Co-owned	Husband should reenter Part 4b and name beneficiaries for the property.
Husband's	Co-owned	Wife should reenter Part 4a and name beneficiaries for the property.

5. After Completing and Printing Your Trust Document

There are important tasks you must complete after finalizing and printing your trust. Be sure to read Chapters 18 and 19 of the Legal Manual to learn the additional steps to take to make your trust legally binding. (To view the Legal Manual, click on the **Legal Manual** icon in the navigation bar or open the **Help** menu.)

C. Amending and Revoking Your Living Trust

Other Quicken WillMaker Plus documents can be revised or modified at any time, and you can safely print out the new version. The living trust documents, however, are different.

After they are printed and signed, you can make revisions only by either amending or revoking them. These processes are explained below.

1. Opening a Trust Document That You've Already Printed or Exported

After you print out a copy of your trust document, the next time you open that document you'll be asked if you have signed your trust document.

If you open a trust document that has been printed, you'll see the "Welcome Back" screen. Here you're asked whether you have signed the trust document that you previously printed.

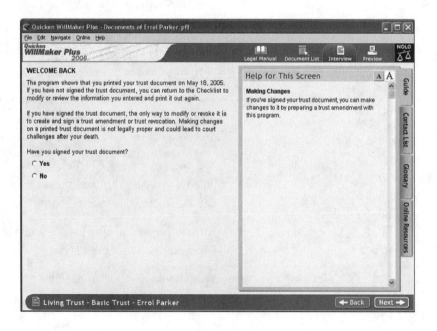

Why This Question Is Important

As explained in Chapter 18 of the Legal Manual (to view the Legal Manual, click on the **Legal Manual** icon in the navigation bar or open the **Help** menu), your declaration of trust has no legal effect until you print it and sign it. If you have not signed your declaration of trust, you can tear it up and print out a new copy at any time, with no legal consequences. Think of the unsigned copies as drafts.

On the other hand, if you have signed your declaration of trust, you can make changes to your trust only by printing and signing a separate document called a trust amendment. (See Section 2, below.) You can also revoke your trust by printing and signing a document called a trust revocation. (See Section 3, below.)

If you click **No** (you have not signed the document), the program assumes that you have printed only a draft copy and returns you to the checklist. From there you can make further modifications or print a final copy.

If you click **Yes** (you have signed the document), you'll be asked to enter the date on which you signed it.

This date is used to identify and name the trust you are about to amend or revoke. For example, if the Glicks signed their declaration of trust on June 29, 2005, the title of their first amendment to the trust would be "Amendment to the Glick Revocable Living Trust Dated June 29, 2005."

Once you enter the date you signed the document and click **Next**, the program saves that information in your documents file and "freezes" the original trust data that was used in your signed, legally binding declaration of trust.

From this point on, you cannot modify your original declaration of trust or print out another signable version of the original document. You can, however, print out unsignable duplicates of your original. (See Section 4, below.) Any additional changes you make to your trust data are used to generate new trust amendments.

⚠️ **If you exported your original trust document.** If you exported your original trust document, changed some of its language and signed the modified copy (see Part 7, Section E), then you cannot use the program to make amendments to your living trust.

Trust amendments must be precisely worded to exactly match the text of the original document. If you modified the exported document, the amendments you make with the program won't match the trust document you signed and may cause legal problems for you and your heirs.

Next, you must choose whether to amend, revoke or print out a duplicate of your original trust. If you are revoking your trust, skip ahead to Section 3, below.

2. Amending Your Living Trust

Making trust amendments involves entering the same kind of information as you did in the trust document interview. If you choose to amend your trust document, you'll come to the "Amendment Menu" screen.

a. Using the "Amendment Menu" Screen

The "Amendment Menu" screen is similar to the checklist you used to create your original trust document. The options available on the "Amendment Menu" screen correspond to Parts 2 through 6 of the Living Trust checklist. Note, however, these important differences:

- The parts where you entered your name and state are not listed, so you cannot change these by amendment. If you need to change one of these parts, you will have to revoke your trust and create a new one.

- All remaining parts are available for selection at all times. You can make as few or as many changes as you want, in any order you wish. The **Preview and Print** item, however, remains dimmed and unavailable until you have changed or added new information to your trust document.

- Checkmarks do not appear next to the parts on the Amendment Menu after you've made a change or entered new information.

To amend any part of your trust document:

1. Select the part where you want to make the change.

2. Click **Next**.

3. Find the interview screen with the answer you want to change, and make your change.

4. Click **Next** to save that revision.

Repeat those steps to make additional revisions. When you're done, you can print the amendment by first selecting **Preview and Print** on the Amendment Menu and then clicking **Next**.

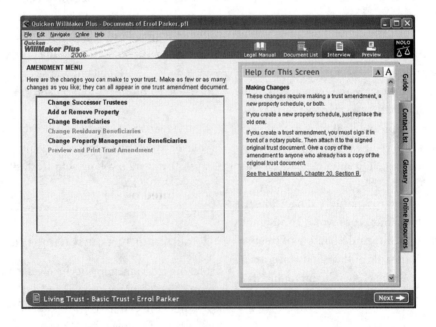

b. Adding or Removing Property

Adding or removing items of property by amendment (or editing a property description) involves the same basic steps you took when you listed the property in Part 4 of the original document interview. There are, however, some notable differences:

- If you add an item of property by amendment, it is listed on screen with an indicator to show that it was not included in your original schedule(s) of trust property.
- You cannot edit the description of an item that was included in your original trust document. If you want to change a property description, you'll need to first delete that item from the property list and then add a new item with the correct description. If you do this, be sure to name a beneficiary for this property item.
- You can, however, change the ownership designation of an item that was included in your original trust document. For example, you can change the ownership designation from Husband to Co-owned or from Co-owned to Wife. (See Section B4, above.)

Make sure you carefully read all the information and warning screens before you make any changes.

If You Add or Remove Property

Remember to Transfer the Property

- If you add property to your living trust, you must transfer ownership of it to your living trust.
- If you remove property from the list, remember to transfer it out of the living trust. (See Chapter 20 of the Legal Manual. To view the Legal Manual, click on the **Legal Manual** icon in the navigation bar or open the **Help** menu.)

Review All the Gifts Made in the Original Trust Document

- If your living trust is set up to give different property to different beneficiaries, you can name beneficiaries for the items of property that you are adding to the trust. To do this, select **Change Beneficiaries** from the Amendment Menu.
- If you delete all items of trust property, you won't be able to display or print an amendment. Your trust must contain at least one item of trust property owned or co-owned by each trust maker.

---

c. Opening an Amended Trust Document That You've Already Printed or Exported

The next time you open your amended trust document by selecting it from the document list, you will be asked if you have signed the trust amendment that you printed.

- If you answer **No**, you will be able to modify this amendment further and print it out again.

- If you answer **Yes**, you'll be asked to enter the date you signed the amendment. At that point, the trust document data will again be "frozen," incorporating the changes in your signed trust amendment. You will then be asked if you want to revoke or amend your trust. If you select the latter, any further changes to your trust document will generate a new trust amendment.

3. Revoking Your Living Trust

Be sure to read Chapter 20 of the Legal Manual before you revoke your trust. (To view the Legal Manual, click on the **Legal Manual** icon in the navigation bar or open the **Help** menu.)

After you choose to revoke your trust, read the preliminary information screens.

If the trust you are revoking is a shared basic trust or an AB trust, select who will sign the revocation, then click **Next**.

You'll next see the "Review and Print Your Trust Revocation" screen. Use this screen to display and print your revocation. (See Part 7 for more on printing and displaying your completed documents.)

4. Printing a Duplicate of the Original Trust

If you select **Print Original Trust Document**, you'll go to Quicken WillMaker Plus's "Print Preview" screen, where your original trust document is displayed. To print a duplicate copy of your original trust document:

1. Click the **Print** icon on the left. You'll then see a standard Print dialog box.
2. Click **OK**.

The printout will have a "Duplicate" watermark on it to show that it is not the original document that you signed earlier. *Don't sign this duplicate.* Because trusts are commonly referred to by the dates on which they are signed—for example, "The Harold R. Smith Revocable Living Trust, dated January 27, 20xx"—signing a duplicate trust document (even though it's identical to the original) would create confusion.

For more on using the "Print Preview" screen and printing documents, see Part 7.

D. Creating a Certification or Abstract of Trust

A certification or abstract of trust is a shorter version of your trust document that can be used to show a bank or other financial institution that your trust exists. (For more on certificates of trust, see Chapter 19 of the Legal Manual. To view the Legal Manual, click on the **Legal Manual** icon in the navigation bar or open the **Help** menu.) You can only create a certification or abstract *after* you've completed the actual trust document.

After selecting to create this document at the "Document List" screen, you will be asked to enter information about the living trust document for which you will be creating the certification. ∎

Part 7: Displaying and Printing Your Completed Documents

Once you have completed all parts of a document interview, the program has the information it needs to assemble and print your document. When this happens, you'll come to a "Congratulations" screen informing you that your document is complete.

Note: If the document interview uses a checklist, you must select **Preview and Print** (the last item on the checklist) and click **Next** in order to view the "Congratulations" screen.

At this point, you can view your completed document and print it out.

Additional Printing Instructions

- For instructions on how to print out topics displayed in the Guide tab, see Part 4, Section A.
- For instructions on how to print out the Contact List, see Part 5, Section F5.
- For instructions on how to print out topics in the online manual, see Part 4, Section B.

A. Displaying Your Final Documents

Before you print your final document, you can review it on the screen to be sure it's correct. To do this, click the **Preview and Print** button (on the left) or the **Preview** icon (in the navigation bar) on the "Congratulations" screen.

1. What Documents Are Displayed

Each document interview actually produces a set of related documents, including instructions on how to sign the document and make it legal. Signing instructions, however, are not shown in the "Print Preview" window; you can see the signing instructions only when you print your document.

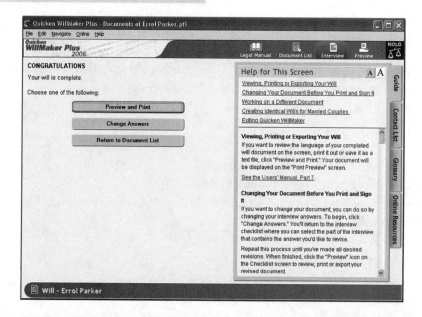

Choosing Which Will, DPAF or Living Trust Documents to Print, Preview or Export

When you print your documents after completing the will, power of attorney for finances or living trust interviews, you'll see a dialog box asking which specific documents in the document set you want to assemble for reviewing, printing or exporting. If you don't want to preview or print all the listed documents, uncheck the ones you don't want before clicking **OK**.

Be sure to include *all* the documents in the set when you print out your final documents (that is, the documents you intend to sign and make legal).

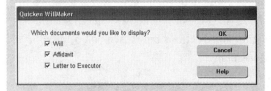

2. Viewing Your Documents

When a document is displayed on the "Print Preview" screen, you can view each page of it, but you cannot edit it. Read it thoroughly, and make sure that the information is correct. If you'd prefer to proofread from paper, print out a draft. (See Section D, below.) Note that the previewed version might not look exactly like the printed version; line breaks, page breaks and the number of pages may differ in the actual output from the printer.

Here are some tips on using the "Print Preview" screen:

- **To move through the document,** use the scroll bar or press the Up and Down Arrow keys.
- **If you're satisfied with the document** as it is, click the **Print** icon to the left of the displayed document. (See Section D, below.)
- **To change how the document looks**, click the **Print Options** icon to the left of the displayed document. (See Section B, below.)
- **To revise your document** by changing answers to interview questions, click the **Close Preview** icon to the left of the displayed document. Then, at the "Congratulations" screen, click **Change Answers**. (See Section C, below.)
- **To create and save a version that can be used with a word processor,** click the **Export** icon to the left of the displayed document. (See Section E, below.)
- **To leave the "Print Preview" screen** and return to the "Congratulations" screen, click the **Close Preview** icon to the left of the displayed document.
- **To work on a different document** without printing the current one, click the **Document List** icon in the navigation bar in the upper right.

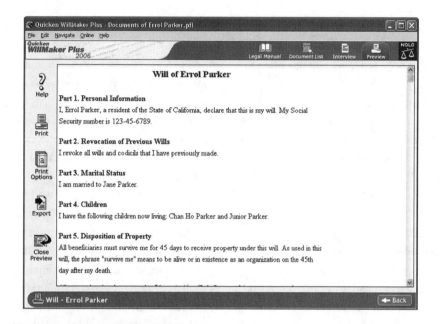

These "hash" marks are both a precaution and a legal necessity—they prevent someone from inserting additional language into blank spaces in the document after you have signed it. Hash marks are used when the page that precedes the document's signatures contains less than a full page of text.

If you print an exported document (see Section E, below), make sure that any hash marks in the version you print match those in the version displayed in Quicken WillMaker Plus's "Print Preview" window.

B. Changing How Your Document Looks

You can change a document's font, font size and page margins by choosing **Print Options...** from the **File** menu. (On the "Print Preview" screen,

you can also click the **Print Options** icon.) You'll then see the Print Options dialog shown below.

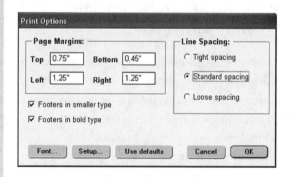

- **Page Margins.** These margins are measured in inches. To fit more text on each page, decrease the margin sizes by typing in the margins you want.
- **Line Spacing.** These options let you control how tightly spaced the printing of the document will be. To fit more text on a page, select **Tight spacing**.
- **Footers in smaller type.** When this option is checked, the type size of the footers at the

bottom of each printed page will be smaller than that of document text.

- **Footers in bold type.** When this option is checked, the footers at the bottom of each printed page are in bold type.
- **Font....** Click to change the font, or its size, in a Windows Font dialog box. (**Note:** Style attributes are ignored. Styles are applied by Quicken WillMaker Plus when the document is assembled.)
- **Setup....** Click to change the paper size or orientation in a Print Setup dialog box.
- **Use defaults.** Click to restore all print options to the default values.

Change the settings you want, then click **OK**. When you return to the displayed document, your changes will be reflected.

C. Reviewing or Changing Your Answers

If, after reading your document, you find something that you want to change, you must first return to the "Congratulations" screen from the "Print Preview" screen. To do this, click the **Close Preview** icon (left), the **Back** button (lower right) or the **Interview** icon (navigation bar).

Next, click **Change Answers** at the "Congratulations" screen. What happens next depends on whether or not that document interview uses a checklist. (For more on checklists, see Part 5, Section B.)

1. If the Interview Uses a Checklist

If the current document interview is for an estate planning document that uses a checklist, you'll

return to that checklist. All items are available for selection.

To review or change information in a particular part, first select it, then click the **Next** button. For example, to go back to the segment of the will interview concerning where you live, click **2. You and Your Residence**, then click **Next**. You'll return to the screen where you entered your name, and your answer is shown.

If you want to change an answer, you can do so. At this point, you will usually cycle through the remaining screens for that part of the interview and eventually return to the checklist screen.

When you're done changing answers, click the **Preview** icon in the navigation bar in the upper right (above the Guide). This will display your newly revised document in the "Print Preview" screen. Now you can read it and print it out, following the directions in Section D, below.

> **Changing your living trust document after you've printed or exported it.** As explained in Chapter 20 of the Legal Manual, there are special legal issues involved in changing a trust document that you've already printed and signed. (To view the Legal Manual, click on the **Legal Manual** icon in the navigation bar or open the **Help** menu.) For more on how you can use Quicken WillMaker Plus to change the terms of your signed trust document, see Part 6, Section C.

2. If the Interview Does Not Use a Checklist

If the current document interview does not use a checklist, you'll return to the first interview screen for the current document. You can then step through every screen in the interview and make your desired changes.

After you've changed a previously given answer, you may need to go through the rest of the interview before you can assemble and print the document.

Once you've completed the document interview, you'll be able to read and print out the document, following the directions in Section D, below.

view" screen. (See Section A, above, on displaying your documents.)

To print your displayed document:

1. Click the **Print** icon. You'll then see a standard Print dialog box.
2. Click **OK** to send the displayed document to your printer.

If You Can't Preview After Making a Change

Quicken WillMaker Plus "knows" when it has all the information it needs to assemble and display your document. You can change your answers on some interview screens without affecting others; however, some changes can have ripple effects that will require you to review previously entered information or provide answers to questions you haven't answered before.

For this reason, there are times when you will not be able to use the **Preview** icon to leave a completed interview and view your document in the "Print Preview" screen until you click **Next** on each screen to reach the "Congratulations" screen. This ensures that you enter the necessary information on the appropriate screens. When you're back at the "Congratulations" screen, you will be able to use the **Preview** icon to leave the interview and view your document in the "Print Preview" screen.

Printing a Draft or Duplicate Copy

There's a way to ensure that the copy you print is used as a draft, rather than as a final, signable document.

To print a draft of your displayed document:

1. Click the **Print** icon. You'll then see a standard Print dialog box.
2. In the **Watermark** box in the lower left of the Print dialog, select **Draft**.
3. Click **OK** to send the displayed document to your printer.

Each page of your printed document will now be clearly labeled as a draft.

You can also label your printed copy as a duplicate. To do so, follow the steps above, except, in Step 2, click **Duplicate**.

Do not sign these draft or duplicate versions.

⚠ Your document begins with instructions on page 1. If you enter page numbers in the **From** and **To** boxes of the **Print Range** section of this dialog box, keep in mind that Quicken WillMaker Plus counts from the first page actually printed, which is the first instruction page (some documents have more than one instruction page). Be sure to factor this in if you only want to print certain pages of a specific document.

D. Printing Your Documents

You can print a Quicken WillMaker Plus document only while it is displayed in the "Print Pre-

Note that the printed version might not look exactly like the previewed version—line breaks, page breaks and the number of pages may differ in the actual output from the printer.

After you print out your document, read the printed instructions for information on how to sign and formalize your document.

Printing Topics From the Guide or the Manual

- For instructions on how to print out a topic displayed in the Guide tab, see Part 4, Section A2.
- For instructions on how to print out topics displayed in the Quicken WillMaker Manual window, see Part 4, Section B3.

E. Exporting Your Documents

You can create a version of your document that anyone can view, edit or print in a word processor. You do this by exporting your document or saving your document to a text file. You have the option of exporting to a plain ASCII text (TXT) or Rich Text Format (RTF) file.

⚠ **Don't edit your exported document.** Making changes to the language of Quicken WillMaker Plus documents can create confusion, contradictions and legal problems that you may not be aware of. (See "Tips to Help You Create Your Export File," below.) Therefore, we strongly advise against exporting your documents unless:

- you are experiencing problems printing from Quicken WillMaker Plus, or

- you need to email a copy of your document.

Do not export for the purpose of using your word processor to edit your document. If you want to change how your document looks, remember that most formatting, including font, font size and page margins can be done from within Quicken WillMaker Plus itself. (See Section B, above.)

If you have questions about the language in your documents, or if you would like to change the language in them, take the documents to an experienced estate planning attorney and get advice on how to accomplish your goals.

To export your document:

1. If you're not there already, go to the "Congratulations" screen for the document you want to export.

2. Click **Preview and Print** to view the document on the "Print Preview" screen.

3. If appropriate, check which documents in the set you want to assemble. (See Section A1, above.) Your document will be assembled and displayed on the "Print Preview" screen.

4. Next, click the **Export** icon on the "Print Preview" screen. After you see a warning message and click **OK**, you'll see the Export Document dialog box.

5. Give the exported file a name.

6. Select the file type for the exported document—either ASCII text (.txt) or rich text format (.rtf). If your word processor can read .rtf files, you should select that file type, as it contains more formatting.

7. Click **Save**.

8. You'll then see a dialog box asking if you'd like to view the exported file. Click **Yes** to open the file in your default word processor. If you click **No**, you'll need to use your word processor, My Computer or Windows Explorer to locate and open your export file.

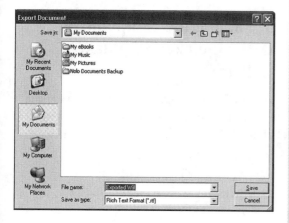

To view and print out the exported document, you will have to open the exported file with your word processor.

Tips to Help You Create Your Export Files

- Give each exported file a unique name. (See Step 5, above.) If you don't, any file you have previously made with the same name will be erased.

- You must use a word processing or text editing program to open your exported file. Consult your word processor's manual if you are not sure how to do this. All computers running Windows have word processors that can read these exported files.

- Do not call Nolo Technical Support for instructions on how to operate your word processor. Consult the manual that came with your word processor for instructions on how to do the necessary operations.

- Carefully read any instructions in the exported file about how to place the proper headers and footers to correctly format your document. Be sure to remove these instructions from the exported file before printing out your final document. ■

Part 8: Troubleshooting

In this section, we briefly discuss some common technical difficulties you might encounter when running the program.

Onscreen help is also available by choosing **Quicken WillMaker Users' Manual Help** from the **Help** menu. If you have a problem that you can't clear up using this Users' Manual or onscreen help, contact Nolo Tech Support. (See Section F, below.)

A. Displaying the "Welcome to Quicken WillMaker Plus Installation" Screen

To install Quicken WillMaker Plus, follow the instructions in Part 2, Section A. When you insert the Quicken WillMaker Plus CD, the "Welcome to Quicken WillMaker Plus Installation" screen should open automatically. If this does not happen, do the following:

1. Click the Windows **Start** button and select **Run....**
2. Click the **Browse** button.

3. Type D:\AUTORUN (you may have to substitute the letter of your CD-ROM drive for "D").
4. Click **OK**.

B. Finding the Setup File on the Quicken WillMaker Plus CD

The installation program QWP2006_SETUP.EXE is located in the root directory of the Quicken WillMaker Plus CD-ROM. If you want to start this program from the Run command line, enter D:\QWP2006_SETUP (you may have to substitute the letter of your CD-ROM drive for "D").

C. Error Messages

Here's a table of error messages, what they mean, and what you should do if you see one.

Error Messages

Error	What It Means	What You Should Do
[CD-ROM drive] is not accessible. The device is not ready.	The CD you inserted is not being read.	Reinsert the CD. Wait ten seconds and double click the CD-ROM drive icon. If that doesn't solve the problem, contact Nolo Technical Support.
An error occurred: couldn't find the requested path name.	Quicken WillMaker Plus couldn't find the path for a file it wants to open.	Contact Nolo Technical Support.
An error occurred while assembling the document.	The resource files of the program might be damaged.	Reinstall all program files. Try again. If that doesn't work, contact Nolo Technical Support.
Internal error: attempt to overwrite existing file.	Quicken WillMaker Plus is attempting to overwrite an existing file without permission.	Try to remember the steps you did before the error appeared, then contact Nolo Technical Support.
Sorry, an internal error occurred.	Something very serious is wrong with the program, either because of a disk error, memory error or (gasp!) bug.	Quit, restart the program and attempt to repeat what you did. The problem may clear up on its own. If not, try reinstalling Quicken WillMaker Plus. If that doesn't work, contact Nolo Technical Support.
Sorry, an internal data-module error occurred.	Something very serious is wrong with the internal data structures.	Contact Nolo Technical Support.
Sorry, a needed resource cannot be found.	The resource files of the program might be damaged.	Reinstall all program files and try again. If that doesn't work, contact Nolo Technical Support
Sorry, this file has been corrupted and cannot be read.	Your data file has been seriously corrupted and cannot be read.	Use the backup file with the same name, located in the **Nolo Documents Backup** subfolder of your **My Documents** folder.

Error Messages

Error	What It Means	What You Should Do
Sorry, Quicken WillMaker Plus can open only one documents file at a time.	You attempted to open more than one Quicken WillMaker Plus file.	Open only one documents file at a time.
Sorry, this file cannot be read by Quicken WillMaker Plus.	You are trying to open a file that is not recognized by Quicken WillMaker Plus.	If you are sure the file you are attempting to use is a Quicken WillMaker Plus data file, try a backup copy. If that doesn't work, contact Nolo Technical Support.
Quicken WillMaker Plus cannot open that file (because it is read-only).	Quicken WillMaker Plus was not allowed to open a file because it didn't have permission to open it, either because it is in use or because it is read-only.	Check that the file (or the disk) is not locked.
Sorry, but this version of Quicken WillMaker Plus requires Internet Explorer version 5.0 or greater. Please install Internet Explorer 5.0 or later on your machine. Quicken WillMaker Plus will now exit.	Your system does not meet the minimum requirements to run Quicken WillMaker Plus.	If you don't run Internet Explorer, install it. If you run an old version, upgrade. You can download Internet Explorer free from Microsoft.com's download center.
Please select a part or option.	You clicked "Next" (or pressed "Enter") before you made a checklist selection.	Make a selection before clicking "Next" (or pressing "Enter").
Quicken WillMaker Plus was not shut down properly the last time it was run. Please run Web Update to make sure your copy of the program is up-to-date. If this problem continues, contact Nolo Tech Support.	Either (1) a bug in Quicken WillMaker Plus caused the program to crash the last time you used it, or (2) you turned off your computer while Quicken WillMaker Plus was still running.	Run Web Update. If the problem was Quicken WillMaker Plus, an update to fix the problem may be available. Also, make sure that you exit Quicken WillMaker Plus before shutting down your computer. If this problem continues, contact Nolo Tech Support.

Error Messages

Error	What It Means	What You Should Do
[Name you're trying to edit information about]'s [name or gender] can't be changed. It's probably being used in a critical place in some document—for example, a frozen trust.	Editing this information could affect the legality of another document you've made.	Think about whether this change really needs to be made. If so, check other documents to see whether they require the same revision. If so, you need to do so by creating a new document file and creating new versions of those documents. Please carefully read the appropriate sections of the Legal Manual before you start recreating documents this way.
Your document is not yet complete. Please complete the interview before printing your document.	The program has determined that it does not have all the information it needs to print your document.	Review all interview screens and enter any missing information. If you still can't print, contact Nolo Tech Support.
A check on your interview answers revealed that some of your data is out-of-date or missing. Please review your answers by clicking "Change Answers" and reviewing the entire interview.	The program has determined that some of your data is out-of-date or missing.	Review all interview screens and make the necessary entries and revisions. If this problem continues, contact Nolo Tech Support.
An error exists in this Help file. Contact your application vendor for an updated Help file.	There's a problem opening the topic you selected in the program's Help system.	First, close the Help file and any open Help files from other programs; keep Quicken WillMaker Plus open. Then, repeat what you did that caused the error message. If the problem persists, contact Nolo Technical Support.

D. Printing Problems

Most Windows printing problems can be corrected by resetting the options in Print Setup. To do this, select **Print Setup...** from the **File** menu. Check to make sure the settings for your printer are correct. For example, if your printer uses a sheet feeder, make sure the print setup for your printer is set for sheet feeding.

If your problems continue, you can export your document and print it using your word processor. See Part 7, Section E, on how to export a document.

E. Problems Updating From the Web

If you are having a problem with Web Update (see Part 2, Section C), read the following.

Firewall and security application users. If you use a firewall and security application and receive warnings, you'll need to add "f1.nolo.com" to the "trusted site" list. If you are unable to complete the update after adding f1.nolo.com to the trusted site list, you may need to completely turn off your firewall program in order to retrieve the update. Once the update is downloaded and installed, you can turn your firewall back on.

If you are a Windows XP Service Pack 2 user, the built-in "Windows Firewall" feature could prevent you from using Web Update. If, when you run Web Update, you see a Windows Security Alert asking you whether you want to keep blocking or unblock your Quicken program's Internet connection, select "Unblock." Once you have unblocked the Quicken program, you should be able to download future Web Updates.

If the problem persists, contact Nolo Tech Support. (See Section F, below.) Please include the following details so we will be able to help you:

- the type of Internet connection you have (modem dial up, DSL, and so on)
- the version of Windows you are running (for example, Windows 98 or XP Home), and
- the name of your Internet service provider.

Corporate proxy server users. If you are trying to update the program behind a corporate proxy server and get various error messages, you won't be able to use Web Update. Web Update was designed for the home user with a basic firewall. Unfortunately, we cannot support proxy servers and other corporate VPN security configurations.

F. Contacting Nolo Technical Support

If you have problems that are not addressed by this troubleshooting section, we may have the answer on our website. Nolo's Technical Support posts FAQs with answers to common user questions or problems. You can find the FAQ page for this program by going to Nolo's Technical Support page at www.nolo.com/support/software_faq.cfm.

If you can't find a solution there, contact Nolo's Technical Support directly.

Email: support@nolo.com

Phone: 510-549-4660 between 9:00 a.m. and 5:00 p.m. Pacific Time, Monday through Friday. When you call, try to be in front of the computer with which you are having the problem.

Please remember that Tech Support can only help registered users with problems running the Quicken WillMaker Plus application and cannot provide legal advice concerning drafting your documents.

Please include the following information in your email (or have it ready before you call):

- the version of Quicken WillMaker Plus (should be 5.0 or higher)
- the point in the program where the problem occurred
- whether you can duplicate the problem
- the brand and model of computer you are using
- the brand and model of printer (if you are having trouble printing)
- the operating system and the version you are running—for example, Windows 2000 version 5.00.2195 or XP Home, and
- the amount of RAM on your computer.

To get most of this information about your system:

1. Right click on the **My Computer** icon on your desktop.
2. Select **Properties**.
3. Choose the tab that contains the information you need. ■

Appendix 1: Menus

File Menu

New Documents File

Use this command to create a new Quicken WillMaker Plus documents file. See Part 3, Section A.

Open Documents File...

Use this command to open documents files made with Quicken WillMaker Plus 2004 and other compatible programs. See Part 3, Section A.

Save

Use this command to manually save your currently open documents file. You do not need to use this command if Automatically Save Changes is on.

Save As...

Use this command to rename your documents file and/or save it to another location on your computer.

Save for Spouse...

Use this command to save a copy of your documents file that can then be used to make an identical will for your spouse. For details on how married couples can use this command to create identical wills, see Appendix 3.

Lock/Unlock Documents File

Use this command to lock your documents file and give it a password. If your documents file is locked, no one can open it without first entering the password. If you want to unlock a file you've locked, you'll need to first enter the password you assigned it. See Part 3, Section A4.

Change Documents File Password

Use this command to change your password. This command is available only if you have pre-viously locked your documents file. See Part 3, Section A4.

Print Options...

Use this command to change the formatting for your documents, including page margins, line spacing, font type and font size. We recommend keeping the default settings. See Part 7, Section B.

Print Setup...

Use this command to open the standard print setup dialog for the currently chosen printer.

Print Guide Topic...

Use this command to print out the help topic that is currently displayed in the Guide. If you don't see this command, click the **Guide** tab and then try opening the **File** menu. See Part 4, Section A2.

Print Contact List...

Use this command to print out the Contact List for the documents file you have opened. If you don't see this command, click the **Contact List** tab and then try opening the **File** menu. See Part 5, Section F5.

Export Document

Use this command to save your document as a text file that you can view, edit or print with a word processor. See Part 7, Section E.

Recent Files

Use this command to open a recently used documents files (*.pfl). This submenu lists up to five files.

Exit

Use this command to quit the Quicken WillMaker Plus program. See Part 2, Section D.

Edit Menu

Undo

Use this command to undo the last typing or editing you did, provided you haven't left the screen on which the changes were made.

Cut

Use this command to remove selected text and place it on the clipboard.

Copy

Use this command to copy selected text to the clipboard, without removing it.

Paste

Use this command to insert text that you have previously cut or copied at the blinking cursor, or to replace selected text with text that you have previously cut or copied.

Delete

Use this command to delete selected text without putting it on the clipboard. The selected text will not be saved.

Select All

Use this command to select all the text in the currently active text field.

Manage Contact List...

Use this command to add names to, modify names in or delete names from the Contact List, and to enter additional information about names previously entered. See Part 5, Section F.

Duplicate Document

Use this command to create a new document by duplicating one you've already created. To use this command, you must select the document you want to duplicate on the "Document List" screen. See Part 5, Section C.

Delete Document

Use this command to delete a document you've already created. To use this command, you must select the document you want to delete on the "Document List" screen.

Preferences...

Use this command to customize your version of Quicken WillMaker Plus. You can use the Preferences command to change the following:

- whether your data will be saved automatically or manually (Part 3, Section A3)
- whether the program will automatically check for Web Updates when you start it up
- if names are to be automatically completed (Part 5, Section E3)
- if related fields are to be automatically filled in after you enter a name (Part 5, Section E3)
- the font size of the Guide text (Part 4, Section A)
- how the names in the Contact List are sorted, and
- the folder where your backup files are stored (Part 3, Section A2).

Navigate Menu

Back

Use this command to go back to the previous screen. See Part 5, Section D.

Next

Use this command to move ahead to the next screen. See Part 5, Section D.

Go to Document List

Use this command to switch to a different Quicken WillMaker Plus document interview. This command takes you to the "Document List" screen, from which you can start a new document or work on one you've already created. See Part 5, Section C.

Go to Introduction

Use this command to view the series of introductory screens you saw the first time you viewed the program.

Go to Interview

Use this command to start the interview of a document you've selected on the "Document List" screen, or to return to the interview if you're previewing it on the "Print Preview" screen.

Preview Document

Use this command to preview your completed document. You can use this command only after you have completed the document interview. See Part 7, Section A.

Online Menu

Web Update

Use this command to update your copy of Quicken WillMaker Plus by downloading the latest updated files from the Web. Before you use this command, you must have a live Internet connection. For more on using Web Update, see Part 2, Section C.

Online Registration

Use this command to register your copy of Quicken WillMaker Plus. You'll need a Web browser and an Internet connection to use this command.

Nolo on the Web

Use this command to access Nolo's website at www.nolo.com. You'll need a Web browser and an Internet connection to use this command.

Help Menu

Quicken WillMaker Users' Manual

Use this command to display a Help file containing a complete version of this manual. This file includes both the Users' Manual and the Legal Manual. See Part 4, Section B.

Quicken WillMaker Legal Manual

Use this command to display the table of contents for the Legal Manual portion of the Help file.

Keyboard Shortcuts

Use this command to see how to operate the program using a keyboard rather than a mouse. See Appendix 2.

About Quicken WillMaker Plus 2006

Use this command to see information on what version of the program you're running and detailed information about all the program files you've installed. ■

Appendix 2: Keyboard Commands

To see this information when you're running the program, choose **Keyboard Shortcuts** from the **Help** menu.

Common Keyboard Shortcuts	
Press ...	**To ...**
ENTER	Trigger the default button (if one exists).
ESC	Trigger **Cancel**, **Close** or **No** button in pop-up dialog boxes.
F1	Open the Quicken WillMaker Users' Manual.
CTRL+O	Open an existing documents file.
CTRL+S	Save the current documents file when the Automatically Save Changes function is turned off.
ALT+LEFT ARROW	Go back to previous interview screen.
ALT+RIGHT ARROW	Go to next interview screen.
TAB	Move to the next text box, list, button or group of option buttons.
SHIFT+TAB	Move to the previous text box, list, button or group of option buttons.
DOWN ARROW	Highlight the next option button (in a group when one option button is selected) or the next item (in a selected list).
UP ARROW	Highlight the previous option button (in a group when one option button is selected) or the previous item (in a selected list).
ALT+F4	Exit the program.

Moving Around an Interview Screen

Press ...	To ...
TAB	Move to the next part of the screen, text box, list, button or group of option buttons.
SHIFT+TAB	Move to the previous part of the screen, text box, list, button or group of option buttons.
DOWN ARROW	Highlight the next option button in a group when one option button is selected, or the next item in a selected list.
UP ARROW	Highlight the previous option button in a group when one option button is selected, or the previous item in a selected list.
ALT+LEFT ARROW	Go back to the previous interview screen.
ALT+RIGHT ARROW	Go to the next interview screen.
CTRL+SHIFT+G	Show **Guide** tab at the right of the screen.
CTRL+SHIFT+C	Show **Contact List** at the right of the screen.
CTRL+SHIFT+L	Show **Glossary** tab at the right of the screen.
CTRL+SHIFT+O	Show **Online Resources** tab at the right of the screen.
ENTER	Activate the default button (as indicated by a thicker outline) or the selected button (if there is no default).

If Cursor Is in a Text Entry Field

Press ...	To ...
ENTER	Start a new line, if the field allows more than one line of text.
LEFT ARROW	Move one character to left.
RIGHT ARROW	Move one character to right.
UP ARROW	Move one line up.
DOWN ARROW	Move one line down.
HOME	Move to beginning of line.
END	Move to end of line.
CTRL+HOME	Move to beginning of a field.
CTRL+END	Move to end of a field.
CTRL+LEFT ARROW	Move one word to left.
CTRL+RIGHT ARROW	Move one word to right.
CTRL+Z	Undo the most recent text editing you have done on the current screen if the change has not yet been saved.
CTRL+X	Cut selected text to the clipboard.
CTRL+C	Copy selected text to the clipboard.
CTRL+V	Paste contents of clipboard.
DELETE	Delete selected text.
CTRL+A	Select all text in current text box.

Appendix 3: Creating Identical Wills for Married Couples

Some married couples may want to create identical wills. By this we mean that all the provisions in the will—such as beneficiaries, alternate beneficiaries and children's guardians—are the same. The only difference is that the spouses' names are reversed. For example, if you make a will and name your spouse as your executor, when your spouse makes an identical will, you will be named as his or her executor.

Married couples are not required to create such identical wills. But, if you do want to create wills that are identical, there's a simple way to do it.

> **⚠ Work on the will interview together.** Since the first spouse to write a will is in effect creating the will for both spouses, we suggest that the two of you complete the will interview together, discussing and agreeing to all decisions and choices.

Here are the steps:

1. One spouse creates a documents file and completes his or her will. (In order to create identical wills, the first spouse must complete his or her will before the second spouse creates his or her own documents file.)

2. When the first will is done and you're at the "Congratulations" screen (see Part 7 of the Users' Manual), choose **Save for Spouse...** from the **File** menu.

3. This brings up a dialog box explaining what you're about to do. Click **OK**.

4. You'll then see a Save As... dialog box asking you to save a copy of your documents file under your spouse's name. Note the location on your computer to which this file will be saved, then click **Save**. If your documents file contains documents other than the will, only the will information is saved to this file.

5. Now it's the other spouse's turn. While running Quicken WillMaker Plus, choose **Open Documents File** from the **File** menu.

6. You'll then see an Open File dialog box asking you to locate the documents file you want to open. Find and select the file that your spouse saved in Step 4, then click **Open**.

7. You'll next see the introductory section of the program. Keep clicking Next until you see the "Document List" screen.

8. At the "Document List" screen, the **Documents You've Created** are listed. The Will is the only document listed, and the will of the second spouse—identified by his or her name—is also selected.

9. Click **Open Document**. At the "Will Checklist" screen, none of the parts are checked, even though this will contains all the information that was in your spouse's will. You are required to review all screens before you can display or print this will document. This ensures that you understand and agree with the choices your spouse has made. You can change any answers you want—these changes, however, will only be reflected in your will and not in the will of the first will-writing spouse.

10. Use the checklist to review all screens. When this is done, print out a copy. (See Part 7 of the Users' Manual.) ▪

Index

Users' Manual Index